A Companion to
Thomas Hardy

Blackwell Companions to Literature and Culture

This series offers comprehensive, newly written surveys of key periods and movements and certain major authors, in English literary culture and history. Extensive volumes provide new perspectives and positions on contexts and on canonical and post-canonical texts, orientating the beginning student in new fields of study and providing the experienced undergraduate and new graduate with current and new directions, as pioneered and developed by leading scholars in the field.

For more information on the Blackwell Companions to Literature and Culture series, please visit www.wiley.com

A COMPANION TO

THOMAS HARDY

EDITED BY

KEITH WILSON

WILEY-BLACKWELL

A John Wiley & Sons, Ltd., Publication

This edition first published 2009
© 2009 Blackwell Publishing Ltd except for editorial material and organization © 2009 Keith Wilson

Blackwell Publishing was acquired by John Wiley & Sons in February 2007. Blackwell's publishing program has been merged with Wiley's global Scientific, Technical, and Medical business to form Wiley-Blackwell.

Registered Office
John Wiley & Sons Ltd, The Atrium, Southern Gate, Chichester, West Sussex, PO19 8SQ, United Kingdom

Editorial Offices
350 Main Street, Malden, MA 02148-5020, USA
9600 Garsington Road, Oxford, OX4 2DQ, UK
The Atrium, Southern Gate, Chichester, West Sussex, PO19 8SQ, UK

For details of our global editorial offices, for customer services, and for information about how to apply for permission to reuse the copyright material in this book please see our website at www.wiley.com/wiley-blackwell.

The right of Keith Wilson to be identified as the author of the editorial material in this work has been asserted in accordance with the Copyright, Designs and Patents Act 1988.

Library of Congress Cataloging-in-Publication Data
A companion to Thomas Hardy / edited by Keith Wilson.
      p. cm. – (Blackwell companions to literature and culture)
   Includes bibliographical references and index.
   ISBN 978-1-4051-5668-4 (hardcover : alk. paper)
   1. Hardy, Thomas, 1840-1928–Criticism and interpretation–Handbooks, manuals, etc.
   I. Wilson, Keith (Keith G.)
   PR4754.C56 2009
   823'.8–dc22
                              2008047634

A catalogue record for this book is available from the British Library.

Set in 11 on 13pt Garamond 3 by SNP Best-set Typesetter Ltd., Hong Kong
Printed in the United Kingdom

1   2009

Contents

Notes on Contributors

Tim Armstrong is Professor of Modern Literature at Royal Holloway College, University of London. His recent publications include *Modernism, Technology and the Body: A Cultural Study* (1998), *Haunted Hardy: Poetry, History, Memory* (2000), and *Modernism: A Cultural History* (2005). His *Thomas Hardy: Selected Poems* (Longman Annotated Texts) will appear in a new edition in 2009.

Penny Boumelha is Deputy Vice-Chancellor (Academic) at Victoria University of Wellington in New Zealand and a Fellow of the Academy of the Humanities in Australia. She is the author of *Thomas Hardy and Women: Sexual Ideology and Narrative Form* (1982), has edited a Casebook on *Jude the Obscure* (2000), and published essays on Hardy, including introductions for Penguin and Oxford World's Classics editions of three of the novels. She has published widely on nineteenth-century writers, realism, and issues of gender and narrative, including a monograph on Charlotte Brontë (1990).

J. B. Bullen is Professor Emeritus of English at the University of Reading. He has had a longstanding interest in interdisciplinary studies, and his books include *The Expressive Eye: Vision and Perception in the Work of Thomas Hardy* (1986), *The Myth of the Renaissance in Nineteenth-Century Writing* (1995), *The Pre-Raphaelite Body* (1998), *Byzantium Rediscovered* (2003) and *Continental Crosscurrents* (2005). He has published articles on Coleridge, Ruskin, Dickens, George Eliot, Browning, Pater, and has edited Roger Fry's *Vision and Design* (1981), Clive Bell's *Art* (1987), and *Post-Impressionists in England* (1988). He is editor of *Cultural Interactions*, a series of interdisciplinary monographs for the publisher Peter Lang, and his critical biography of Dante Gabriel Rossetti appears in 2009.

Pamela Dalziel is Associate Professor of English and Distinguished University Scholar at the University of British Columbia. She has edited *Thomas Hardy: The Excluded and Collaborative Stories* (1992), *Thomas Hardy's "Studies, Specimens &c." Notebook* (with Michael Millgate, 1994), *An Indiscretion in the Life of an Heiress and Other Stories*

(1994), and *A Pair of Blue Eyes* (1998). Her most recent books are *Thomas Hardy's "Poetical Matter" Notebook* (with Michael Millgate, 2009) and *Visual Hardy: Representing Gender and Genre in the Illustrated Novels* (forthcoming).

Tim Dolin is an Associate Professor in the School of Media, Culture and Creative Arts at Curtin University of Technology in Perth, WA. He is the author of a short biography, *Thomas Hardy* (2008), and editor of three of Hardy's novels for Penguin. He is presently working on narrative and performance in Hardy.

Roger Ebbatson is Emeritus Professor at the University of Worcester, and was formerly Visiting Professor at Loughborough University. His publications include *The Evolutionary Self: Hardy, Forster, Lawrence* (1982), *Hardy: The Margin of the Unexpressed* (1993), *An Imaginary England: Nation, Landscape and Literature, 1840–1920* (2005), and *Heidegger's Bicycle: Interfering with Victorian Texts* (2006).

Simon Gatrell, Professor of English at the University of Georgia, has published widely on Victorian literature in general and Thomas Hardy's work in particular. He is currently working on a study of Hardy's fiction and poetry through dress.

William Greenslade is Professor of English at the University of the West of England. He is the author of *Degeneration, Culture and the Novel 1880–1940* (1994) and has edited *Thomas Hardy's "Facts" Notebook* (2004), George Gissing's *The Whirlpool* (1997), and (co-edited with Terence Rogers) *Grant Allen: Literature and Cultural Politics at the Fin de Siècle* (2005). He has written a number of essays on late nineteenth-century British literature and culture, including "Socialism and Radicalism," in Gail Marshall (ed.), *The Cambridge Companion to the Fin de Siècle* (2007).

Margaret R. Higonnet, Professor of English and Comparative Literature at the University of Connecticut, has served as President of the American Comparative Literature Association and the American Conference on Romanticism. Her publications range over German Romantic theory, feminist theory, children's literature, and the First World War. She has edited *The Sense of Sex: Feminist Perspectives on Hardy* (1992) and contributed introductions to editions of *Tess of the d'Urbervilles* and *The Return of the Native*.

Michael Irwin is Emeritus Professor of English, University of Kent. His academic publications include numerous essays on Hardy, and a book, *Reading Hardy's Landscapes* (2000). He was chairman of the Thomas Hardy Society from 2004 to 2008.

George Levine is Professor Emeritus, Rutgers University, and Distinguished Scholar in Residence, New York University. Among his books are *The Realistic Imagination* (1981), *Darwin and the Novelists* (1988), and *Dying to Know: Narrative and Scientific Epistemology in Victorian England* (2002). He has edited many volumes of essays, including *Aesthetics and Ideology* (1994) and *The Cambridge Companion to George Eliot* (2001). His most recent publications are *Darwin Loves You: Natural Selection and the Re-enchantment of the World* (2006), *How to Read the Victorian Novel* (2007), and *Realism, Secularism and Ethics: Essays in Victorian Literature* (forthcoming).

Charles Lock has held the Chair of English Literature at the University of Copenhagen since 1996; he was previously Professor of English at the University of Toronto. Among his publications are *Thomas Hardy: Criticism in Focus* (1992) and some two hundred scholarly articles.

Phillip Mallett is Senior Lecturer in English at the University of St Andrews. His work on Hardy includes the Norton editions of *The Mayor of Casterbridge* (2000) and *The Return of the Native* (2005), and four edited collections of essays, including *The Achievement of Thomas Hardy* (2000) and *Palgrave Advances in Thomas Hardy Studies* (2004). His *Rudyard Kipling: A Literary Life* appeared in 2003.

J. Hillis Miller is UCI Distinguished Research Professor of Comparative Literature and English, University of California at Irvine. His most recent book is *Literature as Conduct: Speech Acts in Henry James* (2005). His *For Derrida* is forthcoming in Spring 2009 from Fordham University Press. He is currently writing two books on communities in literature, one to be entitled *The Conflagration of Community: Fiction Before and After Auschwitz*. His *The Medium is the Maker: Browning, Freud, Derrida, and the New Telepathic Ecotechnologies* is forthcoming from Sussex Academic Press in September 2009. He is a Fellow of the American Academy of Arts and Sciences, a member of the American Philosophical Society, and received the MLA Lifetime Scholarly Achievement Award in 2005.

Michael Millgate is University Professor of English Emeritus at the University of Toronto. In addition to publications in American literature, he has written *Thomas Hardy: His Career as a Novelist* (1971), *Thomas Hardy: A Biography* (1982), *Testamentary Acts: Browning, Tennyson, James, Hardy* (1992), and *Thomas Hardy: A Biography Revisited* (2004). He has also edited *The Life and Work of Thomas Hardy* by Thomas Hardy (1984), *Selected Letters of Thomas Hardy* (1990), *Letters of Emma and Florence Hardy* (1996), and *Thomas Hardy's Public Voice* (2001), and co-edited *The Collected Letters of Thomas Hardy* (7 vols., 1978–88), *Thomas Hardy's "Studies, Specimens &c." Notebook* (1994), and *Thomas Hardy's "Poetical Matter" Notebook* (2009).

William W. Morgan is Professor Emeritus of English at Illinois State University. He has published two co-edited books on Hardy as well as Hardy-related essays in such journals as *PMLA, JEGP, Victorian Poetry, Victorians Institute Journal, Victorian Newsletter*, the *Thomas Hardy Journal*, and the *Hardy Review*. For ten years he wrote the annual review of Hardy studies for *Victorian Poetry*. He is a vice-president of both the Thomas Hardy Society and the Thomas Hardy Association, and was for several years director of the Association's Hardy Poetry Page. He has also published two chapbooks of poems, *Trackings: The Body's Memory, The Heart's Fiction* (1998), and *Sky With Six Geese* (2005), and over thirty poems in various journals.

Richard Nemesvari is Professor and Chair in the Department of English at St. Francis Xavier University. He is editor of *The Trumpet-Major* (1991) and *Jane Eyre* (1999). His article "Fetishism and the Pathology of Class Status in 'Barbara of the House of Grebe'" was published in the *Hardy Review*, 9 (Spring 2007), and his essay

"'Judged by a Purely Literary Standard': Sensation Fiction, Horizons of Expectation, and the Generic Construction of Victorian Realism" appeared in the collection *Victorian Sensations: Essays on a Scandalous Genre* (2006). Along with numerous essays on Hardy he has also published on Emily Brontë, Wilkie Collins, Joseph Conrad, and Mary Elizabeth Braddon.

Ralph Pite published *Thomas Hardy: The Guarded Life* in 2006 and *Hardy's Geography* in 2002. He is Professor of English at the University of Bristol and currently working on a study of Edward Thomas and Robert Frost. He is also researching twentieth-century poetry and the environment.

Andrew Radford is a Lecturer in the Department of English Literature at the University of Glasgow. He is the author of *Thomas Hardy and the Survivals of Time* (2003) and *The Lost Girls: Demeter-Persephone and the Literary Imagination, 1850–1930* (2007). He is currently at work on a book-length study of Victorian sensation fiction.

Stephen Regan is Professor of English and Head of the Department of English Studies at Durham University, where he is also director of the Basil Bunting Centre for Modern Poetry. His publications include *Irish Writing: An Anthology of Irish Writing 1789–1939* (2004), *The Nineteenth Century Novel: A Critical Reader* (2001), *The Eagleton Reader* (1998), *The Politics of Pleasure: Aesthetics and Cultural Theory* (1992), and *Philip Larkin* (1992). He is the founding editor of *The Year's Work in Critical and Cultural Theory*, published annually by Oxford University Press. His latest book (co-edited with Richard Allen) is *Irelands of the Mind: Memory and Identity in Modern Irish Culture* (2008).

Angelique Richardson is Senior Lecturer in English at the University of Exeter. She has published widely on nineteenth-century culture and science and is the author of *Love and Eugenics in the Late Nineteenth Century: Rational Reproduction and the New Woman* (2003), editor of *Women Who Did: Stories by Men and Women, 1890–1914* (2005), and co-editor of *Eugenics Old and New*, a special issue of *New Formations* (2007). She is now completing *The Pull of Biology: Hardy, Nature, and Culture*.

Mary Rimmer is Professor of English at the University of New Brunswick. She has edited Hardy's *Desperate Remedies* (1998), published articles on Hardy, and collaborated on editions of four early Trinidad novels: E. L. Joseph's *Warner Arundell: The Adventures of a Creole*, Mrs. William Noy Wilkins' *The Slave Son*, the anonymous *Adolphus: A Tale*, and Stephen N. Cobham's *Rupert Gray: A Study in Black and White*. She is writing a book on Hardy's allusions.

Claire Seymour teaches English at Queen's College London, and is a tutor in English and music for the Open University, and in opera studies for Rose Bruford College. She was the editor of the *Thomas Hardy Journal* from 2005 to 2008, and has introduced several Wordsworth Classics editions of Hardy, including *Under the Greenwood Tree*, *The Return of the Native*, and *Life's Little Ironies*. She is the author of *The Operas of Benjamin Britten: Expression and Evasion* (2004).

Dennis Taylor is a professor of English at Boston College, and editor emeritus of the journal, *Religion and the Arts*. His books include *Hardy's Poetry 1860–1928* (1981; revised edition 1989), co-winner of the 1990 Macmillan/Hardy Society Prize, *Hardy's Metres and Victorian Prosody* (1988), and *Hardy's Literary Language and Victorian Philology* (1993; revised edition 1998). He is the editor of the Penguin edition of *Jude the Obscure* (1998), and also the editor (with David Beauregard) of *Shakespeare and the Culture of Christianity of Early Modern England* (2003).

Jane Thomas is Senior Lecturer in English at the University of Hull, where she specializes in Victorian literature and the work of Thomas Hardy. Her publications include *Thomas Hardy: Femininity and Dissent. Reassessing the Minor Novels* (1999) and editions of *The Well-Beloved* and *Life's Little Ironies*, as well as numerous articles. She has additional research interests in nineteenth-century literature and art, twentieth-century literature, gender, and women's writing and has published chapters and articles on the changing Victorian canon, Thomas Woolner, William Morris, Carol Anne Duffy, Caryl Churchill, and Michèle Roberts. She is currently writing a monograph for Palgrave on *Thomas Hardy and Desire*. She is a member of the council of management of the Thomas Hardy Society and of the editorial board of the *Thomas Hardy Journal*.

G. Glen Wickens is Professor of English at Bishop's University, where he teaches Victorian and modern British literature as well as film studies. He is the author of *Thomas Hardy, Monism, and the Carnival Tradition* (2002) and of articles on Hardy, Tennyson, and various aspects of Victorian thought. His current research interests include a book-length study of the films of Marlon Brando.

Peter Widdowson is Professor of Literature at the University of Gloucestershire. He has written extensively on Thomas Hardy since publishing *Hardy in History* in 1989 – most recently on silent film versions of Hardy's fiction in T. R. Wright (ed.), *Thomas Hardy on Screen* (2005). He has also published *Literature* (1999), *The Palgrave Guide to English Literature and its Contexts, 1500–2000* (2004), *Graham Swift* (2005), and (with Peter Brooker and Raman Selden) *A Reader's Guide to Contemporary Literary Theory* (5th edn., 2005).

Keith Wilson is Professor of English at the University of Ottawa. His Hardy-related publications include *Thomas Hardy on Stage* (1995), editions of *The Mayor of Casterbridge* (1997, 2003) and *The Fiddler of the Reels and Other Stories* (2003, co-edited with Kristin Brady), the edited collection *Thomas Hardy Reappraised: Essays in Honour of Michael Millgate* (2006), and numerous essays. He has published widely on nineteenth- and twentieth-century British literature, the representation of London, and Victorian and Edwardian music hall.

Julian Wolfreys is Professor of Modern Literature and Culture in the Department of English and Drama, at Loughborough University. The author and editor of numerous books on nineteenth- and twentieth-century literature and literary theory, his most recent publications include *Transgression: Identity, Space, Time* (2008). He is currently compiling the Jacques Derrida concordance, and working on two other books, one on English diaspora, the other on death in the text of Jacques Derrida.

Terry R. Wright is Professor of English Literature at Newcastle University. He has written several books on Hardy, including *Hardy and the Erotic* (1989) and *Hardy and his Readers* (2003), and edited *Thomas Hardy on Screen* (2007). He has also written *The Religion of Humanity* (1986), *Theology and Literature* (1988), *George Eliot's "Middlemarch"* (1991), and *D. H. Lawrence and the Bible* (2000).

Abbreviations

The following short-form designations are used for frequently cited texts. In the case of Hardy's novels, citations in the text refer to the edition of the novel listed in a chapter's individual "Reference and Further Reading" list.

AL   *A Laodicean*

CL   *The Collected Letters of Thomas Hardy*, ed. Richard Little Purdy and Michael Millgate, 7 vols. (Oxford: Clarendon Press, 1978–88)

CPV   *The Variorum Edition of the Complete Poems of Thomas Hardy*, ed. James Gibson (London: Macmillan, 1979)

CPW   *The Complete Poetical Works of Thomas Hardy*, ed. Samuel Hynes. 5 vols. (Oxford: Clarendon Press, 1982–95)

D   *The Dynasts*

DR   *Desperate Remedies*

FFMC   *Far From the Madding Crowd*

GND   *A Group of Noble Dames*

HE   *The Hand of Ethelberta*

JO   *Jude the Obscure*

LLI   *Life's Little Ironies*

LN   *The Literary Notebooks of Thomas Hardy*, ed. Lennart A. Björk, 2 vols. (Basingstoke: Macmillan, 1985).

LW   *The Life and Work of Thomas Hardy*, ed. Michael Millgate (London and Basingstoke: Macmillan, 1984)

MC   *The Mayor of Casterbridge*

MV   *Moments of Vision*

PBE   *A Pair of Blue Eyes*

RN   *The Return of the Native*

TD   *Tess of the d'Urbervilles*

THPV   *Thomas Hardy's Public Voice: The Essays, Speeches, and Miscellaneous Prose*, ed. Michael Millgate (Oxford: Clarendon Press, 2001)

TM   *The Trumpet-Major*

TT   *Two on a Tower*

UGT   *Under the Greenwood Tree*

W   *The Woodlanders*

WB   *The Well-Beloved*

WT   *Wessex Tales*

Introduction

Keith Wilson

The life and work of Thomas Hardy – to appropriate the phrase that he adopted as the title for his disguised autobiography, published under the name of his second wife, Florence Emily Hardy – intersect in a complex of paradoxes that make him a key transitional figure, perhaps *the* key transitional figure, in nineteenth-century literature's movement towards modernism. The most obvious of these was born of the good fortune of longevity: the last surviving of the great Victorian novelists, in the last thirty years of his life he turned away from fiction towards poetry and lived long enough to become one of England's most important twentieth-century poets. In returning to the medium that he claimed had always been his first love, he began the process that would ultimately establish his secure status as that rarest of literary phenomena: a writer whose achievements are defined equally by work in both prose and verse. Critical acceptance of a parity of importance between his writings in the two very different genres took some time to emerge. While a scattering of critical work was published on the poetry in the forty years after his death, it was as late as 1972 before Donald Davie, in his book *Thomas Hardy and British Poetry*, advanced the then deliberately provocative claim, though it seems tame enough now, that "in British poetry of the last fifty years . . . the most far-reaching influence, for good and ill, has not been Yeats, still less Eliot or Pound or Lawrence, but *Hardy*." Once the assertion had been made, it seemed a judgment whose time had inevitably come. Within a year, Philip Larkin's *Oxford Book of Twentieth-Century English Verse* had found space to include more poems by Hardy than by any other single poet.

This familiar view of Hardy's bifurcated literary position, one foot lodged firmly in nineteenth-century fiction and the other planted just as securely in twentieth-century poetry, is a reading that many of the essays in this collection seek to qualify by bringing the fiction and the verse into more seamless relationship with each other. The essays gathered together here range confidently between the two, an ease of movement that testifies not only to the natural imaginative reciprocity between Hardy's work in prose and poetry, but also to the critical assurance that comes from the long immersion these scholars have all had in their subject: rarely if ever have quite so many distinguished

Hardyans been brought together between one set of book covers. While undermining the conventional genre-based way of viewing their subject, they also cumulatively foreground the complex array of paradoxes that Hardy's life and work suggest.

He was a writer whose sensibility and subject matter were shaped by intimate experience in formative years of south-west England's rural life, knowledge of whose rhythms and ways allowed him to create a whole imaginatively consistent world that restored to currency the evocative regional designation "Wessex." Along with Wordsworth, he is probably England's best-known "nature" writer, and even Wordsworth is not quite so inextricably associated with a particular area of rural England as Hardy, who by reimagining Wessex reinvented it. But he also relished his secure place in the socially and intellectually sophisticated world of contemporary London, translating his early reputation as a benign regional pastoralist into one as a dangerous, at times almost subversive, freethinker, so given to challenging social and religious orthodoxies as to become the kind of writer whose books a bishop might burn. A non-believer, confident only in the bleak faith that after a fifty-year search he would have discovered God had a God been there to discover, he remained throughout his life more responsive to the traditions, liturgy, tunes, buildings, and ingrained community rituals of the Anglican Church than is many a convinced Christian. An acute recorder of fleeting circumstantial minutiae – the fascinated muser on the mysteries embodied in the most ephemeral of earth's creatures – he also, perhaps more insistently than any other Victorian or modern writer, viewed the world and everything within it against the immensities of a daunting spatial and temporal infinitude. A consummate lyricist, and creator of one of the most poignantly personal elegiac sequences in the language, he believed his major poetic work to be an epic drama chronicling the public history of Napoleonic Europe across a whole decade, in this making a judgment with which many of his contemporaries agreed.

Even his supposed "pessimism," seized on by early commentators as manifesting an almost perverse desire to exact, in his own words, "a full look at the Worst," was conveyed in works that had, and still have, the capacity to generate in countless non-academic readers (and a good few academic ones) a surprisingly celebratory affirmation of the intensity of life's pleasures: love, community, music, dance, humor, and, perhaps above all, wonder in the face of nature's incandescent beauties and mysteries. Admittedly it sometimes seems like a predictable stock of Hardyan favorites that will be invoked in testimony to his capacity to capture and relish life's riches, enduring traditions, and whimsical humor: the Christmas dance at the tranter's from *Under the Greenwood Tree; Far From the Madding Crowd*'s sheep-shearing in the "Great Barn," a secular cathedral celebratory of community rituals that "had suffered no mutilation at the hands of time"; that breathless paean to erotic anticipation, "Lalage's Coming"; "The Ruined Maid," the respectable world's risqué nod to the enlightened self-interest of sexual opportunism; and supremely, "Great Things," whose last-stanza acknowledgment of the inevitable passing of fleshly pleasures – drink, dance, love – cannot undermine the intensity of their antecedent celebration. But for all the predictability of these favorite exhibits for the defense, those earlier commentators who saw Hardyesque pessimism as a determinative charge that required answering no longer seem even to begin to do justice to the rich complexity of Hardy's responses to human circumstance.

For perhaps the most significant paradoxes that Hardy's work embodies are those relating to what are unanswerable, finally moral, questions about humanity's place in the world. On the one hand, he was a thinker who found life to offer so few and limited consolations as recurrently to figure consciousness as an ironic burden without which humanity might well have been far better off. From this perspective, the post-Darwinian human lot seems sufficiently harrowing as to make Michael Henchard's desire to be wiped from human memory, or Tess's lament to "have my life unbe," or Little Father Time's horrific solution to economic deprivation and social exclusion appear as rational as they are tragic. But on the other hand, there is an equally enduring sense in Hardy's work that the world's only hope of ultimate betterment resides entirely in that same questionable gift of consciousness.

Too often mere lip service has been paid to this aspect of Hardy's thinking by reflex identification of the somewhat cold comfort to be found in the closing lines of *The Dynasts*, which offer the hope, expressed by the Chorus of the Pities, that consciousness may come to inform the Will "till It fashion all things fair." The comfort feels all the colder for Hardy's subsequent apparent retraction of this possibility in the claim that, had he written *The Dynasts* after the First World War, its last words, which proved nothing anyway, would not have gone to Pities. The speculative inclination that lay behind those words has been reduced to mere tokenism in much critical commentary, perhaps because that routinely invoked pessimism has in literary critics long since hardened into the cynicism for which contemporaries mistook it in Hardy. In differing ways many of the essays in this collection address important aspects of the meliorative impulse in Hardy's thinking. Behind, for example, George Levine's notion that "Hardy looks with Darwinian eyes and re-enchants" the world and Angelique Richardson's conclusion that "for Hardy, to be a good human at the end of the nineteenth century was to be close to, and acknowledge kinship with, animals" lies recognition of that affirmativeness to which so many Hardy enthusiasts instinctively respond. While he may have been unable to assert with the confidence of Browning's Fra Lippo Lippi that "This world's no blot . . . / Nor blank; it means intensely, and means good," he does recognize a vital role for humanity in finding a "way to the Better" that gives genuine philosophical purchase to that most quintessentially Hardyan of human virtues: loving-kindness.

These new essays by thirty of the world's foremost Hardy scholars engage with many of the contradictory but densely interfused aspects of Hardy's genius. They provide the fullest exploration of the immense variety and intellectual range of Hardy's work to be found within a single volume. I am very grateful to all those contributors who have helped bring it to completion. In addition, I would like to record special thanks, for a variety of scholarly kindnesses, to Pamela Dalziel, April London, Michael Millgate, and Mary Rimmer, and at Blackwell to Emma Bennett, Al Bertrand, Ally Dunnett, Hannah Morrell, and Janet Moth, whose copy-editing was exemplary.

PART I
The Life

1
Hardy as Biographical Subject

Michael Millgate

Thomas Hardy was, for the greater part of his life, an actively publishing author and a prominent public figure, frequently written about, interviewed, and photographed. By his final decades he had become one of the most famous men in the world, and his death in the early days of 1928 prompted widespread national and international mourning, culminating in the ceremonial interment of his ashes in Westminster Abbey. Because of Hardy's fame, the obituarists, reporters, and other commentators of the day had only to turn to the standard biographical sources – most notably the *Who's Who* entry that Hardy had himself written and kept up to date (*THPV* 142–3, 473–4) – in order to be able to produce confident if brief accounts of his personal history and literary career. A few poorly informed biographies had already appeared – Hardy having reacted to the best of them with angry comments in the margins of his own copy – but it was only after his death that knowledge about his life was immensely enhanced and expanded by his widow's publication of a full-scale two-volume biography, *The Early Life of Thomas Hardy 1840–1891* appearing before the end of 1928, *The Later Years of Thomas Hardy 1892–1928* just two years later. The *Life of Thomas Hardy* – so called long before its first single-volume publication in 1962 – immediately became the standard work of biographical reference and has inevitably remained the foundation document for all subsequent Hardy biography.

Inevitably, but by no means unproblematically. Although the two volumes of the *Life* were published over Florence Hardy's name and initially accepted as being of her own composition, it was always recognized that she must have depended largely upon Hardy's prior assistance, and following her own death in 1937 it became known that the work had been almost entirely ghost-written by Hardy himself in his late seventies with the specific intention of its being posthumously published over the name of his widow. Florence Hardy's actual role, though certainly important, was essentially secondary, Hardy having first written the manuscript pages in secret and then handed them successively to Florence to be typed up in triplicate – at which point the manuscript pages themselves would be destroyed in order to remove all traces of Hardy's participation. The typescripts then became the project's working papers, subject as such to Hardy's further and sometimes extensive revisions and, when necessary, to his wife's retyping. After Hardy's death it fell to Florence to write up the two final chapters, largely on the basis of notes that her husband had left, and then see through the press the two volumes bearing her name. Ironically enough, it was her failure to destroy the working typescripts, many of them containing corrections and revisions in Hardy's hand, that facilitated the subsequent discovery of the work's true authorship.

For Hardy himself, writing at the pinnacle of his fame and out of a profound opposition to all invasions of his own and his family's privacy, the composition of the *Life* had been a largely self-protective hence minimally revelatory exercise that drew with deliberate caution on personal memories and correspondence and on the rich store of anecdotes and observations contained within the numerous notebooks, small and large, that he had accumulated over the course of a lifetime. Written in the distancing third person, the work was clearly intended to find its place within the well-recognized tradition of family-generated memorializations as an "authorized" and as it were official biography, capable as such of anticipating and, ideally, pre-empting the production of more intrusive biographies written by outsiders. After Hardy's death, however, and before its first publication, the *Life*'s underlying autobiographical character was significantly compromised by the additions, deletions, and alterations introduced by Florence Hardy on the advice and under the influence of Sydney Cockerell and James Barrie, whose assistance she had sought and whose male assertiveness she found difficult to resist.

The term "autobiography" does, however, sit somewhat better – if still imperfectly – with the comprehensively re-edited one-volume edition of 1984 that restored Hardy's intended title, *The Life and Work of Thomas Hardy*, and sought to reconstruct his originally intended text on the basis of those working typescripts that his widow had so remarkably failed to destroy (*LW* x–xxix). As thus purged of post-Hardyan interventions, *Life and Work* can fairly claim autobiographical status as Hardy's own account of his own life – the personal information he felt able to share with his readership, the self-image (to put it another way) he wished to project. So considered, it certainly has value, especially since the dates and details supplied for public events customarily jibe with those ascertainable from contemporary sources – Hardy having evidently worked through his old notebooks in chronological sequence – and the references to friendships and social occasions mesh well enough with Hardy's own correspondence, both outgoing and incoming, and with the recollections of the journalists, admirers, friends, and fellow writers who encountered him in London clubs, on social occasions, or over tea at Max Gate. It also provides unique insights into Hardy's pre-adult and early adult years, although it necessarily defers to the endnotes the four expressive letters written from London to his sister Mary that were introduced into *The Early Life of Thomas Hardy* only after his death.

Biographers – and all students of Hardy – are clearly better off with *Life and Work* than without it, but they can only regret its failure, or refusal, to address a large number of central issues. Almost nothing of significance is said about Hardy's political and religious beliefs and values or about either of his marriages, and although his publicly acknowledged friendship with Florence Henniker is mentioned a few times, as is his elderly attraction to Agnes Grove, there are no references, direct or indirect, to his earlier relationships (such as they may have been) with Cassie Pole, Eliza Bright Nicholls, and Rosamund Tomson, while his cousin Tryphena Sparks, though briefly invoked, is not actually named. Events and quotations are sometimes inadequately described or dated, and while there's nothing in *Life and Work* even remotely comparable to Henry James's wholesale rewriting, in *Notes of a Son and Brother*, of those letters by his brother William that provided the book with its ostensible *raison d'être*, it's nevertheless clear that Hardy was from time to time perfectly willing to stretch the truth a little in order to enforce a point. Indeed, his snide assertion that Henry James had at first been excluded from the Rabelais Club because his writings lacked "virility" (*LW* 136) must have been made in despite of the knowledge that James had been, like himself, one of the club's original members.

Especially disturbing is Hardy's insistence upon the destruction of the materials used in the composition of *Life and Work*, including what must have been those extraordinarily interesting diary-notebooks, dating back at least to the early 1860s, of which only a few detached leaves containing penciled sketches or rough drafts of never-completed poems were allowed to survive. It is true that a good many individual entries from the diary-notebooks were copied by Hardy himself – with or without revision – into one or other of the "accumulative" notebooks (sometimes called commonplace books) that he continued to use during his highly creative final years. Hardy had also included these more substantial notebooks among the documents that were to be destroyed following his death, but while Sydney Cockerell, as one of his literary executors, was ready and even eager to comply with that directive, Florence Hardy, as the other literary executor, succeeded in preventing the destruction of at least some of them – notably "Literary Notes" I and II, "Memoranda" I and II, "Facts", and "Poetical Matter" – on the grounds that she would need them when writing the closing chapters of "her" biography. She may also have openly or clandestinely protected one or two other notebooks – including "Studies, Specimens, &c." – simply because she could not bear to see them consigned to the flames that had already consumed so much that had been deemed precious and vital during her husband's last years.

These surviving notebooks are of particular and almost unique importance as allowing direct and fully authenticated access to Hardy's thoughts and ideas – even (if to a much lesser degree) to his beliefs – and it is very helpful to the biographer to have them all accessible in satisfactory and sometimes excellent editions, specifically C. J. P. Beatty's edition (recently revised) of *The Architectural Notebook of Thomas Hardy*, Richard H. Taylor's edition of *The Personal Notebooks of Thomas Hardy* (including the two "Memoranda" notebooks, the brief "Schools of Painting" notebook, and the preparatory notebook for *The Trumpet-Major*), Lennart Björk's two-volume edition of *The Literary Notebooks of Thomas Hardy*, William Greenslade's edition of *Thomas Hardy's "Facts" Notebook*, and the editions of the "Studies, Specimens &c." and "Poetical Matter" notebooks co-edited by Pamela Dalziel and Michael Millgate. The Dorset

County Museum, where the originals of most of the notebooks are preserved, also has pages surviving from Hardy's early pocket-books, other scraps of paper containing notes and occasionally drawings of his plans for the building of Max Gate and – no less importantly – the largest and most significant accumulation of books from Hardy's dispersed library. Other substantial collections of books once owned (and often annotated) by Hardy exist on both sides of the Atlantic, information as to the inclusion and location of individual titles being readily accessible through the comprehensive online reconstruction of the Max Gate library available at http://www.library.utoronto.ca/fisher/hardy/.

Although the destruction of the materials drawn upon for *Life and Work* was in practice somewhat less than comprehensive, it was sufficient to reinforce both the indispensability of the work itself and its effectiveness as a barrier to further and deeper knowledge – resembling as such Hallam Tennyson's *Memoir* of his father, also based very largely upon unique documents that were themselves promptly and irretrievably destroyed. Whereas biographers of, say, Virginia Woolf or Robert Louis Stevenson have rich resources for the narration of their subject's early lives, both having been born into families already highly literate (Stevenson's mother even kept and preserved a diary of his babyhood), biographers of Hardy start out with little more than the early pages of the so largely uncheckable *Life and Work*, a tithe map for Higher Bockhampton, an 1853 auctioneers' catalogue for the Kingston Maurward estate, some miscellaneous family documents (including a copy of Hardy's father's will, a few calculations related to the family's building business, and the receipt for his own instruction in Latin), the official records of births, marriages, and deaths, and the successive national censuses – the first conveniently dating from 1841, a couple of months before Hardy's first birthday, and the fourth, in 1871, unkindly revealing his fiancée, Emma Lavinia Gifford, as having claimed to be four years younger than she actually was. Also regrettably sparse are the additional Hardy family memorabilia, preserved by the family's last representative, Hardy's sister Kate, and now part of the Lock Collection on deposit in the Dorset County Museum. Together with the same museum's holdings of the few books that Hardy owned as a child and a further group of family items, mostly of later date, that were originally collected by Hardy's cousin James Sparks and are now in the library at Eton College, these comprise very nearly the totality of what physically survives from Hardy's early background. Although genealogists – Brenda Tunks above all – have successfully traced both sides of his family back through several Dorset generations, almost nothing is known of them as individuals.

There is a significant if sometimes superficial enhancement of biographical resources as Hardy grows older, produces successful novels, attracts attention, becomes the subject of journalistic articles and interviews, makes famous friends, and writes personal and business letters that are kept by their recipients. Such letters are of particular importance as bearing demonstrably authentic witness to Hardy's thoughts, feelings, and relationships throughout his adult life, and they are copiously available in *The Collected Letters of Thomas Hardy*, published in seven volumes with a supplementary eighth volume currently in progress. Sadly, this plenitude, though biographically crucial, sometimes yields less than might have been hoped: no more than fourteen Hardy letters dating from before his thirtieth birthday are currently known to exist – one of the most important of them, to his sister Mary, having been reproduced in facsimile in *The Early Life of Thomas Hardy* – and there are few enough from any period of his life that could be described as genuinely intimate or self-revelatory. Hardy's transcriptions of two fragments from letters received from Emma Gifford are all that remains of the active correspondence they evidently maintained during their long and mostly long-distance courtship – Emma having apparently burned both sets of letters one angry afternoon well into their marriage. Florence for her part seems to have burned, if in a somewhat different spirit, the bulk of the exceptionally relaxed and interesting letters that Hardy was writing to her during the later stages of their pre-marital friendship, and although the collected edition includes all that survive of Hardy's sometimes painful letters to Florence Henniker it's possible to suspect that others may have been thrust into the fire by Mrs. Henniker at the time of their arrival – or even by Hardy himself in 1923 after they had been sent to Max Gate under the terms of Mrs. Henniker's will.

Hardy in his late seventies certainly disposed of many of the incoming letters he had thus far preserved, with the result that few items of substantial biographical importance are to be found among the 5,000 or so letters written to Hardy that are now in the Dorset County Museum (see Weber and Weber 1968). Appearing on a good many of those letters, however, are draft replies in Hardy's hand – subsequently to be typed and sent by Florence or by May O'Rourke, the part-time typist sometimes employed at Max Gate – and the correspondence as a whole usefully supplements the *Collected Letters* in documenting his dealings with publishers and witnessing to the character and importance of some of his personal friendships. Beyond Hardy's power to control or destroy – presumably beyond his knowledge – were the thoroughly indiscreet letters written by Emma Hardy (especially to Rebekah Owen) and, later, by Florence Hardy (especially to Edward Clodd and Sydney Cockerell). Extensively – though by no means exhaustively – represented in *Letters of Emma and Florence Hardy*, these are useful documents for understanding life at Max Gate, the many hours that Hardy spent working alone in his study having supplied his wives with both motive and opportunity for the writing of long letters of domestic complaint. Such missives were often regretted afterwards – "I *hope* you burn my letters," Florence wrote rather unhopefully to Rebekah Owen, "Some are, I fear, most horribly indiscreet" (Millgate 1996: 114) – but likely to be followed by others equally indiscreet. The secret diaries to which Emma confided her resentments against her husband are now beyond reach, having been discovered and destroyed by Hardy following her death, but her autobiographical *Some Recollections*, including an account of her first meeting with her future husband, has been published (subsequently to Hardy's having adapted a portion of it for inclusion in *Life and Work*) and her capacity for outspokenness is reflected in the extraordinary letter in which she accused Hardy's sister Mary of being "a witch-like creature & quite equal to any amount of evil-wishing & speaking – I can imagine you, & your mother & sister on your native heath raising a storm on a Walpurgis night" (Millgate 1996: 8).

The diaries kept by Emma during some of the Hardys' European holidays, including the honeymoon in France in 1874, are among the important papers of hers, apparently overlooked by both Hardy and Florence, that Florence's executor, Irene Cooper Willis, discovered in an old ottoman in the Max Gate attic Emma had formerly occupied. Subsequently deposited in the Dorset County Museum and now published in facsimile (Taylor 1985), the diaries are fascinating both as reflective of Emma's personality and as constituting the nearest thing we have to a first-hand account not just of the travels themselves but of the ways in which she and Hardy related to each other on a day-to-day basis. It is not known just what diaries Florence Hardy may have kept during her marriage, nor whether those diaries at all extensively survive (Irene Cooper Willis had several at one time and an actual example, apparently devoted largely to household matters, was featured in a BBC *Antiques Roadshow* television program a few years back), but during her widowhood she certainly talked about Hardy to a number of deeply interested visitors – including Frederick Baldwin Adams, Jr., the American Hardy collector, and Richard Little Purdy, Hardy's scholarly bibliographer. Purdy in particular, working extensively on Hardy's papers while they were still in place in the Max Gate study, became over time very friendly with Florence and made a private record (now in the Beinecke Library) of some of their conversations. Florence's observations on these occasions, especially as reflected in the more discursive segments of Purdy's bibliography, have had a significant influence upon Hardy biography as upon other aspects of Hardy studies, and it's necessary to keep in mind that she could on occasion have misconstrued or misremembered what Hardy said and that her remarks must in any case have been colored by her own emotions and biases, even by a concern for her own place in literary history.

It was during the course of Hardy's career as a novelist that the literary interview became a prominent journalistic genre, and Hardy himself became a frequent target for its practitioners. Some of them did capture something of Hardy's manner and record occasional passages of interest, but the vulnerability of interviews to manipulation and consequent misrepresentation always renders them somewhat suspect as source materials: in Hardy's day, for instance, an interviewer who did not have shorthand would have had to depend upon a doubtful combination of notes, memory, and imagination. William Archer's interview for the *Pall Mall Magazine* of April 1901 (Ray 2007: 28–37) is certainly important, Hardy having had the opportunity to correct or revise the record before publication, but because gossip about books was the staple of numerous newspaper columns and cheap magazines in the late Victorian and early Edwardian years it became common enough for interviews to be plagiarized, repackaged, or invented outright. Stuck as cuttings into one of Hardy's scrapbooks in the Dorset County Museum are the published texts of several interviews that he has annotated as having been either partly or wholly faked. Printed along with some of the interviews – and often included among the illustrations to the growing number of books about "Hardy's Wessex" – were sketches and photographs of Hardy himself, interesting in themselves and as forerunners of the many images of him that eventually came into existence.

Hardy seems essentially to have stopped granting interviews round about 1912, and although he always remained quite visible as a public figure – attending productions of plays made from his novels, accepting public honors, welcoming at Max Gate visitors as various as Lawrence of Arabia, Leonard and Virginia Woolf, and the Prince of Wales – he seems neither to have been filmed nor had his voice recorded. But when he died early in 1928 he was of course outlived by many people who had known him to different degrees and in different roles, and witnesses both reliable and unreliable were from time to time prevailed upon, or came eagerly forward, to share their Hardyan memories. Hardy's younger sister Kate, whose surviving diary for the years 1915–39 is itself of occasional interest, was interviewed on at least two occasions, by Donald Winslow (Winslow 1970) and by another well-informed American scholar, Harold Hoffman (Rabiger 1981: 46–8), who in 1939–40 did remarkable research in England for a biography of Hardy he did not live to complete. Hoffman's surviving papers (at Miami University, Ohio) remain largely disorganized and unworked as a result of his early death, but – as is clear from the detailed account given by their discoverer, Michael Rabiger (Rabiger 1981: 6–39) – they are of considerable interest because of the witnesses then alive with whom he spoke or corresponded. Even in the 1960s and early 1970s the bookseller and publisher James Stevens Cox was able to conduct and publish quite an extensive series of interviews with people still living who had encountered Hardy in some way – as friends, servants, tradespeople, actors in stage versions of the novels, and so forth – and while the questions were often loaded, the answers concocted out of the faintest of memories, the sheer unrepeatability of the series guarantees its remaining of permanent value.

The recorded impressions of those who encountered Hardy on a more equal footing, as fellow writers, or as friends of long standing, are in general disappointing, perhaps in part because he rarely risked intimacy and tended to become genuinely close to, hence perceptively readable by, only those friends, whether male or female, whom he thought capable of respecting and reciprocating his own intense instinct and need for privacy. In the 1950s, however, the poet Henry Reed, himself a devoted Hardyan and the author of an acerbic Hardy-related radio play about biographical research called *A Very Great Man Indeed*, put together an excellent radio program (BBC Archives) in which Dorothy Allhusen, Middleton Murry, Walter de la Mare, Lady Cynthia Asquith, and others spoke interestingly and at some length about the Hardy they had known. Other rewarding reminiscences are conveniently gathered into *Thomas Hardy Remembered*, edited by Martin Ray, and it is striking that several of those who wrote most memorably about Hardy – for example, Edmund Blunden, Elliott Felkin, Siegfried Sassoon, and especially Virginia Woolf – did so as relatively youthful figures encountering an ancient and hugely famous sage whose character and manners had long become settled and established and who had accumulated much experience of dealing graciously with visiting admirers, especially during the tea-parties for friends and pilgrims that became during the 1920s almost daily features of the Max Gate summers.

Max Gate itself (now a National Trust property) was of course designed by Hardy and built under his supervision, and although many have found the house difficult to admire it makes better sense from the inside than from the outside and perhaps needs to be "read" like one of the more idiosyncratic of the Hardyan texts. Hardy's drawings for the house, like his other architectural drawings, testify to the persistence of his interest in his first career – later still, in 1893–4, he was the architect, his brother the contractor, in the restoration of the little Dorset church of West Knighton (Beatty 2007: 41–5) – and it is impossible to ignore the importance, at once direct and symbolic, either of Max Gate or of the nearby National Trust property known as the "Birthplace," the Hardy family cottage in Higher Bockhampton in which Hardy was born. Scarcely less significant are Stinsford church and churchyard, where Hardy's heart now lies, and those Dorset villages (e.g., Puddletown and Melbury Osmund) associated with family ancestors and relatives. Appreciation of Hardy's distinctiveness as a specifically regional writer, often using identifiable settings for his novels, stories, and poems, similarly mandates a degree of familiarity with that wider area of southern England, centered upon Dorset and still largely rural, to which he gave the name of Wessex. Dorchester in particular, the county town, where Hardy received his schooling and his earliest architectural training, remained a central point throughout his life and became the model for the Casterbridge of *The Mayor of Casterbridge*. Also located within Dorset are two homes from the early years of Hardy's first marriage: "Riverside," Sturminster Newton, the beautifully situated house in which he and Emma spent what Hardy – in a rare confidential moment – called their "happiest time" (*LW* 122), and "Lanherne" in Wimborne, perhaps the most attractive of the houses in which the couple lived, even though they didn't take to Wimborne itself.

The most zealous of biographers might well draw the line at checking out all the London addresses at which Hardy stayed at different periods of his life. The house in Surbiton in which he and Emma lived when first married is no longer standing, but 16 Westbourne Park Villas, in which he lived so intensely as a young architect and earnestly self-educating poet, is readily identifiable – it can even be glimpsed from the train at a point just short of the Paddington terminus – as is the house in Tooting (marked with an official plaque) in which Hardy endured a long period of illness. Especially suggestive from a biographical point of view are the church and rectory at St. Juliot in Cornwall, where Emma Gifford created for Hardy when they first met a magic that he would re-create in poems written after her death. The church itself and nearby Boscastle remain fully responsive to whoever comes with the poems and their occasion already in mind, and it is an illuminating experience to stay in the rectory, as one now very comfortably can (it currently offers accommodation to paying guests), and realize the closeness of the bedrooms in which Hardy and Emma must respectively have slept.

There are of course other sources that biographers might conceivably draw upon, but none of them seem sufficient to substitute or even greatly compensate for the evasions and blanknesses of *Life and Work* and the limitations of so many of the other potential source-materials. It can be reasonably said that, just as Tennyson biographers have learned to accommodate themselves to the problems presented by Hallam Tennyson's memoir, so Hardy biographers must find – without desperate recourse to outright speculation – a way or ways around *Life and Work*. But it is one thing to question the available evidence or even the accepted interpretive wisdom, quite another to arrive at demonstrably satisfactory answers. *Life and Work*'s highly positive presentation of the childhood years, for example, has often prompted the suspicion – sharpened by knowledge of how the book was written – that Hardy may have deliberately exaggerated his family's social and economic status. As already noted, the sources for an exploration of such issues are few and largely indirect, and while the fragments of available evidence tend to indicate that the Hardy family may indeed have had marginal claims to social superiority over most of its neighbors, there is little in those same fragments to justify the romantic aura thrown over the entire place and period by emotional retrospections rooted in Hardy's domestic loyalties and inflected by his familiarity with Theocritus and with Dryden's translations of Virgil. That aura has for modern readers been effectively validated and even exaggerated by the association of Higher Bockhampton with the irresistible appeal of *Under the Greenwood Tree* and the much-exploited photogenic charm of the Hardy cottage itself, and yet it is clear from early notes of Hardy's (Millgate 2004: 37–8) that he vividly remembered the drunkenness and sexual license that had characterized the life of the hamlet during his childhood years and was keenly aware of the harsh living and working conditions endured by most of its inhabitants.

In a similarly problematic category, therefore, are the other references to those Bockhampton days that Hardy incorporated into his own writings, some entirely specific and incontestable, as in such poems as "Domicilium," "Friends Beyond," "A Bird-scene at a Rural Dwelling," and "Childhood Among the Ferns," others that may seem to the biographer equally authentic yet remain utterly incapable of proof. The domestic exchanges, for example, between Mr. and Mrs. Dewy in *Under the Greenwood Tree* are remarkably similar to those between Mr. and Mrs. Smith in *A Pair of Blue Eyes*, and seem in both instances very likely to have been closely – and affectionately – based upon Hardy's memories of the ways in which his own parents characteristically interacted. Also suggestively present in the early writings are youngish male characters with surnames – Strong, Mayne, Oak – that seem echoes of Hardy's own, if less clearly so than Emma Hardy's choice of During as the surname of the distinctly undashing hero of her story "The Maid on the Shore." A more fundamental biographical challenge, however, is presented by Hardy's having so clearly made emotional, socially conscious, and essentially autobiographical investments in such novels as *The Return of the Native*, *Tess of the d'Urbervilles*, and *Jude the Obscure*.

Although it may be straightforward enough to acknowledge, say, the connection of *Tess* to issues of women's rights, or of *Jude* to issues of educational reform, it is altogether more difficult even to begin to take the measure of the personal anger and pain underlying Hardy's fictional explorations of such issues. Because his first novel, *The Poor Man and the Lady*, was never published, the class-based hostility that led to its rejection has remained invisible, hence largely disregarded. But while Hardy, as a professional novelist, may well have learned from that experience to temper his texts to his desired audience, it is less clear that he significantly modified a fundamental radicalism that may have derived in part from exposure to the comprehensive social anger of his shoemaker uncle John Antell but was also fed by a personal sense of class inferiority and educational deprivation – above all, his not going to university – that even his untold youthful hours of laborious private study could never make good in respect of personal status or even of social and intellectual self-confidence. Here again, however, it is precisely the lack of clarity, of specifically documentable evidence, that so complicates and even obfuscates the task of responsible biography. The many articles, speeches, letters to newspapers, etc. reproduced in *Thomas Hardy's Public Voice* sufficiently testify to Hardy's having spoken out in his own person on such issues as censorship, cruelty to animals, and the hypocrisy of the marriage laws, but for some indication of the full scope of his continuing radicalism it becomes necessary to turn to the private letter to Millicent Garrett Fawcett, dated November 30, 1906, in which he described his support of the women's suffrage movement as grounded in the belief that

> the tendency of the woman's vote will be to break up the present pernicious conventions in respect of manners, customs, religion, illegitimacy, the stereotyped household (that it must be the unit of society), the father of a woman's child (that it is anybody's business but the woman's own, except in cases of disease or insanity), sport (that so-called educated men should be encouraged to harass & kill for pleasure feeble creatures by mean stratagems), slaughter-houses (that they should be dark dens of cruelty), & other matters which I got into hot water for touching on many years ago. (*CL* III: 238)

The conclusion of Hardy's sentence, though lightly phrased, is clearly indicative of a continuing sensitivity and even anger in respect of the brutal criticism that had been directed at some of the novels, notably *Jude*, in which his emotional investment had been particularly strong. As such, it could be taken as lending a general – though not necessarily a particular – plausibility to recent critical studies of Hardy that have tended to emphasize perceived elements of personal subversiveness in his works. On the other hand, it's impossible to calculate – perhaps even to overestimate – the importance that Hardy always placed upon the maintenance of his personal privacy. The publication of reissues and new editions of the novels throughout Hardy's last decades offered successive opportunities both for textual revision and for the alteration, addition, or replacement of authorial prefaces, but while he occasionally took advantage of such occasions to stress the socio-political implications of a particular work, it was only in rare instances (such as *Under the Greenwood Tree*) that he touched upon the possibility of the fiction's being in any sense reflective of his own or his family's experience. His concern with privacy, at once instinctive, reinforced by experience, and shrewdly politic, became over the years increasingly intense, leading almost ineluctably to the destruction in old age of working notebooks, incoming correspondence, corrected proofs, and other personal records, the writing of a distinctly disastrous will (see Millgate 1992: 153–61), and the ghosting of a deceptively bland biography that sought to combine decorously positive self-projection with effective deterrence of alternative biographical intrusions from elsewhere.

It is of course true that the assiduously accumulated knowledge of a biographer can never account for more than a fraction of the life actually lived and never be entirely secure. No sources are entirely unproblematic, and sources of any kind may remain comprehensively deficient for those periods or aspects of a life – childhood, for example, or sexual relationships – that are commonly considered to be of particular significance. There are always gaps and puzzles and thickets to be negotiated, decisions taken as to the riskworthiness of sense-making but unproven speculations, and difficult choices to be made, some complex, others as basic as deciding – as seems crucially to have occurred with certain biographies of Emma, Florence, and even Hardy himself – whether the subject should be positively or negatively characterized and represented. All biographies, clearly, are to a greater or lesser degree shaped by their authors' personalities, life-experiences, and acknowledged or unacknowledged biases. But a biographer's degree of knowledge and depth of first-hand research is of even greater importance, given that knowledge of the biographical subject – especially of one deceased as recently as Hardy – is always likely to expand and render obsolete the speculations with which earlier biographers had sought to create narrative coherence.

Reviewers sometimes speak of biographer and subject as either sympathetically or antipathetically – and in any case ineluctably – intertwined. Leon Edel, the biographer of Henry James, used to speak of his life *with* Henry James, of their living together over many years much as Boswell lived with Dr. Johnson. But it seems questionable whether the relationship between dead subject and living biographer can usefully be figured in such comfortably domestic terms, especially since the sense of *not* being on entirely familiar terms with the subject would seem more likely to keep the biographer more persistently and productively alert. The biographical process might perhaps be more appropriately compared to the experience of reading a Jamesian or, better, a Faulknerian novel and of arriving through gradual and often hard-won increments of knowledge, perception, and sympathy at a progressively richer apprehension of significant moments from a past that can never be known except in fragments and never understood except in broad outline. When writing about Hardy and other creative figures there is of course the further difficulty – the ultimate frustration – that the most important events in their lives, their acts of creativity, are precisely those most resistant to biographical explication. Whatever fresh information about Hardy's life may be gained in the future, biographical understanding of the man himself may never get much beyond what Edmund Gosse, the oldest and closest of his literary friends, concluded after visiting Max Gate in 1912: "He remains what he has always been, a sphinx-like little man, unrelated, unrevealed, displaying nothing that the most affectionate solicitude can make use of to explain the mystery of his magnificent genius" (Gosse 1991: 106).

References and Further Reading

Beatty, C. J. P. (2004). *The Part Played by Architecture in the Life and Work of Thomas Hardy*. Dorset: Plush Publishing.

Beatty, C. J. P. (ed.) (2007). *The Architectural Notebook of Thomas Hardy*, rev. edn. Dorchester: Dorset Natural History and Archaeological Society.

Björk, Lennart A. (ed.) (1985). *The Literary Notebooks of Thomas Hardy*, 2 vols. London and Basingstoke: Macmillan.

Cox, J. Stevens (ed.) (1968). *Thomas Hardy: Materials for a Study of His Life, Times and Works*. St. Peter Port, Guernsey: Toucan Press.

Cox, J. Stevens (ed.) (1971). *Thomas Hardy: More Materials for a Study of his Life, Times and Works*. St. Peter Port, Guernsey: Toucan Press.

Dalziel, Pamela, and Michael Millgate (eds.) (1994). *Thomas Hardy's "Studies, Specimens &c." Notebook*. Oxford: Clarendon Press.

Dalziel, Pamela, and Michael Millgate (eds.) (2009). *Thomas Hardy's "Poetical Matter" Notebook*. Oxford: Oxford University Press.

Gatrell, Simon (1988). *Hardy the Creator: A Textual Biography*. Oxford: Clarendon Press.

Gittings, Robert (1975). *Young Thomas Hardy*. London: Heinemann.

Gittings, Robert (1978). *The Older Hardy*. London: Heinemann.

Gosse, Edmund (1991). *Portraits from Life*, ed. Ann Thwaite. Aldershot: Scolar Press.

Greenslade, William (ed.) (2004). *Thomas Hardy's "Facts" Notebook: A Critical Edition*. Aldershot: Ashgate.

Hardy, Emma (1961). *Some Recollections*, ed. Evelyn Hardy and Robert Gittings. London: Oxford University Press; rev. edn., 1979.

Hardy, Florence Emily (1928). *The Early Life of Thomas Hardy 1840–1891*. London: Macmillan.

Hardy, Florence Emily (1930). *The Later Years of Thomas Hardy 1892–1928*. London: Macmillan.

Hardy, Thomas (1984). *The Life and Work of Thomas Hardy*, ed. Michael Millgate. London: Macmillan.

Millgate, Michael (1971). *Thomas Hardy: His Career as a Novelist*. London: Bodley Head; reissued Basingstoke: Macmillan, 1994.

Millgate, Michael (1992). *Testamentary Acts: Browning, Tennyson, James, Hardy*. Oxford: Clarendon Press.

Millgate, Michael (ed.) (1996). *Letters of Emma and Florence Hardy*. Oxford: Clarendon Press.

Millgate, Michael (1999). Thomas Hardy: The Biographical Sources. In Dale Kramer (ed.), *The Cambridge Companion to Thomas Hardy* (pp. 1–18). Cambridge: Cambridge University Press.

Millgate, Michael (ed.) (2001). *Thomas Hardy's Public Voice: The Essays, Speeches, and Miscellaneous Prose*. Oxford: Clarendon Press.

Millgate, Michael (2004). *Thomas Hardy: A Biography Revisited*. Oxford: Oxford University Press.

Purdy, Richard Little (1954). *Thomas Hardy: A Bibliographical Study*. Oxford: Clarendon Press. Reissued, with supplementary material, Delaware: Oak Knoll Press; London: British Library, 2002.

Purdy, Richard Little, and Michael Millgate (eds.) (1978–88). *The Collected Letters of Thomas Hardy*, 7 vols. Oxford: Clarendon Press.

Rabiger, Michael (1981). The Hoffman Papers: An Assessment and Some Interpretations. *The Thomas Hardy Year Book*, 10, 6–50.

Ray, Martin (ed.) (2007). *Thomas Hardy Remembered*. Aldershot: Ashgate.

Taylor, Richard H. (ed.) (1978). *The Personal Notebooks of Thomas Hardy*. London and Basingstoke: Macmillan.

Taylor, Richard H. (ed.) (1985). *Emma Hardy Diaries*. Manchester: Mid Northumberland Arts Group and Carcanet New Press.

Tunks, Brenda (1990). *Whatever Happened to the Other Hardys?* Poole: Brenda Tunks.

Weber, Carl J., and Clara Carter Weber (1968). *Thomas Hardy's Correspondence at Max Gate: A Descriptive Check List*. Waterville, Maine: Colby College Press.

Wilson, Keith (1995). *Thomas Hardy on Stage*. Basingstoke: Macmillan.

Winslow, Donald J. (1970). A Call on Thomas Hardy's Sister. *The Thomas Hardy Year Book*, 1, 93–7.

PART II
The Intellectual Context

2
Hardy and Philosophy

Phillip Mallett

In his essay on "The Profitable Reading of Fiction," published in 1888, Hardy distinguished between imaginative "representations of life," which are capable of "self-proof" – that is, the reader is immediately convinced of their justice – and "views *about* life," which are open to debate. A representation, he argued, "is less susceptible of error than a disquisition; the teaching, depending as it does upon intuitive conviction, and not upon logical reasoning, is not likely to lend itself to sophistry" (*THPV* 78). In the same vein, the General Preface to the Wessex Edition of 1912 contrasts "imaginative writings," expressing the "mere impressions of the moment," and the pursuit of "a coherent scientific theory of the universe" – even supposing such a theory to be possible. A passage in the *Life and Work*, written in 1920, insists that "I have no philosophy – merely what I have often explained to be only a confused heap of impressions, like those of a bewildered child at a conjuring show" (*LW* 441). The Introductory Note to *Winter Words*, Hardy's "last appearance on the literary stage," repeats that "no harmonious philosophy is attempted in these pages – or in any bygone pages of mine, for that matter" (*CPV* 834).

Such comments might seem to preclude a discussion of "Hardy and Philosophy," or at least limit it to a series of glosses on his self-characterization in the poem "Nature's Questioning": "No answerer I . . . " (*CPV* 67). Michael Millgate suggests that Hardy's mind was "not naturally equipped to move easily in realms of philosophical discourse" (Millgate 1971: 176). Perhaps not: few minds are. But throughout his life Hardy read widely if unsystematically in philosophy, and that reading informed the "representations of life" in the novels. The first entry in his *Literary Notebooks*, dated 1863, derives from an analysis of the human passions by the French utopian socialist Charles Fourier (*LN* I: 3–4). Here, amidst much that was fantastic, including the speculation that the sea might yield lemonade, Hardy might have found two key claims he was to explore in the fiction: that feeling rather than reason governs human life, and that the existing order of society failed to satisfy human passions. More than sixty years later, the final entries in the *Notebooks* return to another concern of the novels, the relation of free will and determinism, taken this time from an article on "The Possibility of Man's Freedom" in the *Journal of Philosophical Studies* in 1927 (*LN* II: 249). In 1876, before embarking on *The Return of the Native*, his first self-consciously tragic novel, Hardy allowed himself a sabbatical year, during which he read and made notes on Plato's *Dialogues*, seemingly as part of a wider investigation of Hellenism, and on Auguste Comte's *Social Dynamics*. A series of entries made in 1901, while he was preparing for *The Dynasts*, is headed "Notes in Philosophy," and cites Spinoza, W. K. Clifford and Eduard von Hartmann. In 1906 he found support for his long-held belief that "If God is omnipotent, it is impossible that he can be good" in the work of the Cambridge Hegelian John McTaggart (*LN* II: 206), and the two became friends. In addition, he read and corresponded with contemporaries such as Leslie Stephen, John Morley, and Frederic Harrison, whose work addressed in a non-technical manner those questions about "the origin of things, the constitution of matter, the unreality of time," which he and Stephen discussed together in 1875, and to which, despite his disclaimers, Hardy was to return in both novels and verse (*LW* 109).

Hardy's early reading, even after he had given up his dreams of university life, was largely shaped by Horace Moule, and it was at Moule's suggestion that he read John Henry Newman's *Apologia Pro Vita Sua*. He found Newman's logic "really human," based as it was on "converging probabilities" instead of syllogisms, but this was only to say that it was essentially not logic at all: "there is no first link to his excellent chain of reasoning, and down you come headlong" (*LW* 50–1). He was more taken with another of Moule's recommendations, Comte's *A General View of Positivism*, which he studied closely in 1865. The excesses of Comte's later work have caused him to be more often derided than read – Huxley described it as a "mixture of bad science with eviscerated papistry" (Huxley 1893–4 V: 255) – but a writer admired by both George Eliot and John Stuart Mill, whatever their eventual reservations, must command some attention (Wright 1986). Certainly Hardy engaged closely with his ideas. When he told Agnes Grove in 1903 that "I am not a Positivist" he added that "no person of serious thought in these times could be said to stand aloof from Positivist teaching & ideals" (*CL* III: 53). He acknowledged the influence of Comte's writing on *Far from the Madding Crowd*, took extensive notes on his *Social Dynamics*, attended Positivist lectures at Newton Hall, and kept up a long friendship with Frederic Harrison, Comte's leading British advocate; Harrison welcomed *Tess* as "a Positivist allegory or sermon" (Harrison 1891), while Hardy wrote to him that the first volume of *The Dynasts* presented a "Positive view of the Universe" (*CL* III: 98).

What comprises such a view, according to Comte, begins with his Law of the Three Stages in the evolution of human understanding. In the Theological stage, natural phenomena and events are ascribed to the will of a supernatural being, and the political order to divine governance. In the Metaphysical stage, supernatural accounts give way to the notion of abstract "virtues" or "powers" supposed to inhere in the physical world, "God" dissolves into "Nature," and political authority is referred to theories of rights, popular sovereignty, and the social contract. In the Positive stage, the notion of a supra-human deity is rejected as untenable, questions of first and final causes are dismissed as fruitless, and speculation about things-in-themselves is superseded by inquiry into the regularities governing the relation of phenomena to each other. The natural sciences had already arrived at this stage; it was Comte's task to show that sociology – a term he was the first to use – should be studied in the same way as physics or biology. The key to Comte's thought at this point (and a main reason why he and Mill parted company) is that society transcends the individual; any claim to stand outside society is self-defeating, since the language in which it is couched is already a social form. Individuals within society are like cells within the human body, in that as each dies it is replaced by another, without detriment to the whole. Hence all human beings, past and present, can be seen as "Humanity," or the "Great Being," and in the absence of a deity can be regarded as a proper object of reverence. The rejection of the Christian doctrine of our fallen nature, allied to a Lamarckian theory of evolution, allows Comte to argue that "the gradual development of humanity must bring about the preponderance of the noble inclinations" (Andreski 1974: 169), and moral progress come slowly but necessarily into line with the advances already made in scientific understanding. The pace and dynamics of this development could be affected by human intervention, but its direction and outcome were inevitable: as one of the passages Hardy copied has it, "The empire of the past is one which the present can modify but can never escape" (*LN* I:73; Hardy's underlining).

There is much here with which Hardy could have agreed. One of the notes he made from Comte in 1876 asserts that the concept of a single God is a "self-contradiction" in a radically imperfect world, and this view is repeated throughout his work (*LN* I: 69). In 1902 he wrote to Edward Clodd, whose own intellectual journey had taken him through three stages, from Christian belief to agnosticism and thence to militant rationalism:

> If the doctrines of the supernatural were quietly abandoned to-morrow by the Church, & "reverence & love for an ethical ideal" alone retained, not one in ten thousand would object to the readjustment, while the enormous bulk of thinkers excluded by the old teaching would be brought into the fold, & our venerable old churches & cathedrals would become the centres of emotional life that they once were. (*CL* III: 5)

It is not only the rejection of the supernatural here that chimes with key tenets of Comtean thought. The suggestion that even when dogmatic theology was set aside there would remain a need for "centres of emotional life," of the kind once provided by the Church, echoes Comte's argument that since human nature was essentially unchangeable it would continue to seek some form of religious expression; in different inflections, this thought underlies both the description of the Great Barn in *Far from the Madding Crowd* (*FFMC* 150–1), and Sue's claim in *Jude* that the railway station is more representative of modern life than the cathedral (*JO* 139). The hope that "'reverence and love for an ethical ideal'" could substitute for older forms of worship has a near-affinity with Comte's "religion of humanity": near rather than complete, since the quoted words are from Huxley's essay on "Agnosticism," and Huxley was too gloomy about humanity to make it an object of worship (Huxley 1893–4 V: 249). The change from an old form of religion, based on dogma and the supernatural, to a new one celebrating the "nobler feelings towards humanity and emotional goodness and greatness" (*LW* 358), is seen in Comtean terms as a "readjustment": that is, the bringing into harmony of two areas of human thought, metaphysics and morality, which had developed and must develop along similar paths, but had done so at different speeds. Angel Clare reaches the same conclusion in Brazil, when having previously "discredited the old systems of mysticism" he now begins to question "the old appraisements of morality": "He thought they wanted readjusting" (*TD* 328). To Comte, sure that he had glimpsed the future, such an adjustment seemed easy; Hardy, intent on the actual, explores the pain and isolation it entails in the stories of Clym, Angel, Sue, and Jude.

Comte's hostility to Christian doctrines of salvation, which in his view encouraged individuals to become "absorbed in celestial objects" at the expense of "sympathy for others," was qualified by his regard for its teaching on altruism (*LN* I: 70). In a Positivist society, this teaching would devolve upon a strengthened family unit, which by fostering love of parents, siblings, and children would both bind together the past, present, and future, and reach out to the wider human race. Over time, altruistic feeling would become an organic improvement, transmissible to future generations. In the same Lamarckian vein, Angel Clare expects that "improved systems of moral and intellectual training" will gradually "elevate the involuntary, and even the unconscious, *instincts* of human nature" (*TD* 167; italics added). Despite his misgivings about Comte, John Stuart Mill was similarly persuaded that it was possible for education to extirpate bad instincts, "or rather (what can be done even to an instinct) to starve by disuse" (Mill [1874] 1904: 29).

Here too Hardy was less confident. Even when they are most eagerly embraced, family ties in his fiction are more often fraught than enabling. Warned by Arabella of the imminent arrival of Father Time, Jude takes Comte's arguments to their next logical level by dismissing "the beggarly question of parentage," along with patriotism, class-feeling, and Christian "save-your-own-soulism," as merely "a mean exclusiveness at bottom": "'All the little ones of our time are collectively the children of us adults of the time, and entitled to our general care'" (*JO* 288). The "ennobling and unselfish" interest he and Sue feel in caring for the child is similarly Comtean in spirit, as is Jude's effort "to link his present with his past" by inviting Widow Edlin to the planned wedding (*JO* 303, 295). But the past Mrs. Edlin brings with her is the tale of his and Sue's hanged and gibbeted ancestor, a child who died, and a mother who went mad, which projects into the future as a disabling vision of "weltering humanity," unhappy with itself and grown "afraid to reproduce" (*JO* 301). In extending the reach of human sympathy to the whole of society, Hardy recognized, altruism also opened new possibilities for human suffering. More than that, by revealing that "all organic creatures are of one family," the theory of evolution had "shifted the centre of altruism from humanity to the whole conscious world" (*LW* 373). Jude and Sue feel pain on behalf of rooks, earthworms, pigs, rabbits, and pigeons, even lopped trees, as well as for humankind. Hardy was too tough-minded ever to wholly abandon his belief in "the gradual ennoblement of man," but he could not help fearing that the human race was already "too extremely developed," its nerves too highly evolved, to endure not just its own existence, but the suffering of others in an imperfect world (*LW* 398, 227).

Hardy's response to Comte, as every other area of his intellectual life, was bound up with his interest in evolutionary ideas (Beer 1983: 220–41). He described himself as "one of the earliest acclaimers" of Darwin's *Origin of Species* – though precisely how he acclaimed it, as an architectural pupil barely 19 years of age, is left unclear – and notes taken from such different sources as Symonds' *Studies of the Greek Poets*, Leslie Stephen on Mill, and Conrad Guenther on Darwinism show that he was quick to understand that post-Darwinian thinking challenged the assumption that "Man's Place in Nature" was one of priority:

Man – The very ground-thought of Science is to treat man as part of the natural order[.] (*LN* I: 65)

History depends upon the relation between the organism & the environment. (*LN* I: 132)

In the eyes of science man is not "higher" than the other animals. (*LN* II: 225)

These and similar notes reveal Hardy's continuing interest in the affective psychology he had found in Fourier. One of the entries from Comte reads: "Feeling – the great motor force of human life" (*LN* I: 68). This force takes its origin in the body (another note from Comte remarks the dependence of the "cerebral functions" on the "nutritive economy"), and in the interaction of the body and the ambient world: "Man is entirely subordinate to the World – each living being to its own environment" (*LN* I: 74).

Comte was so persuaded of the physical basis of our affective life that he saw no need for a science of psychology, since physiological explanation would suffice: to which Mill objected, fairly enough, that if the study of psychological phenomena was disallowed, it was unclear just what physiology would be asked to explain. Hardy does not declare himself on the issue, but his at least partial sympathy with Comte is suggested by the tendency of the novels to register subjectivity not through introspection, or free indirect discourse – the typical means of the psychological novelist, such as Eliot or James – but somatically, in terms of immediate physical sensation, or changed perception of the outer world: hence the recurrence in his work of such words as palpitating, trembling, listless, flushing, librating, irradiated, dazzled, tremulous, and the frequent references to the movement of the blood, and the quickening of the pulse, or of the breath. Gilles Deleuze understandably suggests that Hardy's characters are not so much "people or subjects" as "collections of intensive sensations" (Deleuze and Parnet 1987: 39–40). So, of Bathsheba, kissed by Troy in the hollow amid the ferns:

That minute's interval had brought the blood beating into her face, set her stinging as if aflame to the very hollows of her feet, and enlarged emotion to a compass which quite swamped thought. It had brought upon her a stroke resulting, as did that of Moses in Horeb, in a liquid stream – here a stream of tears. She felt like one who has sinned a great sin. (*FFMC* 196–7)

Or this, when Angel kisses the inside of Tess's arm:

> she was such a sheaf of susceptibilities that her pulse was accelerated by the touch, her blood driven to her finger-ends and the cool arms flushed hot. Then, as though her heart had said, "Is coyness longer necessary?" . . . she lifted her eyes, and they beamed devotedly into his as her lip rose in a tender half-smile. (*TD* 178)

Somatic manifestation and emotional response – the feet aflame and the sense of sin, the accelerated pulse and the repudiation of coyness, or in a simpler instance the two terms of Elfride Swancourt's "flush of triumph" (*PBE* 67) – while analytically distinct, are treated by Hardy as all but identical.[1]

The intimacy of the relation between the physiological and the affective in Hardy's work is unprecedented in English fiction. It enters so deeply into his writing that it can hardly have come from a single source, but its consonance with Comte's ideas is indicated by a note taken in 1877 from G. H. Lewes, another exponent of Positivist thought:

> Physiology began to disclose that all the mental processes were (mathematically speaking) <u>functions</u> of physical processes, i.e. – varying with the variations of bodily states; & this was declared enough to banish for ever the conception of a Soul, except as a term simply expressing certain functions. (*LN* I: 92)

Stripped of the teleological element given it by Comte, this is the materialist philosophy that Carlyle and Ruskin denounced as Mechanism, and Max Weber described as "the disenchantment of the world": a vision of a morally indifferent universe, subject to determining laws, in which human consciousness is the unintended by-product of accidental organizations of matter. It is also the vision that underlies most of Hardy's fiction (Green 1996: 3). But as Sinéad Garrigan-Mattar argues in her forthcoming study of animism in modern English literature, it is not the only account of the relation between humankind and the earth we inhabit that Hardy took from his reading of Comte. More than a dozen entries in the *Literary Notebooks* relate to "Fetichism," defined as the frame of mind which "looks on all objects in nature as animate." Comte might have been expected to treat Fetichism, as the first phase of the Theological stage of human development, still more severely than the Polytheism and then Monotheism which succeeded it, but in fact the reverse is the case. Fetichism is "the most spontaneous mode of philosophising, & useful even now, giving animation to language &c–"; its hypotheses conform to Positivist principles "in being the most simple that will account for the facts"; if it overstates the resemblances between humankind and the rest of organic nature, it does so both less, and less dangerously, than "Theologism" exaggerates the differences: "<u>Fetichist method</u> starts in the normal path of <the> true logic, while the Theological method goes radically astray from it" (*LN* I: 77).

The Fetichist belief that "all objects are alive, and concern themselves with Man" is not, for Hardy, simply an error to be outgrown, but a recurring human intuition (*LN* I: 76). In *The Return of the Native*, as Gillian Beer notices, present and past belief systems coexist rather than succeed each other. Eustacia's death is both psychologically motivated and the result of Susan Nunsuch's sympathetic magic: "Neither form of explanation drives out the other" (Beer 1996: 43). In 1877 Hardy reflected in his journal: "I sometimes look upon all things in inanimate nature as pensive mutes" (*LW* 117); when Edward Clodd referred the superstitions of the Dorset peasants to "the barbaric idea which confuses persons and things," Hardy added that this idea is "also common to the highest imaginative genius – that of the poet" (*LW* 241). There is something more than the pathetic fallacy in the "harmony" between the chaos in Eustacia's mind and that of the world without during her last night on the heath, or in the "marvellous power" of "sympathy" between Giles and the trees he plants in *The Woodlanders* (*RN* 358; *W* 58). When the narrator says of Jude's attempt to feed the rooks in Farmer Troutham's field that "A magic thread of fellow-feeling united his own life with theirs," the link between the boy and the birds is not merely an evolutionary one: it is also, at least for the moment, magical (*JO* 9). The spiritual connection between humankind and nature, pushed out by materialist philosophy, is allowed to edge its way back.

Hardy's reading of Comte was, as one might expect, critical as well as sympathetic. Clym Yeobright, "the nicest of all my heroes" (*CL* IV: 212), is thoroughly Comtean in his desire to serve his kind, his resignation in the face of suffering, and the undogmatic nature of his teaching; but the novel also makes clear the undercurrent of egotism in his self-appointed role as tutor to the Egdon eremites, his secret relief when blindness forces him to abandon his efforts, and the irony that he is listened to not because he is teaching the social sympathies, but because those he is addressing already feel sympathy for him. One ground of dissent for Hardy must have been Comte's explicit and extreme anti-individualism, as it was for John Stuart Mill, who argued in the essay *On Liberty* (1859) that Comte's system, if ever it were introduced, would establish "a despotism of society over the individual" unmatched in history (Mill 1975: 19–20). Hardy, who admired Mill's essay, and took the chapter "Of Individuality" as one of his "Cures for despair," was of the same mind (*LW* 59). Comte's prescriptions for women show him at his most despotic. Women were to renounce all forms of public life outside marriage, including the ownership of property, the better to fulfill their natural role as priestesses of Humanity; marriage ties were to be indissoluble even after death. Mill's essay on *The Subjection of Women*, published ten years after *On Liberty*, offers a compelling rebuttal of such views, and here too Hardy stands closer to Mill than to Comte: Sue plainly has the narrator's support when she quotes Mill's defense of the right of individuals to choose their own "plan of life" (*JO* 234). Comte's ideas, wrote Mill, meant "*liberticide*" (Ten 1980: 159); and Hardy, like Mill, valued liberty.

But it remains difficult to place Hardy in relation to Mill: in particular, the Hardy who admired Darwin. Mill's thinking about sexuality offers a starting-point. Harriet Taylor Mill regretted that "all men with the exception of a few lofty minded, are sensualists more or less," though she was undecided whether this was a fact of nature or the result of education (Rossi 1970: 84). In like manner John Stuart Mill, one of the "lofty minded," habitually dismisses the urgencies of sexual feeling as low, coarse or swinish, "a degrading slavery to a brute instinct" which is to be kept in check by higher ideals (Mill [1848] 1926: 358). Underpinning what might otherwise seem a merely personal view – and at the personal level, a view clearly not shared by Hardy – are two more substantive claims: first, that humanity as a natural kind is radically separated from the animal kind by the possession of reason and the moral sense; and second, that human advance depends upon the control of those qualities which link us with animals, and more broadly of those considered natural or instinctive. This is the central argument of Mill's essay "On Nature" (1874):

> Without touching upon any disputed theoretical points, it is possible to judge how little worthy is the instinctive part of human nature to be held up as its chief excellence . . . [N]early every respectable attribute of humanity is the result not of instinct, but of a victory over instinct. (Mill [1874] 1904: 25)

Civilization, art, the social virtues, if in any sense "natural" to humanity, are so only because the processes of education have made them "a second nature." All that is best and noblest in human beings has been "artificially created"; we progress morally not by trusting to instinct, but by "intentional self-modelling according to an ideal" (Mill [1874] 1904: 28, 26).

Some parts of Mill's view on "Man's Place in Nature" can, with a little wrestling, be reconciled with Darwin's account in *The Descent of Man* (1871). Both, for example, trusted in education; both allowed that behaviors initially learned might, over generations, become instinctive. But there remain clear and important differences. In sum, Darwin argues that much that at first glance seems instinctual in animal behavior in fact shows evidence of reason, while much that appears to be the product of reason in humankind has its origins in instinct. Unlike Mill, Darwin was persuaded that the social instincts could be found even in the lower animals, and since these instincts formed the basis of morality, it was possible that over time animals could "acquire a moral sense or conscience" (Darwin [1871] 2003: 98). Hardy seems to have picked up on this in *Far from the Madding Crowd*, published three years after the *Descent*. As the exhausted and heavily pregnant Fanny crawls her way to the Casterbridge workhouse, she is progressively stripped of her human autonomy, while the dog who comes to her aid "thoroughly [understands] her desire and her incapacity," and becomes "frantic in his distress" on her behalf (*FFMC* 278). That the dog is of no recognizable breed, while Fanny is left unnamed (she is simply "the woman"), allows the chapter to be read as a virtual test case for Darwin's speculation that some of the higher animals, like dogs, might already exhibit "something very like a conscience" (Darwin [1871] 2003: 103).

To ascribe moral qualities to animals was to blur the distinction between human and animal kinds on which Mill placed such importance. There was for Darwin "no fundamental difference between man and the higher animals in their mental faculties," and what difference there was "certainly one of degree and not of kind" (Darwin [1871] 2003: 66, 126). It was also to propose, again *contra* Mill, that the moral sense was innate, or at least, so "deeply planted" as to be "an impulsive power" rather than the product of reflection (Darwin [1871] 2003: 120). That metaphor, nicely poised between culture and nature, is suggestive. When, in *The Woodlanders*, Grace Melbury

feels a sudden need to throw off "the veneer of artificiality" (*W* 186), the phrase contrasts with other images used for her education. The timber-dealers have walking-
sticks twisted into corkscrew shapes, "brought to that pattern by the slow torture of
an encircling woodbine during their growth, as the Chinese have been said to mould
human beings into grotesque toys by continued compression in infancy" (*W* 49).
Grace is such a toy: "tilled" into a more fashionable view of the world, with newly
"implanted tastes," so that "cultivation" is "advanced in the soil of her mind" (*W* 100,
77, 40). The dividing line between the natural and the cultural, the instinctual and
the acquired, which Mill was anxious to see firmly drawn, is in Hardy's work more
often an uncertain one (Richardson 2002).

The difference between Hardy and Mill on this point is part of a wider disagree-
ment in their understanding of human nature. Mill's view of society as composed of
rational, self-governing human beings entails two related claims, to both of which
Hardy gives only qualified assent. First, Mill argues in *On Liberty* that individuals
have the right, even the duty, to choose their own "plan of life" rather than allow it
to be dictated to them by society; and second, he maintains in his *System of Logic*
(1843) that they have the capacity to do so, that is, that they have free will. In Book
VI of the *Logic*, "On the Logic of the Moral Sciences," Mill insists that the doctrine
that the law of causality applies to human actions as to other phenomena – a doctrine
he sees as fundamental to any serious account of moral and social life – is not, despite
contemporary anxieties, inconsistent with our freedom to choose one line of conduct
rather than another. To argue that our actions are caused is not to claim that they are
compelled: while it is true that "our volitions and actions are invariable consequents
of our antecedent states of mind" (Mill [1843] 1987: 23), it does not follow that we
could not act otherwise if we wished, since that wish would itself be a new antecedent. Except in cases of monomania, the causes on which action depends – our motives
– "are never uncontrollable" (Mill [1843] 1987: 25). It is, for example, acutely difficult for Tess to reveal her past to Angel before their marriage, but not impossible;
her discovery that her letter has gone astray serves to draw our attention to her power
to decide which of two conflicting motives, the wish to confess her "faults and blun-
ders" and the "desire . . . to make herself his," she will allow to operate. As the narrator
insists, and Tess herself realizes, "there was still time" (*TD* 209–10).

But while allowing that the doctrine of causation is compatible with freedom of
the will, Hardy does not go on to accept, as Mill does, and as George Eliot does after
him, that we can choose not only our actions but also to some extent our character
(Levine 1962). For Mill, that a man's character is

> in the ultimate resort, formed for him, is not inconsistent with its being, in part, formed
> *by* him as one of the intermediate agents. His character is formed by his circumstances
> . . . but his own desire to mould it in a particular way is one of those circumstances,
> and by no means one of the least influential. (Mill [1843] 1987: 26)

But as J. Hillis Miller has noticed, Hardy's characters are not shown as choosing
to be what they are: "Their distinctive natures are imposed upon them, willy-nilly.

They cannot help being what they are, and acting accordingly" (Miller 2006: 171). Theirs is a world of impulse rather than premeditation. In Mill's rationalist account, motive or intention typically exists prior to and separate from action, and is available to scrutiny (Dale 1989: 71); in Hardy's, it is typically discovered only from or after the action, or indeed not discovered at all, at least by the agent. In moments of crisis, Henchard is left baffled by his own actions, Fitzpiers and Tess act as if asleep or in a trance, and Elfride, Eustacia, and Angel each abandon will, desire, and agency, and become instead passive spectators of their own lives. There is nothing like this in Mill, who despite his own mental crisis in 1825–6 seems to have had no conception of that dark "outer chamber of the brain" of which Hardy writes in *The Mayor of Casterbridge*, into which wander "thoughts unowned, unsolicited, and of noxious kind" (*MC* 285). Not only that: Hardy's most thoughtful characters, those most committed to "self-modelling according to an ideal," appear wounded by the very act of trying to "mould" themselves. For Clym, Angel, Sue, and Jude, thought in the way Mill construes it, as a mental process dissociated from feeling and instinct, is self-destructive: "a disease of flesh" rather than an achievement of mind (*RN* 138). Hardy's fiction, notably *Tess* and *Jude*, echoes *On Liberty* in its protest against the tyranny of public opinion, but is wholly unlike Mill in its sense that the springs of human action may be inaccessible even to the actors. If Hardy valued the essay *On Liberty* as a prophylactic against despair, it may have been because it represented what he hoped about our power to shape our own nature, and not what he in fact believed.

Hardy's sense that character is given rather than chosen, and that we are as much motivated by instinct and the body as by reason and the intellect, aligns him more closely with Darwin, and indeed with Freud, than with Mill. It also suggests his point of contact with Schopenhauer, whose ideas he is likely to have encountered in the periodical press in the 1870s, well before he began reading him in translation in 1883 (Asquith 2005: 39). Complex in detail, and in their derivation from Kant, these ideas are in summary form relatively simple. My own body is known to me in the same way as all other material objects, as something that occupies time and space (in Schopenhauer's terms, as *Vorstellung* or Idea), but I also have immediate, non-sensory knowledge of it from within, in the form of appetency: those primal sensations of longing, hunger, fearing, desire, and aversion, including the action of the bodily organs, which Schopenhauer identifies as the will to life. While it is only of myself that I can know directly that I have both an external and an interior existence, I can infer that the whole phenomenal world, even inorganic or seemingly inert matter, exists in the same two aspects, as both an object of perception and an expression of the blind, ceaseless urging that Schopenhauer denotes the Will. Individual phenomena, including human beings, are merely the form in which the Will reveals itself in space and time. Each empirical event, each separate human desire, can be referred to a sufficient cause or motive, but the totality of event and desire – the question of why one desires at all, even to exist, why *anything* exists – can be explained only in terms of the "endless striving" of a Will with no other goal than to find its "objectivity" or "mirror" in the phenomenal world: "Eternal becoming, endless flux, belong to the revelation of the essential nature of the Will" (Schopenhauer [1819] 1969 I: 164–5).

The work in which these theories were first set out, *The World as Will and Idea*, was little noticed on its publication in 1819, but the apparent affinity between Schopenhauer's account of the world as a seething turmoil of mutually antagonistic elements and post-Darwinian descriptions of the struggle for existence gave it a new resonance in the 1870s. Schopenhauer's is, however, the darker vision. He portrays the Will as originally an undivided unity, now broken up into the multiplicity of separate phenomena in the effort to realize itself. Since it exists as fully in the predator as in the prey, its striving is essentially a process of self-rending: "the Will must live on itself, since nothing exists beside it, and it is a hungry Will" (Schopenhauer [1819] 1969 I: 154). "Nature's logic," as young Jude discovers in the field at Marygreen, is indeed "horrid" (*JO* 13). This logic also entails a disregard for the individual: since each being is equally a manifestation of the Will, it follows that in a world of "infinite time, infinite space, and the infinite number of possible individuals," the individual not only has but *can* have no value (Schopenhauer [1819] 1969 I: 276). To intuit, as Tess does, that your "life and doings" are no different from and of no more account than those of thousands before and after you, that you exist as a vehicle through which an indifferent Will seeks to manifest itself, is to recognize birth as "an ordeal of degrading personal compulsion," and life itself as Sorrow (*TD* 130, 344). Life is merely "an ever-deferred death," a "soap-bubble" blown as large as possible, but always in the knowledge that it will burst.

Because the Will consists of endless striving, its essence "is need, lack, and hence pain, and by its very nature and origin it is therefore destined to pain"; should it attain a temporary satisfaction, "a fearful emptiness and boredom come over it": "Hence life swings like a pendulum to and fro between pain and boredom" (Schopenhauer [1819] 1969 I: 311–12). The same dynamic, of hunger, satiety, and disillusion, informs most of Hardy's love plots, in which desire is welcomed as an alternative to ennui, only to dissipate when the goal of love is obtained (Miller 1970: 176). That Hardy had arrived at this view at least as early as 1867 is evident from poems such as "Neutral Tones," but his reading of Schopenhauer sharpened his sense that the pain of existence was not contingent, but built into its very structure. No outcome in life, not even the ecstasy of love, can compensate for the sheer gratuitousness of our coming into being.

Schopenhauer's account of human action, motive, and self-knowledge, even more than his metaphysics, bears comparison with Hardy's. Like Mill, Schopenhauer allows that we are free to *do* as we will, but his emphasis falls on the fact that we are not free to *will* as we will. For him as for Hardy, character is a given. We cannot choose to be other than we are; the patterns of our conduct and personality are not open to rational suasion; they will remain essentially unchanged throughout our lives. What Schopenhauer calls the man of "acquired character" is not, as the phrase might suggest, one who has become what he determined to be, but one who has come to understand what he is, and has learned to play the part allotted him (Gardiner 1963: 257): such characters, perhaps, as Gabriel Oak or Elizabeth-Jane, or even Arabella. To thus accept the necessities of our nature has been construed by some thinkers as freedom; Schopenhauer concedes only that as the line of least resistance it is the most reasonable path to take.

Implicit in such arguments is the refusal of all claims that what we are and do lies within our conscious control. In Schopenhauer's account, our will-to-live – our desires, hopes, and fears – is primary, "the real core, the being-in-itself, of man," and the intellect merely secondary, a feeble latecomer unable to "penetrate into the secret workshop of the will's decisions" (Schopenhauer [1819] 1969 II: 208–9). Far from being guided by our reason, we are often entirely mistaken as to the real motive as to why we do or omit to do something. Schopenhauer's analysis here brilliantly antici-pates Freud's view in his *Psychopathology of Everyday Life* that our seemingly accidental behavior embodies unrecognized intentions (Freud [1901] 1914: 192). The same insight shapes many of the episodes in Hardy's fiction – the letters misdirected or imperfectly sealed, sent too late or read by the wrong person; or, for example, Mrs. Yeobright's decision to entrust the guineas she is sending to Clym to Christian Cantle, with the predictable but not consciously chosen result that they go astray, casting her again in the role which allows her to do most harm to Eustacia, that of neglected mother. For Schopenhauer, it is our actions which reveal our nature, not our inten-tions, which he regards as little more than unreliable guesses at our future behavior. When Angel Clare learns in Brazil that the moral "beauty or ugliness" of a character lies in "aims" rather than "achievements," he makes a distinction that Schopenhauer would repudiate (*TD* 330). We are what we do.

Angel has, however, attained a partial truth. In so far as he also comes to see that what divides him from Tess is less than what unites them as alike victims of the "universal harshness," he approaches Schopenhauer's definition of the good man as one who "makes less distinction than is usually made between himself and others." This is to offer an account in metaphysical terms of the "shifted centre of altruism" Hardy had derived from his understanding of evolution, in which we are asked to recognize that the same will-to-live we find within ourselves "constitutes the inner nature of everything, and lives in all . . . [extending] even to the animals and to the whole of nature" (Schopenhauer [1819] 1969 I: 372). The direct, inward sense of pity and compassion for another, obscurely recognized as in some sense part of ourselves, which Schopenhauer calls *Menschenliebe*, is a near-equivalent to what Hardy calls "loving-kindness." Severe moralist though he is, Schopenhauer writes at times as though he would have agreed with Hardy's Elizabeth-Jane, that in a "brief transit through a sorry world . . . neither she nor any human being deserved less than was given" (*MC* 310).

Nowhere does Schopenhauer find the predominance of the will over the intellect more evident than in sexual feeling, on which he writes searchingly as well as coldly. Sexual desire is at once a "trifle," "a question of every Jack finding his Jill," and the strongest of all motives, "a malevolent demon" which confuses, perverts, and wounds all who experience it. Man is "concrete sexual impulse," the genitals are "the focus of the will" (Schopenhauer [1819] 1969 II: 534, 514). So it is that Jude is driven to Arabella by "a compelling arm of extraordinary muscular power" (*JO* 40–1), and the dairymaids at Talbothays are left writhing in desire for Angel Clare: "each was but portion of one organism called sex" (*TD* 149). Desire precedes and overrides individuation: in Schopenhauer's terms, it represents itself to the lover wearing "the mask of an objective admiration," but the reality, "the true end of the whole love-story," is the urge to propagate the species (Schopenhauer [1819] 1969 II: 535). Human sexuality, no less than the "rush of juices" or the "hiss of fertilization" at the dairy, is the means whereby the Will can continue to realize itself (*TD* 151); romantic love is merely the "stratagem" used by Nature, a "voluptuous delusion" which lures the individual on to procreation (Schopenhauer [1819] 1969 II: 535, 540). Hardly less cynically, this is close to the narrator's "scientific" account in *The Well-Beloved* of Jocelyn Pierston's conversation with the second Avice Caro about his laundry: "Nature was working her plans for the next generation under the cloak of a dialogue on linen" (*WB* 90). Both are unwitting instruments of the species' need to maintain itself.

In other respects too *The Well-Beloved* seems to draw on Schopenhauer's analysis (Bullen 1994). When Pierston speculates that one or another Avice Caro might furnish the "individual nature" destined to "supplement his own imperfect one and round it out with the perfect whole" (*WB* 99), he is echoing Schopenhauer's view of love as an unconsciously eugenic process, in which two dissimilar beings are brought together in answer to "the will-to-live" of the as yet uncreated child "they can and want to produce" (Schopenhauer [1819] 1969 II: 536). On the face of it, Nature is unsuccessful in *The Well-Beloved*: Pierston does not mate with any of the three Avices. But while the second Avice rejects Jocelyn, she mates instead with Ike Pierston; the two family lines, Caro and Pierston, are brought together, and produce the child that the species rather than the individual has demanded. What Hardy describes in his poem "Heredity" as "The eternal thing in man, / That heeds no call to die," and Schopenhauer identifies as the Will, achieves its end (*CPV* 434).

Despite the sardonic "Ho-ho-ho!" which ended *The Well-Beloved* in its original serial version, Hardy's account of sexual desire is less reductive and less biologically driven than Schopenhauer's. His heroes and heroines leave no offspring; rather than seek to perpetuate themselves in their children, they are drawn to their own destruction, if not in the form of suicide then in a resolution against life. In his essay "On Suicide," which Hardy read in 1891, Schopenhauer defends the right to take one's own life, but insists that to do so represents a moral failing. The highest ethical achievement is the denial of the will to live; but the suicide "wills life, and is dissatisfied merely with the conditions on which it has come to him" (Schopenhauer [1819] 1969 I: 398). Suicide is thus a flight from suffering, not a liberation from desire. The moral condemnation aside, some such idea seems to inform Hardy's fiction. Eustacia chooses death rather than face the choice of life on Egdon or flight as Wildeve's mistress. Jude's death, deliberately brought about, is a protest against the injustice of the world, and the ideology which has ensnared Sue. Even Henchard, who demands "that no man remember me," compels our regard with his last words: "To this I put my name. Michael Henchard" (*MC* 309). Suicide, for each of them, becomes a form of self-assertion. On Schopenhauer's terms, only Tess finds the right way to die, as she rises from the altar at Stonehenge with the words "I am ready" (*TD* 382). She has acquired "the ocean-like calmness" of those who are content to let go of themselves and the world, "and who then merely wait to see the last trace of the will vanish with the body that is animated by that trace" (Schopenhauer [1819] 1969 I: 410). The title of the last phase of the novel, "Fulfilment," is not wholly ironic (Kelly 1982: 187).

Yet this is not quite Hardy's emphasis, since his narrative traces the arc of the individual life, and with the end of that comes the end of the novel. The "true end of the story" may be the onward movement of the species (as, perhaps, Liza-Lu moves into the place left empty by her sister's death), but for the novelist it cannot be the whole story; there is always another side, another way to tell the tale. The modest aim of this essay has been to suggest that Hardy's reading of four thinkers – Comte, Darwin, Mill, and Schopenhauer – informed and enriched his "representations of life." Yet in the end, as all his disclaimers acknowledge, what he shares with the philosophers is not the desire for analytic consistency, but an urgent need to question the terms on which we hold our existence:

> for a being who thinks, it is a precarious position to stand on one of those numberless spheres freely floating in boundless space, without knowing whence or whither, and to be only one of innumerable similar beings that throng, press, and toil, restlessly and rapidly arising and passing away in beginningless and endless time. (Schopenhauer [1819] 1969 II: 3)

NOTE

1   Whether or not Hardy knew Darwin's study of blushing in *The Expression of the Emotions in Man and Animals* (1872), *A Pair of Blue Eyes*, published a year later, offers a virtual typology of the male and female blush. Elfride, Stephen, and Knight blush, flush or turn pale with pique, triumph, jealousy, perplexity, embarrassment, vexation, anger, mortification, gladness, and shame; their faces become rapid red, vivid scarlet, crimson, vermilion, an angry color, lively red, lily-white, pale, livid, cold, heated, and bright.

REFERENCES AND FURTHER READING

Andreski, Stanislav (ed.) (1974). *The Essential Comte*. London: Croom Helm.

Asquith, Mark (2005). *Thomas Hardy, Metaphysics and Music*. Basingstoke: Palgrave Macmillan.

Beer, Gillian (1983). *Darwin's Plots: Evolutionary Narrative in Darwin, George Eliot and Nineteenth-Century Fiction*. Cambridge: Cambridge University Press.

Beer, Gillian (1996). *Open Fields: Science in Cultural Encounter*. Oxford: Clarendon Press.

Björk, Lennart A. (ed.) (1985). *The Literary Notebooks of Thomas Hardy*, 2 vols. London and Basingstoke: Macmillan.

Bullen, J. B. (1994). Hardy's *The Well-Beloved*, Sex, and Theories of Germ Plasm. In Phillip Mallett and R. P. Draper (eds.), *A Spacious Vision: Essays on Hardy* (pp. 79–88). Newmill: Patten Press.

Dale, Peter Allan (1989). *In Pursuit of a Scientific Culture: Science, Art and Society in the Victorian Age*. Madison: University of Wisconsin Press.

Darwin, Charles ([1871] 2003). *The Descent of Man, and Selection in Relation to Sex*, ed. Richard Dawkins. London: Gibson Square Books.

Darwin, Charles ([1872] 1998). *The Expression of the Emotions in Man and Animals*, ed. Paul Ekman. New York: HarperCollins.

Deleuze, Gilles, and Claire Parnet (1987). *Dialogues*, trans. Hugh Tomlinson and Barbara Habberjam. New York: Columbia University Press.

Freud, Sigmund ([1901] 1914). *Psychopathology of Everyday Life*, trans. A. A. Brill. London: T. Fisher Unwin.

Gardiner, Patrick (1963). *Schopenhauer*. Harmondsworth: Penguin.

Garrigan-Mattar, Sinéad (2008). *The Return of the Native*: Animism, Fetichism, and the Enchanted Heath. *Thomas Hardy Journal*, 24.

Green, Brian (1996). *Hardy's Lyrics: Pearls of Pity*. London: Macmillan.

Hardy, Thomas ([1873] 1998). *A Pair of Blue Eyes*, ed. Pamela Dalziel. London: Penguin.

Hardy, Thomas ([1874] 1993). *Far from the Madding Crowd*, ed. Suzanne B. Falck-Yi. Oxford: Oxford University Press.

Hardy, Thomas ([1878] 1990). *The Return of the Native*, ed. Simon Gatrell. Oxford: Oxford University Press.

Hardy, Thomas ([1886] 2004). *The Mayor of Casterbridge*, ed. Dale Kramer. Oxford: Oxford University Press.

Hardy, Thomas ([1887] 2005). *The Woodlanders*, ed. Dale Kramer. Oxford: Oxford University Press.

Hardy, Thomas ([1891] 1988). *Tess of the d'Urbervilles*, ed. Juliet Grindle and Simon Gatrell. Oxford: Oxford University Press.

Hardy, Thomas ([1895] 1985). *Jude the Obscure*, ed. Patricia Ingham. Oxford: Oxford University Press.

Hardy, Thomas ([1897] 1986). *The Well-Beloved*, ed. Tom Hetherington. Oxford: Oxford University Press.

Hardy, Thomas (1979). *The Variorum Edition of the Complete Poems of Thomas Hardy*, ed. James Gibson. London: Macmillan.

Hardy, Thomas (1984). *The Life and Work of Thomas Hardy*, ed. Michael Millgate. London: Macmillan.

Harrison, Frederic (1891). Letter to Thomas Hardy, Dec. 29, 1891. Dorset County Museum.

Hughes, John (2001) *"Ecstatic Sound": Music and Individuality in the Work of Thomas Hardy*. Aldershot: Ashgate.

Huxley, Thomas H. (1893–4). *Collected Essays*, 8 vols. London: Macmillan.

Kelly, Mary Ann (1982). Hardy's Reading of Schopenhauer: *Tess of the d'Urbervilles*. *Colby Library Quarterly*, 28, 183–98.

Levine, George (1962). Determinism and Responsibility in the Works of George Eliot. *PMLA*, 77, 268–79.

Mill, John Stuart ([1843] 1987). *The Logic of the Moral Sciences*, ed. A. J. Ayer. London: Duckworth.

Mill, John Stuart ([1848] 1926). *Principles of Political Economy*, ed. W. J. Ashley. London: Longman, Green.

Mill, John Stuart ([1859], [1861], [1869] 1975). *Three Essays: On Liberty, Representative Government, The Subjection of Women*, ed. Richard Wollheim. Oxford: Oxford University Press.

Mill, John Stuart ([1874] 1904). *Nature, The Utility of Religion and Theism*. London: Rationalist Press.

Miller, J. Hillis (1970). *Thomas Hardy: Distance and Desire*. Cambridge, MA: The Belknap Press of Harvard University Press.

Miller, J. Hillis (2006). Individual and Community in *The Return of the Native*. In Keith Wilson (ed.), *Thomas Hardy Reappraised: Essays in Honour of Michael Millgate* (pp. 154–73). Toronto: University of Toronto Press.

Millgate, Michael (1971). *Thomas Hardy: His Career as a Novelist*. London: Bodley Head; reissued Basingstoke: Macmillan, 1994.

Millgate, Michael (ed.) (2001). *Thomas Hardy's Public Voice: The Essays, Speeches, and Miscellaneous Prose*. Oxford: Clarendon Press.

Purdy, Richard Little, and Michael Millgate (eds.) (1978–88). *The Collected Letters of Thomas Hardy*, 7 vols. Oxford: Clarendon Press.

Richardson, Angelique (2002). Hardy and Biology. In Phillip Mallet (ed.), *Thomas Hardy: Texts and Contexts* (pp. 156–79). Basingstoke: Palgrave Macmillan.

Rossi, Alice S. (ed.) (1970). *Essays on Sex Equality: John Stuart Mill and Harriet Taylor Mill*. Chicago: University of Chicago Press.

Schopenhauer, Arthur ([1819] 1969). *The World as Will and Representation*, trans. E. F. J. Payne. 2 vols. New York: Dover Publications.

Ten, C. L. (1980). *Mill on Liberty*. Oxford: Oxford University Press.

Wright, T. R. (1986). *The Religion of Humanity: The Impact of Comtean Positivism on Victorian Britain*. Cambridge: Cambridge University Press.

3

Hardy and Darwin: An Enchanting Hardy?

George Levine

In place of the usual gloomy reading of Darwin's influence on Hardy's thought and art, I want to offer a happier (if not a better) one. The influence is more nuanced, more complex, and more interesting than that usual reading allows. To make the case, however, it's necessary to begin by premising that the critical consensus is correct: what everybody says – an idea that Hardy surely encouraged – is that Hardy was profoundly and pervasively influenced by Darwin. Virtually all commentators cite Hardy's notation in his autobiographical biography that he was "among the earliest acclaimers of *The Origin of Species*" (*LW* 158) and note that, in his list of thinkers who influenced him, Hardy includes Darwin prominently. Carl Weber may have been the first to note Hardy's now often repeated observation in a letter: "My pages show harmony of view with Darwin, Huxley, Spencer, Comte, Hume, Mill" (Weber [1940] 1965: 246–7).

I am, however, just a little tired of the inevitable catching of Darwinian strains in Hardy just where there is stress, competition, chance, struggle, and suffering. There is by now little need to elaborate or refine this side of the argument. Darwin is there in the embedded fossils into whose eyes Henry Knight stares as he clings for life to the side of the cliff in *A Pair of Blue Eyes*; we hear him again as the trees scrape against each other in the crowded forest of *The Woodlanders* and again in the squealing of the trapped rabbit in *Jude the Obscure*; and again, alas, in virtually every phase of Jude's painful career and in his young son's suicide and murders.

From my point of view – enormously valuable as connections of this kind have been – enough is, well, enough; there are other ways to hear Darwin in Hardy's works, less obvious but perhaps even more fundamental. A. Dwight Culler was right many years ago when he wrote that "to trace the way in which . . . writers derive from Darwin their views of nature, man, God, and society does not seem to me quite to get at the heart of the problem" (Culler 1968: 225) of the relation of Darwin to the literature that followed him. It is, says Culler, the *form* of Darwin's argument that counts most. Culler meant, in particular, the form of paradox and irony, parallel to Darwin's reversal of natural theology, explaining adaptation as the creation not of a guiding Intelligence but of chance (although Darwin did not believe in "chance"). I would want to amend Culler's important suggestion that we must pay attention to the *way* Darwin wrote by attending as well to moral inferences Hardy drew from Darwin's theory, and to the way Darwin *looked* at the natural world, particularly his modes of attention to the minutest details and his almost instinctive reading of history into apparently static particulars, and, finally, to the implicit feeling and moral energy that his intensely sought objectivity never fully disguised.[1] The Darwin I want to consider in Hardy's art is reflected in what I would call their mutually loving, meticulous, and ethically intense attention to the whole range of nature, organic and inorganic, in their discovery of narratives latent in all things. All of these are at the root of Hardy's aesthetically self-conscious and risky engagement with literary forms. He was more in love with life – and in Darwinian ways – than most typical Darwinian readings suggest.

Through all the darkness of a chance-driven, mindless world against which thought-endowed animals like humans have to struggle hopelessly, there glimmers steadily a strong moral vision and even a life-affirming Hardy. Others have noticed this. In her attempt to give an adequate sense of the complication of the connections between Hardy and Darwin, Gillian Beer has argued, "Alongside the emphasis on apprehension and anxiety, on inevitable overthrow long foreseen, persistingly evaded, there is another prevailing sensation in Hardy's work equally strongly related to his understanding of Darwin. It is that of happiness" (Beer 2000: 241). I am not sure that "happiness" is quite the word, although it is true that even in its crudest formulation, natural selection requires a world of organisms sufficiently content with their lives to desire to sustain and propagate them (I will, in fact, be adopting a word out of Charles Taylor and Jane Bennett, "fullness," in place of "happiness"). Beer is certainly right to recognize that Darwin's vision of the world – certainly Darwin's interpretation of his own vision – is hardly as gloomy as most of his interpreters make it; she is right too that Hardy's world implies an underlying vision of the possibilities (rarely if ever, it is true, fulfilled) of human flourishing and fullness.

Although my subject is the way Darwin's thought and language manifested themselves in Hardy's work, the underlying concern here is with two large ideas that have become critically important to contemporary thinking and that should help suggest the significance of this narrower subject. One of these is developed by Charles Taylor (2007). Taylor insists that, historically and universally, humans have aspired to a condition of "fullness" (a word too rich, subtle, and various to submit to easy definition) that religion has traditionally satisfied. A crucial question in Taylor's book is whether "fullness" is a condition that can be achieved through secularity. My consideration here of Hardy and Darwin is in effect an exploration of how Hardy imagined and answered the question. The idea of fullness is connected directly to the second framing idea, of "enchantment," and I consider this concept in relation to Hardy's art, largely through the focus of the work of Jane Bennett.

I don't pretend that it's always easy to catch that glint of life-affirmation that accompanies Hardy's better known and more overt and aggressive Darwinian pessimism. Yet, working with the idea of "enchantment," as Max Weber developed it and, recently, Jane Bennett has modified it, I too want to insist on the life-affirming implications of Hardy's work. There is a Hardyesque enchantment that continues to make Hardy worth reading and that redeems him from his often relentless exploitation of chance, not, as in most other earlier Victorian writers, to bring hero and heroine to comic fruition, but to guarantee their frustration, their pain, and their deaths. Yes, there are many times when it seems as though Hardy's stories were written just to substantiate Max Weber's claim that the "rationalization and intellectualization" of the world, largely by the way of science, has disenchanted it, has made it seem as though there are no "mysterious incalculable forces," and has thus driven wonder from the world (Weber 1958: 138, 139). But just as a sympathetic reading of Darwin makes clear that for him the world remained enchanted, so too should it do for Hardy. For both Darwin and Hardy the naturalization and rationalization of the world did not disenchant, did not close out the pursuit of "fullness," did not exclude the possibility of an ethics not grounded in religion. In my *Darwin Loves You: Natural Selection and the Re-enchantment of the World* (Levine 2006a), I try to make this case for Darwin's writing. I want to extend that argument to Hardy here.

The Weberian disenchantment so insistently asserted in the novels and poems reveals Hardy subject to and struggling with a widely held Victorian (and even modern) view: when religion is lost, morality, value, hope, and "fullness" disappear from the world; no secular alternative could possibly fill these needs. Without some all-inclusive religious or mythic scheme, the "enchantment" that infused all aspects of one's life with spiritual significance, with "meaning," would seem to be unattainable. Yet I want to take Hardy, perhaps the gloomiest of the post-Darwinians, as evidence for what Jane Bennett has argued, that the world does not suddenly empty of value when religion disappears. She criticizes the argument that with the loss of religion and teleology the here and now, our very material lives, come to seem without meaning and ethics and value, which always ultimately depend upon a transcendent power: "The depiction of nature and culture as orders no longer capable of inspiring deep attachment infects the self as a creature of loss and thus discourages discernment of the marvelous vitality of bodies human and nonhuman, natural and artifactual" (Bennett 2001: 4). To be sure Hardy saw and exploited the dark possibilities of Darwin's ideas, but few Victorian writers saw so clearly "the marvelous vitality of bodies human"; few saw so intensely that Darwin's world is full of the spirit of place, that place has its history, its Wordsworthian memories, and that nature, in its quite literally sublime complexity and variety, still has the power to evoke excitement and wonder and awe.[2] It is essential to the experience of Hardy's fiction that, despite his bleak narratives, his novels are imbued with a sense of nature that does indeed "inspire deep attachment." Equally important for my purposes here is Bennett's effort to explain what enchantment really is: "To be enchanted is to be struck and shaken by the extraordinary that lives amid the familiar and the everyday" (2001: 4). This amounts almost to a description of Hardy's "realist" enterprise and a description as well of Darwin's repeated "wonder" and awe at the ordinary ways of nature, the variety of growth in a cup of soil, the woodpecker adapting to life outside of the woods, or the extraordinary efficiency of bees.

"The overall effect of enchantment," Bennett says, "is a mood of fullness, plenitude, or liveliness, a sense of having had one's nerves or circulation or concentration powers tuned up and recharged" (2001: 5). Such a mood is surely what Hardy is after when he describes, say, the strange, squared-off geography of Casterbridge across which a bird might fly on its way from field to field, or Diggory Venn's firefly-lit gambling, or Gabriel Oak fighting off the storm and protecting the harvest, or Giles Winter-borne disappearing into the green of the tree he is shrouding, or Tess's hunt with the other farm laborers crawling through the mead in search of the tiny shoots of garlic that have been spoiling the butter. The almost paranoiac quality of so many of Hardy's narratives, in which no secret act is ever left unobserved, no past act ever left without its effects, no possibility of ignoring the presence of others, even in the deepest, remot-est places, keeps life on edge, reminds every reader of the profound consequences of every ordinary act. Everywhere in Hardy, even when the effects are unhappy, there are energizing moments of these sorts, along with such moments of fullness and plenitude. Hardy's work makes one recognize a sort of universal connectedness – both material and moral – and takes the realist ideal of attributing to the "ordinary" the values appropriate to tragedy and epic to levels so extreme, in certain respects, that his novels begin to move beyond the confines of realism. Bennett's sense of "enchant-ment" is particularly relevant to Hardy's because it is experienced inside a world that has lost both god and teleology while yet being morally significant and sustaining. Hardy's world is quite literally *wonder*ful, even if the wonder is often evoked (as in the heavens that Swithin and Lady Constantine observe) by what Weber would have called ultimately "calculable" forces. There is no avoiding the shiver of wonder and excitement as Swithin and Lady Constantine recognize in the vast depths of the heavens the infinitesimal smallness of their own lives. And yet from that scene the little lives emerge as significant. Awe and even horror at the vastness of the universe play out bathetically, and even perhaps almost comically, in the recognition that Swithin's activity of showing Lady Constantine the heavens through his telescope activates a recognizable drama in the little world of the novel – it is a form of love-making, with the cosmos, the apparent focus of interest, *less* important than the narrative consequences.

The world Bennett describes is not "purposive" nor is it "meaningful" in the way religious experience makes life "meaningful." Its powers of enchantment, however, load it with feeling and value and encourage love and attachment to life itself, without which, she asserts, there can be no attachment to anything. Finally, Bennett claims that she "pursues a life with moments of enchantment rather than an enchanted way of life" (2001: 10). Such a way of being is consonant with the effects, both on readers and characters, of Hardy's fiction. Enchantment as a way of life would, in both Dar-win's and Hardy's terms, sentimentalize and falsify a nature that from moment to moment in the course of human life is thrilling and awesome but that goes its way without reference to how we human observers feel about it. Not Bennett nor, certainly, either Darwin or Hardy wants to minimize the difficulties or the pain; yet all value this life, here and now, intensely.

Beyond their Bennett-like relation to enchantment, the lives and works of Darwin and Hardy might be seen in interesting parallels. The first and most striking is the similarity of their posthumous reputations as bringers of bleak news. "Darwinian," though literally it means only "related to Darwin or Darwin's ideas," usually means "fierce, selfish, competitive, relentless struggle for survival." One doesn't hear much about "Darwinian love" (unless, of course, it means the urge to reproduction and self-perpetuation. In recent years, the connection between Hardy's narratives and the theory of sexual selection has been made several times [see Beer 2000 and Kaye 2002]). One doesn't hear much about "Darwinian selflessness" (unless it means "reciprocal altruism" – you scratch my back, I'll scratch yours). Of course, "Hardyesque" is nothing like as common a word as "Darwinian," but insofar as it is used it is likely to imply a tragic and chance-driven fatality. But as against these popular understandings there is the Darwin that Robert Richards describes: a Darwin who was before all other things a "romantic," a thinker whose ideas emerged from a sense of a value-laden world progressive (à la Tennyson) and perfectible, and fraught with meaning (the Wordsworthian and Miltonic echoes are everywhere). Of course, neither "progress" nor "perfectibility" plays any role at all in "Darwin's dangerous idea," as it is interpreted by writers as widely diverse as Daniel Dennett and Stephen Jay Gould.[3] But Richards calls our attention to a rather different Darwin, one whose prose "vibrated with the poetic appreciation of nature's inner core." (I want to catch those vibrations in Hardy, too.) He wanted, says Richards, "to deliver to the reader an aesthetic assessment that lay beyond the scientifically articulable" (Richards 2002: 521). I hope that the implicit parallel with Hardy's prose is clear: *he* wanted to deliver to the reader an aesthetic assessment that lay beyond the merely rational understanding of nature that issues in his work inevitably in the pessimism he kept trying to deny. I hope it is true, though I have not seen a great deal of evidence to confirm it, that, as Keith Wilson claims, "it is to the life-affirming qualities of Hardy's writing that Hardy scholars and enthusiasts always seem to find themselves vigorously attesting, even in the face of copious textual evidence of his skeptical view of a universe that seems to offer limited possibilities for human felicity" (Wilson 2006: xx–xxi). In any case, I want here to turn from the more or less official responses to Darwin and Hardy to what I take to be a fuller response, one that sees in them both a deep feeling for life itself and a deep sense of the value of this nether world, so darkened by ruthless competition and chance.

Beyond this initial parallel in the nature of the interpretation of their works, there are others. First, neither Hardy nor Darwin began heterodox. Hardy was, the evidence suggests, almost evangelically pious down through the 1850s and 1860s. Darwin – given his upbringing as grandchild of Erasmus Darwin and with his very large rationalist father – was never, to be sure, really pious, but he *was* conventionally religious and, if only for practical reasons, did not, when he left for Cambridge, exclude the possibility of becoming a clergyman. Second, though both fell famously away, neither became hostile to the Church. Victorian literature is distinctive for its narratives of spiritual crisis and conversion, but neither Hardy nor Darwin seems to have gone through such a crisis. Gradually their faith eroded. Hardy, obsessively concerned both in life and art with "respectability," and so remaining socially very restrained and conservative, disclaiming (sometimes perhaps disingenuously) any disruptive intention in his writings, felt deeply the loss of the traditional God and loved the Church even if he could not believe its dogma. Darwin, sensitive to his wife's piety and socially and morally conservative, always supported (without, however, attending) the church at Downe, and did not participate in the kind of anti-clerical battles that marked the career of his "bulldog," T. H. Huxley. And, of course, Darwin was buried in Westminster Abbey.

Third, for both Hardy and Darwin the most telling criticism of Christian theism was the fact of human suffering. Neither could believe that an all-loving and all-knowing God could have been responsible for the horrors and tragedies of human (and animal) experience. It is one thing to explain death and suffering as part of the necessary process of natural selection (or, as William Paley had justified it, as essential to human "probation"); it is another to feel the deaths not as a general fate but as a particular one, not vaguely and statistically but personally and individually – as fictional narrative must. Fourth, as I have already suggested, their sensitivity to the pervasiveness of pain, waste, loss, and suffering gave them both reputations as disenchanters of the world, subjecting it to a coruscating rationalism that must lead to a universal sense that life is not worth living.[4] Such a vision is often read into the tired eyes revealed by the last photographs of the long-bearded Darwin. But, fifth, it is just this deep sensitivity to the pains of this world that presses them to a sense that life here and now – a fully secular life – is indeed worth living. Their works are marked by an astonishing and wonder-inducing attentiveness to the particularities of life, from "ephemera" and barnacles and worms and ants and slugs to rabbits to horses to birds and grass and trees and people. Sixth, that sharp eye for particularities that makes Darwin's work so convincing and Hardy's work so gorgeously painful is closely connected to an intensely ethical relation to the social and natural worlds (and, of course, a recognition that "social" and "natural" are not radically distinct), each driven in his own way into sympathetic engagement with the creatures they describe – a "feeling for the organism" – as if they loved them. And seventh: they *did* love them.

Given these odd (and obviously debatable) parallels and assertions, it is best to take a good look at the worst before proceeding – a perfectly Hardyesque thing to do. And here is Hardy looking hard:

A woeful fact – that the human race is too extremely developed for its corporeal conditions, the nerves being evolved to an activity abnormal in such an environment. Even the higher animals are in excess in this respect. It may be questioned if Nature, or what we call Nature, so far back as when she crossed the line from invertebrates to vertebrates, did not exceed her mission. This planet does not supply the material for happiness to higher existences. (*LW* 227)

Yes, this is pretty bleak. And yet its bleakness depends on attention to the anomalous hyperactivity of human nerves, a quality that we might say is registered in the plots and the narrative voice of most of Hardy's novels. And when we encounter such "nerves," we are confronted with sensibilities of rare quality.

It is worth thinking about this unmistakably Hardyesque pessimism in relation to another question: what is it that makes so many of Hardy's novels, despite the often grotesquely exaggerated fatality that descends upon heroes and heroines, so movingly beautiful? The clue is partly here, though the difference between fictional narrative and "non-fiction" philosophizing must also be part of the answer. It is just this extreme development of the "nerves" that he complains about here, the "recharging" of the nerves, as Bennett puts it. Hardy's narrators are uncannily perceptive, and their perceptions are not directed at utility or adaptiveness. In fact, as the quotation shows, Hardy imagines this hyperactivity of the nerves as distinctly *not* utilitarian. His narrators repeatedly teach us to see beyond the limits of any of the individual consciousnesses that populate his narratives, reminding us of connections the characters cannot recognize, implying mutual dependencies and possible dooms and suggesting patterns of life and change and movement that it is art's function to discover and create: "yet . . . their lonely courses formed no detached design at all, but were part of the pattern in the great web of human doings then weaving in both hemispheres, from the White Sea to Cape Horn" (*W* 22). The aesthetic sensitivity that this pessimistic little journal entry laments is a condition both of Hardy's art and of his ethics.

So the remarkable beauty of his books lies ultimately not in his embittered insistence that "nobody did come, because nobody does" (*JO* 31) but in his astonishing attention to the widest possible range of life, from the great patterns weaving among the hemispheres to the most minute particularities. The narrator, wise, distant, even self-protected from the imaginative clarity of his own perceptions, dramatizes a profound recognition of and compassion for the extraordinary varieties of life forms. This sweeping range, from macroscopic to microscopic vision, is centrally Darwinian. Darwin, to take a familiar example, reminds his readers that "the face of nature bright with gladness," in which "the birds . . . are idly singing round us" doesn't immediately reveal to us that the happy birds are happy in part because they are. Our concern is shifted to the insects who are destroyed. And the singing birds themselves are likely at some point to be destroyed by beasts of prey. And everything will be changing as we move through "all seasons of each recurring year" (Darwin [1859] 1964: 62).

It is a passage that, if not quite as poetically focused, might have been written by Hardy himself: it forces us to see more than is immediately visible, worries the calm with portents of change, and sets the particular scene in the context of constantly altering time and a broadening range of life. "I find no grain," cries the rook in winter" ("Winter in Durnover Field," *CPV* 149), and yet the Darkling Thrush, out of season too, breaks out in "full-hearted evensong / Of joy illimited" (*CPV* 150). Although we hear in Darwin's paragraph this Darwinian connection to the impending gloomy ironies of Hardy's narratives, it almost always comes as a surprise to first-time readers of *The Origin* just because it seems so poetic, or novelistic. The passage leaps off its scientific page because it is built on a feeling for the textures of life; its drama depends on a prior very strong attachment to life. It is not a long way from here to Jude's innocent concern for the crows, the narrator's alertness to the destruction of the snails on which Tess trod, or the sudden revelation of other life – the "ephemera" – when the match for a moment illuminates the evening in *A Pair of Blue Eyes*. Some of the peculiar beauty of Hardy's fictions depends on his Darwinian attentiveness to the finest nuances of landscapes (in which he finds history written) and to the weather and the circumambient conditions that touch upon the amazingly various individualities living centrally in, or on the margins of, his narratives. It depends on his often painful concern for life itself, and for the individuals who populate it.

The sensitivity that Hardy sometimes laments and that I believe is built thematically and stylistically into the very texture of most of his writing is both curse and blessing. Much of Hardy's life and art is aimed at protecting himself from it and celebrating it at the same time. His novels are full of characters who risk reaching for the intense joys and satisfactions – moral, sexual, material – of life just because they matter so much. In different ways, these are the stories even of Jude, but certainly of Henchard, and slowly, awkwardly, of Giles Winterborne. Clym Yeobright has tasted the possibility of fullness of life and returns to bring it to Egdon Heath (but loses part of that excessive sensibility in his blindness, forced to settle into a simpler life). Tess and Angel surrender to the deep sensuousness of their mating season. We know, of course, that in these novels, all ultimate aspirations to fullness are frustrated (just as Darwin's birds will be preyed upon by winter and hawks); but the power of the books is largely in the profound sense of possibility that inheres in life, and the deep disappointment that the evanescence and transmutation of those moments provokes – the deep moral outrage.

Hardy's fiction might be seen as both expression of and homage to what the "nerves" reveal, almost, as it were, to the "nerves" themselves, for they are nature's excess, what gives humans their eccentric, self-conscious power to see and feel beyond where the utility that would seem essential to natural selection takes them. They are homage to and also expression of the human capacity to feel, react, and imagine intensely and yet, through the voices of the narrators and behind them through Hardy himself, to give shape even to the apparently random and chancy movements of life, to create an art that will trace the figure in the carpet and embody a series of "seemings."[5] By creating narrators who see intensely but remain, in their language and style, outside the dramas that ensnare and inflict pain on those who yield to the call of their desires and passions, Hardy might be thought almost to approximate in fiction the "objectivity" that Darwin sought in his science. (For an early and still very useful discussion of the strategy of Hardy's distancing narrators, see Miller 1970.)

The staid, defensive, conservative Victorian gentlemen, Hardy and Darwin, are reputedly radical in their work, each one in effect reimagining the world just by explaining apparent order as a consequence of something like disorder and inattention, and then by extraordinary efforts of reason and imagination restoring order, perhaps as a tangled bank of infinite connections governed by fundamental laws, so that each vital body is dependent on each, perhaps by turning the old order upside down and ascribing it to a mindless world whose structure of resistance to imagination and feeling is imaginatively and feelingly narrated. If one reflects for a moment on their concern for respectability and conventional social conservatism as against the way their writing upset conventional moral and spiritual expectations, or hopes, it seems evident that both of them were strongly attached to the forms their thoughts and imagination were invalidating. Both lived inside the paradoxical condition of being revolutionaries without wanting to be, *malgré eux-mêmes.*

And both had seriously entertained the possibility of becoming clergymen. It is well known that Darwin, though never attending church services, participated importantly in the charitable activities partly run by the church at Downe, and that he retained strong friendships with some local clergy (see Browne 2002: 452–7). Michael Millgate notes that Hardy "was never to lose entirely his imaginative adherence to the Church, his love of its music and its services, and his belief in its civilizing and socializing functions" (Millgate 1982: 91; see also Hands 1989).

It is certainly no accident, then, that the unbeliever Hardy was strongly attracted to Comte's Positivism. Comte's late efforts to establish a Positive Church would, Hardy noted, help disenchanted believers, who know in "their heart of hearts" that Positivism contained "the germs of a true system . . . to modulate gently into the new religion" (*LW* 151). His notebooks contain many citations from his Positivist friend Frederic Harrison, and one is particularly to the point: "Religion does not mean a metaphysical doctrine about the origin of the Universe & man's condition after death: it means the combination of beliefs & emotions which train him to live the best life in the completest way" (*LN* II: 4). Harrison, as an active Positivist, felt what Hardy also felt (and what Weber would later describe), that a fully rationalized view of the world threatened to be disenchanted, to lose just those values of feeling and moral engagement and hope that the culture had previously found in religion.[6] As I have already suggested, this is a central Victorian preoccupation, and although there seems something slightly mad about Comte's form of religious Positivism, the movement represented a central aspect of the Victorian experience. It seems to me that Basil Willey was right many years ago when he claimed that "Comte is, in a sense, the century in epitome" (Willey 1949: 188). It is one thing to be able to see the world turned upside down; it is quite another, as disenchanted Victorians certainly felt, to *live* the irony such a vision produced. The comforts and sanctions and hopes that the world right side up had provided are reflected in the ways in which Hardy and Darwin actually lived.

In *Jude the Obscure*, in the figure of Sue, Hardy dramatizes some of the consequences and weaknesses of the Positivist religion. Beginning with a kind of Positivist secular worship, she converts Jude (and it matters that the conversion is not the result of proselytizing but of Jude's attraction to Sue, just as Lady Constantine's thrilling to the vision of a huge cosmos is driven in part by attraction to Swithin). He is immediately enamored of her, despite – not because of – her beliefs. Even here, it is not ideas but feelings that triumph. Sue and Jude are doomed just because they try to live the ironies in which they believe, both in attempting to cross class lines and, more important yet, in rejecting the convention of marriage. With bitter irony, the book traces Sue's reversion to a savagely self-punishing, masochistic religiosity that leaves her at the end to a misery that makes Jude's terrible death almost attractive (see Gittings 1975: 94–6). The horrifying force of this turn depends upon the ideal that Hardy read about in Harrison – the ideal of finding a way "to live the best life in the completest way," to achieve what Bennett and Taylor call "fullness."

There is a moral force that lies behind this kind of narrative in Hardy, aimed at the conditions, both cultural and natural, that allow for the establishment of the idea and then persistently frustrate it. The novel felt angry to its early audiences; even now it is difficult not to feel Hardy's moral outrage against the merely conventional and pained registration of the distance between natural processes and human sensibilities. A nightmare version of what rectitude and propriety mean (written by a man who insisted on rectitude and propriety in his life), *Jude*, working itself out in a deliberately symmetrical form while deliberately inverting the form of the Victorian *Bildungsroman*, gives vivid shape to the irrational, weaving that figure in the carpet to which, Hardy said, art is dedicated. Its supremely formal balance shapes a story that dramatizes Hardy's conviction that rationality cannot trump all. Lives are shaped by desire and chance, and by cultures whose civilizing restraints are incongruous with the realities of natural process. The rejection of mere rationality (think of Angel Clare in *Tess*, who becomes almost an allegory of the failure of abstract thought to engage well with desire, the determining force in Hardy's world) is part of what drives many of Hardy's narratives.

His fictional worlds are places of thought, yes, but, unlike George Eliot, he is not a philosophical novelist. It is notorious that Hardy rejected the idea that he was a "pessimist," but yet more interesting, he rejected the idea that his art was governed by ideas, Darwin's or Schopenhauer's or Spencer's or Comte's or Mill's. They are "seemings." He dramatizes Jude's reverence for the great voices of the nineteenth century as Jude wanders about Christminster and then, chased away, as he lies in bed thinking of them. But when he awakes, "[t]he ghostly past seemed to have gone, and everything spoke of to-day" (*JO* 83). The ideas are dreams from which, quite literally, he is excluded; "to-day" he feels the pull toward Sue. As for Hardy, as for his novels, the great figures Jude is so moved by and who in most cases had influenced Hardy himself, remained inadequate, even with their grand ideas, to the realities of the life he lived and the life he saw and created in a fictional world called Wessex.

Hardy creates and "thinks" in images and sensuous responses to the natural world, and this instinct of sensuous response is one Darwinian quality, usually not noticed, or not noticed as Darwinian, that emerges in Hardy. For Darwin, of course, the very form of his discourse entailed a full commitment to exclusive rationality, although his prose, as Robert Richards and Gillian Beer demonstrate, is loaded with feeling. His work is part of the continuing effort of modern science to naturalize everything, in the end, to naturalize human spirit itself – it is part of the great "rationalization and intellectualization" of life that Weber describes as the fundamental source of "disenchantment." But part of that work, as clear in Darwin as it was to be in Freud, was the work of recognizing and trying to understand the irrational – rationally. This entailed his intense alertness to the affective (and therefore moral) implications of his arguments. A careful reading of Darwin reveals not only the outlines of the world-historical theory but a deep moral engagement with its significance. The efforts at full rational explanation are often couched in language that responds to the deep emotional needs and moral commitments that drove his work and his life. There is a point in *The Origin*, when he is confronting the full significance of "the Struggle for Existence" in speciation, where he feels obliged to pause, and for what seem unscientific reasons. It is not one of Darwin's strong moments, but it is revelatory of the kinds of feelings and moral questioning that underlay his whole enterprise. Darwin concludes the chapter in language implying awe at natural selection's power to notice even the minutest particularity of any organism and to set to work upon it. In comparing the power of natural selection to the power of humans he evokes, very effectively, and with an implicit twist that is quite literary, I believe, just the sort of language religious writers might use in comparing the power of God to human power. But, arrived at this point, Darwin finally recognizes that he must come to terms with the implications of the process he is metaphorizing, and he concludes: "When we reflect on this struggle, we may console ourselves with the full belief, that the war of nature is not incessant, that no fear is felt, that death is generally prompt, and that the vigorous, the healthy, and the happy survive and multiply" (Darwin [1859] 1964: 79). It is an odd feature of this justification that it sounds very much like the kind of justification Darwin would have found in Paley's *Natural Theology*, a book that very much influenced his thinking, even as he attempted to overturn Paley's argument.

Written by Hardy, this would be bitterly ironic, and my guess is that Hardy read it that way. But what's important here is that Darwin, like Hardy, was seeing the terrible, disenchanting, possible implications of his theory and was trying, however feebly, to head them off. Hardy's strategy was a very different one: to take "a full look at the Worst," and confront it head on. Though committed to a kind of "objective" or "disinterested" rendering of their subjects, refusing to allow moral priorities to shape what they saw or how they would describe it, both Hardy and Darwin felt the urgency of the ethical problems their visions provoked. Darwin tried again in *The Descent of Man* to reintroduce consolatory moral considerations into his arguments, and with more success.[7] But it appears that Hardy's reading of this "struggle for existence" was as bleak as Darwin feared, and the novels might be read in one respect as controlled rages on behalf of the suffering *individuals* caught up in this universal struggle in which, Darwin had claimed, death is quick.

Darwin never raged against the universe, but for him as well as for Hardy moral framing of that amoral world was critical. As Pamela Dalziel has put it, "the existence of pain remained the insurmountable problem in Hardy's desire to believe in an omnipotent, loving power" (Dalziel 2006: 15). Both Darwin and Hardy put their arguments for unbelief in such terms, and they are moral terms. The Christian God can't exist as he is described because no God could be so immoral as to produce the system whose horrors Darwin tries to minimize in the passage I have just quoted. One can doubt that his own consoling paragraph provided him with much consolation. There was no easing the pain or justifying the death of his beloved and innocent daughter Annie at 10 years old. He looked back in his memoir of her by emphasizing her capacity for life and joy – "the main feature in her disposition which at once rises before me is her buoyant joyousness tempered by . . . her sensitiveness . . . and her strong affection." Darwin proceeds to record with quite tender particularity the various ways Annie behaved, helped, loved, cuddled. Concluding the memoir, he returns to the theme: "But looking back, always the spirit of joyousness rises before me as her emblem and characteristic: she seemed formed to live a life of happiness" (Darwin 1990: 540, 542). With the eyes that saw Annie die, he was describing a world in which life depended on death. And yet, though it was written out of great loss, the vivid impression of the life-bearing child renders, for readers of Darwin at least, a moment of enchantment, attention to the life lost, deep feeling for the writer, a sense of the wonders of life, even as it encounters, inevitably, death.

Hardy too writes of figures who seem formed to live a life of happiness, though of course they do not and cannot. The happy ending is not part of Hardy's vision, but happiness is. One of the crises of Victorian secularizing was the difficulty of finding a way to represent the world truthfully, as scientist or novelist, and imagining it as Robert Richards and Gillian Beer claim Darwin did (though most interpreters do not), as laden with value. The very move of Victorian realism away from its initial grounding in comic form toward the kinds of tragedies we find in, say, *The Mill on the Floss*, is tightly related to this problem. It is striking in George Eliot's work, which is virtually obsessed with telling the truth, that she struggles to imagine a secular world in which, after all, there is at least a rough justice, where Nemesis catches up with Arthur Donnithorne or with Bulstrode or with Tito Melema. Eliot builds her worries about the evacuation of justice and redemption from the world after Strauss's *Das Leben Jesu*, or Feuerbach's *Essence of Christianity*, or Darwin, right into her narratives. She finds the traditional happy endings very hard to replicate, but she builds a secular theory of consequences that is both empiricist and ethical: our deeds determine us as much as we determine our deeds.

For Hardy, to put it simply, that game was up: his narratives seem to imply that there is no relation, in moral value at least, between deeds and their consequences. If there is something like spiritual value and balance in the world it is behind those "nerves," that is, in human consciousness. That does not mean that his books are any less morally urgent and self-conscious than George Eliot's. Behind them lies not only a longing for a traditional understanding and justice, but also an enhanced sense of the possibilities of fullness – that life of happiness and joy Darwin saw in the daughter he lost.

Rather than reading the consequences of Darwinian thinking as amoral (and disenchanting), Hardy derived from Darwin an even more intensely moral understanding. In a letter to the Secretary of the Humanitarian League in 1910, he wrote:

> Few people seem to perceive fully as yet that the most far-reaching consequence of the establishment of the common origin of all species is ethical; that it logically involved a re-adjustment of altruistic morals by enlarging as a *necessity of rightness* the application of what has been called "The Golden Rule" beyond the area of mere mankind to that of the whole animal kingdom. Possibly Darwin himself did not wholly perceive it, though he alluded to it. (*LW* 376–7)

Hardy's "nerves" and Darwin had led him to this – the Golden Rule. Hardy was obviously *not* a moralist in his fiction, and Ruth Bernard Yeazell, in her recent exploration of the relation between Dutch painting and Victorian realism, reminds us of Hardy's resistance to moralism, quoting Reuben Dewy of *Under the Greenwood Tree* as saying, "If the story-tellers could ha' got decency and good morals from true stories, who'd have troubled to invent parables?" As Yeazell argues, Dewy's "contention that 'all true stories have a coarse touch or a bad moral' provides a working definition of realism that . . . seems very close to Hardy's own" (Yeazell 2008: 137). It is not that reality's narratives yield the moral Hardy draws from Darwin but that the exigencies of material life require from the human mind and spirit yet greater moral energies – an extension of the Golden Rule. If Darwin was right, that we are all quite literally related, then the Christian ideal of loving one's neighbor as one's brother becomes unmetaphorical, becomes literal. Your neighbor is biologically your brother, and you owe to the trapped rabbit that Jude hears or the horse killed when Tess falls asleep at the reins a deep moral debt. Although through Dewy Hardy may be arguing that truthful art must always have something coarse about it (we know Hardy's relation to the unofficial censorship of polite literature), this does not, certainly not from Hardy's way of looking, at all diminish the moral function of art. It is a part of the morality of art to register the ordinary with the most vivid particularity, to honor it, to recognize the wonder in its ordinariness, and finally to feel our own connection to it.

Many of these qualities of Hardy's work and life, as they reflect as well the sensibility and the attitudes of Darwin, are present in the wonderful sheep-shearing scene in *Far From the Madding Crowd*. It is worth pausing over this scene for a moment to get a feel for that capacity for joy to which Gillian Beer alludes, and that is implicit in Darwin's sad celebration of his daughter's life. The sheep-shearing takes place in a building as old as the medieval churches in the area, perhaps once part of the "conventual buildings" of the era. The architect Hardy celebrates the structure of these simple buildings, which show "the origin of a grandeur not apparent in erections where more ornament has been attempted" (*FFMC* 150). The place is steeped in its own history, which is reflected in its perfect adaptation to the work being done there: "the purpose which had dictated its original erection was the same with that to which it was still applied" (*FFMC* 150). It is a human construction, but "natural" as well – "the spirit of the ancient builders was at one with the spirit of the modern beholder" (*FFMC* 150). It is, in effect, a holy place, and if one wonders how Hardy's persistent feeling for religion expressed itself, it was in such places and passages as this, where the secularity is deeply religious:

> Standing before this abraded pile the eye regarded its present usage, the mind dwelt upon its past history, with a satisfied sense of functional continuity throughout, a feeling almost of gratitude, and quite of pride, at the permanence of the idea which had heaped it up. The fact that four centuries had neither proved it to be founded on a mistake, inspired any hatred of its purpose, nor given rise to any reaction that had battered it down, invested this simple grey effort of old minds with a repose if not a grandeur which a too curious reflection was apt to disturb in its ecclesiastical and military compeers. . . . The defence and salvation of the body by daily bread is still a study, a religion and a desire. (*FFMC* 150–1)

If one can hear some Positivist notes here, one senses more those characteristics I've already alluded to, the sense of the past deeply embodied in the objects of the present, the sense of the sanctity of the body and of the possibilities of creation in the human mind. It is an image of adaptation, and it suggests an evolutionary story – it is the "church" that is "battered down," while this brilliant structure, adapted to humans' natural needs, survives, however picturesquely modified by time. There is a genuine joy in life itself in this peculiar instance of adaptation – "the barn was natural to the shearers, and the shearers were in harmony with the barn" (*FFMC* 151). It is, in a way, a secular church, surviving because it answers to the needs Darwin had laid out in his theory, but, more importantly, because it harbors and sustains life.

"What are my books," Hardy asked, "but one plea against 'man's inhumanity to man' – to woman – and to the lower animals?" (Archer [1901] 2007: 35). This is, certainly, one of Hardy's deliberate, defensive and perhaps oversimplifying explanations of his art. And yet there is a very clear sense in which this is also true. Art, for Hardy, is the place where those "nerves" we shouldn't need for simple natural selection have important work to do, in particular because the Darwinian world he was living with and imagining was so far beyond the fundamentally anthropocentric explanatory modes of traditional religion and even of science. Those "seemings," which describe in such bleak and brilliantly formal organization the way nature and society seemed to Hardy, gave shape to the tangled bank, and made a new kind of meaning, resulting from Hardy's intense and singular attention to the ordinary.

His books do not feel moralized at all, despite the implicitly angry subtitle of *Tess*, "A Pure Woman Faithfully Presented." They are "enchanting" as the earlier *Far From the Madding Crowd* is enchanting, and celebratory of life and the body. This is so even in the last heavily ironic moments of *Tess*, the extraordinary scene in which Tess falls asleep as a kind of sacrifice on a Stonehenge slab:

> The band of silver paleness along the east horizon made even the distant parts of the Great Plain appear dark and near; and the whole enormous landscape bore that impress of reserve, taciturnity, and hesitation which is usual just before day. The eastward pillars and their architraves stood up blackly against the light, and the great flame-shaped Sun-stone beyond them, and the stone of sacrifice midway. Presently the night wind died out, and the quivering little pools in the cup-like hollows of the stones lay still. (*TD* 381)

Here, twenty years after the sheep-shearing, life is celebrated in a secularly holy setting. This is, of course, the moment when the police arrive to take Tess off, but the moment is loving and enchanted, sweeping from the vast views bringing the distant world close on the horizon to the brilliantly assonant image of the "wind" dying down over the "quivering" pools as they grow "still." And if setting up Tess on an ancient sacrificial stone is perhaps another of the excesses of Hardy's narrative ironies, it nevertheless appropriately honors both her "purity" and the sanctity of the body and of the secular. The dawn follows on a very rare sequence in Hardy when, however briefly, the doomed protagonists achieve that fullness of love that escapes almost all the others. It is an enchanted moment, even if implicit with anger for the inevitable violation of that secular purity; it is full of love for the movement of the heavens, for the subtle coming on of the silver light, and for the quivering of the pools; it is full of love for the gently breathing and very corporeal sacrifice, Tess, and full of love for the deep past that those stones represent.

It is but one of many such moving moments in Hardy, though a particularly striking one. The novel is doing the work that Bennett discusses in her insistence on the possibility of secular enchantment, and it is clear from images and moments such as this that the religious strain in Hardy's life did not die away. It just took different shape. Hardy continued to seek "fullness," and human flourishing, and he wrote, "let us magnify good works and develop all means of easing mortals' progress through a world not worthy of them" (*LW* 358). Hardy's "good works" are his art, his novels, his poems. It may be ironic that one of the ways that Hardy found to "ease mortals' progress through the world" was to write stories that described how very difficult that progress is. But it is in the language Hardy found, in what feels like reverent, intense attention to the material world in all its vital detail, in all its inevitable pain, and in all the complexity of that tangled bank in which we are all involved in one another, that Darwin takes on another, gentler life. It is the moral sense growing from Hardy's recognition of the implications of Darwin's theory — we are all, quite literally, brothers and sisters under the skin — that gives to Hardy's full look at the worst its profound force. Like Darwin, Hardy could not look at the mindless processes of the world without feeling. Against the interpretation that Darwin's rationalization and intellectualization of the world had stripped it of meaning and value, Hardy looks with Darwinian eyes and re-enchants it.

NOTES

1 I want to note here, in addition, a few other such connections made in earlier scholarship. A very important one that has not received through the years the attention it deserves is Perry Meisel's (see Meisel 1972). Meisel takes the emphasis on the external determinism suggested by Darwin as something that Hardy largely outgrew and argues that, for Hardy, the most important aspect of Darwin's thought was his extension of biological cause and effect to the internal, to the workings of consciousness. Through this turn, Meisel argues, Hardy makes connections with new Paterian aestheticism *and* with modernist explorations of individual consciousness. Obviously, a crucial and influential study of the Darwin–Hardy connection is Beer's *Darwin's Plots* (2000), which refuses to reduce either Darwin or Hardy to the ideas of struggle, survival, and a relentlessly determinist and naturalistically understood world. In my recent "The Woodlanders and the Darwinian Grotesque" (Levine 2006b) I attempt to follow up Culler's insight, connecting Darwin with the generic instability and formal plasticity of Hardy's novel.

2 One of the great nature writers of the twentieth century, Loren Eiseley, writes of nature with something of Hardy's attentiveness and awe, but, of course, with a kind of explicit reverence that Hardy, in his carefully adopted detachment and disillusion, seems to attempt to disguise. For a sense of the kind of "enchantment" (I don't think Eiseley uses the word) that Bennett is evoking and that I think inheres in Darwin's work, see among others Eiseley's *The Immense Journey* (1957), and *The Night Country* (1971). There is something of the mystic in Eiseley, a condition Bennett eschews. But all of his readings of nature are both "scientific," honoring in all its particulars the objects of his description, and resistant to the idea that a strictly scientific explanation of life, even if it were possible, can get at its full significance. His prose, in any case, is often a model of the way one can detect the wonderful in the ordinary.

3 See Daniel Dennett (1995). Stephen Jay Gould discusses the problem of "progress" and perfectibility in many of his books, and he, as a scientist and thinker, comes down on the side of the idea that Darwin rejected the notion of progress although he was culturally impelled to affirm it occasionally. One point of reference is Gould's huge posthumous study, *The Structure of Evolutionary Theory* (2002). See, for one starting point, pp. 467–8.

4 Note this famous passage from *The Origin of Species*: "We behold the face of nature bright with gladness, we often see superabundance of food; we do not see, or we forget, that the birds which are idly singing round us mostly live on insects or seeds, and are thus constantly destroying life; or we forget how largely these songsters, or their eggs, or their nestlings, are destroyed by birds and beasts of prey; we do not always bear in mind that though food may be now superabundant, it is not so at all seasons of each recurring year" (Darwin [1859] 1964: 62). One notices here not only George Eliot's "roar on the other side of silence," but also and yet more directly, the sensibility of Hardy himself. His narratives *and* his particular perceptions of the natural world and human lives are often almost built on this kind of revelation of the difficult struggles that lie outside our normal sensible perception of the life around us.

5 Hardy's comments on his art can suggest another very complicated connection with Darwin, though this is not the place to develop it. But I think one needs to take seriously his insistence that what interests him is art, what he cares about is art, and what he does with the materials from life that he brings to art is turn them into art. This does not turn him into one of the aesthetes of late nineteenth-century England, but it does connect him with them. In this well-known passage, for example, there is obviously something Paterian, as the moral and aesthetic are virtually elided:

> As, in looking at a carpet, by following one colour a certain pattern is suggested, by following another colour, another; so in life the seer should watch that pattern among general things which his idiosyncrasy moves him to observe, and describe that alone. This is, quite accurately, a going to Nature; yet the result is no mere photograph, but

purely the product of the writer's own mind. (*LW* 158)

Hardy moves here to Pater's formulation: to see the thing as in itself it seems to me to be – there are Hardy's "seemings." In Pater, in fact, the famous "Conclusion" to the Renaissance comes almost as a moral injunction, if a hedonist one. The moral injunction remains in Hardy, but note his insistence that it *is* a "going to nature," yet the order of nature, following Darwin, easily becomes a creation of the mind since the real thing, if we can so call it, has neither rhyme nor reason, being only a tangled bank that requires either Darwin or Hardy to interpret. As Perry Meisel put it in his excellent study of Hardy (he too noting a Paterian connection), "headquarters was slowly seen to shift to the inner life of the individual" (1972: 159), and the Darwinian Hardy joins that movement in late Victorian literature that was throwing the drama inside.

6 We are here on the grounds of the great questions of secularism that became so critical among the Victorians – not least for writers like Hardy and Darwin – and that continue to worry Western cultures. In his *Why I Am Not a Secularist*, William Connolly (who *is* a secularist) rejects a secularism that affirms its rational authority while, at the same time, failing to come to terms with the almost universal

human needs that religions have traditionally filled, and he affirms secularism's need to recognize the part of the brain called the "amygdala" – "the site of thought-imbued intensities." Charles Taylor counts Comte's Positivism as one of many European attempts "to hold on to some of the force of Christian piety, while dropping the Christian God of personal agency." These movements, says Taylor, could "win minds, but not hearts" (2007: 389), and they were all short-lived. Lying behind much of my argument here is Taylor's idea of "fullness" and of human "flourishing."

7 There, it will be remembered, facing the question of what distinguishes human from other animals, he attempts to show how the moral sense derives from a combination of developments, the development of intelligence, group selection (a much-debated and embattled concept in modern evolutionary biology), and, as Darwin puts it, "the social instincts, including in this term family ties." It is useful to note Darwin's later point that "the activity of mind in vividly recalling past impressions is one of the fundamental though secondary bases of conscience." The point is directly relevant to my argument here about the way Hardy's and Darwin's vivid (indeed often Wordsworthian) impressions of the particulars of nature tend to imply a strongly moral relation to the world. See Darwin [1871] 1981: 391.

REFERENCES AND FURTHER READING

Archer, William ([1901] 2007). Real Conversations. In Martin Ray (ed.), *Thomas Hardy Remembered* (pp. 28–37). Aldershot: Ashgate.

Beer, Gillian (2000). *Darwin's Plots: Evolutionary Narrative in Darwin, George Eliot and Nineteenth-Century Fiction*, 2nd edn. Cambridge: Cambridge University Press.

Bennett, Jane (2001). *The Enchantment of Modern Life: Attachments, Crossings, and Ethics*. Princeton: Princeton University Press.

Björk, Lennart A. (ed.) (1985). *The Literary Notebooks of Thomas Hardy*, 2 vols. New York: New York University Press.

Browne, Janet (2002). *Charles Darwin: The Power of Place*. New York: Alfred A. Knopf.

Connolly, William (1999). *Why I Am Not a Secularist*. Minneapolis: University of Minnesota Press.

Culler, A. Dwight (1968). The Darwinian Revolution and Literary Form. In George Levine and William Madden (eds.), *The Art of Victorian Prose* (pp. 224–46). New York: Oxford University Press.

Dalziel, Pamela (2006). The Gospel According to Hardy. In Keith Wilson (ed.), *Thomas Hardy Reappraised: Essays in Honour of Michael Millgate* (pp. 3–19). Toronto: University of Toronto Press.

Darwin, Charles ([1859] 1964). *On the Origin of Species: A Facsimile of the First Edition*. Cambridge, MA: Harvard University Press.

Darwin, Charles ([1871] 1981). *The Descent of Man, and Selection in Relation to Sex* Princeton: Princeton University Press.

Darwin, Charles (1990). *The Correspondence of Charles Darwin*: vol. V: *1851–1855*, ed. Frederick H. Burckhardt. Cambridge: Cambridge University Press.

Dennett, Daniel (1995). *Darwin's Dangerous Idea: Evolution and the Meanings of Life*. New York: Simon & Schuster.

Eiseley, Loren (1957). *The Immense Journey*. New York: Vintage.

Eiseley, Loren (1971). *The Night Country*. New York: Charles Scribner.

Gittings, Robert (1975). *Young Thomas Hardy*. Boston: Little, Brown.

Gould, Stephen Jay (2002). *The Structure of Evolutionary Theory*. Cambridge, MA: Harvard University Press.

Hands, Timothy (1989). *Thomas Hardy: Distracted Preacher? Hardy's Religious Biography and its Influence on his Novels*. Basingstoke: Macmillan.

Hardy, Thomas ([1874] 1993). *Far From the Madding Crowd*, ed. Suzanne B. Falck-Yi. Oxford: Oxford University Press.

Hardy, Thomas ([1887] 1998). *The Woodlanders*, ed. Patricia Ingham. London: Penguin.

Hardy, Thomas ([1891] 1988). *Tess of the d'Urbervilles*, ed. Juliet Grindle and Simon Gatrell. Oxford: Oxford University Press.

Hardy, Thomas ([1895] 1998). *Jude the Obscure*, ed. Dennis Taylor. London: Penguin.

Hardy, Thomas (1979). *The Variorum Edition of the Complete Poems of Thomas Hardy*, ed. James Gibson. London: Macmillan.

Hardy, Thomas (1984). *The Life and Work of Thomas Hardy*, ed. Michael Millgate. Athens: University of Georgia Press

Kaye, Richard A. (2002). *The Flirt's Tragedy: Desire without End in Victorian and Edwardian Fiction*. Charlottesville: University of Virginia Press.

Levine, George (2006a). *Darwin Loves You: Natural Selection and the Re-enchantment of the World*. Princeton: Princeton University Press.

Levine, George (2006b). *The Woodlanders* and the Darwinian Grotesque. In Keith Wilson (ed.), *Thomas Hardy Reappraised: Essays in Honour of Michael Millgate* (pp. 174–98). Toronto: University of Toronto Press.

Meisel, Perry (1972). *Thomas Hardy: The Return of the Repressed*. New Haven: Yale University Press.

Miller, J. Hillis (1970). *Thomas Hardy: Distance and Desire*. Cambridge, MA: The Belknap Press of Harvard University Press.

Millgate, Michael (1982). *Thomas Hardy: A Biography*. New York: Random House.

Richards, Robert (2002). *The Romantic Conception of Life: Science and Philosophy in the Age of Goethe*. Chicago: University of Chicago Press.

Taylor, Charles (2007). *A Secular Age*. Cambridge, MA: Harvard University Press.

Weber, Carl ([1940] 1965). *Hardy of Wessex: His Life and Literary Career*. New York: Columbia University Press.

Weber, Max (1958). Science as a Vocation. In H. H. Gerth and C. Wright Mills (eds.), *From Max Weber: Essays in Sociology* (pp. 129–58). New York: Oxford University Press.

Willey, Basil (1949). *Nineteenth-Century Studies: Coleridge to Matthew Arnold*. New York: Columbia University Press.

Wilson, Keith (ed.) (2006). *Thomas Hardy Reappraised: Essays in Honour of Michael Millgate*. Toronto: University of Toronto Press.

Yeazell, Ruth Bernard (2008). *Art of the Everyday: Dutch Painting and the Realist Novel*. Princeton: Princeton University Press.

4

Hardy and the Place of Culture

Angelique Richardson

When Hardy was writing *Far from the Madding Crowd*, "sometimes indoors, sometimes out," we are told in *The Life and Work of Thomas Hardy*,

> he would occasionally find himself without a scrap of paper at the very moment that he felt volumes. In such circumstances he would use large dead leaves, white chips left by the wood-cutters, or pieces of stone or slate that came to hand. He used to say that when he carried a pocket-book his mind was barren as Sahara. (*LW* 98–9)

It is an intriguing image: a writer possessed by a curious disregard for the materials of culture. When he carries a pocket-book, his imagination leaves him. He takes an image from nature to express this vacancy. Constrained somehow by his pocket-book, a utilitarian reminder of the need to produce (Leslie Stephen had just seen and approved rough drafts of the first two to three monthly installments of the novel and decided to accept it "at once"), his mind is desert. Deserted. The next paragraph finds him describing the "sweet smells and oozings" of cider-making in crisp autumn air. How are we to read this moment? Is it partly ironic? Is Hardy sending up, no less than accepting, the notion that he was a pastoral writer, embedded in nature? A couple of years later he went further in unsettling preconceptions with his London satire *The Hand of Ethelberta*, noting that he had "not the slightest intention of writing for ever about sheepfarming, as the reading public was apparently expecting him to do, and as, in fact, they presently resented his not doing" (*LW* 105). Nonetheless, in order to write – a fairly uncontestable expression of culture – Hardy needs nature. Or, at best, cultivated nature, chips left by the wood-cutters. He turns to nature to produce culture, bringing the two into fertile reciprocity.

Then he was in his early thirties. In his late seventies, months before the First World War was to end, when the manuscript of *Far from the Madding Crowd* was brought from the offices of the *Cornhill Magazine* and sold at Christie's Red Cross Sale on April 22, 1918, "Hardy's rather whimsical regret," we are told, "was that he had not written it on better paper, unforeseeing the preservation" (*LW* 416).

What is culture? For some it would seem to be all-encompassing, so that even nature is its product, its construct. But nature is not a derivative of culture but an independent source of value. And after all, etymologically, culture is allied with cultivation, the tending of nature. And is culture something to be acquired, or is it inside us, potentially even inside all of us? This rather depends on whether the word is wielded by broad-minded anthropologists or specialists in rather more narrow-minded thinking.

These have never been easy questions to resolve. But, after Darwin, they became even less so. Hardy was well aware that nature was not simply a discourse. Living in rural Wessex as well as in Tooting in south London, it could hardly have been otherwise. It goes almost without saying but, as I have heard it disputed at academic conferences, I shall say it. And Hardy did, after all, point out explicitly in *The Trumpet-Major* (1880), set in the time of the Napoleonic Wars, the malleability of discourses on the natural: "Nature was hardly invented at this early point of the century" (*TM* 139). Hardy is ambivalent, conflicted, contradictory on the place of culture, and in being so he engages in a deep and pressing late nineteenth-century quandary. Easy definitions, boundaries, and categories were in serious disarray. Humans were integrated into the natural economy. Was nature or culture a source of value? Or both? Each was looked to as ill or panacea. If it had ever been possible to draw a neat line between humans and nature, between culture and nature, it wasn't now.

It is well known to Hardy scholars that Hardy declared himself to have been among the earliest acclaimers of *On the Origin of Species* (1859). The work contained a simple hypothesis: species were not fixed but mutable. The implication: humans were part of the evolving animal kingdom. It is also well known that *On Liberty*, Mill's great philosophical plea for civic freedom, published the same year as the *Origin*, was one of Hardy's cures for despair, in particular the chapter on Individuality (*LW* 59). Writing to *The Times* on the centenary of Mill's birth, Hardy referred to *On Liberty* as a treatise "which we students of that date knew almost by heart" (*THPV* 239). In a letter of 1924 to the American literary critic Ernest Brennecke, Hardy remarked "my pages show harmony of view with Darwin, Huxley, Spencer, Comte, Hume, Mill" (*CL* VI: 259). But these influences were not an easy fit. Hardy was caught between biology and philosophy, between, in essence, Darwin and Mill, and not always able to accommodate both.

Thomas Henry Huxley, in *Man's Place in Nature* (1863), his follow-up to Darwin's *On the Origin of Species* (Darwin had greeted it with the words "Hurrah, the Monkey Book has come . . . I long to read it. The Pictures are splendid" [Darwin 1863]) remarked: "the simplest study of man's nature reveals, at its foundations, all the selfish passions and fierce appetites of the merest quadruped" (Huxley 1863: 131). In his lecture on "A Liberal Education and Where To Find It" (1868), given first to the South London Working Men's College, nature and culture are seen as being in close-knit cooperation. Education is presided over by a benevolent if exacting nature:

> Education is the instruction of the intellect in the laws of Nature, under which name I
> include not merely things and their forces, but men and their ways; and the fashioning

of the affections and of the will into an earnest and loving desire to move in harmony
with those laws. (Huxley [1868] 1900: 83)

> a liberal education is an artificial education [that education in which man intervenes]
> which has not only prepared a man to escape the great evils of disobedience to natural
> laws, but has trained him to appreciate and to seize upon the rewards, which Nature
> scatters with as free a hand as her penalties. (Huxley [1868] 1900: 86)

But Huxley became less optimistic. A quarter of a century later, in his Romanes
Lecture of 1893, "Evolution and Ethics," he warned that "the ethical progress of
society depends, not on imitating the cosmic process, still less in running away from
it, but in combating it"; man was to "subdue nature to his higher ends" (Huxley
[1893] 1989: 83). This shift reflects wider unease as to the value of nature.

How natural are Hardy's characters? On the opening page of what he referred to
as his "somewhat frivolous narrative," *The Hand of Ethelberta*, Hardy observes that
"many people" forget "that a bear may be taught to dance" (*HE* 1). The remark is
made of Ethelberta, who walks with "diadem-and-sceptre bearing" (*HE* 1). It is a
telling one. They forget, he explains, partly because they choose to read what is social
in biological terms: "for reasons of heredity discovering such graces only in those
whose vestibules are lined with ancestral mail" (*HE* 1). Culture, in the metaphorical
sense of refinement, rather than the archaeological or anthropological sense of general
human development or way of life, was at this time increasingly becoming associated
with class distinction. By the 1870s, the adjective "cultural" had emerged; by the
1890s it was in common usage (Williams [1976] 1988: 92). Hardy, acutely sensitive
to social and economic shifts and inflections in language, is quick, in this novel of
1876, to point out this tendency to assume the cultural is biological, an attribute of
breeding (itself a term conflating the biological and the social) rather than something
acquired. In one neat swoop, he rejects the reading of history as nature, and the class
implications of such readings.

Culture, then, the image of the dancing bear reminds us, can change nature. It can
develop it, alter it, counter it. As a bear can dance, a working-class woman can acquire
the culture – the manners, mannerisms, and peculiar behaviors – of the upper classes.
The image, suggesting that nature (as bear) is susceptible to culture, implies also that
class is not a fixed or natural category, however it may be read as one. The moment
warns against biologistic readings of character, against a belief in heredity as determining, in nature over nurture, that, the reader is reminded, would obscure Ethelberta's story. The passage encapsulates Hardy's class politics, his commitment to freedom
from the biological determinism (by which I mean determinism in a strictly heredi-
tarian sense – through generations, impervious to environmental influence) that was
escalating as the century progressed. It was the same politics, the same objection to
the misuse of culture, that some twenty years later would drive an incensed and
whiskied Jude to rail at a group of privileged Oxford undergraduates "every fool
knows, except you, that the Nicene is the most historic creed!" (*JO* 172).

The idea of the dancing bear is not a comfortable one. Culture can be an imposition. Some years later, in December 1913, Hardy would write to *The Times* on the cruelty of performing animals: "Quite possibly some animals may be, and are, trained for performances without discomfort to themselves, but there is ample evidence to show that many trainers prefer short cuts to attain their ends, and that these short cuts are by the way of cruelty" (*THPV* 346). If this is what nurture, or culture, can offer nature, how are we to read that contribution? A cautionary note about the relation of culture to nature is struck, calling into question the value of the breeding Ethelberta has acquired.

The Hand of Ethelberta is on one level a socialist-leaning account of rise through the British class system, a satire on, and challenge to, class hierarchy and prejudice, showing how a bright young woman can climb its ranks if she is willing to conceal her background. A butler's daughter, widowed soon after her marriage into the wealthy Petherwin family where she was working as a governess, she is living now with her mother-in-law as daughter and companion. Ethelberta is, largely, a self-made woman. Trained as a teacher, she completed her education on the continent, spending "two or three years in a boarding-school at Bonn" (*HE* 1), acquiring a culture that appears to be innate. As she so clearly demonstrates, there is much talent to be found in the working class. Nurture, in the nature–nurture pairing coined in 1874 by Darwin's cousin Francis Galton (who also coined the term eugenics in 1883), has triumphed. However, the narrator confides to us, "her claim to distinction was rather one of brains than of blood," "a fact not generally known" (*HE* 1). Both brains and blood are part of nature, though "blood" in this sense is a conflation of the biological and the social. Ethelberta's individual biology (her nature) and her ancestry (her history) are separated. In referring to her ability as her brains, Hardy situates her intelligence in her body; it is part of her immediate nature. In this way, then, an antithetical opposition between nature and culture is challenged, for while Ethelberta has acquired culture, it is her nature that has allowed her to do so, enabling and motivating her. Ethelberta uses her brains to alter her environment – her physical make-up moves her towards a new form of culture. The culture she acquires, though, is not necessarily enviable – it is revealed as repressive and shallow. In the exchange Ethelberta loses, like the dancing bear, something of her natural bearing.

At this point, Darwin was refusing the boundary and the rigid hierarchies that lie between nature and culture, or at least pulling at them somewhat, and calling into question the idea that the relation between the two is antithetical, positioning them as two coexisting, possibly equal, forces. When Darwin considers the relations between humans and animals in *The Descent of Man, and Selection in Relation to Sex* (1871), he gives several examples of animals acquiring culture. The use of tools was one example. He remarked: "I have myself seen a young orang put a stick into a crevice, slip his hand to the other end, and use it in the proper manner as a lever." (Darwin [1871] 1981 I: 51) In an addition to the second edition of *The Descent* a bear figures in these scientific observations:

A well-known ethnologist, Mr. Westropp, informs me that he observed in Vienna a bear deliberately making with his paw a current in some water, which was close to the bars of his cage, so as to draw a piece of floating bread within his reach. (Darwin 1882 I: 76)

Darwin charged his friend, the biologist George Romanes, to do for psychology what he had done for biology, to bridge, and also to problematize, the gaps between humans and animals. In *Animal Intelligence* (1882), challenging through the title any uniquely human claim for intelligence, Romanes devoted a chapter to "the psychology of all the Mammalia which present any features of psychological interest." In this, he quoted these observations of Westropp from *The Descent*, adding an example of his own and concluding: "the fact of bears reaching the high level of intelligence which the fact implies can hardly be doubted" (1882: 352). Intelligence and reason are not exclusive attributes of culture. Romanes quoted the same passage in his later study, *Mental Evolution in Man: Origin of Human Faculty* (1888: 51). Anxious to show that reason was not a prerogative of humans, Darwin had stressed the reasoned behavior of dogs, elephants and bears, remarking of Westropp's observations: "These actions of the elephant and bear can hardly be attributed to instinct or inherited habit, as they would be of little use to an animal in a state of nature" (Darwin 1882 I: 76). Here is a bear that seeks out aspects of culture necessary to its survival. While the image of the dancing bear initially posits nature and culture as separate, closer reading suggests a much more complex relationship. "Now," Darwin asks, "what is the difference between such actions, when performed by an uncultivated man, and by one of the higher animals?" (Darwin 1882 I: 76–7). In this way he asserts the continuum between humans and animals. The bear is not without reason, and thus the capacity to acquire culture, in the sense of behaviors that are not innate.

Hardy's dancing bear draws an analogy between the human and animal worlds, but, at a time when the capacity of the bear for reason, and, more broadly, the kinship between humans and animals, was being revealed by evolutionary scientists, the imposition of the dance on a reasoning animal seems especially inappropriate. The questioning of the value of culture that the image provokes continues through Hardy's novels and is in rich dialogue with contemporary debate. Nature in *The Hand of Ethelberta* is not just a backcloth, one of the oldest subjects and resources of the writer, but signals a more profound, if indirect, comment on the animal aspects of human nature.

Humans were revealed by Darwin to be motivated as much by instinctive patterns of behavior as by reason. Arthur Schopenhauer and Eduard von Hartmann, whom Hardy also read avidly, said as much too (see CHAPTER 2, HARDY AND PHILOSOPHY; see also Richardson 2002, 2004), and August Weismann, in his dismissal of the idea of the hereditary transmission of acquired characters, argued that instinct was innate, the product not of environmental influence acting over generations, but of natural selection (Weismann 1889: 91); Hardy professed to have "dipped into" (*LW* 240) these essays as soon as they appeared in English. And heredity is present in the novels, with the language of degeneration marking *Tess of the d'Urbervilles* and *Jude the Obscure* especially. In *Jude the Obscure* a psychological heredity enters, a decade after Hardy had taken assiduous notes from Henry Maudsley's *Natural Causes and Supernatural Seemings* (1886) (on Hardy's interest in Maudsley see Gallivan 1979; Shuttleworth 2002) and recorded: "The individual brain is virtually the consolidate embodiment of a long series of memories; wherefore everybody, in the main lines of his thoughts, feelings & conduct, really recalls the experiences of his forefathers" (*LN* I: 201, from Maudsley 1886: 319). But heredity for Hardy is only one of many, and competing, narratives of explanation (see Richardson 2002, 2004).

Likewise, animals were recognized to be capable of reason. On this, Darwin wrote:

> of all the faculties of the human mind, it will, I presume, be admitted that *Reason* stands at the summit. Few persons any longer dispute that animals possess some power of reasoning. Animals may constantly be seen to pause, deliberate, and resolve. It is a significant fact, that the more the habits of any particular animal are studied by a naturalist, the more he attributes to reason and the less to unlearnt instincts. (Darwin [1871] 1981 I: 46, emphasis in original)

He continued: "in future chapters we shall see that some animals extremely low in the scale apparently display a certain amount of reason" ([1871] 1981 I: 46). The evolutionary anthropologist Edward Clodd, chair of the Rationalist Press Association, president of the Folklore Society, and close friend of Hardy, quoted from this passage when urging "The artificial lines drawn between instinct in the animal and reason, as the prerogative of man, have vanished" (Clodd [1905] 1996: 15).

In his notebooks Darwin criticized the practice of grading one species higher than another – "it is absurd to talk of one animal being higher than another" (*Notebooks* B46, 74, cited in Desmond and Moore 1992: 232). He remarked in *The Descent* of "man and all other vertebrate animals" that "we ought frankly to admit their community of descent . . . It is only our natural prejudice, and that arrogance which made our forefathers declare that they were descended from demigods, which leads us to demur to this conclusion" ([1871] 1981 I: 32–3), writing of the second chapter, "Comparison of the Mental Powers of Man and the Lower Animals," "my object in this chapter is solely to show that there is no fundamental difference between man and the higher mammals in their mental faculties"; "all have the same senses, intuitions and sensations – similar passions, affections, and emotions, even the more complex ones" ([1871] 1981 I: 35, 48). Hardy copied out and pasted into his notebook extracts from Conrad Guenther's *Darwinism and the Problems of Life* (1906): "in the eyes of science man is not 'higher' than the other animals" (*LN* II: 225). Hardy's notebooks also contain the assertion from John Addington Symonds' *Studies of the Greek Poets* (1873) "<u>Man</u> – The very ground-thought of Science is to treat man as part of the natural order" (*LN* I: 65) and from Havelock Ellis' *The New Spirit* (1890) (where T is Tolstoy): "the first condition of happiness, he (T.) tells us, is that the link between man & nature shall not be broken" (*LN* II: 16).

As Darwin established that animals had reason, he found a commonality of instincts between humans and other animals, writing in "The Notebooks on Man, Mind and Materialism": "A child crying, frowning, pouting, smiling just as much instinctive as a bull calf, just born butting, or young crocodile snapping" (Gruber and Barrett 1974: 351). Instincts, for Darwin, were simply part of the natural order. By contrast, Mill deplored the validation of instincts, a development which he saw as a retrogressive validation of unmediated nature:

> the vein of sentiment so common in the modern world (though unknown to the philosophic ancients) which exalts instinct at the expense of reason; an aberration rendered still more mischievous by the opinion commonly held in conjunction with it, that every, or almost every, feeling or impulse which acts promptly without waiting to ask questions is an instinct. (Mill 1874: 44)

On this, Hardy parted company with Mill, plunging his characters into a primal world of unconscious drives, unreason and impulse. In *Tess of the d'Urbervilles* the sex instinct propels the milkmaids forward, without reference to consciousness and entirely without consent; they are bewildered, anguished vessels to biological impulse. Retty,

> The poor child torn by a feeling which she hardly understood, turned to the other two girls who came upstairs just then. . . . The air of the sleeping-chamber seemed to palpitate with the hopeless passion of the girls. They writhed feverishly under the oppressiveness of an emotion thrust on them by cruel Nature's law – an emotion which they had neither expected nor desired. (*TD* 149)

Hardy's women were, according to the sexologist Henry Havelock Ellis, writing in the *Westminster Review* in 1883, "made up of more or less untamed instincts"; "they have an instinctive self-respect, an instinctive purity. . . . One feels compelled to insist on the instinctiveness of these women" ([1883] 1979: 126, 106).

Havelock Ellis here follows the greater association of women with unreason that predominated in the nineteenth century and continues today (in, for example, sexist discourse which can include essentialist feminism); "it is generally admitted," Darwin had remarked,

> that with women the powers of intuition, of rapid perception, and perhaps of imitation, are more strongly marked than in man; but some, at least, of these faculties are characteristic of the lower races, and therefore of a past and lower state of civilisation. (Darwin [1871] 1981 II: 327)

But at times Hardy's men, no less than his women, are driven wholly by instinct. When Maybold the young vicar in *Under the Greenwood Tree* (1872) feels himself falling for Fancy in church on Christmas morning, he is moved, like Dick, by "the same instinctive perception of an interesting Presence"; his instincts are unconscious, surprising – his emotions can't keep up: "his emotion reached a far less developed stage" and "surprised at his condition" he "sedulously endeavoured to reduce himself to his normal state of mind" (*UGT* 43).

Jude's scholarly endeavors are described as his attempt to show himself "superior to the lower animals," but the possibility of contributing to "the general progress of his generation" is lost through his capitulation to "a momentary surprise by a new and transitory instinct." His story is set in motion by an inescapable biological drive:

> In short, as if materially, a compelling arm of extraordinary muscular power seized hold of him – something which had nothing in common with the spirits and influences that had moved him hitherto. This seemed to care little for his reason and his will, nothing for his so-called elevated intentions. (*JO* 87)

Instinct can so overwhelm Hardy's characters that they lose access to reason. Certainly, at these moments they do not seem to have the option of self-discipline that Mill counseled, or the will to subdue nature which Huxley would urge but which for Hardy does not necessarily seem to have been possible or desirable. Mill continued resolutely suspicious of instincts:

> Allowing everything to be an instinct which anybody has ever asserted to be one, it remains true that nearly every respectable attribute of humanity is the result not of instinct, but of a victory over instinct; and that there is hardly anything valuable in the natural man except capacities – a whole world of possibilities, all of them dependent upon eminently artificial discipline for being realised. (1874: 46)

For Hardy, contrastingly, instinct is often related to a greater authenticity of feeling and action, a greater truth value: "a complexity of instincts," for example, "checked Elfride's conventional smiles of complaisance and hospitality" (*PBE* 211).

Champion of individualism, of self-government and autonomy, Mill gave Hardy a way to a more defiant individuality, an alternative to biology that was liberating but, at the same time, limiting, relying as it did on a faith in human progress and reason (see Mill 1836). Hardy's own faith in reason was neither constant nor confident. While Mill kept animals in their prior place, Darwin gave Hardy access to nature that was a source of value, of moral and aesthetic meaning. Mill is more circumspect. For him, nature is an altogether more suspect and slippery idea. He gives two definitions: an entire system of things, or things as they would be without human intervention. And nature without intervention was bleak for Mill. While actively seeking to resist biological determinism in favor of the autonomous, self-governing individual, he risked underemphasizing nature, and, paradoxically, the sociality of humans, their links to communities. For an unintended or unforeseen consequence of the refutation of biological determinism and its rigid restraints is to refute biology itself, and, with that, at the most extreme end, material reality, or at least the bodily foundations of both selfhood and human social relations.

For Mill self-government was of overriding importance, and uniquely available to humans through deliberate choice and reflection. In interrogating contemporary enthusiasm for biologistic readings of humans and human difference Mill offered an environmentalist challenge to the idea that nature determined the development of individuals or the development of society. In "On Nature," written in the 1850s and published posthumously in 1874 as the first of three essays in the volume *Nature, The Utility of Religion and Theism*,[1] Mill treats all moral associations as social, arguing that moral associations are "wholly of artificial creation"; nature was to be countered at every turn. In the "Utility of Religion," begun soon after "Nature," Mill writes "the power of education is almost boundless: there is not one natural impulse which it is not strong enough to coerce, and, if needful, to destroy by disuse" (1874: 82).

Herbert Spencer, in an approbative piece on Mill, alluded to his turning from nature; his downplay, or expulsion, even, of the bodied, referring to Mill's "unusual predominance of the higher sentiments, – a predominance which tended, perhaps, both in theory and practice, to subordinate the lower nature unduly"; he was, Spencer regretted, a man who "too little regarded his bodily welfare" (1873: 42). Like Mill, Matthew Arnold sought in culture an antithetical retreat from the bodily, the instinctive. In 1869 in *Culture and Anarchy* he impressed upon his readers the dangers of the "bodily senses"; instincts were to be expunged, "the obvious faults of our animality" to be subdued; "the very principle of the authority which we are seeking as a defence against anarchy is right reason, ideas, light" ([1869] 1996: 37, 55, 85). But, the centrality, the inevitability and the morality, even, of animality, and the limits of culture were finding expression in Hardy and evolutionary scientists.

Darwin's argument in relation to the moral sense is "that any animal whatever, endowed with well-marked social instincts" (at this point, in the second edition, he adds, widening the ambit of social instincts, "the parental and filial affections being here included") "would inevitably acquire a moral sense or conscience, as soon as its intellectual powers had become as well, or nearly as well developed, as in man" (Darwin [1871] 1981: 71–2). He was quite clear:

> the moral sense is fundamentally identical with the social instincts; and in the case of the lower animals it would be absurd to speak of these instincts as having been developed from selfishness, or for the happiness of the community. They have, however, certainly been developed for the general good of the community. ([1871] 1981: 97–8)

This is a significant moment in the conception of the relation of humans to animals.

Darwin, a good Whig, believed in the effects of education as well as natural selection, remarking on his voyage on the *Beagle* in his diary entry for March 17, 1832 that education was "the mainspring of human actions" (Darwin [1831–6] 2001: 46). But he was ambivalent. Musing on his difference from his brother Erasmus, he observed that he was inclined to agree with his cousin Galton "in believing that education and environment produce only a small effect on the mind of any one, and that most of our qualities are innate" (Darwin 1887 I: 21). Here, Darwin privileges nature, or biology, over culture, or nurture. This was part of his investment in nature, which Hardy shared with him, at times finding nature adequate to human needs.

While Hardy resists biologistic understandings of character, suggesting education has a larger influence, the negative effects of education signal a disillusion with a culture that separates individuals from their environment and represses their animal spirits. The education Jude so covets is denied him, but also shown to be part of a wider culture of discrimination; equally, education sets Grace Melbury and Clym apart from their communities without giving them new ones.

One of the questions on which Darwin and Mill were at odds was the source of morality. The vexed question of the moral sense in animals was key to a much bigger question, the respective value of nature and culture. If animals had a moral sense, then nature, not culture, was ultimately the source of value. Darwin had been quite clear that humans were not alone in possessing moral instincts. In 1909 his son William Erasmus remarked that Darwin had been "an ardent liberal" who had "a very great admiration for John Stuart Mill and Mr. Gladstone" (Darwin and Darwin 1909: 12). But they remained divided on the question of the moral sense. Frances Power Cobbe, the feminist social reformer and founder, in 1875, of the Society for the Protection of Animals Liable to Vivisection and, in 1898, of the British Union for the Abolition of Vivisection, recalls disagreeing loudly with Darwin on Mill on sex on a Welsh hillside; she recorded in her diary that Darwin had said "Mill could learn some things from physical science; and that it is in the struggle for existence and (especially) for the possession of women that men acquire their vigor and courage" (Cobbe 1894 II: 445). She then offered him a copy of Kant on the "moral sense" (he declined). As it happens, Mill was not unversed in biology. In a letter to Comte of March 26, 1846 he remarked, "As for my meditations, they are most often devoted to questions of biology" (Haac 1995: 366).

In *The Descent* Darwin expressed regret at his necessary divergence from Mill:

> It is with hesitation that I venture to differ at all from so profound a thinker but it can hardly be disputed that the social feelings are instinctive or innate in the lower animals; and why should they not be so in man? Mr. Bain (see, for instance, "The Emotions and the Will," 1865, p. 481) and others believe that the moral sense is acquired by each individual during his lifetime. On the general theory of evolution this is at least extremely improbable. (Darwin [1871] 1981 I: 71)

In the same footnote, Darwin notes:

> Sir B. Brodie, after observing that man is a social animal ("Psychological Enquiries" . . .), asks the pregnant question, "ought not this to settle the disputed question as to the existence of a moral sense?" Similar ideas have probably occurred to many persons, as they did long ago to Marcus Aurelius. Mr. J. S. Mill speaks, in his celebrated work, "Utilitarianism" . . . of the social feelings as a "powerful natural sentiment," and as "the natural basis of sentiment for utilitarian morality"; but on the previous page he says, "if, as is my own belief, the moral feelings are not innate, but acquired, they are not for that reason less natural."

At this point Mill admits into nature that which is acquired through culture.

For Darwin the social instincts were the "prime principle of man's moral constitution" ([1871] 1981 I: 106). For Mill, only civilization (uniquely human) can produce goodness:

> It is only in a highly artificialised condition of human nature that the notion grew up, or, I believe, ever could have grown up, that goodness was natural: because only after a long course of artificial education did good sentiments become so habitual, and so predominant over bad, as to arise unprompted when occasion called for them. In the times when mankind were nearer to their natural state, cultivated observers regarded the natural man as a sort of wild animal, distinguished chiefly by being craftier than the other beasts of the field; and all worth of character was deemed the result of a sort of taming; a phrase often applied by the ancient philosophers to the appropriate discipline of human beings. The truth is that there is hardly a single point of excellence belonging to human character which is not decidedly repugnant to the untutored feelings of human nature. (Mill 1874: 46)

In his concern to expose the conflation of history and nature, to show that what was deemed natural was historical, Mill risked dislodging meaning and value altogether from nature: "There is hardly a bad action ever perpetrated which is not perfectly natural" (1874: 63).

In Hardy's novels, nature is frequently a source of good, humans often thrive where civilization is least developed, and animals show sympathy, empathy – reason, even: in *Far From the Madding Crowd*, George's puppy-dog son, in chasing Gabriel Oak's entire flock of sheep off a cliff, provides "another instance of the untoward fate which so often attends dogs and other philosophers who follow out a train of reasoning to its logical conclusion, and attempt perfectly consistent conduct in a world made up so largely of compromise" (*FFMC* 42). In several ways, Hardy was departing from Mill.

"Animals," wrote Romanes, "habitually and accurately interpret the mental states of other animals" (Romanes 1888: 198; see also 407). In *Far From the Madding Crowd* the contrast between human inhumanity and a dog's fellow-feeling is stark. On delivering Fanny safely to her destination the dog receives an unceremonious stoning from one of the workhouse men. The dog seems entirely free from the more limited, immediate, concerns that Mill attributes to animals; he may act from a shared position of homelessness, a fellow outcast, but there is nothing in it for him. While there is a clear hierarchy in Darwin between the higher and lower animals, differences are in degree rather than kind, and his thesis contains the potential to undo hierarchy. Frequently if not consistently Hardy could find space through biology for individuality and for morality, for sociality.

Mill's views on the individual appeal to Hardy, likewise his resistance to the use of nature as a way of explaining the cultural and social. His notebooks contain a cutting on Mill that suggests an overemphasis on individualism:

"Individualism," perhaps in a necessarily exaggerated form, had been both the lever and the stumbling-block of the Utilitarians. To Mill the external world was a series of isolated "facts" mechanically strung together by "causation"; and the consequent impossibility of asserting any universal truth about phenomena thus individualised . . . left him without any philosophical basis for science. (*LN* II: 357–8; unidentified newspaper cutting from a review of Leslie Stephen's *The English Utilitarians* [1900])

His attempt to find a basis for social science failed,

as most thinkers, including Mr. Leslie Stephen, agree, through his insistence on the very Bentham-like view that to know the characters of individuals (and could we say that Shakespeare knew them?) is to know the character of the society they constitute – a view which ignores alike his own theory of chemical action and the simple experience that a crowd is something often terribly different from the people in it. (*LN* II: 358)

It is no accident that the objections to Mill are couched in the language of chemistry, which speaks of elements changed by their interaction. Cohesive biological sociality, rather than individual minds, was lacking in Mill. The piece would have resonated with Hardy's own ambivalence on the relation of the individual to the group.

Biology, then, through Darwin, could provide Hardy with sufficient scope for individuality, without his having to adhere to Mill's bleak view of nature. In *The Hand of Ethelberta* it is outside of civilization that his characters are most free. Hardy wryly observed of this novel in *The Life and Work* that it was received with a "general disappointment at the lack of sheep and shepherds" (*LW* 136). There is, though, no absence of animal characters. Ethelberta (whose squirrel hair is frequently alluded to), cannot, we are told, be counted on to behave with her contrived dignity once she is outside the constraints of civilization, which demand the "repression of animal spirits" (*HE* 1). Happiest outdoors, she is drawn beyond the highway and railway, symbols of modernity, to the heath. When she races impulsively alongside a hawk chasing a duck she is caught up in this animal world; in her intent to see the end of the struggle her veneer of culture – "her stateliness" (*HE* 5) – goes away, she is breathless and excited, an entirely bodied creature; all we have to remind us of her out-of-placeness in the habitat of the birds are "her patent heels" which "punched little D's in the soil" (*HE* 5). A hybrid of impulse and patent shoes she is both part of, and an intruder upon, this natural world.

If bears are reluctant dancers, humans in *The Hand of Ethelberta* are not. Ethelberta "danced freely, and with a zest that was apparently irrespective of partners" (*HE* 27). Here is a dance quite different from the dancing bear of the opening pages, an expression not of culture imposed but of freewill, of exuberance, before she moves to the constraints of London. Humans dance when they are least repressed, quickly growing "full of excitement and animal spirits" (*HE* 27) – the moment is quite different from the enforced dancing of the bear, showing a culture that returns humans to a freeing, animal state; later they are compared to insects: "the couples whirl and turn, advance and recede as gently as spirits, knot themselves like house-flies and part again" (*HE* 28).

Civilization for Hardy is, at best, a mixed bag, regularly pitted against nature. In an entry for April 1884 in *The Life and Work* he recalled a scene of itinerant musician-sisters playing the song "In the gloaming," in the High Street. "*Now* they were," he remarks, "what Nature made them, before the smear of 'civilization' had sullied their existences" (*LW* 171, emphasis in original). It is a telling image. In the opening of *The Mayor of Casterbridge*, when Susan Henchard "looked down sideways to the girl she became pretty," at other times she is lost to introspective thought: "The first phase was the work of Nature, the second probably of civilization." (*MC* 6). Her prettiness is the result of immediate and unmediated sensory experience of affection, at a time when Darwin had established beauty as essential to the functioning of the biological world; the second contemplative phase Hardy ascribes to civilization, though with a moment of hesitation, for the faultlines between nature and culture trouble him. While Hardy repeatedly stated that his work provided a series of impressions, rather than a single outlook, there is nonetheless sufficient consistency to the politics of his thinking for moments of hesitancy, of genuine confusion, to be, at the very least, noticeable.

"You always was fond o' books, I've heard," remarks Tinker Taylor the church ironmonger to Jude in the tavern, "and I don't doubt what you state. Now with me 'twas different. I always saw there was more to be learnt outside a book than in; and I took my steps accordingly, or I shouldn't have been the man I am" (*JO* 171). He speaks as one whose assumptions about the limitations of print culture have already been proven, and there is a sense in which Taylor's position is the one borne out by the novel; the world of introspection makes Jude unsatisfied, seeming to take him from his happier, bodied, self; we find him "walking somewhat slowly by reason of his concentration," his initial disappointment that there is no simple way to translate, no law of transmutation, overcome. Though his choice of lover is entirely unsuitable, there is something celebratory about his falling in love, which takes him from his studies:

> He walked as if he felt himself to be another man from the Jude of yesterday. What were his books to him? what were his intentions, hitherto adhered to so strictly, as to not wasting a single minute of time day by day? "Wasting!" It depended on your point of view to define that: he was just living for the first time: not wasting life. (*JO* 92)

When he is in nature, he questions, perhaps rightly, the value of his studies: "There were no brains in his head equal to this business; and as the little sun-rays continued to stream in through his hat at him, he wished he had never seen a book."

The education on which they have been able to lay their hands assists Sue and Jude in their individual development, but they cannot be accommodated. Clym does return, after his education, pulled back towards the heath, but his education repeatedly distances him from it. One of the ideas that emerges from this early novel, which

Jude the Obscure would take on and develop, is the at-oddsness between the life of the mind and the life of the body. The heath natives see Clym as separated from them by his education, remarking: "they say he can talk French as fast as a maid can eat black-berries" (*RN* 107); the idea of speaking French is foreign to them, but they make it comprehensible through a familiar, bodied, image which paradoxically serves to high-light his distance from them. There is a similar moment in *Jude*, when the workmen refer to Christminster growing parsons like radishes (*JO* 64); the unfamiliar, the intellectual, is made comprehensible through natural analogy.

Clym's body is marked, scarred, by thought; the narrator observes "he already showed that thought is a disease of flesh, and indirectly bore evidence that ideal physi-cal beauty is incompatible with growth of fellow-feeling and a full sense of the coil of things" (*RN* 138); Clym is caught between mind and body in ways which are dra-matized through the novel and make him unable to find a lasting home on the heath. His erstwhile fellow natives associate him with a culture he has rejected and bear witness to his seeming inability to fit back into rural life; they are at home in nature, he is not: "Yes, Paris must be a taking place," observes Humphrey. "Grand shop-winders, trumpets, and drums; and here be we out of doors in all winds and weathers –" (*RN* 173). As the narrator remarks, "The rural world was not ripe for him" (*RN* 174); again, the language of nature, of harvest, serves only to highlight Clym's separateness, his renewed alienation.

The tension between the natural and the intellectual culminates in Clym's physical affliction. His reading takes place against nature, in the dark, and reacts against his body – another instance of the novel suggesting the *unnatural* nature of learning, pushing Clym further towards the heath (literally, so that at times he merges with his environment, becoming inseparable from it). For Eustacia "it is so dreadful – a furze-cutter; and you a man who have lived about the world, and speak French, and know the classics, and who are fit for what is so much better than this" (*RN* 258). But in one sense Clym's body's reaction to reading leads directly to furze-cutting – he moves from a life of the mind to one in nature, unable to belong fully in either. His damaged vision means he has to read large-print books; again, this is a dramatization of his body's refusal of the written word. And, in a foreshadowing of *Jude the Obscure*, it is bodily instinct that pulls Clym away from his studies; he divides his day between "sitting slavishly over his books" (*RN* 203) and meeting Eustacia; through her, his instincts for life, for the bodily, are roused.

Eustacia has her own discontents. A quest for culture pulls her away from her habitat, at a time when Clym has no choice but to move increasingly into his. Both exist between the poles of nature and culture, taken out of nature by books, by thought, and yet moving in opposite directions, amid the contented heath dwellers who live with the rhythms of nature, on a heath which is unusually resistant to culture. The anthropomorphism of the opening description of the heath jars with its meaning: "Civilization was its enemy. Ever since the beginning of vegetation its soil had worn the same antique brown dress, the natural and invariable garment of the formation" (*RN* 6). The characters who suffer in the novel are those who aspire towards culture.

When Clym works the heath, merging with nature, one among the insects, it is
no accident that he is singing a French opera song, a pastoral about shepherds. In
nature, he turns to culture, but culture has turned to nature. The reciprocity of the
two is vital. He can merge with the heath while he is able to distinguish himself from
it. The novel dramatizes the incompleteness of nature and culture for the modern man
or woman, but points, ultimately, to the greater failings of civilization.

What, then, was nature, evolution, capable of meaning for Hardy? Darwin has an
interest in finding continuity between humans and animals which Mill palpably does
not, for it is too close to innatism. Often Darwin underplays the significance of his
observations – *On the Origin of Species* famously underplayed its implications for humanity, leaving Huxley to write "the monkey book." In *The Descent* he affirms (albeit
hesitantly) human difference – "The moral sense perhaps affords the best and highest
distinction between man and the lower animals" – but proceeds to remind his reader
of the instinctive basis of this sense:

> I need not say anything on this head, as I have so lately endeavoured to shew that
> the social instincts, – the prime principle of man's moral constitution – with the aid
> of active intellectual powers and the effects of habit, naturally lead to the golden rule,
> "As ye would that men should do to you, do ye to them likewise;" and this lies at the
> foundation of morality. ([1871] 1981: 106)

In 1890 Hardy wrote:

> Altruism, or The Golden Rule, or whatever "Love your Neighbour as Yourself" may be
> called, will ultimately be brought about I think by the pain we see in others reacting
> on ourselves, as if we and they were a part of one body. Mankind, in fact, may be, and
> possibly will be, viewed as members of one corporeal frame. (*LW* 235)

In a letter to the Humanitarian League in 1910 he spelt out what he saw as the greatest implication of Darwin's work:

> Few people seem to perceive fully as yet that the most far-reaching consequence of the
> establishment of the common origin of all species, is ethical; that it logically involved
> a readjustment of altruistic morals by enlarging as a *necessity of rightness* the application
> of what has been called "The Golden Rule" beyond the area of mere mankind to that
> of the whole animal kingdom. Possibly Darwin himself did not wholly perceive it,
> though he alluded to it. (*LW* 376–7)

Hardy's interest in Darwin was quite different from that of some of his literary contemporaries, who drew on *The Descent* in their biologistic arguments against the
working class (whom they deemed both morally and biologically defective), and in
favor of the middle class, who embodied for them the good human. These writers
urged humans to subordinate their instincts and passions to their reason, distancing

themselves from their animal natures through recourse to reason and intervening eugenically in nature (see Richardson 2003). By contrast, for Hardy, to be a good human at the end of the nineteenth century was to be close to, and acknowledge kinship with, animals; in essence, to follow Phillotson's advice to Jude to hold on to the necessity of both nature and culture: "Be a good boy, remember; and be kind to animals and birds, and read all you can" (*JO* 49).

NOTE

1 Helen Taylor in her foreword to "Nature" notes that the first two of these essays were written between the years 1850 and 1858, during which interval three other essays – on justice, on utility, and on liberty – were also composed. The essays on justice and utility were afterwards incorporated, with some alterations and additions, into one, and published under the name of *Utilitarianism*.

REFERENCES AND FURTHER READING

Arnold, Matthew ([1869] 1996). *Culture and Anarchy*, ed. J. Dover Wilson. Cambridge: Cambridge University Press.

Barrett, P. H., P. J. Gautry, S. Herbert, D. Kohn, and S. Smith (eds.) (1987). *Charles Darwin's Notebooks, 1836–1844*. Cambridge: Cambridge University Press.

Beer, Gillian (1996). *Open Fields: Science in Cultural Encounter*. Oxford: Clarendon Press.

Björk, Lennart A. (ed.) (1985). *The Literary Notebooks of Thomas Hardy*, 2 vols. London and Basingstoke: Macmillan.

Clodd, Edward ([1905] 1996). *Animism: The Seed of Religion*. Kessinger Publishing.

Cobbe, Frances Power (1894). *Life of Frances Power Cobbe by Herself*, 2 vols. Boston: Houghton Mifflin.

Darwin, Charles ([1831–6] 2001). *Darwin's Beagle Diary*, ed. R. D. Keynes. Cambridge: Cambridge University Press.

Darwin, Charles (1863). Letter to Huxley, Feb. 18, 1863. Thomas Huxley Papers 5: 173. London: Imperial College of Science and Technology. Reprinted in *The Correspondence of Charles Darwin*, ed. Frederick Burkhardt and Sydney Smith. Cambridge: Cambridge University Press (1985), 148.

Darwin, Charles ([1871] 1981). *The Descent of Man, and Selection in Relation to Sex*, 2 vols. Princeton: Princeton University Press.

Darwin, Charles (1882). *The Descent of Man*, 2nd edn., 2 vols. London: John Murray.

Darwin, Charles (1887). *The Life and Letters of Charles Darwin: Including an Autobiographical Chapter*, ed. Francis Darwin, 2 vols. New York: D. Appleton.

Darwin, George, and Francis Darwin (eds.) (1909). *Darwin Celebration Speeches Delivered at the Banquet Held on June 23rd 1909*. Cambridge: Cambridge Daily News.

Desmond, Adrian, and James Moore (1992). *Darwin*. Harmondsworth: Penguin.

Ellis, Henry Havelock ([1883] 1979). Thomas Hardy's Novels. *Westminster Review*, 99 (NS 63), 334–64. In R.G. Cox (ed.), *Thomas Hardy: The Critical Heritage* (pp. 103–32). London and New York: Routledge.

Gallivan, Patricia (1979). Science and Art in *Jude the Obscure*. In Anne Smith (ed.), *The Novels of Thomas Hardy* (pp. 126–44). New York: Barnes & Noble.

Galton, Francis (1874). *English Men of Science: Their Nature and Nurture*. London: Macmillan.

Galton, Francis (1883). *Inquiries into Human Faculty and its Development*. London: Macmillan.

Gruber, Howard E., and P. H. Barrett (1974). *Darwin on Man. A Psychological Study of Scientific Creativity; together with Darwin's Early and Unpublished Notebooks*. Transcribed and annotated by Paul H. Barrett, commentary by Howard E. Gruber. London: Wildwood House.

Haac, Oscar A. (ed. and trans.) (1995). *The Correspondence of John Stuart Mill and Auguste Comte*. New Brunswick, NJ: Transaction Publishers.

Hardy, Thomas ([1872] 1985). *Under the Greenwood Tree*, ed. Simon Gatrell. Oxford: Oxford University Press.

Hardy, Thomas ([1873] 1986). *A Pair of Blue Eyes*, ed. Roger Ebbatson. Harmondsworth: Penguin.

Hardy, Thomas ([1874] 1993). *Far From the Madding Crowd*, ed. Suzanne B. Falck-Yi. Oxford: Oxford University Press.

Hardy, Thomas ([1876] 1975). *The Hand of Ethelberta*, ed. Robert Gittings. London: Macmillan.

Hardy, Thomas ([1878] 1990). *The Return of the Native*, ed. Simon Gatrell. Oxford: Oxford University Press.

Hardy, Thomas ([1880] 1991). *The Trumpet-Major*, ed. Richard Nemesvari. Oxford: Oxford University Press.

Hardy, Thomas ([1886] 2004). *The Mayor of Casterbridge*, ed. Dale Kramer. Oxford: Oxford University Press.

Hardy, Thomas ([1895] 1985). *Jude the Obscure*, ed. C. H. Sisson. Harmondsworth: Penguin.

Hardy, Thomas ([1891] 1988). *Tess of the d'Urbervilles*, ed. Juliet Grindle and Simon Gatrell. Oxford: Oxford University Press.

Hardy, Thomas (1984). *The Life and Work of Thomas Hardy*, ed. Michael Millgate. London: Macmillan.

Huxley, Thomas Henry (1863). *Evidence as to Man's Place in Nature*. New York: D. Appleton.

Huxley, Thomas Henry ([1868] 1900). A Liberal Education and Where To Find It. In *Collected Essays*. 9 vols. (III: 76–110). London: Macmillan.

Huxley, Thomas Henry ([1893] 1989). *Evolution and Ethics*, ed. James Paradis and George C. Williams. Princeton: Princeton University Press.

Maudsley, Henry (1886). *Natural Causes and Supernatural Seemings*. London: Kegan Paul, Trench & Co.

Mill, John Stuart (1836). Civilization. *London and Westminster Review*, 25, 160–205.

Mill, John Stuart (1874). *Nature, The Utility of Religion and Theism*, introd. Helen Taylor. London: H. Holt.

Millgate, Michael (ed.) 2001. *Thomas Hardy's Public Voice: The Essays, Speeches, and Miscellaneous Prose*. Oxford: Clarendon Press.

Purdy, Richard Little, and Michael Millgate (eds.) (1978–88). *The Collected Letters of Thomas Hardy*. 7 vols. Oxford: Clarendon Press.

Richardson, Angelique (2002). Hardy and Biology. In Phillip Mallett (ed.), *Thomas Hardy: Texts and Contexts* (pp. 156–79). Basingstoke: Palgrave Macmillan.

Richardson, Angelique (2003). *Love and Eugenics in the Late Nineteenth Century: Rational Reproduction and the New Woman*. Oxford: Oxford University Press.

Richardson, Angelique (2004). Hardy and Science: A Chapter of Accidents. In Phillip Mallett (ed.), *Palgrave Advances in Thomas Hardy Studies* (pp. 156–80). Basingstoke: Palgrave Macmillan.

Romanes, George (1882). *Animal Intelligence*. London: Kegan Paul, Trench & Co.

Romanes, George (1888). *Mental Evolution in Man: Origin of Human Faculty*. London: Kegan Paul, Trench & Co.

Shuttleworth, Sally (2002). "Done because we are too menny": Little Father Time and Child Suicide in Late-Victorian Culture. In Phillip Mallett (ed.), *Thomas Hardy, Texts and Contexts* (pp. 133–55). Basingstoke: Palgrave Macmillan.

Spencer, Herbert (1873). His Moral Character. In Herbert Spencer, Henry Fawcett, Frederic Harrison, and Other Distinguished Authors, *John Stuart Mill: His Life and Works. Twelve Sketches*. Boston: James R Osgood.

Weismann, August (1889). On Heredity. In *Essays Upon Heredity*. Oxford: Clarendon Press.

Williams, Raymond ([1976] 1988). *Keywords: A Vocabulary of Culture and Society*. London: HarperCollins.

5

"The Hard Case of the Would-be-Religious": Hardy and the Church from Early Life to Later Years

Pamela Dalziel

although invidious critics had cast slurs upon him as Nonconformist, Agnostic, Atheist, Infidel, Immoralist, Heretic, Pessimist or something else equally opprobrious in their eyes, they had never thought of calling him what they might have called him much more plausibly – churchy; not in an intellectual sense, but in so far as instincts and emotions ruled. As a child, to be a parson had been his dream; – moreover, he had had several clerical relatives who held livings; while his grandfather, father, uncle, brother, wife, cousin, and two sisters had been musicians in various churches over a period covering altogether more than a hundred years. He himself had frequently read the church-lessons, and had at one time as a young man begun reading for Cambridge with a view to taking Orders. (LW 407)

Any discussion of "Hardy and the Church" must begin by defining which Church – or church – is under consideration. Is it the Church as an institution, and, if so, is it the Church of England or the Church of Rome? Or is it the church of the orthodox churchman, the church of the radical reformer Jesus, or the church as the centre of village life? Perhaps it is the parish church of Stinsford, or the church as embodied in its buildings, music, or liturgy? Hardy had views on all of these churches, and many of his views evolved during the course of his life.

Before attempting to define these diverse and sometimes contradictory views, scholars must come to terms with the autobiographical *The Life and Work of Thomas Hardy*, written by Hardy during his late seventies and early eighties, and destined to be published after his death over Florence Hardy's name as *The Early Life of Thomas Hardy, 1840–1891* and *The Later Years of Thomas Hardy, 1892–1928*.[1] Most of the factual details of *Life and Work* can be shown to be accurate enough, if inevitably selective (see *LW* xiv–xvi); however, Hardy's interpretation of those facts, especially his representation of his personal views during his early and middle years, does not always stand up to scholarly scrutiny. The elderly Hardy was, after all, consciously seeking to construct a public image of himself as he chose to be remembered, and the creation of this essentially consistent narrative persona "Thomas Hardy" inevitably required the privileging of certain biographical details and the misrepresentation or omission of others. *Life and Work* thus provides an excellent account of Hardy's later views – including his response to the Church in its many manifestations – but is sometimes less than reliable in its representation of his early beliefs and attitudes.

Hardy was baptized in the Church of England and brought up "according to strict Church principles" (*CL* I: 259). As a child he regularly attended the parish church of Stinsford, with which his family had longstanding connections. In the early 1800s his grandfather had revitalized the Stinsford choir by gathering together a small group of instrumentalists; some thirty years later the choir – affectionately evoked as the "Mellstock quire" in *Under the Greenwood Tree* and elsewhere – included Hardy's grandfather, father, and uncle. From 1837 until 1891 – i.e., from three years before Hardy's birth until the final year recalled in *Early Life* – the vicar of Stinsford was the Reverend Arthur Shirley, a High Church clergyman of old family and Oxford education, who, undeterred by Dorset's reputation for Low churchmanship, brought to Stinsford the energetic commitment to Tractarianism and keen sense of duty characteristic of such early Oxford Movement leaders as Keble and Newman (see Hands 1989: 6–11). Timothy Hands has ably challenged the *Life and Work* portrait of Shirley, particularly Hardy's suggestion that the vicar "seemed bewildered" by questions about paedo-baptism, but what can be accepted with some confidence – in keeping with the distinction outlined above between the recounting of factual details and the interpretation of those details – are Hardy's accounts of himself as a young boy wrapping himself in a tablecloth before reading the Morning Prayer and preaching a sermon ("a patchwork of the sentences used by the vicar"), of his knowing "the Morning and Evening Services by heart," and of his subsequently teaching Sunday school with Shirley's two sons (Hands 1989: 8–9; *LW* 33, 20, 23, 30). More suspect is Hardy's downplaying of his religious seriousness as a boy when, for example, he suggests that it was (merely) his "dramatic sense of the church services" which led him to imitate Shirley, or dismissively notes that "Everybody said that Tommy would have to be a parson, being obviously no good for any practical pursuit" (*LW* 20).

Whatever Hardy's childhood enthusiasms, it is certain that as a youth he aspired to enter the Church and that on at least one occasion he experimented with sermon-writing. On October 24, 1858, when he was in the third year of his articles to the Dorchester architect John Hicks and counted among his personal friends his fellow pupil Henry Bastow, an ardent Baptist, and several of the sons of Henry Moule, the Evangelical vicar of Fordington, Hardy wrote a theologically orthodox, if uninspired, sermon based on Galatians 3: 13: "Christ hath redeemed us from the curse of the law, being made a curse for us" (printed in Dalziel 2006: 8–9). The sermon is remarkable for its evangelistic fervor and distinctly Evangelical tone; when considered in conjunction with Hardy's early Bible markings and Bastow's surviving letters (see Dalziel 2006: 10–12), it suggests that during the late 1850s and early 1860s Hardy had a personal faith that was ardent, orthodox, and Evangelically inflected, hence fundamentally different in order and magnitude from the gentlemanly, unimpassioned churchmanship defined by the *Life and Work* accounts of the young Hardy's determining to "stick to his own [Church] side" when debating paedo-baptism, or his "curious scheme" of combining poetry and the Church by becoming "a curate in a country village" (*LW* 33, 53).

Hardy's youthful sympathy with Evangelicalism did not, however, mark a break with his High Church upbringing. From the late 1850s until the mid-1860s he was worshiping at both High and Low churches (see Hands 1989: 16–27), and indeed shortly after moving to London in 1862 he wrote to his sister Mary Hardy that the distinctly High St Mary's, Kilburn, was "rather to my taste[,] and they sing most of the tunes in the Salisbury hymn book there" (*CL* I: 1). Hardy's lifelong love of traditional church music is already in evidence here, but there is nothing to suggest that the High Church ritualism and preaching were not also to his taste. Hardy subsequently referred to the years of his late teens and early twenties as his "theological days," when he was an "orthodox Churchman" (*CL* III: 197, 308),[2] and his active participation in both types of churchmanship, though somewhat unusual for a mid-Victorian, could simply reflect a tendency towards theological openness or even eclecticism.

In any case, Hardy never had to align himself with a single church party, since at some point during his mid-twenties he began to question Christian orthodoxy. Almost nothing is known of what led to Hardy's loss of faith. The only *Life and Work* reference to this critical philosophical shift is the vague and somewhat disingenuous statement that his plan of matriculating at Cambridge and becoming a country curate "fell through less because of its difficulty than from a conscientious feeling, after some theological study, that he could hardly take the step with honour while holding the views that on examination he found himself to hold" (*LW* 53). Those "views" are never specified, and there is no suggestion that, as his 1866 letter to Mary Hardy clearly indicates, practical considerations figured prominently in the decision to abandon his long-cherished dream of a university education: "I find on adding up expenses and taking into consideration the time I should have to wait, that my notion is too far fetched to be worth entertaining any longer" (*CL* I: 7).

Life and Work also states that Hardy was one of the "earliest acclaimers" of Darwin's 1859 *On the Origin of Species* (see CHAPTER 3, HARDY AND DARWIN) and that he had been "impressed . . . much" by the notorious 1860 Broad Church collection, *Essays and Reviews* (*LW* 158, 37); however, if it was the reading of these works which led to his rejection of orthodoxy in the mid-1860s, his reaction was of rather slow gestation, requiring some five years. Moreover, if, as *Life and Work* suggests, Hardy's heterodoxy, originating in "theological study," was primarily intellectual, it is somewhat surprising that he did not align himself with the Broad Church, many of whose defining liberal principles he endorsed during his later years.

Intellectual sympathy in itself, however, would have been insufficient to keep Hardy within the Church if, as seems probable, he underwent some kind of personal crisis of faith in the mid-1860s. It is also possible that during these London years he became disillusioned with the contemporary Church, since by the summer of 1867 he was at work on *The Poor Man and the Lady*, that lost first novel which evidently included "modern Christianity" among its numerous objects of satire (*LW* 63). But presumably the most significant factor – quite possibly the determining factor – both in establishing Hardy's new philosophical position and in maintaining it throughout the remainder of his life was his inability to be persuaded by theodicean arguments (see, e.g., *LW* 338–9). His acute identification with the world's suffering rendered him incapable of belief in a benevolent, omnipotent God, and ultimately led him to conclude that the Cause of Things must be unconscious, "neither moral nor immoral, but *un*moral" (*CL* VI: 54), not unlike the "purblind Doomsters" in his poem "Hap," dated 1866. Some forty years later, responding to a suggestion in the *Daily News* of March 14, 1908 that his "pessimism" must lead to despair, Hardy confessed:

> What does often depress me is the sight of so much pain in the world, constant pain; & it did just as much when I was an orthodox Churchman as now; for no future happiness can remove from the past sufferings that have been endured. (*CL* III: 308)

Little documentary evidence of Hardy's attitude towards the Church – or towards Church doctrine – survives from the mid-1860s, when he ceased to subscribe to Christian orthodoxy, to the early 1880s, when he began to engage more actively in philosophical speculation, or at least began to formulate and to record the philosophical ideas that he later considered worthy of preservation. "Literary Notes I" includes four leaves from an earlier notebook that testify to his having read Newman's *Apologia Pro Vita Sua* on July 2, 1865; the identically dated *Life and Work* note suggests that by this time Hardy had already ceased to concur with Newman's fundamental initial premise, the certainty of "the being of a God" (*LN* I: xxxii, 5–7; Newman 1864: 376):

> Style charming, and his logic really human, being based not on syllogisms but on converging probabilities. Only – and here comes the fatal catastrophe – there is no first link to his excellent chain of reasoning, and down you come headlong. (*LW* 50–1)

Life and Work also states that in May 1870 Hardy was reading Comte, and that in January 1874 the *Spectator* reviewer's tentative identification of George Eliot as the author of *Far from the Madding Crowd* could perhaps be attributed to Hardy's "latterly" having read "Comte's *Positive Philosophy*, and writings of that school, some of whose expressions had thus passed into his vocabulary" (*LW* 79, 100). In 1876 Hardy transcribed into "Literary Notes I" numerous passages from Comte's *Social Dynamics*, thereby providing further support for his claim nearly twenty years later that, although he was not himself a Positivist, "no person of serious thought in these times could be said to stand aloof from Positivist teaching & ideals" (*LN* I: 64, 66–78; *CL* III: 53). The influence of Positivism on Hardy's thought and writing, particularly during the 1870s, has long been acknowledged (see Björk 1987: 79–98; Wright 1986: 202–17; and CHAPTER 2, HARDY AND PHILOSOPHY), and indeed, as one of the "Literary Notes I" entries demonstrates, Hardy found in *Social Dynamics* another articulation of his own position with respect to "God" as conventionally defined: "A self-contradiction in the conception of a single God. 'For omnipotence, omniscience, & moral perfection are irreconcilable' with a radically imperfect world" (*LN* I: 69).

According to *Life and Work*, the most significant influence on Hardy's thought during the 1870s and beyond was not Comte, however, but another writer much indebted to him: Leslie Stephen, "the man whose philosophy was to influence . . . [Hardy's] own for many years, indeed, more than that of any other contemporary" (*LW* 102). In 1873 Hardy read and, as he told Stephen, admired "Are We Christians?" (*Fortnightly Review*, March 1873), with its questioning of "whether the doctrines preached by many admirable men are really Christian doctrines reconciled to reason, or rationalism thinly veiled under Christian phraseology" (*THPV* 260; Stephen 1873a: 302). Stephen was "gratified" by Hardy's approbation of his article, remarking that he would "have some more to say upon that matter" in his forthcoming *Essays on Freethinking and Plainspeaking*, which would "shock the orthodox" (*THPV* 260). Several of the volume's essays, most notably "The Broad Church" (originally published in *Fraser's Magazine*, March 1870), enabled Stephen to contextualize and to justify his 1862 decision to cease performing his clerical responsibilities at Trinity Hall, Cambridge, though it was not until 1875 that he formally renounced his Orders, asking Hardy to witness his signature. Stephen's choice of Hardy as witness suggests that their conversation that evening about "theologies decayed and defunct, the origin of things, the constitution of matter, the unreality of time, and kindred subjects" (*LW* 109) was probably not the first of its kind, and indeed Hardy's *Life and Work* justification of the abandonment of his own clerical ambitions – "he could hardly take the step with honour while holding the views that on examination he found himself to hold" (*LW* 53) – sounds rather like an anachronistic assignment to his mid-1860s self of Stephen's views as articulated in the 1870s.

Life and Work includes no philosophically speculative entries for the 1865–80 period, a time when Hardy kept up some outward appearance of orthodoxy, at least to the point of regular church attendance while at Stinsford and St. Juliot, and presumably also after his marriage to Emma Gifford in 1874. A note of 1877, when he and Emma were living in Sturminster Newton – their "happiest time" (*LW* 122) – suggests that he was a regular church-goer at that date: "Sunday. Grannys with round spectacles seen reading the lessons for the day. You see them this year, & the next, & the next, & then you see them no more" (Dalziel and Millgate 2009: 6).

It is not known when Hardy ceased attending services regularly – or for that matter when he began to attend more frequently in his later years – though irregular attendance in itself would not have negated his "churchy" self-identification (see epigraph), since, as he noted in 1876, "There are two sorts of church-people; those who go, and those who don't go" (*LW* 116). Conceivably his serious illness, necessitating his being confined to bed from late October 1880 to early May 1881, marked a practical as well as a philosophical turning point. Certainly it seems significant that the earliest philosophically speculative entry in *Life and Work*, emphasizing the "cruel injustice" of "Law" in creating "emotions . . . in a world of defect," is both dated May 9, 1881 and defined as the culmination of "infinite" attempts "to reconcile a scientific view of life with the emotional and spiritual" (*LW* 153). Moreover, Hardy's "Scheme of the Universe" diagram in the "Poetical Matter" notebook specifies "? 1880" as the commencement of his conviction that the "Prime Force" – no longer the "Crass Casualty" of "Hap" – is neither "Beneficent" nor "Maleficent" but "Neutral" (Dalziel and Millgate 2009: 36).

How Hardy at the age of 45 envisioned the role of the Church in such a universe is recorded in his November 20, 1885 letter to John Morley, lamenting that in the current public discussions of disestablishment "the thinkers – the literary multitude – whose nature it is to cry aloud, are the dumb section of the population" (*CL* I: 136). Hardy clearly hoped that Morley would promote the evolutionary development of the Church into an institution which would satisfy the "religious wants" of "thoughtful people who have ceased to believe in supernatural theology," including "the growing masses . . . who for conscientious reasons can enter neither church nor chapel":

> I have sometimes had a dream that the church, instead of being disendowed, could be made to modulate by degrees (say as the present incumbents die out) into an undog-matic, non-theological establishment for the promotion of that virtuous living on which all honest men are agreed – leaving to voluntary bodies the organization of whatever societies they may think best for teaching their various forms of doctrinal religion. (*CL* I: 136–7)

Hardy's vision of a new Church, while differing somewhat in its details, remained remarkably consistent in its essentials throughout the remainder of his life. Thus in 1902, having just read his friend Edward Clodd's biography of T. H. Huxley, Hardy wrote:

> What is forced upon one again, after reading such a life as Huxley's, is the sad fact of the extent to which Theological lumber is still allowed to discredit religion, in spite of such devoted attempts as his to shake it off. If the doctrines of the supernatural were quietly abandoned to-morrow by the Church, & "reverence & love for an ethical ideal" alone retained, not one in ten thousand would object to the readjustment, while the enormous bulk of thinkers excluded by the old teaching would be brought into the fold, & our venerable old churches & cathedrals would become the centres of emotional life that they once were. (*CL* III: 5)

Similar pronouncements figure in the *Life and Work* accounts of 1907, 1917, and 1922 (*LW* 357–9, 407, 448–9), all of which refer specifically to Hardy's "energetic preface" (*LW* 448), the 1922 Apology to *Late Lyrics and Earlier*, containing the only sustained exposition of his views on religion and the Church published during his lifetime. In the Apology, after claiming that "poetry, pure literature in general," and "religion, in its essential and undogmatic sense," are "often but different names for the same thing," Hardy insisted:

> these . . . visible signs of mental and emotional life, must like all other things keep moving, becoming; even though at present, when belief in witches of Endor is displac-ing the Darwinian theory and "the truth that shall make you free", men's minds appear . . . to be moving backwards rather than on. (*CPW* II: 323–4)

Hardy's hope – perhaps "a forlorn hope, a mere dream" – was that through poetry an alliance would be created "between religion, which must be retained unless the world is to perish, and complete rationality, which must come, unless also the world is to perish" (*CPW* II: 325). If this hope were to be realized, then the current "ominous moving backward" would prove to be *"pour mieux sauter*, drawing back for a spring," in accordance with Comte's theory that "advance is never in a straight line, but in a looped orbit" (*CPW* II: 325). Hardy also identified specific groups of people as the forerunners of intellectual and emotional advance:

[the] many thoughtful writers in verse and prose; also men in certain worthy but small bodies of various denominations, and perhaps in the homely quarter where advance might have been the very least expected a few years back – the English Church – if one reads it rightly as showing evidence of "removing those things that are shaken", in accordance with the wise Epistolary recommendation to the Hebrews. (*CPW* II: 324)

Clearly Hardy was looking to the Church of England to grasp the "chance of being the religion of the future" lost by Rome a generation earlier when it had rejected "the little band of New Catholics who were making a struggle for continuity by applying the principle of evolution to their own faith, joining hands with modern science":

what other purely English establishment than the Church of sufficient dignity and footing, with such strength of old association, such scope for transmutability, such architectural spell, is left in this country to keep the shreds of morality together? (*CPW* II: 324)

Not surprisingly, response to the Apology was often uncomprehending. Indeed, shortly after Hardy's death on January 11, 1928, the Dean of Canterbury quoted the Apology, which he defined as "a tribute . . . lately paid to the Church of England," in defense of the decision to bury Hardy in Westminster Abbey (Bell 1928: 13). As Hardy had lamented to Lady Grove several years earlier in his letter of October 20, 1922:

one never can tell beforehand how a writer's meaning may be misapprehended, & I find some people gather from it [the Apology] that I have become strictly orthodox (rather funny, this!) when I thought my meaning to be clear enough that some form of Established ritual & discipline should be maintained in the interests of morality, without entering into the very large question of what that form should be: I should say offhand that it might be some ethical service based on the old liturgy. (*CL* VI: 162)

What all these public and private articulations of Hardy's vision of a new Church share, predictably enough, is his fundamental conviction – held at least from the mid-1880s to the mid-1920s – that "rational religion" (*CL* VII: 32) would ultimately prevail. When it did not, he was keenly disappointed: "I fear that since the 'Apology' . . . [was written] some years ago, no advance whatever has been shown: rather indeed a childish back-current towards a belief in magic rites" (*LW* 359). Hardy had hoped that the new Prayer Book, proposed in 1927, would include a revised, rationalistic liturgy, but the revision was in fact largely in the opposite direction, "towards Roman sacerdotalism," resulting at a national level in the House of Commons' rejection of the Prayer Book, and at a personal level in Hardy's loss of "all expectation of seeing the Church representative of modern thinking minds" (Murry 1928b: 195; *LW* 448–9).

The reassertion of sacerdotalism – whether Roman or English – and the continuing Prayer Book proclamation of "dogmatic superstitions" confirmed Hardy's view, articulated in his July 1, 1926 letter to Clodd, that "the movement of thought seems to have entered a back current" (*LW* 359; *CL* VII: 32). Four years earlier, in the above-cited letter to Lady Grove, Hardy had been quite specific about his concerns:

> the Romanists had a fine chance, but let it slip: & I fear the English Church may do the same if it doesn't mind. The mediaevalists are the danger: if they succeed in harking back to transubstantiation, plenary inspiration, etc. the Church becomes a sect, & all is undone. I don't know whether you are old enough to have known a friend of mine now long dead – St George Mivart – He was one of the new Catholics; but was extinguished. (*CL* VI: 162)

Mivart, the well-known zoologist and Roman Catholic polemicist, had died in 1900, shortly after having been denied the sacraments, hence effectively excommunicated. For many years his primary goal had been to demonstrate "the essential harmony which exists between the truths of science and the dictates of religion" (Mivart 1885: 47). Hardy's friendship with Mivart provides further evidence of his support – also articulated in the Apology – for the promulgation of a more rational religion wherever it might be found, be it within the Roman Catholic Church, the Church of England, or the Nonconformist chapel.[3]

On February 24, 1907, a month before completing the first draft of *The Dynasts*, Part Third, Hardy thanked Clement Shorter for introducing him to "that interesting man Mr. Campbell" (Hardy 1938). R. J. Campbell was the popular minister of the City Temple, London, whose sermons, as preached and published, attracted considerable controversy. His "New Theology," expounded in his 1907 book of the same name, advocated the union of Christianity and socialism, re-emphasized "the Christian belief in the Divine immanence," insisted that the "Infinite Cause" was unknowable, "except as we read Him in His universe and in our own souls," and, most significantly as far as Hardy was concerned, challenged "antiquated dogmatic theology," while denying that "there is, or ever has been, or ever can be, any dissonance between science and religion" (Campbell 1907: 8, 4, 5, 2, 15). Hardy found much to commend in Campbell's theology:

> If the Nonconformists have the good sense to follow his lead I think they will steal a march upon the English & R. Catholic Church, & capture the great mass of thinking people who at present want to be religious but do not want superstitions. His ingenuity in retaining Christian terms for what plain People call common morality is very amusing; however it is a step in the right direction. (Hardy 1938)

Hardy perhaps had Campbell, among others, in mind when on November 13, 1913 he suggested to the Positivist Frederic Harrison that *The Positive Evolution of Religion* was "a trifle hard upon the Dissenters": "Their horn of revelation dilemma is not so bad as the Roman Catholic one. They did go half way across the stream towards truth & reasonableness" (*CL* IV: 319).

While Hardy supported all efforts to promote "truth & reasonableness," regardless of denominational affiliation, he also remained convinced – as his letters, the Apology, and *Life and Work* make abundantly clear – that the most effective way forward would be through the Church of England, with its "dignity, strength, and solidity . . . all due to the ancient traditions," not to mention its "scope for transmutability" (Lefèvre 1925: 101; *CPW* II: 324). For Hardy, "to keep a church of some sort afoot" was "a thing indispensable," as was "meeting together at least once a week in the cause of some religion or other" (January 1907 entry, *LW* 358; November 12, 1923 letter to Clodd, *CL* VI: 222). In a conversation of October 21, 1922, recollected by J. H. Morgan, Hardy said:

> I believe in going to church. It is a moral drill, and people must have something. If there is no church in a country village, there is nothing. . . . I believe in reformation coming from *within* the Church. The clergy are growing more rationalist, and that is the best way of changing. (Morgan 1928: 8; Morgan's ellipsis)

Moreover, unlike Leslie Stephen, John Morley, and other writers whom he admired, Hardy did not condemn those who subscribed to Articles of Religion in which they did not believe; as he told Morgan, "I think . . . that the clergy feel in such cases that it is only by joining the Church that they can hope to reform it" (Morgan 1928: 8). Hardy in turn hoped that that reform would be part of a "new enthusiasm," revitalizing the Church and enabling it to reacquire the position and influence it had enjoyed during its medieval (Roman Catholic) prime (Dalziel and Millgate 2009: 40). Responding on April 27, 1926 to Roy McKay, a young ordinand who had publicly pointed out that many members of the Church of England could not give literal assent to all elements of the creeds, Hardy wrote:

> a simpler plan than that of mental reservation in passages no longer literally accepted (which is puzzling to ordinary congregations) would be just to abridge the creeds & other primitive parts of the Liturgy, leaving only the essentials. Unfortunately there appears to be a narrowing instead of a broadening tendency among the clergy of late, which if persisted in will exclude still more people from church. But if a strong body of young Reformers were to make a bold stand, in a sort of New Oxford Movement, they would have a tremendous backing from the thoughtful laity, & might overcome the retrogressive section of the Clergy. (*CL* VII: 21)

Hardy's reference to "broadening" in a letter advocating Church reform seems particularly apt. That he was in many respects sympathetic to Broad Church theologies is suggested not only by his consistent rejection of belief in plenary inspiration, "magic rites," and "dogmatic superstitions" but also by such remarks as the following, written to Clodd on January 17, 1897:

The older one gets, the more deplorable seems the effect of that terrible, dogmatic ecclesiasticism – Christianity so called (but really Paulinism *plus* idolatry) – on morals & true religion: a dogma with which the real teaching of Christ has hardly anything in common. (*CL* II: 143)

Hardy clearly recognized the fundamental discrepancy between orthodox Christian dogma and the radical teaching of that "young reformer . . . in the humblest walk of life" (*LW* 353). As early as 1880, on seeing a Calvary rocking in the wind at Honfleur, Hardy had imagined Christ exclaiming, "Yes, Yes! I agree that this travesty of me and my doctrines should totter and overturn in this modern world!" (*LW* 143). The fact that some of Hardy's views seem distinctly Broad Church must be situated, however, within the larger context of his stated convictions, especially his inability – much as he sometimes wished otherwise – to subscribe to the essential premise underlying all liberal Christian theologies: belief in a benevolent God.

Perhaps the most comprehensive statement of Hardy's position with respect to the Church and Church doctrine during his later years can be found in his notes, dated January 1907 and subsequently included in *Life and Work*, for an "ephemeral article," entitled "The Hard Case of the Would-be-Religious," "By Sinceritas":

"Synopsis. – Many millions of the most thoughtful people in England are prevented entering any church or chapel from year's end to year's end.

"The days of creeds are as dead and done with as the days of Pterodactyls.

"Required: services at which there are no affirmations and no supplications.

"Rationalists err as far in one direction as Revelationists or Mystics in the other; as far in the direction of logicality as their opponents away from it.

"*Religions, religion*, is to be used in the article in its modern sense entirely, as being expressive of nobler feelings towards humanity and emotional goodness and greatness, the old meaning of the word – ceremony, or ritual – having perished or nearly.

"We enter church, and we have to say, 'We have erred and strayed from thy ways like lost sheep', when what we want to say is, 'Why are we made to err and stray like lost sheep?' Then we have to sing, 'My soul doth magnify the Lord', when what we want to sing is, 'O that my soul could find some Lord that it could magnify! Till it can, let us magnify good works, and develop all means of easing mortals' progress through a world not worthy of them.'

"Still, being present, we say the established words full of the historic sentiment only, mentally adding, 'How happy our ancestors were in repeating in all sincerity these articles of faith!' But we perceive that none of the congregation recognizes that we repeat the words from an antiquarian interest in them, and in a historic sense, and solely in order to keep a church of some sort afoot – a thing indispensable; so that we are pretending what is not true; that we are believers. This must not be; we must leave. And if we do, we reluctantly go to the door, and creep out as it creaks complainingly behind us." (*LW* 357–8)

When read in conjunction with the personal and public statements Hardy made from the 1880s until his death in 1928, "The Hard Case of the Would-be-Religious" – an apt designation for Hardy's own position – points up some of the contradictions inherent within both his views and his practice. Although metaphorically Hardy might have aligned himself with those who could no longer enter a church, his letters and *Life and Work* include numerous references to his occasional attendance through-out his life at church and especially cathedral services, his love of the Church of England liturgy and music not infrequently having drawn him to evensong at Salis-bury Cathedral and elsewhere. During at least the last decade of his life his church attendance became more frequent, if far from regular (see, e.g., Graves 1929: 375; Millgate 1996: 121, 167; Ray 2007: 201).

As for the insistence on the days of the creeds being past and on the necessity of services without affirmations or supplications, even Hardy seems to have realized that he was contradicting himself, since "The Hard Case of the Would-be-Religious" is followed by a disclaimer – "it should be added here that he sometimes took a more nebulous view, that may be called transmutative" – and a note, written "some years" after the 1922 Apology, suggesting, among other things, that the liturgy be "recast" rather than abolished (*LW* 358–9). Clearly of central significance here is Hardy's lifelong love of the Book of Common Prayer liturgy, as opposed to what Florence Hardy described as his hatred of all "new services and new prayers" (F. Hardy 1940: 299). In 1922 he told Morgan: "The liturgy of the Church of England is a noble thing. So are Tate and Brady's Psalms. These are the things that people need and should have" (Morgan 1928: 8). It is difficult to imagine, however, the liturgy's being simultaneously preserved and revised, as would be required for an "ethical service based on the old liturgy" (*CL* VI: 162). Even Hardy's suggestion to McKay that "the creeds & other primitive parts of the Liturgy" be abridged, "leaving only the essen-tials" (*CL* VII: 21), raises more questions than it answers. Which sections of the liturgy would be considered essential, and would an advocate of rational religion be able to subscribe to them?

On the other hand, the critique in "The Hard Case of the Would-be-Religious" of extremists of any persuasion – rationalist, revelationist, or mystic – is in fact consistent with Hardy's stated convictions. If he was not, as he phrased it, "a normal Church-man" (*CL* III: 273), he was not a "normal" rationalist either. In 1920 he declined an invitation to be included in Joseph McCabe's *A Biographical Dictionary of Modern Rationalists*, claiming not only that he was "rather an irrationalist than a rationalist, on account of his inconsistencies," but also that "no man is a rationalist, and that human actions are not ruled by reason at all in the last resort" (*CL* VII: 162; also included at *LW* 432). Five years earlier, commenting on Henri Bergson's *Creative Evolution*, Hardy had written to Caleb Saleeby:

> You must not think me a hard-headed rationalist . . . Half my time (particularly when I write verse) I believe – in the modern use of the word – not only in things that Bergson does, but in spectres, mysterious voices, intuitions, omens, dreams, haunted places, &c., &c. (*CL* V: 79; also included at *LW* 400)

The inclusion in *Life and Work* of the letters to McCabe and Saleeby indicates that Hardy wanted them, along with his numerous pronouncements on the Church, past, present, and (as he hoped) yet to come, to be part of the public record of his convictions. Also in *Life and Work* is the frequently cited passage, used as the epigraph to this essay, lamenting that "invidious critics" had labeled Hardy "Nonconformist, Agnostic, Atheist, Infidel, Immoralist, Heretic, Pessimist or something else equally opprobrious in their eyes," but never "what they might have called him much more plausibly – churchy; not in an intellectual sense, but in so far as instincts and emotions ruled" (*LW* 407). While the defensiveness of this declaration is obvious, not least in its placement immediately following Hardy's assertion that "no modern thinker can be an atheist in the modern sense" (*LW* 406), it is nonetheless true that Hardy was in many respects "churchy."

Hardy's instinctual and emotional "churchiness" manifested itself in a variety of ways. His regard for the Church, particularly as it had been and as it could be, is evident in his recognition that for many years it was "the centre of all the musical, literary and artistic education in the country village" (Graves 1929: 375), and in his continuing hope for the evolutionary development of a new Church, embodying the best of the traditional and the modern. His delight in church music and the language of the Bible and the Book of Common Prayer found its creative expression in the rhythms of his language and the numerous allusions throughout his prose and verse (see Rimmer 2006; Taylor 1988; Vance 2007). His early attachment to the parish church of Stinsford was renewed during his later years, in part because of the burial in its churchyard of so many of his family members. In 1916, following the death of Mary Hardy the preceding year, he told the vicar of Stinsford, "we all feel ourselves your parishioners still – I suppose from our family's 100 years association with the parish & church-music" (*CL* V: 180). In 1920 Hardy was actively involved in restoring the Norman font at Stinsford, having recommended its restoration in 1908 and then again the following year in an architectural report on the church for the Restoration Committee (*CL* VI: 36, III: 346, IV: 18–20). Throughout his life Hardy remained fully alive to the "architectural spell" of "our venerable old churches & cathedrals," and from the 1880s onwards regretted his own youthful participation in church "restoration," which had frequently resulted in destruction rather than preservation (*CPW* II: 324; *CL* III: 5; see *LW* 35, 82; Beatty 2004).

The element of nostalgia needs to be acknowledged in all these manifestations of "churchiness," and also in Hardy's wistful expression, in such poems as "The Impercipient" and "The Oxen," of a desire for some form of traditional Christian belief. Hardy's intellectual convictions, however, were not nostalgic but modern, hence his insistence that he was not "churchy . . . in an intellectual sense." In a 1904 conversation with W. Smithard, Hardy made a similar statement, claiming that Christianity appealed "very powerfully" to his "emotional and artistic faculties," but that "intellect cannot be stifled, and we cannot ignore the revelations of geology and history" (Ray 2007: 40). Such convictions did not, however, negate his assertion in *Life and Work* that if the Bishop of Wakefield, who had supposedly burnt *Jude the Obscure*, "could have known him as he was, he would have found a man whose personal conduct, views of morality, and of the vital facts of religion, hardly differed from his own" (*LW* 295).

"Churchy," "Christian," "the vital facts of religion": clearly terminology is a fundamental issue here. Hardy and the Bishop of Wakefield would presumably not have agreed in their respective definitions of "the vital facts of religion." What Hardy nonetheless recognized – as had Stephen years earlier in "Are We Christians?" – was the extent to which rationalism had influenced all forms of modern thought, including Christian theology. In a note of 1899 he observed: "It would be an amusing fact, if it were not one that leads to such bitter strife, that the conception of a First Cause which the theist calls 'God', and the conception of the same that the so-styled atheist calls 'no-God', are nowadays almost exactly identical" (*LW* 326). Having aligned himself with the "no-God-ists," Hardy's intellectual integrity prevented him from transferring his allegiance, even while he defined himself as "churchy," advocated a rational Church of England, and recognized that Christianity in the mid-1920s – or at least some manifestations of it – had evolved into an ethical system of belief not unlike the one he himself had envisioned for some forty years:

> Christianity nowadays as expounded by Christian apologists has an entirely different meaning from that which it bore when I was a boy. If I understand, it now limits itself to the religion of emotional morality and altruism that was taught by Jesus Christ, or nearly so limits itself. (*LW* 358)

Shortly after Hardy's death, his friend John Middleton Murry articulated a similar definition of Christianity and summarized, more accurately than he perhaps realized, several aspects of that complex relationship between "Hardy and the English Church" (*New Adelphi*, March 1928). Murry's editorial remains a fitting tribute to "the Would-be-Religious" Hardy:

> it was felt, and rightly felt in this country that there was no incongruity in the burial of the great "pessimist" in the central shrine of the English Church. The feeling may have been inarticulate but it was widespread that in Hardy we have lost one of the most Christian minds of our time. We may refine and refine in our definitions of what Christianity is, but we have not much doubt in our hearts that the true Christian is he
>
> > To whom the miseries of the world
> > Are misery, and will not let him rest.
>
> Of this high compassion Hardy and his works were full. And not the least reason why the Christian Church is fallen into disrepute among us is that it is felt that it tithes the mint and cummin and neglects this weightier matter of the law, and that those who do not neglect it – like Hardy – are generally to be found not within the Church, but outside it.
>
> Yet not wholly outside. I remember in the summer of last year [1927] Hardy's saying to me one afternoon that, when he was a boy, there had been a possibility of his entering

the Church. Circumstance decided otherwise. "But I," he said, "have often regretted it." I was, for the moment, astonished; but when, in the evening, I came to think over his words, I felt that they showed a faith in the English Church which I would give much to share. Whether or not Hardy was right in supposing that room could have been found for his beliefs within the Church – and the difficulties are not so great as they at first sight appear – he paid the Church a noble tribute in "hoping it might be so." And I have little doubt that all through his life Hardy in a real sense regarded himself as a member of the Church of England. (Murry 1928a: 194)

Notes

1 Most of *Life and Work* was written 1917–19, but the process of composition and revision concluded only with Hardy's death; see *LW* xii–xviii.

2 Although in *Life and Work* Hardy assigned his "curious scheme" of combining poetry and the Church to the summer of 1865 and gave as an example of his beginning "to practise orthodoxy" his attending the morning service and staying to the sacrament at Westminster Abbey on "July 5. Sunday" of that same year, he also acknowledged that "he had long had a leaning" towards the Church (*LW* 52–3). His clerical ambitions would have been present from at least the late 1850s when he was engaged in theological debate and studying the Greek Testament (see *LW* 33–5; Hardy replaced his old Greek Testament with Griesbach's text in February 1860). His

inscription of "W. Abbey. 5.7.63" at the conclusion of the Order of Holy Communion in his Book of Common Prayer (Dorset County Museum) indicates that the date of his abbey visit was not July 5, 1865 (a Thursday) but July 5, 1863, when he would have been continuing, rather than beginning, to practice orthodoxy.

3 The sole exception seems to be Hardy's expression of disdain in his May 17, 1888 letter to Frederic Harrison for "the New Christians (or whatever they are) who, to use Morley's words 'have hit their final climax in the doctrine that everything is both true & false at the same time'" (*CL* I: 176). Hardy was referring specifically to "the 'Robert Elsmere' school"; he had recently read Ward's *Robert Elsmere* and Morley's *Voltaire*, both of which are excerpted in "Literary Notes I" (see *LN* I: 211–18).

References and Further Reading

Beatty, Claudius J. P. (2004). *The Part Played by Architecture in the Life and Work of Thomas Hardy*. Dorchester: Plush Publishing.

Bell, G. K. A. (1928). Mr. Hardy. Poetry and Religion. Tribute to the English Church. *The Times*, Jan. 16, 1928, 13.

Björk, Lennart A. (ed.) (1985). *The Literary Notebooks of Thomas Hardy*, 2 vols. London and Basingstoke: Macmillan.

Björk, Lennart A. (1987). *Psychological Vision and Social Criticism in the Novels of Thomas Hardy*. Stockholm: Almqvist & Wiksell.

Campbell, R. J. (1907). *The New Theology*. London: Chapman & Hall.

Dalziel, Pamela (2006). The Gospel According to Hardy. In Keith Wilson (ed.), *Thomas Hardy Reappraised: Essays in Honour of Michael Millgate* (pp. 3–19). Toronto: University of Toronto Press.

Dalziel, Pamela, and Michael Millgate (eds.) (2009). *Thomas Hardy's "Poetical Matter" Notebook*. Oxford: Oxford University Press.

Graves, Robert (1929). *Good-bye to All That*. London: Jonathan Cape.

Gregor, Ian (1986). Contrary Imaginings: Thomas Hardy and Religion. In David Jasper (ed.), *The Interpretation of Belief: Coleridge, Schleiermacher and Romanticism* (pp. 202–24). Basingstoke: Macmillan.

Hands, Timothy (1989). *Thomas Hardy: Distracted Preacher? Hardy's Religious Biography and its Influence on his Novels*. Basingstoke: Macmillan.

Hands, Timothy (2000). Religion. In Norman Page (ed.), *Oxford Reader's Companion to Hardy* (pp. 360–5). Oxford: Oxford University Press.

Hardy, Florence (1940). Letter, Aug. 4, 1918, to Sydney Carlyle Cockerell. In Viola Meynell (ed.), *Friends of a Lifetime: Letters to Sydney Carlyle Cockerell* (p. 299). London: Jonathan Cape.

Hardy, Thomas (1938). Extract from letter, Feb. 24, 1907, to Clement Shorter. *Maggs Brothers*, catalogue 664, item 254.

Hardy, Thomas (1982–95). *The Complete Poetical Works of Thomas Hardy*, ed. Samuel Hynes, 5 vols. Oxford: Clarendon Press.

Hardy, Thomas (1984). *The Life and Work of Thomas Hardy*, ed. Michael Millgate. London: Macmillan.

Jędrzejewski, Jan (1996). *Thomas Hardy and the Church*. Basingstoke: Macmillan.

Lefèvre, Frédéric (1925). An Hour with Thomas Hardy. *The Living Age*, 325, 98–103. Reprinted in Ray 2007 (pp. 282–6).

Millgate, Michael (ed.) (1996). *Letters of Emma and Florence Hardy*. Oxford: Clarendon Press.

Millgate, Michael (ed.) (2001). *Thomas Hardy's Public Voice: The Essays, Speeches, and Miscellaneous Prose*. Oxford: Clarendon Press.

Mivart, St. George (1885). Modern Catholics and Scientific Freedom. *The Nineteenth Century*, 18, 30–47.

Morgan, J. H. (1928). Mr. Hardy and the Church. A Reminiscence. *The Times*, Jan. 19, 1928, 8. Reprinted in Ray 2007 (pp. 259–60).

Murry, John Middleton (1928a). Hardy and the English Church. *The New Adelphi*, NS 1, 194.

Murry, John Middleton (1928b). The Church of England and the Nation. *The New Adelphi*, NS 1, 195–7.

Newman, John Henry (1864). *Apologia Pro Vita Sua*. London: Longman, Green, Longman, Roberts & Green.

Purdy, Richard Little, and Michael Millgate (eds.) (1978–88). *The Collected Letters of Thomas Hardy*, 7 vols. Oxford: Clarendon Press.

Ray, Martin (2007). *Thomas Hardy Remembered*. Aldershot: Ashgate.

Rimmer, Mary (2006). "My Scripture Manner": Reading Hardy's Biblical and Liturgical Allusion. In Keith Wilson (ed.), *Thomas Hardy Reappraised: Essays in Honour of Michael Millgate* (pp. 20–37). Toronto: University of Toronto Press.

Roberts, Jon (2003). Mortal Projections: Thomas Hardy's Dissolving Views of God. *Victorian Literature and Culture*, 31, 43–66.

Stephen, Leslie (1873a). Are We Christians? *The Fortnightly Review*, NS 13, 281–303. Collected in Stephen 1873b (pp. 110–54).

Stephen, Leslie (1873b). *Essays on Freethinking and Plainspeaking*. London: Longman, Green & Co.

Taylor, Dennis (1988). *Hardy's Metres and Victorian Prosody*. Oxford: Clarendon Press.

Vance, Norman (2007). George Eliot and Hardy. In Andrew Hass, David Jasper, and Elisabeth Jay (eds.), *The Oxford Handbook of English Literature and Theology* (pp. 483–98). Oxford: Oxford University Press.

Wright, T. R. (1986). *The Religion of Humanity: The Impact of Comtean Positivism on Victorian Britain*. Cambridge: Cambridge University Press.

6

Thomas Hardy's Notebooks

William Greenslade

I

Most aspiring and successful Victorian writers were prolific, regular, and well-organized note-makers, whether in the spirit of self-education, or as part of a disciplined process for what would later serve their trade. Notebooks by mid- to late Victorian novelists are especially instructive, such as George Eliot's "quarry" for the making of *Middlemarch* and *Daniel Deronda* (Rignall 2000: 288–9) or George Gissing's notebooks, re-entered into a large "scrapbook" and maintained for more than twenty years (Postmus 2007). Hardy, likewise, carried about him a series of what he variously described in the *Life and Work of Thomas Hardy* as his "notebooks," "pocket-books," "diaries," and "memoranda," most, in their original state, destroyed. Some tantalizing glimpses of those destroyed pocket-books can be gained from observing four leaves from a small notebook which Hardy began in 1865 and which were pasted onto the second flyleaf of his notebook "Literary Notes I"; its extent can be gauged from its pagination on the recto leaves, beginning "520" (*LN* I: xxxii, 5–7). The "Facts" notebook contains three pasted-in leaves from another destroyed notebook, probably compiled 1876–81, of at least eighty-one leaves (Greenslade 2004: 25–38). Such surviving fragments, with their paginations, tell us something of the sheer magnitude of Hardy's private note-taking and of what was lost to us in the Max Gate incinerations and bonfires.

All of the twelve surviving notebooks of Thomas Hardy have now been edited: *The Architectural Notebook of Thomas Hardy*, edited by C. J. P. Beatty ([1966] 2007); the "Memoranda I," "Memoranda II," the "Schools of Painting Notebook," and the "Trumpet-Major Notebook," collected in *The Personal Notebooks of Thomas Hardy*, edited by Richard H. Taylor (1978); "Literary Notes I," "Literary Notes II," "Literary Notes III," and the so-called "1867" notebook, collected in *The Literary Notebooks of Thomas Hardy*, edited by Lennart A. Björk (1985); *Thomas Hardy's "Studies, Specimens &c." Notebook*, edited by Pamela Dalziel and Michael Millgate (1994); *Thomas*

Hardy's "Facts" Notebook, edited by William Greenslade (2004); and, most recently, *Thomas Hardy's "Poetical Matter" Notebook*, edited by Pamela Dalziel and Michael Millgate (2009).

The notebooks can be categorized in various ways. Firstly we can distinguish between, on the one hand, the "synthetic" or composite notebooks, that is, those that are largely made up from earlier destroyed sources – the two "Memoranda" notebooks and the "Poetical Matter" notebook – and, on the other hand, the remaining notebooks which survive as, in the main, "raw" rather than "cooked" productions. Of these "raw" notebooks, three – "Literary Notes I," the "1867" notebook, and the "Facts" notebook – are partly "cooked" insofar as they include items gathered from earlier, destroyed notebooks, either pasted in or recopied. The notebooks can also be grouped in relation to specific phases of Hardy's life as a writer: the "Architectural," "Studies, Specimens &c.," and the "Schools of Painting" notebooks derive from the mid-1860s to early 1870s, the "Trumpet-Major" and the "Facts" notebooks from the late 1870s to the 1880s, while "Memoranda I," "Memoranda II," and "Poetical Matter" date variously from the period 1917–27. An alternative distinction between the notebooks as "personal" and "commonplace" is offered by Barbara Rosenbaum in her entry on Hardy in the *Index of English Literary Manuscripts* (1990).

When ten of the notebooks are set out together in the Dorset County Museum where they are held, they range from the pocket-book size of the "Trumpet-Major" and "Memoranda" notebooks through to the bulkier library style of "Literary Notes I," "II," and "III" and the "Facts" notebook. Of the other two, "Studies, Specimens &c.," held in the Beinecke Library at Yale, is also pocket-book size, while "Poetical Matter" survives only as a microfilm copy (also in the Beinecke Library) of the original document whose leaves are said to have been 8 x 6¼inches in size (Dalziel and Millgate 2009: xvi).

II

What do we have from the young Hardy of the 1860s and early 1870s, those crucial years during which he was building up the resources for the literary career to which, in 1872, he entirely devoted himself on abandoning his chosen profession of architecture? What survive are the "Architectural," "The Schools of Painting," and the "Studies, Specimens &c." notebooks, and a number of notes in the "Memoranda I," "Literary Notes I," "1867," and "Poetical Matter" notebooks. Much else, it can be assumed, has been destroyed.

Architecture was a defining creative resource in Hardy's life. At the age of 16 he was an articled pupil with the Dorchester architect John Hicks. In his early twenties he was an assistant for five years with the London architect Arthur Blomfield, again with Hicks after returning to Dorchester, and with Crickmay in Weymouth after Hicks's death in 1869. Until 1872, when he left the profession, Hardy was a respected and needed collaborator in London school-building schemes. But he continued "in an advisory capacity at least, to make use of his professional skill for the rest of his life" (Beatty [1966] 2007: 15). Few major poets or novelists could match Hardy's devotion to a sister art. The "Architectural" notebook is a densely and elegantly composed representation of Hardy's professionalism, dating mainly from 1862–72, but with entries also from 1893–4, and as late as 1920. It displays the wide range of Hardy's architectural activities, from ecclesiastical buildings to public and domestic commissions. Its extraordinarily detailed, clear pencil drawings and sketches – of structures, alternative patterns and decorations, sectional drawings of windows, pew "Seat Ends," fonts, plans for houses – all reveal a masterly draughtsmanship. There are passages (in ink) about color and materials, drainage, roofs, arithmetical calculations about, for example, the proportion of treads and risers of stairs and the dimensions of laborers' cottages "wh experience teaches to be advisable" (Beatty [1966] 2007: 38, 23, 33, 89, 163). The "Architectural" notebook highlights the importance of church restoration for Hardy. To the fore is his retrospective reconstruction of Stinsford church prior to its major restoration of 1842. The recording of the restoration of St. Juliot, Cornwall, 1870–2, and of West Knighton in 1893–4, suggests a substantial personal and professional investment. The range of his architect's commitments, from domestic and engineering concerns to ecclesiastical Gothic, resulted in an ever-productive tension: the pull between modernity and tradition, between the functional and the aesthetic, would emerge in *A Laodicean*, but most acutely in *Jude the Obscure*, for which this notebook remains a key document.

Hardy's "sensibility to architectural forms and devices," as Sir John Summerson put it, is a "thing which, once acquired, can never be lost. Hardy had it and no study of him as a man, novelist and poet can be complete without recognition of this fact" (Beatty [1966] 2007: 1). Hardy himself recognized this aspect of his "sensibility" when authorizing the following entry for inclusion in the *Life*:

> He knew that in architecture cunning irregularity is of enormous worth, and it is obvious that he carried on into his verse, perhaps unconsciously, the Gothic art-principle in which he had been trained – the principle of spontaneity, found in mouldings, tracery, and such-like – resulting in the "unforeseen" (as it has been called) character of his metres and stanzas. (*LW* 323; Beatty [1966] 2007: 45)

The importance of Hardy's study of the Gothic for his poetic practice has been widely recognized in recent years; "the imagery, structure, atmosphere, and aesthetic issues of Gothic architecture," as Dennis Taylor observes, "nurtured Hardy's novels, poems, and finally his theory of metre and 'verse skeletons'" (Taylor 1988: 47; see also Armstrong 1993: 31–2).

During those London architect years, 1862–7, among the most intensely formative of his life, Hardy sought to equip himself, in a variety of ways, with the wider aim of becoming a poet and a man of letters. He worked phenomenally hard, studying early and late, attending French classes, concerts, and plays and visiting art galleries on a regular basis, and during this period he compiled a modest "Schools of Painting" notebook of seventeen pages, dating from May 1863. For this he was probably using a guidebook to the history of painting, from which he listed, in detail, painters from "School of Florence – Cimabue" onwards (Taylor 1978: 105), with summarized comments on individual painters, continuing systematically through Italian, German, Spanish, French, and Dutch schools, to the "British School" of Constable, Bonington, and Stothard. Pedestrian though it may appear, here is an early and characteristic example of Hardy's powers of tireless application, compressing much into little. More than fifty years later he showed the same formidable intellectual energy in condensing a lifetime's note-taking into the "materials" for *Life and Work*.

Of the notebooks that survive from the 1860s, the "Schools of Painting" notebook is the most limited in aim and function, but the most significant contrast offered by notebooks of these years is between the professional assurance and sophistication of the "Architectural" notebook and the laborious exploration of new territory at a level of linguistic innocence pursued in "Studies, Specimens &c." This notebook, composed probably 1865–9, is best seen as a self-constructed poet's primer; at the same time, as Hardy later recorded, he was writing verse "constantly" (*LW* 51). It is a crucial document for an understanding of Hardy's poetic development. Much of it is taken up by vocabulary-building lists based on quotations taken from a miscellany of authors, including particularly numerous entries from Shakespeare, Milton, Scott, and Swinburne. It proceeds by stages, first from the simplest gathering and emphasizing of words in order to increase his stock of poetical vocabulary without regard to any semantic or metrical context in his source. This develops towards experimentation with words that can displace or alternate with those found in his sources. From William Barnes, for example, he garners "the wild daisies a-spread in a sheet," then improvises: "the wide sheet of stars, sheets of moonlight" (Dalziel and Millgate 1994: 67).

Yet this deliberate, painstaking recording of phrases can mask the presence of deeper attachments at work. Troubling doubts about religion and sex thread through the annotations, stirred, primarily, by the example of Swinburne, to whom Hardy devotes twelve groups of entries and who, in Pamela Dalziel's view, is primarily responsible for "the liberation of Hardy's erotic imagination" (Dalziel 1993: 148). His testing out of erotic feeling extends, startlingly, to the language of Old Testament prophets such as Habakkuk or Ezekiel, from whom, as Ralph Pite suggests, Hardy mines language which "might enrich possible erotic writing of his own" (Pite 2006: 120). Ezekiel's "hand of the Lord" becomes "the hand of love"; "I have made thee a watchman" transmutes into "love made me a watcher" (Dalziel and Millgate 1994: 51). The most surprising source for the language of passion is Thomas Rickman's study, *An Attempt to Discriminate the Styles of Architecture in England, from the Conquest to the Reformation* (6th edition 1862), from where "two sets of mouldings" becomes "the set of thy head" and "fine hollow mouldings" becomes "fine-drawn / kisses" (Dalziel and Millgate 1994: 62, 141–2, xix–xx). A system of abbreviations is deployed (there are shorthand notations for "love," "lips," "cheek," "kisses") that disguises the very erotic charge his investigations detonate. One of the undoubted pleasures of "Studies, Specimens &c." is to be able to observe, in Hardy's detailed accumulations, his development from self-education to creative expression.

III

The "fullest extant record" of Hardy's "reading for his career as a writer" (Björk 2000: 291) is to be found in "Literary Notes I" (entered from 1876 to 1888) and "Literary Notes II" (1888 to 1927), together comprising 2,481 summarized or copied-out extracts and passages from books and essays. The "1867" notebook (mid-1870s to mid-1880s) delivers a further 245 items. Together with a volume of cuttings, "Literary Notes III" (1906–10), these notebooks were collected in *The Literary Notebooks of Thomas Hardy*, edited by Lennart A. Björk (1985) (the first 1,339 entries of "Literary Notes I" having appeared in Björk's edition, *The Literary Notes of Thomas Hardy* [Göteborg, 1974]). Taken together these materials comprise items dating from the 1860s right through to the year before Hardy's death.

The program of reading and note-taking which Hardy initiated in 1876 contributed in a substantial way to a new creative phase in his work, leading directly into the preparations for his prospective novel, *The Return of the Native* (1878), and on into the period of his last great novels from the 1880s through to the mid-1890s. This note-making phase, in any case, signals a significant change in tempo. With the completion of *The Hand of Ethelberta* in 1876 Hardy decided to take his foot off the pedal of literary production: he had, after all, written virtually a book a year during the preceding five years. The project of the Literary Notes, probably begun that spring, was carried through intensively once Hardy and Emma had completed their move to Sturminster Newton that July. Their twenty months at Sturminster were later recalled as their "happiest time" (*LW* 122), partly because of their very success in working enterprisingly together. Emma, under Hardy's direction, was responsible for entering over 200 items from earlier notes, including extracts from Clarendon and Macaulay, from G. H. Lewes's translation of Goethe and from the lives of Michelangelo and Raphael, going on to record Hardy's new reading of newspapers and magazines (Millgate 2004: 176). Hardy proceeded to compile entries on his own through the summer and autumn of 1876; then, by August 1877, seven chapters of *The Return* had been completed (Purdy [1954] 1968: 27), Hardy's program of enforced intellectual stock-taking having evidently prompted a new level of ambitiousness in fictional structure, allusion, and symbolism.

His note-making draws on a very wide range of sources – from popular educational works to current periodicals and key works of Victorian criticism, history, and philosophy. While the *Literary Notes* contain a significant number of entries from Fourier, Taine, Spencer, John Morley, and, particularly, Matthew Arnold, the single most productive writer for Hardy was Auguste Comte: Hardy enters 130 extracts from his *System of Positive Philosophy*. Positivism was one of the "ethical systems popular at the time," studied in Paris by Clym Yeobright, whose subsequent experience of course calls its efficacy into question. Comte's idea that societies evolve by passing through definable stages, from a religious to a scientific view of the world, is frequently noted, as are ideas about "continuous [human] development," evolution, and "biological dependence" (*LN* I: 74) – all put to the test in the trials of Clym and Eustacia and in the suffering figures of Henchard, Tess, Jude, and Sue. The decisive influence of Comte's law of psychological development on Hardy's later tragic fiction has been thoroughly examined by Björk (Björk 1980: 109–11).

As the notes chart his reading through the 1880s and 1890s, Hardy pays increasing attention to aesthetic questions, particularly of representation in art and literature. The evidence is found in his underlining of words and phrases, usually heading an item: "Realism and Idealism," "Tragedy," "Impressionism," "Naturalisme," "Imaginative Literature," "The Imaginative Faculty." He quotes from suggestive sources such as Havelock Ellis's *The New Spirit*, and from other writers and critics, very much *au courant*, such as Stevenson, Symons, Ibsen, Maeterlinck, George Egerton, and Sarah Grand, as well as taking from Walter Pater and Schopenhauer eloquently brief quotations that capture the aesthetic and philosophical preoccupations of the *fin de siècle*. "[T]he transcript of his sense of fact rather than the fact," he notes from Pater. "Man is a burlesque of what he should be," he enters from Schopenhauer's *Studies in Pessimism* (*LN* II: 17, 29).

There is a noticeable increase in the entry of cuttings from his sources, rather than of new transcriptions, in the latter part of "Literary Notes II." By the turn of the century, Hardy, now in his sixties, is rather less inclined to copy and more apt to resort to the pasting in of cuttings. This procedure dominates the scrapbook "Literary Notes III" (compiled probably from 1906 to 1910), together with substantial entries which were carefully typed up by Florence and pasted in. Hardy's alertness to developments in literature, philosophy, and science, well into the 1920s, is evident in his copying into "Literary Notes II" sections of T. S. Eliot's "Prufrock" in 1917; he also deals with work by and commentary on Bergson and James, Einstein and Spengler, pasting in a *TLS* review of *The Decline of the West* in 1926 (*LN* II: 226–7, 215–22, 201, 223–4, 240, 228–9, 246, 233–7).

A less remarked feature of Hardy's note-taking process is his cryptic summarizing, in his own words (often underlined), of the content of the notes themselves. He heads a note from Clarendon's *The History of the Rebellion* with his own comment, "Different estimates of Doing." Hardy also appends parenthetical asides: to a note from a cleric in 1893 urging that "Pessimism has had its day," he adds "[comforting, but false]" (*LN* II: 55). "[I quite agree with the above criticism]" he adds to a subtle essay on *The Bacchae* which includes a phrase he part-underlines: "we can see the virtue of Paganism in making a virtue of joy" (*LN* II: 54–5) – both these items entered as he is preparing *Jude*.

The so-called "1867" notebook, while grouped together with the other "Literary Notebooks," has a good claim to stand apart and be considered separately. Its title is, in fact, misleading. Walter F. Wright in 1967 referred to it as "the Book of Observations" (Wright 1967: 24–5), and although it does begin with a series of notes probably recopied from the 1860s most of the entries were taken from sources available to Hardy from the mid-1870s to the mid-1880s and the notebook was, for the most part, composed during those years. "1867" also differs from the other "Literary Notebooks" in its concentration on aesthetic and stylistic prose experiment; in this respect it is something of a prose counterpart to "Studies, Specimens &c." Extracts from Carlyle, Hugo, Browne, Bunyan, de Musset, Johnson, and Zola sit alongside quotations (amounting to about a quarter of the total) from Shakespeare, Gray, Shelley, Swinburne, and other poets. But the entries are also instructive about the volume and range of Hardy's current interests, particularly in contemporary French literature and criticism. Indeed, Hardy's entries from Zola combine these two threads of the notebook in a revealing clutch of correspondences between *Abbé Mouret's Transgressions* (trans. 1886), which Hardy read in 1886 or 1887 (*LN* II: 473–5, 571), and *The Woodlanders* (1887). There is a striking parallel between one entry from *Abbé Mouret* that describes an intense visualization of the Darwinian struggle in nature ("The rust-hued lichens gnawed away at the rough plaster like a fiery leprosy. The thyme followed on, & thrust their roots between the bricks like so many iron wedges," *LN* II: 474) and a scene in the novel in which "arms of ivy . . . were pushing in with such force at the eaves as to lift from their supports the shelves that were fixed there" (*W* 20). Hardy here derives a surprising and striking aesthetic resource from this naturalistic "slow-mo" of organic life.

IV

Hardy's own interest in facts about his local past was as developed a faculty as one might expect to find in an imaginative writer. He had been soaked in stories about his family, their friends, and immediate neighbors, as well as about famous – sometimes infamous – local figures, be they titled women, smugglers, or horse-stealers. From an early age Hardy actively prompted and subsequently recorded stories told to him by his parents, particularly by his mother, Jemima, and by his paternal grandmother, Mary Head, whose memories, dating back to the inception of the French Revolution, were shared with her grandson, and commemorated in his poem "One We Knew" (1902). This facility for immersion in the local past is the impetus behind a perceptible quest, dating from the late 1870s, for documentation of that past. "I am wishing to consult the 'Sherborne Journal,' or the old 'Sherborne Mercury' mentioned in Hutchins, for the early part of the present century," he wrote to the Reverend Charles Bingham in September 1877. "Can you tell me where . . . I could see any county records, notes, or memoranda relating to that time?" (*CL* I: 51). Perhaps sensing that the local past with which he had been so familiar was becoming increasingly remote in time, Hardy turned to the period of the Napoleonic Wars, and to the years in which Dorset personalities and Dorset itself were particularly, even intimately, involved in the national emergency.

More than any other notebook the "Trumpet-Major" notebook, described by Hardy as "Notes taken for 'Trumpet Major' & other books of time of Geo III in (1878–1879–)," was given an almost exclusive focus: to record details which could be used for a forthcoming novel and for any future narrative centering on the Napoleonic Wars. Hardy's research involved numerous and sustained periods of study in the British Museum over an eighteen-month period, spring 1878 to autumn 1879. The

General Catalogue led him to standard bibliographies, such as Watts's *General Index to British and Foreign Literature*, and numerous "Periodical Publications." He investigated books of military statutes, regulations and standing orders, mid-century memoirs such as George Landmann's *Adventures and Recollections* (1852), local histories such as George Bankes' *The History of Corfe Castle* (1853), and, most conspicuously, contemporary magazines and newspapers, particularly the *Morning Post*.

What Linda Shires terms the "minute particulars of early nineteenth century custom" (*TM* 339) are to be found in sketches of teapots and notes on military drill and uniforms as well as on fashions, male and female. For Bob Loveday's exaggerated sartorial appearance at the theater in Weymouth, "the perfection of a beau in the dog-days [of hot August]" (*TM* 217), he draws on a report headed "the Modern beaus in the Dog-days," reproducing terminology and a metaphor from within the report. The "yards and yards of muslin wound round [Bob's] neck, forming a sort of asylum for the lower part of his face" (*TM* 217) are anticipated in a fashion observation from the *St James's Chronicle*: "neck surrounded with yards of muslin, which forms an asylum for the lower part of the face" (Taylor 1978: 132). Then, as if compensating for this over-dependence, Hardy takes imaginative possession of the scene: "Nobody would have guessed . . . that he had ever been aloft on a dark night in the Atlantic, or knew the hundred ingenuities that could be performed with a rope's end and a marling-spike as well as his mother tongue" (*TM* 217). Elsewhere in the notebook he makes careful notes about the early morning journey of the king's coach party en route for Weymouth, awaited keenly by the villagers, and the precise timing of the king's troop review on Bincombe Down (Taylor 1978: 126, 131; *TM* 86, 92). Details on topics such as press-gangs and military drilling are likewise based on entered notes (*TM* 339). The creative use to which he puts some of the material ranges far beyond what was needed for his prospective novel: entries on the subject of rules for the baptism of infants (Taylor 1978: 180–3) find issue in *A Laodicean*, and notes about soldiers shot for desertion on Bincombe Down make their way into his story of 1889, "The Melancholy Hussar of the German Legion."

To judge from other notes, subsequently written up for *Life and Work* and invoked in "Poetical Matter" and "Memoranda I," Hardy had fostered from the 1870s through to the end of his career what Millgate calls his "active and outgoing appetite for whatever was lively, local, and curious" (Millgate 2004: 172). This element of his note-taking supplies the realist texture of precisely those philosophically freighted novels *The Mayor of Casterbridge*, *The Woodlanders*, *Tess of the d'Urbervilles*, and *Jude the Obscure*, on which his reading had such a profound influence. That "appetite" for the "lively, local and curious" finds its satisfaction, most fully, in the notebook "Facts From Newspapers, Histories, Biographies, & other chronicles – (mainly Local)."

The date of the inception of "Facts" is clear from the source of the first entry, dated July 1883. Early on, Emma performed a clearing-up exercise, entering various items from other papers, or cuttings from them that dated back at least until 1876 and had probably been taken from another notebook. But the greater part of the "Facts" notebook is as first entered; it is not in the main a synthetic or edited compilation. After about ninety entries of its total of 690, Hardy set himself the task of copying items from the *Dorset County Chronicle* with the project of *The Mayor of Casterbridge* immediately in view. Of the items entered by Hardy and Emma, a good proportion originated in newspaper reports (in mainly local, but also national, papers). Over a concentrated two-month period, March to May 1884, he took items from issues of the *Dorset County Chronicle* for 1826–9. It is significant that he chose to work on material which presents itself as an indisputably public account of local events. No matter how banal or trivial they might be, their claim on his attention was that they had some kind of independent existence as a matter of record. The notebook is also unusual in showing the note-maker at work, introducing interjections, comments, and so forth (the later "Poetical Matter" notebook is also characterized by this). Hardy's reading in sources other than newspapers prompted poems such as "The Duel," "Barthélémon at Vauxhall," and "Panthera."

For Hardy there was evident satisfaction in getting the facts right, even though, as he conceded in the General Preface to the Wessex Edition (1912), "nobody would have discovered . . . errors [he might have committed] to the end of Time" (Orel 1967: 46). But the "Facts" notebook shows a new commitment to the recreation of the past, with less emphasis on a given historical situation than on a cultural collision, historically located, but framed by the struggle (and it is also a secular, epic struggle) between the customary values of pre-Victorian England (obsolescent, amoral, primitive), and those hegemonic values of mid-Victorian respectability (scientific, progressive, disciplined). These tensions are bountifully exemplified by the anonymous and near-anonymous social actors who live them out in the details of their everyday lives, as recorded by Hardy from the "old papers."

The very first entry to be selected from "old D.C.C." (to use Hardy's abbreviation) is suggestively emblematic of a brutal struggle between old and young and of a state of lawlessness in which humankind is rendered more brutal than the animals it tames:

> Dog – fighting. Man owned bull terrier, wh. beat every dog of its size in neigh[d]. He fought it with a much stronger dog, wh. it beat after severe struggle. As it lay panting on the ground he hounded on it a young dog, saying his dog still had pluck for another battle. Feeble & lacerated his dog had for the first time to yield. Owner so enraged at loss of match that he killed his dog. (Greenslade 2004: 41–2)

Such shocking narratives as these (about half of which are excerpted from old copies of the *Dorset County Chronicle* for 1826–30) offered Hardy a kind of "cultural poetics" in their attentiveness to the texture of the everyday life – pre-dating the world of his childhood, but doubtless also a component of it – that he wished to recapture. And it was precisely the everyday quality of the reports (even if in other respects brutal and sensational) which met Hardy's requirements in the early 1880s for a novel, powerfully grounded in a medium framed by a detailed cultural seeing, which would both validate the ordinary life and, at the same time, play off – against the frame of the ordinary – the extraordinary, the baffling, and, ultimately, the tragic.

The cultural-historical condition is now subject to an intense theatricality. Hardy entered into the notebook a newspaper report for September 1826 of a Private Quin who committed suicide having been forced to go on parade undressed after over-sleeping. Hardy must have seen at once the potential of this incident for the dramati-zation, in *The Mayor of Casterbridge*, of the conflict between the customary practice of Henchard and the rational polity of Farfrae in their contrasting attitudes to an employee, Abel Whittle, who is invariably late for work. While Henchard's response is to drive Abel out of bed and up the street in a state of undress, Farfrae, with an eye to Abel's dignity, and thus his productivity as a worker, tells him to return to work, properly dressed. A phase of conflict in social relations is here dramatized through Hardy's imported use of farce, since it is not present in the news story from which this episode is fashioned (*MC* 99–100; Greenslade 2004: 335–6). Indeed, the mixed spec-tacle offered in this notebook of comedy, farce, and fabliau, and of pathos, passive suf-fering, and tragedy, is strikingly placed at the service of his cultural-historical imagination. There is the recognition of poverty and crime: "Great distress & pover-ty . . . at this period (1826) – suicides: horse-stealing: highway robbery frequent" (Greenslade 2004: 76). But there is also a range of effects which the narratives of everyday life can elicit, from several examples of low comedy of the "biter bit" kind to the tragic consequences of misunderstandings and accidents. Hardy is captured both by the social and cultural "real" and by their shape, how they are performed in narrative.

The recall of a past bearing witness to the protean elements in human experience is encapsulated in the scene in *Two on a Tower* where Swithin's grandmother

> was gazing into the flames, with her hands upon her knees, quietly re-enacting in her brain certain of the long chain of episodes, pathetic, tragical, and humorous, which had constituted the parish history for the last sixty years. . . . "I've had a nap, and went straight back into my old country again, as usual. The place was as natural as when I left it, – e'en just three-score years ago!" (*TT* 41–2)

Hardy's "old country" was now made newly familiar to him through his retrieval of a culture from public sources, still vividly alive in the imagination.

V

Superficially, the first "Memoranda" notebook and the "Poetical Matter" notebook have much in common. Both are composite, synthetic, compilations largely derived from earlier notebooks that were later destroyed. They are the products – "Memoranda I" immediately, "Poetical Matter" retrospectively – of Hardy's extensive overview of all his many notebooks, when he at last turned to the gathering of "materials" that would be needed for the composition of what was, in effect, his authorized biography, known, since Michael Millgate's edition of 1984, as *The Life and Work of Thomas Hardy*. That revisitation process was probably initiated in 1917, and was being actively pursued in conjunction with Florence until the materials for the "Early Life" were complete. It is worth noting that readers of the *Life and Work*, and previously of *The Early Life* and *The Later Years*, would have become unsuspectingly familiar with some of the contents of Hardy's own assiduous note-making through his frequent citation of these earlier materials. Indeed, more than a quarter of *Life and Work* for the years 1867–80 is taken from notebooks, lending this text much of its sense of immediacy.

It was partly with that biography in mind that from January 1921 Hardy kept up a third notebook through the final decade of his life, "Memoranda II." Together with a separate typescript, "T.H. / Memoranda & Notes towards completing / the remainder of Vol. II (to end of book)," this notebook was intended to provide Florence with the materials she needed for composing the account of the years up to 1927 for the *Later Years* and on which she then drew extensively for chapters 37 and 38 (*LW* xvii, xxiv; Millgate 2004: 521). It has largely the character of a diary, recording day-to-day events up to and including 1927 (Millgate 1999: 15). While some of the discursive notes resemble those in "Memoranda I," "others are distinctly more personal and domestic" (Taylor 1978: 43), as will be familiar to readers of the closing sections of *Life and Work*. With its lists of modest outings, many now by chauffeured car, of engagements and of visitors to Max Gate – from the Shaws to Siegfried Sassoon and Colonel Lawrence, from Lady Ottoline Morrell to the composer Rutland Boughton – Hardy reveals himself through his final decade as, quite unconsciously, a generous host, particularly friendly to the young. He welcomes, in July 1924, the "Balliol Players," who arrive by bicycle to stage "The Oresteia" on the Max Gate lawn, "their theatrical properties" having been sent on "a lorry that sometimes broke down" (Taylor 1978: 81).

The form of "Memoranda I" was established by an extensive process of culling and sifting from earlier notes and pocket-books (far more extensive than either the selection of old material at the beginning of "Literary Notes I" or that which featured at the start of the "Facts" notebook) that both preceded and accompanied a process of destruction of what Hardy called (in a letter of 1919) "papers of the last 30 or 40 years" (*CL* V 303–4; *LW* xiv). Compiled probably 1917–20, "Memoranda I" comprises extracts covering the years 1867–1920, from "old papers, notebooks and diaries" which were then discarded or destroyed in the course of sorting out material for inclusion in the *Life* (Taylor 1978: xiii–xiv). Such an enterprise, with the evidence in front of him of his life-long accumulation of diaries, notebooks, and memoranda, had the effect of prompting re-immersion in what Gillian Beer has called "that shared past, as well as those many and separate individual pasts . . . [which] . . . becomes the most intense question of Hardy's creativity" (Beer 2002: 18). Its full title, "Memoranda of Customs, Dates, &c – (viz: Prose Matter)," evidently distinguishes it from "Poetical Matter," the notebook that Hardy probably began once most of the work for *Life and Work* had been completed "in late 1920 or early 1921" (Dalziel and Millgate 2009: xviii). Yet notwithstanding this formal differentiation of material, there are instances of correspondence between items recorded in each of the notebooks: for example, an early entry in "Memoranda I" reads "1876. Aug. Rain: like a banner of gauze waved in folds across the scene" (Taylor 1978: 19), while in "Poetical Matter" there is an almost verbatim entry: "At S. Newton 1876. Rain, like a banner of gauze waved in folds across the scene" (Dalziel and Millgate 2009: 5). Many of the prose entries are full of precisely felt life (and perhaps selected for this reason). An 1872 entry in "Memoranda I" records returning from Dorchester on a wet night: "The town . . . is circumscribed by a halo like an aurora: up the hill comes a broad band of turnpike road, glazed with moisture, which reflects the lustre of the mist" (Taylor 1978: 11). An 1879 note reads: "July. Rainy sunset: the sun streaming his yellow rays through the wet atmosphere like straying hair. The wet ironwork & wet slates shine" (Taylor 1978: 20). Elsewhere in the same notebook there are plots for possible stories, items recording old customs and local characters and aspects of social history, such as a story about a mail-coach guard living in Higher Bockhampton "in the eighteen thirties" who supplemented his wages by taking "small packages to London on his own account by collusion with the coachman" (Taylor 1978: 16). Such material, already historically remote in Hardy's experience when first noted, was now doubly removed in time, suggesting a still powerful impulse on his part to refamiliarize and live out memories of his local past.

It is, though, the "Poetical Matter" notebook that emerges as the most intensely revealing product of this exercise of reaffirmation of his creative powers in the 1920s. In particular it provides compelling evidence, as Millgate puts it, "of his continuing activity as a poet on into such future as might remain" (Millgate [1992] 1995: 133). Apparently surviving only as a microfilm, it was almost completely unknown until it was described and quoted from in Michael Millgate's *Thomas Hardy: A Biography* (1982). In part transferred from earlier notebooks going back to the late 1860s, "Mostly copied from old notes of many years ago," it is deliberately titled "POETICAL MATTER" (Dalziel and Millgate 2009: 76, 3). Some of these notes had only been recently extracted from old pocket-books for inclusion in *Life and Work* and were now recopied, presumably as potential sources for further, unwritten poems: "May 1. A man comes every evening to the cliff in front of our house to see the sun set. . . ." (*LW* 117) is further recopied as "Man comes to terrace to see the sun set (S. Newton)" (Dalziel and Millgate 2009: 6). A lengthy item (abbreviated here) is closely reworked: "March 9. British Museum Reading Room. Souls are gliding about here in a sort of dream – screened somewhat by their bodies, but imaginable behind them . . ." (*LW* 215) re-emerges as: "Souls gliding about in the B. M. They are in a sort of dream, screened by their bodies somewhat, but imaginable . . ." (Dalziel and Millgate 2009: 16).

Images recorded from Hardy's seven months at Swanage, his Sturminster Newton months, and the Tooting period are frequent in its early stages. But the notebook's function to record, in the editors' words, "materials and ideas in which he perceived some clear or latent promise of creative stimulation or exploitation" is unmistakable from the outset (Dalziel and Millgate 2009: xix). "Poetical Matter" includes notes for series of poems on specific topics, such as "God poems" and "Ghost poems" (Dalziel and Millgate 2009: 50, 39–41) and several items involving ghosts and "somnambulism," while ballads and/or narrative poems figure prominently, one ballad referred to being "The Banks of Allan Water," sung by Bathsheba in *Far from the Madding Crowd* (Dalziel and Millgate 2009: 30, 98). As the notebook develops, quotation from "old notes" becomes less prominent, new matter becomes more frequent: "from personal reflections, extracts from books and articles about poetry, and quotations from other poets, to ideas, themes, narrative outlines, metrical schemes, working notes, and even drafts for individual poems" (Dalziel and Millgate 2009: xix). Indeed, "Poetical Matter" shows us clearly Hardy's undiminished appetite for and interest in poetic method and experimentation: "<u>As to rhyme & rhythm</u> – let the lyric get more in tune as the song goes on, by increasing the rhymes . . . This might be elaborated to a system of <u>growing rhyme</u>" (Dalziel and Millgate 2009: 49). The drafts for poems which never reach the point of completion include the seven rough stanzas for a ballad, "Woodyates Inn. or The Bagman's Story" (Dalziel and Millgate 2009: 67–9), and recovered erasures, recorded in the annotations, reveal words and images subsequently incorporated into poems published in *Winter Words*. Dennis Taylor has noted how in one of the incomplete fragments in "Poetical Matter" Hardy "shows how he would work into a poem with a sense of rhythmical idioms felt before their content was entirely established" (Taylor 1993: 310); the poem is "Thoughts at Midnight."

There is in "Poetical Matter," particularly in the early pages, much "nature observed" comprising possible material for poems, even when apparently far-fetched for the purpose, and offering abundant evidence of how Hardy, in Dennis Taylor's words, "kept his poetical hand in during the novel-writing years" (Taylor 2002: 36). A good example is "Rushy Pond in August. To lie among the camomiles, Shep[ds] thyme, & wild strawberries. Pigeons come to drink. Almost every bird on the heath has gone afield" (Dalziel and Millgate 2009: 5). There are fragments about the weather, of great intensity and variety of tone, such as "Extraordinary gale & rain. Wind pulls at trees like a termagant seizing another termagant's hair; whizzes like a relaxing spring, combs the grass violently" (Dalziel and Millgate 2009: 18) or "Windy evening at Swanage. The wind shrieks an aria round angles & posts, & the chimney growls a bass accompaniment" (Dalziel and Millgate 2009: 4). Then, conversely, the near-absence of wind (again at Swanage): "Calm day. The air only moving enough to make a faint drone through the crevices of the window" (Dalziel and Millgate 2009: 5) or a note from 1887 (pointing to a formative pocket-book entry for descriptions of Talbothays in the "Rally" phase of *Tess*) which evokes the Frome valley in September: "Silent afternoon – gnats. Bell-metal sun – stream stealing noiselessly on: haze: private conversations audible afar: the murmur of Lewell Mill below" (Dalziel and Millgate 2009: 15).

The notebook's editors have tentatively concluded that "everything in the second half of the notebook was entered during the last fourteen months of Hardy's life," and that "Hardy began using 'Poetical Matter' early in the 1920s and continued to do so, with increased intensity from the autumn of 1926 onwards, until the beginning of his final illness, less than five weeks prior to his death in January 1928" (Dalziel and Millgate 2009: xviii).

VI

Following Hardy's death, his co-executor, Sydney Cockerell, zealously destroyed "almost all of the still surviving notebooks" (Rosenbaum 1990: 192). Michael

Millgate's *Testamentary Acts* provides an exhaustive account, based on the available evidence, of these vexatious transactions (Millgate [1992] 1995: 156–61). Those notebooks that remained, together with all other of Hardy's papers, passed, on Florence Hardy's death in 1937, to her executor, the solicitor Irene Cooper Willis, for eventual housing (as her will stipulated) in the Thomas Hardy Memorial Collection at the Dorset County Museum, Dorchester. The one significant exception was the "Studies, Specimens &c." notebook, entrusted to the Hardy bibliographer and editor Richard Little Purdy and now in the Beinecke Library at Yale. Cooper Willis was, however, extremely dilatory in delivering certain documentary materials to the Dorset County Museum, some of the deposits of papers, including the notebooks, being made only in "1957, in 1958, and 1962, and even subsequently to Cooper Willis's death in 1970," Millgate noting, diplomatically, that Cooper Willis "seems to have found trusteeship a satisfaction as well as a burden" (Millgate [1992] 1995: 171–2). Cooper Willis, herself, had drawn on "Memoranda I" for an essay, "Thomas Hardy," written in 1940 but published posthumously (Cooper Willis 1971: 266–79), and Evelyn Hardy (no relation) had drawn on the two Memorandum notebooks for her *Thomas Hardy's Notebooks and Some Letters from Julia Augusta Martin* (1955) which, while offering a quite inadequate bibliographical account of the notebooks, provided a valuable commentary on them.

By 1962 the museum had finally made available all four of the so-called "Commonplace Books" – the designation appears to have been Cooper Willis's – to three of which Hardy had given the titles "Literary Notes I," "Literary Notes II," "Facts from Newspapers, Histories, Biographies & other chronicles (mainly Local)" (marked "III" on the cover), while he had marked only "IV" on the cover of what has subsequently become known as the "1867" notebook (Rosenbaum 1990: 193–4). The scrapbook-style notebook, entitled by Hardy "Literary Notes III," was found amongst further papers of Cooper Willis after her death, and was delivered to the museum in July 1972 (*LN* xxxi and Dorset County Museum papers). This notebook did not figure in the microfilm collection of Hardy materials produced by E. P. Microform in 1975, but it was edited by Björk as "Literary Notes III" in 1985.

One notebook, however, "Poetical Matter" has never been received by the Dorset County Museum and is not now thought to exist. The introduction to the Dalziel and Millgate edition provides a fascinating reconstruction of what can be discovered of the notebook's history and records the good fortune of Richard Purdy's having had microfilm copies made of all of the major Hardy notebooks, including "Poetical Matter," when they were temporarily on loan to him from Cooper Willis from September 1949 until July 1952. Of course, we have little exact knowledge of how and why any of the notebooks survived when so many were destroyed, but taken together, as they can be now, they provide a striking and sometimes surprising representation of what was going on in the creative and quotidian working life of a great novelist and poet, from early manhood through to old age. Coming across an entry that Hardy made in "Memoranda I" for a remedy for diarrhea (Taylor 1978: 37), Philip Larkin mused that it was "odd to think of Hardy carefully transcribing it for posterity," concluding that "the concern he had for his surviving image was refreshingly free from any desire to inflate it" (Larkin 1979: 643). This is neatly and, in its way, sensitively said, but nonetheless manages to miss the point. Hardy kept up his notebooks for his own various purposes and not for the satisfaction of prospective readers, let alone tidy-minded critics and editors.

Each of the notebooks is inevitably and necessarily a mixed production to a greater or lesser degree. That notes copied from Horace Walpole make their appearance in "Studies, Specimens &c.," with little to do with the notebook's lexical focus (Dalziel and Millgate 1994: 82), or that a reference to the distribution of "Chuppaties" as a signal for the Indian Mutiny should appear in "Literary Notes I" (*LN* I: 12), should not really surprise us. The notebooks reflect both the purposeful activity of the mind of a poet-novelist and the distillation of a lifetime's reading, and inferences drawn from what we find in them may be both suggestive and deceptive. What is certain is that they provide a remarkable and unique record of the predispositions and habits, the growth and the discoveries, of the mind of Thomas Hardy.

REFERENCES AND FURTHER READING

Armstrong, Tim (ed.) (1993). *Thomas Hardy, Selected Poems*. London: Longman.

Beatty, C. J. P. (ed.) ([1966] 2007). *The Architectural Notebook of Thomas Hardy*, revised edn. Dorchester: Dorset Natural History and Archaeological Society.

Beer, Gillian (2002). Hardy: The After-Life and the Life Before. In Phillip Mallett (ed.), *Thomas Hardy: Texts and Contexts* (pp. 18–30). Basingstoke: Palgrave Macmillan.

Björk, Lennart A. (1980). Hardy's Reading. In Norman Page (ed.), *Thomas Hardy: The Writer and his Background* (pp. 102–27). London: Bell & Hyman.

Björk, Lennart A. (ed.) (1985). *The Literary Notebooks of Thomas Hardy*, 2 vols. London and Basingstoke: Macmillan.

Björk, Lennart A. (2000). Notebooks. In Norman Page (ed.), *Oxford Reader's Companion to Hardy* (pp. 290–2). Oxford: Oxford University Press.

Dalziel, Pamela (1993). Hardy's Sexual Evasions: The Evidence of the "Studies, Specimens &c." Notebook. *Victorian Poetry*, 31(2), 143–55.

Dalziel, Pamela, and Michael Millgate (eds.) (1994). *Thomas Hardy's "Studies, Specimens &c." Notebook*. Oxford: Clarendon Press.

Dalziel, Pamela, and Michael Millgate (eds.) (2009). *Thomas Hardy's "Poetical Matter" Notebook*. Oxford: Oxford University Press.

Greenslade, William (ed.) (2004). *Thomas Hardy's "Facts" Notebook: A Critical Edition*. Aldershot: Ashgate.

Hardy, Evelyn (ed.) (1955). *Thomas Hardy's Notebooks and Some Letters from Julia Augusta Martin*. London: Hogarth Press.

Hardy, Thomas ([1880] 1997). *The Trumpet-Major*, ed. Linda M. Shires. London: Penguin.

Hardy, Thomas ([1882] 1975). *Two on a Tower*, ed. F. B. Pinion. Basingstoke: Macmillan.

Hardy, Thomas ([1886] 1987). *The Mayor of Casterbridge*, ed. Dale Kramer. Oxford: Oxford University Press.

Hardy, Thomas ([1887] 1985). *The Woodlanders*, ed. Dale Kramer. Oxford: Oxford University Press.

Hardy, Thomas (1984). *The Life and Work of Thomas Hardy*, ed. Michael Millgate. London: Macmillan.

Larkin, Philip (1979). Review of *The Personal Notebooks of Thomas Hardy* (ed. Richard H. Taylor). *New Statesman*, May 4, 642–3.

Millgate, Michael (1982). *Thomas Hardy: A Biography*. New York: Random House.

Millgate, Michael ([1992] 1995). *Testamentary Acts.* Oxford: Clarendon Press.

Millgate, Michael (1999). Thomas Hardy: The Biographical Sources. In Dale Kramer (ed.), *The Cambridge Companion to Thomas Hardy* (pp. 1–18). Cambridge: Cambridge University Press.

Millgate, Michael (2004). *Thomas Hardy: A Biography Revisited.* Oxford: Oxford University Press.

Orel, Harold (ed.) (1967). *Thomas Hardy's Personal Writings.* London: Macmillan.

Pite, Ralph (2006). *Thomas Hardy: The Guarded Life.* London: Picador.

Postmus, Bouwe (ed.) (2007). *George Gissing's Scrapbook.* Amsterdam: Twizle Press.

Purdy, Richard Little ([1954] 1968). *Thomas Hardy: A Bibliographical Study.* Oxford: Clarendon Press.

Purdy, Richard Little, and Michael Millgate (eds.) (1978–88). *The Collected Letters of Thomas Hardy,* 7 vols. Oxford: Clarendon Press.

Rignall, John (ed.) (2000). *The Oxford Reader's Companion to George Eliot.* Oxford: Oxford University Press.

Rosenbaum, Barbara (ed.) (1990). *Index of English Literary Manuscripts,* vol. IV: *1800–1900,* pt. 2: *Hardy–Lamb.* London: Mansell.

Taylor, Dennis (1988). *Hardy's Metres and Victorian Prosody.* Oxford: Clarendon Press.

Taylor, Dennis (1993). *Hardy's Literary Language and Victorian Philology.* Oxford: Clarendon Press.

Taylor, Dennis (2002). The Chronology of Hardy's Poetry, Part III. *Thomas Hardy Journal,* 18(1), 35–53.

Taylor, Richard H. (ed.) (1978). *The Personal Notebooks of Thomas Hardy.* London and Basingstoke: Macmillan.

Willis, Irene Cooper (1971). Thomas Hardy. *Colby Library Quarterly,* 9(5), 266–79.

Wright, Walter F. (1967). *The Shaping of "The Dynasts": A Study in Thomas Hardy.* Lincoln: University of Nebraska Press.

7

"Genres are not to be mixed. . . . I will not mix them": Discourse, Ideology, and Generic Hybridity in Hardy's Fiction

Richard Nemesvari

I

Jacques Derrida begins his essay "The Law of Genre" with the categorical statements quoted in my title (Derrida 1980: 55) only to immediately and characteristically repudiate the certainties they appear to imply. The critic, inviting his readers to consider the opposite position to his opening declarations, asks us to "suppose for a moment that it were impossible not to mix genres," and to contemplate the questions "What if there were, lodged within the heart of the law itself, a law of impurity or a principle of contamination? . . . suppose the condition for the possibility of the law were the *a priori* of a counter-law, an axiom of impossibility that would confound its sense, order, and reason?" (Derrida 1980: 57). In this typically deconstructive move Derrida not only invokes one of the issues central to contemporary discussions of genre, but also reveals why Thomas Hardy's novels are forceful illustrations of current theories exploring genre and literary analysis. Hardy's technique of generating generic expectations within his fiction, only to then subvert those expectations by introducing contrasting and at times contradictory genre discourses into his narratives, is arguably his most consistent novelistic method. Texts such as *Under the Greenwood Tree: A Rural Painting of the Dutch School* or *The Hand of Ethelberta: A Comedy in Chapters* provide explicit genre identifiers in their subtitles, yet they at best partially fulfill their promised forms, while a novel like *Far From the Madding Crowd*, with its allusive title and early, literal representation of a shepherd and his flock, prepares its audience for a pastoral idyll but then juxtaposes this with the harsh materialism of agricultural economics and a sensational love triangle resulting in murder and madness. *Tess of the d'Urbervilles* is even more eclectic, containing as it does elements of the realist, the tragic, the sensational, the pastoral, the Gothic, the melodramatic, and the didactic – a whirl of generic hybridity that destabilizes reader response by refusing any firm position from which to develop a secure interpretive stance.

And it is this effect that reinforces Hardy's ideological purpose. While Hardy was negotiating with Alexander Macmillan over his unpublished first novel, *The Poor Man and the Lady*, Macmillan said of the book that it "meant mischief" (*LW* 64), and one way the author continued to make "mischief" throughout his career as a novelist was by manipulating genre to disrupt the complacency of his Victorian middle-class audience. But it was not just nineteenth-century readers who found themselves discomfited by this refusal to provide the stability of genre guidance. As Gérard Genette notes, "The whole history of genres . . . is imprinted with . . . fascinating patterns that inform and deform the often irregular reality of the literary field – patterns whose designers claim to have discovered a natural 'system' precisely where they are constructing a factitious symmetry" (Genette 1992: 45). The desire for pure forms and naturalized literary structures pre-dates and post-dates the Victorians, providing in itself a powerfully attractive ideology of reading. Thus a modern audience, encountering Hardy's problematized grounds of reference, continues to find its easy assumptions and reactions challenged.

Now of course one apparently straightforward way to simplify this discussion is to state the obvious: Hardy is writing prose fiction, and therefore the genre in which he is working is the novel. As we shall see, it is precisely this that creates the possibility for Hardy's aggressive hybridity; however, it is also necessary to note that during the period in which he is writing, the dominant trend in fiction did not support his type of overt genre-blending. The rising influence of realism encouraged a unity of novelistic effect, for example through the mediating control of George Eliot's authoritative third-person narrator or through the tightly constrained center of consciousness of Henry James, whose purpose was at least partly to create the naturalized cohesion deemed necessary for a legitimate formalist genre. Hardy's manipulation of genre demonstrates his refusal to fully commit himself to this aesthetic project, and identifies the anti-realist nature of his fiction. The multi-modal quality of Hardy's narratives reveals the artifice necessary for realism's illusion of mimetic coherence, and because of this his fiction provides an apt model for Mikhail Bakhtin's theorizations about the novel. According to Bakhtin,

> The novel can be defined as a diversity of social speech types (sometimes even diversity of languages) and a diversity of individual voices, artistically organized. . . . Authorial speech, the speeches of narrators, inserted genres, the speech of characters are merely those fundamental compositional unities with whose help heteroglossia [*raznorečie*] can enter the novel. . . . These distinctive links and interrelationships between utterances and languages, this movement of the theme through different languages and speech types, its dispersion into the rivulets and droplets of social heteroglossia, its dialogization – this is the basic distinguishing feature of the stylistics of the novel. (Bakhtin 1981: 262–3)

The question thus becomes not *whether* any given novel is dialogic, but *how willing* that novel is to acknowledge the divergent voices and forms it employs – whether it embraces the multiplicity of its stylistics or aligns itself with a unitary language that

constitutes "the theoretical expression of the historical processes of linguistic unifica-
tion and centralization, an expression of the centripetal forces of language . . . opposed
to the realities of heteroglossia" (Bakhtin 1981: 270).

Hardy's unsublimated incorporation of "inserted genres" into the rubric of his
novels is just one element that establishes them firmly as dialogic discourse, since the
diversity that results precludes any possibility of a single, monologic response. If
Alastair Fowler is correct in his claim that "genres adjust a reader's mental set and
help in selecting the optimally relevant associations that amount to a meaning of the
literary work" (Fowler 2003: 190), then Hardy's method amounts to a process of dis-
association which, if it does not absolutely defer meaning, certainly complicates the
manner in which it may be derived. Because modern conceptualizations of genre no
longer focus on classificatory formal features, but instead insist on a dynamic generic
negotiation between reader, author, and social constructions of literary horizons of
expectation, Hardy's encouragement and indeed insistence on such a process provides
numerous examples of how these kinds of mixed discourses work. In this way he fulfills
"the law of the law of genre . . . precisely a principle of contamination, a law of impurity, a parasitical economy" (Derrida 1980: 59) that insists on an interdependent play
of forms as the only way to adequately represent the complexities of class and gender
interaction which dominate his texts.

Hardy's employment of genre disjunction, therefore, often takes on a more specifically ideological role. Various critics have commented on the impact of prose realism's
increasing cultural dominance, and Fredric Jameson's observations may stand as a
useful summary:

> Indeed, as any number of "definitions" of realism assert . . . mimesis or realistic repre-
> sentation has as its historic function the systematic undermining and demystification,
> the secular "decoding," of those preexisting inherited traditional or sacred narrative
> paradigms which are its initial givens. In this sense, the novel plays a significant role
> in what may be called a properly bourgeois cultural revolution – that immense process
> of transformation whereby populations whose life habits were formed by other, now
> archaic, modes of production are effectively reprogrammed for life and work in the new
> world of market capitalism. The "objective" function of the novel is thereby also implied:
> to its subjective and critical, analytic, corrosive mission must now be added the task of
> producing as though for the first time that very life world, that very "referent" . . . of
> which this new narrative discourse will then claim to be the "realistic" reflection.
> (Jameson 1981: 152)

It is precisely this "process of transformation," as characters and societies based on
"traditional . . . paradigms" and "archaic" experience find themselves confronted by
antithetical historical/materialist forces, that repeatedly drives Hardy's narratives.
Whether it is the quasi-comic replacement of the Mellstock church musicians by
Fancy Day and the vicar's up-to-date cabinet-organ in *Under the Greenwood Tree*, or
the tragedy of Tess Durbeyfield's inability to negotiate the deracinated "ache of modernism" (*TD* 177) in *Tess*, many of his novels foreground the transition from an older,
established order to corrosive new ways of being. Jameson might maintain that in

doing so Hardy, especially because his representations of such shifts imply their inevitability, simply reinforces the ideological purpose of nineteenth-century fiction. I would suggest, however, that it is his refusal to naturalize the processes portrayed as "reality" that acts to prevent such a result. Hardy's insertion of, for example, melo-drama and sensationalism into his texts disrupts the detachment of realist rhetoric by insisting on affective response, while at the same time strategically undercutting the realist novel's claims to generic purity by introducing "low" forms of popular entertainment into his texts. Elaine Hadley argues that "the melodramatic mode emerged in the early and mid-nineteenth century as a polemical response to the social, economic, and epistemological changes that characterized the consolidation of market society" (Hadley 1995: 3), so that this particular type of genre manipulation serves as a specific resistance to the normalization of bourgeois assumptions, and to the new system of cultural referents they seek to establish.

But the mixing of such explicitly literary forms is only the initiating strategy upon which Hardy's hybridity rests. Within such expansive categories his complex employ-ment of what Bakhtin calls "speech genres" also contributes to his heteroglossia. For Bakhtin it is crucial to recognize that

> the study of verbal art can and must overcome the divorce between an abstract "formal" approach and an equally abstract "ideological" approach. Form and content in discourse are one, once we understand that verbal discourse is a social phenomenon – social throughout its entire range and in each and every of its factors, from the sound image to the furthest reaches of abstract meaning. (Bakhtin 1981: 259)

This, in turn, leads to his idea of "the utterance," a formulation that in its foreground-ing of the verbal expands the contextualization inherent in abstract concepts of dis-course by insisting on the vocalized element of language. An utterance is always contingent on the circumstances in which it occurs so that, while it partakes of ines-capable linguistic elements, its meaning can only be determined by the framework in which it appears. The bridge between utterance and genre lies, according to Bakhtin, in the fact that, while the expression of particular utterances may be unique, their use in social situations leads inevitably to quasi-standardized conventions, so that while "Each separate utterance is individual . . . each sphere in which language is used develops its own *relatively stable types* of these utterances. These we may call *speech genres*" (Bakhtin 1990: 60, italics in original). It is, however,

> especially important here to draw attention to the very significant difference between primary (simple) and secondary (complex) speech genres (understood not as a functional difference). Secondary (complex) speech genres – novels, dramas, all kinds of scientific research, major genres of commentary, and so forth – arise in more complex and com-paratively highly developed and organized cultural communication (primarily written). . . . During the process of their formation, they absorb and digest various primary (simple) genres that have taken form in unmediated speech communion. These primary genres are altered and assume a special character when they enter into complex ones. (Bakhtin 1990: 62)

Incorporated into the secondary speech genres of his novels Hardy provides a wide variety of primary speech genres, including songs, hymns, sermons, ballads, folk tales, and dialect expressions, which create further opportunities to complicate any expectations of formal unity his reader might hold. Such utterances, removed from their status quo contexts and realigned by their employment inside the secondary speech genre's textual economy, become fruitful sites for the exposure of conventional belief through pastiche, parody, and satire, thus feeding back into additional secondary (literary) genres in a type of self-reinforcing loop. The various levels of irony generated are effective because they force a re-evaluative exchange between Hardy and his audience that encourages a flexibility of generic response that translates into a flexibility of ideological reaction.

This, in turn, fosters an unavoidably dialogic give-and-take, since "Each utterance is filled with echoes and reverberations of other utterances to which it is related by the communality of the sphere of speech communication. . . . Each utterance refutes, affirms, supplements, and relies on the others, presupposes them to be known, and somehow takes them into account" (Bahktin 1990: 91). Or, as Hans Robert Jaus puts it, "Just as there is no act of verbal communication that is not related to a general, socially or situationally conditioned norm or convention, it is also unimaginable that a literary work [can] set itself into an informational vacuum" (Jaus 1982: 79). The strength of Hardy's novels lies in their refusal to elide the essential interdependence of textuality, so that by embracing genre heteroglossia and making it a part of his narrative practice he insists that there is no "norm or convention" that can stand outside of textual interrogation. By defamiliarizing his plots through a radical undercutting of generic unity Hardy disrupts not only the smooth flow of predictable story-telling but also the presuppositions upon which that predictability rests, providing a series of utterances whose startling juxtapositions verge on the kind of fragmentation he would develop further in his poetry. To illustrate what I am suggesting I have chosen to concentrate on two specific elements of Hardy's genre manipulation in his fiction, starting with a literary form fitting Bakhtin's designation of a secondary speech genre and concluding with his employment of a primary speech genre. In this way Hardy's use of melodrama and dialect reveal an approach to novel writing which, in its assertive demonstration that "A genre, whether literary or not, is nothing other than the codification of discursive properties" (Todorov 1991: 18), provides a unique system for social observation and commentary.

II

By the time Hardy entered the world of Victorian letters in 1871, with the publication of the sensational *Desperate Remedies*, melodrama was firmly established as a nineteenth-century cultural force through its domination of Victorian theater. Its influence on prose fiction, however, was increasingly seen as problematic. The 1860s debate over sensationalism and melodrama in the novel resulted in the triumph of realist fiction as "serious" literature, and the concomitant relegation of the melodramatic sensation novel to the status of merely "popular entertainment." This illustrates nicely Thomas O. Beebee's contention that "the act of canonizing is one of the potential use-values associated with certain genres" (Beebee 1994: 17), since the clear purpose of this bifurcation creating competing sub-genres within the genre of the novel was to establish a hierarchy of literary value. And on the whole this system appeared to achieve its goal. Realist authors such as Eliot, Meredith, and James were granted legitimacy denied to melodramatic writers like Collins, Braddon, and Reade so that, "purified" of the low-status elements that might weaken its claim to generic validity, a certain kind of novel was prepared to take its place as a significant arbiter of social values. Hardy, however, refuses to fit this neat schema, and thus calls the whole enterprise into question.

Hardy's fiction is pervaded by the effects of melodrama. His emphasis on plot over psychology, his willingness to explore extreme situations and reactions, and his use of stock characters, tableaux, and sensation scenes provide a constant challenge to realist assumptions about how "high" literature should work, a challenge made increasingly sharp by his eventual, undeniable status as the predominant English novelist of the last quarter of the nineteenth century. Hardy's mixing of realism with melodrama was a direct repudiation of the sensation fiction debate's attempt to create generic purity in the Victorian novel, and the transcription into his literary notebooks of a passage from Trollope's *Autobiography* is suggestive:

> The division of novels into sensational & anti-sensl. ⟨or realistic,⟩ a mistake – wh. arises from the inability of the imperfect artist to be at the same time realistic & sensl. A good novel shd be <u>both</u>, & both in the highest degree. Horrors heaped on horrors are not tragic, but dull. But he who can deal adequately with tragic elements is a greater artist than the writer whose efforts never carry him above the mild walks of everyday life.
>
> No novel is anything, for comedy or tragedy, unless the reader can <u>sympathize</u> with the characters. If the author can thus touch his reader's heart, & draw his tears, he cannot be too sensl. (*LN* I: 163–4)

This direct call for hybridity, with its specific evocation of melodrama's affective goals of touching the heart and drawing tears placed in the context of realism, sensationalism, comedy, and tragedy, reinforces Hardy's full commitment to genre-blending. A focused example of just how discomfiting his use of the melodramatic mode could be, and a good demonstration of the way Hardy employs melodrama to advance his cultural critique, is found in his most overt (some critics might say most egregious) evocation of a melodramatic figure in his entire oeuvre – Alec in *Tess of the d'Urbervilles*.

From the moment of his first appearance Alec Stoke-d'Urberville is described as a melodramatic villain. His "almost swarthy complexion, with full lips, badly moulded, though red and smooth" (*TD* 52) invokes the dark features of melodrama's antagonists and the destructive sexuality which often underlies their wrongdoing, while his "well-groomed black moustache with curled points" (*TD* 52) pushes him close to caricature.

Even his opening words to Tess, " 'Well, my Beauty, what can I do for you?' " (*TD* 53), replicate the salacious assurance common to this theatrical type, something the February 1892 issue of *Punch* recognizes when it says of Alec that he "would be thoroughly in his element in an Adelphi Drama of the most approved type. . . . He is just the sort of stage-scoundrel who from time to time seeks to take some mean advantage of a heroine in distress" (Clark 1993: 201). Yet in a subsequent and considerably less good-natured review for *Blackwood's Magazine* in March of 1892, Margaret Oliphant is forced to concede the manifest realist strengths of *Tess*:

> But with all this, what a living, breathing scene, what a scent and fragrance of the actual, what solid bodies, what real existence. . . . We feel inclined to embrace Mr. Hardy, though we are not fond of him, in pure satisfaction with the good brown soil and substantial flesh and blood, the cows, and the mangel-wurzel, and the hard labour of the fields – which he makes us smell and see. Here is the genuine article at least. Here is a workman who . . . knows how to use his colours, and throw his shadows, and make us feel the earth under our feet. (Cox 1970: 204)

It is precisely the insertion of Alec's melodramatic villainy into such a realistic context that disturbs the reader's comfortable sense of narrative predictability, thus foreshadowing the additional disruptive challenges soon to follow. Along with this direct generic "contamination" (in Derridean terms) of opposed rhetorical modes, Hardy also invokes and then subverts the accustomed scenario of melodrama. Within the usual plot line a seductively sensual man of aristocratic background pursues an economically vulnerable young woman, despite her devotion to a stalwartly virtuous man of lower social status. The narrative twists and turns around her attempts to maintain her virtue despite the pressures brought to bear by the upper-class cad, until finally through a providential intervention she is saved from succumbing, the threatening male character is vanquished, the heroine marries her true love, and all ends happily. Variations on this story were ubiquitous on the nineteenth-century stage, so that, as Judith Walkowitz puts it, "A familial drama was . . . entwined with a class drama, as represented by the erotic triangle of upper-class male villain, passive plebeian hero . . . and passive, victimized heroine" (Walkowitz 1992: 87). Having generated the expectation of this familiar progression through its introduction of Tess and Alec's relationship early in the story, *Tess of the d'Urbervilles* proceeds to deny the genre satisfactions of melodrama on every level, ironizing its effects in order to advance Hardy's repudiation of Victorian class and gender assumptions.

To start with the text's most obvious subversion, Alec, despite his wealth, manifestly does *not* possess the aristocratic background of the standard melodramatic seducer. As the son of "an honest merchant (some said money-lender)" (*TD* 51) whose father, "Conning for an hour in the British Museum the pages of works devoted to extinct, half-extinct, obscured and ruined families," appropriated the name "d'Urberville" because it "looked and sounded as well as any of them" (*TD* 52), Alec is a product of the most crass kind of bourgeois false gentility. Melodrama's rise as a genre in the late eighteenth and early nineteenth centuries occurred while most social power still resided in the hands of a landed nobility whose purported corruption was used to dramatize the opposed virtues of a growing urban laboring class and, increasingly, the nascent middle class. By the late nineteenth century, however, cultural capital and influence had passed to that very middle class, which continued attending the theater to confirm its righteousness by despising upper-class villains whose power, beyond the footlights, was more and more circumscribed.

Hardy's refusal to support this comfortable illusion of moral superiority directly attacks his middle-class audience by providing it with a novelized version of the melodramatic villain, and then insisting that he is one of *them* – a "gentleman" whose (questionably) accumulated, market-derived wealth allows him to misuse lower-status young women as ruthlessly as any roué possessed of actual rank. Further, Angel Clare, the novel's putative hero, is shown engaged in a similarly hollow exercise of status displacement only, as it were, in the opposite direction. Working at Talbothays dairy as part of his goal of "learning farming in all its branches," he nonetheless remains, by bourgeois standards, "quite the gentleman-born" as "a pa'son's son" (*TD* 163), so that his attempt to join the ranks of agricultural workfolk is as empty as Alec's attempt to mimic the aristocracy. Angel can no more be the "plebian" protagonist of melodrama than Alec can be its "upper-class" antagonist, but by setting up these two points of his central erotic triangle to echo this theatrical trope, and then refusing to follow its pattern, Hardy drives home his critique of middle-class exploitation, rigidity, and hypocrisy by insisting that it is the values of this group alone that encompass and destroy his heroine. As a Durbeyfield, Tess is a mere "cottage girl" (*TD* 73) available for Alec's phallic predation while, as a d'Urberville, she is the "belated seedling of an effete aristocracy" (*TD* 330) available for Angel's fastidious rejection. In both cases bourgeois arrogance, which constructs itself as superior to those both "below" and "above" it, comes under blistering exposure as the two male characters representing its expression stand revealed as more destructive than any melodramatic blackguard.

On another level, Hardy's presentation of Tess herself also feeds into his genre manipulation. Whether Tess exhibits the kind of passivity often associated with melodrama heroines has been the subject of extended critical debate, and that discussion does not need to be replicated here. What matters is that Alec's campaign to overwhelm her sexual resistance, based as it is on a relentless pursuit employing emotional and financial coercion, fits precisely the kind of female jeopardy that played itself out over and over again on the Victorian stage. Michael R. Booth, in his foundational study *English Melodrama*, notes that a "cardinal rule of melodrama is that at some point, usually early in the play, the heroine begins to suffer" (Booth 1965: 24), and also that it is "the heroine, who is the emotional core of melodrama and very often the storm centre of its action" (Booth 1965: 30), two observations that clearly apply to *Tess of the d'Urbervilles*. In this way Hardy quickly establishes a plot which would appear thoroughly familiar to his audience, so that Amy J. Devitt's broader comments on how such narrative evocations work is telling: "Since genre responds to recurring situations, a text's reflection of genre indirectly reflects situation. Thus the act of constructing the genre – of creating or perceiving the formal traces of a genre – is also the act of constructing the situation" (Devitt 1993: 578). The text appears to replicate a standard melodramatic situation for its heroine, only to then shockingly have the villain succeed in his sexual conquest as Tess moves from being "The Maiden" of "Phase the First" to being "Maiden No More" in "Phase the Second." This breaks the implied genre contract between reader and author because the novel insists on a continuing sympathetic engagement with Tess even after she has surrendered what melodrama constructs as a woman's most prized possession. Hardy's assertion in his title page that Tess remains "A Pure Woman Faithfully Presented" creates a definition of female purity that completely repudiates the Manichean values of the nineteenth-century stage, as does her eventual execution. Tess's death moves melodrama into tragedy, and by pushing her victimization to its full conclusion Hardy's didactic challenge to his audience's complacency exchanges the sometimes too-easy affective responses to melodramatic suffering for the deeper reactions of catharsis.

The genre-blending in *Tess of the d'Urbervilles* achieves the same effect that Bakhtin argues is characteristic of Tolstoy's fiction – its "discourse harmonizes and disharmonizes (more often disharmonizes) with various aspects of the heteroglot socio-verbal consciousness ensnaring the object, while at the same time polemically invading the reader's belief and evaluative system, striving to stun and destroy the apperceptive background of the reader's active understanding" (Bakhtin 1981: 283). By generating a potential horizon of expectation through character and situation, and then disrupting the standard patterns usually followed, Hardy disturbs automatic understandings and prepares the way for potentially liberating insights. That many readers were disturbed by this technique is understandable, since what appears to be an unthreatening, predictable form turns into a controversial device for exposing unexamined assumptions. The use of melodrama to achieve this partakes of a general cultural movement of his time, but Hardy's employment of dialect in his novels is a perhaps more distinctive way of achieving something similar. This issue is briefly touched upon in *Tess*, when we are told of the heroine that "The dialect was on her tongue to some extent, despite the village school" (*TD* 23), and that she "spoke two languages; the dialect at home, more or less; ordinary English abroad and to persons of quality" (*TD* 29), both statements suggesting the class indeterminacy that plays such a large part in her downfall. In other novels, therefore, Hardy employs dialect to once again generate hybridity and subvert assumptions about cultural status.

III

Hardy's efforts to incorporate the Dorset vocabulary, inflections, and pronunciations of his family background into the fictional world of Wessex required a deft balancing act. If, like his mentor and friend William Barnes (who wrote his poetry solely in West Country dialect), Hardy attempted linguistic fidelity, he ran the risk of alienating an urban middle-class readership that would mostly be unable to follow what was being said. If, on the other hand, he quasi-standardized his dialect constructions, what he gained in intelligibility might be lost in the perception of his characters as bumpkins whose quaint ways of expressing themselves merely represented an uneducated inability to speak "properly." That Hardy was aware of this dilemma is clear from the letter of November 30, 1878 that he wrote to the *Athenaeum*, in which he states: "An author may be said to fairly convey the spirit of intelligent peasant talk if he retains the idiom, compass, and characteristic expressions, although he may not encumber the page with obsolete pronunciations of the purely English words" (*THPV* 14). The assertion that non-standard English may nonetheless communicate intelligent thought (peasant or otherwise) is his way of insisting that, as he put it in a later letter to the *Spectator* of October 15, 1881, dialects are "varieties of English which are intrinsically as genuine, grammatical, and worthy of the royal title as is the all-prevailing competitor which bears it; whose only fault was that they . . . were worsted in the struggle for existence, when a uniform tongue became a necessity among the advanced classes of the population" (*THPV* 29). Of course it is precisely the assumed superiority in the "advanced classes" that Hardy intends to challenge through his representation of his rural characters, and his use of dialect advances this purpose.

In discussing how such a primary speech genre functions when it is incorporated into a secondary speech genre like the novel, Bakhtin is explicit about the dialogic effect produced:

> As they enter literature and are appropriated to literary languages, dialects in this new context lose, of course, the quality of closed social-linguistic systems; they are deformed and in fact cease to be that which they had been simply as dialects. On the other hand, these dialects, on entering the literary language and preserving within it their own dialogical elasticity, their other-languagedness, have the effect of deforming the literary language; it, too, ceases to be that which it had been, a closed socio-linguistic system. Literary language is a highly distinctive phenomenon, as is the linguistic consciousness of the educated person who is its agent; within it, intentional diversity of speech [*raznorečivos*] (which is present in every living dialect as a closed system) is transformed into diversity of language [*raznojazyčie*]; what results is not a single language but a dialogue of language. (Bahktin 1981: 294)

Dialect in a novel creates heteroglossia not only because it forces into congruence different versions of the same language, but also because it demonstrates the need for that congruence in order for speech value to be assigned. As a primary speech genre used within prose fiction, dialect provides an additional reinforcement to the law of genre, in that by contaminating the Standard English of literary discourse it becomes "neither separable nor inseparable" from its supposed opposite, and forms "an odd couple of one without the other in which each evenly serves the other a citation to appear in the figure of the other" (Derrida 1980: 56). The attempt to naturalize one form of English as correct and another as incorrect is exposed as ideological and artificial, confirming that in reality the concept "dialect" applies to both. Hardy uses this linguistic dangerous supplement to explore the moments of cultural transition mentioned earlier, and to qualify his town-bred audience's belief that "progress," as represented by the erasure of localized customs and speech through the spread of standardized behavior and language, is as unremittingly positive as it might like to think. Given the importance of this theme to Hardy, and given his intense awareness of the role dialect would play in his own professional and class aspirations, it is unsurprising that this device should appear early in his canon, so that if his broad use of generic hybridity is best illustrated in a late work such as *Tess of the d'Urbervilles*, his employment of dialect to achieve genre-blending is already apparent in his second published novel, *Under the Greenwood Tree*.

Hardy's original name for this work was *The Mellstock Quire*, and although the revised title with its romance implications seems to focus the reader's attention on the advances in, and obstacles to, the relationship between Dick Dewy and Fancy Day, Ruth Bernard Yeazell is right to insist that "Though the courtship plot seems to have gained in prominence as Hardy revised, almost half the published novel still concentrates on the musicians and their activities" (Yeazell 2006: 146). This, in turn, provides multiple opportunities for dialect expression in the text, and indeed such expressions are not exempt from the courtship narrative. The result is that dialect discourse comes to be a marker for the traditional ways being supplanted by the modernizing tendencies of the newly appointed vicar, Mr. Maybold, and of Fancy herself. It is no coincidence that, as schoolmistress, it is Fancy's job to "improve" her students by inculcating in them the form of speech that is intended to replace the local dialect, just as happened (partially) with Tess. Like other speech genres, therefore, dialects serve to create hierarchical relationships, since "Social stratification is also and primarily determined by differences between the forms used to convey meanings and between the expressive planes of various belief systems" (Bahktin 1981: 290). Hardy recognizes his audience's tendency to patronize his rustic characters, and through his comic representation of some of them occasionally even reinforces it. But by bringing their dialect into direct confrontation with the language of the novel's more educated characters he refuses to accept the inferiority of either their mode of expression or the values it represents. *Under the Greenwood Tree* thus demonstrates that "at any given moment of its historical existence, language is heteroglot from top to bottom: it represents the co-existence of socio-ideological contradictions between the present and the past, between different epochs of the past, [and] between different socio-ideological groups in the present" (Bahktin 1981: 291). It is the novel's presentation of this heteroglot reality that drives its subdued critique of the cultural changes that are about to sweep the church musicians from their posts, and the scene in which they accost the vicar about their replacement acts as a condensed illustration of Hardy's use of dialect as socio-linguistic commentary.

In his 1896 preface to the novel Hardy observes that "One is inclined to regret the displacement of these ecclesiastical bandsmen by an isolated organist," because "With a musical executive limited . . . to the parson's wife or daughter and the school-children, or to the school-teacher and the children, an important union of interests has disappeared" (*UGT* 3). This fragmentation and all it implies about modern individualization and isolation is central to Hardy's sense of what is at stake in his narrative. Significantly, although the tranter Reuben Dewy acts as their spokesperson, it is as the maidservant says, "'all the quire . . . except the boys'" (*UGT* 79) who enter the vicarage and fill the hall outside Maybold's study, a polite but nonetheless startling moment of class transgression which leaves the "astonished vicar" (*UGT* 80) quite nonplussed. This act of solidarity symbolizes the communal coherence that is about to be weakened by the disbanding of their group, and Reuben's most often repeated dialect phrase to describe the other band members, appearing in the very first sentence he speaks – "'Hello my sonnies, here you be, then!'" (*UGT* 16) – clearly marks the camaraderie that characterizes their fellowship. The suggestion that they form a kind of family, that their bond with each other approaches kinship, communicates the intimacy of what is about to be displaced as effectively as any more formal or poetic construction. It is for this reason that when Thomas Leaf, the "'terrible silly'" member of the choir, declares he would like to enter the vicar's study with Reuben and William Dewy, because he "'never in [his] life seed a quire go into a study to have it out about the playing and singing,'" Reuben's response is "'You'll be like chips in porridge, Leaf – neither good nor hurt. All right, my sonny, come along'" (*UGT* 81). The good nature displayed here and elsewhere in the narrative can only come from long and understanding acquaintance, again suggesting what may be lost when the connection creating these qualities is severed. The fact that the choir both teases Thomas about his foolishness and yet accepts him as one of them, an acceptance emphasized by the shared discourse in which they communicate, hints at a patience with weakness and imperfection that might provide a useful lesson to the novel's urban Victorian readership.

It is interesting, therefore, to contrast Maybold's reaction to this member of his parish. Although their entire exchange is too long to reproduce fully, its conclusion is suggestive.

"You live with your mother I think, Leaf?"

The tranter looked at Leaf to express that the most friendly assistant to his tongue could do no more for him now, and that he must be left to his own resources.

"Yes sir: a widder sir. Ah, if brother Jim had lived she'd have had a clever son to keep her without work."

"Indeed, poor woman. Give her this half-crown. I'll call and see your mother."

"Say thank you sir," the tranter whispered imperatively towards Leaf.

"Thank you sir" said Leaf.

"That's it then: sit down Leaf," said Mr Maybold. (*UGT* 82)

Although there is little doubt that Thomas and his mother will appreciate an additional half-crown, Maybold's recourse to purely formulaic responses and the dispensation of cash demonstrates little real desire to know the details of this family's situation, and his language suggests a status detachment from the group and its concerns that is unlikely to be recognized or addressed.

Throughout the exchange between Reuben and Maybold that follows, the direct, forceful speech of the tranter is contrasted with the vicar's proper but prevaricating language, so that the subaltern dialect of the one becomes a comment on the hegemonic speech of the other. Here is Reuben making the choir's central appeal:

> "All we thought was that for us old ancient singers to be choked off quiet at no time in particular, as now, in the Sundays after Easter, would seem rather mean in the eyes of other parishes sir. But if we fell glorious with a bit of a flourish at Christmas, we should have a respectable end, and not dwindle away at some nameless paltry second-Sunday-after or Sunday-next-before something, that's got no name of his own." (*UGT* 84)

And here is Maybold's response, after admitting that one of the reasons he is removing the choir is because an influential churchwarden has pressured him to do so:

> "Quite, quite, and I shouldn't think of refusing to listen to such a reasonable request. . . . You know Dewy, it is often said how difficult a matter it is to act up to our convictions and please all parties. It may be said with equal truth that it is difficult for a man of any appreciativeness to have convictions at all. Now in my case – I see right in you, and right in Shiner. I see that violins are good, and that an organ is good. And when we introduce the organ it will not be that fiddles were bad, but that an organ was better. That you'll clearly understand, Dewy?" (*UGT* 86)

With his nervous opening repetition and passive constructions the vicar's speech does not really represent anything "clearly," except that his decision is unilateral and final; and of course what he fails to "see" is the most important thing of all: he is about to destroy a significant church tradition without giving his action any serious thought. Further, the fact that the choir recognizes much better than he what is going on – that the churchwarden Shiner "'is for putting forward that young woman . . . in the sight of the congregation, and thinking he'll win her by showing her off'" (*UGT* 89) – demonstrates the kind of awareness rooted in a sense of place which dialect both reflects and expresses.

Hardy juxtaposes speech genres to deconstruct the hierarchical assumptions underlying linguistic assignments of value, which in turn calls into question the dominant class's entire social/cultural project, even as the text retrospectively acknowledges its inevitability. Although Fancy eventually marries Dick Dewy and follows the village's customs to celebrate that event, it is clear that this victory for the old ways is at best a temporary reprieve. As Michael Millgate puts it, "By the end of the novel something real if scarcely tangible has been lost, something detectable in the contrast between the air of unease and restraint which hangs over the dance under the greenwood tree and the comfortable enjoyment which marked the party at the tranter's in the opening pages" (Millgate [1971] 1994: 54). The quick dissolution of the Mellstock choir presages the more gradual disappearance of the speech forms that characterize it, and Hardy's regret at the implications of uniformity these changes generate illustrates the "scarcely tangible" benefits of heteroglossia by showing the variety and unique perceptiveness erased by monologic cultural expression.

Finally, then, melodrama and dialect are just two in a broad range of primary and secondary genres that Hardy uses to disrupt and resist established assumptions about how fiction should work: about how it should "mean" at the most basic level. Although he was not positioned to utilize the more radical disturbances of novelistic modernism which were preparing to appear as he turned from prose to poetry, Hardy also provides the type of writing whose goal is to aggressively challenge horizons of expectation rather than fulfill them. His accomplished ability to both provide and withhold what his audience wants helps explain his (continuing) popularity, since through it he manages to balance the centripetal and centrifugal forces of language to create an exhilarating sense of narrative force. In Hardy genre both establishes the dialogic nature *of* his texts and encourages a dialogic response *to* his texts. In this way his fiction becomes a fully executed Bahktinian utterance, although in written rather than spoken form, for the intellectual and artistic challenge it provokes matches the description precisely:

> The utterance is addressed not only to its own object, but also to other's speech about it . . . the utterance is related not only to preceding, but also to subsequent links in the chain of speech communion. When a speaker is creating an utterance, of course, these links do not exist. But from the very beginning, the utterance is constructed while taking into account possible responsive reactions, for whose sake, in essence, it is actually created. . . . From the very beginning, the speaker expects a response from them, an active responsive understanding. The entire utterance is constructed, as it were, in anticipation of encountering this response. (Bahktin 1990: 94)

By the time Hardy decided to leave fiction behind he had become famous (or notorious) for exploring topics which were considered by some to be improper or inappropriate – for being more than willing to anticipate and incite a "response" from his audience. Within his particular style of utterance, however, generic hybridity contributes significantly to the ideological challenge, for "At the heart of the social function of the notion of genre lies the problem of the proper. What forms, attributes, characteristics, acts, actions, or means of expression are proper . . . for 'literary' writing. What does it mean to be proper or to act properly?" (White 2003: 373). Hardy's testing of the boundaries of genre's formal proprieties is the foundation of his testing of accepted cultural proprieties, and it is this powerful union of method and content that continues to fascinate readers as they negotiate the shifting complexities of his narrative discourse.

REFERENCES AND FURTHER READING

Bakhtin, Mikhail (1981). Discourse in the Novel. In *The Dialogic Imagination: Four Essays by M. M. Bakhtin*, ed. Michael Holquist, trans. Caryl Emerson and Michael Holquist (pp. 259–422). Austin: University of Texas Press.

Bakhtin, Mikhail (1990). The Problem of Speech Genres. In *Speech Genres and Other Late Essays*, ed. Caryl Emerson and Michael Holquist, trans. Vern W. McGhee (pp. 60–102). Austin: University of Texas Press.

Beebee, Thomas O. (1994). *The Ideology of Genre: A Comparative Study of Generic Instability*. University Park: Pennsylvania State University Press.

Björk, Lennart A. (ed.) (1985). *The Literary Notebooks of Thomas Hardy*. 2 vols. London and Basingstoke: Macmillan.

Booth, Michael R. (1965). *English Melodrama*. London: Herbert Jenkins.

Clark, Graham (ed.) (1993). *Thomas Hardy: Critical Assessments*, vol. I: *The Contemporary Response*. Mountfield: Helm Information.

Cox, R. G. (ed.) 1970. *Thomas Hardy: The Critical Heritage*. London: Routledge & Kegan Paul.

Derrida, Jacques (1980). The Law of Genre. *Critical Inquiry*, 7(1), 55–81.

Devitt, Amy J. (1993). Generalizing about Genre: New Conceptions of an Old Concept. *College Composition and Communication*, 44(4), 573–86.

Fowler, Alastair (2003). The Formation of Genres in the Renaissance and After. *New Literary History*, 34, 185–200.

Genette, Gérard (1992). *The Architext: An Introduction*, trans. Jane E. Lewin. Berkeley: University of California Press.

Hadley, Elaine (1995) *Melodramatic Tactics: Theatricalized Dissent in the English Marketplace, 1800–1885*. Stanford: Stanford University Press.

Hardy, Thomas ([1872] 1985). *Under the Greenwood Tree*, ed. Simon Gatrell. Oxford: Oxford University Press.

Hardy, Thomas ([1891] 1983). *Tess of the d'Urbervilles*, ed. Juliet Grindle and Simon Gatrell. Oxford: Clarendon Press.

Hardy, Thomas (1984). *The Life and Work of Thomas Hardy*, ed. Michael Millgate. London: Macmillan.

Jameson, Fredric (1981). *The Political Unconscious: Narrative as a Socially Symbolic Act*. Ithaca, NY: Cornell University Press.

Jaus, Hans Robert (1982). *Towards an Aesthetic of Reception*, trans. Timothy Bahti. Minneapolis: University of Minnesota Press.

Millgate, Michael ([1971] 1994). *Thomas Hardy: His Career as a Novelist*. Basingstoke: Macmillan.

Millgate, Michael (ed.) (2001). *Thomas Hardy's Public Voice: The Essays, Speeches, and Miscellaneous Prose*. Oxford: Clarendon Press.

Todorov, Tzvetan (1991). *Genres in Discourse*, trans. Catherine Porter. Cambridge: Cambridge University Press.

Walkowitz, Judith R. (1992). *City of Dreadful Delight: Narratives of Sexual Danger in Late-Victorian London*. Chicago: University of Chicago Press.

White, Hayden (2003). Commentary: Good of their Kind. *New Literary History*, 34, 367–76.

Yeazell, Ruth Bernard (2006). Hardy's Rural Painting of the Dutch School. In Keith Wilson (ed.), *Thomas Hardy Reappraised: Essays in Honour of Michael Millgate* (pp. 136–53). Toronto: University of Toronto Press.

8

Hardy and his Critics:
Gender in the Interstices

Margaret R. Higonnet

He was lying on his back in the sun, thinking how useless he was, and covered his face with his straw hat. The sun's rays streamed through the interstices of the straw, the lining having disappeared. Reflecting on his experiences of the world so far as he had got he came to the conclusion that he did not wish to grow up. Other boys were always talking of when they would be men; he did not want at all to be a man, or to possess things, but to remain as he was, in the same spot. (LW 20)

Jude went out, and, feeling more than ever his existence to be an undemanded one, he lay down upon his back on a heap of litter near the pig-sty. The fog had by this time become more translucent, and the position of the sun could be seen through it. He pulled his straw hat over his face, and peered through the interstices of the plaiting at the white brightness, vaguely reflecting. Growing up brought responsibilities, he found. Events did not rhyme quite as he had thought. Nature's logic was too horrid for him to care for. (JO 18)

Thomas Hardy's description of his dreamy boyhood in the *Life and Work of Thomas Hardy* connects his resistance to the pressures of growing up male with his resistance to the pressures of a system based on property rights and economic privilege. Recording the boy's anxieties about his modest class origins and his masculinity, the scene vividly responds to the difficulties of identity formation. An early feminist reading of Hardy related to the vulnerable masculinity described in this autobiographical passage focused on the testing of manhood in *The Mayor of Casterbridge* (1886): Elaine Showalter found that the virile Henchard's "unmanning" led to his self-discovery and ultimate maturity (Showalter 1979: 102). Yet most feminist discussions of Hardy have started not from masculinity but from femininity, attracted by the extraordinary power of his portrayals of women and their often tragic fates. Today gender and queer theory redirect us toward a more complex understanding of the social as well as psychological and perhaps even biological situatedness of conflicts and consonances among such terms. Penny Boumelha and Patricia Ingham have found Hardy's interrogation of gender – as a web of relations, an unstable process, and an artificial construct – to be present everywhere in his writings, whether we consider his "unorthodox women" such as Eustacia Vye or their counterparts such as Eustacia's blinded husband Clym Yeobright (Boumelha 1985; Ingham 1990: 136). The *Life and Work* reveals that themes centered on gender were rooted in Hardy's experiences as a boy and helped shape his artistic vision.

Parallel to Hardy's image of himself as a boy in the *Life and Work* is a passage in the second chapter of *Jude the Obscure* (1895), as J. Hillis Miller has noted (1970: 7). The Wordsworthian child Jude Fawley has been punished after allowing rooks to feed in Farmer Troutham's field because "A magic thread of fellow-feeling united his own life with theirs" (*JO* 15). He seeks the rewards and harmony of wise passivity as he looks through his hat deep into the flawed life of things. "Nature's logic was too horrid for him to care for" (*JO* 18). Jude's empathetic gifts point toward his thwarted artistic yearnings. In both the autobiography and the semi-autobiographical fiction, then, a hypersensitive youth must screen his vision, taking in the blinding white brightness of the world through the interstices of a worn straw hat. The budding artistic temperament needs a protective mask and filter, like the grid which helped Renaissance painters develop a realist perspective. If the hat harks back to a Romantic poetic vision that half creates and perceives, in the words of "Tintern Abbey," the image looks forward as well to more modern preoccupations with blindness as a source of artistic insight, with events that do not "rhyme," and with the need to find the "interstices" within which a new art may be located. Hardy will break up the unified perspective of an omniscient or an individualized narrator, fragmenting the narrative line and multiplying the windows through which the fictional world is seen.

Jude uses the coordinates of social geography and gender to map the difficulty of shaping a new vision: "As you got older, and felt yourself to be at the centre of your time, and not at a point in its circumference, as you had felt when you were little, you were seized with a sort of shuddering, he perceived" (*JO* 18). Passing out of himself to generalize about "you," Jude concludes that those displaced from the sources of power (such as children or women) possess a sense of harmonious fellow-feeling that contrasts with the violently jarring perceptions (social, philosophical, erotic) that shake and scorch a young man forced to occupy a masculine site of social responsibility. The process of sobering insight, reinforced by the lifting fog, is emphatically gendered – and the child resists it: "If he could only prevent himself growing up! He did not want to be a man" (*JO* 18). Such socially imposed roles threaten to imprison the orphan in contradictions. As Elisabeth Langland writes, "Part of the novel's brilliance derives from Hardy's ability to represent Jude's battle with the class and gender self-constructions his culture offers him" (Langland 1993: 32). The importance of the margin to Hardy has made his work important to feminists.

It should be remembered that the *Life and Work* itself was written behind a multi-layered, feminized straw screen: Hardy largely dictated it in the third person to his second wife, Florence, starting from notes and diaries that he then burned, and she published it for him posthumously under her name (*LW* xviii–xix). The ghostwriting of his own autobiography in effect reconstructs a textual self via a displaced narrator, whose distanced female voice mediates and authorizes Hardy's self-invention. More-over, Hardy projected images of authorship through female figures, most ironically through Ethelberta Petherwin, in *The Hand of Ethelberta* (1876). The "hand" of the title points to her performances as a poet and public improviser; it also inscribes her private performance as a gentlewoman concealing her family of servants and stone-masons, as she strives to secure marriage to a wealthy husband in order to support them all (Boumelha 1993: 251; Ingham 1990: 34). Perhaps the masks of the author correspond in another register to the masks worn by women to perform a gender role, while watching themselves in a mirror, as his heroines Bathsheba and Tess do, albeit in quite different ways.

Life and Work suggests Hardy felt that to become "a man" (within current social expectations) meant to be active and penetrative rather than passive and absorptive. To become an adult at the center of the social map meant "to possess things" and to possess people as well. We might speculate that for Hardy to become an *artist* required an ability to occupy both center and margin, both masculinity and femininity, to penetrate and to absorb, to inscribe and to embrace. It is in this sense that writers from Coleridge to Virginia Woolf have praised the "androgyny" of creative minds that possess the power of imagination and yet adapt chameleon-like to the tones and colors of a manifold world.

The inconsistent use of gender terms to describe style, creative functions, or actual characters may reflect Hardy's own ambivalence toward contemporary conventions as well as broader tensions in Victorian discourse. Generalizations about gender, however, are often treated as suspect in Hardy's novels. Thus in *A Pair of Blue Eyes* (1873) the pedantic and prudish reviewer Henry Knight boasts that he writes successfully about women because "All I know about women, or men either, is a mass of generalities" (*PBE* 131). In his view, the best story to be told about a woman is "that she has married," and when Elfride Swancourt asks him what follows, he responds that it is best "to hear no more about her" (*PBE* 158). The narrative that frames these remarks demonstrates that this "best" plot leads logically to Elfride's silencing and death. Generalization about the female sex also points to error in *The Well-Beloved* (1897), written near the end of Hardy's career as a novelist. There he similarly depicts the writer Jocelyn Pierston as blinded by his own imagination. When Pierston passes Avice, the second of the three women who incarnate his ideal, he sees "for the moment an irradiated being, the epitome of a whole sex: by the beams of his own infatuation '. . . robed in such exceeding glory That he beheld her not;' beheld her not as she really was" (*WB* 256). Pygmalion-like, Pierston creates, essentializes, and adores Avice as "the epitome of a whole sex" in a gesture that comes close to self-infatuation in this highly ironic novel.

Although it is often suggested that the Victorian era calcified gender distinctions especially within the middle classes, this view obscures a lively debate over gender that prepared the way for *fin-de-siècle* New Women and for the ambiguities of Decadence, whose orientalizing, iridescent images paradoxically depend on gender distinctions. Like Hardy, other Victorians found the artificiality of social gender codes and hierarchies increasingly apparent. Thus John Stuart Mill in *The Subjection of Women* (1869) wrote "What is now called the nature of woman is an eminently artificial thing." For Mill, "the natural differences between the two sexes" was "a subject on which it is impossible in the present state of society to obtain complete and correct knowledge" (Mill 1998: 493–4). In his 1877 lecture on the idea of comedy George Meredith, known for depicting androgynous heroines, advocated "some degree of social equality of the sexes" (Meredith 1897: 14). The complex way in which gender distinctions may survive their blurring governs the conclusion of Tennyson's "The Princess," where the narrator proposes: "Yet in the long years liker must they grow; / The man be more of woman, she of man." Similarly, in a notebook Tennyson jotted that "men should be androgynous and women gynandrous, but men should not be gynandrous nor women androgynous" (Ricks 1972: 215). Hardy's narrative turns, shifts in voice, and dramatization of unstable gender relations translate inquiries like these that preoccupied his contemporaries.

In the *Life and Work* Hardy traced his career as a struggle to attain literary "manhood" in the face of doubts and social obstacles. Internalizing the literary culture's stylistic gender code, he recalled that his poetic growth in about 1866–7 required him to abandon the "jewelled line" of poetry "as being effeminate" (Millgate 2004: 100). Personal doubts may have fed his professional doubts, for he remembers (perhaps tongue in cheek) a "lateness of development in virility, while mentally precocious" (*LW* 37). Likewise, he takes care to tell us of his invitation in 1879 to join the Rabelais Club, a group formed to cultivate "virility in literature." "Hardy was pressed to join as being the most virile writer of works of the imagination then in London; while, it may be added, Henry James, after a discussion, was rejected for the lack of that quality, though he was afterwards invited as a guest" (*LW* 136). To defend himself against an attack in 1924 by George Moore, he turned to jocular slander: "Somebody once called him a putrid literary hermaphrodite, which I thought funny, but it may have been an exaggeration" (Millgate 1982: 553). Thus, even in his maturity, Hardy's literary rivalries played themselves out as competition over sexual status and as an anxiety to develop "a more virile type of novel," as opposed to the "doll" of fiction (*CL* I: 250).

The doubts about gender identity that Hardy remembered in his boyhood were perhaps revived by the reception of his first published novels. Was the anonymous writer a man or a woman? Hardy's first books provoked debate about his sex, just as the first works of the Brontës, George Eliot, and George Sand aroused critics' imaginings about their pen(wo)manship. He reports that his friend Anne Thackeray protected his anonymous authorship of *Far From the Madding Crowd* (1874) by referring to him tongue in cheek as "it" (*LW* 101). The bemused reviewer in *The Athenaeum* found "unpleasant" power in *Desperate Remedies* (1871), presumably masculine, but could not reconcile it with precise details about female apparel, presumably the signature of femininity:

> We cannot decide, satisfactorily to our own mind, on the sex of the author; for while
> certain evidence, such as the close acquaintance which he or she appears (and as far as

we can judge, with reason) to possess with the mysteries of the female toilette, would appear to point to its being the work of one of that sex, on the other hand there are certain expressions to be met with in the book so remarkably coarse as to render it almost impossible that it should have come from the pen of an English lady. (Lerner and Holmstrom 1968: 12)

Yet since "all the best anonymous novels" are undoubtedly by female writers, the reviewer inclines to ascribe Hardy to that class. Contemporaries of the young Hardy thus occasionally noted the pre-eminence of women, often anonymous or wearing a masculine pseudonym, in the arena of novel-writing. Hardy's very gifts assimilated him to skills that were tagged on the title page as masculine but marked in the literary marketplace as feminine. In response, Hardy at first was proud to repeat a comparison to George Eliot (Lerner and Holmstrom 1968: 15–16). Later reviewers rejected the mistaken conjecture that *Far From the Madding Crowd* was Eliot's work (Lerner and Holmstrom 1968: 23, 25). Hardy's reversal of Victorian norms of conduct for men and women provoked a reader to denounce Bathsheba as "an incorrigible hussy" whom Oak is not "manly" enough to reject, and to accuse Hardy of travestying "Eliotism" (Lerner and Holmstrom 1968: 35, 36). Ironically, then, Hardy's entry into the marketplace engendered queries about the sex of his pen, accusations of theft, and laments about his implied lacks, by comparison with established women writers (see Higonnet 1994: 31).

Issues of class likewise dogged the heels of the young author. His first manuscript, "The Poor Man and the Lady," had announced its class consciousness in its title. Alexander Macmillan admired its description of "country life among working men," but was dismayed by the "wholesale blackening" of the aristocracy. Lacking intimate knowledge of this world, Hardy had no right to make such an attack. Unlike Thackeray, whose satire was in "fun," Hardy meant "mischief." Mowbray Morris condemns him for experimenting "in a style for which he was assuredly not born" (Lerner and Holmstrom 1968: 87). A similar critic in the *Spectator* (1871) mocked Hardy for his poverty and dismissed his work as "a desperate remedy for an emaciated purse" (Cox 1970: 4). Publishers, in short, used explicitly classist criteria of review and exclusion.

Hardy, whose sensitivity about his class origins placed him at the mercy of such publishers' views, decided therefore to pursue "the safest venture" – pastoral. Ironically, this "safe" mode was shaped in the mid-nineteenth century by the very foremothers from whom he increasingly wished to distinguish himself. Thus an ideology of class impelled Hardy to experiment in a genre that was already highly gendered as feminine. Hostile reviewers treated Hardy's subject matter with a condescension to which women writers were well accustomed: *Far From the Madding Crowd*, one complained, is concerned with "no deeper mysteries than women's hearts" (Lerner and Holmstrom 1968: 26).

Questions about gender and class status, we may speculate, fed the deepest contradictions as well as the strengths of Hardy's art. Invoking the multifarious social codes of his time, Hardy may thus casually label his art in gender terms as "virile," as we have seen, thereby showing "residual signs of sexist thinking" (Kramer 1979: 7), or he may strenuously contest the gendering and labeling tendencies of conventional thought. Both in the *Life and Work* and in the novels, he wrestles against pigeonholing and against authorities who presume to fix where the "centre" lies. Like a straw screen held up for the reader, his complex narrative voice alternates between challenging and authoritatively repeating the social schemes of class and gender within which his protagonists struggle, in order to define their shifting identities. The narrative voice itself has long been considered problematic – whether double, multiple, inconsistent, or incoherent – especially in its gendered relationship to female protagonists. While characters' misreadings of the Other most often seem to affect women in his texts, Hardy in "The Dorsetshire Labourer" condemns the erasure of poor country laborers under a generalization such as "Hodge." Angel must quickly learn in *Tess of the d'Urbervilles* that the dairy folk are not mere Hodges, but he nonetheless translates Tess into his own idealized image of Artemis. So too, Tess falls into "idolatry" of Angel, as J. Hillis Miller noticed in his landmark study of repetition as pattern in Hardy (Miller 1982: 143). At times, textual doubt and debate over gender foster artistic play with projections, mirrorings, and inversions of paired characters, as when Jocelyn Pierston perceives the moon, a metaphor for mutability and for his muse, the "migratory Well-Beloved," as "his wraith in a changed sex" (*WB* 292).

Inversions that emerge at the intersection of gender and class can be traced back to the very first book Hardy wrote, as suggested by its title: "The Poor Man and the Lady: A Story with No Plot." That unpublished work, cannibalized as he wrote other novels and stories, opened up a recurrent theme in his fiction. A poor man, a young architect from a peasant family, becomes betrothed to the daughter of the local squire, who thwarts his daughter's love-match in favor of marriage to a man of her own class. Artistic ambition and class origins conspire to feminize the male protagonist by norms that assume power is masculine. In later novels such slippages mark the representation of femininity as well as masculinity. Patricia Ingham has suggested that Hardy's narrative voices and plots developed over time, increasingly interrogating conventional judgments of female behavior and subverting the stock plots of nineteenth-century fiction (Ingham 1990: 19, 28). Kristin Brady agrees, distinguishing the romance heroines of his early novels from the heroines who challenge romance plots in his final novels (Brady 1993: 87).

As Hardy explored these themes over the years, he unsettled the codes of masculinity and femininity within relationships that cross shifting class lines, sometimes compounded by differences in age and experience as well as wealth that attribute a power of action to the woman, as in *Far From the Madding Crowd*, *The Hand of Ethelberta*, *Two on a Tower* (1882), and *The Woodlanders* (1887). The ambiguities and potential inversions of gender relations, for example, become manifest in *Far From the Madding Crowd* when Bathsheba asks of her maid Liddy, "I hope I am not a bold sort of maid – mannish?" and receives the reply, "O no – not mannish; but so almighty womanish that 'tis getting on that way sometimes" (*FFMC* 174). Peter Casagrande explains that Bathsheba occupies here "the conventionally masculine role of aggressor and seducer" (Casagrande 1979: 62). As if on a Möbius strip, according to Liddy's reply, hyperfemininity may overflow into an apparent masculinity. Similarly, in *The Return of the Native* (1878), the innkeeper Damon Wildeve, who courts two women at once, has a lithe grace that is "the pantomimic expression of a lady-killing career" (*RN* 45). He explains his social status as a fall from engineering to innkeeping because the "curse of inflammability" forces him to "take any snub from a woman" (*RN* 63) Thus his sexual excitability and powers make him ironically dependent on the women he courts, entailing a loss of social power.

In the lighter novels of social satire the effect of such inversions may seem carnivalesque, echoing the folk rituals in which masquerades that cross sexual lines are performed in order to enforce the social order. Yet for Hardy, the performative element in these folkloric slippages tends to satirize the social order itself. When a skimmity ride targets Lucetta in *The Mayor of Casterbridge*, the pathos of her death highlights the malice of the mockers; in *The Return of the Native* Thomasina's return from church unmarried also exposes her to a "skimmity"-like wedding celebration or "nunny-watch," from which she barely escapes, and which eventually forces her into a loveless marriage. Dark consequences also shadow performance in a midwinter ritual in the same novel. When Hardy depicts the "fossilized survival" of the St. George play, he contrasts the stolid performance by boys carrying the tradition forward to the erotic thrill of cross dressing, which affords the sensual and bored Eustacia Vye the possibility of meeting Clym Yeobright without a formal introduction. Drawn by the "charm of adventure" Eustacia in Charley's costume becomes "changed in sex, brilliant in colours, and armed from top to toe"; her distinctively dramatic performance succeeds in capturing Clym's attention, giving individual life to the reversal embedded in the solstice celebration (*RN* 125). Hardy the artist fuses a dramatic turning point in his plot with mythic elements as well as a flamboyant performance crossing gender assignment in a scene that is sexually charged and psychologically revealing.

The moment when he depicts the attraction between the two offers Hardy an opportunity to explore gender as a factor in psychology, as Eustacia and Clym both experience "depression," but each in a different way. Clym foreshadows Jude's meditative pathos: while he displays a strange power, the beauty of his face is also "wasted" by the "wearing habit of meditation" and by his preparation for a life as a teacher. Hardy explains with a generality, that "ideal physical beauty is incompatible with growth of fellow-feeling and a full sense of the coil of things" (*RN* 135) – the very thoughts that preoccupy Jude as he lies under his straw hat. Clym's reflections also prefigure the "ache of modernism," which Angel and Tess share in *Tess of the d'Urbervilles*. When Eustacia catches sight of Clym's face, she observes a tension that captures her attention and seems to correspond to her own "hypochondria": "a natural cheerfulness striving against depression from without" (*RN* 136). Eustacia responds to this man returned from Paris, "exceptional" within the rural scene, as she feels herself to be, with palpable excitement. When he therefore asks her why she joined the mummers, something girls never do, she replies, "To get excitement and shake off depression" (*RN* 142). Hardy builds up the verbal echoes in the chapter that describes their first exchange, to lend weight to Eustacia's infatuation with

Clym as her appointed mate. Yet he also makes clear that Clym's sorrows spring from his philosophic reflections and his idealistic desire to serve humanity that "shone out of him like a ray" (*RN* 136), while Eustacia's smoldering rebelliousness and frustrated sensuality burn like a nocturnal flame (*RN* 66). Thus even in shaping these two characters as exceptions, distinguished from more stereotypical figures on Egdon Heath, Hardy reinscribes the association of masculinity with intellect, and femininity with the body.

Hardy tests the boundaries of cultural definition by making social hierarchies interact with and interrogate gender hierarchy. In a musical structure of motif and counter-motif, he builds a number of his plots on shifts in social and economic status that alter the relationship of power in a couple and thus invert relationships of gender: "their sexes were thus reversed," reflects the narrator, when Christopher Julian shyly if eagerly visits Ethelberta Petherwin after her success as a performer (*HE* 124). Clym Yeobright's return to Egdon Heath from Paris puts his masculinity at risk along with his financial status, in his mother's eyes: while he considers Parisian jewelers to be "effeminate," she scolds him on the ground that "men" "who deserve the name" do not "go backward in the world" (*RN* 173). Economic power constructs masculinity. For Hardy the artist, social definitions of gender were neither abstract intellectual problems nor essential truths, but resources for character representation, turns of plot, and social critique.

The problematic nature of gender is especially marked in its assimilation to the theme of writing itself. This cannot surprise us, given Hardy's experiences as an anonymous writer under review. After his publisher urged him to trim pages of rural dialogue from *Under the Greenwood Tree* as a "trifle," he translated his own experience as an author into that of a fictive female author. In *A Pair of Blue Eyes*, Elfride Swancourt's first publication is faintly praised for "a murmuring of delicate emotional trifles," which the reviewer Knight considers "occasionally felicitous" on "matters of domestic experience" (*PBE* 149). Knight's arrogant aesthetic criteria, in short, deprecate materials drawn from women's lives or from "lower" social strata. Condescension was accompanied by censorship: Hardy's editors, especially when he began serial publication, insisted on the omission of any material that might appear improper in the family circles to which lending libraries catered. Hardy commented at length on his own self-censorship in order to get texts such as *Tess of the d'Urbervilles* into print before a "middle-class female readership" (Gatrell 1988: 8). Nonetheless, throughout his career Hardy defended the "honest portrayal" of "the relations of the sexes" (Orel 1967: 127). If decorum was a serious matter for Hardy, it is even more so for his fictive author Ethelberta, whose precarious social situation makes the success of her artistic projects especially important. Hardy's editor Leslie Stephen objected to her using the word "amorous" – at precisely the point in the narrative when Ethelberta explains the fundamental distinction between author and text, or between her own condition and what may seem to be the "amorous" content in her volume of verse *Cancelled Words* (*HE* 437n2). So Hardy cancelled her word.

Links between writing and sexuality run through many of Hardy's novels, where the metaphor of writing often stands for the taking of a woman's body, as in the narrator's comment on the "coarse pattern" traced on Tess Durbeyfield in the Chase while she sleeps, ending her maidenhood. In the following chapter, eyeing Tess, a hell and brimstone follower of the Reverend Clare equipped with a red paint pot writes the "tex" of biblical commandments for her benefit on barns, as if he could read the "trace" that had been inscribed on her body by Alec d'Urberville; but the painter's truncated term "tex" points to the incompleteness of a verbal art that strives to capture the fullness of being implied by a figure such as Tess. In the course of her harvesting work Tess's body will be scarified by stubble, and on her long walk into exile from happiness she will clip off her eyebrows in a vain attempt to unsex herself and make her body illegible. Not only does the writer seem to write upon the characters' bodies, so too do society and the characters themselves.

Here again, Hardy's rhetorical figure of writing invites the question whether the metaphoric transfer of writing to the body is itself gendered. In *The Return of the Native*, for example, Clym's absorption in reading philosophy ("a real perusing man," *RN* 106) has marked his face and drawn the attention of those around him:

> The face was well shaped, even excellently. But the mind within was beginning to use it as a mere waste tablet whereon to trace its idiosyncrasies as they developed themselves. . . . people who began by beholding him ended by perusing him. His countenance was overlaid with legible meanings. Without being thought-worn he yet had certain marks derived from a perception of his surroundings . . . He already showed that thought is a disease of flesh. (*RN* 135)

In a variation on the realistic theme of "reading" a character's body, Hardy tells us that "The observer's eye was arrested, not by his face as a picture, but by his face as a page; not by what it was, but by what it recorded. His features were attractive in the light of symbols, as sounds intrinsically common become attractive in language, and as shapes intrinsically simple become interesting in writing" (*RN* 165). Clym thereby becomes a figure for modernity, whose face records his perceptions and ideas rather than his physical beauty; his intellectualism marks him off from the heathfolk, who read the outside world through him. By contrast, the women's bodies in the novel seem to symbolize physically their status as women, yet in characteristically resistant ways. Clym's dying mother is assimilated to writing but its meaning is not "legible": in her last trek across the heath she is accompanied by little Johnny Nunsuch, who studies her face like an old manuscript, "the key to whose characters is undiscoverable" (*RN* 277). Her complex emotions of desire and revulsion must shape a palimpsest impossible for the child to sort out, which the narrator leaves the reader free to interpret. Eustacia notoriously acquires so many allusive attributes in the chapter introducing her as "Queen of Night" that she resists any reading at all. Insofar as she too is linked to modernity, it is primarily through her interest in a consumer culture from which she has been exiled. She likewise appears blank in an intoxicated moment of escape from her dreary life with Clym when she runs off to dance with Damon Wildeve: "her face rapt and statuesque; her soul had passed away from and forgotten her features, which were left empty and quiescent" (*RN* 253). In her death, when she has ceased speaking, her "more than whiteness," the narrator observes, eclipses her and unwrites the phases or pages of her life (*RN* 361).

Such metanarrative passages, in which female figures may take on allegorical roles, correspond to the turn among modern critics toward an anti-realist reading of Hardy's work. Linda Shires, for example, finds multiplicity and incongruity at every narrative level, undercutting the realist premises of coherent causality, perspective, and genre (Shires 1999: 147–8). The issue of realism intersects directly with the representation of sexuality and of gender. While Hardy himself called for the frank representation of "the position of man and woman in nature," and described a novel as a living structure or "organism" that "reflected life, revealed life, criticised life" (Orel 1967: 121, 127), he also emphatically rejected photographic realism and any assumption that an accumulation of factual details could produce truth. In "The Science of Fiction" (1891) he defined "realism" as "an artificiality distilled from the fruits of closest observation" and rejected "complete copyism" (Orel 1967: 136). Rather, he suggests, an author such as Sir Walter Scott seduces us: "the reader is illuded to believe the personages true and real like himself. Solely to this latter end a work of fiction should be a precise transcript of ordinary life" (*LW* 154).

Yet Hardy teasingly insisted on the reality of his characters, talking of Tess, for example, as a living person he had known, and many readers continue to respond as if his characters possess recognizable life. From the first, reviewers emphasized this effect, especially among his female characters. The *Saturday Review* of 1879 found in *Far From the Madding Crowd* characters who were made "living and breathing realities" (Cox 1970: 51). The *British Quarterly Review* in 1881 admired Hardy for "creating personages which live, and become even more real than many historic phantasms" (Cox 1970: 78). Of Tess, we read in *The Speaker* of 1891, that she is "the portraiture of a living woman" (Lerner and Holmstrom 1968: 60). For some readers the eroticism of Hardy's texts has been an anchor of their realism. One of the first critics to praise Hardy for his "feminine realism," Edmund Gosse, maintained: "Mr. Hardy's women are moulded of the same flesh as his men . . . they are not always constant . . . some of them are actually 'of a coming-on disposition'" (Cox 1970: 170).

Precisely that sexual aspect of Hardy's heroines has attracted some of the women reading his novels today. While we may consider this response to rest on a critical fallacy, it bears witness to the power of Hardy's fictions across time, from their scandalousness for their first readers to their pathos and persuasiveness today. The issue of a realistic treatment of sexuality may also point us toward the complexity of our own operations as critics. Thus a sensitive essay on *Tess* by Mary Jacobus implies just such a "real" Tess whom Hardy more or less succeeds in representing faithfully. With a perhaps unconscious pun on "the making of a pure woman," Jacobus explores the differences between a sensuous "Ur-Tess" seduced by Alec and the "purified" and more conscious Tess produced by later revisions of the manuscript and printed text. What concerns Jacobus, at least initially, is the problem of turning a female protagonist into a passive victim: "To regard Tess as unimplicated is to deny her the right of participation in her own life. Robbed of responsibility, she is deprived of tragic status

– reduced throughout to the victim she does indeed become. Worst of all, she is stripped of the sexual autonomy and the capacity for independent being and doing which are among the most striking features of Hardy's conception" (Jacobus 1976: 320). Tess, in this kind of analysis, not only is a "conception" but has a "life" separable from its framing in narrative language.

As Patricia Ingham has pointed out, mimetic criticism points to difficulties that feminist critics have sometimes encountered in assessing artistic representation (Ingham 1990: 1–8). It is hazardous, for example, to measure manuscript changes to test a later version's truth to an original, privileged conception. Textual criticism shows us that no such authority can be found in a quest for origins, even though the process of creative transformation certainly merits investigation. The conception of the "real," set against the social attitudes that "ticket" us, brings into play problematic stereotypes about gender and class, because truth to "nature" obscures our understanding of the social representations that lie at the center of Hardy's art and his treatment of gender. Near the surface in discussions of realism lie assumptions about the relationship between literature and art that continue to color the way we read today.

Not only do readers seem impelled to compare the vivid images they draw from the books with the images they perceive in the world around them, they also often seek role models or lessons in those books. Thus P. D. Edwards admires Hardy's depiction of a "heroine capable of abandoning herself to raw sexual passion" in *Far From the Madding Crowd*, above all in the scene where Troy's sword plucks a caterpillar from Bathsheba's bodice, evoking "the turbulent oscillations of excitement and fear, male sadism and female masochism" and symbolically enacting Bathsheba's sexual initiation (Edwards 1988: 148). Rosemarie Morgan defends Hardy by arguing that he aims to show that his female protagonists are "strong, sexually vital, risk-taking rebels"; she reads Eustacia Vye as "a potential woman-on-the-barricades" (Morgan 1988: 78). Framing such analyses of Hardy's heroines is the hypothesis that our reading shapes us and might even change the world. Perhaps this is so. That impulse, however, is one that Hardy rejected out of hand as reading for "hygienic purposes" (Orel 1967: 111). Indirectly he tackles the practice of judging texts by their moral impact in *Under the Greenwood Tree*, whose Reuben Dewy explains that "all true stories have a coarseness or a bad moral, depend upon't. If the story-tellers could have got decency and good morals from true stories, who'd ha' troubled to invent parables?" (*UGWT* 46).

Hardy's condemnation of didacticism directly responded to the laws of decorum brought to bear by editors to whom he proposed his manuscripts. Mowbray Morris, of *Macmillan's Magazine*, for example, rejected *Tess* on the grounds of "rather too much succulence" (Millgate 2004: 277). It was not "convenient" for him as an editor to have Hardy present a protagonist who stirs up or might even gratify sexual feelings. As Hardy complained in his essay on "Candour in English Fiction" (1890), the artist's adaptation of his narratives to the demands and needs of (male) editors and (female) readers, subscribers to serials or to lending libraries, forced him into self-censorship and mutilation of his materials. "Life being a physiological fact, its honest portrayal must be largely concerned with, for one thing, the relations of the sexes" (Orel 1967: 127). Not the "regulation" happy ending of marriage but "catastrophes based upon sexual relations" (Orel 1967: 128) guarantee candor. And the substitutions to satisfy "the social forms and ordinances" dictated by serial magazines could only lead away from "eternal verities" toward "indescribably unreal and meretricious" forms (Orel 1967: 130). Tellingly, in the way the story of Hardy's serial publications has been cast it is not the male editors or male reviewers but the hypothetical female readers who were responsible for his difficulties. The nameless "ladies" who took fright at "broken commandments" imposed censorship in incident, plot, characterization, and diction. The castrating power of these female readers lends melodrama to studies of Hardy's complex revisions. R. G. Cox, for example, as editor of the critical responses to Hardy's books, comments on the bowdlerization of Fanny's death in *Far From the Madding Crowd*, of *Tess*, and of *Jude* as a consequence of publication in "an emasculated serial form" (Cox 1970: xxxii).

In sum, gender has played a role in the criticism surrounding Hardy's fiction as well as in his own construction of imaginative worlds. As we reflect upon the limits of our methodologies, the shift from "feminist" readings focused on single characters to "gender" readings of narrative and rhetorical relationships may help us avoid some obvious pitfalls. The structuralist approach that makes the narrator into a creature of the plot lends autonomous force to plot, itself a critical abstraction from the verbal sequence of a narrative that theoretically is controlled by the narrative voice. Likewise, the semiotic approach to gender as a system of social signs incorporated into a text may not altogether escape the mimeticist fallacy. We need to inquire how the translation from social discourse to literary text is operated: many generative social discourses are grafted onto competing literary conventions. When we treat characters as "signs" of a social discourse about gender or class, we may neglect their imaginative force. If we allegorize novels as readings of Romantic myths or as parables about "cultural intercourse," our very success in identifying recurrent patterns may blur our awareness of a text's specificity. The continuing richness of Hardy criticism corresponds to the dense textures and disruptive tensions within his works.

REFERENCES AND FURTHER READING

Boumelha, Penny (1985). *Thomas Hardy and Women: Sexual Ideology and Narrative Form*. Madison: University of Wisconsin Press.

Boumelha, Penny (1993). "A complicated position for a woman": *The Hand of Ethelberta*. In Margaret Higonnet (ed.), *The Sense of Sex: Feminist Readings of Hardy* (pp. 242–59). Urbana: University of Illinois Press.

Brady, Kristin (1993). Textual Hysteria: Hardy's Narrator on Women. In Margaret Higonnet (ed.), *The Sense of Sex: Feminist Readings of Hardy*

(pp. 87–106). Urbana: University of Illinois Press.

Casagrande, Peter (1979). A New View of Bathsheba Everdene. In Dale Kramer (ed.), *Critical Approaches to the Fiction of Thomas Hardy* (pp. 50–73). London: Macmillan.

Cox, R. G. (ed.) (1970). *Thomas Hardy: The Critical Heritage*. New York, Barnes & Noble

Edwards, P. D. (1988). *Idyllic Realism from Mary Russell Mitford to Hardy*. New York: St Martin's.

Gatrell, Simon (1988). *Hardy the Creator: A Textual Biography*. Oxford: Clarendon Press.

Hardy, Thomas ([1872] 1998). *Under the Greenwood Tree*, ed. Tim Dolin. London: Penguin.

Hardy, Thomas ([1873] 1998) *A Pair of Blue Eyes*, ed. Pamela Dalziel. London: Penguin.

Hardy, Thomas ([1874] 2000). *Far From the Madding Crowd*, ed. Rosemarie Morgan, with Shannon Russell. London: Penguin.

Hardy, Thomas ([1876] 1997). *The Hand of Ethelberta: A Comedy in Chapters*, ed. Tim Dolin. London: Penguin.

Hardy, Thomas ([1878] 2005). *The Return of the Native*, ed. Simon Gatrell, introd. Margaret Higonnet. Oxford: Oxford University Press.

Hardy, Thomas ([1891] 2003). *Tess of the d'Urbervilles*, ed. Tim Dolin, introd. Margaret Higonnet. London: Penguin.

Hardy, Thomas ([1895] 1998). *Jude the Obscure*, ed. Dennis Taylor. London: Penguin.

Hardy, Thomas ([1897] 1997). *The Pursuit of the Well-Beloved* and *The Well-Beloved*, ed. Patricia Ingham. London: Penguin.

Hardy, Thomas (1984). *The Life and Work of Thomas Hardy*, ed. Michael Millgate. London: Macmillan.

Higonnet, Margaret (1994). Telling Thefts: Authenticity, Authority, and Male Anxieties. *LIT*, 5, 119–34.

Ingham, Patricia (1990). *Thomas Hardy*. Atlantic Highlands, NJ: Humanities Press.

Jacobus, Mary (1976). Tess's Purity. *Essays in Criticism*, 26, 318–38.

Kramer, Dale (ed.) (1979). *Critical Approaches to the Fiction of Thomas Hardy*. London: Macmillan.

Langland, Elisabeth (1993). Becoming a Man in *Jude the Obscure*. In Margaret Higonnet (ed.), *The Sense of Sex: Feminist Perspectives on Hardy* (pp. 32–48). Urbana: University of Illinois Press.

Lerner, Laurence, and John Holmstrom (eds.) (1968). *Thomas Hardy and his Readers: A Selection of Contemporary Reviews*. London: Bodley Head.

Meredith, George (1897). *An Essay on Comedy and the Uses of the Comic Spirit*. Westminster: Constable.

Mill, John Stuart (1998). *On Liberty and Other Essays*, ed. John Gray. New York: Oxford University Press. *The Subjection of Women*. Consulted June 26, 2008. <http://www.constitution.org/jsm/women.htm>.

Miller, J. Hillis (1970). *Thomas Hardy: Distance and Desire*. Cambridge, MA: The Belknap Press of Harvard University Press.

Miller, J. Hillis (1982). *Fiction and Repetition: Seven English Novels*. Cambridge, MA: Harvard University Press.

Millgate, Michael (1982). *Thomas Hardy: A Biography*. Oxford: Oxford University Press.

Millgate, Michael (2004). *Thomas Hardy: A Biography Revisited*. Oxford: Oxford University Press.

Morgan, Rosemarie (1988). *Women and Sexuality in the Novels of Thomas Hardy*. London: Routledge.

Orel, Harold (ed.) (1967). *Thomas Hardy's Personal Writings*. London: Macmillan.

Purdy, Richard Little, and Michael Millgate (eds.) (1978–88). *The Collected Letters of Thomas Hardy*, 7 vols. Oxford: Clarendon Press.

Ricks, Christopher (1972). *Tennyson*. New York: Macmillan.

Shires, Linda (1999). The Radical Aesthetic of *Tess of the d'Urbervilles*. In Dale Kramer (ed.), *The Cambridge Companion to Thomas Hardy* (pp. 145–63). Cambridge: Cambridge University Press.

Showalter, Elaine (1979). The Unmanning of the Mayor of Casterbridge. In Dale Kramer (ed.), *Critical Approaches to Thomas Hardy* (pp. 99–115). London: Macmillan.

PART III
The Socio-Cultural Context

9

"His Country": Hardy in the Rural

Ralph Pite

Biographers rely on anecdotal evidence; they sift anecdote for evidence – the reports of first-hand witnesses whenever possible, of relatives and friends, and of children and grandchildren handing on the family stories. In Hardy's case, very little from his intimates survives, and much of that has been sanitized either by Hardy himself or by his loyal second wife, Florence, and her overbearing adviser Sydney Cockerell. The received image of the man remains stubbornly hard to dislodge even now, and much has to be made out of little hints Hardy "accidentally" let fall or from the sidelights provided by, mostly, marginal figures. Unimportant events and actions he neglected to edit or erase become the focus of what can seem disproportionate attention. One of these minor incidents that is biographically revealing helps also to disrupt the assumptions usually made about Hardy and place – assumptions that are almost as deeply entrenched as those surrounding the man himself.

The first number of the *Thomas Hardy Journal* was published in January 1985, and it contained an article by William W. Morgan entitled "Verses Fitted for a Monument: Hardy's Contribution to the Dudley War Memorial." This recounts how Hardy, soon after the end of the First World War, was asked by James Smellie, the mayor of Dudley (an unglamorous industrial town near Birmingham in the West Midlands of England), to improve his proposed inscription for the town's war memorial. Hardy, by return of post, suggested changes to the wording of the four-line verse inscription, changes that Smellie adopted. Morgan's work is a detailed, scrupulous piece of biographical research, which is characteristic of the *THJ* in its concern for the unconsidered aspects of Hardy's life and work. Morgan also gives an insightful account of how Hardy's changes benefited the inscription and how closely they correspond with the interests and intelligence of his other war poetry.

The incident reveals qualities in Hardy that might easily surprise us: in place of the dreamy, unworldly character he presented in his ghost-written *Life* (published posthumously but composed during the First World War – that is, in the years just prior to the events Morgan describes), Hardy's action reveals a different side of his personality, a more conscientious, public-spirited aspect of him, as he willingly placed his poetic craft in the service of the community. Hardy comes across as brisk too, and businesslike. His letters to Smellie are not particularly warm – they show instead the buttoned-up, Edwardian reserve that was Hardy's usual manner in his life as an author and public figure; on the other hand, the reclusive, private poet of legend, wrapped up in his half-imaginary world of Wessex or lost in his memories of youth, this character did in reality, and at a moment's notice, transform himself into a useful member of post-war English society.

Active engagement with public affairs recurs in Hardy's later life. *Moments of Vision* (1917), like *Poems of the Past and the Present* (1901), contains, for example, sections devoted to war poetry and many of these were originally published (unusually for Hardy) in newspapers and journals during, respectively, the Boer War and the Great War.[1] Disregarding or downplaying this side of the man goes along with seeing him (as he encouraged people to do) as unambitious and by temperament passive, and with regarding his works as concerned to preserve as much as possible of Wessex and its vanishing way of life. Hardy cannot have been simply and entirely the kind of person he presented himself as being; drive and ambition, in fact, are two of his most pronounced characteristics. Similarly, his relationship to his home territory in and around Dorchester was never as straightforward as he tried to make it appear.

Hardy's landscapes were made into a tourist attraction while he was still alive; his works, similarly, have been adopted by ruralist critics and co-opted into their traditions; in fact, Hardy's hostility was very marked (see, for instance, Gervais 1993: 16–19). He defined himself early on against the idyllic realism (as P. D. Edwards has cleverly termed it) of mid-Victorian ruralist writing, as it developed from Mary Russell Mitford and Edward Bulwer-Lytton and culminated (for Hardy most powerfully) in George Eliot.[2] The genuinely rural was, for him, what was compelled (by location and class position) to resist the unwitting predations of an urbanized middle class, who were building cottages in the country and both writing and reading books about the delights of rustic life. Simultaneously, Hardy's continuing belief that something (and somewhere) genuinely rural could be found and should be valued gave him common ground with the ruralists whose sentimentalities and pieties he disliked. Out of that tension arose his conflicted relation with his readership, his insistence on disturbing their assumptions without straightforwardly satirizing or dismissing them; for the same set of reasons, he consistently refused to become the author they saw him as being, though he did actively cultivate that image. This was in part for good commercial reasons but only in part; Hardy was also concerned that some at least of his readers, through growing familiarity with him and his writings, might find grounds for questioning their expectations.

Clear instances of this intent can be found in two of his male protagonists: Angel Clare in *Tess of the d'Urbervilles* and Henry Knight from the much earlier and less well known novel, Hardy's third published book, *A Pair of Blue Eyes*. Both these figures are educated, middle-class, and in many respects attractive – Angel seems honorable and interesting by comparison with his complacent brothers; Henry is accomplished and upstanding, scrupulous and hard-working. They are figures, particularly Angel because of the contrast with Alec, whom Hardy's readers would be likely to sympathize with and admire. Unfortunately, however, both prove cruelly judgmental towards the women they seem to love. Angel cannot come to terms with Tess's sexual history; Henry Knight seeks to dominate Elfride intellectually (showing himself insensitive to the vulnerabilities in her character) and then, just like Angel, insists upon her sexual purity, rejecting her when he learns of her past. Knight insists that Elfride be "pure" – unsullied and intact both sexually and intellectually – in just the same way that Angel Clare sees in and makes of Tess an emblem of natural innocence. Projecting innocence onto these two female characters seems, moreover, to produce violence towards them – Knight and Clare both cruelly mistreat the women – and that is worrying on several levels.

Noticing and responding to this aspect of the books, readers have accused Hardy of sharing his characters' contradictory feelings. Particularly in relation to Tess and *Tess*, Hardy has been seen idealizing his women and simultaneously punishing them, the one impulse arising out of the other. Maybe he is such an insightful analyst of masculine contradictoriness (and masculine perversity) because he shared in it; complicity though leads in Hardy's case to critique (at points a critique that is the more violent for being partly directed at himself) and in particular it leads him to attack men's desire to idealize women (as is most fully explored in Angel Clare).

In Clare, desiring purity goes along with imagining innocence and, following Henry Knight's example, goes along with insisting upon that quality as well (even though this insistence opposes its object since innocence cannot be required any more than it can be regained or restored or the clock turned back). Hardy's judgmental, legalistic characters turn out, in other words, to be sentimentalists as well. The violence and oppressiveness of the male domineering impulse is seen as deriving from the fantasy of innocence, because violence comes into play whenever the real woman (inevitably – and quite forgivably) fails to live up to the fantasy. These characters and their behavior suggest that literary language (which Knight is master of) and educated aesthetic terminology (which Angel deploys) are dangerous sources of potential oppression – that these progressive, enlightened accomplishments can align themselves with moralism and prejudice and the forces of social control. Furthermore, Hardy implies that people will use the power of literature and education in this way just at the moment when they start to imagine a state that is free from all those things – that they oppress people into (what they call) innocence.

Hardy, then, perceives two extremes as being bound together – perfect freedom and ruthless cruelty; pastoral innocence and invasive, conquering violence. If you imagine the first, you will, like Knight and Clare, end up performing the second. Furthermore, there is another way – an alternative mode of relating to objects of desire. Though Elfride is caught between two unsatisfactory men (ultimately succumbing to the affectionate admiration of a third, the lord of the manor), the younger of the two, Stephen Smith, understands her better than Knight does, is more tolerant of her faults and more affectionate towards her foibles. Smith is a local boy and, strikingly, his sense of her and her value is increased by his going away – to India, to make his fortune and make himself, ironically, worthy of her by the standards of her snobbish father. There is no equivalent to Smith in *Tess*, unless it is Hardy himself as narrator (or possibly Alec d'Urberville in the earliest draft versions of the story; see Jacobus 1976), though Clare when he comes back from abroad sees Tess with greater understanding and more genuine love than he had done before. Similarly, in *The Return of the Native* the reader who finds Eustacia caught between Clym and Wildeve would not have her choose either. No other alternative is open to Eustacia herself but Thomasin and Venn imply another way forward, if only for other people – people better suited to the current environment. Venn is in truth just as much a native of the heath as Clym although he moves in and out of it continually, and likewise his loyalty to Thomasin does not get translated into a fetishization of place. The couple at the end marry and move away, to the richer cattle pastures of the river valley. Clym, in other words, appears, like Clare and Knight, to be another sentimentalist who becomes cruel, whose imaginings of a return to innocence produce outbursts of rage, which are directed against Eustacia although they are prompted more by the discovery that he cannot regain what he has parted from – that he cannot re-enter stillness.

The pattern in these novels, then, is one you would not necessarily expect to find in Hardy, just as it may be surprising to discover the historian of a rural world that was rapidly passing away writing patriotic war poetry for the London newspapers or verse inscriptions for memorials in Dudley. Smith and Clare both see the local more truly by leaving it behind. Clym, though obsessed with the local, appears less closely in touch with it than Diggory Venn, who comes and goes and then moves on in life. The values Hardy is often taken to oppose – mobility, cosmopolitanism, aspiration, progress – are being mutedly affirmed by the stories he tells. Localism (particularly delight in the simple life of pastoral England) is seen as at best paradoxical and at worst poisonous.

If the novels, then, suggest a more cosmopolitan Hardy whose views are more broadly sympathetic and more willing to modernize than readers and critics usually assume, something similar can also be found in his poetry. Hardy's poem "Geographical Knowledge" exemplifies the cosmopolitanism apparent in his depiction of the local and the rural.

GEOGRAPHICAL KNOWLEDGE

(*A Memory of Christiana C——*)

Where Blackmoor was, the road that led
    To Bath, she could not show,
Nor point the sky that overspread
    Towns ten miles off or so.

But that Calcutta stood this way,
    Cape Horn there figured fell,
That here was Boston, here Bombay,
    She could declare full well.

Less known to her the track athwart
    Froom Mead or Yell'ham Wood
Than how to make some Austral port
    In seas of surly mood.

She saw the glint of Guinea's shore
    Behind the plum-tree nigh,
Heard old unruly Biscay's roar
    In the weir's purl hard by . . .

"My son's a sailor, and he knows
    All seas and many lands,
And when he's home he points and shows
    Each country where it stands.

"He's now just there – by Gib's high rock –
    And when he gets, you see,
To Portsmouth here, behind the clock,
    Then he'll come back to me!"

                          (*CPV* 287–8)

The poem was first published in volume form in *Time's Laughingstocks* (1909), after appearing in the journal *Outlook* (April 1, 1905). In the journal version, there was an additional stanza between stanzas 4 and 5:

At last came explanation why
    Her mind should be so clear
On distant scenes, and blank wellnigh
    On places that were near.

                          (*CPV* 288n)

There are probably accidental but still risky suggestions of condescension in this stanza (arising from "At last," as if perhaps she was too slow to answer more readily, and from the judgmental quality of "blank"). Hardy avoids these dangers by cutting the stanza and avoids distracting the reader with questions about the narrator's point of view and assumptions. Without the word "explanation," we are not confronted with the issue of whether what she says is an explanation exactly and, following on from that, what might motivate a listener to call what she says an explanation, instead of responding to her less analytically. Furthermore, without this interruption, stanza 4 is not so widely separated from what the woman says, and one result of that is to extend the poem's reflection on the "knowledge" of the title.

    The initial gesture of the poem is to disrupt the reader's assumptions about rural seclusion and provincial narrowness. The woman remembered (and therefore claimed as real) does not conform to stereotype: she is not ignorant of the outside world and neither, interestingly, is she intimate with the local. Both aspects of the received idea are denied. One might respond to the first stanza by supposing that to some rustics (like Christiana perhaps) places moderately distant (such as Bath or Blackmoor Vale) would be unfamiliar. If so, the third stanza raises the stakes by saying that she knew little even about places right on her doorstep, the Froom valley meadows down the hill from Bockhampton or Yellowham Wood, only a mile or so north-west. The reader's possible strategies for missing the point are countered by this sequence, which is assisted by Hardy's use of the real place names instead of Wessex ones. One cannot dismiss her ignorance as a quaint piece of rusticity, charming but somewhat exaggerated. Helpful too in this process is the contrasting zoom out towards the most remote parts of the globe – the "Austral port" of stanza 3 – as the writing zooms in on her local ignorance.

What she knows about is probably surprising to Hardy's readers (then and now), and the poem therefore issues a challenge to established expectations of rural culture – the limits assumed to exist in its knowledge and the special advantages subsequently located in such limited knowledge. Following on from this, however (and particularly in the absence of the excised stanza), the poem reveals the partiality of Christiana's knowledge. That she "saw the glint of Guinea's shore" carries within it the double sense of seeing riches, prospects, and wealth. Her geography lacks scientific disinterestedness, I think we can say; it is not objective knowledge but knowledge rising from hope, just as her son's journeying arises in all probability out of financial need. And if that line allows the reader to disdain the woman's vulgar, mercenary interest, the ending rebukes disdain: "Then he'll come back to me!" again identifies hope as an enduring motive behind her acquiring geographical knowledge. Anxious concern is hinted at earlier in her hearing "old unruly Biscay's roar" in the sound of the weir – a roar that worries the confidence of its rhyme-word "shore" ("sure"). Yet there is a sailor's bravado in calling it "old unruly Biscay," and a hint that the phrasing is one she has learned. Certainly the last line is, by contrast, emphatically in her own voice, imitating in that verbal change the mother's will to reclaim her son when he comes home.

If her knowledge is interested, then, so might others' be; all geographies may be just as personal as hers and not the objective knowledge that the terms would seem to imply. Such "knowledge" may therefore be a product of (and a producer of) other cultural forces – colonial ambition, or the agricultural "improvement" that strips the countryside of jobs, or familial and personal bonds. The poem is concerned, in other words, first to counter metropolitan assumptions about the countryside – showing how rustic folk are becoming global citizens whether they travel abroad themselves or stay at home. Consequently, actual rural places and people no longer inhabit (if they ever did) the secluded, tranquil space of the ruralist imaginary. Neither do they attain special knowledge. Hardy's attack on metropolitan assumptions extends into a sense of assumptions operating in the construction of all geographies and in the locating of places. The enlightened, scientific outsider enjoys neither an advantage nor a disadvantage in respect of the primitive, pre-rational insider because both these figures are fantastical – both stereotypes are produced by a pastoral view of the countryside and serve to reinforce it.[3]

In *Time's Laughingstocks*, "Geographical Knowledge" follows "The Man He Killed," a poem written in 1902 at or near the close of the Boer War. Hardy's internationalist loyalties appear explicitly in this piece, where they are voiced by a Dorsetshire figure, speaking in dialect. Both poems suggest, therefore, that local distinctiveness is not violated by experience of the outside world, and at a deeper level that a certain kind of "knowledge" resembles war, both being destructively oppositional as they transform diversity into strangeness. Similarly, "His Country," one of the "Poems of War and Patriotism" Hardy included in *Moments of Vision*, casts the English soldier fighting abroad as a version of Coleridge's Ancient Mariner, who like the Mariner discovers kinship where his expectations (his cultural training) had been leading him to expect foreignness. Instead of an alien world, his finds that his "country seems to have kept in sight / On my way everywhere" (*CPV* 540).[4] In the same way that "Geographical Knowledge" implicitly challenges the cultural superiority of the readership, "His Country" sets against the speaker's experience (narrated directly in the first person) a marginal gloss that summarizes it in rather flat prose. The gloss and its layout suggest Coleridge's poem, confirming the link to the Ancient Mariner and his redemptive narrative. Meanwhile, the words of the gloss seem perplexingly literal about the experience described in the verse – their plainness ('He travels | southward, | and looks | around; ‖ and cannot | discover the | boundary ‖ of his native | country" [*CPV* 539]) comes across as simultaneously obtuse and respectful, with something of a scholar's arid, reserved precision. The consequence is that the poem juxtaposes fervor and removed observation of fervor, experience and the inevitable diminishment it suffers when represented. In that respect the poem reflects Hardy's frequent feeling that the "original irradiated conception" (*CL* I: 157) of his books could only ever be transcribed imperfectly.

In this instance, the clash created by the juxtaposition of verse and prose gloss brings out the intensity of attachment that the speaker feels towards "His" country, even as it extends around the globe. Impartial third-person observation cannot properly register this love of place and views the expansion of loyalty as necessarily involving a loss of particular attachments. The prose of the gloss, indeed, regards the poem's narrative as a process in which naive, childlike fondness for the scenes of home is supplanted by a mature and abstract benevolence, that regards everywhere as equally deserving of affection. The relentlessly prosaic quality of Hardy's prose (in part by implied contrast with Coleridge's expansively poetic marginal gloss and in part as an immediate effect) shows the limits of this rationalizing perspective and, therefore, suggests the persistence of old, primitive local feeling within the distinctively modern experience of discovering universal brotherhood.

The ironies Hardy achieves within these two poems parallel the effects of his prose style, whose learnedness is so often at the expense of learnedness and whose abstract nouns seem habitually to be setting a challenge to the authority of abstract thought. Moreover, the poems' ideas correspond with their style, as both aspects show unease with the opposition between a secluded rural world in which the instincts and affections survive and a post-Enlightenment, rational urban world and world-view that sees itself as having outgrown both localism and instinctual feeling. Both poems work to disrupt the outsider's mixture of condescension and idealizing when he or she looks in on the rural world. And this is an act of disruption that needs continually to be performed.

Jonathan Bate, in his ecocritical survey *The Song of the Earth*, generalized about Hardy that "He placed mobile new men and advanced ideas in opposition to rooted types and traditional ways." Consequently, in *The Woodlanders*:

> For the old woodlanders, there is no division between human intercourse and local environment. The presence of memory means that the countryside is inhabited rather than viewed aesthetically. The condition of the modern man, with his mobility and his displaced knowledge, is never to be able to share this sense of belonging. . . . Fitzpiers is never without his eyeglass; he peers fitfully at his environment instead of dwelling steadily within it. (Bate 2000: 14, 18)

Likewise Lawrence Buell writes, in *The Future of Environmental Criticism*:

> In the Little Hintock of Hardy's late nineteenth-century novel *The Woodlanders* (1887), people's lives get traumatically disrupted or extinguished, but the villagers' basic life-rhythms have scarcely changed for years and seem unlikely to do so in the future. Graham Swift's late twentieth-century regional novel *Waterland* (1983) tells the long history of the East Anglian fenlands as a series of reshapings of landscape and social arrangements. . . . The difference in perception of the stability and porosity of local cultural arrangements between the two worlds stems largely from the increasing sense that regions remain permeable to shock waves potentially extending worldwide. (Buell 2005: 88)

Buell's historical assumptions are dubious, since Hardy evidently was aware of "the porosity of local cultural arrangements" and the presence within secluded rural communities of "shock waves potentially extending worldwide." He was selective in referring to these (the slave trade, for instance, although important in nineteenth-century Dorset, is never referred to as far as I know). Nonetheless, the comparison of Swift and Hardy does not convincingly show a greater degree of global awareness in late twentieth-century writing. Swift's novel shows, by contrast, modern characters fixated on and disabled by the traumas of their rural past; though he writes a history of anthropogenic environmental change (in the draining of the fens), the local cultural arrangements of childhood seem unalterable.[5]

Bate treats Hardy's novel as Buell does, essentially, and to do so he relies on polarizing sentence structures: the woodlands are "inhabited *rather than* viewed," Hardy places "advanced ideas *in opposition to* rooted types," his modern protagonist "peers fitfully . . . *instead of* dwelling steadily" (my emphases). The tricksy identification of a pun in Fitzpiers' name (he peers fitfully because he is called Fitzpiers) does not obscure the crudity of Bate's own style – an insistent quality in the writing that matters because his oppositions keep up a reductively straightforward separation between town and country, old and new, mobile and rooted – a separation that the novel (despite its attractiveness to ecocritics) does little to affirm.

In Bate's account, in other words, Hardy presents a countryside that is pre-aesthetic and pre-conscious, and he unambiguously valorizes such an innocent rural world while lamenting his own (and our) modern alienation from it. This, though, is much closer to Fitzpiers' sense of the country than it is to Hardy's. Not only can you find – constantly find – links between the primitive and modern groups within Hardy novels, such that no one and nothing is insulated from the modern, Hardy also suggests that the idealization of countryside (its idyllification, if you like) is itself an act of modernity – a feature of tourism – and one furthermore that disguises disdainful superiority behind celebration.[6]

Similarly, but on the positive side, Hardy's rustics are rarely if ever straightforwardly innocent or pastoral. They are not simply wheeled on as a rustic chorus, whom the reader can feel superior to and also nostalgic about, as if they were children. Nearly always, his rustics reveal preferences, character, awareness, limitation, and personal taste. The novels bear out the visitor's experience as Hardy describes it in his essay "The Dorsetshire Labourer" (1883). Although the yokel Hodge is assumed by the metropolitan visitor to be "a degraded being of uncouth manner and aspect, stolid understanding and snail-like movement," he emerges over time and with familiarity as "somehow not typical of anyone but himself," and "disintegrated into a number of dissimilar fellow-creatures" (*THPV* 38, 40). The essay narrates the chastening and enlivening experience of finding personality emerge from stereotype, as idiosyncrasy, history, and distinctiveness gradually reveal themselves despite the best efforts of the visitor's customary presumption to obscure these qualities.

Thus Tess of the d'Urbervilles persists in the reader's mind as herself, as not typical of anyone but herself, despite the stereotypings of her that are performed by the novel's male protagonists, both Alec and Angel. The book (perhaps to counter the danger of nostalgia present in *The Woodlanders*) is an endeavor to reach an unidealizing regard for and of Tess – an effort to regard her as someone who is pure despite impurity, and as a person who represents "country" values not so much despite her being tainted by the modern as amidst that (historical and personal) process of metamorphosis. It may be that the modern will crush those humane instincts, present in Tess, in the same way that the plot has her executed – this modern threat is something the plot suggests; but at the same time one way the modern has of crushing Tess is to claim that she simply cannot survive – in the grandiose plangency of modernity's self-pity, the modern says it cannot touch the pristine, primitive world of Wessex without corrupting it. Gendering the modern as male and the primitive as female allows this mythic narrative to support a masculinist self-image of the man as (tragic) conqueror and the woman as violated creature. It shows and shows up the colonizer's (self-)pathos.

Hardy, though, never disguised the fact that women experienced desire, and he saw Wessex as resilient. Grace Melbury in *The Woodlanders* not only proves (*contra* Bate) that that novel contains and celebrates figures who are both mobile and traditional, both inhabitant and aesthetic viewer of the landscape, she also shows herself to be a sturdy Wessex girl. Her decision at the end to take Edred Fitzpiers back, despite his infidelity, is usually read as a further piece of misfortune and a further reason to lament the passing of Giles, who truly and loyally loved her. That feeling is balanced, though, by Giles' stubborn hesitancy about acting on his feelings (even when he knows they are reciprocated) and, in line with this, by the novel's reservations about self-sacrifice. Grace opts instead to take herself and her natural sexual instincts forward into a miscegenated future, and into a life of intimacy with both the modern spirit and the modern body of Fitzpiers. Alongside an elegy for the vanishing way of life, therefore, led by Giles (now dead) and Marty South (destined to be childless), the novel includes the idea of Grace finding ways and means to carry that way of life on, in a modified (and adulterated) form. In doing so, she is following out the impulse to joy and to adaptation which underlay the life of "old woodlanders" from the beginning.

The limitations in both these ecocritical accounts of Hardy center around their concern for what Bate terms "dwelling," the pre-modern and untroubled relation to place that Fitzpiers cannot attain and that seems to depend upon a "sense of belonging," rootedness, and the avoidance of aesthetic appreciation in favor of inhabiting. Bate's use of "dwelling" originates in Heideggerian thought and, whether or not he makes good use of Heidegger's ideas, he assumes that they fit neatly onto Hardy. For J. Hillis Miller, tracing the same line of thought, this is a basic error:

> Heidegger is beguiled by the dream of a harmonious and unified culture, a culture rooted in one particular place. Hardy knows, and shows in his novels, that such an apparent unity, even in rural cultures, is riven by divisions and disharmonies. (Miller 1995: 55)

This comment arises out of Miller's analysis of *The Return of the Native*. *The Woodlanders*, written a decade later, "shows" not only rifts in the fabric of rurality's "apparent unity" but a willingness to embrace dividedness and the possibility that rural values may persist amidst dislocation and deracination. It is not clear what the "future of environmental criticism" will be, and Buell's book responds to a fairly widespread suspicion that ecocriticism has already run its course. If so, this is principally because, to judge from Buell and Bate, its practitioners are so wedded to non-viable and outdated accounts of how people inhabit the natural world. Hardy is (in my opinion) an environmental writer more because he refuses to idealize rustic ways of life than because he unambiguously celebrates them. His refusal of the ecocritical dichotomy between aesthetic viewing and unselfconscious dwelling is precisely the reason why he is valuable now to reflection about humanity, the environment, and what literature may have to contribute to the adjustments in our cultural assumptions that the present environmental crisis requires. Study of his work should spell, in other words, both the end of ecocriticism and its possible new beginning.

Furthermore, the perspective on rurality that emerges from Hardy is shared by many subsequent writers about provincial experience and, characteristically, erased from their work by established critical preferences. In the case of Norman Nicholson, a post-war British poet whose work focuses almost exclusively on his "home" in the English Lake District, that erasure of a ranging cosmopolitan outlook from writing based in rustic experience is something he has performed himself. Nicholson's *Selected Poems 1940–1982* (1982) selects only two poems from his second collection, *Five Rivers*, published nearly forty years earlier in 1944. It is not of course unusual for poets in later life to be harsh editors of their earlier verse; in this instance, however, the selections and exclusions seem to be based upon a concern on Nicholson's part to sustain an image of himself as a provincial poet, within quite a narrow definition of provinciality. His chooses for the *Selected Poems* "Cleator Moor" and "To the River Duddon," the second particularly intent upon Nicholson's relations with Wordsworth, his great predecessor as poet of the Lake District. He leaves out the ambitious sequence "The Bow in the Cloud" that echoes Christopher Smart in style and in its sense that the universals of (spiritual) experience can be found amidst the mundane life of a backwater. Nicholson backs away from the 1944 collection's stylistic eclecticism, its range and boldness, with the claim to equality such stylistic ambition makes. Similarly, he excludes a poem like "The Evacuees," which observes the heterogeneity of a rural population, its inclusion and assimilation of people from far-away places.

Nicholson also excludes the excellent short poem, "The Blackberry" (Nicholson 1944: 37). Perhaps its exclusion was because he (rightly) found the phrase "nigger fists" to describe the fruit of the title unacceptable by 1982, or perhaps the poem's note of religious devotion at the close seemed quaint or inauthentic in retrospect. It is just as likely, though, that the oddity of its similes grated with him. A blackberry as a fly's compound eye or the world found repeated in its shining surfaces "like / Coupons in a ration book": both of these are startling and bold comparisons. They fit with the poem's evocation of A. E. Housman at the beginning ("Between the railway and the mine / Brambles are in fruit again"), an evocation of English pastoral that the industrial scenery of the poem challenges in the same way that the poem's celebrating a blackberry, a bramble, at all is a decision that already upsets the hierarchy in which cherry-blossom stands high. Similarly, "Rockferns," the poem facing this one in *Five Rivers*, begins: "On quarry walls the spleenwort spreads / Its green zipfasteners and black threads" (Nicholson 1944: 36).[7]

Mannerism is one danger here, an impression of contrivance and conscious novelty being pursued at the expense of naturalness. The surrealism of these early poems can become introverted, and cease to achieve the effects of defamiliarization that it seeks. Consequently, to tone down ambition, as Nicholson's later more colloquial and "confessional" poetry often does, and to exclude the more daring work from his *Selected Poems*, might seem a natural result of talent maturing. On the other hand, the ambition of "The Blackberry" achieves a distinctive sense of what this poem terms "the large condensed within the small [. . .] The sky within the blackberry" – a sense of the provincial environment providing scope, in the same way that the poem finds the modern, industrial world within places assumed to be rustic and delightful. The poem delights in the oddness of the plant, bringing that forward through the strangeness of the similes, and delights equally in the unique landscapes of a particular place. What Hardy accomplishes via clashes of register and voice, Nicholson achieves through remote analogies. And in that, too, he follows a pattern set (among others) by Hardy, whose writing, prose and verse, is characterized by a willingness to make unexpected and even disturbing comparisons.

Both "The Blackberry" and "Rockferns" imply therefore a cosmopolitan sensibility existing within the provincial environment. Partly through their intertextuality, their modernism, they rebuke assumptions often brought to provincial poetry; they over-turn hierarchies within which both provincial and center have their allotted place, their assigned style, and their stereotypical mindset. By disturbing these structures, they also unsettle the division that their readership is accustomed to create (accultur-ated to create) between center and margin, city and country, urban and rural. Cer-tainly, too, these poems declare that the splendors of the living world cannot be reduced to pastoral, refusing as they do the familiar representational strategies that preserve the sanctity of pastoral and ensure that the actual becomes passively stylized through it and within it.

Hardy's style as both poet and novelist similarly disrupts pastoral assumptions, just as his narratives contest the opposition of country and city, and the purposes that opposition serves. He, like Nicholson, tailored his work at times so that it appears to fit more easily into his readership's and wider culture's patterns of expectation. He presented himself as the historian of Wessex partly because his audience wanted him to be such a figure. Fortunately, though, Hardy never obscured the writer of his earlier works, developing instead, within his collected editions and through the multilayered ironies of his *Life and Work*, a skilled obliquity that allows his texts both to welcome and disconcert their readers. His locations become, in consequence, "His Country," somewhere it is easy to label and identify, and somewhere too that makes labeling appear a trivial, shallow pursuit. Hardy does not reject the visitors who come to his books and their landscapes looking either for Dorset itself or the idyllic world of rural England. Though he did make fun of them and weary of their intrusions, he also helped his friend Hermann Lea to compose first *A Handbook to the West Country of Hardy's Novels and Poems* (1905) and then its more comprehensive version, *Highways and Byways in Hardy's Wessex* (1913). How those places are "His," and the kind of attachment that this possessive implies, are, however, the more profound questions that his work always seeks to raise.

NOTES

1 See Pite 2007. It's paradoxical that the *Life and Work* emphasizes the importance of *The Dynasts* (stressing Hardy's long gestation of the project and investment in it) while also presenting an image of Hardy as passive and impressionable – an image that makes the epic drama seem an anomaly, considering its admiration for mili-tary heroism and its explicit "philosophy."

2 Edwards (1988). Keith (1988: 85ff) develops a subtle account of Hardy's relation to the nine-teenth-century tradition of (what Keith terms) regional writing.

3 Christiana was "Christiana Coward," postmis-tress in Lower Bockhampton: see Ray 2006: 54–5.

4 Again Hardy revised the poem in successive versions, excluding from 1919 onwards an additional final stanza published in *Moments of Vision* (1917). Originally the ending included an alternate, conventional voice (of "a wise man" who "set[s] right" the speaker, calling his extended sympathies "blindness" and viewing them "with pitying eye"). As with "Geographical Knowledge," the revised version removes contention, leaving the speaker unchallenged and the responsibility for possi-ble dissent with the reader. See *CPV* 540.

5 See Pite 2002: 4–9 for an account of the Oxford school of regional geography that, late in the nineteenth century, established within the

newly emerging discipline a model of regions as isolated, autonomous areas. The rest of the study argues that this model postdates Hardy's work, differs profoundly from Hardy's own sense of region, and has exerted a powerful influence over readings of Hardy.

6 Evidence for this appears from the beginning and not only in *A Pair of Blue Eyes* (see above). In Hardy's "An Indiscretion in the Life of an Heiress," published 1878 but based on his first, unpublished novel, *The Poor Man and the Lady* (1867–8), the heroine is roundly rebuked for treating the poor schoolchildren in her estate school (where the poor man is their teacher) as "poor things," objects of her sentimental pity, and not as persons in their own right.

7 "Rockferns" ends by imagining that if after death the poet's "subtler part may cruise / Twice round the sun and Betelgeuse" then "My soul shall detonate on high / And plant itself in cracks of sky"; these ideas curiously echo Hardy's in poems such as "In a Museum," "Apostrophe to an Old Psalm Tune," and "To Shakespeare" (see *CPV* 430–2, 439–40).

References and Further Reading

Bate, Jonathan (2000). *The Song of the Earth*. London: Picador.

Buell, Lawrence (2005). *The Future of Environmental Criticism: Environmental Crisis and Literary Imagination*. Oxford: Blackwell.

Dean, Tacita, and Jeremy Millar (2005). *Place*. London: Thames & Hudson.

Edwards, P. D. (1988). *Idyllic Realism from Mary Russell Mitford to Hardy*. Basingstoke: Macmillan.

Gervais, David (1993). *Literary Englands: Versions of "Englishness" in Modern Writing*. Cambridge: Cambridge University Press.

Howe, Irving (1985). *Thomas Hardy*. Basingstoke: Macmillan.

Jacobus, Mary (1976). Tess's Purity. *Essays in Criticism*, 26, 318–38.

Keith, W. J. (1988). *Regions of the Imagination: The Development of British Rural Fiction*. Toronto: University of Toronto Press.

Lea, Hermann (1905). *A Handbook to the West Country of Thomas Hardy's Novels and Poems*. London: Macmillan.

Lea, Hermann (1913). *Thomas Hardy's Wessex*. London: Macmillan.

Maxwell, Donald (1928). *The Landscape of Thomas Hardy*. London: Cassell.

Miller, J. Hillis (1995). *Topographies*. Stanford: Stanford University Press.

Millgate, Michael (ed.) (2001). *Thomas Hardy's Public Voice: The Essays, Speeches, and Miscellaneous Prose*. Oxford: Clarendon Press.

Morgan, William W. (1985). Verses Fitted for a Monument: Hardy's Contribution to the Dudley War Memorial. *Thomas Hardy Journal*, 1(1), 25–32.

Nicholson, Norman (1944). *Five Rivers*. London: Faber & Faber.

Nunokawa, Jeff (1992). Tess, Tourism and the Spectacle of the Woman. In Linda M. Shires (ed.), *Rewriting the Victorians: Theory, History, and the Politics of Gender* (pp. 70–86). New York and London: Routledge.

Pite, Ralph (2002). *Hardy's Geography: Wessex and the Regional Novel*. Basingstoke: Palgrave Macmillan.

Pite, Ralph (2006). *Thomas Hardy: The Guarded Life*. London: Picador.

Pite, Ralph (2007). "Graver things . . . braver things": Hardy's Martial Zest. In Tim Kendall (ed.), *The Oxford Handbook of British and Irish War-Poetry* (pp. 34–50). Oxford: Oxford University Press.

Ray, Martin (2006). The Collected Letters of Thomas Hardy: Some Additional Notes. *Thomas Hardy Journal*, 22, 48–71.

Widdowson, Peter (1989). *Hardy in History: A Study in Literary Sociology*. London and New York: Routledge.

Williams, Merryn (1972). *Thomas Hardy and Rural England*. London and Basingstoke: Macmillan.

10

Thomas Hardy of London

Keith Wilson

The first six items in volume I of Hardy's *Collected Letters*, all written to his sister Mary between 1862 and 1866, exist because he had spent most of that period separated from his family, living in London and experiencing to the full the pleasures and challenges of getting to know a capital that by the second half of the nineteenth century was already being routinely described, and not just by Londoners themselves, as the foremost city in the world. This was his first extended separation from his family and from Dorset, at that time the still remote area of rural England that shaped his sensibility and with which he and his writings will always be most inextricably connected. This reflex association was well established even during his lifetime. By the turn into the twentieth century it had already begun to generate a plethora of tourist guides to an area, part real part imaginary, variously designated "Hardy's Wessex," "Hardy Country," "Hardy-land," "Hardy's Wessex Scene," or "The Landscape of Hardy's Novels." "Hardy of Dorset" in life, "Hardy of Wessex" in art, he has since been reified as rural icon by the numerous enterprises that have with growing sophistication adapted to their own ends the resonances of both Hardy's name and those he bestowed on the towns, villages, and major topographical features of Dorset (see Widdowson 1989, particularly 55–72). These appropriators of the evocative power of the term "Wessex" include not only publishing but also the cinema, television, and stage industries; journalism; tourism; town planning; calendar, postcard, commemorative chinaware, tea-cloth, and beer manufacture; and even the royal family – although whoever persuaded Sophie Rhys-Jones to become the first actual countess of Wessex had presumably only titular familiarity with Hardy's account of the bizarrely unconventional life of the first fictional one. In that loosely defined arena of consciousness known as the public mind, Hardy is "Hardy of Wessex" as surely as Dickens is "Dickens of London," both securely rooted in their respective literary bailiwicks long before Carl Weber or Wolf Mankowitz thought to conflate authorial name, domicile, and imaginative setting into eponymous book titles.

Despite this automatic association of Hardy's name with the West Country, it has also long been recognized (although the implications of that recognition relatively little explored) that London had a significance to both his life and his work that was in its way as important as that of Dorset. If Dorset fed his imagination and provided the primary subject matter and settings for his writing, London enabled the processes that brought his work before a reading public and allowed this most regional of writers to develop such a trans-regional, world-wide reputation. Of letters that survived to follow those to Mary Hardy in the first volume of the *Collected Letters*, the overwhelming majority, right down to the 1880s, comprise communications with publishers, virtually all of them based in London. Its dominance as either source or destination for so much of Hardy's early surviving correspondence anticipates the beginning of a lifetime of professional and social connection to the capital. In fact after his July 1867 return to Dorset from those first years in London, and notwithstanding the assumption among some of his neighbors that return must signal failure of his professional ambitions, more than forty years would pass before the disinclinations and infirmities of old age would begin to stand in the way of his making regular, often extended, visits there.

The evidence of *Life and Work* suggests that from the earliest stage of his introduction to the city Hardy was aware of the importance it would come to have for him. Initially he envisaged that importance in relation to the development of a career as an architect rather than to the furthering of literary ambitions. Under the heading "A New Start," *Life and Work* somewhat portentously describes his departure from Dorchester for the capital:

> On Thursday, April 17, 1862, Thomas Hardy started alone for London, to pursue the art and science of architecture on more advanced lines. . . .
>
> The Great Exhibition of that year was about to be opened, and this perhaps influenced him in the choice of a date for his migration. His only previous journey to the capital had been made with his mother in 1848 or 1849, when they passed through it on the way to and back from Hertfordshire, on a visit to a relative . . . (*LW* 40)

The recollection of the precise date and day of the week, the emphasis on the solitariness of his starting out, the solemn articulation of his architectural aspirations, and the ancillary detailing that this was only the second occasion on which he had ever visited the capital all suggest that this departure for London was remembered throughout Hardy's life as a formative experience of immense significance. Its association (and, in its solitariness, contrast) with his vivid memories of the childhood visit with his mother is particularly suggestive, almost as if the journey that brought the first significant separation from family is lodged in his mind with that other cherished recollection of filial–maternal intimacy. While the precise year of the earlier visit had apparently been forgotten – it is in Millgate's biography that Hardy's own tentative "1848 or 1849" becomes a more confident 1849 (Millgate 2004: 46) – some of its circumstantial detail had proved indelible, including the overnight stay on the return journey at the Cross-Keys in Clerkenwell, "the inn at which Shelley and Mary Godwin had been accustomed to meet on week-ends not two-score years before." The further observation that the inn "was at this time unaltered from its state during the lovers' romantic experiences there – the oval stone staircase, the skylight, and the hotel entrance being untouched," with its speculation that shared impecuniousness meant that the room in which Hardy and his mother stayed "may have been the same as that occupied by our most marvellous lyrist" comes presumably from the ruminations of the mature rather than the 9-year-old Hardy. But the extent of what the 9-year-old remembered – sights of the Pantheon, of the Cumberland Gate entry to Hyde Park, of the "mud, curses, and cries of ill-treated animals" at Smithfield, and of the distant view at Swiss Cottage of "the *outside* of London creeping towards them across green fields" (*LW* 22) – is in itself very revealing of early responsiveness to the grandeur, the squalor, and the invasive organic growth of the city.

Hardy recollected his arrival in London as an aspiring young architect with similarly striking precision (indeed, it has to be said, in somewhat implausible detail given the confidence with which direct speech from half a century earlier is quoted):

> Hardy used to relate humorously that on the afternoon of his arrival he called to inquire for lodgings at a house where was employed a bachelor some ten years older than himself, whose cousin Hardy had known. This acquaintance, looking him up and down, was sceptical about his establishing himself in London. "Wait till you have walked the streets a few weeks," he said satirically, "and your elbows begin to shine, and the hems of your trousers get frayed, as if nibbled by rats! Only practical men are wanted here." Thomas began to wish he had thought less of the Greek Testament and more of iron girders. (*LW* 40)

Notwithstanding these initial apprehensions, and their partial vindication five years later in the increasing enervation and deteriorating health that caused his retreat to Dorset, Hardy proved rapidly to be both at home and at ease in London, soon developing the detailed familiarity with it that continued throughout his life, and that was ended only by the incapacities of age. In fact, one of the most striking impressions given by the substantial body of information available about Hardy's introduction to London is the apparent effortlessness with which this quite sheltered young man from the country made a life for himself there. Arriving in mid-April 1862 with nowhere to live and nothing more substantial in the way of social or professional connections than two letters of introduction (only one of which proved of much use to him), by May 5 he had already found a position and started work in the architectural offices of Arthur Blomfield. Between them, *Life and Work*, the *Collected Letters*, and Michael Millgate's *Thomas Hardy: A Biography Revisited* (to all of which this summary is indebted) have documented many of the key experiences in Hardy's first engagement with London.

Well placed to attend the opera, the concert hall, and the theater, to benefit from a self-directed course in the history of European art during regular lunchtime visits to the National Gallery, and to witness at first hand many of the major public events taking place in 1860s London, Hardy made full use of the opportunities the capital offered. Caught up in the crowds viewing the illuminations celebrating the 1862 wedding of the Prince of Wales, and notwithstanding the fact that "my waistcoat buttons were torn off and my ribs bent in before I could get into a doorway" (*LW* 42), he gave early service to the cause of literature by contriving not to be crushed to death, as were half a dozen people standing close to some of his office colleagues. He saw one of Palmerston's final appearances in the House of Commons, and in October 1865 attended his burial in Westminster Abbey (*LW* 53). He attended some of Dickens' later dramatic readings. Famously clutching his edition of the plays for consultation during performances, he claimed to have attended all productions in Samuel Phelps' "series of Shakespeare plays at Drury Lane" (*LW* 54). Behind and informing these more public moments is a relationship with the city founded upon scrupulous, at times almost obsessive, attention to circumstantial detail, an attentiveness that would be reflected, as we shall see, in the perspectival strategies of Hardy's writing.

A summary of the broad outline of Hardy's times in London will help to establish their centrality in his life. After that first extended stay between 1862 and 1867, he was back in London again in the early months of 1869, energetically, if in the end fruitlessly, negotiating with Chapman & Hall over the fate of his first, never to be published, novel, *The Poor Man and the Lady*. Of this he wrote with some heat:

> the most important scenes were laid in London, of which city Hardy had just had between five and six years' constant and varied experience – as only a young man in the metropolis can get it – knowing every street and alley west of St. Paul's like a born Londoner, which he was often supposed to be; an experience quite ignored by the reviewers of his later books who, if he only touched on London in his pages, promptly reminded him not to write of a place he was unacquainted with, but to get back to his sheepfolds. (*LW* 63–4)

He took lodgings in London again between May and August of 1870, and returned there for a third extended stay between April and July of 1872, assisting the architect T. Roger Smith with his designs for new London School Board schools. He spent much of the spring and summer of 1874 in London, a period culminating in his marriage there in September. On returning from their honeymoon, he and Emma set up home there for nine months before moving to Dorset in the summer of 1875. After a somewhat peripatetic three years (including their two-year "idyll" at Sturminster Newton), they returned to London again, Hardy having "decided that the practical side of his vocation of novelist demanded that he should have his head-quarters in or near London" (*LW* 121). In furtherance of these plans to establish himself as a metropolitan literary presence, Hardy rapidly secured election to membership in the Savile Club (June 1878), whose literary focus guaranteed opportunities to socialize with influential writers, editors, and publishers.

Millgate's sense of Hardy's social proclivities and professional ambitions in these years is that London's opportunities may have had a distracting effect, and "tempted

him with journalistic opportunities, invited him to be trivial, exacerbated his vulnerability to contemporary opinion, undermined him with sheer occupation – an excess
of gossip, shop-talk, dining out, and 'keeping up'" (Millgate 2004: 183). Certainly
the evidence of *Life and Work* is that, despite Hardy's claim that the initial return to
Dorset from London indicated that "He constitutionally shrank from the business of
social advancement, caring for life as an emotion rather than for life as a science of
climbing" (*LW* 54), no small part of the appeal of London derived from the opportunity it afforded to establish himself in a fashionable social milieu to which Dorset
alone could never have given him access, whatever his literary talents.

Even after the Hardys made Dorset their home again – this time for good – in
June 1881 (a move necessitated, like Hardy's earlier withdrawal from London, by
anxieties about his health), they regularly took a flat in London for between two and
four months a year. On the many occasions when Hardy was in London alone, the
terms of his sometimes daily letters to Emma make almost embarrassingly clear what
London had to offer that Dorset hadn't:

> I lunched (did I tell you?) with Lady Londonderry Saturday, & met there the Ld.
> Chancellor, & others. He is, as you know, a son in law of Mr Kindersley's, of Clyffe.
> To day at Lady J.'s Ld Randolph Churchill lunched – also T. P. O'Connor & Mrs T. P.,
> Ld Morris (Judge of Appeal) &c. &c. . . .
>   In addition to the above-named I have met – Lady Hilda Broderick, Sir E. Lawson
> (proprietor of D. Telegraph), Buckle (Times) Lady Dorothy Nevill . . . Hon. George
> Curzon, Sir Redvers Buller, Sir F. Lockwood. (*CL* II: 52–3)

Even if one discounts here what to an unsympathetic ear might sound like egregious
tuft-hunting as a possible desire merely to keep Emma informed of his doings as much
as to impress her, or perhaps to use letters to her as a kind of aide-memoire for himself,
such recurrent roll-calls of influential, and in many instances titled, names may
suggest a Hardy too soon made glad by his inclusion in such circles.

Certainly by the time he was elected in 1891 to membership of the Athenaeum,
London's most intellectually eminent club (an election that took nearly three years
from his own first approach to Lord Carnavon with a view to bringing it about), he
occupied an assured place in fashionable London life. Indeed, in its way, it was a more
assured place than the one he occupied in Dorchester, and for paradoxically complementary reasons: the more famous he became, the more secure his position in London
society, but also the greater his distance from the provincial inhabitants of small-town
Dorchester, some of whom regarded his literary eminence with a mixture of suspicion,
envy, and malice. Although with advancing age, Hardy inevitably found travel to
London more difficult, causing the pattern of extended stays to end around 1910, for
another decade after this he still periodically visited there, for both professional and
social reasons. When growing frailty meant he was no longer able to do so at all,
London not infrequently came to him, in the shape of visits by friends and acquaintances from a metropolitan world in which he had by that point been at home for

half a century. On one memorable occasion, this reversal of roles took the form of the whole cast of the London production of his adaptation of *Tess of the d'Urbervilles* coming down to perform for him at Max Gate.

I want to consider Hardy's enduring relationship with London from two main perspectives: first, London as a complex point of vantage offering perspectives exemplary of some of those strategies of observation that one thinks of as being most distinctively Hardyan; and secondly, London as an imaginative site in its own right – that is, London as urban complement to Wessex rather than London as urban complement to Dorset. I am not concerned here with the topographical specifics of Hardy's experience of London (for a detailed account of his residences, including all London addresses at which he is known to have stayed, see Chalfont 1992–3), or with the social circles in which he moved and the London society figures who became his good friends, but with what the combined actuality and imaginative idea of London contributed to the subject matter and techniques of his writing.

Hardy himself was less than confident about what that contribution may have been. He describes the reason for the final 1881 decision to make Dorset his permanent home as his arrival at the conclusion

> that it would be better to make London a place of sojourn for a few months only in each year, and establish their home in the country, both for reasons of health and for mental inspiration, Hardy finding, or thinking he found, that residence in or near a city tended to force mechanical and ordinary productions from his pen, concerning ordinary society-life and habits. (*LW* 154)

Given that the two novels most associated with London, apart from the ill-starred *The Poor Man and the Lady*, were *The Hand of Ethelberta* and *The Well-Beloved*, this harsh self-judgment carries also the ring of self-knowledge. The social comedy of *The Hand of Ethelberta*, in particular, generates a somewhat formulaic approach to the rendering of fashionable urban life, in a cursorily established setting that for much of the time might almost as easily do service for Bath or Cheltenham as for London. But those points at which London is evoked most originally in the novels that evoke it at all are also the points at which distinctively Hardyan perspectival strategies appear most pronounced. Here, for example, is Ethelberta anticipating the excursion to Cripplegate church to view Milton's tomb:

> There is nowhere I like going to so much as the depths of the city. The absurd narrowness of world-renowned streets is so surprising – so crooked and shady as they are too, and full of the quaint smells of old cupboards and cellars. Walking through one of them reminds me of being at the bottom of some crevasse or gorge, the proper surface of the globe being the tops of the houses. (*HE* 197)

The translation of metaphorical urban depths into literal ones imaged as gigantic fissures in the earth's surface already takes one some distance from that human world of "ordinary society-life and habits" that Hardy felt London forced from his pen. In fact, far more frequently Hardy presents London in impressionistic, or even expressionistic, proto-modernist terms, as the embodiment of a collectivity that denies individual identity, subsuming it within the inchoate, the illimitable, and even the grotesque (for fuller discussion of Hardy's London and impressionism, see Gilmore 2004).

This recurrent representational tendency can be found even as early as *A Pair of Blue Eyes*, a novel not particularly associated with evocations of London at all. Here is the view that greets Stephen Smith from Henry Knight's window in Bede's Inn, a view to which Knight has directed attention as manifestation of what he calls his "Humanity Show." It offers a suggestive anticipation of what will be (in a generically completely different work as yet thirty years in Hardy's future) the vantage point enjoyed by that other impresario of a "Humanity Show," *The Dynasts*' Spirit of the Years:

> Beneath them was an alley running up to the wall, and thence turning sideways and passing under an arch, so that Knight's back window was immediately over the angle, and commanded a view of the alley lengthwise. Crowds – mostly of women – were surging, bustling, and pacing up and down. Gaslights glared from butchers' stalls, illuminating the lumps of flesh to splotches of orange and vermilion, like the wild colouring of Turner's later pictures, whilst the purl and babble of tongues of every pitch and mood was to this human wildwood what the ripple of a brook is to the natural forest. (*PBE* 132)

The crowds' "surging, bustling, and pacing" may not be as developed an image of human matter in the undifferentiated organic mass as that presented in the Fore Scene of *The Dynasts*, where "the peoples, distressed by events which they did not cause, are seen writhing, crawling, heaving, and vibrating in their various cities and nationalities" (*CPW* IV: 20). But the representational terms are very similar in their diminution of individual human particularity. Indeed, for a moment the reader is as inclined to associate "the lumps of flesh" illuminated "to splotches of orange and vermilion" with those pacing women as with the actual inanimate but once living referent, the meat on the butchers' stalls.

A similar alienating effect is achieved in *The Well-Beloved* with Jocelyn Pierston's agonized apprehensions that a mischance may have befallen Avice II as a result of his having unthinkingly sent her on an errand into the immensity of an unknown, and finally unknowable, city:

> Pierston went to the window. . . . Over the opposite square the moon hung, and to the right there stretched a long street, filled with a diminishing array of lamps, some single, some in clusters, among them an occasional blue or red one. From a corner came the notes of a piano-organ strumming out a stirring march of Rossini's. The shadowy black figures of pedestrians moved up, down, and across the embrowned roadway. Above the roofs was a bank of livid mist, and higher a greenish-blue sky, in which stars were visible, though its lower part was still pale with daylight, against which rose chimney-pots in the form of elbows, prongs, and fists.

From the whole scene proceeded a ground rumble, miles in extent, upon which individual rattles, voices, a tin whistle, the bark of a dog, rode like bubbles on a sea. The whole noise impressed him with the sense that no one in its enormous mass ever required rest.

In this illimitable ocean of humanity there was a unit of existence, his Avice, wandering alone. (*WB* 268–9)

As it happens, Pierston's apprehensions are not Avice's, and when she eventually turns up she perkily reveals herself to have been utterly unaffected by his brand of night-thoughts, having merely taken a delaying detour through "the fashionable streets, where folks are all walking about just as if it were daytime!" and "were more respectable than they are anywhere at home!" (*WB* 270). But an impression of the city as a site that dwarfs the individual "unit of existence" and translates aural distinctions of form into a "ground rumble" upon which distinguishable sounds "rode like bubbles on a sea" constitutes a denial of all formal properties, and hence of meaning. It is an experience that is surely closer to Adela Quested's traumatic penetration into the distinctly non-urban, elemental depths of the Marabar Caves in Forster's *A Passage to India* than to, say, Catherine Morland's merely social engagements, however disconcerting these may be, with fashionable Bath in Austen's *Northanger Abbey*.

Thus Hardy's versions of the actual ambience of London are striking precisely because they do not limit themselves to the rendering of "ordinary social-life and habits." They reach instead towards mediation of those aspects of urban experience that within a decade or two younger contemporaries would be attempting to convey by changing the language of literary discourse. Even that apparently incidental registering of "the notes of a piano-organ strumming out a stirring march of Rossini's" seems anticipatory of the deployment of musical leitmotifs by writers as various as Conrad, Joyce, Woolf, Forster, or T. S. Eliot, in ways that will become almost definitional of modernist strategies for shaping quotidian experience into ironizing moments of vision or epiphanic insight.

In fact, Hardy as modernist and Hardy as Londoner are typifications near-allied. Stephen Smith's and Jocelyn Pierston's discomfiting experiences of London here are very close to aspects of Hardy's own. This is his memory of taking Emma in November 1879 to see the Lord Mayor's Show, which they watched from above, "from the upper windows of *Good Words* in Ludgate Hill," thereby being granted a view of the assembled masses that, if not as exalted as that enjoyed by the spirit overworld in *The Dynasts*, was exalted enough to elicit from Emma the felicitous if unflattering observation that "the surface of the crowd seemed like a boiling cauldron of porridge":

as the crowd grows denser it loses its character of an aggregate of countless units, and becomes an organic whole, a molluscous black creature having nothing in common with humanity, that takes the shapes of the streets along which it has lain itself, and throws out horrid excrescences and limbs into neighbouring alleys; a creature whose voice exudes from its scaly coat, and who has an eye in every pore of its body. The balconies, stands, and railway-bridge are occupied by small detached shapes of the same tissue, but of gentler motion, as if they were the spawn of the monster in their midst. (*LW* 134)

Gathered in sufficient numbers and seen from a sufficient distance, humanity, though consisting only of combined units of itself, comes to have nothing in common with humanity, becomes a formless "organic whole" and evocation of the monstrous. Among the things that London may well have given Hardy are the earliest inklings of what eventually emerges in his most conceptually ambitious work, *The Dynasts*, as the acting out of the imperatives of the Immanent Will (see Sherman 1948). Thus it could be argued that London – *pace* his own early judgment – takes Hardy about as far as his work ever gets from a merely mechanical preoccupation with "ordinary society-life and habits."

   This is also a "view" of London in the most literal of perspectival senses, which reflects that attention to circumstantial detail in Hardy's earliest adult experience of the city mentioned earlier. The central locations occupied by Blomfield's office, first at St. Martin's Place next to St. Martin-in-the Fields and Trafalgar Square, subsequently in the even more panoptically privileged viewing ground of Adelphi Terrace overlooking the Thames, meant that what London provided him with from the outset was the opportunity simply to view, whether from the expansive perspective of the panoramatist (or privileged observer of the Lord Mayor's procession) or from the narrowed focus encouraged by his remarkable eye for situational detail. This was compounded by his Bockhampton-instilled proclivity for energetic walking, from lodgings that certainly in these early years were at the very edge of London's urban reach: he records bus conductors about to depart from Kilburn still calling out "Any more passengers for London!" (*LW* 44). Towards the end of his life, in a poem often taken for the epitaph it would have been had *Moments of Vision* become the final volume of poetry that Hardy suspected it might, he chose to imagine himself remembered as a man who "used to notice such things" ("Afterwards," *CPW* II: 309). The things in question in that instance were the fleeting phenomena of a natural world seen with such intensity and relish for detail as almost to substitute for mystical apprehension of the divine purposiveness in which Hardy could not believe. The further refinement in the arts of noticing provided by his time in London was arguably as important to Hardy's subsequent imaginative development as the formative years spent in Dorset.

   The contribution made by questions of perspective – by point of view in both literal and metaphorical senses – to Hardy's narrative techniques and the situational contrivances of both his fiction and his poetry has long been recognized, and often associated with his early experience as an architect. Framing, foreshortening, overseeing, and overhearing – with a consequent blurring of borders between the private and the public through the tendency of private perception and public event mutually to inform each other – are the perspectival stock-in-trade of the Hardy plot, as they are of the distinctively Hardyan "satire of circumstance," "moment of vision," "human show," or "little irony." Familiar Hardyan moments of quasi-epiphanic insight depend for their apprehension on the presence of an eye-witness, actual or notional, to record contingent process unfolding and hardening in the mind of the onlooker into the fixity that gives it a meaning that transcends the moment. Hardy's memories of London abound in such moments of translation, moments in which an event is simultaneously both private and public, with its significance located finally in generative interaction between the two.

Here, for example, is part of his description, again for his sister Mary's benefit, of the burial of Lord Palmerston in Westminster Abbey, a striking enough occasion for a 25-year-old trainee architect from Bockhampton to have gained access to:

> Yesterday Lord Palmerston was buried – the Prime Minister. I & the Lees got tickets through a friend of a friend of Mr B's, & we went of course. Our tickets admitted to the triforium, or monk's walk, of Westminster Abbey, & we got from there a complete view of the ceremony. . . . All the Cabinet ministers were there as pall bearers. The burial service was Purcell's. The opening sentences "I am the resurrection &c" were sung to Croft's music. Beethoven's Funeral March was played as they went from the choir to the vault, & the Dead March in Saul was played at the close. I think I was never so much impressed with a ceremony in my life before, & I wd not have missed it for anything. The Prince of Wales and Duke of Cambridge were present.
>
> . . . Only fancy, Ld P. has been connected with the govt off and on for the last 60 years, & that he was contemporaneous with Pitt, Fox, Sheridan, Burke &c. I mean to say his life overlapped theirs so to speak. I sent father a newspaper containing an account of his life, & to day one with an account of the funeral. As you are not a politician I didn't send you one, but since father has taken to reading newspapers these things interest him. (*CL* I: 6)

The translation of unfolding experience into text, even if the texts in this case are only letters and newspaper reports, lifts it above the fleeting and quotidian and locates it within the trans-temporal permanence of an expansive past. This has the double effect of contemporizing Pitt, Fox, Sheridan, and Burke while historicizing Palmerston, and by extension Hardy, his correspondent Mary, and even his father, who, via the newspaper accounts, is associationally brought into this scene as it plays out in Hardy's mind. London was to prove recurrently for Hardy a place in which public and private, like the past and the present, would interfuse with each other in even more complex and resonant ways than the less publicly charged environment of Dorset could generate, central as such apprehensions were in Hardy's experience of Dorset also.

One can see this impulse to engage with a very public (or even mythic) past through the capturing and documentation of important moments in a private present as lying behind what for a few years became something of a London ritual for Hardy. On at least four occasions – July 1870, Waterloo Day (June 18) 1875, Waterloo Day 1876, and October 27, 1878 (less than a week after Trafalgar Day) – he went to Chelsea Hospital to talk with Waterloo veterans. In part this was early preparation for work on Napoleonic projects – most immediately composition of *The Trumpet-Major* but ultimately of *The Dynasts* also, which in *Life and Work* Hardy specifically associates with the 1875 visit to Chelsea. The emphasis in Hardy's accounts of these meetings, rendered almost in a tone of wonder, is on himself seeing those who have seen, on vicarious witnessing:

on Waterloo Day he and his wife went to Chelsea Hospital – it being the 60th
anniversary of the Battle – and made acquaintance with the Waterloo men still surviving
there. Hardy would tell that one of these – a delightful old campaigner named
John Bentley whom he knew to the last – put his arm round Mrs. Hardy's waist, and
interlarded his discourse with "my dear young woman", while he described to her his
experiences of that memorable day, one rather incisive touch in his tale to her being
that through the haze of smoke all that could be discerned was "anything that shined",
such as bayonets, helmets, and swords. (*LW* 109)

Three years later, Hardy's fascination with this kind of visual mediation of the past
through those who have witnessed it is equally apparent:

October 27. – Sunday. To Chelsea Hospital and Ranelagh Gardens: met a palsied
pensioner – deaf. He is 88 – was in the Seventh (?) Hussars. He enlisted in 1807 or
1808, served under Sir John Moore in the Peninsula, through the Retreat, and was at
Waterloo. It was extraordinary to talk and shake hands with a man who had shared in
that terrible winter march to Coruna, and had seen Moore face to face. (*LW* 127)

London provided Hardy with countless opportunities for seeing public figures, on
occasion even rather disreputable ones, "face to face":

On his way to Adelphi Terrace he used to take some short cut near Seven Dials, passing
daily the liquor saloons of Alec Keene and Tom King (?) in West Street (now demolished), and Nat Langham at the top of St. Martin's Lane, when he could sometimes
discern the forms of those famous prize-fighters behind their respective bars. (*LW* 44)

On one of Hardy's visits to Chapman and Hall, Chapman pointed out an elderly
Thomas Carlyle: "Have a good look at him. . . . You'll be glad I pointed him out to
you some day" (*LW* 62). It even seems very possible that lying behind some of those
epistolary name-droppings and lists in *Life and Work* of dignitaries met is nothing
more blameworthy than a fascination with seeing those who have seen.

    Within London's packed historical density an analogous time-transcending effect
was achievable for Hardy from the mere resonance of particular locations; hence the
advantages of a perch atop Adelphi Terrace:

I sat there drawing, inside the easternmost window of the front room on the first floor
above the ground floor, occasionally varying the experience by idling on the balcony. I
saw from there the Embankment and Charing-Cross Bridge built, and of course used
to think of Garrick and Johnson. (*LW* 42)

Hardy would have been witnessing not just the creation of the Victoria Embankment
and Charing Cross Bridge but much of late nineteenth-century imperial London, in
considerable part as we still know it. But there is an important qualification to how
a contemporary viewer, particularly one with as elegiac a cast of mind as Hardy's,
would at the time have experienced such a process. What is for the modern eye, even

after the ravages of the Blitz and modern property development, an iconic institutional core suggestive of the enduring power of fixed architectural form had to have been for Hardy an inchoate, still evolving cityscape undergoing, like those masses of humanity caught within it, almost organic metamorphosis. During just those early pre-marriage periods in London he would have been able to see the construction, in whole or in part, of Holborn Viaduct (1863–9), the Victoria Embankment (1863–70), Queen Victoria Street (1867–71), St. Thomas's Hospital (1868–71), the Royal Courts of Justice (1873–82), Charing Cross Station and Hotel (1863–4), Hungerford Bridge (1863), Cannon Street Station (1865–6), St. Pancras Station (1868–76), the Albert Memorial (1863–75), the Royal Albert Hall (1867–71), the Public Record Office (1851–66), the University of London (1866–9), the Natural History Museum (1873–81), the India Office (1863–8), and the Home and Foreign Offices (1868–73) (see Bradley and Pevsner 2002, 2003; Port 1995). A few years later he would see whole areas swept away as new roads were driven through former slums: Shaftesbury Avenue (opened 1886), Charing Cross Road (opened 1887), the Aldwych and Kingsway (opened 1905), and the completely redesigned ceremonial route of the Mall with the Queen Victoria Memorial at one end and Admiralty Arch at the other (1903–4). The construction of the Embankment had even been responsible for pushing back the Thames itself, rendering the term "Strand" meaningless and marooning some 150 yards from the river the last of the water-gates servicing the former aristocratic houses that had once bordered the Strand. And all that is just a cross-section of what was happening at London's core, without taking into account the relentless continuation of the process of suburbanization that Hardy remembered from childhood as "the *outside* of London creeping towards them across green fields."

In fact London was undergoing during the whole period at which Hardy was most familiar with it the most radical changes it had experienced at any time since the Great Fire, and the wholesale rebuilding that had given rise to. What Hardy must have felt he was witnessing was not so much the birth of modern London as the death of late-medieval London. This was a transformation far more profound and wide-ranging than that undergone by Dorchester, whose changes were pragmatically (but no less regretfully) commented on by Hardy in the speech he gave on the occasion of his being granted the Freedom of the Borough:

> though we may regret the disappearance of many of these old buildings, I cannot be blind to the difficulty of keeping a town in what may be called working order while retaining all its ancient features. . . . Old houses . . . have a far larger commercial value than their owners always remember, and it is only when they have been destroyed, and tourists who have come to see them vow in their disappointment that they will never visit the spot again, that this is realised. . . . if . . . the original All Saints' and Trinity Churches, with their square towers, the Castle, and the fine mansion of the Trenchards at the corner of Shirehall-lane, the old Three Mariners Inn, the old Greyhound, the old Antelope, Lady Abingdon's house at the corner of Durngate-street, and other medieval buildings were still in their places, more visitors of antiquarian tastes would probably haunt the town than even haunt it now. Old All Saints' was, I believe, demolished

because its buttresses projected too far into the street. What a reason for destroying a record of 500 years in stone! I knew the architect who did it. A milder-mannered man never scuttled a sacred edifice. Milton's well-known observation in his *Areopagitica*, "As well kill a man as kill a good book," applies not a little to a good old building, which is not only a book, but a unique manuscript that has no fellow. (*THPV* 320–1)

London in the second half of the nineteenth century was by these lights destroying whole libraries of unique manuscripts. The rapid disappearance of what remained of late-medieval London was one of the stimuli that encouraged the foundation in 1877 by William Morris and Philip Webb of the Society for the Protection of Ancient Buildings. Two years earlier, attempts at least at photographic preservation had begun that would result in the formation of the Society for Photographing Relics of Old London, hurriedly constituted before wholesale development swept the past away so completely as to leave no visual record of what was being lost (see Bush 1975). Many of these threatened buildings were located in wards that had escaped the ravages of the Great Fire, and hence themselves pre-dated it. Appropriate to the prominence of medieval inns in Hardy's list of lost Dorchester buildings and his enduring childhood memory of the Cross-Keys at Clerkenwell, this innovative exercise in early archival photography was initially provoked by the desire of a handful of enthusiasts to pre-serve a record of the famous Oxford Arms in Warwick Lane (first threatened in 1873 and eventually demolished in 1878), one of the last London coaching inns – rendered redundant by the railways whose relentless expansion Hardy had both watched and, during one memorable period, helped enable.

When Hardy supervised the exhumation of human remains during the Midland Railway's construction of a cutting through Old St. Pancras churchyard, the principle of dissolution governing both human beings and the structures they create was brought macabrely home to him in what became an enduring memory, recalled in the writing of "In the Cemetery" (*Satires of Circumstance*, *CPW* II: 143):

> There after nightfall, within a high hoarding that could not be overlooked, and by the light of flare-lamps, the exhumation went on continuously of the coffins that had been uncovered during the day, new coffins being provided for those that came apart in lifting, and for loose skeletons; and those that held together being carried to the new ground on a board merely; Hardy supervising these mournful processions when present – with what thoughts may be imagined. . . . In one coffin that fell apart was a skeleton and two skulls. (*LW* 47)

Hardy's London, at both human and infrastructural levels, made manifest relentless processes of dissolution necessitated by what would today be termed "urban renewal." It would have encouraged him to view destruction and creation as complementary principles, displaying that process of protean matter keeping on keeping on that the Spirit of the Years displays in the Fore Scene of *The Dynasts* as the operation of the Immanent Will.

The "penetrating light" that Years conjures up exhibits "as one organism the anatomy of life and movement in all humanity and vitalized matter." The fuller description that Years offers of this organism echoes central aspects of Hardy's descriptions of London:

> These are the Prime Volitions, – fibrils, veins,
> Will-tissues, nerves, and pulses of the Cause,
> That heave throughout the Earth's compositure.
> Their sum is like the lobule of a Brain
> Evolving always that it wots not of;
> A Brain whose whole connotes the Everywhere,
> And whose procedure may but be discerned
> By phantom eyes like ours; the while unguessed
> Of those it stirs, who (even as ye do) dream
> Their motions free, their orderings supreme;
> Each life apart from each, with power to mete
> Its own days measures; balanced, self-complete;
> Though they subsist but atoms of the One
> Labouring through all, divisible from none.
>
> (*CPW* IV: 21–2)

If not exactly Emma's Lord Mayor's Day "boiling cauldron" of human "porridge," this is very close to Hardy's viewing on the same occasion of the crowd as "an organic whole, a molluscous black creature having nothing in common with humanity . . . whose voice exudes from its scaly coat, and who has an eye in every pore of its body." Thus London was for Hardy a place of disparate and finally irreconcilable phenomena that, far from generating "mechanical and ordinary productions . . . concerning ordinary society-life and habits," evoked haunting visions of dislocation, of relentless impersonalization, and of individual identities subsumed within the molluscous black organism of which they formed part.

For the consciousnesses experiencing them, Hardy's cityscapes are often as drained of meaning and purposiveness as the streets passed through by J. Alfred Prufrock, in a poem in which Hardy, in his late seventies, took sufficient interest to transcribe more than twenty lines into his literary notebooks (*LN* II: 226–7). In light of his noting of work by Eliot – identified as "a poet of the vers-libre school" (*LN* II: 227) – Hardy's own poem "Coming Up Oxford Street: Evening" provides fitting encapsulation of London's profound influence on a sensibility that younger modernist writers (though, ironically, not Eliot himself) often found sympathetic – to a perhaps surprising degree given Hardy's secure status as eminent Victorian. This poem is a good example of what was described earlier as the passing epiphanic moment stopped in time, of form being imposed on contingent process in its translation into text. In fact we even know on what day the moment occurred since the poem, not published until 1925, has the appended notation "As seen 4 July 1872." The fifty-year gap between conception and public appearance may explain the change from the first-person stance used in the manuscript to the poem's eventual adoption of a third-person perspective. Its structure counterposes the dominating elemental sun – like Egdon Heath, "having been ere man was" – against the bleakly ruminative mind of Hardy's version of Eliot's prematurely old, disenchanted, and communicatively challenged young man.

Even without the textual evidence of the change from first to third person, and the standard Hardyan feint of transposing a poem's ratiocinative burden onto the convenient shoulders of a substitute persona, this surely impresses itself on the reader as a recollection of aspects of Hardy's own young self:

> The sun from the west glares back,
> And the sun from the watered track,
> And the sun from the sheets of glass,
> And the sun from each window-brass;
> Sun-mirrorings, too, brighten
> From show-cases beneath
> The laughing eyes and teeth
> Of ladies who rouge and whiten.
> And the same warm god explores
> Panels and chinks of doors;
> Problems with chymists' bottles
> Profound as Aristotle's
> He solves, and with good cause,
> Having been ere man was.
>
> Also he dazzles the pupils of one who walks west,
> A city-clerk, with eyesight not of the best,
> Who sees no escape to the very verge of his days
> From the rut of Oxford Street into open ways;
> And he goes along with head and eyes flagging forlorn,
> Empty of interest in things, and wondering why he was born.
>   *As seen 4 July 1872 (CPW III: 25)*

As we know, although he could not have known it himself at the time, Hardy was about to escape from the ruts of both Oxford Street and architecture into "open ways." His London society novel *The Poor Man and the Lady* might have failed to find a publisher, and less than three months before his Oxford Street experience Tinsley had returned him the £59. 12s. 7d. that was all he would ever see of his £75 investment in the publication of *Desperate Remedies*. But *Under the Greenwood Tree* had just been published the previous month, and he was about to sign a £200 contract with Tinsley for *A Pair of Blue Eyes*. Professionally at least, the sunny uplands were about to beckon. But this cameo London moment snatched from temporal oblivion – "head and eyes flagging forlorn, / Empty of interest in things, and wondering why he was born" – takes us straight back to the Bockhampton child, face covered by a straw hat, "lying on his back in the sun, thinking how useless he was . . . [r]eflecting on his experiences of the world so far as he had got" and forced "to the conclusion that he did not wish to grow up" (*LW* 20). They are poignantly complementary moments in the evolution of a richly creative sensibility to which London finally contributed almost as much as Dorset.

References and Further Reading

Björk, Lennart A. (ed.) (1985). *The Literary Notebooks of Thomas Hardy*, 2 vols. London and Basingstoke: Macmillan.

Bradley, Simon, and Nikolaus Pevsner (2002). *London I: The City of London*. New Haven: Yale University Press.

Bradley, Simon, and Nikolaus Pevsner (2003). *London VI: Westminster*. New Haven: Yale University Press.

Bush, Graham (1975). *Old London: Photographed by Henry Dixon and Alfred & John Bool for the Society for Photographing Relics of Old London*. London: Academy Editions.

Chalfont, Fran (1992–3). Hardy's Residences and Lodgings: Parts One, Two, and Three. *Thomas Hardy Journal*, 8(3), 46–56; 9(1), 41–61; 9(2), 19–38.

Gilmore, Dehn (2004). Vacuums and Blurs: The Related Responses of Thomas Hardy and the French Impressionists to the Modern City. *Literary London: Interdisciplinary Studies in the Representation of London*, 2 (1), <http://www.literarylondon.org/london-journal/march2004/gilmore.html>.

Hardy, Thomas ([1873] 1985). *A Pair of Blue Eyes*, ed. Alan Manford. Oxford: Oxford University Press.

Hardy, Thomas ([1876] 1996). *The Hand of Ethelberta*, ed. Tim Dolin. London: Penguin.

Hardy, Thomas ([serialized 1892; 1897] 1997). *The Pursuit of the Well-Beloved* and *The Well-Beloved*, ed. Patricia Ingham. London: Penguin.

Hardy, Thomas (1982–95). *The Complete Poetical Works of Thomas Hardy*, ed. Samuel Hynes, 5 vols. Oxford: Clarendon Press.

Hardy, Thomas (1984). *The Life and Work of Thomas Hardy*, ed. Michael Millgate. London: Macmillan.

Millgate, Michael (2004). *Thomas Hardy: A Biography Revisited*. Oxford: Oxford University Press.

Page, Norman (2000). London. In Norman Page (ed.), *Oxford Reader's Companion to Thomas Hardy* (pp. 243–6). Oxford: Oxford University Press.

Port, M. H. (1995). *Imperial London: Civil Government Building in London 1851–1915*. New Haven: Yale University Press.

Purdy, Richard Little, and Michael Millgate (eds.) (1978–88). *The Collected Letters of Thomas Hardy*, 7 vols. Oxford: Clarendon Press.

Sherman, George Witter (1948). The Influence of London on *The Dynasts*. *PMLA*, 63(3), 1017–28.

Sherman, George Witter (1949). The Wheel and the Beast: The Influence of London on Thomas Hardy. *Nineteenth-Century Fiction*, 4(3), 209–19.

Slater, Michael (1994). Hardy and the City. In Charles P. C. Pettit (ed.), *New Perspectives on Thomas Hardy* (pp. 41–57). London and Basingstoke: Palgrave Macmillan.

Widdowson, Peter (1989). *Hardy in History: A Study in Literary Sociology*. London and New York: Routledge.

11

"A Thickness of Wall": Hardy and Class

Roger Ebbatson

> *Separate individuals form a class only insofar as they have to carry on a common battle against another class.*
>
> (Karl Marx [1846] 1996: 82)

> *A great storyteller will always be rooted in the people, primarily in a milieu of craftsmen.*
>
> (Walter Benjamin [1955] 1999: 100)

Our examination of Hardy's responsiveness to issues of social class might begin with a characteristically illusory "moment of vision":

> Some way within the limits of the stretch of landscape, points of light like the topaz gleamed. The air increased in transparency with the lapse of minutes, till the topaz points showed themselves to be the vanes, windows, wet roof slates, and other shining spots upon the spires, domes, freestone-work, and varied outlines that were faintly revealed. It was Christminster, unquestionably; either directly seen, or miraged in the peculiar atmosphere. (*JO* 17)

As a trainee mason, Jude Fawley begins to "see his way to living comfortably in Christminster in the course of a year or two, and knocking at the doors of one of those strongholds of learning of which he had dreamed so much" (*JO* 33). As an autodidact scholar, however, he sees those same doors opening onto a clerical career which would elevate him into the upper echelons of Victorian society – in his own mind, he is set to become at least an archdeacon. The arrival of the pig's pizzle over the hedge at this moment of class aspiration, with its hints of boundaries and transgression, notates not only an investment in "false consciousness" on the hero's part, but also signposts the culmination of the novel when, after the deaths of the children, Jude returns to work in Christminster, mounting "the parapets and copings of colleges he could never enter" (*JO* 363). Hardy's treatment here is unremittingly determinist: despite the momentary class solidarity of his Remembrance Day homily as "Tutor of St. Slums" (*JO* 343),

Jude remains isolated, a victim of what Georg Lukács would identify as "status-consciousness," "a real historical factor" which "masks" class consciousness and in effect "prevents it from emerging at all" (Lukács [1923] 1971: 58). *Jude the Obscure* traces those processes which would lead, in a Lukácsian analysis, to "the veiling or the exposure of the class character of society" ([1923] 1971: 59). In the nineteenth century as a whole, as Gary Day has argued in terms applicable to both Jude and his creator,

> the concept of class functions both as a way of understanding the organisation of society and as a means of transcending it. It can thus be seen as an idea that combines two contradictory elements: the principle of form – society as composed of classes – and the principle of the transcendence of form – the move beyond the present class-divided society to a "classless" one. (Day 2001: 100)

Jude and Sue are destined never to achieve such transcendence; to the contrary, on their return to Christminster they take lodgings in Mildew Lane, "a narrow lane close to the back of a college," but significantly "having no communication with it" (*JO* 347). The houses here are "darkened to gloom by the high collegiate buildings," ultimate sign of class separation and oppression. Within these walls, "life was so far removed from that of the people in the lane as if it had been on opposite sides of the globe," and yet "only a thickness of wall divided them" (*JO* 348).[1] It is in this ambience, dominated by the "silent, black and windowless" outer walls of Sarcophagus College (*JO* 351), that the couple are plunged into crisis by the actions of Little Father Time. The institutionalization of class privilege at Christminster stands as evidence of what Lukács terms "the utter sterility of an ideology divorced from life" – Oxford here embodying "the world-historical irrelevances and nullities of its own existence" marked by "an unfailing sign of decay" (Lukács [1923] 1971: 67).

Narratives of class in Hardy take two countervailing forms: first, in both the art and the life, as a story about self-culture in an upward trajectory in which the subjects – Hardy or his fictional avatars – become agents rather than objects of history. Secondly, class consciousness widely operates to shape a story of separation, exclusion, and failure. The sense of unavailing class struggle which pervades *Jude* is largely absent in the unruffled affiliations of earlier novels, where the stress falls upon homogeneity and solidarity, as for instance in the emergence of the Mellstock Quire, in *Under the Greenwood Tree*, from the imperviosity of nature:

> Scuffling halting irregular footsteps of various kinds were now heard coming up the hill, and presently there emerged from the shade severally five men of different ages and gaits – all of them working villagers of the parish of Mellstock. They too had lost their rotundity with the daylight, and advanced against the sky in flat outlines, which suggested some processional design on Greek or Etruscan pottery. They represented the chief portion of Mellstock parish choir. (*UGT* 12)

Yet even here, in the sociality of rural Dorset, it is the promptings of sexuality and social ambition which disturb the even tenor of rural life and custom, a disturbance registered in the reception of Fancy Day's boot, Mr. Penny perceiving that "the interest the object had excited was greater than he had anticipated," sign and referent of "'as neat a little figure of fun as ever I see'" (*UGT* 24, 25). As Rosemary Jann argues, frequently Hardy's rustics "function as agents of class rivalry," their characteristic behavior serving "to define by contrast the kinds of subjectivity that justify the higher social positions of the more central characters" (Jann 2000: 411).

This essay seeks to examine the class implications of the trajectory from the comedy of *Under the Greenwood Tree*, a text founded in the history and culture of the folk, to the tragedy of *Tess of the d'Urbervilles*, in which the suffering female field-laborers stand cut off from the promise of happiness. It is at Flintcomb-Ash that the former milk-maids fall victim to the class divisions inherent in the exigencies of landownership and capital:

> The swede-field, in which [Tess] and her companion were set hacking, was a stretch of a hundred odd acres, in one patch, on the highest ground of the farm, rising above stony lanchets or lynchets – the outcrop of siliceous veins in the chalk formation, composed of myriads of loose white flints in bulbous, cusped, and phallic shapes . . . Every leaf of the vegetable having already been consumed the whole field was in colour a desolate drab; it was a complexion without features, as if a face from chin to brow should be only an expanse of skin. (*TD* 277)

The girls live upon "memories of green, sunny romantic Talbothays," in a moving embodiment of Walter Benjamin's theory of the decline of the aura, defined as the "unique phenomenon of a distance" (Benjamin [1955] 1999: 216), under the impress of modernity:

> "You can see a gleam of a hill within a few miles o' Froom Valley from here when 'tis fine," said Marian.
>
> "Ah – can you?" said Tess, awake to the new value of this locality. (*TD* 278)

In Benjamin's account, "The decline of the aura and the waning of the dream of a better nature – this latter conditional on its defensive position in the class struggle – are one and the same" (Benjamin [1982] 2002: 362). The class antagonism which motivates the momentum of *Tess* and leads to this "calvary of labour" is already enunciated at the outset, in the refusal of the Clare brothers to join in the Marlott May-dance: "Dancing in public with a troop of country hoydens – suppose we should be seen!" (*TD* 22).

Hardy is, indeed, in such stories as "The Son's Veto" or "To Please His Wife," a keen vivisectionist of that snobbery which would mark and mar his own life – Max Gate was to become ultimately off-limits to his own family down the road at Stinsford – while the reader is at a loss as to what to make of many revealing passages in his covert autobiography:

In London this spring [the Hardys] again met many people, the popularity of Hardy as an author now making him welcome anywhere. For the first time they took a whole house, 70 Hamilton Terrace, and brought up their own servants, and found themselves much more comfortable under this arrangement than they had been before.

While getting into the house, however, Hardy stayed with their friends the Jeunes, and met there among many others "the Bancrofts, Miss Mary Moore, Mr Goschen, Lord and Lady Wimborne, Miss Julia Peel, Lady Louisa Loder, Lady Hilda Brodrick and her husband, Sir Spencer Ponsonby Fane, Lord Sudeley, and Mr Peel." (*LW* 268)

These class-inflected reminiscences refer to the Hardys' social life in the spring of 1893, not long after the publication of *Tess*, with its portrayal of the lives of the immiserated field-workers. Peter Widdowson is surely right to argue that this "is not simply snobbery of some sort, but the irresistible result of class mobility"; in this reading, Hardy is rendered *déclassé* by virtue of his profession, "and within that position, as a *petit-bourgeois arriviste*, he could not speak of his social origins" (Widdowson 1989: 141). The corollary of this is everywhere evident in the *Life and Work*, not least in the heightened status accorded to Hardy's own family, in the guarded silence concerning his political views, and in the circling around the fascinatingly eroticized topic of aristocratic young women.

In *Tess* itself, the devotion of the two Clare brothers to the perusal of *A Counterblast to Agnosticism* is ultimately less disastrous than Angel Clare's determination to broach class barriers in his pursuit of the heroine. The brothers "leant over the gate by the highway" (*TD* 22), but it is Angel who proceeds to open it, the entanglements of class and sex rendered in a moment of textual density to be reduplicated in the heroine's later encounter with Alec d'Urberville. While "Sir" John Durbeyfield claims to be "head o' the noblest branch of the family" (*TD* 39), it is Alec who, benefiting from his father's "annexation" of the aristocratic d'Urberville name, will stage the "tragic mischief" of the action, functioning as "the blood-red ray in the spectrum of [Tess's] young life" (*TD* 45). This is nothing other than a drama of class misrecognition, the inheritor of a northern merchant "passing" as a minor aristocrat. Tess, having "dreamed of an aged and dignified face, the sublimation of all the d'Urberville lineaments," finds herself confronted with a dandy displaying a "swarthy complexion," "full lips" and "well-groomed black moustache with curled points" (*TD* 43). The notation here is of a class ambivalence already signaled in Tess's assumption of both dialect and standard speech patterns, and further exploited in Alec's transformation into evangelical preacher. These slippery markers of class distinction stem from the temporizing inherent in the author's own situation. The instance of class oscillation offered by Alec d'Urberville is a sign of conflict between the psyche and the economic structure in a formation which transmutes people into "types." Social identity is transformed by means of a doubling between inner and outer worlds, as in the phenomenon of Alec as "ranter" and "converted man," which is "less a reform than a transfiguration," his former "riotousness" "evangelised today into the splendour of pious rhetoric" (*TD* 297). These inconsistencies in Alec's demeanor serve to interrogate the social construction of identity by demonstrating that the self may be counterfeited in ways peculiarly available to the middle class.

Tess's putative passage into that class is signposted by her command of "two languages," "the dialect at home" and "ordinary English abroad and to persons of quality" (*TD* 26). As a writer for the English Dialect Society observed in 1888, the rural poor were now, under the influence of the Board Schools, "learning two distinct tongues," so that a child who could "read correctly, giving accent, aspirates (painfully), intonation, and all the rest of it, according to rule," would at home "go back to his vernacular" (cited in Phillipps 1984: 87–8). This bilingualism is also practiced by the "well-trained and even proficient masters," Phillotson and Gillingham, who "occasionally used a dialect-word of their boyhood to each other in private" (*JO* 240). Such linguistic slippage confirmed the fact that language was "a principal, precise, pragmatic, and subtle way of defining one's position, or of having it defined by others" (Phillipps 1984: 3). While such characters inhabit a linguistic transition zone, it is clear that in the overall picture, as John Barrell observes, "there occurred a large-scale subjugation of provincial English, and the modes of expression of the different social classes, to the norms of the elite" (Barrell 1983: 112). That process is dramatized in Michael Henchard's expostulations with Elizabeth-Jane over her slipping into the very dialect forms gradually removed from the mayor's own speech patterns in successive versions of the text. Henchard fires up at his supposed daughter's usage of folk idioms in which he hears her "talk like a clodhopper" (*MC* 136), and the result is an immediate gentrification of her spoken idiom:

> The sharp reprimand was not lost upon her, and in time it came to pass that for "fay" she said "succeed"; that she no longer spoke of "dumbledores" but of "humble bees"; no longer said of young men and women that they "walked together," but that they were "engaged"; that she grew to talk of "greggles" as "wild hyacinths"; that when she had not slept she did not quaintly tell the servants next morning that she had been "hagrid," but that she had "suffered from indigestion." (*MC* 130)

Despite the injustices of class difference to which Hardy is alert, as Jann suggests, "certain middling characters" are seen as possessing "the emotional, moral, and intellectual distinction that justifies their upward social mobility from the border class in which they begin" (Jann 2000: 413). Hardy moves, under the pressures of the literary market, and the class-inflected nuances of his own mystified social origins and upwardly mobile marriage, from the stable social formations of the early work towards the conflictual model of *The Mayor of Casterbridge*, *Tess*, or *Jude the Obscure*. His texts grow increasingly self-conscious about the ways in which their characters relate to one another via the productive forces of Victorian rural society. In this bleak scenario systems of exchange come to dominate human relations, in ways elaborated by Gary Day:

Abstract labour power, in the form of money, is exchanged for actual labour power, the worker's concrete capacity to produce commodities. However, this is an unequal exchange since . . . its essence is the extraction of surplus value. Exchange, in short, reflects the dominance of the bourgeoisie. (Day 2001: 136)

While the village worthies of the early texts produce their means of subsistence within a humane environment, the later fiction refracts Marx's notion that circumstances make men (and women), individuality being subsumed within the logic of capital, just as the field-laborers become enslaved to the steam-threshing machine. The highly developed consciousness, in Hardy's diagnosis, leads to separation from the community – a process which commences with Clym Yeobright on Egdon Heath and culminates in Christminster.

In the subtext of Hardy's work the power of one class to oppress another gains momentum with inexorable force: the class representing the advancement of the productive elements of the society stands as inheritor of political power. It was this class which Hardy, in a creative state of self-division, both envied and critiqued, and it is his ambivalence which motivates the fiction, a body of work in which use-value – the unmediated relation of the worker to his or her product – gives place to exchange-value. This was a transition frequently masked by a new moral terminology, so that, from the mid-century onwards, as Geoffrey Crossick has argued, there is "less talk of 'working class' and 'middle class,' and more of 'deserving' and 'undeserving poor,' of 'respectable artisans' and 'gentlemen,' as a good proportion of society (including much of the working class) came to concentrate on divisions which emphasised moral rather than economic criteria" (Crossick 1991: 161–2). Michael Henchard, in taking his vow of abstinence, subscribes to this moral scheme and rises socially as a consequence; however, in gambling upon the effects of the harvest weather, the mayor transforms himself from a non-capitalist to a capitalist form of economy, moving from the direct satisfaction of wants towards a desperate ploy for creating profit. It is, indeed, the pursuit of profit which marks both the capitalist (Donald Farfrae, Farmer Groby, et al.) and the miser (Uncle Benjy in *The Trumpet-Major*). While in the eighteenth century class carried implications of rank, in Victorian England it was determined by one's place in the productive system. This is the crucial problematic for Hardy himself as a member of a village artisanal class fraction with ambitions to join the professionalizing middle class, first as architect then as author. Torn between loyalty to a vanishing rural life-world and the pressures of a metropolitan culture, Hardy himself speaks two dialects; and, like the author, the workers who bring their labor to market, despite the richness of their folk heritage, are drawn into the equations of labor power and surplus value desiderated by Marx, becoming subject to the exploitation of their labor by capital. Marx noted that, beside the "physical element of labour," which was determined by "a *traditional standard of life*," "It is not mere physical life, but it is the satisfaction of certain wants springing up from the social conditions in which people are placed and reared up" (Marx 1969: 71). It is these cultural satisfactions to which Hardy was both acutely sensitive and symptomatically inattentive:

Here is the ancient floor,
Footworn and hollowed and thin,
Here was the former door
Where the dead feet walked in.

She sat here in her chair,
Smiling into the fire;
He who played stood there,
Bowing it higher and higher.

Childlike, I danced in a dream;
Blessings emblazoned that day;
Everything glowed with a gleam;
Yet we were looking away!

("The Self-Unseeing," *CPV* 166–7)

The novels trace a course from the village economies of *Under the Greenwood Tree* or *Far From the Madding Crowd* to the immiseration of the workfolk in *Tess* or *Jude*, in which the Great Depression functions to produce a "reserve army" of itinerant labor. As the accumulation of productive capital increases, so do this surplus population and its misery. The craftspeople celebrated for their skills are gradually reduced in this historic movement, transformed into unskilled components of the productive process, in ways Marx had predicted: "as the division of labour increases, labour is simplified. The special skill of the worker becomes worthless. He [sic] becomes transformed into a monotonous productive force . . . His labour becomes a labour that anyone can perform" (Marx 1977: 265). Elsewhere, Marx observed how the "automaton consists of a number of mechanical and intellectual organs, so that the workers themselves can be no more than conscious limbs of the automaton" (Marx [1925] 1971: 132):

> Close under the eaves of the stack, and as yet barely visible was the red tyrant that the women had come to serve – a timber-framed construction, with straps and wheels appertaining – the threshing-machine, which, whilst it was going, kept up a despotic demand upon the endurance of their muscles and nerves. (*TD* 315)

Thus it comes about, for instance, that Farfrae's vaunted seed-drill, "a sort of agricultural piano" in Lucetta's view (*MC* 167), is set to evolve, in Engels' definition, into a "powerful weapon in the war of capital against the working class," so that "the very product of the worker is turned into an instrument for his subjugation" (Marx 1970: 140). K. D. M. Snell has argued that Hardy's novels "rarely enter seriously and sympathetically into the area of labourers' values, priorities, and subjective experience," and that they are "reticent on the actual conditions of life in Dorset":

> On the low wages and unemployment; on the prevalence of and reasons for religious nonconformity; on the reality and character of political belief; on the agricultural union-ism and bitterness of class antagonism; on labourers' attitudes to work and the use of

the land; on working-class sexuality; on familial relationships and the treatment of the elderly; on the notorious hostility to the New Poor Law and its administrators. (Snell 1987: 392)

This is worth pondering, but is perhaps an overly simplified reading of the literary text with its gaps and indeterminacies. However, it is certainly the case that Hardy's most direct treatment of the predicament of the rural working class lies not in his novels but in his non-fiction essay, "The Dorsetshire Labourer," which first appeared in *Longman's Magazine* in July 1883.

Hardy suggests that the image of "Hodge" does not do justice to the variety of working folk, and he proposes that a "pure atmosphere and a pastoral environment are a very appreciable portion of the sustenance which tends to produce the sound mind and body, and thus much sustenance is, at least, the labourer's birthright" (*THPV* 41). Hardy is insistent that the Dorset dialect, "instead of being a vile cor- ruption of cultivated speech, was a tongue with a grammatical inflection": "Having attended the National School they would mix the printed tongue as taught therein with the unwritten, dying, Wessex English" (*THPV* 40). A false view of agricultural workers has arisen from the vantage point of "philosophers who look down upon that class from the Olympian heights of society," often mistaking cleanliness for dirt in the cottages they choose to visit (*THPV* 41). Anyone wishing to observe the field- laborer *in extremis* should visit a wet hiring-fair at Candlemas (February 2), Hardy notes, and he proceeds to give a grim portrait of a superannuated shepherd waiting hopelessly for employment (a passage reworked in *The Mayor of Casterbridge*). Hardy suggests that the clothing adopted by the field-workers has become more compatible with that of the townsfolk, and contrasts it with the smock frocks, shepherds' crooks, and appurtenances of earlier times. There is now a general post in the countryside on Old Style Lady Day (April 6), when the laborer's furniture, belongings, and family are piled on a wagon sent by his new employer. At such times the roads are full of movement, reflecting Hardy's sense of an increasing migratory tendency in the rural economy. He concedes a loss of the picturesque, but argues that "Change is also a certain sort of education": "Many advantages accrue to the labourers from the varied experience it brings, apart from the discovery of the best market for their abilities" (*THPV* 48–9). The laborer is losing his individuality and an "increasing nomadic habit" is inevitably leading to "a less intimate and kindly relation with the land he tills" (*THPV* 49–50). On the land, the laborer is becoming more independent, thanks largely to the agricultural union movement. Hardy concludes his essay by describing the extensive nature of female labor, and lamenting the depopulation going on in the villages. As he remarks, "the question of the Dorset cottager here merges in that of all the houseless and landless poor" (*THPV* 57). In my critique of this essay, I have suggested that it "simultaneously speaks for, and silences, a social group which lacks its own public articulation, and in its descriptive fullness notably fails to provide the kind of analysis which would expose and examine the structuration of consciousness through material conditions." The essay, in this reading, "represents an aestheticised response to its subject" (Ebbatson 1993: 134). However, it remains the case that consideration of "The Dorsetshire Labourer" is crucial to an understanding of class in Hardy's work and to his sense of the crisis and amelioration which accompanied the Great Depression. Pauperism is one of the concomitants of capital, as both the Durbeyfields and the Fawleys would attest. The external character of work, for the milkmaids at Flintcomb-Ash, or for Jude at Christminster, means that they labor not for themselves but for an other. As we see in the steam-threshing scene, or in Jude's bird-scaring, the human body functions as the site of both signification and labor: in the labor-process, the hired laborer is stripped of a sense of purpose as surely as the trouserless Abel Whittle is compelled to report for work by Michael Henchard.

However, the implications of class issues in Hardy's work are not susceptible to explication solely through the overtly rational frame of Marxian theory. In two aspects, the depiction of familial relations and the portrayal of women, Hardy's life and work are furrowed by lines of indirection and secrecy, not least in relation to his own family background and history: "Behind the eminent author . . . there lurked the ghosts of those lower-class relations consigned to silence" (Ebbatson 2004: 115). Hardy's studious evasion of social origins leads towards that return of the repressed which is so marked a feature of his work, from Stephen Smith's revisiting his native Cornwall to the more portentous returns of Clym Yeobright or Susan Henchard. As early as *A Pair of Blue Eyes*, Rosemary Jann observes, we see the complications inherent in the distinctions between the older gentry and the rising professional: "Stephen's correspondence-course versions of chess and Latin suggest how difficult it is for one in his position to carry off gentlemanly accomplishments" (Jann 2000: 418). The characters thus enact the function of the double, a figure generated by the uncanny in a complex of the homely/unhomely which this writing circles around. The disturbances in Hardy's texts are related to this act of class repression and the consequent return of that which is, in Freudian terms, all too familiar. The narrative trajectory of social improvement, the aesthetic self-help which dominates Hardy's motivation, is counteracted by that countervailing trajectory of failure and exposure dramatically staged by the furmity-woman in relation to Michael Henchard and the wife-sale. Having put together the fanciful "Hardy Pedigree" and toyed with altering his name to "Le Hardy," the novelist concluded, "So we go down, down, down" (*LW* 224). The splitting of the self that begins with Smith/Knight and culminates with Angel/Alec or Jude/Sue is the signature of an author who is self-divided in respect to social class.

The figure of the double in Hardy emerges not out of the penumbra of the Gothic but from the writerly attempt to contain elements of social shame and impoverishment in his own family history. The revenant or the phantom here inhabits not the Gothic castle but Mixen Lane or Rolliver's. In Freud's definition, the uncanny "is that class of the frightening which leads us back to what is known of old and long familiar" (Freud [1919] 1985: 340). Hardy's texts explore that complex in simultaneously opening up and censoring the issue of class origins: in his case the uncanny is precisely "something which is familiar and old-established in the mind and which has become alienated from it only through the process of repression" ([1919] 1985: 363–4). Both the construction of Max Gate and the cultivation of aristocratic connections bear witness to the anxiety of that which "ought to have remained secret but has come to light" ([1919] 1985: 345) – in Hardy's case his kinship with the disreputable Hands and Antells in Puddletown. From the idea of the home, as Freud puts it, the sense of "belonging to the house," the further idea is developed "of something withdrawn from the eyes of strangers, something concealed, secret" ([1919] 1985: 346), and he even cites as an instance of the uncanny, "a *hand* cut off at the wrist" ([1919] 1985: 366, italics added). Under pressure of circumstance, Hardy produces a series of haunted texts in which the "dread and horror" to which Freud's essay alludes is triggered by the anxiety concerning social "death." The forbidding architectural redoubt of Max Gate embodied this social contamination of the uncanny. In existential terms, the writer lives in the "house of Being" constituted by language in a state neither living nor dead, haunted by dread of the return of a revenant traced by an undefined social stigma:

> We two kept house, the Past and I,
>   The Past and I;
> Through all my tasks it hovered nigh,
>   Leaving me never alone.
> It was a spectral housekeeping
>   Where fell no jarring tone,
> As strange, as still a housekeeping
>   As ever has been known.
>
> ("The Ghost of the Past," *CPV* 308)

Thus Thomas Hardy's career, in ways which John Goode, Joe Fisher, and Peter Widdowson have fruitfully explored, involved a complicated negotiation with the literary market. Writing is indeed, as Goode argues, "both an institution which has to be negotiated and an agency of self-improvement" (Goode 1988: 142). For Widdowson, Hardy's village artisanal origins are important, "but only within the frame of the upwardly-mobile professional writer operating in a metropolitan, upper-class dominated, social and literary culture" (Widdowson 1989: 130). The pauper background of Hardy's mother and his own partly autodidactic motivation worked to produce the writer's accommodations with, and scorn for, editorial constraints, and served to elicit what Widdowson defines as "an inferiority complex, in which a disdainful superiority protects Hardy from admitting the desired participation" in a constant process of "many-layered and schizophrenic deception" (1989: 147).

Hardy's writing is haunted by the invisible presence of the rural poor, most notably that of his own familial relations in Dorset, in ways which might be related to Marxian political economy. As Jacques Derrida has shown, Marx's work is dominated by a kind of "hauntology": in the exordium to the *Communist Manifesto* we are told, "A spectre is haunting Europe." Derrida points, in terms applicable to the action of *A Laodicean*, to ways in which an "alliance of the worried conspirators assembles, more or less secretly, a nobility and a clergy, in the old castle of Europe, for an unbelievable expedition against what will have been haunting the night of these masters" (Derrida 1994: 40). As Hardy's writing project evolves from the delineation of the use-value economies towards the exchange-value society of modernity, we may be prompted to demand, with Derrida, how "living men, temporal and finite existences, become subjected, in their social relations, to these spectres that are relations, *equally social* relations among commodities." In the course of this process, "ghosts that are commodities transform human producers into ghosts" (Derrida 1994: 154, 156). "'Ought I to be afeard o'nights, Master Fairway?'' demands Christian Cantle on Egdon Heath, and receives the disturbing information that it is "'but to single sleepers that a ghost shows himself when 'a do come.'" "'The heth isn't haunted,'" Christian reassures himself, adding, "'but we'd better get home'" (*RN* 24, 27). This dislimning of the body of the folk under the pressure of capitalization is "a production of ghosts, illusions, simulacra, appearances, or apparitions" (Derrida 1994: 45). And, as Tim Armstrong suggests, it is the ghost which is, paradoxically, "the product of modernity and the modes of historicity which the modern gives birth to" (Armstrong 2000: 2). In accommodating himself to the market and entry into the professional middle classes, Hardy was haunted by voices from the past in ways which demonstrate the inevitability of spectral revenance, that return of the repressed which is most marked in connection with his own occluded class relations. Across the entire writing project falls the shadow of that which is lost (memory of the folk) and the heavy responsibility of recording that loss – a responsibility that Hardy, in his negotiation with modernity, both sought and evaded.

The past in Hardy is always destined to be lost and is entailed in a sense of history as motivated class struggle in which nature functions as unregenerate and unchanging:

> His daily life was of a curious microscopic sort, his whole world being limited to a circuit of a few feet from his person. His familiars were creeping and winged things, and they seemed to enroll him in their band. Bees hummed around his ears with an intimate air, and tugged at the heath and furze-flowers at his side in such numbers as to weigh them down to the sod. The strange amber-coloured butterflies which Egdon produced . . . quivered in the breath of his lips, alighted upon his bowed back, and sported with the glittering point of his hook as he flourished it up and down. (*RN* 253–4)

Clym Yeobright's furze-cutting offers a finely tuned registration of class and labor; the goggles he is obliged to don because of his loss of sight would have secured dismissal for a worker, but in this instance partial blindness is a sign of knowledge. Seeing him working in this way, Eustacia chooses to construct her husband as "a poor afflicted man, earning money by the sweat of his brow" (*RN* 254), and appeals to him to "leave off this shameful labour" (*RN* 255). At such a juncture Eustacia registers the distinction between Clym's gentlemanly espousal of agricultural work and the economic necessity which drives the workers on Egdon. Such a potent scene is complicated by the ironies and anguish of Hardy's own class position in ways articulated in Tim Armstrong's analysis of the mode in which, in Hardy, "inheritance is experienced as haunting" (Armstrong 2000: 35–6). *The Dynasts*, Armstrong observes, depicts characters "sleepwalking through the dream of reality, with the 'real' forces driving history invisible to them" (2000: 36). This imbrication of class and ghostliness is tellingly projected in a late poem, "The Little Old Table":

> Creak, little wood thing, creak,
> When I touch you with elbow or knee;
> That is the way you speak
> Of one who gave you to me!
>
> You, little table, she brought –
> Brought me with her own hand,
> As she looked at me with a thought
> That I did not understand.
>
> – Whoever owns it anon,
> And hears it, will never know
> What a history hangs upon
> This creak from long ago.
>
> (*CPV* 648–9)

The "thought" which Hardy "did not understand" relates to the aspirations which Jemima Hardy focused upon her son, aspirations rendered the more intense by her harsh upbringing in Melbury Osmond, where her own mother was in receipt of Poor Law dole. Jemima began work as a servant at the age of 13, and her experiences frame and complicate the history of the table. Derrida, in his reading of Marx's table, defines the seismic change involved in the switch from use-value to exchange-value as a moment of spectrality:

> To say that the same thing, the wooden table for example, comes on stage as commodity after having been but an ordinary thing in its use-value is to grant an origin to the ghostly moment. Its use-value, Marx seems to imply, was intact. It was what it was, use-value, identical to itself. The phantasmagoria, like capital, would begin with exchange-value and the commodity-form. It is only then that the ghost "comes on stage." (Derrida 1994: 159)

The Thomas Hardy who discerns "the ghost of a perished day" ("A Procession of Dead Days," *CPV* 644) is one who is preternaturally conscious of the "other me" ("He Follows Himself," *CPV* 646) – that loss of self-identity and doubling of the personality which generates a guilt both personal (the death of Emma) and social (the betrayal of his own roots). The proletarian body of the folk and the female body of desire are both suppressed or subject to transformations in the act of writing in a process of acculturation which is simultaneously enabling and disabling for the author. This nexus of feeling is present in embryonic form, as it were, in the incident of the youthful Hardy's "adoption" by Julia Augusta Martin of the Kingston Maurward estate, and by Jemima's jealous intervention in the burgeoning relationship. Years later, Hardy could still resuscitate "throbs of tender feeling" and the memory of "the thrilling 'frou-frou' of her four grey silk flounces when she had used to bend over him, and when they brushed against the font as she entered church" (*LW* 104–5). The origins of the entire "poor man and the lady" syndrome are to be located here, and would be ultimately worked out with numbing effect within the walls of Max Gate. The theme of the poor man and the lady is an expression of relationships between marginality, sexual identity, social class, and language in which the aspirant male seeks to cross a boundary. A story like "An Indiscretion in the Life of an Heiress" functions as a border-text in which the schoolmaster insists that his public role does not accord with his real self and seeks to escape the classroom through romantic involvement with an heiress. Giving up teaching for writing, Egbert Mayne attempts to raise himself socially through literary production in a way which refracts the experience of his creator. Geraldine Allenville's only role is to energize her literary admirer, after which she dies in a deathbed scene whose lack of motivation underlines the contradictions thrown up by class aspiration. The sense of radical difference, Hardy acknowledges here, can only be represented as an experience of borders, and the question of gender is bound up with that of social class – the high-born lady etherealized and rendered immobile by a phallocentric awareness of sexual and social "difference." The ellipses so prevalent in Hardy's writing stem from this problematic, characteristically rendered as an abortive marriage plot. Himself living upon a border, Hardy struggled to envisage a different cultural terrain for the women of his imagination, and yet it may be argued that Tess or Sue participate in a newly transgressive narrative pattern, alert to those possibilities of "passing" emblematized in Sue's adoption of Jude's clothing after her escape from the training college. Emerging out of the linguistic borderland of Wessex, Hardy increasingly speculates about appropriate sexual and class representation in a period when public and private spheres began to collapse inwards to elicit a sense of shifting positionality.

Essentialism is undoubtedly part of Hardy's world-view, but it is continually eroded or challenged in his work by a sense of lack – lack of a literary "place" ("the good little Thomas Hardy"), of an assured social position, or even of a stable aesthetic realm (the oscillation between fiction and poetry). Like Henry Knight on the cliff, Thomas Hardy occupies a perilous "limit-situation" in both class and gender terms, and it is this quasi-existential sense of crisis which generates the depth of his imaginative work – a sense of a social and gender void proleptically staged in a moment from Emma's memoirs:

> I often dream of the dangerous pathways over cliffs and rocks leading to spots almost inaccessible. Once I hung over the "devil's hole" by a tuft of grass whilst my schoolfellow shouted to a mussel-seeking man far below, who rushed up the steep ascent and rescued me and who was never rewarded. (Emma Hardy 1979: 3)

This scenario offers a densely registered "involute" of characteristic Hardyesque themes – the sense of a risky borderline existence, the voyeuristic quality, and the man climbing up the "steep ascent" who (like her future husband?) is to be "never rewarded." The touting of aristocratic connection in the autobiography is the dialectical counterpart to Hardy's blindness and insight as to his own origins. Language is furrowed by traces of power and agency, and Hardy's idiolect is saturated with the complexities of social origins which would be mystified into the "Hardy Pedigree." In Mikhail Bakhtin's account language inhabits a boundary between self and other, and the novel specifically is a form which crosses boundaries between dialectal groups, high and low cultures, to produce a dialogical discourse. The language of the Other is thus beyond our control – a concept which is pertinent to Hardy's delineation of both the rural poor and of women. Boundaries are imperialistic and tend to denigrate the Other, just as dialect is "worsted in the struggle for existence" by the "uniform tongue" of Standard English (*THPV* 29). At this historical conjuncture language refracted many of the tensions inherent in conceptions of society and difference, and yet regional dialects could also express a sense of class solidarity and radicalism to which Hardy is often inattentive. It is, however, unarguable that the largely comedic deployment of dialect forms in the early work gives way to a more deeply pondered usage in later texts, where notions of popular justice, equality, and class unity become more explicitly elaborated. From the outset of his career, with *The Poor Man and the Lady*, written "By the Poor Man," Hardy would recognize the unequal distribution of power inherent in language use, an inequality of both class and gender, while his later work contains utopian elements working towards a realization of Bakhtinian polyphony in its handling of social or sexual identity.

It may be appropriate, in concluding, to glance at a symptomatic text in which Hardy with superb insight examines the class issues of his day. "A Tragedy of Two Ambitions" (1888) was to embody "present day aspirations – i.e., concerning the ambitions of two men, their struggles for education, a position in the Church, & so on, ending tragically" (*LLI* 236, as quoted from *CL* I: 178). In delineating the ambition of the two Halborough youths, the deployment of their sister as a pawn in the marriage market, and the shame elicited by the irregular appearances of their scapegrace father, Hardy offers a registration of the way, in Max Weber's terms, in which bureaucratization entails a hierarchy of offices and an unrelenting devotion to means–ends rationality. Modern culture, Weber argued, would demand calculability as the key to social success and class ambition, and the consequent elimination of the type of emotional instability embodied in the wayward Miller Halborough. The brothers, while espousing a clerical career, evince little genuine faith, seeing the Church rather as an instrument for entering a higher class: "'we are in for Christianity, and must stick to her,'" as Joshua remarks doggedly (*LLI* 72). The Protestant ethic of worldly asceticism, as classically expounded by Weber, is lived out in the brothers' renunciatory self-discipline, their repressed characters offering a stark contrast to the attractive lawlessness of the father, whose charismatic personality, in line with Weber's thesis, is fated to recede with the development of permanent institutional structures. Both the brothers and their sister Rosa are bound to an irresistible social force and are consequently unable to adhere to the religious view cited by Weber that material possessions should be worn "like a light cloak, which can be thrown aside at any moment." With the onset of modernity, materialism and class interest dictate that "the cloak should become an iron cage" (Weber [1905] 1958: 181). Rosa, eagerly on her way to her first meeting with the squire, flirtatiously pulls up "the edge of her skirt under her cloak" (*LLI* 79), but later, Cornelius demands, " 'Do you think human hearts are iron-cased safes?' ", to which Joshua ominously responds, " 'Yes – I think they are, sometimes' " (*LLI* 91). In contradistinction the father, whom the brothers guiltily allow to drown, is resurrected in the natural transmutation of his walking-stick into "a straight little silver-poplar," the leaves of which shimmer with a "flicker of whiteness" (*LLI* 92). (It is a Hardyesque satire of circumstance that Max Weber had himself participated in a patricidal quarrel when, in June 1897, he expelled his father from his home, an event shortly followed by the death of Max Weber senior.)

In such a text, and widely elsewhere in his work, one might conclude, Hardy crystallizes and refracts those complex and deeply submerged issues of class, shame, and ambition which mark out his progress as a "native" who could never truly "return."

NOTE

1   The function of the wall as signifier of social class here is interestingly modified in "The Melancholy Hussar," where it acts as an amatory/national barrier, Hardy remarking that the stone wall "of necessity made anything like intimacy difficult," so that the lovers' conversation "had been overtly conducted across this boundary" (*WT* 45).

REFERENCES AND FURTHER READING

Armstrong, Tim (2000). *Haunted Hardy: Poetry, History, Memory*. Basingstoke: Palgrave Macmillan.

Bakhtin, Mikhail (1986). *The Dialogic Imagination*, trans. C. Emerson and M. Holquist. Austin: University of Texas Press.

Barrell, John (1983). *English Literature in History: 1730–80*. London: Hutchinson.

Benjamin, Walter ([1955] 1999). *Illuminations*, trans. Harry Zohn. London: Pimlico.

Benjamin, Walter ([1982] 2002). *The Arcades Project*, trans. Howard Eiland and Kevin McLaughlin. Cambridge, MA: Harvard University Press.

Crossick, Geoffrey (1991). From Gentlemen to the Residuum. In P. J. Corfield (ed.), *Language, History and Class* (pp. 150–78). Oxford: Blackwell.

Day, Gary (2001). *Class*. London: Routledge.

De Vine, Christine (2005). *Class in Turn-of-the-Century Novels of Gissing, James, Hardy, and Wells*. Aldershot: Ashgate.

Dentith, Simon (1998). *Society and Cultural Forms in Nineteenth-Century England*. Basingstoke: Macmillan.

Derrida, Jacques (1994). *Specters of Marx*, trans. Peggy Kamuf. London: Routledge.

Ebbatson, Roger (1993). *Hardy: The Margin of the Unexpressed*. Sheffield: Sheffield Academic Press.

Ebbatson, Roger (2004). Hardy and Class. In Phillip Mallett (ed.), *Palgrave Advances in Thomas Hardy Studies* (pp. 111–34). Basingstoke: Palgrave.

Fisher, Joe (1992). *The Hidden Hardy*. Basingstoke: Macmillan.

Freud, Sigmund ([1919] 1985). The Uncanny. In *Art and Literature*, trans. James Strachey. Pelican Freud Library vol. 14 (pp. 339–76). Harmondsworth: Penguin.

Gittings, Robert (1975). *Young Thomas Hardy*. London: Heinemann.

Goode, John (1988). *Thomas Hardy: The Offensive Truth*. Oxford: Blackwell.

Hardy, Emma (1979). *Some Recollections*, ed. Evelyn Hardy and Robert Gittings. Oxford: Oxford University Press.

Hardy, Thomas ([1872] 1985). *Under the Greenwood Tree*, ed. Simon Gatrell. Oxford: Oxford University Press.

Hardy, Thomas ([1878] 1998). An Indiscretion in the Life of an Heiress. In *An Indiscretion in the Life of an Heiress and Other Stories*, ed. Pamela Dalziel (pp. 43–113). Oxford: Oxford University Press.

Hardy, Thomas ([1878] 1990). *The Return of the Native*, ed. Simon Gatrell. Oxford: Oxford University Press.

Hardy, Thomas ([1886] 1987). *The Mayor of Casterbridge*, ed. Dale Kramer. Oxford: Oxford University Press.

Hardy, Thomas ([1888] 1991). *Wessex Tales*, ed. Kathryn R. King. Oxford: Oxford University Press.

Hardy, Thomas ([1891] 1988). *Tess of the d'Urbervilles*, ed. Juliet Grindle and Simon Gatrell. Oxford: Oxford University Press.

Hardy, Thomas ([1894] 1996). *Life's Little Ironies*, ed. Alan Manford. Oxford: Oxford University Press.

Hardy, Thomas ([1895] 1985). *Jude the Obscure*, ed. Patricia Ingham. Oxford: Oxford University Press.

Hardy, Thomas (1979). *The Variorum Edition of the Complete Poems of Thomas Hardy*, ed. James Gibson. London: Macmillan.

Hardy, Thomas (1984). *The Life and Work of Thomas Hardy*, ed. Michael Millgate. London: Macmillan.

Ingham, Patricia (1996). *The Language of Gender and Class*. London: Routledge.

Jann, Rosemary (2000). Hardy's Rustics and the Construction of Class. *Victorian Literature and Culture*, 28(2), 411–25.

Joyce, Patrick (ed.) (1995). *Class*. Oxford: Oxford University Press.

Lukács, Georg ([1923] 1971). *History and Class Consciousness*, trans. Rodney Livingstone. London: Merlin Press.

Marx, Karl ([1846] 1996). *The German Ideology*, ed. C. J. Arthur. London: Lawrence & Wishart.

Marx, Karl ([1925] 1971). *Grundrisse*, trans. David McLellan. Oxford: Oxford University Press.

Marx, Karl (1977). *Selected Writings*, ed. David McLellan. Oxford: Oxford University Press.

Marx, Karl (1969, 1970). *Selected Works*, vols. 2 and 3. Moscow: Progress Publishers.

Millgate, Michael (ed.) (2001). *Thomas Hardy's Public Voice: The Essays, Speeches, and Miscellaneous Prose*. Oxford: Clarendon Press.

Millgate, Michael (2004). *Thomas Hardy: A Biography Revisited*. Oxford: Oxford University Press.

Phillipps, K. C. (1984). *Language and Class in Victorian England*. Oxford: Oxford University Press.

Pite, Ralph (2006). *Thomas Hardy: The Guarded Life*. London: Picador.

Purdy, Richard Little, and Michael Millgate (eds.) (1978–88). *The Collected Letters of Thomas Hardy*, 7 vols. Oxford: Clarendon Press.

Sayer, Karen (1995). *Women of the Fields*. Manchester: Manchester University Press.

Snell, K. D. M. (1987). *Annals of the Labouring Poor*. Cambridge: Cambridge University Press.

Tomalin, Claire (2006). *Thomas Hardy: The Time-Torn Man*. London: Penguin.

Weber, Max ([1905] 1958). *The Protestant Ethic and the Spirit of Capitalism*, trans. Talcott Parsons. New York: Scribner's.

Widdowson, Peter (1989). *Hardy in History: A Study in Literary Sociology*. London: Routledge.

Wiener, Martin J. (1981). *English Culture and the Decline of the Industrial Spirit*. Cambridge: Cambridge University Press.

Williams, Raymond (1970). *Keywords*. London: Croom Helm.

Wotton, George (1985). *Thomas Hardy: Towards a Materialist Criticism*. Dublin: Gill & Macmillan.

12

Reading Hardy through Dress: The Case of *Far From the Madding Crowd*

Simon Gatrell

No nineteenth-century writer is more fully aware of the multiplicity of ways that dress informs, shapes, patterns our lives than Thomas Hardy, and none has a more profound variety of insights into the relationships amongst mind, body, and dress. It is impossible in so short a space to justify these contentions completely, so rather than give a sort of universal but necessarily superficial field-guide to Hardy's uses for dress, I have chosen to explore how he works in a single novel. *Far From the Madding Crowd* is only representative in that, as with every other of his novels, it is possible to read it through dress. It seemed the most appropriate novel to choose for this chapter because it is one of his more familiar texts, and also because it is in his earlier novels that Hardy was most direct and generous with theoretic generalizations about dress.

The essence of his conception is that women's bodies extend into their dress, and that in being put on their clothes become an integral part of their nervous system, as they do not for men. Readers of his first novel, *Desperate Remedies*, will be particularly aware of this, where, for example, we hear of "delicate antennae, or feelers," bristling on every frill of a dress, but there are other fascinating examples in *A Pair of Blue Eyes*. So, when the narrator of *Far From the Madding Crowd* pronounces that "A woman's dress [is] a part of her countenance and any disorder in the one [is] of the same nature with a malformation or wound in the other" (p. 77), he continues to educate us in aspects of an established theory. Through the ambiguity inherent in "countenance" he also indicates economically the essential double nature of the power of clothing, in its effect on the observer and on the self – a torn skirt is a malformation of the identity a woman presents to the world, but to her it comes with the physical pain of a slash to her face.

The same bodily quality of dress is evident when Bathsheba first enters the Corn-market in Casterbridge:

> The numerous evidences of her power to attract were only thrown into greater relief by a marked exception. Women seem to have eyes in their ribbons for such matters as these. Bathsheba, without looking within a right angle of him, was conscious of a black sheep among the flock. (p. 95)

Hardy might have written the more conventional "eyes in their backs," but instead there is again the powerful, here almost surreal, indication that a woman's dress is part of her sense-organization.

What are the consequences in *Far From the Madding Crowd* of this conception? Well, consider one of the more significant incidents in Bathsheba's life: Hardy required his heroine to experience a powerful and instantaneous sexual attraction to a man; there were hundreds of possibilities for a first encounter with such passionate implications, but he chose that the skirt of the woman's dress should become involved with a projection from the man's clothing. He has taught us to recognize at once that when the rowel of Frank Troy's spur becomes caught in the gimp decoration on Bathsheba's dress, not only has fabric become entangled but her sensibility also – gored, raked, twisted, implicated.

As the metal teeth take hold on the cord Bathsheba is physically and psychically destabilized by the force of the check to her progress, by the shock to her senses through the material. Instinctively her body moves to recover her physical equilibrium, but as it does so it receives another shock: "In recovering she struck against warm clothes and buttons" (p. 170). It is characteristic that Hardy represents Frank by the clothes he is wearing, but also that, in the most economical manner possible, through the adjective "warm," he makes us aware of the body within the clothes. The verb, too, "struck against," is precise: more violent than any casual contact in passing, such as touching, brushing, or grazing; it is a ship in a fog colliding with another, or foundering on a rock. And yet the rock is warm, though it has those small and perhaps chilly metal projections; we are forced to register the sensation as physically as Bathsheba does. It is a further irony that in recovering her physical balance she crashes into the body that will destabilize her emotional balance for years.

The unknown man is also surprised to find himself "hitched" to a woman somehow (pun presumably intended), and the entanglement of their clothes is presented as an image of their future together: "The unfastening was not such a trifling affair. The rowel of the spur had so wound itself among the gimp cords in those few moments that separation was likely to be a matter of time" (p. 171). As Bathsheba is anxious to go, the soldier first proposes cutting the skirt (or the relationship) at once, but we know that it's not just the material or the relationship he would thus sever – the knife would inflict a deep wound to Bathsheba's sensibility. It is a testament to her urgency that she begs him to do it. But then he suggests (driven by his own sexual instinct to prolong the connection) that she be patient; and under pretense of unraveling the material connection, complicates it further, while at the same time twining himself into her mind by flirting with her.[1] As a consequence she tries again to extricate herself: "and the gathers of her dress began to give way like liliputian musketry" (p. 172); the military simile works on several levels, enhancing her association with the soldier, but also indicating the sharp pain inflicted on Bathsheba by the damage to her dress. Despite this, again "Bathsheba was revolving in her mind whether by a bold and desperate rush she could free herself at the risk of leaving her skirt bodily behind her" (p. 173) – abandoning the skirt of her dress would be like leaving part of her body in the hands of the soldier with the twinkling eye and the strong sexuality. No wonder the narrator continues: "The thought was too dreadful." And in describing the dress (not its appearance but its status) he augments the bodily imagery: "The dress – which she had put on to appear stately at the supper – was the head and front of her wardrobe." Since the psychic price of "bold and desperate" action would be dearer than the material destruction of a dress, she stoops to untwist the cords herself.

Everything in the scene turns on dress, even the *coup de théâtre* at its heart, the moment when light shines on the darkness that has obscured the initial impact:

> The man to whom she was hooked was brilliant in brass and scarlet. He was a soldier. His sudden appearance was to darkness what the sound of a trumpet is to silence. Gloom, the *genius loci* at all times hitherto, was now totally overthrown, less by the lantern light than by what the lantern lighted. The contrast of this revelation with her anticipations of some sinister figure in sombre garb was so great that it had upon her the effect of a fairy transformation. (p. 171)

The red and gold radiance of Troy's uniform causes yet another destabilization in Bathsheba's psyche. It remains imprinted on her consciousness after she is freed, when she runs indoors, to ask Liddy about the man who has called her beautiful: "'is any soldier staying in the village – Sergeant somebody – rather gentlemanly for a sergeant, and good looking: a red coat with blue facings?'" (p. 174). And Hardy is careful to ensure that on every subsequent occasion Frank appears, until after the Harvest Home, he is wearing his military red. It might hardly seem worth pointing out that red is traditionally the color of sexual passion – the connection between Troy's habitual dress and the passion he inspires in Bathsheba is too obvious – were it not that Hardy has created a larger pattern through illuminated red (and reddish) dress, of which this revelation of Troy's uniform is the heart.

The pattern begins in the first chapter of the novel; the first time we (and Gabriel) see Bathsheba she too is dressed in red intensified by an effect of light: "the sun lighted up to a scarlet glow the crimson jacket she wore, and painted a soft lustre upon her bright face and dark hair" (p. 10). A little later in her stay at Norcombe she is the center of another theatrical moment. It is night; Gabriel is lying on a bank into which a hut is built, and he looks down through a chink in the roof at the illuminated scene within. Inside there is a girl about whom he can tell little: "She wore no bonnet or hat, but had enveloped herself in a large cloak, which was carelessly flung over her head as a covering" (p. 18). "Oak . . . became more curious to observe her features, but this prospect being denied him by the hooding effect of the cloak, and by his aërial position, he felt himself drawing upon his fancy for their details" (p. 19). As if on cue, the girl at that moment flings off her cloak "and forth tumbled ropes of black hair over a red jacket. Oak knew her instantly . . ." (p. 20); and that ends the chapter. Neither Frank nor Bathsheba intends the effect they produce upon the observer – Troy opens the lantern because he wants to see Bathsheba, Bathsheba is unaware that there is anyone watching – but none the less they inspire a red emotion that endures as long as its object does.

The pattern extends and is modified to include Gabriel's dress also: he slips off the back of a wagon on its way to Weatherbury, and sees a fire. As he approaches,

> His weary face now began to be painted over with a rich orange glow, and the whole front of his smockfrock and gaiters was covered with a dancing shadow pattern of thorn twigs – the light reaching him through a leafless intervening hedge – and the metallic curve of his sheep-crook shone silver-bright in the same abounding rays. (p. 48)

His smock is white, the glow the fire casts on it is orange not red, and it is flickeringly shadowed with black; but still, this is Bathsheba's farm, and though there is no one but the narrator to observe him, the effect of light is striking. In only a brief time he will be before his lost beloved again; but Hardy is also careful to note that in this specimen the true red that inspires the most passionate sexual desire is in Gabriel now somewhat damped down to orange.

The same effect may be observed when Frank Troy greets Gabriel Oak and Jan Coggan from an upper window of Bathsheba's farmhouse on the morning after he has taken up residence there:

> "Why – they *may* not be married!" suggested Coggan. "Perhaps she's not there."
> Gabriel shook his head. The soldier turned a little towards the east, and the sun kindled his scarlet jacket to an orange glow. (p. 247)

This "orange glow" is altogether less brilliant than the effect created by Bathsheba's lantern in the dark, and Hardy is preparing us for Frank's cynical assessment of passion later in the novel: "'All romances end at marriage'" (p. 281).

The last element in the design comes soon afterwards when, during the cataclysmic thunderstorm, Bathsheba comes to assist Gabriel in saving the ricks. Her new husband is asleep in the barn, drunk – he has rejected the idea that a storm is coming or that the farm's wealth will thereby be lost, because it interferes with his pleasure of the moment. The juxtaposition thus of the two men she has run after presents Bathsheba with a striking contrast. There comes a tremendous bolt of lightning:

> Gabriel was almost blinded, and he could feel Bathsheba's warm arm tremble in his hand – a sensation novel and thrilling enough . . . Oak had hardly time to gather up these impressions into a thought, and to see how strangely the red feather of her hat shone in this light . . . (p. 261)

This intensely illuminated feather is surprising, even eccentric, and has been deliberately placed in connection with Gabriel's consciousness of Bathsheba's body to leave a small reminder for the reader that he is not just her faithful guardian; the phrasing too – "Oak had hardly time to gather up these impressions into a thought" – remembers his response to waking in his lambing hut with his head in Bathsheba's lap (see note 1). And this is where the pattern, the passion, ends.

Outside the pattern lies William Boldwood, whose clothes never reach towards passionate illumination, even when they might. When he receives Bathsheba's valentine, it is the insistent red seal on the envelope with its message "marry me" that transfixes him. The following morning, still disturbed, he is up at sunrise leaning on a gate looking east. Hardy describes the scene: "the only half of the sun yet visible burnt rayless, like a red and flameless fire shining over a white hearthstone" (p. 104). But the radiance doesn't touch the farmer with its color, and there is in the opposite sky even a similarly negative anticipation of Troy's gleaming buttons: "Over the west hung the wasting moon, now dull and greenish-yellow, like tarnished brass." It is not that Boldwood has not the potential for passion within him; it is that he has no power to inspire such intense feeling in others, in Bathsheba – just as the emotion Gabriel can stir is more moderate, less burning, than that which Frank provokes, in Fanny as in Bathsheba.[2]

This pattern of illuminated red dress is perhaps the most sustained that Hardy weaves with dress in the novel, but a return for a moment to the fire in Bathsheba's rick-yard will provide an example of how he works on a smaller scale. Gabriel directs the rescue effort, then climbs up on one of the ricks that has just caught alight to beat out the flames. Once the fire is contained he inquires for the farmer, hoping the place needs a shepherd: " 'That's she back there upon the pony,' said Maryann; 'wi' her face a covered up in that black cloth with holes in it' " (p. 51). As the woman farmer's face is veiled in a "black cloth with holes in it," so Gabriel's dress approximates to the same condition, and his face is veiled in blackness. He approaches her, "his features smudged, grimy, and undiscoverable from the smoke and heat, his smockfrock burnt into holes and dripping with water, the ash stem of his sheep-crook charred six inches shorter" (p. 52). He raises his hat to her, and in a parallel response she "lifted the wool veil tied round her face, and looked all astonishment. Gabriel and his cold-hearted darling Bathsheba Everdene were face to face." The situation is ostensibly one in which we are made conscious of Bathsheba's superiority – we've just been told anecdotally how rich she is, and there she sits above Gabriel elegant on her horse, while he is humble beneath her, singed and filthy from the fire. But the emphasis on the holes in the cloth each wears and the shared action with the hat and veil run as a counterpoint suggesting that beneath the substantial surface distinction there is a subterranean harmony, which may or may not emerge before the end of the story.

It is, indeed, towards the conclusion of the novel that the most concentrated patterning in relation to dress occurs. This is chapter 52, entitled "Converging Courses," in which Bathsheba, Frank, and Boldwood are preparing themselves for the Christmas party at Little Weatherbury Farm. The chapter is a montage of three intercut narratives of dressing, and there is very little of significance in the sequence that is not communicated through attention to dress, mediated in part through the confidant to whom each protagonist looks for advice, and who acts as a kind of opinionated mirror, providing the two-way exchange of dress – the desire of the wearer to mean and the interpretive response of the observer.

A pervasive uneasiness characterizes the chapter, and the first section describing the unfestivity of the festivities planned – the *mise-en-scène*, to continue the cinematic perception – sets the mood. There is not enough space here to follow in detail the intricate dance of dress Hardy choreographs. What we experience is Bathsheba in front of her mirror simultaneously reluctant and excited, in a plain black silk dress, but with hair that won't lie down. She tells Liddy to "'finish me off.'" Boldwood, for the first time in his life more fastidious than his tailor over the cut of his coat, feels agitated excitement unalloyed, at its clearest when he asks Gabriel (of all people) if there is a new knot in fashion for him to tie at his neck; then we see him rapt in contemplation of the diamond ring with which he intends to bind Bathsheba. Troy too is agitated, bent upon a theatrical revelation of himself at Boldwood's, to which end he dresses so as to disguise himself, using his confidant the dishonest bailiff Pennyways as a mirror to test the effectiveness of his costume.

So there is Boldwood, in new, festive, and perfectly fitting clothes, wrapped in visions of a shining future of his own fabrication, waiting for the woman who, he intends, will be the material in which he will realize the visions; there is Bathsheba, traveling towards him in plain black that goes beyond the convention of mourning to represent her fears, but with a contradictory air of excitement in her countenance – *something*, at least, is going to happen to break the monotony of her days; and there is Frank also traveling, more slowly, towards him, disguised in dull grey, ready to be the corpse at the feast.

The next chapter provides the resolution, and just to emphasize that there are small as well as large patterns of dress throughout the novel, we might consider three striking images here. The first is of Bathsheba sitting on a chair, weeping, with her face buried in the handkerchief that she holds in one hand, while the other, with a new ring on one finger, is somewhere above her head, captured by Boldwood. The second is of Bathsheba sitting on the floor beside the body of her husband, his head pillowed in her lap, while with one hand she holds her handkerchief to his breast and covers the wound there, and with the other she tightly clasps one of his. The third is of Boldwood who, having shot Frank, fastens his handkerchief to the trigger of his gun, places his foot on the other end, and is in the act of turning the second barrel upon himself.

The narrator says of Bathsheba that she had been "fairly beaten into non-resistance" by Boldwood (p. 388), that he has forced her into the pattern of his vision of the future. The irony is fierce that has her attempt futilely to preserve her husband's life with the handkerchief still damp from the tears shed over his final abandonment; and is further twisted by the deliberate placement of a second handkerchief on the trigger of the weapon that has in reality released Bathsheba from her marriage, and simultaneously ripped apart the fabric of his vision of a brilliant future with her. Gabriel's sadness is prescient.[3]

In fact, though Frank Troy had been attracted to Bathsheba's body, he was never able to see that her dress was part of her self; this is true of neither Gabriel nor Boldwood. When Gabriel begins to love Bathsheba he imagines her beside the hearth of her aunt's house "in her outdoor dress; for the clothes she had worn on the hill were by association equally with her person included in the compass of his affection" (p. 30). On the Saturday after Boldwood receives Bathsheba's valentine, he was in Casterbridge market-house as usual, when the disturber of his dreams entered and became visible to him. Adam had awakened from his deep sleep, and behold! there was Eve. The farmer took courage, and for the first time really looked at her. . . .

He saw her black hair, her correct facial curves and profile, and the roundness of her chin and throat. He saw then the side of her eyelids, eyes, and lashes, and the shape of her ear. Next he noticed her figure, her skirt, and the very soles of her shoes. (p. 122)

Both the flesh and the dress constitute her individuality and her beauty for him, as for Gabriel – this is so even for the man on whom £20-worth of new clothes has been wasted by a girl who has previously tried to attract his sleeping attention. Adam's experience did not involve clothes, and by invoking Adam's amazement, the narrator also brings simultaneously into play, for the reader if not for Boldwood, the sense of Bathsheba's shaping body within her dress.

Or consider the sequel to Bathsheba's swoon on hearing that Frank has drowned: Boldwood "lifted her bodily off the ground, and smoothed down the folds of her dress as a child might have taken a storm-beaten bird and arranged its ruffled plumes, and bore her along the pavement to the King's Arms Inn" (p. 339). If more evidence is needed of Boldwood's instinctive understanding of the relationship between dress and identity, at the end of the novel, when Boldwood is in prison, his locked closet is gone through:

There were several sets of lady's dresses in the piece, of sundry expensive materials; silks and satins, poplins and velvets, all of colours which from Bathsheba's style of wear might have been judged to be her favourites. There were two muffs, sable and ermine. . . . They were all carefully packed in paper, and each package was labelled "Bathsheba Boldwood," a date being subjoined six years in advance in every instance. (p. 397)

The narrator, anxious to provide a justification for the stay of execution thought appropriate for a family magazine, asserts that these are "somewhat pathetic evidences of a mind crazed with care and love"; but what they really show is that the mind responded with love and insight to the individuality of the woman he loved, and who herself loved dress. These are potential dresses, awaiting the shaping hand of the dressmaker and the animating body of his beloved – they are ideals, dreams.

There is, however, in this novel a particular desolation to dress without a body to fill it. Most ordinary is the pile of Frank's clothes found on the beach, the circumstantial evidence that he has drowned. When they are brought back to Bathsheba the narrator comments that it "was so evident to her in the midst of her agitation that Troy had undressed in the full conviction of dressing again almost immediately that the notion that anything but death could have prevented him was a perverse one to entertain" (p. 341). I suppose the reader is to infer that the bundle includes his under-linen, and no one could imagine that he would (even in the midst of *his* agitation) have walked off naked. We learn long before any character in the novel that he has been picked up by members of a ship's crew in a small boat, who cover his naked body with "what little clothing they could spare among them." (In the manuscript and in the Oxford World's Classics edition of the novel the crew agrees to row back to the beach on which Troy left his clothes – but they have already been taken as evidence of his drowning.) But he has lost for the time being his outward identity – he is a melange of miscellaneous dress – and instead of making an attempt to restore that self, he is content to adopt another, suggested by his temporary gear, and signs up for a transatlantic voyage. Shedding the outer layer of self frees the body and the mind to fill other selves.

A more poignant disappearance of the body from dress is metaphorical. When Fanny finally arrives at Casterbridge workhouse she collapses, and the gatekeeper "discerned the panting heap of clothes" (pp. 278–9). Fanny is disembodied here, even to the degree that it is the heap of clothes that is panting. She has, for the moment, no identity, no self, no existence. The same is true of Bathsheba after preparing Frank's body for the grave: "as if at that instant to prove that her fortitude had been more of will than of spontaneity she silently sank down between them and was a shapeless heap of drapery on the floor" (p. 395). In her case we witness the process; her body is gradually abstracted from her dress as she slides to the floor. Hardy thus for both women shows the extremities to which they have been driven, extremities that their bodies can no longer sustain.

The absences I have drawn attention to so far have been temporary, but there is one – an almost thrown-away description – that if examined at all closely is frighteningly permanent. In giving sketches of some of the workfolk on Bathsheba's farm the narrator says of Matthew Moon that he was "a singular framework of clothes with nothing of any consequence inside them, which advanced with the toes in no definite direction forwards, but turned in or out as they chanced to swing" (p. 82). This is the self as dress – the framework moves, not the man; and the toes may as well be of boots as feet. It is true that there is something inside the shape, but there is no hint that it is human – it seems more likely that it is sawdust; there is certainly no hint of will guiding the movement, and the voice that speaks its name must be ventriloquism – it is described as "the rustle of wind among dead leaves." It comes as a shock that this Gothic horror can perform a week's work worth ten shillings and twopence halfpenny.

The description of Moon is the more disturbing in that it is female dress in mid-Victorian England that normally provides a framework to structure the body, an observation made in a striking way by a most unlikely reporter. Gabriel's youthful under-shepherd Cainy Ball has been to Bath on holiday and seen Frank and Bathsheba: "she wore a beautiful gold-colour silk gown, trimmed with black lace, that would have stood alone 'ithout legs inside if required" (pp. 232–3). Cainy's picture begins conventionally enough, but ends in the grotesque – it is the "if required" that works to cut Bathsheba off at the hips in our imagination; but also, by the juxtaposition, he superimposes disembodied on bodied dress.

Hardy finds dress a source of flexible and powerful images in the representation of character and emotion, but he's also thoroughly aware of dress as a social force.

Here I'd like to consider three strands: the question of uniforms (defined very broadly), habits, and customs in the wearing of hats, and the wielding of staffs of various kinds.

Troy's is the only officially sanctioned uniform in the novel, but throughout his fiction Hardy is interested in exploring ideas about the proper way to do things, and this includes the proper way to dress in a given social circumstance. The mourning that Bathsheba wears on her uncle's death, and then reluctantly puts on again after Frank goes missing, and does not remit thereafter, is the most generally accepted instance of this in the novel; it is almost inevitable that her wearing of black towards the end of the novel coincides with a new somberness in her demeanor, staidness in her behavior. But Hardy identifies other, less universally recognized, approaches to uniform: among the first things that we learn about Gabriel is that "on working days he was a young man of sound judgment, easy motions, proper dress":

> He wore a low crowned felt hat, spread out at the base by tight jamming upon the head for security in high winds, and a coat like Doctor Johnson's, his lower extremities being encased in ordinary leather leggings, and boots emphatically large, affording to each foot a roomy apartment so constructed that any wearer might stand in a river all day long and know nothing of damp – their maker being a conscientious man who endeavoured to compensate for any weakness in his cut by unstinted dimension and solidity. (p. 7)

These clothes are proper to his station as a modest sheep-farmer; there is no implication that all such men will dress exactly like this, but rather that there is an understood but also undefined range of dress that is appropriate to one in his social circumstances. Utility rather than fashion is proper – and in making boots for such a man the boot-maker is right to privilege solidity over elegance.[4]

When Gabriel loses his farm and tries for a position as bailiff on someone else's farm, these clothes are no longer proper, they misinform, they're too good: others searching for a place ask him if he has one to offer, call him "sir." Ultimately, finding himself unemployable as a bailiff, he's reduced to purchasing the shepherd's uniform, smockfrock, and crook – thus announcing his diminished qualifications to all and sundry.

Hardy also shows us Gabriel dressing for a different social situation. He's preparing to go to ask Bathsheba to marry him:

> He thoroughly cleaned his silver watch-chain with whiting, put new lacing-straps to his boots, looked to the brass eyelet holes, went to the inmost heart of the plantation for a new walking-stick and trimmed it vigorously on his way back, took a new hand-kerchief from the bottom of his clothes-box, put on the light waistcoat patterned all over with sprigs of an elegant flower uniting the beauties of both rose and lily without the defects of either, and used all the hair-oil he possessed upon his usually dry, sandy, and inextricably curly hair till he had deepened it to a splendidly novel colour between that of guano and Roman cement, making it stick to his head like mace round a nutmeg, or wet seaweed round a boulder after the ebb. (pp. 30–1)

Gabriel's preparations seem marked – the details of watch-chain, eyelet-holes and handkerchief, the expedition for a new walking-stick, and above all the arduous work undertaken to force his hair to conform to the respectable fashion for elegant males of 1874, suggest something quite out of the ordinary. If Hardy has in mind the mock-heroic, the arming of the hero about to go into battle, then his choice of objects for comparison – the one bird-shit and the other mortar – though perhaps exact in their way, significantly enhance the effect; and we may suspect irony, in a text of Ruskinian, post-pre-Raphaelite times, in any "elegant flower uniting the beauties of both rose and lily without the defects of either." The effect of the description, of its tone in particular, is to make Gabriel seem at least a little foolish to the reader; the question, though, is whether he would have presented a foolish appearance to his chosen observer, Bathsheba. The hair must have been rather striking to anyone who had seen it in its unoiled state, but otherwise surely he would simply have looked smarter than usual – he would have announced his special purpose before he spoke, had such an opportunity occurred.

When Gabriel needed to turn shepherd again at the hiring-fair in Casterbridge, he had a crook made for him by a blacksmith, who threw a staff into the bargain; but he also wanted a smockfrock to cover the no longer proper clothes he inhabits. He "went to a ready-made clothes shop, the owner of which had a large rural connection. As the crook had absorbed most of Gabriel's money he attempted, and carried out, an exchange of his overcoat for a shepherd's regulation smockfrock" (p. 44). The crook and smockfrock were a shepherd's uniform at any time in the nineteenth century before 1873 in the south of England – in Wessex. What makes this passage particularly interesting is that Gabriel gets his smockfrock from a ready-made clothes shop. Lying behind this bare detail is the as yet under-researched history of the machine production of smockfrocks in England. Rachel Worth, in her study of rural working-class dress, points out that by the 1860s Gurteen in Haverhill in Suffolk were mass-producing smockfrocks on powered looms and sewing-machines, though the patterned smocking was still outwork (Worth 2002: 109). What are the chances that a man in Dorchester in Gabriel's position would have acquired a smockfrock made in Suffolk? The question cannot be answered without more research. But the possibility throws an interesting light on one of the better-known generalizations in *Far From the Madding Crowd*:

> In comparison with cities, Weatherbury was immutable. . . . nothing less than a century set a mark on its face or tone. Five decades hardly modified the cut of a gaiter, the embroidery of a smockfrock, by the breadth of a hair. . . . In these Wessex nooks the busy outsider's ancient times are only old; his old times are still new; his present is futurity. (p. 151)

It may be that smockfrocks made in Weatherbury did still follow a traditional pattern, but when Hardy points out that the clothes shop in Casterbridge had "a large rural connection," one implication is that some of the Weatherbury workfolk will there have purchased what amounts to alien dress, and will in this respect at least be thoroughly in tune with the present.

This celebrated passage is further placed into context by a consideration of dress in the novel as a whole. It is evident that Hardy's claim for the timelessness of Wessex dress can only apply to those without sufficient surplus income to be interested in the fashions of London or Paris. As soon as Troy leaves off his uniform he's dressed in a "farmer's marketing suit of unusually fashionable cut" (p. 269); when Gabriel is made bailiff of both Bathsheba's and Boldwood's farms, he's accused by Susan Tall of "coming it quite the dand" (p. 343) and hardly knowing the name of smockfrock. There is a fundamental uneasiness in the novel between claims of timeless pastoralism and evidence of mid-Victorian cultural modernity which dress illuminates.

Bathsheba certainly keeps up; take, for instance, the clothes she wears to ride in. Gabriel first sees her while she is part of the rural poor:

> The girl, who wore no riding-habit, looked around for a moment as if to assure herself that all humanity was out of view, then dexterously dropped backwards flat upon the pony's back, her head over its tail, her feet against its shoulders, and her eyes to the sky. (p. 21)

Her dress adds to the implicit eroticism of her unconventional position; fashionable mid-Victorian riding habits differed primarily from day-dresses by being particularly long in the skirt and of heavy material, draping over the foot so that there would be little chance of an ankle emerging. Lying back on the horse in her ordinary dress would inevitably be revealing of fringes of petticoat. (For an account of Victorian riding-habits, see Matthews 2002.)

After she inherits her uncle's farm, in this respect as in others, she eagerly adopts the habits of the fashionable world. We see her at the sheep dip contrasted with her work-folk: "Shepherd Oak, Jan Coggan, Moon, Poorgrass, Cain Ball and several others were assembled here all dripping wet to the very roots of their hair – and Bathsheba was standing by in a new riding-habit – the most elegant she had ever worn" (p. 131). Boldwood comes up, and as she leaves he follows, to ask her for the first time to marry him. It is then striking that, during a second high point in the ovine year, the sheep-shearing, again she leaves with Boldwood dressed in a riding-habit – and this time, like the glove she was straining to put on when her sheep strayed, it is so close-fitting as to be almost a second skin: "she reappeared in her new riding habit of myrtle green which fitted her to the waist as a rind fits its fruit" (p. 154).[5]

It is a commonplace of Victorian dress that both men and women wore headgear out of doors as a matter of course. The particular interest of *Far From the Madding Crowd* in this respect is that Hardy shows just how essential a hat was considered, even in remote rural areas. As we have seen, the first description of Gabriel begins with his hat. When he observes Bathsheba looking at herself in her mirror at the tollgate, the narrator implies surprise that she did so not to "adjust her hat" (p. 10); and it is this very hat, perhaps, that is the means of introducing the two. The wind blows it off as she is on her way with her aunt at night to tend to a sick cow, and the next day Gabriel finds the lost hat and takes possession of it, returning with it to his lambing-hut, where (for the third time) he begins to look from a place of concealment at the bare-headed girl (approaching on the back of a pony). As she comes towards his hut he is about to emerge and return the hat, when he is stopped in his tracks by the unconventional flexibility she suddenly shows. He has to take the next opportunity of accosting her with the hat:

> She came, the wood-handled pail in one hand, hanging against her knee. The left arm was extended as a balance, enough of it being shown bare to make Oak wish that the event had happened in the summer when the whole would have been revealed. (p. 22)

His opening gambit is direct to the point of brusqueness: "'I found a hat,' said Oak" (p. 23). To which she responds: "'I wanted my hat this morning. . . . I had to ride to Tewnell Mill'" (p. 24). And we understand that her riding bare-headed is as unconventional, and might have been as stimulating to Gabriel, as her riding with a male saddle.

There are other indications of the omnipresence of headgear – Jan Coggan wears his hat while harvesting oats in the height of the summer heat; when Liddy finds Bathsheba after she has run from Frank and Fanny's body into the night, the first thing she brings is a hat. It is a measure of her distress that she leaves without one, for even when going to Casterbridge to give himself up after shooting Frank, Boldwood remembers to put on his hat. And remember that Fanny deliberately left the farm to go to Frank without a hat in order to persuade that she was going nowhere.

Hats are also indicators of status; Boldwood rides up to the door of Bathsheba's house, and Liddy looks out an upper window: "''What impert'ence,' said Liddy in a low voice. 'To ride up the footpath like that. Why didn't he stop at the gate. Lord! 'Tis a gentleman! I see the top of his hat'" (pp. 76–7). His tall hat, presumably – the sort that Gabriel wears on Sunday once he has become bailiff on Bathsheba's farm and partner in Boldwood's, and that forces Susan Tall to "stand dormant with wonder" (p. 343). Hats are receptacles – Billy Smallbury carries a handkerchief in his – and they can be vehicles of insight into the wearer's very nature:

> He saw the square figure sitting erect upon the horse, the head turned to neither side, the elbows steady by the hips, the brim of the hat level and undisturbed in its onward glide, until the keen edges of Boldwood's shape sank by degrees over the hill. To one who knew the man and his story there was something more striking in this immobility than in a collapse. (p. 249)

And then there is the broad-brimmed hat Bathsheba puts on to protect herself when she starts out to hive bees that have just swarmed. The occasion comes soon after she has encountered Frank Troy, and it raises issues that go beyond the conventional hat-wearing – it involves cross-dressing of a sort, though not as dramatically as, say, Sue Bridehead putting on Jude Fawley's Sunday clothes.

There are small transgressions of gender norms throughout the incident. The bees have flown to the top of a tall apple tree and there they "defy all invaders" who do not "come armed with ladders, veils, and staves to take them" (p. 189). Everyone else is out saving the hay, so Bathsheba decides to try to take on this mock-military exercise by herself. In preparation she

> had dressed the hive with herbs and honey, fetched a ladder, brush, and crook, made herself impregnable with armour of leather gloves, straw hat, and large gauze veil – once green but now faded to snuff colour – and ascended a dozen rungs of the ladder. (p. 189)

In continuing the military metaphor, and in giving Bathsheba both a brush and a crook, Hardy is making it clear that she is taking on a traditionally male role, and so when Frank Troy turns up and offers to hive the bees in her stead he is, we might think, simply attempting to restore the conventional balance of things. When in a similarly conventionally feminine dress-response, "Bathsheba flung down the brush, crook and empty hive, pulled the skirt of her gown tightly round her ankles in a tremendous flurry, and, as well as she could, slid down the ladder" (pp. 188–9), this estimate seems to be confirmed, especially when she responds to his offer thus: "'What and will you shake them in for me?' she asked, in what, for a defiant girl, was a faltering way, though, for a timid girl it would have seemed a brave way enough" (p. 190). The narrator tries rather feebly to save some of Bathsheba's strength and independence here, but the sequel disturbs expectations again. Frank first "flung down his crop and put his foot on the ladder to ascend" (p. 190); but Bathsheba tells him: "'you must have on the veil and gloves, or you'll be stung fearfully!'" And though earlier the hat and veil have been described as armor, now they are decisively feminized, as Bathsheba dresses him in them:

> So a whimsical fate ordered that her hat should be taken off, veil and all attached, and placed upon his head, Troy tossing his own into a gooseberry bush. Then the veil had to be tied at its lower edge round his collar, and the gloves put on him. (p. 190)

The passive voice, the hat being "her" hat, the tying of the veil around his neck – it is as if he is a lady being dressed by her maid. And the temporary emasculation of Troy restores Bathsheba's usual state of mind: "she could not avoid laughing outright." When he descends, having achieved the goal unscathed, he asks her: "'Would you be good enough to untie me and let me out? I am nearly stifled inside this silk cage.'" One might say that this is the only time she has Frank caged in the course of their relationship, unless marriage itself is a cage for him. On the other hand perhaps he is begging her to restore his masculinity – and she obligingly does so, not only by untying the veil, but by taking up something mentioned earlier: "'holding up this hive,'" he has said, "'makes one's arm ache worse than a week of sword-exercise.'" As the two negotiate over his performing the display, Bathsheba says: "'Not with a walkingstick – I don't care to see that. It must be a real sword'" (p. 191).

The flashing blade in the hollow amid the ferns is the high point of what might be called stick-phallicism in the novel. It is a feature of *Far From the Madding Crowd* that male characters carry and sometimes use rods and staffs of all kinds. Some of them, like the pitchfork, the sheep-crook, the implement that relieves sheep of their killing gas, the implement that assists them through the sheep-dip, the rick-stick, are farming equipment, but others are in more general use: walking-sticks, canes, crops, whips; and then, of course, there is a sword, a cudgel, and a gun.

One or two examples are particularly interesting. To begin with there is a passage that generalizes in an amusing way on the prevalence of sticks. Just before Bathsheba's first entry, Hardy describes the Casterbridge Corn Exchange. It

> was thronged with hot men who talked among each other in twos and threes . . . The greater number carried in their hands ground-ash saplings, using them partly as walking-sticks and partly for poking up pigs, sheep, neighbours with their backs turned, and restful things in general . . . (p. 93)

The reserved Boldwood, it seems, might be one of the few who did not carry such a stick, but later in the novel Poorgrass relates the progress of a conversation with the farmer, in the course of which "'Mr. Boldwood turned round . . . and left off spitting a thistle with the end of his stick'" (p. 288) (a gesture akin to Frank's sword exercise, or Gabriel's puncturing the side of the bloated sheep) – so perhaps not. But Gabriel is rarely without some functional supporting implement or other, some tool for dealing with sheep, or covering a rick; and when he doesn't have the right tool he improvises:

> Oak seized the cut ends of the sheaves, as if he were going to engage in the operation of "reed-drawing," and digging in his feet and occasionally sticking in the stem of his sheep-crook he clambered up the beetling face. He at once sat astride the very apex, and began with his crook to beat off the fiery fragments which had lodged thereon . . . (p. 50)

The one time when he is identified as carrying an ordinary, perhaps redundant, stick is when he goes courting Bathsheba, when (as we have seen) he "went to the inmost heart of the plantation for a new walking-stick and trimmed it vigorously on his way back" – but we hear no more of it.

Frank, however, is never without one, and he flourishes it – he twirls a crop, flicks a whip, wields a hay-fork, flashes a sword, and almost the last words he speaks to Pennyways before leaving Casterbridge in disguise for Boldwood's Christmas party are: "'Well what is there besides? A stick – I must have a walking-stick'" (p. 379). The phallic symbolism is clear enough; Frank is all display, flashing his sexuality about; Gabriel is driven into preoccupation with his work, and only carries what he can use in it; while you have to search through the novel to find instances of Boldwood wielding a stick at all, the most striking (potentially striking) of which is the cudgel he carries during his attempt to persuade Frank to marry Fanny, then Bathsheba – a weapon he doesn't use, even when provoked to physical violence. There is a clear correlation here with the sexual potential of each of the men as a mate for Bathsheba – so clear, indeed, that it is a matter of surprise that Frank does not have his sword buckled by his side when his spur catches in Bathsheba's skirt. It is utterly appropriate that Boldwood kills Frank with the discharge at close quarters from the barrel of a shotgun.

A different interpretation of these staves scattered around the male parts of the text might focus on the idea that they are material props for psychic uncertainty – that Frank is so determined to carry something as evidence of his potency because he is fundamentally unsure about his sexuality. Such a view could draw for support upon the beekeeping scene, might consider that his uniform is an official rather than a customary one, that there is something mechanical, unwilled, automatic about his red dress – as if the passion he inspires he only feels on the surface; and might wonder why he wears this conspicuous scarlet uniform *all* the time, even when on leave.

The novel comes to a close with Gabriel and Bathsheba holding each other and each another similar accessory:

> Ten minutes later a large and a smaller umbrella might have been seen moving from the same door and through the mist along the road to the church. . . . An observer must have been very close indeed to discover that the forms under the umbrellas were those of Oak and Bathsheba, arm in arm for the first time in their lives – Oak in a great coat extending to his knees, and Bathsheba in a cloak that reached her clogs. (p. 413)

The umbrellas are like all of Gabriel's staffs, functional, demanded by the weather. So too are the anonymously concealing clothes, but they are also demanded by the narrator's account of the muted passion of their coming together at last. We have no idea what they wear in the way of wedding attire, but Gabriel has asked Bathsheba to do her hair as she used to do it at Norcombe when he first met her, and so the narrative comes full circle, and "she seemed in his eyes remarkably like the girl of that fascinating dream." [6]

NOTES

1   Earlier in the novel Bathsheba has stood (or rather sat) in Frank's place, flirting with Gabriel, whose life she has probably just saved. There is a similar intimacy between the two, indicated through clothing: Gabriel wakes from near-suffocation to find his head on the lap of Bathsheba's dress, her fingers unbuttoning his collar. The narrator enters his mind: "He was endeavouring to catch and appreciate the sensation of being thus with her – his head upon her dress – before the event passed on into the heap of bygone things" (p. 26).

2   Even Bathsheba's raven hair is (by inference) capable of taking on the brilliance of the rising

sun, and shining it out at Gabriel. He has just returned the hat she lost, and she makes polite conversation, "swinging back her hair, which was black in the shaded hollows of its mass; but it being now an hour past sunrise the rays touched its prominent curves with a colour of their own" (pp. 23–4).

3   There is another detail in this sequence of events worth noting. After being psychologically beaten into submission by Boldwood, Bathsheba "cloaked the effects" of the scene on her face, and "in a few moments came downstairs with her hat and cloak on, ready to go" (p. 388). It's rare that Hardy writes with such

apparent awkwardness as to use the same word both metaphorically and realistically in the same sentence, and he does so to draw our particular attention to the double covering-up that Bathsheba achieves; Frank is about to fling off his covering and precipitate the action that will render vain all Bathsheba's efforts at cloaking.

4　As far as Dr Johnson's coat is concerned, it was told of him by Sir John Hawkins in his *Life of Samuel Johnson* (1787), 45–50, that he was "dressed in a loose horseman's coat, and such a great bushy uncombed wig as he constantly wore."

5　When Hardy first describes Bathsheba, he shows himself in the same way aware of fundamental differences in urban and rural perceptions of dress:

> From the contours of her figure in its upper part, she must have had a beautiful neck and shoulders, but since her infancy nobody had ever seen them. Had she been put into a low dress, she would have run and thrust her head into a bush. Yet she was not a shy girl by any means; it was merely her instinct to draw the line dividing the seen from the unseen higher than they do it in towns. (p. 23)

The only question is whether Hardy is here in fact noting a distinction in class as well as in place – whether, when she inherited her uncle's farm, she became more accustomed to wear urban fashions, whether, for instance, the black silk dress she wore to Boldwood's Christmas party bared her shoulders. It seems likely.

6　The Victorian fascination with hair as a memorial of the beloved and the dead is something Hardy also works with in this, as in many other, novels. Unfortunately there is no space here to consider the issue.

References and Further Reading

Carter, Michael (2003). *Fashion Classics from Carlyle to Barthes*. Oxford and New York: Berg.

Flügel, J. (1930). *The Psychology of Clothes*. London: Hogarth Press.

Gatrell, Simon (2006a). Dress, Body and Psyche in "The Romantic Adventures of a Milkmaid," *Tess of the d'Urbervilles* and *The Mayor of Casterbridge*. *Thomas Hardy Journal*, 22, 143–59.

Gatrell, Simon (2006b). The Erotics of Dress in *A Pair of Blue Eyes*. In Keith Wilson (ed.), *Thomas Hardy Reappraised: Essays in Honour of Michael Millgate* (pp. 118–35). Toronto: University of Toronto Press.

Hardy, Thomas ([1874] 1993). *Far From the Madding Crowd*, ed. Suzanne B. Falck-Yi. Oxford: Oxford University Press.

Harvey, John (1995). *Men in Black*. London: Reaktion Books.

Hollander, Anne (1975). *Seeing through Clothes*. Berkeley: University of California Press.

Kaiser, Susan (1990). *The Social Psychology of Clothing*. New York: Macmillan.

Matthews, David A. (2002). Elegant Amazons: Victorian Riding Habits and the Fashionable Horsewoman. *Victorian Literature and Culture*, 30(1), 179–210.

Steele, Valerie (1985). *Fashion and Eroticism: The Ideals of Feminine Beauty from the Victorian Era to the Jazz Age*. New York: Oxford University Press.

Steele, Valerie (1996). *Fetish: Fashion, Sex, and Power*. New York: Oxford University Press.

Steele, Valerie (2005). *Fashion Theory*. Oxford and New York: Berg.

Summers, Leigh (2001). *Bound to Please: A History of the Victorian Corset*. Oxford and New York: Berg.

Taylor, Lou (2002). *The Study of Dress History*. Manchester: Manchester University Press.

Warwick, Alexandra, and Dani Cavallaro (1998). *Fashioning the Frame*. Oxford: Berg.

Wilson, Elizabeth (2003). *Adorned in Dreams: Fashion and Modernity*, 2nd edn. New Brunswick, NJ: Rutgers University Press.

Worth, Rachel (2002). Rural Working-Class Dress, 1850–1900: A Peculiarly English Tradition? In Christopher Breward, Becky Conekin, and Caroline Cox (eds.), *The Englishness of English Dress* (pp. 97–112). Oxford and New York: Berg.

13

Hardy and Romantic Love

Michael Irwin

Romantic love is Hardy's central theme: the dominant topic in his poetry and the narrative mainspring for his fiction. While most of the major Victorian novelists were concerned above all with relationships, for Hardy the issue was love itself, love as an overwhelming and capricious power, the great source of human joy and grief. His stock-in-trade is the progress of that emotion, from dramatic onset, through development and change, to eventual grief and disillusion. J. Hillis Miller states the case definitively in *Distance and Desire*: "Hardy's fiction has a single theme: 'fascination.' Novel after novel tells the story of a love affair which emerges from the dreaming background of Wessex life and is followed to its predestined end" (Miller 1970: 114). In his poetry he regularly uses terms which seem to suggest that the aspects and phases of this progress might even be codified: "love's brink" ("A Musical Incident," *CPV* 909); "love's young rays" ("Beyond the Last Lamp," 314); "Love's blossoming" ("I Look in Her Face," *CPV* 631); "Love's fresh-found sensation" ("A Second Attempt," *CPV* 753); "Love's unbroken smile" ("The Child and the Sage," *CPV* 611); "Love's fitful ecstasies" ("In a Eweleaze near Weatherbury," *CPV* 70); "love's decline" ("She to Him II," *CPV* 15); "love's grim hue" ("Two Serenades," *CPV* 604); "Love's sepulchring" ("The Christening," *CPV* 261). Love is seen as a *condition* to be illustrated, scrutinized, anatomized.

When Hardy tells a love-story, whether in poetry or fiction, he is likely to punctuate it with diagnostic generalizations:

"there is a hair's breadth of time at which the question of getting into love or not getting in is a matter of will – quite a thing of choice." (*HE* 55)

a delicate poise between love and friendship – that period in the history of a love when alone it can be said to be unalloyed with pain. (*MC* 175)

To be conscious that the end of the dream is approaching, and yet has not absolutely come, is one of the most wearisome as well as the most curious situations along the whole course between the beginning of a passion and its end. (*RN* 100)

In such passages – and there are many of them in his work – Hardy seems to speak almost as a Naturalist distinguishing recognizable stages of a measurable emotional condition. His beliefs concerning the workings of that condition are idiosyncratic, strongly held, and remarkably consistent. Commentators have often attempted to explain his views on sex and marriage in the light of inferences drawn from his personal life. It is more revealing to reverse this approach. Hardy's reactions to his wives and lovers were anticipated in the attitudes towards love expressed even in the earliest of his writings.

The first of the novels, *Desperate Remedies*, provides particularly telling evidence in that, as a Gothic mystery story, it scarcely afforded obvious occasion for general comments about the workings of love. The youthful author, however (Hardy was not yet 30 when he began work on the novel), chose to volunteer regular pronouncements on the subject, of the kind to become familiar in his later work:

> Perhaps, indeed, the only bliss in the course of love which can truly be called Eden-like is that which prevails immediately after doubt has ended and before reflection has set in . . . (*DR* 41)

> Springrove had long since passed that peculiar line which lies across the course of falling in love . . . a longing to cherish; when the woman is shifted in a man's mind from the region of mere admiration to the region of warm fellowship. (*DR* 250)

These are the observations of a man who is interested in love as a predictable sequence of moves and moods. By implication he himself has traversed this "course" more than once. It is strongly suggested that the sensation experienced when "falling in love" is irrational, and probably doomed to burn itself out. Owen Graye quotes the opinion of his workmate, Edward Springrove:

> "He says that your true lover breathlessly finds himself engaged to a sweetheart, like a man who has caught something in the dark. He doesn't know whether it is a bat or a bird, and takes it to the light when he is cool to learn what it is." (*DR* 26)

Miss Aldclyffe generalizes about the male lover in not dissimilar terms: "He sees a beautiful face and thinks he will never forget it, but in a few weeks the feeling passes off and he wonders how he could have cared for anybody so absurdly much" (*DR* 84).

Hardy, as narrator, seems to endorse these comments. He appeals to common experience when suggesting how emotional self-deception might come about:

> We pass the evening with faces lit up by some flaring illumination or other: we get up the next morning – the fiery jets have all gone out, and nothing confronts us but a few crinkled pipes and sooty wirework, hardly even recalling the outline of the blazing picture that arrested our eyes before bedtime. (*DR* 89–90)

Within the narrative he provides detailed illustrations of the workings of such delusion. Cytherea, the heroine, displays a particularly marked susceptibility in that she begins to be attracted towards Edward Springrove before she has even set eyes on him. Her brother's account of his new friend is sufficient to rouse her interest. The impression is so strong that when Edward seems likely to leave the town without her ever meeting him "An indescribable feeling of sadness shot through Cytherea's heart" (*DR* 27). In the event they do meet, and do fall in love.

A little later in the narrative, while temporarily separated from Edward, she experiences another abrupt romantic encounter. Having just met Aeneas Manston for the first time, in the course of a walk, she is obliged to retreat indoors with him to take shelter from a violent storm. He lives in a dilapidated old manor, which we have already been told is "just the house for a nice ghastly hair-on-end story" (*DR* 60). Hardy clearly relishes the mock-Gothic situation, stoking up the storm to maximum fury: "The thunder, lightning, and rain had now increased to a terrific force. The clouds, from which darts, forks, zigzags, and balls of fire continually sprang, did not appear to be more than a hundred yards above heir heads" (*DR* 130). Profiting from the situation, Manston begins to play, with demonic skill, an organ that he happens to have in the house. Moved by the power of the storm and the power of the music Cytherea

> was swayed into emotional opinions concerning the strange man before her; new impulses of thought came with new harmonies, and entered into her with a gnawing thrill. A dreadful flash of lightning then, and the thunder close upon it. She found herself involuntarily shrinking up beside him, and looking with parted lips at his face. (*DR* 132)

Cytherea is enthralled only temporarily. By the time the storm abates and Manston ceases to play she has recovered herself. Brushing aside various blandishments, she leaves him on relatively cool terms. But she recognizes that she has been "spellbound," and asks herself "O, how is it that man has so fascinated me!" (*DR* 133).

It was bold, in the Victorian period, to permit your heroine to display such emotional and sexual vulnerability. Hardy perhaps got away with it because the episode in question is plainly something of a melodramatic joke; but the emotional psychology of the scene he was to recapitulate again and again. Mop Ollamoor, in "The Fiddler of the Reels," has a musical potency yet greater than Manston's. Car'line Aspent falls subject to "fascination" the first time she hears him play, and (unlike Cytherea) is "unable to shake off the strange infatuation for hours" (*LLI* 140). In subsequent weeks the mere sound of his passing footfall outside her house is sufficient to make her leap from her seat as though receiving "a galvanic shock" (*LLI* 140). Given this susceptibility it is hardly surprising that she rejects her worthy lover, Ned Hipcroft, and is seduced by the wily musician. When Elfride Swancroft has sung at the piano to Stephen Smith she is "startled to find that her harmonies had fired a small Troy, in the shape of [his] heart" (*PBE* 24). Other Hardy characters emotionally swayed by the power of music include Elizabeth-Jane, "enraptured" by the singing of Farfrae, and Anne Garland, moved in Bob Loveday's favor by the plaintive sounds of the Aeolian harp he has erected for her. The most telling episode of this kind comes in *Tess*, when the heroine, like a fascinated bird, is transfixed by the harp-playing of Angel Clare (see CHAPTER 15, HARDY AND MUSIC).

Although Hardy himself, as he records in *The Life and Work* (*LW* 19, 27, 28), was comparably sensitive to music, he uses such scenes to make a wider point. They figure what he sees as the irrational and magical nature of "falling in love." It is rare for any of his characters to be gradually attracted to a member of the opposite sex: they catch love suddenly, almost as one catches an illness. To certain temperaments, including Hardy's, music could be a powerful ancillary agent in this infiltration. Dancing could be another, as when Eustacia yields to the "fascination" and "enchantment" of a moonlit encounter with her former lover:

> Wildeve by himself would have been merely an agitation; Wildeve added to the dance, and the moonlight and the secrecy, began to be a delight.
>
> Whether his personality supplied the greater part of this sweetly compounded feeling, or whether the dance and the scene weighed the more therein, was a nice point upon which Eustacia herself was entirely in a cloud. (*RN* 264)

Such emotion may also be sparked off by an unusual incident or encounter. Dick Dewy has only to see Fancy Day at her window, illuminated by candlelight, to be transfixed (*UGT* 34ff). In *Far From the Madding Crowd* alone, Oak is stirred by the sight of Bathsheba boldly supine on horseback, Boldwood is disorientated by a mysterious valentine card, and Bathsheba is seduced by Troy's swordplay. It is not merely a matter of being drawn to an attractive member of the opposite sex; in each case what is imaged as the prelude to falling in love involves a *complex* of emotions and ideas. Only in one notable case in Hardy's fiction is the catalytic element a simple physical one, and that is because the work in question is structured round contrasts. Jude Fawley has so confined himself to the claims of mind and spirit that the irruption of sex, in the crude form of a barrow-pig's penis, throws him into confusion.

As in the quoted episode from *Desperate Remedies*, Hardy invokes a storm in his last novel, *The Well-Beloved*, to precipitate an erotic encounter. Jocelyn Pierston and Marcia Bencomb are thrust into physical proximity only minutes after they have first met. Faced by a "raking fusillade" of rain, the two are forced to take shelter, huddling together beneath an upturned boat. Later, as they struggle on again, Pierston

> became conscious of a sensation which, in its incipient and unrecognised form, had lurked within him from some unnoticed moment when he was sitting close to his new friend under the lerret. Though a young man, he was too old a hand not to know what this was, and felt alarmed – even dismayed. It meant a possible migration of the Well-Beloved. (*WB* 29)

In the context of Victorian fiction the hint is a remarkably explicit one. The sudden surge of desire has been triggered partly by contiguity, partly by agitations deriving from the storm.

Hardy's beliefs about the onset of love are illustrated in diagrammatic terms by Dare's successful attempt, in *A Laodicean*, to get Captain De Stancy to fall in love with Paula Power. He conducts what amounts to a naturalistic experiment. Having first persuaded the captain to take a stiff drink, breaking a vow of abstinence, he leads him to a spy-hole through which he can watch Paula in her private gymnasium, "bending, wheeling, and undulating in the air" (*AL* 173). The "sportive fascination" of the girl's performance keeps his eyes fixed on the scene. Dare comments on the process he has set in motion: "'A fermentation is beginning in him . . . a purely chemical process; and when it is complete he will probably be clear, and fiery, and sparkling, and quite another man'" (*AL* 174). His calculations prove correct. We are told in the following chapter that the captain is "a changed man": "The sight of Paula in the gymnasium . . . led up to and heightened by subtle accessories, operated on De Stancy's surprised soul with a promptness almost magical" (*AL* 177).

That episode typifies the workings of numerous others. A man and a woman are thrown into contact in bizarre circumstances that create a sense of intimacy. When Bathsheba first encounters Troy it is because they are physically linked, in total darkness, his spur entangled in her skirt. Farfrae and Elizabeth-Jane are initially drawn together when mysteriously summoned (by Susan Henchard, as it turns out) to keep a rendezvous at a granary. Before they eventually part Farfrae volunteers to blow the chaff off her clothes lest it should be washed in by the rain: "As Elizabeth neither assented nor dissented Donald Farfrae began blowing her back hair, and her side hair, and her neck, and the crown of her bonnet, and the fur of her victorine, Elizabeth saying, 'Oh thank you,' at every puff." (*MC* 95)

A particularly piquant example of such small intimacies is to be found in the short story "On the Western Circuit." Charles Raye has begun to flirt with Anna, a servant-girl he has just met at a fair. When her mistress, Mrs. Harnham, comes to fetch the girl, it so happens that all three are trapped together in the crowd:

> the wine-merchant's wife . . . found herself pressed against Anna's acquaintance without power to move away. Their faces were within a few inches of each other, his breath fanned her cheek as well as Anna's. . . . Mrs Harnham then felt a man's hand clasping her fingers, and from the look of consciousness on the young fellow's face she knew the hand to be his: she also knew that from the position of the girl he had no other thought than that the imprisoned hand was Anna's. What prompted her to refrain from undeceiving him she could hardly tell. Not content with holding the hand, he playfully slipped two of his fingers inside her glove, against her palm. (*LLI* 99)

Although the contact has been unintended, Mrs. Harnham is stirred by it: "There had been a magic in his wooing touch of her hand . . ." (*LLI* 100–1).

The most extravagant exercise in this vein does not concern a first meeting, although it does inspire a courtship. It occurs in *A Pair of Blue Eyes*. Henry Knight, a self-contained intellectual in his thirties and a confirmed bachelor, is by a series of chances reduced to clinging to a cliff-face, in a pelting rainstorm, in imminent danger of plunging to his death. He is rescued when the resourceful Elfride makes a rope from her own undergarments which enables him to scramble to safety. As the two instinctively embrace, he finds that her clothing has been reduced to a single "diaphanous exterior robe" (*PBE* 216).

In all these cases, and many more, the situation concerned has short-circuited social, cerebral, or common-sense considerations. There is immediate instinctual communication. It is in some such way, Hardy insists, that love works, that the "purely chemical process" described by Dare is set in motion.

Apart from its truth to Hardy's beliefs about love this technique has two ancillary advantages. One is that it serves as a convenient shorthand device, concentrating what might otherwise have been a lengthy narrative sequence – acquaintanceship ripening into love – into one or two intrinsically vivid episodes. The second is that the episodes concerned can, and usually do, become a metaphorical means of conveying the intensity of the very emotion that they precipitate. Bathsheba's passion is imaged in the flash of a lantern, a flare of scarlet, a dazzle of sword-blades, that of George Somerset and Paula Power, in *A Laodicean*, by the rush of an express train that nearly kills them. Knight's is distilled into the moments when he is hanging on for dear life, high above the sea, while the driving rain is whirled upwards by the wind that strikes the cliff. The storms in *Desperate Remedies*, *The Well-Beloved*, and several other novels are the most obvious metaphors for strong emotion. As in *King Lear*, the storm without stands for the storm within. These lavish episodes can have an expressionistic force as thrilling as an operatic aria. "Love," they proclaim, "feels something like *this*."

Taken as a whole Hardy's fiction would seem to suggest that anybody, of whatever temperament, might fall prey to such insidious intensities. But he also appears to believe that certain habits of living or states of mind engender an enhanced vulnerability to love. In explaining his attraction towards Grace – whom he has never spoken to – Fitzpiers observes to Giles Winterborne: "people living insulated, as I do by the solitude of this place, get charged with emotive fluid like a Leyden jar with electric, for want of some conductor at hand to disperse it" (*W* 89). Lady Constantine, in *Two on a Tower*, is in a rather similar state before forming her attachment with Swithin, "languishing for want of something to do, cherish, or suffer for" (*TT* 26) So, too, is Ella Marchmill, the "Imaginative Woman" bored by her marriage, and so capable, like Cytherea, of beginning to fall in love with a man she has not met. Staying in the house of the poet, Robert Trewe, she devours his verses and comes to feel a "magnetic attraction" towards him: "that all that moved her was the instinct to specialize a waiting emotion on the first fit thing that came to hand, did not, of course, suggest itself to Ella" (*LLI* 14).

Eustacia Vye is portrayed in comparable terms, a "highly charged woman" (*RN* 116) desperate for love. A few minutes of overheard conversation about the arrival of Clym Yeobright from Paris furnishes her "with visions enough to fill the whole blank afternoon." Again there is an effect akin to a chemical change: "She could never have believed in the morning that her colourless inner world would before night become as animated as water under a microscope" (*RN* 108). A little while later she passes, in darkness, a man she knows must be the newcomer, and hears him say "good-night." Although she has yet to see Clym's face "The perfervid woman was by this time half in love with a vision" (*RN* 118). Her responses seem to answer to Fitzpiers' definition: "Human love is a subjective thing . . . joy accompanied by an idea which we project against any suitable object in the line of our vision." He could be speaking for Eustacia or for Ella Marchmill when he proceeds to admit: "I am in love with something in my own head, and no thing-in-itself outside it at all" (*RN* 89).

Hardy dramatizes just this theory of love in *The Well-Beloved*. Jocelyn Pierston, a young sculptor, is portrayed as being in a chronic state of romantic instability:

> To his Well-Beloved he had always been faithful; but she had had many embodiments. Each individuality known as Lucy, Jane, Flora, Evangeline, or whatnot, had been merely a transient condition of her . . . Essentially she was perhaps of no tangible substance; a spirit, a dream, a frenzy, a conception, an aroma, an epitomized sex, a light of the eye, a parting of the lips. (*WB* 16)

At one point Pierston gives a friend a short history of these encounters. Suggestively enough his description of the first of them strongly echoes Hardy's account of his own early attachments at the end of the first chapter of *The Life and Work* (*LW* 30). Later Pierston stresses the sheer miscellaneousness of the manifestations concerned:

> Four times she masqueraded as a brunette, twice as a pale-haired creature, and two or three times under a complexion neither light nor dark. Sometimes she was a tall, fine girl, but more often, I think, she preferred to slip into the skin of a lithe airy being, of no great stature. (*WB* 39)

If the subsequent narrative had corresponded to this past history it could have proved tiresomely lengthy and fragmented. In the event, however, Pierston's love-life effectively narrows down to three women, Avice Caro, when he is 20, her daughter, when he is 40, and her granddaughter, when he is 60. The device could be seen merely as a convenient way of shaping and tightening the narrative; but it has a further significance. All three Avices come from Pierston's own native place, the isolated and in many ways mysterious Isle of Slingers. All three are repeatedly associated with its characteristic sights and sounds. The implication would seem to be that although Pierston is in general of a romantic temperament he is not as promiscuously volatile as a Fitzpiers. Rather, the sculptor feels a particular attraction towards women linked with his deepest predisposition – his feeling for his home territory, the island made of stone. His "well-beloved," Hardy suggests, is "a subjective phenomenon vivified by the weird influences of his descent and birthplace" (*WB* 16). Similarly Ella Marchmill, herself a writer of verse, is drawn to Robert Trewe because she considers him a superior poet, while the romantic Eustacia is immediately excited by the prospect of meeting "a man whose latter life had been passed in the French capital – the centre and vortex of the fashionable world" (*RN* 109) Less obviously, Angel Clare falls in love with Tess – at least in the first instance – because for him she epitomizes the innocence and beauty of the natural way of life that he has chosen in turning from religion to agriculture. In the dawn light, in particular:

> she impressed him most deeply. She was no longer the milkmaid, but a visionary essence of woman – a whole sex condensed into one typical form. He called her Artemis, Demeter, and other fanciful names, half-teasingly – which she did not like because she did not understand them.
>
>   "Call me Tess," she would say askance; and he did. (*TD* 146–7)

When, following her confession, he tells her that "the woman I have been loving is not you" (*TD* 226), his aloofness may be chilling, but he is speaking the truth.

The message is that most of us are born with, or proceed to acquire, romantic predilections of a certain cast, and that our longing to satisfy them can lead us to project that preferred image onto some unsuitable object. In *The Life and Work*, Hardy approvingly quotes Proust as having further developed "the theory exhibited in *The Well-Beloved*":

> "Peu de personnes comprennent le caractère purement subjectif du phénomène qu'est l'amour, et la sorte de création que c'est d'une personne supplémentaire, distincte de celle qui porte le même nom dans le monde, et dont la plupart des éléments sont tirés de nous-mêmes." (*LW* 466–7)

> ["Few people understand the purely subjective quality of the phenomenon which is love, and the way in which it is a kind of creation of a supplementary person, distinct from her who bears the same name in the real world, and of whom most elements are derived from ourselves."]

As with Fitzpiers, all lovers can be said to be enamored with something inside their own heads. Eventually reality will intrude: they will wake after the firework show, as suggested in *Desperate Remedies*, and find that they have caught bat rather than bird.

What continually renews the process, in defiance of previous disappointments, is the fact that it thrills, that it brings both mental and animal joy. Even the physical reaction may be immediate. Troy's first kiss "brought the blood beating into [Bath-sheba's] face, set her stinging as if aflame to the very hollows of her feet" (*FFMC* 196). When Elizabeth-Jane parts from Farfrae after he has hinted his love for her, "Without any consciousness of what she was doing she started running with all her might till she reached her father's door" (*MC* 111). At Bob Loveday's proposal, "Anne's bosom began to surge and fall like a small tide" (*TM* 338). Such physical manifestations – blushing, trembling, panting, palpitation – are very common in the Wessex novels; but they are, of course, a mere reflex of the essential *emotional* intensity. Love, for Hardy, is a transformative magic which we all crave, instinctively, to be possessed by. The "invincible instinct towards self-delight" (*TD* 104) which revives Tess is a renewed longing to be loved. Eustacia's spontaneous prayer is a plea: "send me great love from somewhere, else I shall die" (*RN* 67). To Hardy such desire for supreme happiness is the very driving force of human existence:

> Show me again just this:
> The moment of that kiss
> Away from the prancing folk, by the strawberry-tree! –
> Yea, to such rashness, ratheness, rareness, ripeness, richness,
> Love lures life on.
>   ("Lines to a Movement in Mozart's E-Flat Symphony," *CPV* 459)

In Hardy's belief, however, the mismatch between the power of the emotion con-cerned, and the inescapable unreality of its object, means that romantic joy cannot last long. Hence the comment in *A Pair of Blue Eyes*: "Rapture is often cooled by contact with its cause" (*PBE* 125). In *The Life and Work* this observation is refined to the bleak aphorism: "Love lives on propinquity, but dies of contact" (*LW* 230). Hardy develops the point in *Far From the Madding Crowd*, when describing the nature of Boldwood's feelings towards Bathsheba after receiving the valentine:

> The great aids to idealization in love were present here: occasional observation of her from a distance, and the absence of social intercourse with her – visual familiarity, oral strangeness. The smaller human elements were kept out of sight: the pettinesses that enter so largely into all earthly living and doing were disguised by the accident of lover and loved-one not being on visiting terms . . . (*FFMC* 130)

In more normal circumstances routine familiarity will ensure that the scales fall from the eyes of the deluded lover. Idealization is at the mercy of domesticity. Given that this must be the case it seems almost unnecessary that Hardy should also put so much emphasis on the transience of physical beauty – particularly of female physical beauty:

> These market-dames, mid-aged, with lips thin-drawn,
> > And tissues sere,
> Are they the ones we loved in years agone,
> > And courted here?
>
> ("Former Beauties," CPV 239)

Viviette, in *Two on a Tower*, Lucetta, in *The Mayor of Casterbridge*, and Mrs. Charmond, in *The Woodlanders*, are among the Hardy heroines who start to worry about aging at an absurdly early stage. But perhaps in the Hardy universe that anxiety is not misplaced. His portrayals of elderly women can be devastating. Marcia Bencomb returns to Pierston after forty years, transformed to

> an old woman, pale and shrivelled, her forehead ploughed, her cheek hollow, her hair white as snow. To this the face he once kissed had been brought by the raspings, chisellings, scourgings, bakings, freezings of forty invidious years – by the thinkings of more than half a lifetime. (*WB* 200)

The narrator of "The Revisitation" encounters a former lover by night – in this case after a mere twenty years of absence. Immediately reconciled, they sink into "a large content." But at sunrise he sees her changed image:

> That which Time's transforming chisel
> Had been tooling night and day for twenty years, and tooled too well,
> In its rendering of crease where curve was, where was raven, grizzle –
> Pits, where peonies once did dwell.
>
> (CPV 194)

She, in turn, perceives how he recoils from these ravages, and the two part, never to meet again. He admires the woman he has lost but, as he bleakly observes: "Love is lame at fifty years" (*CPV* 195). "In the Night She Came" offers a blackly humorous slant on the theme. The speaker has assured his lover that Time will not change his love for her. But

> ... in the night she came to me,
> Toothless, and wan, and old,
> With leaden concaves round her eye,
> And wrinkles manifold.
>
> (*CPV* 228)

When she questions his dismayed reaction: "I faltered: 'Well . . . I did not think / You would test me quite so soon!'"

The poem is obviously concerned with an unnerving premonition rather than an actual visitation, but that scarcely helps the case. Thereafter a shadow falls between the lovers. Little Father Time, in *Jude*, seems to reveal a similarity of outlook when remarking apologetically to his parents: "I should like the flowers very very much, if I didn't keep on thinking they'd be all withered in a few days!" (*JO* 312). Hardy goes over the same ground more seriously, or at least less sardonically, in "At Waking," where the speaker has a sudden mental picture of his lover stripped of the special charms with which he has vested her:

> O vision appalling
> When the one believed-in thing
> Is seen falling, falling,
> With all to which hope can cling.
> Off: it is not true;
> For it cannot be
> That the prize I drew
> Is a blank to me!
>
> (*CPV* 224)

The melancholy inference to be drawn from Hardy's stress on physical aging is that in the unlikely event of love surviving propinquity, the physical ravages wrought by time will finish it off. (There is nothing like the same emphasis on the physical degeneration of the male lover. But in "I Look into My Glass" [*CPV* 81], Hardy poignantly expresses his awareness of his own aging, and the third of the Avices, in *The Well-Beloved*, is courted by the 60-year-old Pierston, who once wooed her grandmother.)

It is hardly surprising therefore that the novels abound in partings – Troy from Bathsheba, Eustacia from Clym, Knight from Elfride, Fitzpiers from Grace, Clare from Tess, Sue from Jude. Love, from its very nature, cannot last. In *The Woodlanders* Mrs. Charmond asks Fitzpiers what would have happened if their initial contact, some years previously, had been followed up:

"I should have seen you again."

"And then?"

"Then the fire would have burnt higher and higher. What would have immediately followed I know not; but sorrow and sickness of heart at last."

"Why?"

"Well – that's the end of all love, according to Nature's law. I can give no other reason."
(*W* 146–7)

It might seem reasonable to attribute this extreme view to the philanderer Fitzpiers alone, had it not already been expressed earlier in the novel, and in terms of the same fiery metaphor. In the woods, by the remains of an open-air fire, Fitzpiers has in effect proposed marriage to Grace Melbury, and has been put off. As the two stand, hesitant:

> A diversion was created by the accident of two large birds, that had either been roosting above their heads or nesting there, tumbling one over the other into the hot ashes at their feet, apparently engrossed in a desperate quarrel that prevented the use of their wings. They speedily parted, however, and flew up with a singed smell, and were seen no more.
>   "That's the end of what is called love!" said some one. (*W* 108)

The snatch of soliloquy comes from Marty South, who has not seen the other two and is presumably speaking from her own sad experience in endorsing Fitzpiers' belief.

Numerous poems reflect the same pessimistic outlook – for example "Neutral Tones," "Her Reproach," "The Dawn after the Dance," and "Lost Love" (*CPV* 12, 135, 230, 318). "The End of the Episode" concludes:

> Though fervent was our vow,
> Though ruddily ran our pleasure,
> Bliss has fulfilled its measure,
>   And sees its sentence now.
>
> Ache deep; but make no moans:
> Smile out; but stilly suffer:
> The paths of love are rougher
>   Than thoroughfares of stones.
>
> (*CPV* 227)

It is hardly surprising that on occasion Hardy seems to accept the logic of his own frequently stated view, and turn away from romance altogether. Such is the burden of "He Abjures Love":

> No more will now rate I
> The common rare,
> The midnight drizzle dew,
> The gray hour golden,
> The wind a yearning cry,
> The faulty fair,
> Things dreamt, of comelier hue
> Than things beholden! . . .
>
> (CPV 237)

Yet this seemingly long-resisted renunciation had been anticipated much earlier in his work – most notably in the sonnet "Revulsion," which is dated 1866. In it the young Hardy suggests that we would do better to avoid romantic attachment altogether:

> For winning love we win the risk of losing,
> And losing love is as one's life were riven;
> It cuts like contumely and keen ill-using
> To cede what was superfluously given.
>
> Let me then never feel the fateful thrilling
> That devastates the love-worn wooer's frame,
> The hot ado of fevered hopes, the chilling
> That agonizes disappointed aim!
> So may I live no junctive law fulfilling,
> And my heart's table bear no woman's name.
>
> (CPV 14)

He did not, of course, keep this vow, no doubt for the reason implied in "He Abjures Love" – that the alternative is too dispiriting:

> But – after love what comes?
> A scene that lours,
> A few sad vacant hours,
> And then, the Curtain.
>
> (CPV 237)

It seems that the delusive joys of love may after all be preferable to the desolation of cold literalism.

In *A Tale of a Tub* Swift limits us, by means of apparently logical argument, to two possible views of life, each uninviting – that of the "fool" and that of the "knave." Hardy offers both himself and his readers a comparable Hobson's choice. Should we surrender to love's blissful but short-lived deceptions, and suffer for so doing, or would we do better to view the world with what he calls, in *Tess*, "the mean unglamoured eye" (*TD* 69)? As Ethelberta remarks, "between continually wanting to love, to escape the blank lives of those who do not, and wanting not to love, to keep out of the miseries of those who do, I get foolishly warm and foolishly cold by turns" (*HE* 55). The lonely Eustacia, however, would not vacillate: "she had mentally walked round love, told the towers thereof, considered its palaces; and concluded that love was but a doleful joy. Yet she desired it, as one in a desert would be thankful for brackish water" (*RN* 66–7).

It was observed earlier that Hardy's somberly consistent views on love can be traced even in his first novel. Equally striking is the fact that what he asserted on this theme in his early fiction he was later to demonstrate that he truly meant. The claim, in *Desperate Remedies*, that "with some natures utter elusion is the one special event which will make a passing love permanent for ever" (*DR* 10) might seem no more than a rhetorical flourish. But in *Far From the Madding Crowd* it is the "utter elusion" produced by Fanny's death that restores Troy's lost passion for her. In *A Pair of Blue Eyes* Smith and Knight experience a similar revival of feeling when they hear that Elfride has died. Much later in his fictional career Hardy has Pierston react even more strongly to news of the death of the first Avice, whom he has not seen for twenty years: "He loved the woman dead and inaccessible as he had never loved her in life" (*WB* 72). This recovered feeling has an "intrinsic, almost radiant, purity": "The flesh was absent altogether; it was love rarefied and refined to its highest attar. He had felt nothing like it before" (*WB* 73).

Neither here nor earlier is Hardy striking an attitude. His response to the death of his first wife, Emma, was to be immediately and precisely of the kind described in *The Well-Beloved*. It seems that he felt, in real life, exactly what his own writings had implied he would feel in such circumstances. For Hardy there would have been an underlying consistency, a kind of emotional logic, in this reaction. A man (or woman) who falls in love, he repeatedly implies, is infatuated by a subjective image. That love is doomed to die once the image is confuted and effaced by the real personality of the individual in question. So Hardy's original "dream" Emma would have been eroded first by simple actualities of "propinquity," later also by physical and mental changes. With her death those effacements are themselves effaced: "The flesh was absent altogether." She could, and did, in his poetry, revert to being "A phantom of his own figuring" ("The Phantom Horsewoman," *CPV* 354). Although love dies it can have an after-life.

"The Fiddler of the Reels" is by no means the only work in which Hardy dramatizes seriously held views on sexual desire in hyperbolic, if not grotesque, terms. In "Barbara of the House of Grebe" the heroine falls out of love with the admirable Edmond Willowes after he has been horribly disfigured in a fire. Years later, when he has long been presumed dead, and she is unhappily married to Lord Uplandtowers, she comes into possession of a life-sized statue of Edmond as he had looked before his accident: "The mutilated features of Willowes had disappeared from her mind's eye; this perfect being was really the man she had loved, and not that later pitiable figure; in whom tenderness and truth should have seen this image always, but had not done so" (Hardy 1997: 246). Soon she gets into the habit of rising in the night to embrace the statue and swear her devotion to Edmond with "an intensity of feeling . . . which Lord Uplandtowers had not dreamed of her possessing" (Hardy 1997: 248). Barbara's reaction to this physical image prefigures with unlikely exactness Hardy's reaction to his restored mental images of the youthful Emma. The psychology he is parodically portraying proves to be his own.

Two further aspects of the topic merit an afterword. For most of us romantic love renews itself, if in altered terms, through parenthood. Hardy himself, of course, to his apparent regret, had no children. (It would have been interesting to see what sort of father he would have been.) In his fiction parenthood never becomes a serious issue. Henchard's daughter dies in infancy. The two (unnamed) children of Jude and Sue are efficiently dispatched by Jude's eldest offspring, who then commits suicide. Car'line Aspent's daughter is abducted. Barbara, quite exceptionally, bears eleven children, but only one (again unnamed) survives into adulthood. The love-affairs with which Hardy is concerned are closed units of symbiotic solipsism, virtually never evolving into a new generation.

There is a more particular bearing of Hardy's portrayal of love – and probably his experiences of it. The subject seems to have been bound up with his sense of himself as an artist. It was suggested earlier that some of his characters are shown to be particularly sensitive to the stresses of love even in quasi-constitutional terms. In the case of Barbara he invokes physical explanations: "her nerves were still much shaken"; "the nerves of the poor lady were quivering in agony" (Hardy 1997: 252). Viviette in *Two on a Tower* reaches a pitch of exquisite misery once she has decided to let Swithin go abroad: "as she heard her feverish heart throb against the desk, she firmly believed the wearing impulses of that heart would put an end to her sad life" (*TT* 78). Both women, in effect, die for love, as do the comparably neurasthenic Ella Marchmill, Eustacia, and Lucetta.

Of Hardy's male characters the one closest in temperament to these hyper-susceptible victims is the poet Robert Trewe, the unseen object of Ella Marchmill's affections. Prior to his suicide he leaves behind a note that makes it clear that he could have been saved had the right woman appeared in his life: "I have long dreamt of such an unattainable creature, as you know; and she, this undiscoverable, elusive one, inspired my last volume . . . She has continued to the last unrevealed, unmet, unwon" (*LLI* 27). There may be an element of self-portraiture, or self-caricature, in this depiction of a fellow-poet, afflicted by something like Ella Marchmill's exaggerated sensibilities. Alternatively, or additionally, the implication may be a connection between artistic creativity and the pursuit of love. As in the case of Pierston the sculptor, Trewe's aesthetic vision has apparently been fueled by dreams of "an unattainable creature." Hardy's presentation of the two men is an interesting anticipation of Robert Graves' *The White Goddess*. Although an admirer of Hardy Graves does not seem to have read *The Well-Beloved*, but his vision of a divine Muse, presiding over an island, and associated with sea, moon, and storms, could almost be an extrapolation from that novel and the poem of the same title. His account of the life of the true poet could readily be applied to Pierston's travails:

A Muse-poet falls in love, absolutely, and his true love is for him the embodiment of the Muse. As a rule, the power of absolutely falling in love soon vanishes; and, as a rule because the woman feels embarrassed by the spell she exercises over her poet-lover and repudiates it. . . . But the real, perpetually obsessed Muse-poet distinguishes between the Goddess . . . and the individual woman whom the Goddess may make her instrument for a month, a year, seven years, or even more. The Goddess abides; and perhaps he will again have knowledge of her through his experience of another woman. (Graves 1961: 490–1)

The formulations are very close to Pierston's own. In both cases the claim is that, for the artist, true creativity is dependent upon the constant renewal of romantic desire. It is a claim perhaps also relevant to Hardy himself. Pierston loves again at 60: Hardy remarks of himself in *The Life and Work*: "I was a child till I was 16; a youth till I was 25; a young man till I was 40 or 50" (*LW* 408).

It so happens that Pierston, unlike either Graves or Hardy, puts the Muse theory negatively to the test. Illness and emotional stress bring to an end his pursuit of the "well-beloved" – but they simultaneously destroy his creativity and his pleasure in his own former work. The change goes even deeper: he no longer enjoys aesthetic responses of any kind. With the search for love now at an end he finds "his sense of beauty in art and nature absolutely extinct" (*WB* 202). Hardy would seem to be asserting that artistic inspiration and sexual vitality are indeed crucially linked: lose the latter and you will lose the former.

The Well-Beloved is subtitled "A Sketch of a Temperament." Hardy told Swinburne that it was "a fanciful exhibition of the artistic nature" (*LW* 305). The words "sketch" and "fanciful" suggest that the work is of limited seriousness. *The White Goddess* itself might be thought to incorporate at least an element of playfulness. None the less, the underlying issue is a serious one. Hardy, Graves, Yeats, Janáček, and Picasso, for example, would all seem to have engaged with it in real life, seeking renewed inspiration, in their later years, through love. Graves implies that emotional instability is a price worth paying for the sake of art. Hardy, by contrast, in remaining studiously neutral about the quality of Pierston's work, leaves open the possibility that the "artistic temperament" may be an expression of, and perhaps an excuse for, emotional immaturity. *The Well-Beloved* ends on what seems to have been intended as a note of cynical realism. There is an agreeable irony in the fact that at the date of publication Hardy had thirty years of life ahead of him, a second marriage (to a much younger woman), and an entire poetic career.

The more general question as to whether the joys of love can be sufficient compensation for its inevitable pains Hardy leaves unresolved. Indeed its unresolvability is the dilemma at the heart of his writings. He offers eloquent and copious evidence on either side of the case. It is left to the reader to decide which of the extreme positions is the more persuasive. On the one hand:

> Joy-jaunts, impassioned flings,
>   Love, and its ecstasy,
> Will always have been great things,
>   Great things to me!
>
> ("Great Things," *CPV* 475)

But on the other:

> "Love is a terrible thing: sweet for a space,
> And then all mourning, mourning!"
>
> ("A Hurried Meeting," *CPV* 829)

REFERENCES AND FURTHER READING

Graves, Robert (1961). *The White Goddess*. London: Faber & Faber.

Hardy, Thomas ([1871] 2003). *Desperate Remedies*, ed. Patricia Ingham. Oxford: Oxford University Press.

Hardy, Thomas ([1872] 1985). *Under the Greenwood Tree*, ed. Simon Gatrell. Oxford: Oxford University Press.

Hardy, Thomas ([1873] 1985). *A Pair of Blue Eyes*, ed. Alan Manford. Oxford: Oxford University Press.

Hardy, Thomas ([1874] 1993). *Far from the Madding Crowd*, ed. Suzanne B. Falck-Yi. Oxford: Oxford University Press.

Hardy, Thomas ([1876] 1996). *The Hand of Ethelberta*, ed. Tim Dolin. London: Penguin.

Hardy, Thomas ([1878] 1990). *The Return of the Native*, ed. Simon Gatrell. Oxford: Oxford University Press.

Hardy, Thomas ([1880] 1991). *The Trumpet-Major*, ed. Richard Nemesvari. Oxford: Oxford University Press.

Hardy, Thomas ([1881] 1991). *A Laodicean*, ed. Jane Gatewood. Oxford: Oxford University Press.

Hardy, Thomas ([1882] 1993). *Two on a Tower*, ed. Suleiman M. Ahmad. Oxford: Oxford University Press.

Hardy, Thomas ([1886] 1987). *The Mayor of Casterbridge*, ed. Dale Kramer. Oxford: Oxford University Press.

Hardy, Thomas ([1887] 1985). *The Woodlanders*, ed. Dale Kramer. Oxford: Oxford University Press.

Hardy, Thomas ([1891] 1988). *Tess of the d'Urbervilles*, ed. Julian Grindle and Simon Gatrell. Oxford: Oxford University Press.

Hardy, Thomas ([1894] 1996). *Life's Little Ironies*, ed. Alan Manford. Oxford: Oxford University Press.

Hardy, Thomas ([1895] 1985). *Jude the Obscure*, ed. Patricia Ingham. Oxford: Oxford University Press.

Hardy, Thomas ([1897] 1998). *The Well-Beloved*, ed. Tom Hetherington. Oxford: Oxford University Press.

Hardy, Thomas (1979). *The Variorum Edition of the Complete Poems of Thomas Hardy*, ed. James Gibson. London: Macmillan.

Hardy, Thomas (1984). *The Life and Work of Thomas Hardy*, ed. Michael Millgate. London: Macmillan.

Hardy, Thomas (1997). *The Complete Stories*, ed. Norman Page. London: J. M. Dent.

Miller, J. Hillis (1970). *Thomas Hardy: Distance and Desire*. Cambridge, MA: The Belknap Press of Harvard University Press.

14

Hardy and the Visual Arts

J. B. Bullen

Writing in *The Speaker* in 1890, Hardy's close friend Edmund Gosse wrote a highly appreciative account of Hardy's novels and short stories. In this he used a strongly pictorial analogy. "Besides his ten great oil-pictures," he said, "Mr. Hardy has occasionally hung up in his gallery a water-colour sketch of extraordinary charm and quality" (Cox 1970: 170). Gosse knew that Hardy would have approved of the parallel between writer and artist. By temperament and talent Hardy was sensitively attuned to visual pleasure. As a child he was responsive to the power of color and form (*LW* 20) and it was his skill as a draughtsman that first directed him towards an architectural career. He continued to paint and draw, albeit on a modest scale, throughout his life, and this lent a strongly practical coloration to his enthusiasm for works of art in many media. In using pictorial terms to describe Hardy's writing, Gosse would have picked up on something that Hardy frequently applied to his own work. For Hardy and his contemporaries the comparison between the aims of the artist and those of the writer was no loose simile. At a period when issues of literary and visual mimesis were widely debated, the two arts seemed to be closely aligned and to come under similar influences. For Hardy the subjects of the painter, the composition, grouping, and lighting of the artist, and even the appreciation and interpretation of the pictorial image all had significance for the writing and understanding of a literary text. Throughout his life he used terms drawn from the visual arts to objectify his own activity as a writer to himself. Art, he wrote in 1890, "is a changing of the actual proportions and order of things, so as to bring out more forcibly than might otherwise be done that feature in them which appeals most strongly to the idiosyncrasy of the artist." "Hence," he added, "'realism' is not Art" (*LW* 239). What Hardy sought most often in the work of painters was expressive power, the capacity to mold and change the material world in accordance with the emotional one. "Nature," he said, referring to a painting attributed to Richard Parkes Bonington, "is played out as a Beauty, but not as a mystery." Bonington offered him only the "simply natural" when he craved "the deeper reality underlying the scenic, the expression of what are sometimes called abstract imaginings" (*LW* 192). This "deeper reality" he found in the work of many, and sometimes unexpected, artists. Turner was still a controversial figure in the late nineteenth century, but Hardy was impressed by what he called "the much-decried, mad, late-Turner rendering," where "The exact truth as to material fact ceases to be of importance" (*LW* 192). He also found the "deeper reality" in some of the Old Masters. "My art," he wrote in 1887, "is to intensify the expression of things, as is done by Crivelli, Bellini, &c. so that the heart and inner meaning is made vividly visible" (*LW* 183).

When Hardy wrote this, he would have been familiar with Crivelli's *Pietà* (c.1472) and Bellini's *Agony in the Garden* (c.1455) both of which had been acquired by the National Gallery not long before he arrived in London as a young man. In style, subject matter, and technique, nothing could be further removed from the work of Turner, yet for Hardy and his contemporaries there was one factor that the artists shared – they used form expressively. Crivelli and Bellini in the Venetian Renaissance, and Turner in the modern period, endowed the objective world with imaginative meaning by altering and changing appearances to express something within. The work of all three involved a form of self-expression, "a disproportioning . . . of realities" (*LW* 239). When T. S. Eliot, who was not an admirer of Hardy's work, said that he seemed to him "to have written as nearly for the sake of 'self expression' as a man well can" (Eliot 1934: 54), the comment was meant to be derogatory, but Hardy would have been flattered. He valued "self-expression" in literature just as he valued expressive form in art.

If, as Hardy told two of his early biographers, "ideas presented themselves to his mind more in the guise of mental pictures than as subjects for writing down" (Brennecke 1928: 113–14), then the images themselves came to him in the first place as the result of his passionate interest in the art of painting and from his lifelong habit of drawing and sketching. Some of his earliest and happiest memories were bound up with what for him was an enormously pleasurable activity. The benign figure of Henry Moule, for example, "emerges," said Hardy late in life,

> from the obscurity of forgotten and half-forgotten things somewhere between 1856 and 1860, when I recall him as he stood beside me while I was attempting a sketch from nature in water colours. He must have been about thirty, and had already become an adept in out-door painting. As I was but a youth, and by no means practised in that art, he criticized my performance freely. (*THPV* 230)

A few of Hardy's paintings from this period are collected in the Dorset County Museum. Some of them are animal studies, a rabbit and a kingfisher, for example, but most of them are topographical sketches. The area around the cottage at Bockhampton continued to feed Hardy's imagination for the rest of his life, and much of the conviction and authenticity that he brought to his literary settings derives from hours of careful drawing in his youth. An accomplished study of the Old Manor House, Kingston Maurward, painted in 1859, provided him with an image that he transformed into Knapwater House in *Desperate Remedies,* and his drawings of the streets and cottages of Bockhampton and Stinsford found literary expression in the architectural details of Mellstock in *Under the Greenwood Tree*. The close identification in Hardy's mind between fiction and reality, between the visual image and its verbal equivalent, is illustrated by a sketch of his parents' cottage and neighboring Puddletown Heath, where a note on the back of the drawing conflates fiction and reality. It reads "Bockhampton Cottage and Egdon Heath."

When Hardy went to London in 1862 he joined the thriving architectural practice of Arthur Blomfield as a draughtsman, and filled pocket-books with notes and drawings. Most of these have been destroyed, but a few leaves remain to testify to his passion for recording places and scenes in this way. There is a small sketch of St. James's Park and a view from his lodgings at Westbourne Park Villas, a view over Windsor Castle, and a picture of the sun setting over the Channel at Dover, all dating from 1862; in September 1863 he drew Warbarrow Bay, near Lulworth, and Gad Cliff; a visit to his home in 1863 resulted in a drawing of Dorchester from Stinsford Hill and a view of Dogberry Down from the Devil's Kitchen. Later in the same decade he made a study of Denchworth, near Wantage, the country of *Jude the Obscure*, and one of Lulworth Cove, which became Lulwind Cove in *Desperate Remedies*.

His meeting with Emma Gifford in 1870 stimulated his interest in this field. She was an enthusiastic water-colorist, and drawings and sketches appear everywhere in her diaries. In their early years together, she and Hardy frequently went out on painting expeditions. As late as 1893 Sir George Douglas remembered Hardy attempting to correct Emma's painting at the Douglas's home at Springwood Park (Millgate 2004: 292–3). Hardy drew extensively in the Valency valley, near Emma's Cornish home, between 1870 and 1872, and the same valley provided many of the settings for *A Pair of Blue Eyes*. Hardy actually supplied the editor of *Tinsley's Magazine* with a number of drawings to aid the artist in his illustrations (*CL* I: 18), and the text itself often replicates the configurations of a landscape study. For example, the account of "two bold escarpments sloping down together like the letter V," towards "the bottom, [of which] like liquid in a funnel, appeared the sea, grey and small" (*PBE* 25) echoes the visual pattern of one of Hardy's drawings from this same spot in north Cornwall.

The Valency valley appears again in a drawing Hardy made of Emma as she tried to retrieve a glass that had fallen into a pool by a waterfall. In the poem "Under the Waterfall" Hardy recalls how he and Emma went to the valley "to paint the scene," and the drawing shows Emma reaching into the pool, in the words of the poem, "with long bared arms" (*CPW* II: 45–6). Several days later, on August 22, Emma appears again in one of Hardy's drawings, this time on Beeny Cliff. Her visual image continued to haunt him, and in "The Figure in the Scene" from *Moments of Vision* (1917) he remembers how

> It pleased her to step in front and sit
>   Where the cragged slope was green,
> While I stood back that I might pencil it
>   With her amid the scene.

> (*CPW* II: 216)

Some of Hardy's extant drawings were done specifically in preparation for the writing of the novels. In 1873 he drew "smockfrocks, gaiters, sheep-crooks, rick-'staddles,' a sheep-washing pool, one of the old-fashioned malt-houses, and some out-of-the-way things" *(LW* 99) for Helen Paterson, who was illustrating *Far from the Madding Crowd.* His study of an old Wessex milking-pail, now in Dorchester County Museum, may well be one of these. More drawings were done for *The Return of the Native,* and in 1878 he sent studies of mummers' clothing and stage properties to Arthur Hopkins, who was illustrating the novel in *Harper's New Monthly Magazine (CL* I: 54–5). Later, Hardy climbed the downs near Sutton Pointz to sketch the scene for *The Trumpet-Major.* In the 1880s he made drawings of, and extensive notes on, the portraits of Julia and Francis Turberville at Woolbridge Manor House, and on a pencil study of "Old Groves Place" in Shaftesbury (now in Dorchester County Museum) he wrote that it was "sketched on the spot for a novel called 'Jude the Obscure.'"

Some of Hardy's most accomplished graphic work is to be found in the vignettes attached to the *Wessex Poems* (1898). He did these in the late 1890s with a view to publication, and as such they are very different from the drawings that he made for his own private purposes. They do not serve to clarify the visual images of the verse, nor are they illustrations of the incidents in the poems. Instead, they act as enigmatic, economical commentaries on the poetic themes. Many of them are architectural fragments, buildings, street scenes, and townscapes, and a very large number employ one of Hardy's favorite motifs – the road which winds across a landscape disappearing at the horizon into infinity. Most of them are highly symbolic – the vase of dead flowers for the poem "To Outer Nature," the highly stylized conjunction of townscape, earthworks, and graveyard for "Her Death and After," and, most famous of all, the enormous pair of spectacles that appears to be resting in a field for the poem "In a Eweleaze near Weatherbury."

If the vignettes to the *Wessex Poems* represent both the strengths and the limitations of Hardy's technical ability, his talents as a draughtsman were sufficient for him to admire the genius of others, and from an early age he possessed a keen interest in all kinds of painting, ancient and modern. Before going to London in 1862, it was the art journals, particularly the *Illustrated Magazine of Art,* which formed the basis of his art education, and later in life he recommended these same journals as a way of introducing children to the pleasures of painting. But it was London that opened his eyes to the real power and vitality of visual art. In *Life and Work* he says that he was influenced in his decision to "migrate" to the capital by the opening of the International Exhibition *(LW* 40), where the centerpiece was a huge gallery of pictures borrowed from many countries around the world. The British section alone comprised 790 oil paintings, 600 watercolors, and 500 engravings, and there were thousands of pictures from elsewhere. Hardy clearly reveled in this new visual experience. He was constantly traveling to South Kensington to visit and revisit the exhibition. Sometimes he went alone, but sometimes he took his sister Mary or his cousin Martha Sparks, and on at least one occasion went with his friend Horace Moule, whose poem on Gérôme's *Roman Gladiators* was published in the journal *Once a Week.* During this period he began to stock his mind with images which were later to influence his writing, and it was here that he saw for the first time the work of artists whose acquaintance he would make later in life. The British section was the largest, but the greatest revelation of the show for English audiences was the painting that came from France. Ingres's *La Source* and Delacroix's *The Murder of the Bishop of Liège* dominated the French entry, but the "modern" French school was well represented by Meissonier, described as "the idol of the Paris salons," and by the work of the French landscape artists whose techniques Hardy later mentioned in *Desperate Remedies*, Théodore Rousseau, Charles Daubigny, Paul Baudry, and most especially Constant Troyon and Rosa Bonheur. From the earlier English school were Turner's *Falls at Schaffhausen* (1841) and *Fifth Plague of Egypt* (1800), and the work of artists with whom Hardy would later become familiar – G. F. Watts, Frederick Leighton (his *Cimabue's Madonna*, 1853–5), and W. P. Frith (his huge and bustling *Ramsgate Sands*, 1854). Sculpture was also represented, and it was here that Hardy had his first opportunity to see the work of Thomas Woolner, an artist whose images were significantly to influence the writing of *The Return of the Native*. But the most prominent artist in the British section was Sir Joshua Reynolds, and the very large number of Reynolds' portraits – thirty in all – were widely admired and much praised for their technical skill and psychological insight. The most prominent was undoubtedly his study of Sarah Siddons as *The Tragic Muse* – a picture which Hardy later saw on a number of occasions, and which contributed materially to his creation of Eustacia Vye (Bullen 1986: 106–7).

The immediate effect upon Hardy of so much fine painting was that he rapidly and systematically began to make up for his lack of formal art education. The National Gallery was the obvious place to start; so on every day that the gallery was open he devoted "twenty minutes after lunch to an inspection of the masters hung there, confining his attention to a single master on each visit, and forbidding his eyes to stray to any other" (*LW* 53). Anticipating the charge of too earnest autodidacticism, Hardy added that "He went there from sheer liking, and not with any practical object," and, recommending the plan to the young, said that "they would insensibly acquire a greater insight into schools and styles by this means than from any guide books to the painters' works and manners" (*LW* 53). In 1863 he began to keep a notebook entitled "Schools of Painting" containing entries about painters and their works copied from some unidentified source. But, failing to take his own advice, he copied into it remarks that were often misleading, inaccurate, or out of date. In spite, however, of such misdirected information, Hardy's visits to the National Gallery familiarized him with the work of a wide range of painters. It was here that he first saw the work of "Giotto," now thought to be by Spinello Aretino that he mentions in *Tess of the d'Urbervilles* (*TD* 383), of Crivelli and Bellini, of Sebastiano del Piombo, of Moroni and Greuze, allusions to whose works appear in a number of the novels. It was here, too, that he saw what the subtitle to *Under the Greenwood Tree* calls "rural painting of the Dutch school," when, in 1871, the gallery was augmented by a very large number of Dutch paintings from the Peel collection. The National Gallery also possessed a fine collection of paintings by Turner, and there were more Turner canvases in another collection that Hardy frequently visited, in South Kensington. The iron sheds, jokingly known as "The Brompton Boilers," were the temporary home of the paintings collected by the Regency connoisseurs Robert Vernon and John Sheepshanks. These two had left their pictures to the nation, and in 1857 they were made available to the public for the first time before they were moved to South Kensington. There was no finer collection of English paintings of the early nineteenth century than this one, the bulk of the collection comprising genre and narrative painting. Here Hardy had access to works by Mulready, Wilkie, and Webster – works whose lively conjunction of narrative and image made them very popular with English audiences. But the master of this style of painting was very much alive and flourishing, and in 1862 Hardy was almost certainly one of the 83,000 people who crowded into a small gallery in the Haymarket between April and September to marvel at W. P. Frith's *The Railway Station.*

If the National Gallery introduced Hardy to the works of the Old Masters, and the South Kensington collection provided him with his first experience of narrative painting, his art education was further extended by the exhibitions at the Royal Academy. For Hardy, however, the Academy was much more than just an exhibition space. He loved it as an institution, and not only did he regularly attend the annual exhibitions but, from 1887, he was invited to the private views and to the dinners held there. Something of the importance which Hardy attached to the Royal Academy he expressed in *The Hand of Ethelberta.* Ethelberta, like Hardy himself, is "a firm believer in the kindly effects of artistic education" (*HE* 179), so she takes her two humble brothers on a didactic trip to the annual exhibition. With their untutored taste they tend to indulge in "curious speculations on the intrinsic nature of the delineated subject" (*HE* 180), but Ethelberta knows better. "Catalogue in hand" (*HE* 179), she encourages her brothers to see beyond the anecdotal and the curious and to appreciate the pictures "as art" (*HE* 180), and to respond to them in terms of style and technique rather than simply as illustrations. In this episode it is the summer exhibition of modern painting that Ethelberta is attending, but the winter exhibitions were equally important in Hardy's calendar. These were started in 1870, and the pictures were drawn largely from private collections usually closed to the public. In the early years the paintings of Sir Joshua Reynolds featured prominently, and for the first time people began to appreciate the diversity and subtlety of his portraits. In the mid-1880s it was the turn of J. M. W. Turner.

In his early years in London, Hardy's knowledge of art was enlarged from two other sources. During his student days he began to frequent the smaller, private galleries that tended to show paintings of a more ambitious or avant-garde nature. The French Gallery, for example, put on an annual show of works selected from the official Salon of the previous year, and the Grosvenor Gallery opened in 1877 showing works which would not be acceptable at the Academy. It was in these smaller galleries that he was introduced to the work of the Impressionists in the 1880s, the New English Art Club (founded in 1885), and the school of French realist painting led by Bastien-Lepage.

Finally there were the critics. As early as 1862 Hardy had told his sister that he was reading Ruskin's *Modern Painters*; as a young architect he could hardly have failed to read *The Seven Lamps of Architecture* and *The Stones of Venice*. Even though Hardy rarely mentions Ruskin by name, his literary notes show that, throughout his life, he frequently turned to Ruskin's views on the nature of perception, or to his ideas about verisimilitude in painting and literature. Hardy also read the histories of Renaissance painting by Quatremère de Quincy and Richard Duppa, and was a keen student of the works of John Addington Symonds. He made notes from the writings of Francis Palgrave, and the influence of Walter Pater, whom he met in 1886, can often be detected in his writing. In 1863 Hardy had submitted an essay entitled "On the Application of Coloured Bricks and Terra Cotta to Modern Architecture" to the Institute of British Architects. He was presented with a silver medal by Professor T. L. Donaldson and considered the possibility of a career as an art critic specializing in architecture (*LW* 49).

If Hardy's knowledge of painting came from visits to galleries in England and reading books and journals, his understanding was broadened by his numerous Continental journeys. Part of his honeymoon, in 1874, was spent looking at the pictures in the Louvre, and when he and Emma went to Versailles Hardy bought two reproductions of Napoleonic subjects, one by Horace Vernet, the other by Paul Philippoteaux. In the autumn of 1882 he was once again "studying the pictures at the Louvre and the Luxembourg" (*LW* 160), and in 1887 he and his wife passed through Paris yet again. In 1888 they returned to the French capital, and this time went to see the June exhibition of the official Salon and visited an exhibition of the drawings and manuscripts of Victor Hugo (*LW* 217). Another Continental journey, this time taking in Holland, Germany, and Belgium, seems to have been especially important to Hardy, since he makes a number of half-hidden references to it in the novels. It took place in 1876. Hardy's diaries for this period were destroyed, but his wife's have been preserved, and she records many of the towns they visited and the pictures they saw. At The Hague she made a slight sketch of a painting by Paul Potter; in Antwerp she remarks that they saw several pictures by Rubens; but when they reached Brussels, she began to tire. Consequently Hardy went alone "to see the picture gallery which," Emma said, "was closed yesterday" (Emma Hardy 1985: 93). One of his visits was almost certainly to the Wiertz Museum, which Cook's *Handbook* described as "one place that no one must fail to visit" (Cook 1874: 56). The pictures of Antoine Wiertz (1806–65) were profoundly macabre, intensely violent, and highly melodramatic, but they were calculated to appeal to Hardy's temperament, with their penchant for the grotesque. Wiertz's best-known picture, *Deux jeunes Filles,* or *La Belle Rosine* (1847), has a curious affinity with a note Hardy made several years later, and which it may have unconsciously prompted. The juxtaposition of a girl's youthful body and a skeleton in the picture carries with it emotions and sentiments resembling Hardy's strange view of Montmartre cemetery through a window. In front of the window, and with the cemetery as a background, Hardy observed "young women dancing the *cancan*" (*LW* 240). Wiertz's painting was often compared with that of his fellow countryman Jan Van Beers, and in March and April of 1887 an exhibition of what the *Art Journal* described as "one or two new horrors" from Van Beers was held in Bond Street in London. Hardy and his wife stayed in London between April and July of 1887 on their way back from Italy, and, since Hardy made a special point of visiting London exhibitions whenever the opportunity arose, he almost certainly saw this one. The evidence that he did so is contained in *Tess of the d'Urbervilles*. In one brief, but suggestive, sentence, Hardy's memory of the Wiertz Museum, stimulated by his visit to the Van Beers show, is set against his recent experience of Italian art in the galleries and churches of Florence and Venice. Angel and Tess have just separated, and this separation forces Angel to take a new and different view of humanity. It now "stood before him," Hardy wrote, "no longer in the pensive sweetness of Italian art, but in the staring and ghastly attitudes of a Wiertz Museum, and with the leer of a study by Van Beers" (*TD* 254). The Wiertz picture Hardy had in mind may well have been his *The Spirit of the Civilization of the Nineteenth Century* (1864), which was both a profoundly cynical commentary on nineteenth-century values and a highly appropriate image for *Tess of the d'Urbervilles* where some soldiers with cruel, jeering faces chase to her death a beautiful, young, frantic mother, her new-born infant in her arms.

The appearance in a fictional context of the names of Wiertz and Van Beers is curious, because their significance for Hardy was so personal, but the general meaning is clear. Hardy is making a contrast between the stark realities, the cruelty, and the violence of the present, and the gentleness, the dignity, and the humanity of a mythical past. Elsewhere in the same novel Hardy discovers affinities between Italian art with its "pensive sweetness" and the appearance of female field workers in whom "The pensive character which the curtained hood lent to their bent heads would have reminded the observer of some early Italian conception of the two Marys" (*TD* 277). He also finds it in the bent heads of Angel and Liza-Lu; on leaving Wintoncester gaol, the "drooping of their heads" resembles "that of Giotto's Two Apostles" (*TD* 383).

The contrast between modern Belgian art and early Italian art presented itself most forcibly to Hardy's mind when he returned home from Italy in 1887. Genoa impressed him and his wife sufficiently for Hardy to make a comparison between the famous palazzi and the appearance of the buildings in "Chief Street," Christminster, in *Jude the Obscure*. From Genoa they went to Pisa, visiting the Baptistry and the famous Campo Santo, and in Florence they spent some time going "through the galleries and churches" (*LW* 195), including a visit to the "Assisi frescoes" in Santa Croce, where Emma recollected that Ruskin had admired two *basso relievos* near the door. From there they went to Rome, where they spent a large part of the month of March. Hardy confesses that he was rather oppressed by the overwhelming sense of history everywhere in Rome, and was disappointed with the state of preservation and the restoration of much early Italian work. His account of the Italian trip in *Life and Work* is very brief, but Emma's diary is more explicit about what they saw. They went to the Pinacoteca in the Vatican several times, and on April 1 they returned to the Vatican to see the collection of marbles. They also spent time in the Capitoline Museum, where Emma remarked that a figure of Venus had "both little toes crumpled under as if she had worn boots" (Emma Hardy 1985: 149). Hardy bought five photographs of sculptural subjects, including the Belvedere Apollo, a Faustina, and a Juno, which served, no doubt, as aides-memoire for the form of Car Darch, the rustic girl at Chase-borough, "beautiful as some Praxitelean creation" (*TD* 70). He may also have bought in Rome the two busts, one of Caesar, the other of Venus de Milo, which stood for many years in his study at Max Gate. We know for certain that he purchased two further pictures in Rome. They were a St. Bonaventura and a *Head of a Monk*, and they remained at Max Gate until his death.

By April 3 the couple were back in Florence, where Emma noticed "the bridge where Dante first see Biatrice [*sic*] (the etching we have at home)" (Emma Hardy 1985: 127) but she had very mixed feelings about the frescoes which they revisited in San Marco, Santa Croce, and San Giovanni. "Old frescoes are <u>horrid</u> entre-nous," she confided to her diary (1985: 161). The nudity of Michelangelo's *David* shocked her slightly (1985: 162), and the numerous visits to the Uffizi tired her, so when Hardy proposed a visit to Siena, where, presumably, he saw Duccio's *Maestà*, he rose at five in the morning and went alone (1985: 164).

On April 12 they left Florence, arriving on April 15 in Venice, where they immediately began visiting churches and galleries. According to Hardy himself, he "found more pleasure in Venice than in any Italian city previously visited" (*LW* 200), even though the weather was not the best for sightseeing. He thought that San Marco was squat as it stood on "the glassy marble pavement of the Grand Piazza," and remembered Ruskin's description of the church in *The Stones of Venice* as "conventional" in its ecstasy (*LW* 201). Nevertheless, the interior impressed him with its "Mosaics, mosaics, mosaics, gilding, gilding, gilding, everywhere inside and out." He noticed the domes "like inverted china bowls within – much gilt also" (*LW* 201). Emma's diary suggests, as one might expect, that the highlight of this part of the journey was the painting of Giovanni Bellini, with whom Hardy had compared his own "art" in the previous year, and Emma records detailed descriptions of the Bellinis in the Accademia and in the sacristy of the Salute.

Throughout his life Hardy sought out the company of artists, and when he was in Florence he struck up an acquaintance with the American sculptor Richard Henry Park, and went to his studio, presumably to discuss his work. Similarly, back in England he was welcome in the homes of W. P. Frith and Laurence Alma-Tadema, who was Edmund Gosse's brother-in-law. He was on good terms with Helen Paterson, Arthur Hopkins, and George du Maurier, and he struck up acquaintances with some of the illustrators of the later novels. In 1884 he met Edward Burne-Jones (*LW* 173), in 1886 he met Whistler (*LW* 187), in 1887 he sent a copy of *The Woodlanders* to the President of the Royal Academy, Frederick Leighton, and in 1891 he was impressed by the studio of G. F. Watts (*LW* 248). Hardy also made friends with two sculptors. In 1880, thanks to Edmund Gosse, he met Thomas Woolner at the Rabelais Club, and gave him a copy of *The Return of the Native*; in exchange, Woolner sent Hardy some of his verse, and gave Emma a picture attributed to Richard Parkes Bonington. Woolner's well-known busts of modern intellectuals, churchmen, and statesmen almost certainly lay behind the sculptural appearance of Clym Yeobright with his "countenance of the future" (*RN* 169; Bullen 1986:

111–12), though Hardy did not develop further his association with Woolner. Instead, he was much closer to Hamo Thornycroft, whom he met at the same time, and when Thornycroft died in 1925, Hardy recalled all the pleasant hours he had spent in his studio (*LW* 464). Thornycroft was one of the many artists whom Hardy invited to his home at Max Gate. Feeling that the Wessex countryside had been neglected by landscape painters "though within a four hours' journey from London" (*TD* 18), Hardy asked two artists – Alfred Parsons and Arthur Tomson – to rectify the oversight. Tomson did not take up the invitation, but Parsons, whom Hardy called "one of the most promising painters of the English landscape school" (*CL* I: 187), did, and the two men spent much time searching the countryside for suitable subjects. In 1881 Hardy considered writing the text for a series of Dorset landscape illustrations by his first mentor in the art of watercolor, Henry Moule, and in 1905 he attended an exhibition of landscapes by Walter Tyndale, for some of whose pictures Hardy claimed to have offered subjects (*LW* 350).

As for Hardy's own taste in art, the interior of Max Gate suggested a preference for visual objects with personal associations. In 1886 Helen Paterson's drawings for the illustrations to *Far from the Madding Crowd* were placed above one of the principal doors of the house, together with several watercolor paintings by Emma Hardy representing actual spots that are described under fictitious names in the novels. In his study Hardy had life-size profile silhouettes of his family. The sitting room was decorated with various trophies of Continental visits, including the two portrait heads that the Hardys had bought in Rome. Hardy's most prized possessions, however, were several pictures of the Dutch school. An early seventeenth-century canvas portrayed a wooded landscape with figures engaged in an archery contest, and there were two Dutch merry-making scenes showing peasant figures dancing and feasting. He also owned a picture attributed to the Dutch painter Godfried Schalcken (1643–1703) – a candlelit interior with a group of figures. Two other paintings had personal associations for Hardy. Thomas Woolner's present to Emma, the painting ascribed to Bonington, and a study of the "Three Marys," bought from the sale of the estate of his friend William Barnes, the Dorsetshire poet, both of which he kept until his death.

During his career as a novelist Hardy's taste in pictures underwent considerable change. In his early years, up to *Far From the Madding Crowd*, he was much influenced by the genre study, narrative painting, and works which had very clear implications for literary texts. Towards the end of the 1870s, particularly in *The Return of the Native* (Bullen 1986: 88ff), he was drawn to portraiture and to certain kinds of landscape painting that integrated human figures and natural settings. He found the work of Giovanni Boldini and Meindert Hobbema particularly significant, since they exemplified for him the impress of the human presence upon the inanimate, and confirmed the idea that "the beauty of association is entirely superior to the beauty of aspect, and a beloved relative's old tankard to the finest Greek vase. Paradoxically put, it is to see beauty in ugliness" (*LW* 124). When Impressionism made its mark on the London exhibitions he was very struck by its literary potential. From the first he had been fascinated by the fact that the interpretation of visual images was highly subjective. In *Far From the Madding Crowd* he had noted that "in making even horizontal and clear inspections we colour and mould according to the wants within us whatever our eyes bring in" (*FFMC* 19). Both Impressionism (mentioned in *W* 9) and the late works of Turner seemed to him to involve this principle. Turner's many studies of the passage of the sun through the sky, particularly his *The Angel Standing in the Sun* (1846), left their mark on *Tess of the d'Urbervilles* (Bullen 1986: 192–9), and there is some evidence that the images for *Jude the Obscure* were drawn from the new, melancholy realism of Bastien Lepage (Bullen 1986: 244). But the Old Masters also exerted a permanent power over Hardy's imagination, and one factor underlies his attitude to all these paintings and works in sculpture. For Hardy, the visual image, whether a slight sketch of his own or a canvas by Rembrandt, acted as a kind of reservoir of ideas and feelings. Gérôme's *Jerusalem* (1867) (which he saw at the Royal Academy in 1870), was, he said, "a fine conception" (*LW* 79, 215); Gabriel Guay's *Death of Jezebel* (which he saw at the Paris Salon in 1888) was equally important to him, because each told its story "in a flash," as he put it (*LW* 217). These pictures were vivid and economical, and for Hardy they stored their energy in a single image.

Hardy's relationship to the visual arts is a very special one in that he rarely employs ekphrasis. Actual works of visual art rarely appear in his texts, and Tess's inspection of the d'Urberville portraits is unusual in this respect. In his earlier novels his methods have strong elements of the picturesque, in that scenes are composed or framed in painterly terms. "The Great Barn and the Sheep-Shearers" or "The Same Night in the Fir Plantation" in *Far From the Madding Crowd* are both grand set-pieces, carefully composed and lit for the maximum visual and hence psychological effect. In his later novels this device is used much more subtly. Hardy said that he hated "*word*-painting," and added, "I never try to do it; all I endeavour is to give an *impression* of a scene as it strikes me" (Hardy 1892: 6). In other words material reality became less important to him than its impress upon the mind and emotions. For this reason he abandoned the picturesque for another technique which involved pictures, but in a different way. For example the frame of reference in the opening scene of *The Mayor of Casterbridge*, where an anonymous couple with a child walk through the countryside, has strong pictorial overtones. The figure we later come to know as Michael Henchard is distanced in such a way that "he showed in profile a facial angle so slightly inclined as to be almost perpendicular. He wore a short jacket of brown corduroy, newer than the remainder of his suit" (*MC* 5). Similarly the sculptured form of Eustacia Vye appears on Edgon Heath:

> Viewed sideways the closing-line of her lips formed, with almost geometric precision, the curve so well known in the arts of design as the cima-recta, or ogee. . . . One had fancied that such lip-curves were mostly lurking underground in the south as fragments of forgotten marbles. (*RN* 64)

In both these cases Hardy is not replicating a scene in nature; he is reading a representation of that scene already in pictorial or sculptural form. In the case of the opening of *The Mayor of Casterbridge* he is scrutinizing a painting that might be called "The Country Labourer's Walk" and recording his impressions. He often employs this method in his account of landscape effects, perhaps most powerfully in *Tess of the d'Urbervilles*. This is sometimes described as proto-cinematic, but it is more likely that the hugely agile manipulation of distance and perspective derives from the delight that Hardy took in standing before the static image of the painter and filling it with movement as his eye traveled up and across the painted surface. Hardy's most sophisticated importation of the visual into the verbal text, however, is also the hardest to pin down. It transcends the material painted object and involves the assimilation and re-creation of a painterly style in terms of lighting, mood, and subject. The numerous portraits which populate *The Return of the Native*, including a "portrait" of Edgon Heath itself, almost certainly owe something to the contemporary revival of interest in the work of Joshua Reynolds, though neither his name nor his paintings are mentioned in the text. Similarly, the vivid light and color which suffuse the solar drama of *Tess of the d'Urbervilles* are surely indebted to "the much-decried, mad, late-Turner rendering," of the natural world, with whose sensibility Hardy had much in common.

Hardy is sometimes dismissed as an art-dilettante, or a "painter manqué," but neither is quite accurate. His taste was very Victorian, and yet passionate, eclectic, and personal. Above all, it grew out of a faith in the expressive power of the image. In the paintings of Crivelli and Bellini he detected the artist's sensibility operating on, and transforming, the objects of visual perception as vehicles for artistic sensibility. He tired of pictures by Bonington because he felt that Bonington reproduced the "simply natural," and turned, instead, to the unfashionable late Turners because they went beyond mere appearances to the "heart and inner meaning" (*LW* 183) of visual phenomena. For Hardy, these pictures were the quintessence of expressiveness; they were "landscape *plus* a man's soul" (*LW* 225). Every line and every brush stroke was permeated with human consciousness in such a way that, for Hardy, to modify T. S. Eliot's remark about Hardy himself, Turner was a man who seemed to paint as nearly for the sake of self-expression as a man well can.

REFERENCES AND FURTHER READING

Brennecke Jr., Ernest (1928). *The Life of Thomas Hardy*. New York: Greenberg.

Bullen, J. B. (1986). *The Expressive Eye: Fiction and Perception in the Work of Thomas Hardy*. Oxford: Clarendon Press.

Cook, Thomas, and Son Ltd (1874). *Cook's Tourist's Handbook for Holland, Belgium, and the Rhine*. London.

Cox, R. G. (ed.) (1970). *Thomas Hardy: The Critical Heritage*. London: Routledge & Kegan Paul.

Eliot, T. S. (1934). *After Strange Gods*. London: Faber & Faber.

Hardy, Emma (1985). *Emma Hardy's Diaries*, ed. Richard Taylor. Ashington: Mid Northumberland Arts Group/Carcarnet New Press.

Hardy, Thomas ([1873] 1985). *A Pair of Blue Eyes*, ed. Alan Manford. Oxford: Oxford University Press.

Hardy, Thomas ([1874] 1993). *Far From the Madding Crowd*, ed. Suzanne B. Falck-Yi. Oxford: Oxford University Press.

Hardy, Thomas ([1876] 1996). *The Hand of Ethelberta*, ed. Tim Dolin. London: Penguin.

Hardy, Thomas ([1878] 1990). *The Return of the Native*, ed. Simon Gatrell. Oxford: Oxford University Press.

Hardy, Thomas ([1886] 2004). *The Mayor of Casterbridge*, ed. Dale Kramer. Oxford: Oxford University Press.

Hardy, Thomas [[1887] 1985). *The Woodlanders*, ed. Dale Kramer. Oxford: Oxford University Press.

Hardy, Thomas ([1891] 1988). *Tess of the d'Urbervilles*, ed. Juliet Grindle and Simon Gatrell. Oxford: Oxford University Press.

Hardy, Thomas (1892). Letter to *The Bookman*, 2 (Apr.), 6.

Hardy, Thomas (1982–95). *The Complete Poetical Works of Thomas Hardy*, ed. Samuel Hynes. 5 vols. Oxford: Clarendon Press.

Hardy, Thomas (1984). *The Life and Work of Thomas Hardy*, ed. Michael Millgate. London: Macmillan.

Holland, Clive (1933). *Thomas Hardy OM*. London: Jenkins.

Millgate, Michael (ed.) (2001). *Thomas Hardy's Public Voice: The Essays, Speeches, and Miscellaneous Prose*. Oxford: Clarendon Press.

Millgate, Michael (2004). *Thomas Hardy: A Biography Revisited*. Oxford: Oxford University Press.

Purdy, Richard Little, and Michael Millgate (eds.) (1978–88). *The Collected Letters of Thomas Hardy*. 7 vols. Oxford: Clarendon Press.

15

Hardy and Music: Uncanny Sounds

Claire Seymour

There's many a heart now mangled,
And waiting its time to go,
Whose tendrils were first entangled
By my sweet viol and bow!

("The Fiddler," *CPV* 248)

Visitors to the Dorset County Museum at Dorchester who have peered curiously into the "Hardy Memorial Room" will have seen, standing in one far corner, Thomas Hardy's violin and cello – silent now, but tangible reminders of Hardy's passion for, and proficiency in, the art of music.

His practical, theoretical, historical, and bibliographical musical zeal is well documented in *Life and Work*, where we learn of the musical skills and fervor of his father and grandfather, their devoted involvement in the music at Stinsford church, their vigorous fiddle-playing at country dances and weddings – affectionately re-created in the forms of old William Dewy and his son Reuben in *Under the Greenwood Tree* – and of Hardy's own loving preservation of traditional ballads and hymns, his wild fondness for dancing, and his self-hypnotizing performances on the violin. On one occasion, "he was stopped by his hostess clutching his bow-arm at the end of a three-quarter-hour's unbroken footing to his notes by twelve tireless couples in the favourite country-dance of 'The New-Rigged Ship' . . . lest he should 'burst a blood-vessel', fearing the sustained exertion to be too much for a boy of thirteen or fourteen" (*LW* 28).

Hardy's musical tastes were diverse. Enraptured as a young child by such popular jigs and airs as "Enrico," "The Fairy Dance," "Miss Macleod of Ayr," and "My Fancy-Lad" (*LW* 19), Hardy retained his love of dancing and dance tunes. Happily recalling his visits, during the early 1860s, to the balls at Willis's Rooms, he professed to prefer the old-fashioned style, rejoicing in the

pretty Lancers and Caledonians [that] were still footed there to the original charming tunes, which brought out the beauty of the figures as no later tunes did, and every movement was a correct quadrille step and gesture. For those dances had not at that date degenerated to a waltzing step, to be followed by galloping romps to uproarious pieces. (*LW* 45)

Yet in *Life and Work* he also recalls his admiration for "a set of charming new waltzes [the *Morgenblätter*] by Johann Strauss," performed by the town band on the esplanade at Weymouth in the summer of 1869 (*LW* 65); and much later, in July 1896, he was spurred by the strains of the "Blue Danube" waltz, performed at the Imperial Institute by one of the "famous bands of Europe," to take to the floor with "the beautiful Mrs, afterwards Lady, Grove," dancing, with apparent joyful abandon, "two or three turns to it among the promenaders, who eyed them with a mild surmise as to whether they had been drinking or not" (*LW* 298).

As a young apprentice architect in London, Hardy made the most of the musical opportunities available in the capital, frequenting the opera at Covent Garden and Her Majesty's Theatre "two or three times a week." Purchasing a fiddle "in a . . . fit of musical enthusiasm," he practiced, to the piano accompaniment of a fellow lodger, favorite pieces from the Romantic Italian operas he heard, "the foreign operas in vogue [being] those of Rossini, Donizetti, Verdi, Meyerbeer, Bellini" (*LW* 45). Towards the end of his life, on November 3, 1927, Florence Hardy recorded: "While he was having tea to-day, T.H. said that whenever he heard any music from *Il Trovatore*, it carried him back to the first year when he was in London and when he was strong and vigorous and enjoyed his life immensely." The following day, reading an article by the composer Ethyl Smyth, he was pleased to have his opinion confirmed that *Il Trovatore* was "good music" (*LW* 476, 477). Interestingly, Hardy saw in Verdi a parallel with his own artistic development and his "progression" from prose to poetry:

It may be observed that in the art-history of the century there was an example staring them [the skeptical critics] in the face of a similar modulation from one style into another by a great artist. Verdi was the instance, "that amazing old man" as he was called. Someone of insight wrote concerning him: "From the ashes of his early popularity, from *Il Trovatore* and its kind, there arose on a sudden a sort of phoenix Verdi." (*LW* 320–1)

The many folk songs quoted or mentioned in *Life and Work* and in Hardy's writing – such as "The Outlandish Knight," "May Colvine," "The Foggy Dew," and "O Nannie" – are evidence of Hardy's enjoyment of, and desire to preserve, these traditional "orally transmitted ditties of centuries" that were "being slain at a stroke by the London comic songs" (*LW* 25). Similarly, Hardy repeatedly avowed a love of hymn tunes. In 1896, in response to a letter inquiring about "Hymns that have helped me," he replied that the hymns "Thou turnest man, O Lord, to dust," "Awake, my soul, and with the sun," and "Lead, kindly Light" "have always been familiar and favourite hymns of mine as poetry" (*LW* 290–1). Even at the age of 81, the elderly Hardy would make his way to church expressly to hear a particular hymn or service:

About this time [July 1921] he went to St. Peter's Church, to a morning service, for the purpose of hearing sung by the choir the morning hymn, "Awake, my Soul", to Barthélémon's setting. This had been arranged for him by Dr. Niven, the Rector of St. Peter's. Church music . . . had appealed strongly to Hardy from his earliest years. On July 23 a sonnet, "Barthélémon at Vauxhall", appeared in *The Times*. He had often imagined the weary musician, returning from his nightly occupation of making music for a riotous throng, lingering on Westminster Bridge to see the rising sun and being thence inspired to the composition of music to be heard hereafter in places very different from Vauxhall. (*LW* 447)

Such a catalogue of references and cross-references is almost inexhaustible. Hardy's response to musical experience was so obviously deep-rooted that it is not surprising that music is a constant presence and influence in his work. Characters are defined by their musical knowledge and skill: Grandfer Cantle's approach is heralded by "a light step, and a gay tune in a high key" (*RN* 388); Joan Durbeyfield is "a passionate lover of tune" (*TD* 25); the notes of Gabriel Oak's flute "had a clearness which was to be found nowhere in the wind, and a sequence which was to be found nowhere in nature" (*FFMC* 14); the trumpet-major is a "gallant musician" whose soul was "so much disturbed by tender vibrations" (*TM* 95). Musical metaphors express individuality and sensitivity: Farfrae is like a "well-braced musical instrument" (*MC* 147); Sue Bridehead's nervous sensibility is figuratively captured – "the fibres of her nature seemed strained like harp-strings" (*JO* 236); when, in *The Hand of Ethelberta*, Christopher Julian mistakenly kisses Picotee, believing her to be Ethelberta, "Being . . . a complete bundle of nerves and nothing else, his thin figure shook like a harp-string in painful excitement at a contretemps which would scarcely have quickened the pulse of an ordinary man" (*HE* 158); Bathsheba is entranced by the luminous hue of Troy's flashing sword arm, "spread in a scarlet haze over the space covered by its motions, like a twanged harp-string" (*FFMC* 195). At moments of disappointment, Eustacia Vye's mood descends to her "old mournful key" (*RN* 285), while Marian, disregarded by Angel, finds her temperament "tuned to its lowest bass" (*TD* 149).

We find music in Hardy's earliest attempt at fiction: the "deafening harmonies" of the "Hallelujah Chorus" "flying from this group and from that" leave the hero and heroine of "An Indiscretion in the Life of an Heiress" "like frail and sorry wrecks upon that sea of symphony" ("Indiscretion," 86, 87). And it closes the final scene of his last novel, where the dying Jude hears the notes of the organ, "faint as a bee's hum" (*JO* 426), drowned by the crowd's joyful cries and the tolling Christminster bell – the latter merrily ringing out in celebration of Remembrance Day, a bitter reminder of his own disillusionment and failure. Indeed, music mocks Jude even in death: "By ten o'clock that night Jude was lying on the bedstead at his lodging covered with a sheet, and straight as an arrow. Through the partly opened window the joyous throb of a waltz entered from the ball-room at Cardinal" (*JO* 430). Moreover, Trevor Hold (2002: 401–2) has estimated that, of the 900 or more poems that Hardy wrote, at least one in eight has musical associations. Poems such as "In a Museum," "Haunting Fingers," "A Bygone Occasion," "At the Railway Station, Upway," and "Could I but

Will" describe music, respond to music, and record the effects of music; passions, memories, man's spirit, and nature's soul are eternally conjoined in a universal song, "the full-fugued song of the universe unending" ("In A Museum," *CPV* 430). Many of these poems were intended to be, and have been, set to music.

Thus whether it serves to express gentle rustic comedy (as when Fancy Day's arched brows are pictured as resembling "nothing so much as two slurs in music," *UGT* 50) or to underscore life's terrible ironies ("Suddenly there came along this wind something towards him; a message from the place – from some soul residing there, it seemed. Surely it was the sound of bells, the voice of the city; faint and musical, calling to him, 'We are happy here'," *JO* 19), music permeates the form and fabric of Hardy's work.

But music was more than a life-long interest; it was in many ways a consuming, even controlling, passion. His rare sensitivity to music from an early age is documented in a well-known passage from *Life and Work*:

> He was of ecstatic temperament, extraordinarily sensitive to music, and among the endless jigs, hornpipes, reels, waltzes, and country-dances that his father played . . . and to which the boy danced a *pas seul* in the middle of the room, there were three or four that always moved the child to tears. . . . This peculiarity in himself troubled the mind of "Tommy" as he was called, and set him wondering at a phenomenon to which he ventured not to confess. He used to say in later life that . . . he danced on at these times to conceal his weeping. He was not over four years of age at this date. (*LW* 19)

Thus Hardy combined a scholarly knowledge of traditional music and dance with an instinctive and ecstatic response. Describing here his boyhood in the third person, he insists upon his own extreme emotional sensitivity to music but qualifies his response by recalling his sense of shame at his "weakness." The mature Hardy could be similarly swayed by music's power, dashing from his writing room to chase a street organ-grinder in pursuit of an unidentified quadrille tune, a ghost of a whistled melody that had "spread such a bewitching halo more than twenty years earlier" (*LW* 126), or meticulously taking down a nightingale song in musical notation (*LW* 59).

Melodies which he admired make repeated appearances in Hardy's work, aural echoes of past feelings. In *A Pair of Blue Eyes*, Elfride Swancourt's singing enchants Stephen Smith, firing his heart like "a small Troy" (*PBE* 24) as he gazes "wistfully up into Elfride's face" as if in prayer: "so earnestly gazed he, that her cheek deepened to a more and more crimson tint as each line was added to her song" (*PBE* 23). Elfride begins with the Victorian parlor song, "Should he upbraid," which, in *Life and Work*, Hardy recalls being gloriously and sensuously performed on March 5, 1878 by "A Miss Marsh of Sutton [Keinton?] Mandeville. . . . the sweetest of singers – thrush-like in the descending scale, and lark-like in the ascending – drawing out the soul of listeners in a gradual thread of excruciating attenuation like silk from a cocoon" (*LW* 122). Here Hardy emphasizes both the physiological and psychological effect which the music has on the listener; these responses are spontaneous and involuntary, and interestingly he remarks that this "most marvellous old song in English music" is capable of moving the listener even when "executed but indifferently well" (*LW* 122). The song and the memory associated with it resurface in the poem "The Maid of Keinton Mandeville," where the voice once again enters the body of the listener and transfixes the mind:

> I hear that maiden still
> Of Keinton Mandeville
> Singing, in flights that played
> As wind-wafts through us all,
> Till they made our mood a thrall
> To their aery rise and fall,
>   "Should he upbraid!"
>
> (CPV 563)

Music and memory also become infused at this moment in *A Pair of Blue Eyes*. The quasi-devotional image of Elfride's form "in which she was beheld during these minutes of singing" becomes "her permanent attitude of visitation to Stephen's eyes during his sleeping and waking hours in after days":

> The furthermost candle on the piano comes immediately in line with her head, and half invisible itself, forms the accidentally frizzled hair into a nebulous haze of light, surrounding her crown like an aureola. Her hands are in their place on the keys, her lips parted, and thrilling forth, in a tender *diminuendo* . . . (*PBE* 22)

Music takes Hardy in many directions – song, dance, military marches, bird-song, other natural sounds of the earth and elements; and these aspects often intermingle and fuse, intensifying the emotional and sensory experience. In "The Self-Unseeing," which recalls Hardy's own trance-like response to his father's "Bowing it higher and higher," the enraptured boy is also dancing: "Childlike, I danced in a dream" (*CPV* 166–7). Similarly, in "The Dance at the Phoenix" music is mixed with dance, sexuality, and the military, and the poem features at least one of the tunes that so moved the young Hardy. Tempted, after many years of demure married life, the middle-aged Jenny succumbs to the strains of the King's-Own Cavalry and after a night of "beating" out the various dances, she returns home "bosom-beating," lies down at her husband's side and suffers a fatal attack of the heart (*CPV* 46).

The spell cast by music is often most potent when it is associated with memory – the vision of a place, the sound of a voice, the snatch of a melody, the resonances of an emotion – a memory which may be deliberately repressed, consciously recognized, or subconsciously experienced. In this way, Jenny's years of honest, decent marriage are swept away by the "throbbing 'Soldier's Joy', / The measured tread and sway / Of 'Fancy-Lad' and 'Maiden Coy' " (*CPV* 45), as her yearnings of yesterday are resurrected. For the narrator reveals:

> Now Jenny's life had hardly been
>   A life of modesty;
> And few in Casterbridge had seen
>   More loves of sorts than she
> From scarcely sixteen years above;
>
> (CPV 43)

In "The History of the Hardcombes" ("A Few Crusted Characters," *Life's Little Ironies*), the stimulating effect of music and dance is likewise responsible for a moment of irrational infatuation. The cousins Steve and James Hardcombe, engaged to Olive Pawle and Emily Darth respectively, exchange partners during a festive "wedding-randy" and find themselves overcome by a strange attraction for the "wrong girl," a feeling which is reciprocated by the young ladies: " 'Your Emily clung as close to me as if she already belonged to me, dear girl.' 'And your Olive to me . . . I could feel her heart beating like a clock' " (*LLI* 171). So they determine to change partners "for good and all." However, as time passes and these young people grow a little less warm to their respective spouses, the two men come to regret their hasty action, and "would shake their heads together over their foolishness in upsetting a well-considered choice on the strength of an hour's fancy in the whirl and wildness of a dance" (*LLI* 172). The two couples have been "dis-coupled" by the power of dance and music; sadly, the strange fascination which engulfs them results in tragic deaths and a passionless marriage:

> He sees couples join them for dancing,
>   And afterwards joining for life,
> He sees them pay high for their prancing
>   By a welter of wedded strife.
>
> ("The Fiddler," CPV 248)

Music is thus a transforming power. In *Under the Greenwood Tree* Michael Mail describes how he felt obliged to eat in time with a band playing outside the Three Mariners:

> "Once I was a-setting in the little kitchen of the Dree Mariners at Casterbridge, having a bit of dinner, and a brass band struck up in the street. Such a beautiful band as that were! I was setting eating fried liver and lights I well can mind – ah, I was! And to save my life, I couldn't help chawing to the tune. Band played six-eight time: six-eight chaws I, willynilly. Band plays common: common time went my teeth among the liver and lights as true as a hair. Beautiful 'twere! – Ah, I shall never forget that there band!" (*UGT* 59)

Even birds and beasts may be translated by music, as when William Dewy pacifies a bull with his fiddle airs. Dairyman Crick tells Tess:

he pulled out his fiddle as he runned, and struck up a jig, turning to the bull, and backing towards the corner. The bull softened down, and stood still, looking hard at William Dewy, who fiddled on and on; till a sort of a smile stole over the bull's face.

Forced to continue fiddling, to save his breeches from the bull's horns, "he so leery and tired that 'a didn't know what to do. . . . then he called to mind how he'd seen the cattle kneel o' Christmas Eves in the dead o' night." William duly broke into the Nativity Hymn, and "down went the bull upon his bended knees," enabling William to vault to safety over the hedge (*TD* 115).

In *The Mayor of Casterbridge* Elizabeth-Jane is "enraptured" by Farfrae's impassioned singing of "hame, hame fain I would be, / O hame, hame, hame to my ain countree!" – "she could not help pausing to listen" (*MC* 49). Viewed through a "golden haze which the tone of his mind seemed to raise around him," Farfrae "had completely taken possession of the hearts of the Three Mariners' inmates" (*MC* 51). Henchard too is described as one powerfully influenced by music: despairing that there remains "nobody for him to be proud of, nobody to fortify him," he longs to summon music, "for with Henchard music was of regal power. The merest trumpet or organ tone was enough to move him, and high harmonies transubstantiated him" (*MC* 275). Paradoxically, though we are told that "Nothing moved Henchard like an old melody" (*MC* 252), in his desolation, leaving the town by the east road, he is strangely deaf to the music of the moors and the meadows that he traverses, whose waters emit "singular symphonies . . . as from a lampless orchestra":

> At a hole in a rotten weir they executed a recitative; where a tributary brook fell over a stone breastwork they trilled cheerily; under an arch they performed a metallic cymballing; and at Durnover Hole they hissed. The spot at which their instrumentation rose loudest was a place called Ten Hatches . . . (*MC* 275–6)

Henchard arrives at Ten Hatches Weir intent on suicide, but is averted from self-destruction by the startling apparition of an effigy, not simply "a man somewhat resembling him, but one in all respects his counterpart, his actual double" (*MC* 276); at this moment, the "fugue of sounds" which resonates in the air significantly enhances the supernatural nature of the experience. Moreover, the appearance of this inanimate "doppelgänger" and its effect on Henchard accord with Sigmund Freud's explanation for the "uncanny" effect of the "double" (Freud [1919] 1990: 356–8). Although originally "sprung from the soil of unbounded self-love, from the primary narcissism which dominates the mind of the child and of primitive man," and an "insurance against the destruction of the ego, an 'energetic denial of the power of death'" ([1919] 1990: 356), the double, Freud argues, has reversed its aspect and "become the uncanny harbinger of death" ([1919] 1990: 357). Also incorporated in this idea of the double are "all the unfulfilled but possible futures to which we cling in phantasy, all the strivings of the ego, which adverse external circumstances have crushed, and all our suppressed acts of volition which nourish in us the illusion of free will" ([1919] 1990: 358).

Music is also used rather oddly in Part III, Act VI, scene ii of *The Dynasts*, when the festivities in the Brussels ballroom are interrupted by word of Napoleon's imminent attack. The scene commences with two hundred guests dancing joyfully to the strains of "The White Cockade," but the melody diminishes as whispered news of Napoleon's advance threatens to halt the ball. At first, "the sense of looming tragedy carries emotion to its climax," and to the leaping strains of a contemporary favorite, "The Prime of Life," the young officers and their partners, inebriated by the "ecstasizing" air, "abandon themselves to the movement": "Nearly half an hour passes before the figure is danced down. Smothered kisses follow the conclusion. The silence is broken from without by more long hollow rolling notes, so near that they thrill the window-panes" (*D* 622). As fears of the impending battle grow, the officers bid farewell, leaving the women to "mope and murmur to each other" (*D* 622); the dancing becomes "fitful and spiritless" (*D* 623) and the music transmutes into a strange *danse macabre*:

> SPIRIT OF THE PITIES
> When those stout men-at-arms drew doorward there,
> I saw a like grimacing shadow march
> And pirouette before no few of them.
> Some of themselves beheld it; some were blind.
>
> SPIRIT OF THE YEARS
> Which were so ushered?
>
> SPIRIT OF THE PITIES
>   Brunswick, who saw and knew;
> One also moved before Sir Thomas Picton,
> Who coolly conned and drily spoke to it;
> Another danced in front of Ponsonby,
> Who failed of heeding his. — De Lancey, Hay,
> Gordon, and Cameron, and many more
> Were footmanned by like phantoms from the ball.
>
>   (*D* 623–4)

An unsettling effect is produced, as temporality is suspended, the distinction between imagination and reality, between worlds, effaced.

In similar fashion, during the village festivities in *The Return of the Native* (Book Fourth, chapter 3) the "five-and-twenty couples" through which Eustacia and Wildeve thread "their giddy way" are affected by the vital pulse of the dance in the pale evening light, which disturbs the equilibrium of the senses and promotes dangerously tender moods, "reason becoming sleepy and unperceiving":

All the dancing girls felt the symptoms; but Eustacia most of all. . . . The air became quite still . . . the players appeared only in outline against the sky; except when the circular mouths of the trombone, ophicleide, and French horn gleamed out like huge eyes from the shade of their figures. . . . Eustacia floated round and round on Wildeve's arm, her face rapt and statuesque; her soul had passed away from and forgotten her features, which were left empty and quiescent, as they always are when feeling goes beyond their register. (*RN* 263)

Likewise, in *A Laodicean* (Book the First, chapter 15) as Somerset dances with Paula it seems as if "a perfumed southern atmosphere had begun to pervade the marquee, and that human beings were shaking themselves free of all inconvenient gravitation" (*AL* 120). And as Dick Dewy twirls with Fancy Day, "The room became to Dick like a picture in a dream . . . the fiddlers going to sleep as humming-tops sleep, by increasing their motion and hum" (*UGT* 55).

One might describe many of these musical transformations, which captivate and alarm in equal measure, as "uncanny." In his essay "The Uncanny," Freud explores the etymological root of the term, focusing on the inherent ambivalence of the German word *heimlich*, which can mean both "what is familiar and agreeable" and "what is concealed and kept out of sight." *Unheimlich* can be used as a contrary of the first, but not of the second, definition; and thus Freud continues, "According to [Schelling], everything is *unheimlich* that ought to have remained secret and hidden but has come to light" (Freud [1919] 1990: 345).

Rather than attempting to provide an unequivocal definition of the term, most critics resort to describing the uncanny experience, usually by way of the dream-like visions of doubling and death that invariably seem to accompany it. Primitive desires and fears are triggered by these uncanny happenings. According to Freud the uncanny derives its terror not from something externally alien or unknown but – paradoxically – from something strangely or secretly familiar which defeats our efforts to repress it and separate ourselves from it: "the uncanny is that class of the frightening which leads back to what is known of old and long familiar" (Freud [1919] 1990: 340).

Many of the musical experiences presented in Hardy's fiction and poetry seem to possess these qualities. Things – emotions, memories, physical responses – that perhaps "ought to have remained secret and hidden" are brought "to light" by the arch of a fiddler's bow, the rustle of a lover's lyre, the pattern of a rustic dance, the sweet sonority of a voice, real or imagined. Freud ([1919] 1990: 340) notes that Jentsch, in a 1906 study, claimed that people vary greatly in their sensitivity to this quality of feeling, some exhibiting extreme delicacy of perception, and others remaining unmoved. Time and again both Hardy and his fictional characters are seen to experience an intense neurological response to particular sounds, often in association with the resurrection of subdued emotional impulses or memories. There is commonly a sense of the unexpected, a compelling spontaneity, as if the listener is taken unawares by the nature and power of the musical sound, often potently seductive, and submits to its force. The experience is dynamic, overwhelming; the music appears to resurrect a subconscious emotion, knowledge, or experience, or to reawaken a primitive fear or desire.

We witness one such "uncanny" transformation in *Desperate Remedies* (chapter 8), when Aeneas Manston all but seduces Cytherea by playing the organ to her during a thunderstorm, inducing an inexplicable and overmastering attraction to a man she would in other circumstances find disagreeable. Hardy makes much of Manston's appearance. He is an "extremely handsome man" (*DR* 127), whose most striking aspect is the "wonderful, almost preternatural, clearness of his complexion. There was not a blemish or speck of any kind to mar the smoothness of its surface or the beauty of its hue" (*DR* 127–8). Arresting too are his lips, "full and luscious . . . possessing a woman-like softness of curve, and a ruby redness so intense" (*DR* 128). Though he confesses he has not "learnt scientifically" but plays merely for his own amusement, Manston extemporizes "a harmony which meandered through every variety of expression of which the instrument was capable" (*DR* 130). The uncomfortable, even sinister, intensity of the "unearthly weirdness" which surrounds her both thrills and alarms Cytherea. Moved first by the touch of his fingers against the palm of her glove, then by the brush of his clothes against hers as they shelter in the narrow porch, Cytherea is now pierced by the sounds he conjures:

> He now played more powerfully. . . . The varying strains – now loud, now soft; simple, complicated, weird, touching, grand, boisterous, subdued; each phase distinct, yet modulating into the next with a graceful and easy flow – shook and bent her to themselves, as a gushing brook shakes and bends a shadow cast across its surface. The power of the music did not show itself so much by attracting her attention to the subject of the piece, as by taking up and developing as its libretto *the poem of her own life and soul*, shifting her deeds and intentions from the hands of her judgment and holding them in its own.
>
> She was swayed into emotional opinions concerning the strange man before her; new impulses of thought came with new harmonies, and entered into her with a gnawing thrill. A dreadful flash of lightning then, and the thunder close upon it. She found herself involuntarily shrinking up beside him, and looking with parted lips at his face. (*DR* 131–2, emphasis added)

Overwhelmed by the gushing, gnawing emotions which are provoked by his hypnotic running fingers, mesmerized also by the "dark strong eyes" which he fixes firmly upon her, Cytherea is compelled to turn her gaze upon his "too-delicately beautiful face" (*DR* 131). This element of involuntary compulsion reappears in the intoxicating effect of Christopher Julian's organ playing on Ethelberta Petherwin:

> peals broke forth from the organ on the black oaken mass at the junction of nave and choir, shaking every cobweb in the dusky vaults, and Ethelberta's heart no less. She knew the fingers that were pressing out those rolling sounds, and knowing them, became absorbed in tracing their progress. To go towards the organ-loft was an *act of unconsciousness*, and she did not pause till she stood almost beneath it. (*HE* 313, emphasis added)

The closing strains of Manston's performance are accompanied by the subduing of the storm's violence. The clearing of the skies and lightening of the clouds brings relief to Cytherea, desperate to escape the Gothic scene of her detention. Aware that it was "not a thing she wished," she laments her foolishness "to have been excited and dragged into frankness by the wiles of a stranger" (*DR* 132).

Manston's unearthly sounds blend with the natural clamor of the raging storm: the "peal of thunder" and the "low roar of the waterfall . . . rivalled by the increasing rush of rain upon the trees and herbage of the grove" (*DR* 128). The "song of the earth" is a powerful presence in Hardy's fiction, to which birds and insects add their whispering choruses. Places are infused with musical resonances, natural sounds mingle with man-made melodies. Thus, the "soft musical purl of the water through little weirs" (*PBE* 92) accompanies Stephen Smith's evening stroll at Endelstow. More monumental is the "booming tune" of the wind at Stonehenge, "like the note of some gigantic one-stringed harp" (*TD* 379). In *The Return of the Native*, as the five central characters – "wanderers" on the heath in darkness and in rain – draw closer together, Hardy dramatizes the accumulating tension through the music of nature:

> The wind rasped and scraped at the corners of the house, and filliped the eaves-droppings like peas against the panes. . . . Rain was still falling heavily, the whole expanse of heath before him emitting a subdued hiss under the downpour. . . . the drumming of the storm without . . . snapped at the window-panes and breathed into the chimney strange low utterances that seemed to be the prologue to some tragedy. (*RN* 362, 363, 366)

Moreover, this "music" harmonizes with Eustacia'a inner life: "Never was harmony more perfect than that between the chaos of her mind and the chaos of the world without" (*RN* 358).

Aeneas Manston anticipates another mesmerizing musician, Wat Ollamoor ("of the moor," "à l'amour"?), the eponymous "Fiddler of the Reels" (*Life's Little Ironies*) – a Pied Piper-like figure of mystery and inscrutability, of ambiguous name and provenance. Once again, his appearance is described in detail: his "rank . . . dark, and rather clammy" hair is long, curled and scented, in an effeminate manner. He is a dark, romantic archetype – foreign-looking, daemonic: "All were devil's tunes in his repertory" (*LLI* 138, 139). His music is menacing rather than magical, and comparisons to Liszt and Paganini emphasize his wild genius. Though he never speaks, the elfin-shrieks and "unholy music" of his violin are a threat to the stability of the community he haunts:

> His fiddling . . . had . . . a most peculiar and personal quality, like that in a moving preacher. . . . There was a certain lingual character in the supplicatory expressions he produced. . . . He could make any child in the parish, who was at all sensitive to music, burst into tears in a few minutes by simply fiddling one of the old dance-tunes he almost entirely affected . . . (*LLI* 138)

Hardy's account of the extreme powers of expressiveness invested in Mop's music is deliberately detailed. Recalling Manston's profession of amateurism, Ollamoor is said to be indolent and averse to "systematic application," yet his "heart-stealing melodies"

could draw "an ache from the heart of a gate-post" (*LLI* 138). Like a poisonous arach-
nid, he spins a seductive tune, an "insidious thread of semi- and demi-semiquavers"
(*LLI* 139) which could "draw your soul out of your body like a spider's thread . . . till
you felt as limp as withywind and yearned for something to cling to" (*LLI* 141).
While extemporizing he invariably closes his eyes, and Hardy evokes a strong sense
of the grotesque and sinister when he slyly opens just *one* eye, fixing it intently upon
Car'line Aspent:

> The fiddler knows what's brewing
>   To the lilt of his lyric wiles:
> The fiddler knows what rueing
>   Will come of this night's smiles!
>
> ("The Fiddler," *CPV* 248)

Car'line is seized by a peculiar infatuation, lured to renounce normal decorum, gripped
by a wild desire to dance. Even the gentle pad of Mop's distant footfalls is sufficient
to cause her to "start from her seat . . . as if she had received a galvanic shock, and
spring convulsively towards the ceiling" (*LLI* 140), sobbing with emotion.

In the poem "To a Lady Playing and Singing in the Morning," Hardy expresses
his own momentary wish to submit to infatuation, to allow the rapturous sound of a
lady's trilling throat to transport him to, and sustain him in, other worlds: "But let
indulgence be / This once, to my rash ecstasy: / When sounds nowhere that carolled
air / My idled morn may comfort me!" (*CPV* 579). However, in "The Fiddler of the
Reels," the scientifically minded narrator says it would take "a neurologist to fully
explain" Carl'ine's possession (*LLI* 140), and Hardy's language here is quite technical,
ironic, and detached. Emphasizing her nervous disposition and physiological weakness, Hardy refrains from passing moral judgments on Car'line. Yet, in the passage
where she is literally entranced and her daughter kidnapped, Hardy indulges the
sensual and irrational, providing an anguished account of sustained emotional ecstasy
and sexual compulsion:

> The saltatory tendency which the fiddler and his cunning instrument had ever been able
> to start in her was seizing Car'line just as it had done in earlier years. . . . Tired as she
> was she grasped her little girl by the hand, and plunging in at the bottom of the figure,
> whirled about with the rest. . . . she convulsively danced on, wishing that Mop would
> cease and let her heart rest from the aching he caused, and her feet also. (*LLI* 150)

Bliss and despair afflict her in equal measure, as the exquisite torment persists.
Trapped at the apex of a five-handed reel, Carline cannot escape: Mop's "wild and
agonizing sweetness" projects "through her nerves excruciating spasms, a sort of
blissful torture. The room swam, the tune was endless . . ." (*LLI* 151):

He twangs: "Music hails from the devil,
    Though vaunted to come from heaven,
For it makes people do at a revel
    What multiplies sins by seven.

("The Fiddler," *CPV* 248)

The piercing sweetness of his bow awakens her sexuality; it is the aural embodiment of subconscious primordial yearning, which she both celebrates and fears. Perhaps he is not a "person" at all, but rather an erotic music which pulses within her. Yet the feelings aroused are not solely sexual – as Hardy reminds us, Mop's plaintive longing can wring tears from a statue. It is rather her inner life which is stirred to consciousness; she is drawn to dance endlessly, a *perpetuum mobile* which she wishes never to end. In contrast, her eventual husband, Ned Hipcroft "had not the slightest ear for music; could not sing two notes in tune, much less play them" (*LLI* 141). Dance and music are the shape and rhythm of life, the threads and tempi which bind people to each other; hence the significance of the pattern of the five-handed reel: "the five reelers stood in the form of a cross, the reel being performed by each line of three alternately, the persons who successively came to the middle place dancing in both directions" (*LLI* 151).

Freud observed that such hypersensitive responses were typical of neurotics, whose minds were dominated by "the over-accentuation of psychical reality in comparison with material reality" (Freud [1919] 1990: 367). Car'line's intense, uninhibited response to the primitive rhythm of Mop's music is, however, both a virtue and a weakness. His creativity is a liberating, life-giving force; yet Hardy stresses her hysterical nature, spasms, and convulsions. She is "special" in her response to the music – yet this "gift" reveals her as naive and misguided. She disregards conventional manners and customs, which inevitably leads to social conflict and tragedy.

The supernatural elements of this tale transform the excessive emotion into something uncanny. At the Great Exhibition, she sights Mop's "double," a ghostly reflection in a large mirror, "a form exactly resembling Mop Ollamoor's – so exactly, that it seemed impossible to believe anybody but that artist in person to be the original" (*LLI* 147). But on investigation no Mop is to be seen. There is witchery in his probing "gimlet-gaze," in the single orb which he opens and fixes "peeringly upon her . . . smiling dreamily" (*LLI* 152). As Freud recalled, "One of the most uncanny and widespread forms of superstition is the dread of the 'evil eye'" (Freud [1919] 1990: 362). A feeling is betrayed in a look, even though it is not put into words; there is an unusually heightened fear that the perceived intention to harm will be put into action, and a belief that certain signs – here, Mop's disturbing physical appearance and devilish musical prowess – indicate that that intention has the necessary power at its command.

Interestingly, Car'line's second encounter with her seducer is unintentional and undesired, and this factor of involuntary repetition enhances the uncanny atmosphere evoked by Mop's "acoustic magnetism," suggesting something fateful and inescapable, when otherwise it may have simply seemed to be mere "chance." Freud declared that

> it is possible to recognize the dominance in the unconscious mind of a "compulsion to repeat" proceeding from the instinctual impulses and probably inherent in the very nature of the instincts – a compulsion . . . lending to certain aspects of the mind their daemonic character . . . a compulsion, too, which is responsible for a part of the course taken by the analyses of neurotic patients. All these considerations prepare us for the discovery that whatever reminds us of this inner "compulsion to repeat" is perceived as uncanny. (Freud [1919] 1990: 360–1)

Thus, unintended recurrences of an action or situation, "subject to certain conditions and combined with certain circumstances, arouse an uncanny feeling, which, further-more, recalls the sense of helplessness experienced in some dream-states" (Freud [1919] 1990: 359). This sense of "helplessness" accompanies so many of Hardy's moments of musical "hypnotism." For example, in addition to those incidents already described, in *The Trumpet-Major* (chapter 22), Captain Bob Loveday presents Anne Garland with an Aeolian harp whose "weird harmony" blends with "the mournful gales of autumn, the strange mixed music of water, wind and strings . . . swelling and sinking with an almost supernatural cadence," bewitching and molding her emotions, which "flow out yet a little further in the old direction, notwithstanding her late severe resolve to bar them back" (*TM* 183).

Repression, repetition, compulsion, revelation: these elements are also present in *Tess of the d'Urbervilles*, most strikingly in the episode when Tess is overcome by the strumming of Angel's harp (Phase the Third, chapter 19). The atmosphere is one of "such delicate equilibrium and so transmissive that inanimate objects seemed endowed with two or three senses, if not five" (*TD* 127). Interestingly, Freud, quoting Jentsch, identifies the situation or impression where one "doubts whether an apparently animate being is really alive; or conversely, whether a lifeless object might not be in fact animate," as producing a sense of the uncanny. Here, the silence itself becomes animate – "a positive entity," rather than a "mere negation of noise" – and the strummed notes wander in the still air "with a stark quality like that of nudity" (*TD* 127). Induced into a state of heightened sensitivity – tactile and extrasensory – Tess's soul is drawn out of her body. She has heard these sounds before but has not responded in this way. Sensed through a mist of pollen, a fertilizing agent, Clare's music, though poorly executed, takes a form of life within Tess. She is drawn towards it, like a "fas-cinated bird." She experiences a physical oneness with her surroundings, is affirmed as part of raw nature: she "felt close to everything within the horizon," and the bound-aries between near and far dissolve. The fetid pungency of the flowers and the garden, "damp and rank with juicy grass which sent up mists of pollen at a touch; and with tall blooming weeds emitting offensive smells," signifies the gross sexuality both within and without Tess. Primitive, Edenic, she merges with the landscape; her absorption is gestured by the cuckoo-spittle which clings to her skirts, the crack of snails underfoot, and by the thistle-milk and slug-slime which stain her hands. She cannot remove the blemishes, "rubbing off upon her naked arms sticky blights which, though snow-white on the apple-tree trunks, made madder stains on her skin." The symbolism is pointed here, "madder" signifying "blood-red," and the apples perhaps suggesting her unconscious identification with Eve.

In a state of unbidden exaltation, "conscious of neither time nor space," Tess *is* the music; she "undulate[s] upon the thin notes," riding the waves of sound, and their harmonies pass "like breezes through her, bringing tears into her eyes." She floats, literally and metaphorically, in a hypnotic orgy of pain and pleasure. The extremity of her experience is enhanced by her identification with her surroundings: the garden too seems to weep, "the dampness" a visible outpouring of its lamentation. Smell and light, color and sound, are synaesthetically fused in a climactic and spiritual rapture. Clare's music – plaintive but simple, "demanding no great skill" (*TD* 128) – seems insignificant besides Tess's emotional heights, its gentle intimations overshadowed by the powerful energy which surges within her.

What does the "uncanny" sound like? It is surely a melody which is unique to each individual, relating to particular memories, experiences, emotions. In Hardy, the intimation often seems to be that it is an aural rendition of a character's sexual and sensual "self"; and its effects are powerful, startling, alarming. The extra-lingual experiences which Hardy describes call forth the indefinable and indescribable quality which is an integral part of our understanding of the uncanny experience, and which may be terrifying precisely because, while oddly familiar, it cannot be adequately explained. In this way, the poet-persona in "The Voice" questions the source of the voice which calls to him – "Can it be you that I hear? . . . / Or is it only the breeze, in its listlessness," concluding:

> Thus I; faltering forward,
> Leaves around me falling,
> Wind oozing thin through the thorn from norward,
> And the woman calling.
>
> (*CPV* 346)

Most critical explorations of aesthetic experience and perception concentrate upon what is believed to be beautiful, sublime, and attractive, and are concerned with the objects and circumstances which call such responses and judgments forth. However, in his depiction of music and musical experience – both fictional and autobiographical – Hardy goes beyond these parameters and ventures into an aesthetics of emotion, combining perception of beauty with the aesthetics of quality of feeling. The emotional power of his writing at such moments strongly suggests that Hardy believed that there was some sort of quasi-neurological impact producible by particular musical sounds; and, moreover, he seems to relate the potentiality of these tones and harmonies to a hypersensitive, even erotic, response in certain temperaments, such as Car'line Aspent's – or his own.

Hardy thus uses music to express and dramatize his characters', and his own, experience of the world. Significantly, Hardy reveals that his mother, though shocked by her young son's intense responses to music, "did not object to these performances," perhaps believing that "they would help to teach him what life was" (*LW* 28). For Hardy, music is more than a pastime or even an art. It is the very rhythm of life, a perpetual pulse which bears our passions and also our disappointments. It is within us and without – an experience, an identity, as much as a perception. And, so often in his work, external melodies chime with echoes of an inner music, and resonate with primitive notes and pulses, establishing both a welcome familiarity and a feared novelty, a paradoxical sensation which is truly uncanny.

References and Further Reading

Asquith, Mark (2005). *Thomas Hardy, Metaphysics and Music*. Basingstoke: Palgrave Macmillan.

Freud, Sigmund ([1919] 1990). The Uncanny. In Albert Dickson (ed.), *Art and Literature. The Penguin Freud Library*, vol. 14 (pp. 338–76). London: Penguin.

Grundy, Joan (1979). *Thomas Hardy and the Sister Arts*. London and Basingstoke: Macmillan.

Hardy, Thomas ([1871] 2003). *Desperate Remedies*, ed. Patricia Ingham. Oxford: Oxford University Press.

Hardy, Thomas ([1872] 1985). *Under the Greenwood Tree*, ed. Simon Gatrell. Oxford: Oxford University Press.

Hardy, Thomas ([1873] 1985). *A Pair of Blue Eyes*, ed. Alan Manford. Oxford: Oxford University Press.

Hardy, Thomas ([1874] 1993). *Far From the Madding Crowd*, ed. Suzanne B. Falck-Yi. Oxford: Oxford University Press.

Hardy, Thomas ([1876] 1996). *The Hand of Ethelberta*, ed. Tim Dolin. London: Penguin.

Hardy, Thomas ([1878] 1990). *The Return of the Native*, ed. Simon Gatrell. Oxford: Oxford University Press.

Hardy, Thomas ([1878] 1998). An Indiscretion in the Life of an Heiress. In *An Indiscretion in the Life of an Heiress and Other Stories*, ed. Pamela Dalziel (pp. 43–113). Oxford: Oxford University Press.

Hardy, Thomas ([1880] 1991). *The Trumpet-Major*, ed. Richard Nemesvari. Oxford: Oxford University Press.

Hardy, Thomas ([1881] 1991). *A Laodicean*, ed. Jane Gatewood. Oxford: Oxford University Press.

Hardy, Thomas ([1886] 2004). *The Mayor of Casterbridge*, ed. Dale Kramer. Oxford: Oxford University Press.

Hardy, Thomas ([1891] 1988). *Tess of the d'Urbervilles*, ed. Juliet Grindle and Simon Gatrell. Oxford: Oxford University Press.

Hardy, Thomas ([1894] 1999). *Life's Little Ironies*, ed. Alan Manford. Oxford: Oxford University Press.

Hardy, Thomas ([1895] 1985). *Jude the Obscure*, ed. Patricia Ingham. Oxford: Oxford University Press.

Hardy, Thomas ([1903–8] 1978). *The Dynasts*. London: Macmillan.

Hardy, Thomas (1979). *The Variorum Edition of the Complete Poems of Thomas Hardy*, ed. James Gibson. London: Macmillan.

Hardy, Thomas (1984). *The Life and Work of Thomas Hardy*, ed. Michael Millgate. London: Macmillan.

Hold, Trevor (2002). *Parry to Finzi: Twenty English Song-Composers*. Woodbridge: Boydell.

Hughes, John (2001). *"Ecstatic Sound": Music and Individuality in the Works of Thomas Hardy*. Aldershot: Ashgate.

PART IV
The Works

16
The Darkening Pastoral:
Under the Greenwood Tree and *Far From the Madding Crowd*

Stephen Regan

Under the Greenwood Tree (1872) remains immensely popular among Thomas Hardy's readers, but it has rarely been given the serious critical attention it deserves. Too often, it has been dismissed as immature and insignificant – slight in conception and lacking the intellectual vigor and tragic grandeur of the later works. For Lord David Cecil, *Under the Greenwood Tree* was the "light-weight" among Hardy's masterpieces, and his sentiments have been echoed many times in more recent criticism (Cecil 1954: 31). For all its seeming insubstantiality, however, *Under the Greenwood Tree* has won high praise for its stylistic finesse. Michael Millgate has written approvingly of the novel's "nearly flawless" execution (Millgate 1971: 50), and Hardy himself thought highly enough of the book to count it among his "Novels of Character and Environment" in the 1912 Wessex Edition of his works. Even so, its critical reputation rests on its appeal as a rural romance or rural idyll.

It might seem, initially, as if Hardy responded pragmatically to the disappointing reviews of his first published novel, *Desperate Remedies* (1871), and decided to produce a novel that would consolidate and give new concentrated expression to those scenes of rural life that some commentators had responded to favorably. It is clear from the biography and the letters, however, that Hardy salvaged some scenes from his first (unpublished) novel, *The Poor Man and the Lady*, and that the Christmas Eve episode at the tranter's house very likely derives from these. Beneath its rural charm and local color, *Under the Greenwood Tree* reveals a deep and pervasive interest in the destructive effects of social class and class consciousness, and it resorts at times to a sharp-edged satirical antagonism that is only barely contained within the constraints of pastoral comedy. It simultaneously draws on the conventions of pastoral romance and exposes those conventions as an inadequate means of representing rural life, introducing formal and generic elements that contradict each other and complicate what might otherwise seem a pleasant and undisturbing picture of English country life.

That notion of the novel as "picture" – as a pleasing rural painting – might well be responsible for some of the critical objections to *Under the Greenwood Tree* as superficial and devoid of substance. Another complaint to which it is sometimes subjected, however, is not that it is lacking in plot, but rather that it struggles to sustain more than one principal narrative interest. If the title *Under the Greenwood Tree* draws attention to the rustic tale of the lovers in the woods, to the rural romance of Dick Dewy and Fancy Day, the alternative title *The Mellstock Quire* gives prominence to the story of local singers and musicians displaced from their traditional role in church services. These are not, of course, entirely separate narratives. Dick Dewy is a member of the local choir, and the woman whom he falls in love with and eventually marries is Fancy Day, the musician whose talents on the keyboard lead to the superannuation of the instrumentalists and singers in the Mellstock choir. It is in keeping with the elements of pastoral comedy in the novel that the choir should reassemble for the wedding celebrations of Dick and Fancy. Even so, there is some evidence of anxiety on Hardy's part over the competing demands of these related narrative strands. If he was initially inclined to play up the romance of Dick and Fancy, he was later concerned, especially in the prefaces to subsequent editions of the novel, to highlight the passing of the Mellstock choir. In 1912 he expressed regret that he had not given deeper consideration to the role of the musicians in the novel, and he claimed in the same preface that the title of the novel was originally intended to be *The Mellstock Quire*, an assertion that has been challenged by recent editors (see, for example, Simon Gatrell's introduction to *UGT*, xi).

The title *Under the Greenwood Tree* gives the novel a Shakespearian frame of reference, with its allusion to Act II, scene v of *As You Like It*, but it also looks back to a much older provenance in the ballads of Robin Hood and his merry men:

> In somer, when the shawes be sheyne
> And leves be large and long,
> Hit is full mery in feyre foreste
> To here the foulys song,
>
> To se the dere draw to the dale,
> And leve the hilles hee,
> And shadow hem in the levës grene,
> Under the grene-wode tre.
>
> (Hodgart 1965: 81)

Here, the speaker participates in the refreshment afforded by the forest, listening to the birdsong and watching the deer seeking out the shade, but in *As You Like It*, the singer is himself already beneath the greenwood tree, at one with the singing bird and the woodland:

> Under the greenwood tree
> Who loves to lie with me,
> And turn his merry note
> Unto the sweet bird's throat,
> Come hither, come hither, come hither.
> Here shall he see
> No enemy
> But winter and rough weather.
>
> (Shakespeare 1997: 1618)

In both cases, the greenwood tree is a benevolent, sheltering presence, and in Hardy's novel it takes on a similar function, providing a place of nurture and protection for birds and people alike. In keeping with the harmonious resolution of Shakespearian pastoral comedy, the novel closes with wedding celebrations beneath the tree. Shakespeare's bird, transformed into the richly mythological nightingale, calls "come hither," but Fancy Day's furtive response, as she contemplates an earlier offer of marriage from Reverend Maybold, suggests that the winter and rough weather ahead might have more than a literal significance: "'O, 'tis the nightingale,' murmured she, and thought of a secret she would never tell" (p. 198). Even allowing for the somber acknowledgment of "the rain that raineth every day," *Under the Greenwood Tree* goes far beyond the framework of Shakespearian pastoral comedy, repeatedly invoking a range of different and conflicting generic codes and frequently drawing attention to its own highly stylized modes of representation. The self-conscious exploration of multiple ways of seeing and representing rural life gives the novel a formal complexity at odds with its familiar description as a pastoral idyll.

The opening paragraph of *Under the Greenwood Tree* registers an acute sensitivity to the sights and sounds of nature, investing the trees with a powerful acoustic arrangement that strongly anticipates the evocative passages of landscape description in *Far from the Madding Crowd* and *The Woodlanders*:

> To dwellers in a wood, almost every species of tree has its voice as well as its feature. At the passing of the breeze the fir-trees sob and moan no less distinctly than they rock: the holly whistles as it battles with itself: the ash hisses amid its quivering: the beech rustles while its flat boughs rise and fall. And winter, which modifies the note of such trees as shed their leaves, does not destroy its individuality. (p. 11)

As in later novels, Hardy brings competing discourses of nature into play with each other. The passage is striking in its display of what John Ruskin termed "pathetic fallacy," attributing human moods and characteristics to the various trees, but it also demonstrates a knowledge of scientific naturalism (Ruskin 1903–12: 201). The prominent word "species" in the opening line ought to remind us of the close proximity of the novel to the publication of Charles Darwin's *Origin of Species* (1859), a suggestion borne out by the emphasis on a surviving "individuality." If there is romantic imagining in this passage, there is also a keenly scientific awareness. Tim Dolin finds evidence in the novel of Hardy's reading of John Stuart Mill and speculates that individual liberty is being posited against the preservation of communal ways and traditions from the very outset (Dolin 2004: xxxiv). If, at one level, the novel is a celebration of communal life, it also inveighs against the occasional oppressiveness of the community. Dick Dewy is notably apart from his fellow musicians when we first encounter him, and he will pull away from the group even further as his affections for Fancy Day develop.

The opening both acknowledges conventional realist modes of writing and repeatedly evades them. The temporal and spatial coordinates are carefully established and then dissolved as the novel slips into the realm of myth and archetype. We are asked to imagine "a cold and starry Christmas-eve within living memory" (p. 11), as Dick Dewy makes his way along Mellstock Lane, but the texture of the writing soon begins to resemble painting and sculpture. The various trees "all appeared now as black and flat outlines upon the sky" (p. 11) and the men of the Mellstock parish choir are similarly seen "against the sky in flat outlines" (p. 12). Hardy's simple but sublime observation that "all was dark as the grave" (p. 11) further complicates the novel's realist credentials. As Tim Dolin notes, we recognize from the start that "these men are long dead, and that all this is long past" (Dolin 2004: xxix). If the novel is intent on recreating the Mellstock choir in all its living vitality, it also seems simultaneously to memorialize it as already dead and gone. This self-conscious memorializing persists, even while the novel proclaims that its events exist "in living memory," and it helps to explain the otherwise exotic description of the men in terms of "some processional design on Greek or Etruscan pottery" (p. 12) (Assyrian or Egyptian incised work in the first edition). The style here tends towards excess, moving beyond the initial realist observation of actual time and place, but also offering a richness of perception and insight altogether more complicated than "rural idyll" might suggest.

The generic diversity of *Under the Greenwood Tree* becomes more pronounced as it moves into a satirical mode and becomes a highly polished comedy of manners. In the chapter titled "Dick Makes Himself Useful" there are strong indications of Hardy's persistent interest (from *The Poor Man and the Lady* onwards) in class distinctions and their manifestation in speech and behavior. Although the novel is elsewhere at pains to emphasize Dick's educational achievements and his business acumen, he is here given the role of hapless and anxious assistant to the superior Miss Day. Having returned to the schoolhouse with possessions from her father's house, Fancy is presented (like Bathsheba Everdene at the opening of *Far From the Madding Crowd*) as a young woman of property and independent means, with a canary and cage among the furniture and utensils. With brilliant comic effect, Hardy shows how anxieties about social status and standards of polite behavior manifest themselves in an over-zealous concern for cups and spoons, clean hands and towels. The dialogue is sensitively attuned to the nuances and niceties of genteel conduct ("We always use kettle-holders – didn't you learn housewifery as far as that, Mr Dewy?"), while the authorial voice subtly renders Dick's discomfort in the petty proceedings by variously characterizing him as "the agreeable Richard" or "that civil person" (p. 103). At the same time, the chapter registers the physical attraction between the couple through a deft display of sexual innuendo and erotic imagery, culminating in Fancy's invitation to Dick that he dip the tips of his fingers in a basin of water: "Thereupon he plunged in his hands, and they paddled together. It being the first time in his life that he had touched female fingers under water, Dick duly registered the sensation as rather a nice one" (p. 104).

As with Bathsheba Everdene and Grace Melbury, Hardy shows how sexual desire is compromised and complicated for Fancy Day by questions of social and cultural status. His revisions to the novel appear to have been made in the interests of accentuating social and economic status and intensifying the rivalry among the three men vying for Fancy Day's attention. The precise details with which the novel documents the appurtenances of social class suggest once again that "rural idyll" is not the most helpful or exact description of its strangely mixed generic components. The subtitle of the novel, "A Rural Painting of the Dutch School," suggests a willingness to show "a low phase of life" and an emphasis on "the faithful representing of commonplace things," following the example of George Eliot's *Adam Bede* (Eliot [1859] 1996: 177–8), but Hardy's pictorial allusions and techniques are peculiarly his own, tending neither to romantic idealization nor to realist verisimilitude. As Ruth Bernard Yeazell points out, Hardy is clearly familiar with those notions of the Dutch school as an art of the commonplace and the actual, and therefore admitting social and economic differences, but his use of painterly techniques and pictorial analogies is immensely versatile and wide-ranging (Yeazell 2006, 2008).

At the simple level of setting, it seems likely that Hardy had in mind such paintings as Meindert Hobbema's *Wooded Landscape* (1667) or Jan Skeen's *Skittles* (1662), in which trees assume a large thematic and structural significance, serving as an overarching and embowering natural presence under whose benign shadow human activities are played out in the various light of the changing seasons. Hardy draws on many other pictorial devices and situations, however, including the striking interplay of light and shadow in the night-time paintings of Gerard Dou and Godfried Schalcken. Schalcken's *Woman with a Candle* (1660) possibly provides the model for the image of Fancy as "a young girl framed as a picture by the window architrave . . . unconsciously illuminating her countenance to a vivid brightness by a candle she held in her left hand" (p. 34). A passage in the chapter titled "Honey-Taking, and Afterwards" anticipates the dramatic night-time meeting of Bathsheba and Troy in *Far From the Madding Crowd*, and appears to derive its memorable image of a lantern radiating light from Dou's *The Night School*: "The party remaining were now lit up in front by the lantern in their midst, their shadows radiating each way upon the garden-plot like the spokes of a wheel" (p. 146).

One of the most memorable pictorial scenes in the novel, a description of Keeper Day's house, shows Hardy borrowing from Dutch paintings of domestic interiors, but doing so with a high degree of artistic self consciousness:

> It was a satisfaction to walk into the keeper's house, even as a stranger, on a fine spring morning like the present. A curl of wood-smoke came from the chimney and drooped over the roof like a blue feather in a lady's hat; and the sun shone obliquely upon the patch of grass in front, which reflected its brightness through the open doorway and up the staircase opposite, lighting up each riser with a shiny green radiance and leaving the top of each step in shade. (pp. 92–3)

To begin with, there is an assertive realism in the temporality and assumed actuality of "a fine spring morning like the present." Yet along with this comes a highly stylized and overtly artificial rendering of the scene in pictorial terms. The passage invites admiration for its verisimilitude, but the scene is so perfectly framed as to draw attention to its own "make-believe" tendencies. The image of smoke as "a blue feather in a lady's hat" is startlingly novel and perhaps appropriate given Fancy's preference for a hat rather than a bonnet, but it is also excessively ornate. A similar shift in modes of representation and codes of signification occurs in the account of Dick's drive to Budmouth and his unexpected meeting with Fancy. This time, we move from popular Victorian sentimentality ("a bunch of sweets: it was Fancy! Dick's heart went round to her with a rush") to an impeccably aesthetic seascape in which the water is "a brilliant sheet of liquid colour" with "bright tones of green and opal" (p. 117).

What makes *Under the Greenwood Tree* a novel worth reading and re-reading is not that it offers some pleasant and light-hearted rural comedy (though there are certainly elements of that), but rather that it initiates in Hardy's work a series of profound questions about a particular social environment and how best to represent it in fiction. The novel's radical undecidability about the image of rural life that it might convey is matched by an equally radical uncertainty about the question of genre – about the appropriate literary form and means of representation. The novel would later be revised and more fully integrated into Hardy's Wessex group of novels, but for the time being it achieved a modest success and prompted some enthusiastic reviews. Leslie Stephen wrote to Hardy on November 30, 1872 to offer his congratulations and to seek a new novel for the *Cornhill* magazine. Hardy, by this time, was already turning his attention to another pastoral tale, to be called *Far From the Madding Crowd*. He revealed to Stephen that the "chief characters" would be "a young woman-farmer, a shepherd, and a sergeant of cavalry" (Millgate 2004: 140).. Once again, however, the pastoral framework serves a much more complicated purpose than creating a world of antique simplicity. Hardy draws extensively on the close association of pastoral literature with rural occupations, but his version of pastoral is one that functions in dark and unsettling ways. Even though Hardy was undoubtedly persuaded by Stephen to develop the pastoral elements in his writing, it is clear that some of the generic forms he had already experimented with – satire, melodrama, sensationalism – found their way into *Far From the Madding Crowd*, along with a measure of the caustic irony and brooding tragic outlook he had begun to infuse into *A Pair of Blue Eyes* (1872).

The title of the novel suggests that Hardy's vision is by no means simple or straightforward. It has its source in Thomas Gray's "Elegy Written in a Country Church Yard" (1751):

> Far from the madding crowd's ignoble strife,
> Their sober wishes never learn'd to stray;
> Along the cool sequester'd vale of life
> They kept the noiseless tenor of their way.
>
> (Gray 1966: 40)

While the novel certainly has its moments of quiet contemplation and serene composure, it is also riven with powerful and memorable images of destitution, misery, and violence: Gabriel's loss of his flock, Fanny Robin's death in Casterbridge Union (the workhouse), Boldwood's murder of Troy and his subsequent imprisonment. In view of the novel's tendency to provoke and disturb its readers rather than gently lull them, the title's invocation of a pastoral idyll seems heavily ironic.

Most obviously, perhaps, *Far From the Madding Crowd* invokes the pastoral tradition by taking as one of its central characters a shepherd who is also a lover. Like many of his literary predecessors, Gabriel sings and plays the flute. We are told that "Oak could pipe with Arcadian sweetness" (p. 45), a tribute that firmly links him with the classical origins of pastoral literature. Chapter 5, in which Gabriel loses his sheep, announces "a pastoral tragedy," and later we see Gabriel at the hiring fair, having sunk "from his modest elevation as pastoral king" (pp. 38, 43). Gabriel's work as a shepherd provides the basis for much of the action in *Far From the Madding Crowd*. The novel scrupulously observes the seasonal activities going on at Weatherbury Upper Farm, but it gives particular emphasis to the importance of sheep-farming in the agricultural year. The very structure of the novel seems to be determined (like that of earlier pastoral works) according to the shepherd's calendar. There are three pastoral scenes in particular that carry a powerful symbolic resonance: the sheep-washing, the sheep-shearing, and the shearing supper.

While explicitly invoking the pastoral tradition, however, *Far From the Madding Crowd* also departs significantly from some of its familiar conventions. The novel does not simply offer its readers an idealized world of bucolic innocence; nor does it suggest that the life of the country is necessarily preferable to that of the town. Much more provocatively, it presents a series of severe disturbances that threaten to demolish its pastoral affiliations completely. In addition, the novel's generic instability is intensified by the existence of other literary conventions which further complicate and occasionally undermine its realist credentials, so much so that Hardy's writing sometimes seems willfully anti-realist. As well as employing pastoral devices, *Far From the Madding Crowd* also draws in strange and unexpected ways on Gothic fiction, the novel of sensation, and popular melodrama.

Like *Under the Greenwood Tree*, with its evocation of rural painting of the Dutch school, *Far From the Madding Crowd* is a highly pictorial novel which draws extensively on images and ideas from the visual arts. Chapter 1 is a "description of Farmer Oak," but it also involves "an incident" in which Bathsheba Everdene is brought dramatically into view. The passage that follows is remarkable for its highly organized visual design and its subtle articulation of shifting visual perspectives:

> Casually glancing over the hedge, Oak saw coming down the incline before him an ornamental spring waggon painted yellow and gaily marked, drawn by two horses, a waggoner walking alongside, bearing a whip perpendicularly. The waggon was laden with household goods and window plants, and on the apex of the whole sat a woman, young and attractive. Gabriel had not beheld the sight for more than half a minute when the vehicle was brought to a standstill just beneath his eyes. (p. 9)

The arrival of Bathsheba in the yellow wagon is framed by Gabriel's visual perceptions: by the initial casual glance with which he catches sight of the wagon on the incline, and then – as if in quick succession – by the close-up apprehension of the vehicle "beneath his eyes." It is almost as if the movement of the wagon has been filmed, but within that frame we have a geometrical vocabulary more suggestive of eighteenth- and nineteenth-century painting. With all the formality of academy paintings, the wagoner carries his whip "perpendicularly," while the young woman (whose name is not revealed until chapter 4) is seated "on the apex" of the wagon and its chattels. The fetching picture of the woman seated outdoors and yet surrounded by household objects owes much to the popular tradition of genre painting in which figures are painted "as if from life," depicted within a pleasing landscape or within a recognizable domestic setting. Here, Hardy's narrative cleverly conflates the two possibilities. But apart from creating a pleasant "picture," the incident plays ironically with ideas about the ways in which art might be said to mirror life. The young woman blushes at seeing herself blush in the mirror, and the blush, we are told, ended in "a real smile" (p. 10).

As several critics have pointed out (see especially Berger 1990 and Bullen 1986), Hardy's interest in visual design extends beyond the influence of painterly techniques to a concern with the ways in which people perceive themselves and others. In a whimsical anticipation of this aspect of the novel, the narrative draws our attention to a cat in a willow basket, which "gazed with half-closed eyes, and affectionately surveyed the small birds around" (p. 9). As so often in *Far From the Madding Crowd*, the narrative proceeds according to the ways in which people perceive the world around them. The woman looks "attentively downwards" at an oblong package and assures herself that the wagoner is "not yet in sight." Her eyes creep back to the package and what she reveals is the looking-glass in which she proceeds to "survey herself attentively" (p. 10). The passage in which Bathsheba blushes at her own reflection is full of brilliant visual effects:

> It was a fine morning, and the sun lighted up to a scarlet glow the crimson jacket she wore, and painted a soft lustre upon her bright face and dark hair. The myrtles, geraniums and cactuses packed around her were fresh and green, and at such a leafless season they invested the whole concern of horses, waggon, furniture, and girl with a peculiar vernal charm. What possessed her to indulge in such a performance in the sight of the sparrows, blackbirds and unperceived farmer, who were alone its spectators – whether the smile began as a factitious one to test her capacity in that art – nobody knows: it ended certainly in a real smile; she blushed at herself, and seeing her reflection blush, blushed the more. (p. 10)

The subtle gradations of scarlet and crimson in the morning sunshine are seen with a painter's eye, and so too is the vivid contrast between the woman's "bright face" and "dark hair." The green of the plants adds further color to the scene and also sets up a sharp contrast between the spring-like charm of the picture and the "leafless season" in which the incident takes place. Entirely characteristic of Hardy's composition, both in this novel and elsewhere, is the presentation of characters who, unknowingly, are watched by others. Bathsheba conducts her looking-glass "performance" in the sight of the sparrows and blackbirds, but the "unperceived farmer" is also one of the "spectators." We are later told that Gabriel "withdrew from his point of espial" (p. 11).

Hardy's preoccupation with ways of seeing is clearly more than a novelty. The visual relationships established early in the novel have a profound structural importance and also carry a weight of social and cultural meaning. Although Gabriel pays twopence to the turnpike keeper to allow the wagon to pass (the first of several important economic transactions), his initial social distance from Bathsheba is immediately apparent: "He looked up at her then; she heard his words, and looked down" (p. 11). As if to reinforce the impression of condescension and belittlement, the narrator adds that "The red jacketed and dark haired maiden . . . carelessly glanced over him" when she "might have looked her thanks to Gabriel" (p. 11). What Gabriel infers from the picture he has observed is "Vanity" (p. 12), but this is only one perspective among many possibilities, and what Hardy's novel repeatedly suggests is the fallible, tentative nature of human perception. This abiding interest in multiple perspectives and different angles of vision has a powerful impact on Hardy's understanding of what constitutes realism. Instead of an authoritative, single-minded account of what is true or real, we are much more likely to encounter a conflicting and competing series of impressions.

At one level, the narrative structure of *Far From the Madding Crowd* seems very bold and simple. Three suitors compete for the affections of Bathsheba Everdene: a shepherd, a gentleman farmer, and a soldier. The narrative progresses according to the aspirations of each of these lovers, and much of the drama in the novel ensues from the overlapping and competing interests of the three, as well as from Bathsheba's fluctuating responses. This stark outline, however, is given a highly elaborate design by the repeated emphasis on visual codes of conduct and by the shifting degrees of visual attention and discrimination with which the principal characters regard each other. So Gabriel, in declaring his constancy to Bathsheba, remarks: "whenever you look up there I shall be – and whenever I look up there will be you" (p. 35). It is Gabriel who, in the end, sees Bathsheba most clearly, but before they reach the equilibrium he seeks, Bathsheba passes before the surveying gaze of both Farmer Boldwood and Sergeant Troy. In each case, the way in which Bathsheba is seen and appraised differs markedly from the way in which she is perceived by Gabriel.

Farmer Boldwood's first meeting with Bathsheba is delayed when he visits Weatherbury Upper Farm and she refuses to see him. Later, in the corn-market at Casterbridge, Bathsheba is conscious of being the focus of attention: "Women seem to have eyes in their ribbons for such matters as these" (p. 95). She is also conscious, however, of a certain "recusant" who seems to withhold his gaze. The same man, who turns out to be Boldwood, passes her on the way home, "with eyes fixed on the most advanced point along the road," and Bathsheba remarks to Liddy: "I wonder why he is so wrapt up and indifferent, and seemingly so far away from all he sees around him" (pp. 96–7). As with Gabriel, Bathsheba's growing acquaintance with Boldwood is presented as an ocular drama. What seems to induce the fateful decision to send a valentine to Boldwood is Bathsheba's pique at being denied "the official glance of admiration" (p. 100). She finds it "faintly depressing that the most dignified and valuable man in the parish should withhold his eyes" (p. 101). Significantly, it is dusk when Boldwood is presented to us, contemplating the words "marry me" embossed on the seal of the valentine letter. So many crucial scenes, including decisive moments of judgment and confrontation, take place at night or in the half-light, when clear vision is difficult to obtain. We are told that "the bachelor's gaze was continually fastening itself" on the letter, "till the large red seal became as a blot of blood on the retina of his eye" (p. 102). The obsessive and disturbed nature of Boldwood's vision is immediately apparent. He places the valentine in the corner of the looking-glass, as if registering its hold on his psyche, and is conscious of its presence even when his back is turned.

Bathsheba's first meeting with Sergeant Troy takes place at night in the gloom of the fir plantation. She finds herself "hooked" to a soldier "brilliant in brass and scarlet," and the contrast of this "revelation" with her somber expectations has upon her "the effect of a fairy transformation" (p. 171). Troy, in sharp contrast to Boldwood, is brazen in his way of seeing: "He looked hard into her eyes when she raised them for a moment: Bathsheba looked down again, for his gaze was too strong to be received pointblank with her own" (p. 171). Troy's modes of perception and apprehension are sporadic and opportunistic: "His outlook upon time was as a transient flash of the eye now and then" (p. 176). In a sharp reversal of roles, it is Bathsheba who now comes to be dominated, and this is made emphatic in the novel's visual symmetry. At the end of chapter 25 (p. 178), it is Troy who emerges as "a bright scarlet spot" (the color formerly associated with Bathsheba), and his attempted mastery is given a strongly visual manifestation. One indication of Bathsheba's steady divergence from Boldwood and Troy towards the loyal and steadfast Oak is her eventual appreciation not just of his patient forbearance but of his selfless vision. The "simple lesson" Gabriel reveals "by every turn and look" is that the interests most affecting his personal well-being are "not the most absorbing and important in his eyes" (p. 305). His way of seeing is tempered and serene, without any of the agitation that besets the other principal characters in the novel: "Oak meditatively looked upon the horizon of circumstances without any special regard to his own standpoint in the midst" (p. 305).

To the very end, the novel is propelled by this drama of visual attitudes and gestures, but its structure also depends on a skillfully orchestrated series of contrasts and parallels between people, situations, and events, and on a highly dramatic and episodic arrangement of scenes. This undoubtedly owes something to the exigencies of magazine publication, but the result is a series of powerfully concentrated and memorable incidents such as the fire, the sheep-washing and sheep-shearing, the sword exercise, and the storm. While each of these episodes has its own narrative and dramatic interest, the cumulative effect gives the novel a tremendous sense of activity and momentum. Sergeant Troy's sword exercise in chapter 28 lends itself remarkably well to the kind of Freudian psychoanalytical criticism practiced in Richard Carpenter's influential essay (1964), but in fact the episode is so overtly erotic as to render Freud's insights superfluous. Although there is no direct reference to any physical contact beyond a kiss, Hardy's account of Troy's "strange and glorious performance" (p. 191) is one of the most sexually charged and sexually provocative scenes in nineteenth-century fiction. "Yes, I should like to see it very much," Bathsheba confides to Troy earlier in the novel (p. 191), and at the beginning of the chapter entitled "The Hollow amid the Ferns," her anxiety is immediately apparent: "She was now literally trembling and panting at this her temerity in such an errant undertaking: her breath came and went quickly and her eyes shone with an infrequent light" (p. 192). Even before the sword exercise commences, the landscape seems seductively inviting. The heath is dotted with "tall thickets of brake fern, plump and diaphanous from recent rapid growth," while the pit is "floored with a thick flossy carpet of moss and grass intermingled, so yielding that the foot was half buried within it" (pp. 192–3). The sun is described as "a bristling ball of gold" which sweeps "the tips of the ferns with its long luxuriant rays," and Bathsheba appears in the midst of the ferns, "their soft feathery arms caressing her up to her shoulders" (p. 192).

The close and daring cuts of Troy's sword exercise are mimicked at the textual level by a commentary that is equally close and daring. When Troy produces his sword, it is "raised . . . into the sunlight . . . like a living thing" (p. 193). In the act of impressing Bathsheba with his various "thrusts," Troy darts the point and blade of the sword "towards her left side just above her hip," and Bathsheba is conscious of the sword "emerging as it were from between her ribs, having apparently passed through her body" (p. 194). "Have you run me through?", she cries out in fright, to which Troy responds by telling her not to be afraid, "Because if you are I can't perform" (p. 194). Leaving aside the sexually symbolic aspects of the chapter's title, the episode is remarkable not least because of its powerful crescendo of visual and aural sensations. The onomatopoeic effect of the sword exercise is brought to a marvelously sibilant climax: "In short, she was enclosed in a firmament of light, and of sharp hisses, resembling a sky-full of meteors close at hand" (p. 194).

The strong pictorial design of the novel, its intense concentration on visual impressions, and its emphasis on the fallibility of perception give it a distinctive place in nineteenth-century fiction. In a fundamental way, it questions and challenges many of the assumptions that were commonly held about the nature of realism in the later nineteenth century. At the level of genre, too, it both complicates and extends our understanding of how literary realism functions. One of the hallmarks of Hardy's bold enterprise in writing *Far From the Madding Crowd* was the introduction of a bewildering variety of generic forms, many of which might be thought to sit oddly and awkwardly alongside each other: Victorian melodrama, classical tragedy, popular songs and ballads, hymns and sermons, travel writing, nature writing, art criticism, scientific discourse, and political invective. In many ways the success of the novel might be said to be the achievement of a harmonious resolution of these various textual practices within the subtle adaptation and modification of a prevailing realist model; in other ways, though, these multiple discursive forms refuse to coalesce, and reveal the actual diversity and multifariousness of what we commonly refer to as "realism."

The Gothic and sensationalist elements in the novel are strikingly apparent in its depiction of Fanny Robin's seduction and betrayal by Sergeant Troy, and in its unremitting insistence on the sordid circumstances of her death. Reports of Fanny's disappearance and repeated instances of her misery and distress serve to dispel any lingering suggestion of pastoral innocence in the novel. The most shocking revelation, and one that Leslie Stephen was at pains to tone down, occurs in chapter 43, entitled "Fanny's Revenge." The Oxford World's Classics edition usefully reprints the manuscript version of this chapter rather than the version that appeared in the *Cornhill Magazine* and in subsequent editions of the novel. Hardy's original text has Liddy report to

Bathsheba that "a wicked story is got to Weatherbury within this last hour – that – there's *two of 'em* in there!" (p. 303). Bathsheba's opening of the coffin and discovery of two bodies clearly emulates the sensation novel of the time, but the episode also contains stylistic flourishes which even now seem calculatedly perverse, as if challenging conventional moral and aesthetic ideals through a triumphant display of bad taste. In "a miniature wrapping of white linen," Bathsheba perceives "a face so delicately small in contour and substance that its cheeks and the plump backs of its little fists irresistibly reminded her, excited as she was, of the soft convexity of mushrooms on a dewy morning" (p. 43). The same flouting of decorum and respectability is evident in the disturbingly incongruous comparison of the dead woman's hands with those in paintings by the Venetian artist Giovanni Bellini (*c*.1430–1516): "Her hands had acquired a preternatural refinement, and a painter in looking upon them might have fancied that at last he had found the fellows of those marvellous hands and fingers which must have served as originals to Bellini" (p. 308). There is sufficient evidence here to suggest that Hardy was not only intent on manipulating a variety of styles and generic types to suit his purposes, but also strongly inclined towards the use of parody and satire as a way of provoking and engaging his readers.

Hardy's invocation of the visual arts, his self-conscious parading of classical and artistic allusions, his strange mixing of pastoral, Gothic, and sensational modes – all of these threaten to sabotage what we commonly think of as realism, with its scrupulous and consistent observation of actuality. Hardy, by his own admission, sets art against realism. Yet there is a special sense in which his writing is supremely and enduringly realist: in that special sense of being "more truthful than truth." As Alison Byerly has argued, the Victorian novel's self-conscious preoccupation with "art" and various art forms actually reinforces its claims to realism. Hardy's unnerving shifts of perspective and unabashed mixing of genres are not an evasion of "the real" but part of a complex concern with various modes of description and representation. *Far From the Madding Crowd* confronts us with "disjunctive artistic moments that shake our sense of what is real" (Byerly 1997: 12). Ironically, in contrast to those moments of heightened artistic expression, the rest of the narrative might be said to appear "more real."

What lies behind Hardy's preoccupation with visual impressions and different modes of representation in *Under the Greenwood Tree* and *Far From the Madding Crowd* is an idea of novel-writing as an essentially explorative process, a tentative reaching after truths rather than an authoritative and confident declaration of "what is really there." His capacity to "shake our sense of what is real" has important social and political repercussions. In a way that anticipates the more stridently antagonistic vision of the later works, these early novels disturb our familiar perceptions of the way things are: they challenge received opinion and refuse to conform to conventional social and moral values. They have a profoundly important place in a developing body of work concerned with overthrowing complacent and settled views about sexuality, social class, religious belief, community, work, and environment.

If *Under the Greenwood Tree* and *Far From the Madding Crowd* initially present themselves as pastoral romances, what they ultimately reveal is that love and marriage are not simply matters of the heart, but choices and decisions involving complicated economic and cultural factors. Within the chronic insecurity of the changing social order that Hardy depicts, these choices are particularly pressing and acute. So often in Hardy's later novels desire is thwarted and defeated. *Tess of the d'Urbervilles* and *Jude the Obscure* are the bleakest testimonies to this thwarted desire, but *Far From the Madding Crowd* also bears witness to the tragedy of unfulfilled aims, with the lives of Fanny Robin and Farmer Boldwood ending poignantly in terminal collapse and defeat. As Raymond Williams pointed out, the social process in Hardy's novels so often tends towards isolation and separation within a community that might otherwise be nurtured and sustained (Williams 1970). *Under the Greenwood Tree* and *Far From the Madding Crowd* close with an affirmative sense of togetherness and shared endeavor, but already the pastoral vision is darkening and the tentative hopefulness of these early novels will never be found again.

REFERENCES AND FURTHER READING

Berger, Sheila (1990). *Thomas Hardy and Visual Structures: Framing, Disruption, Process*. New York: New York University Press.

Bullen, J. B. (1986). *The Expressive Eye: Fiction and Perception in the Work of Thomas Hardy*. Oxford: Clarendon Press.

Byerly, Alison (1997). *Realism, Representation and the Arts in Nineteenth-Century Literature*. Cambridge: Cambridge University Press.

Carpenter, Richard (1964). The Mirror and the Sword: Imagery in *Far From the Madding Crowd*. *Nineteenth Century Fiction*, 18, 331–45.

Cecil, Lord David (1954). *Hardy the Novelist: An Essay in Criticism*. London: Constable.

Dolin, Tim (2004). Introduction to *Under the Greenwood Tree* (pp. xxi–xli). London: Penguin.

Eliot, George ([1859] 1996). *Adam Bede*, ed. Valentine Cunningham. Oxford: Oxford University Press.

Gatrell, Simon (2003). *Thomas Hardy's Vision of Wessex*. Basingstoke: Palgrave Macmillan.

Gray, Thomas (1966). *The Complete Poems of Thomas Gray*, ed. H. W. Starr and J. R. Hendrickson. Oxford: Clarendon Press.

Hardy, Thomas ([1872] 1999). *Under the Greenwood Tree*, ed. Simon Gatrell. Oxford: Oxford University Press.

Hardy, Thomas ([1874] 1998). *Far From the Madding Crowd*, ed. Suzanne Falck-Yi, introd. Simon Gatrell. Oxford: Oxford University Press.

Hodgart, Matthew, ed. (1965). *The Faber Book of Ballads*. London: Faber & Faber.

Irwin, Michael (2000). *Reading Hardy's Landscapes*. Basingstoke: Palgrave Macmillan.

Miller, J. Hillis (1970). *Thomas Hardy: Distance and Desire*. Cambridge, MA: The Belknap Press of Harvard University Press.

Millgate, Michael (1971). *Thomas Hardy: His Career as a Novelist*. London: Bodley Head.

Millgate, Michael (2004). *Thomas Hardy: A Biography Revisited*. Oxford: Oxford University Press.

Neill, Edward (2004). *The Secret Life of Thomas Hardy*. Aldershot: Ashgate.

Ruskin, John (1903–12). *The Works of John Ruskin*, ed. E. T. Cook and Alexander Wedderburn, vol. V: *Modern Painters*. London: George Allen.

Shakespeare, William (1997). *The Norton Shakespeare*, ed. Stephen Greenblatt et al. New York: Norton.

Williams, Raymond (1970). *The English Novel from Dickens to Lawrence*. London: Chatto & Windus.

Yeazell, Ruth Bernard (2006). Hardy's Rural Painting of the Dutch School. In Keith Wilson (ed.), *Thomas Hardy Reappraised: Essays in Honour of Michael Millgate* (pp. 136–53). Toronto: University of Toronto Press.

Yeazell, Ruth Bernard (2008). *Art of the Everyday: Dutch Painting and the Realist Novel*. Princeton: Princeton University Press.

17

"Wild Regions of Obscurity": Narrative in *The Return of the Native*

Penny Boumelha

Most modern readers will inevitably come to any particular novel by Thomas Hardy with an awareness of the context of the whole of his long career as a nineteenth-century novelist and a twentieth-century poet. However, in 1877–8, the period when he was composing and publishing *The Return of the Native*, Hardy was not yet the well-established and esteemed writer he was to become, and had not embarked on the consistent creation of the imagined Wessex now inseparable from his name. Despite the early success of *Far From the Madding Crowd*, he had still to create a willing and expectant audience. *The Return of the Native* is a novel on which Thomas Hardy rested much hope of success, both as a professional man of letters and as a literary artist with a justified claim to be taken seriously. He took time to prepare himself for this next stage of his assault on fame, reading widely in contemporary science and philosophy, gathering and studying admired models of prose style, reflecting on his reading of classical writers, and generally taking extensive notes. Artistic ambition is perfectly apparent in the novel's generic aspirations and high cultural models (both Greek and Shakespearian tragedy, classical legend, biblical allegory), close to the surface as they are. And it is a novel of which he seems to have remained particularly fond.

Nevertheless, the novel was in its own time close to a failure, both commercially and critically. The response of contemporary editors and reviewers to this long considered and authorially cherished work was not the first occasion on which Hardy had experienced a painful clash between his own artistic vision and the horizon of readerly expectation forming around him, and it would certainly not be the last. Early and late in his career as a novelist, he encountered objections to the supposedly dangerous – or at least questionable – moral tone some saw in his works. As those novels came to be more and more centrally preoccupied with questions of sexuality and marriage – or perhaps, as Jules David Law puts it, with using "the sexual crises in women's life-histories" as the focus and vehicle of an exploration of "an interpretation of social relations" (Law 1998: 224) – the attacks on him on moral grounds came to be more and more virulent. Hardy's characteristic response to them would be twofold: he would comply (albeit bitterly) with the letter of the requirements of such censorship, and at the same time unmistakably (though hardly joyously) flout their spirit.

This perceived moral issue unquestionably shapes some of the responses of the first readers of *The Return of the Native*. The novel was rejected for serial publication in Hardy's first choice of periodical, for example, on these grounds; the editor of the *Cornhill*, Leslie Stephen, detected on the basis of only a short section of an early draft the germ of something "dangerous" in the triangulations of desire and relationship forming around Eustacia, Wildeve, and Thomasin (Dalziel 1996: 85). Similarly, after the novel's first publication in the then dominant three-volume format, early reviewers were widely troubled by the unsympathetic nature of the main characters: "we . . . can scarcely get up a satisfactory interest in people whose history and habits are so entirely different to our own," complained the *Times* reviewer, while the New York journal *The Eclectic* was more forthright than some, but by no means alone, in finding Eustacia Vye to be a "selfish, cruel, unprincipled, and despicable woman" (Pinck 1969: 297 and 302 respectively). But alongside such morally based objections, there is a further element in these earliest reviews that opens up some important questions about the distinctive qualities of this novel.

That is to say, there is to be found in these reviews, interspersed with praise for Hardy's descriptions of the natural world and of Egdon in particular, a marked unease with aspects of the novel's writing. The *Academy* reviewer speaks of "affectation" of style and "arbitrary and accidental" tragic plotting, and is widely echoed by fellow reviewers in the British periodicals, who complain variously of "mannerisms" and "clumsy style," "quaintness of expression" and "eccentricities of language," "eccentric forms of expression" and "strained and far-fetched" figurative language, or an "air of affectation" in the writing (Pinck 1969). Reviewers in the American journals were no more impressed, objecting to the "obscurity" of the title or its "far-fetched and infelicitous" nature, to "padding" in the plot, and generally to unusual vocabulary and affected writing (Pinck 1969: 299–304). In other words, irrespective of the perceived moral tone of the work, there is a sense of discomfort, even shock, at the plotting, imagery, and style of the writing. To a high degree, this sense of unfamiliarity is due to normative expectations about the nature of English provincial realism, with its predominant conventions of complex and coherent characterization, plotting driven by causality and motivation, and objective narration: these are expectations which *The Return of the Native* rather ostentatiously declines to fulfill.

Interestingly, more recent critics too have sometimes manifested their unease with aspects of Hardy's writing, often identifying a kind of doubleness that seems on occasion to subordinate sequential narrative to some other quality. Judith Mitchell, for example, describes the "Queen of Night" chapter of *The Return of the Native* as "a halt in the narrative" for a moment of "rhapsody" (Mitchell 1994: 177), and John Hughes comments tartly of Hardy's first published novel, *Desperate Remedies*, that "he does not know when it is time to stop looking and turn back to the official business of narrative" (Hughes 2004: 231). In a more positive vein, Michael Irwin notes in Hardy's work more generally a tension between "story" and something else that he variously identifies as "vision" (Irwin 1999: 147) and as "melody" (Irwin 1998: 134), an analogue of landscape painting or of opera, remarking that "most lovers of Hardy read him for the 'arias,' those potent, memorable scenes . . . which in many cases may seem extraneous to the narrative proper" (Irwin 1998: 134). Critics may differ over whether these elements in Hardy look back towards sensation fiction and melodrama or forward to the characteristic disruptive gaps and juxtapositions of modernist narrative. The point on which all such critical readings are agreed, surely, is that there resides within Hardy's realism a significant presence of something more like a texture or a rhythm than a narrative impulsion.

In fact, *The Return of the Native* presents its readers with a distinctive fictional universe of an unusual and (it would certainly appear from the early reviewers' comments) an unsettling kind. To begin with, it is a universe of sudden shifts of perspective, in which Clym's dimmed eyesight limits his world to "a circuit of a few feet from his person" (p. 247) and his society to insects and baby rabbits, or his mother switches her vision within the space of a few lines from the colony of ants at her feet – "To look down upon them was like observing a city street from the top of a tower" (p. 282) – to a heron taking flight "away from all contact with the earthly ball to which she was pinioned" (p. 282). It is a world of unexpected continuities between the animate and the inanimate: so, the night "sang dirges with clenched teeth" (p. 85) and "the bluffs had broken silence, the bushes had broken silence, the heather-bells had broken silence; at last, so did the woman; and her articulation was but as another phrase of the same discourse as theirs" (p. 57).

It is a world in which the presence of witches or Mephistophelian visitants seems as plausible as the presence of retired sea captains or innkeepers, and in which a young woman mistakes a returning suitor for "the ghost of yourself" (p. 374). The invisible, the bodiless, the dead, seem to have as much effectivity as the living: the sound of a gate latch in the wind is "as if the invisible shapes of the dead were passing in on their way to visit him" (p. 350), and Clym moves through the world as a "Lazarus" (p. 367), as "the mere corpse of a lover" (p. 383). Personified abstractions act as antagonists of the characters: Adversities "set upon" Clym (p. 241), Eustacia "goes out to battle against Depression" (p. 251), and as Clym passes across the heath, "the past seized upon him with its shadowy hand, and held him there to listen to its tale" (p. 373). Characters, even when intimately known to one another, can pass unnoticed or become oddly unrecognizable. In the episode in which Mrs. Yeobright walks to visit her son's home, fails to be admitted, and walks back to die on the exposed heath, there are three moments of such non-recognition: first, Mrs. Yeobright sees her own son as "nothing more than a moving handpost to show her the way" (p. 271) until she recognizes his walk as like that of her dead husband; then, as she lies collapsed on the heath, Clym returns the favor by "not for a moment" (p. 280) thinking her his mother until recognition is inevitable; while, as Eustacia roams with her sometime lover Wildeve, she comes upon the scene and "did not recognise Mrs. Yeobright in the reclining figure nor Clym as one of the standers by till she came close" (p. 295).

It is, again, a world in which it seems no secrets can be kept, no human actions can go unobserved (except, crucially, the death of Eustacia and Wildeve, to which it will be necessary to return): observers conceal themselves beneath turves, fall back into shadows, peer through windows, spy through telescopes, listen through chimneys. When no human eye is there, animals, birds, even insects, bear witness, as the heathcropping ponies, glow-worms, and moths preside over the midnight gambling of Cantle, Wildeve, and Venn. The heath itself has eyes: a pond like "the white of an eye without its pupil" (p. 183), a "knot of stunted hollies, which in the general darkness of the scene stood as the pupil in a black eye" (p. 265). And such actual observers, animate or inanimate, are profusely supplemented by hypothetical eyes and conditional interpretations posited by the narrative voice (always a favorite narrative device of Hardy's, here employed with near-obsessive frequency): "a keen observer might have been inclined to think . . ." (p. 80), "the natural query of an observer would have been . . ." (p. 14), "had a looker-on been posted in the immediate vicinity of the barrow, he would have learned . . ." (p. 18).

The Return of the Native has been described by Peter Casagrande as at once "cultural drama" and "psychodrama" (Casagrande 1982: 116). It is an accurate description in that the novel presents its reader with a fictional world in which what might be called the daylight plot of familiar social interaction – earning a living and borrowing money, courting and marrying, cutting hair and drinking ale – is shadowed by something altogether stranger, something more at ease in those "wild regions of obscurity which are vaguely felt to be compassing us about in midnight dreams of flight and disaster" (p. 11) said at the opening of the novel to be associated with Egdon. Alongside the familiar sequentiality of social plot runs a psychically motivated universe of repetitions and returns, of doubles and dualisms, of dream and vision, of compulsion and obsession. Eustacia dreams an encounter with a knight in shining armor who falls apart before her eyes, and then meets Clym while herself disguised as a knight. Susan Nunsuch wreaks a displaced violence upon Eustacia, "warping and kneading, cutting and twisting, dismembering and re-joining" (p. 347) the wax to form an effigy that she casts into the fire even as Eustacia embarks on her final disastrous venture across the heath. As Mrs. Yeobright looks hopefully through the window of her son's house, he stirs in his sleep and murmurs "mother" without awakening from his dream of her. Diggory Venn vanishes and then reappears as his own double, the white ghost of his red self. Charley will do anything at all for a few minutes of holding Eustacia's hand, Venn stores the glove of his beloved in his breast, Clym treats every household item of his mother's as a holy relic of the "sublime saint" (p. 395) who is the centre of his "religion" (p. 335). That so many of the novel's key scenes are set at night only further emphasizes this sense that the events of the novel follow as much the unconscious logic of the dream as the intricate interconnections of motivation and intent.

Through some cultural prescience or by chance, the uncanny dimension of *The Return of the Native* has been deepened and strengthened for more recent readers by the elaboration of Freudian concepts. That Hardy and Freud should both have identified Oedipus as the vehicle of an exploration of a son's relationship to his mother is perhaps not astonishing, given the content of the Sophoclean original. In any event, explicit allusions to Oedipus were added by Hardy only in the course of his revisions for the edition of 1895, by which time the emergence of psychoanalytic discourse was more clearly in the air. Yet, though Hardy could hardly have anticipated the emergence of the concept of the "return of the repressed," he has captured something of its cultural resonance in the title he chose for his novel. It puzzled some reviewers, probably accustomed to more typical Victorian titles invoking individual biography (*Jane Eyre, David Copperfield*) or community (*Middlemarch, Villette*). Hardy's title evokes at once a more abstract and a more general significance. He is a writer who has often been associated with an excessive foregrounding of plot, with over-reliance on coincidence and a degree of shapely interconnectedness that many have misread as authorial mimicry of a universe presumed to be ruled by malign fate. Yet his plotting reveals acutely how the accidental and contingent can be used to mark the seam between chance and design, between the individual and the general. What might have been simply the story of Clym Yeobright's homecoming is overlaid with something closer to myth, the parallel tracking of specific event and cultural archetype.

And indeed, the fictional world of *The Return of the Native* is so densely packed with figuration, symbol, and allusion that it significantly blurs the margin between event and metaphor. The novel invokes the natural world of Egdon and its notably permeable boundaries with human society with striking vividness and particularity, but at the same time binds it so inextricably into the notation of event and dialogue that it is not always easy to distinguish between the language of what really happens and the language of figuration. "My life creeps like a snail," says Clym Yeobright (p. 312), and in the next chapter, as he walks toward a fateful confrontation with his wife, it is so early that no one else is stirring and "all the life visible was in the shape of a solitary thrush cracking a snail upon the doorstone for his breakfast" (p. 317). The proximity of metaphor followed so closely by event forms a moment of ambiguous status: clearly saturated with meaning, but not unequivocally a symbol of Clym's life, about to be destroyed before our eyes and his own. As easily as such natural description, human actions in the plot can also perch on this narrow border between the literal and the figurative. Venn, one of the novel's principal survivors, is also the character who makes the most vigorous attempts to save the drowning couple from the water. The narration of his lifesaving efforts brings the two dimensions so closely together that metaphor and incident appear to merge: "As soon as he began to be in deep water," we are told, "he flung himself across the hatch, and thus supported was able to keep himself afloat as long as he chose" (p. 362). The evocation of the consciousness of a character from within is on occasion handled in the same way. Eustacia Vye's particular role in the mumming episode seems to have multiple determinations, including, for example, her exotic status in the closed community of Egdon and the consistent narrative linkage of her with antiquity and defeat. Insofar as the narration depicts the role as her own choice, it is described in these terms: "This gradual sinking to the earth was, in fact, one reason why Eustacia had thought that the part of the Turkish Knight . . . would suit her best. A direct fall from upright to horizontal . . . was not an elegant or decorous feat for a girl. But it was easy to die like a Turk, by dogged decline" (p. 135). Here, the literal notation of the power of decorum in the life of a woman is overlaid with the culturally prominent metaphorical significance of the "fallen" woman, and at the same time with the novel's own elaborate figurative and symbolic chain of significance relating to the vertical and the horizontal, rising and falling.

Such emblematic moments – and there are many of them – are linked in turn to more extended episodes of an allegorical or symbolic kind, with the reader's attention sometimes drawn quite overtly by commentary, reflection, or even lighting effect toward their dual significance as literal event and as figure. Eustacia's passive surrender to the bramble that snags her dress, for example, is noted as "a clue to her abstraction" (p. 59), while the meaningfulness of Mrs. Yeobright's moments of insight into the insignificance of the large and the significance of the microscopically small as she crosses the heath is flagged by the passing comment that she is "a woman not disinclined to philosophise" (p. 270). Dramatic lighting gives the impression of incidents meaningfully isolated against a background of the indistinct, as in the luridly lit scene of the midnight gambling (p. 228), and in Eustacia's momentary irradiation by firelight: "As Eustacia crossed the firebeams she appeared for an instant as distinct as a figure in a phantasmagoria – a creature of light surrounded by an area of darkness: the moment passed, and she was absorbed in night again" (p. 342). Most telling of all, in this connection, is the sequence in which Eustacia and Wildeve drown.

Both the nature of Eustacia's death and the ambiguity with which it is recounted are illuminated by recalling that water in rapid motion – floods, rushing torrents, open sea – has a strong presence in nineteenth-century English fiction as a metaphor and a plot device for resolving the impasse of the unsatisfied woman whose desire for love is metonymic of a wider desire that the world should be otherwise. Like such other water-associated heroines as Charlotte Brontë's Lucy Snowe or George Eliot's Maggie Tulliver, Hardy's Eustacia is a figure whose desires are greater than her environment can encompass. With a varying blend of sympathy and irony, the narrator points up repeatedly just this opposition between the passionate life she perhaps might have lived and "her Hades," Egdon (p. 69), where "coldest and meanest kisses were at famine prices" and no "mouth matching hers" is to be found (p. 71). She talks continually of her desire for escape to somewhere beyond Egdon, and yet the actual opportunities that present themselves – Budmouth as a lady's companion, Wisconsin with Wildeve – no more match her hopes of a larger life fit for the "splendid woman" (p. 346) she seeks to be than does Egdon itself. At the same time, the novel from the outset stresses her inseparability from the heath, from which she seems to emerge at her first appearance and into which she seems to merge once more when last depicted alive. A language of chafing, of imprisonment, and of resentment characterizes Eustacia's accounts of her physical and her social environment alike. Almost from the first, she sees Egdon Heath itself as her enemy, an embodiment of the forces that conspire to keep her in place, and at times the narrative voice appears to endorse this view: "the wings of her soul were broken by the cruel obstructiveness of all about her" (p. 346). However, it is with equal insistence that the narrative voice draws attention to her congruence with Egdon's moods and ways, even as she embarks on her final attempt to leave it: "the tearfulness of the outer scene was repeated upon her face" (p. 346). A dialectic between escape and resignation is central to Eustacia's dilemma: "an impulse to leave the spot, a desire to stay, struggled within her" (p. 332).

In a novel in which everyone is constantly under the eye of their neighbors, Eustacia is the focus of particular community attention to the propriety of her behavior. As the final search for her begins, her grandfather fears for her life: "I only hope it is no worse than an elopement," he suggests. Clym's response is telling: "Worse? What's worse than the worst a wife can do?" (p. 352). A more or less malicious network of local gossip and spying, comment and interpretation, sets the boundaries for the repeated pattern of desire and resignation, fantasied escape and (self-)imprisonment, that forms her story. So it is fitting that the episode in which the boundaries are finally overcome is unseen, even by the narrator or the cast of disembodied hypothetical narrators on which he so regularly draws. All we have to go on is a sound: "the fall of a body into the stream adjoining," with some irony described as "unmistakable" (p. 360). With visual observation for once forsaken, this sound does not permit us to choose finally between a number of possible options: that she has taken control of her life at last by committing suicide, that the heath reclaims her one last time as she seeks to flee with a man she has finally chosen as her lover, that she is doomed by the encompassing social malignity imaged in Susan Nunsuch's wax models and backward recitation of the Lord's Prayer. The novel affords textual evidence to support any of these interpretations, but the most interesting point here is that the novel maintains the plausibility of all of these mutually contradictory versions to the end of the episode rather than employing a "truth-voice" in the narration to endorse any one of them. The undecidability of the moment gives Hardy's drowned heroine a deep resonance, as at once a victim of her society, a heroine who at last takes control of her life, and a consoling image of transcendence of frustrating social circumstance.

This sense that event is not privileged over metaphor, that the logic of the dream shadows the concatenations of causality, is what gives *The Return of the Native* its quality of almost hallucinatory vividness. Further reinforcing it is an unusual aspect of its narrative technique: an insistence on separating out into a kind of slow motion sequence the processes of seeing and interpreting what is seen. At the opening of the human action of the novel, for example, is the scene in which Captain Drew (perhaps more recognizable under the name given to him in later revisions, Captain Vye) meets the reddleman on the road, and discovers that in his van is Thomasin, returning from her failed attempt at a wedding. It is not recounted in these direct terms, however. Instead, we have this: "Along the road walked an old man. . . . One would have said that he had been, in his day, a naval officer of some order or other." As he looks ahead, he sees "a moving spot, which appeared to be a vehicle. . . . When he drew nearer, he perceived it to be a spring van." Leading it is a strikingly red figure: "The old man knew the meaning of this," we are told, as he recognizes the reddleman (p. 13). And so it goes: this process of seeing, reflecting on what it means, identifying, is repeated over and over again. Sometimes it is attributed to the consciousness of a particular character, as in the passage just discussed; at other times, it comes directly in the voice of the narrator.

One of the most extreme examples is to be found in the gradual discovery of Eustacia Vye that immediately follows this earlier passage. The resting Diggory Venn looks at the heath and at its highest point, the barrow. Then he notices that "its summit . . . was surmounted by something higher." That "something higher" is "like a spike from a helmet," in turn identified as "a form" which the hypothetical observer might suppose to be "a sort of last man," imaginary survivor of the Celtic forebears. The "form" in turn becomes a "figure," compared in its relationship to the hills with the "lantern" without which a dome is nothing (p. 17). The "figure" becomes recognizable as a "person," and finally the person reveals a sex: "the movement had been sufficient to show more clearly the characteristics of the figure: it was a woman's" (p. 18). Only three chapters later do more specific features of "The Figure against the Sky" (p. 55) become apparent, in a further lengthy place of progressive discernment. At first, she is no more than a "closely-wrapped female figure," then "all that could be learnt of her just now" is her height and lady-like quality while her stance poses a question – "whether she had adopted that aspect because of the chilly gusts . . . did not at first appear" – and her stillness is "just as obscure" (p. 55). As she lifts her hand, we learn that she holds a telescope, and only when she throws back the kerchief that covers her head does her profile become visible, with a glimpse of "matchless lips" and cheek in the firelight (p. 58). Finally, before the action resumes, her "buoyant bound up the bank" shows that she is young (p. 60).

The reader is led here through a process of progressive bringing into focus of Eustacia, as if not merely present as a spectator but engaged in active interpretation. The sequence, in the course of which Eustacia evolves from a spike on a helmet to a beautiful young woman, is only an unusually lengthy example of a narrative technique prevalent in the novel. Time and again, a perception is reported first while the moment of its understanding – or, almost as often, misunderstanding – is deferred. So the disjunction of vision and interpretation gives particular importance to the very fully developed strain of imagery of sight and blindness in the novel. As well as the constant reference to the onlooking eyes of actual or imagined spectators, the novel offers a symbolic schema of vision in relation to its central characters. Eustacia and Mrs. Yeobright share a kind of long-range vision of which Eustacia's telescope is only the most concrete example. Just as she knows "by prevision what most women learn only by experience" (p. 71), so too Mrs. Yeobright "had a singular insight into life, considering that she had never mixed with it" (p. 188). The narrator generalizes this observation on the basis of gender: it is usually women, we are told, who "can watch a world which they never saw . . . We call it intuition" (p. 188). Just as clearly, Venn's "eye . . . keen as that of a bird of prey" (p. 14) is central to his ability to sum up a situation and to the slightly predatory nature of the tactics that allow him to emerge unscathed from potential disaster. Again, the dimming of Clym Yeobright's sight following his exposure to the "blinding halo" of love (p. 199) also marks the contraction of his social vision, from his original aims of the intellectual and spiritual betterment of the Egdon community to his placid engagement with the "microscopic" world of "creeping and winged things" in his immediate physical vicinity (p. 247).

At the same time, the narrative gives unusually explicit prominence to the processes by which characters reach their interpretation of what they see or hear. They continually ask themselves or one another the significance of what is before them: " 'Isn't there meaning in it?' she said, stealthily" (p. 316); " 'What does it all mean?' " (p. 286); " 'what's the meaning of this disgraceful performance?' " (p. 43). The effort of interpretation is often conveyed through linguistic metaphors, and a good deal of attempted reading goes on (interestingly, in a society in which the value of literacy is contested in conversations among the heath inhabitants). Clym Yeobright's face, for example, is interesting not "as a picture, but . . . as a page" (p. 167), his features attractive "as shapes intrinsically simple become interesting in writing" (p. 168). And as Mrs. Yeobright walks away from the closed door of her son's home, she encounters the child Johnny Nunsuch, whose attempts to understand the situation are conveyed both through a decidedly non-naturalistic passage of dialogue and through the metaphor of frustrated literacy: "He gazed into her face in a vague, wondering manner, like that of one examining some strange old manuscript, the key to whose characters is undiscoverable" (p. 281).

Notably exempted from this complex conjunction of conjectural interpretation, figurative representation, and deferred understanding is the figure of Thomasin Yeobright, who increasingly becomes the narrative and moral centre of *The Return of the Native*. The introduction into the novel of Thomasin, once identified by Hardy (in a letter of guidance to the illustrator of the serial version) as "the *good* heroine" (Dalziel 1996: 96), stands in marked contrast to the obscured and protracted unveiling of Eustacia. " 'Let me see her at once,' said Mrs Yeobright" (p. 41), and the reader shares in her immediate exposure. She is from the first exactly what she appears to be, to the point of metaphorical transparency: "An ingenuous, transparent life was disclosed: it was as if the flow of her existence could be seen passing within" (p. 41). With such transparency goes a matching perspicacity: "She understood the scene in a moment" (p. 41). While others labor to read what they see, Thomasin's power of interpretation appears spontaneous and immediate: " 'It means just what it seems to mean,' " she tells her aunt (p. 43). She even appears to have the ability to arrest the unceasing generation of metaphor that envelops other central characters: "All similes and allegories concerning her began and ended with birds" (p. 209). Importantly, her world is not peopled with the abstractions, metaphors, and symbols that otherwise threaten to engulf Egdon society:

> To her there were not, as to Eustacia, demons in the air, and malice in every bush and bough. The drops which lashed her face were not scorpions, but prosy rain; Egdon in the mass was no monster whatever, but impersonal open ground. Her fears of the place were rational, her dislikes of its worst moods reasonable. At this time it was in her view a windy, wet place, in which a person might experience much discomfort, lose the path without care, and possibly catch cold. (p. 355)

Adopting the figurative scheme of the novel, it could be said that Thomasin is distinguished in the novel by her capacity to see only what is before her eyes.

Thomasin's exceptionality in itself highlights the novel's insistence on the processes of understanding and interpretation. That element is reinforced by the distinctive character of the narrative voice, unusually positioned as it is in relation to the story it tells. It is evident that we are not in the presence of an embodied narrator with a role in the action of the novel, on the model of first-person narration, and yet there are moments of what can only be called intimacy that suggest a parallel kind of narrative inwardness, as in the phrase "our Eustacia – for she was not altogether unlovable" (p. 73). Yet nor do we find the distanced and objective tone that characterizes the omniscient narrative mode typical of Victorian realism. Indeed, *The Return of the Native* is notable for its explicit disavowal of omniscience. Part of what is sometimes considered the awkwardness of the writing derives from the indirectness of its narration. Rather than simply reporting the events of the narrative in the indicative, the narration continually interposes a chink of doubt: things "seem" or "appear" to be the case, hypothetical observers interpret in conditional tenses, and the phrase "it was as if" recurs with notable frequency. The withholding of omniscient narration so particularly marked in the episode of the deaths of Eustacia and Wildeve also characterizes the conclusion to their story:

> The story of the deaths of Eustacia and Wildeve was told throughout Egdon, and far beyond, for many weeks and months. All the known incidents of their love were enlarged, distorted, touched up, and modified, till the original reality bore but a slight resemblance to the counterfeit presentation by surrounding tongues. (p. 371)

Nor is this the only instance in the novel of self-conscious reference to what might be called the generation of community narrative from individual experience. Earlier, in a more humorous version of the same effect, Clym Yeobright is identified as the focus of a similar process. As one "whose fame had spread to an awkward extent" – that is, "at least two miles round" – at an early age, he has become as much the hero of a story as a friend and neighbor: "if he were making a fortune and a name, so much the better for him; if he were making a tragical figure in the world, so much the better for a narrative" (p. 168). This explicit enunciation of the possibility of a gap between what happens and what is understood inevitably invites some reflection on the narrator's own practices.

While this hesitant and conjectural mode of narration is unusual, it is of course by no means unique. That it is close to the core of Hardy's conception of his novel is apparent in its persistence in later, revised editions of *The Return of the Native*, to which he added first a preface (in 1895) and later a note (added in 1912). Both of these occur in what would normally be considered an authorial rather than a narrative voice; that is, they are commonly regarded as Hardy's direct address to his reader. The preface refers to the period "at which the following events are assumed to have occurred" (p. 429): "assumed," in this context, comes as a surprise, where one might perhaps have expected "set" or some synonym reflecting an authorial decision. An intentional blurring of the boundaries between real and imagined histories is an essential element in the whole imagined edifice of the Hardyan Wessex, just as the real geography of nineteenth-century England both underlies and gives the lie to the map of Wessex with which the later editions of his novels are prefaced. Still, "assumed" once again implies a narrative mode lying somewhere between conjecture and legend. More remarkable still is the footnote to *The Return of the Native* which Hardy added in 1912 halfway through Book Sixth, "Aftercourses." Here, he offers his reader a shadowy choice of endings: "the original conception of the story did not design a marriage between Thomasin and Venn. He was to have retained his isolated and weird character to the last . . . Thomasin remaining a widow" (p. 427). It certainly appears to have been the case that Hardy's original intention in writing the novel was that it should have five books, modeled on the five acts of classical tragedy. Book the Sixth in its entirety might well have been a more or less weary recognition of the likely demand from publishers and perhaps readers for a happy ending like that he had given them in *Far From the Madding Crowd*. However, his habit of continually revising his texts for each new edition afforded him many opportunities simply to rewrite the novel as (he says) he wished it to be, according to the more "austere artistic code" (p. 427) that was to have led to the bleaker ending. That he chose not to do so surely means that the note has now to be read as *part* of the text of these later editions of the novel, rather than as a commentary upon it. In any case, that Hardy should have added it to the existing version of the text as an alternative, rather than rewriting his ending, is of a piece with the narrative techniques of the novel from its earliest version. So it is that the conjectural mode of narration, and the disavowal of certainty, extend even to the irresolution of an ending: perhaps Venn returned to Egdon society as a pale-skinned dairy farmer and married Thomasin, but perhaps he didn't. It is just as with the earlier deaths: perhaps Eustacia committed suicide, or perhaps she tried to flee with her lover, or perhaps Susan Nunsuch's Wessex voodoo condemned her to an early death. Does Wildeve leave Thomasin in the hope of eloping with Eustacia? Does he simply wish to help her to escape? Does he also commit suicide, or perhaps die trying to save Eustacia? No authoritative comment is to be found in the text.

Such radical indeterminacy of narration points up Hardy's attentiveness, in *The Return of the Native*, to different sources and forms of knowledge: to local lore and "central town thinkers" (p. 172), to "intuition" (p. 188) and "high doctrine" (p. 109). Traditional snakebite remedies and witchcraft rituals coexist with Clym's Parisian social theory and the Lady's History from which Eustacia draws her models of heroism. Prometheus and St. Sebastian, Mrs. Siddons and Farmer Lynch, the Vale of Tempe and the Garden of Gethsemane, the dodo and the microscope, jostle together in the novel's allusive range. The texture of the writing is just as ecumenical, as Gillian Beer has noted: "His vocabulary rockets across registers, between language close as touch and removed as Latinate legal documents . . . between very old dialect words and very up-to-date references" (Beer 1996: 44–5). The novel does not adjudicate between these different discourses, or between the chains of causality and modes of explanation that are aligned with them. Nor does it require, or even permit, its reader to do so. Rather, it allows these different versions of the action and its meaning to stand together, unresolved into a single and uniform significance. Egdon Heath has multiple functions in the novel: part backdrop, part protagonist, part metaphor, it delimits the narrative space of the action while projecting it endlessly forward and back in time. "Untameable," "primitive," "inviolate" (pp. 11–12), the heath serves as a palimpsest on which human histories can be written, erased, and rewritten. There is undeniably a mythic quality to *The Return of the Native*, and while it derives in part from the proliferation of references to classical myth, it also emerges from the narrative technique. Those early reviewers who found the novel's title far-fetched and its writing obscure were responding above all to a distinctive narrative quality, a quality never quite repeated in Hardy's later fiction: the combination of vivid particularity of observation – the veins in a baby rabbit's ear, Eustacia's mouth lit by the sunlight like the trumpet of a tulip – and the tentative and conditional mode of its narrative voice. Before the reader's eyes, it seems, even the most vibrant of observations modulates into conjecture and gossip, even the most intense and personal of histories melts into legend and fiction.

NOTE

It should be noted that the edition of *Return of the Native* cited in this chapter, edited by Tony Slade, uses as its copy-text the three-volume edition published by Smith, Elder & Co. in 1878. Hardy made substantial changes to the novel for the 1895 Osgood, McIlvaine edition (including changes to the names of characters and places), and more minor changes for the collected Wessex edition of 1912.

REFERENCES AND FURTHER READING

Beer, Gillian (1996). *Open Fields: Science in Cultural Encounter*. Oxford: Oxford University Press.

Casagrande, Peter J. (1982). *Unity in Hardy's Novels: "Repetitive Symmetries."* London: Macmillan.

Dalziel, Pamela (1996). Anxieties of Representation: The Serial Illustrations to Hardy's *The Return of the Native*. *Nineteenth-Century Literature*, 51, 84–110.

DiBattista, Maria (1991). *First Love: The Affections of Modern Fiction*. Chicago: University of Chicago Press.

Fisher, Joe (1992). *The Hidden Hardy*. Basingstoke: Macmillan.

Garson, Marjorie (1991). *Hardy's Fables of Integrity: Woman, Body, Text*. Oxford: Clarendon Press.

Gribble, Jennifer (1996). The Quiet Women of Egdon Heath. *Essays in Criticism*, 46, 234–57.

Hardy, Thomas ([1878] 1999). *The Return of the Native*, ed. Tony Slade, introd. Penny Boumelha. London: Penguin.

Hughes, John (2004). Visual Inspiration in Hardy's Fiction. In Phillip Mallett (ed.), *Palgrave Advances in Thomas Hardy Studies* (pp. 229–54). Basingstoke: Palgrave Macmillan.

Irwin, Michael (1998). From Fascination to Listlessness: Hardy's Depiction of Love. In Charles P. C. Pettit (ed.), *Reading Thomas Hardy* (pp. 117–37). Basingstoke: Palgrave Macmillan.

Irwin, Michael (1999). *Reading Hardy's Landscapes*. Basingstoke: Palgrave Macmillan.

Law, Jules David (1998). Sleeping Figures: Hardy, History, and the Gendered Body. *ELH*, 65, 223–57.

Malton, Sara (2000). "The woman shall bear her iniquity": Death as Social Discipline in Thomas Hardy's *The Return of the Native*. *Studies in the Novel*, 32, 147–64.

Miller, J. Hillis (1981). Topography in *The Return of the Native*. *Essays in Literature*, 8, 119–34.

Mitchell, Judith (1994). *The Stone and the Scorpion: The Female Subject of Desire in the Novels of Charlotte Brontë, George Eliot, and Thomas Hardy*. Westport, CT: Greenwood Press.

Morgan, Rosemarie (1988). *Women and Sexuality in the Novels of Thomas Hardy*. New York: Routledge.

Nemesvari, Richard (2004). Hardy and his Readers. In Phillip Mallett (ed.), *Palgrave Advances in Thomas Hardy Studies* (pp. 38–74). Basingstoke: Palgrave Macmillan.

Paterson, John (1963). *The Making of The Return of the Native*. Berkeley: University of California Press.

Pinck, Joan B. (1969). The Reception of Thomas Hardy's *The Return of the Native*. *Harvard Library Bulletin*, 17, 291–308.

Pite, Ralph (2002). *Hardy's Geography: Wessex and the Regional Novel*. Basingstoke: Palgrave Macmillan.

Rimmer, Mary (2000). A Feast of Language: Hardy's Allusions. In Phillip Mallett (ed.). *The Achievement of Thomas Hardy* (pp. 58–71). Basingstoke: Palgrave Macmillan.

Sumner, Rosemary (2000). *A Route to Modernism: Hardy, Lawrence, Woolf*. Basingstoke : Palgrave Macmillan.

Wright, T. R. (2003). *Hardy and his Readers*. London: Palgrave Macmillan.

18

Hardy's "Novels of Ingenuity"

Desperate Remedies, The Hand of Ethelberta, and A Laodicean: Rare Hands at Contrivances

Mary Rimmer

The "Ingenuity" Label

As he prepared his works for Macmillan's 1912 Wessex Edition, Hardy divided them into groups, one of which – containing *Desperate Remedies* (1871), *The Hand of Ethelberta* (1876) and *A Laodicean* (1881) – became the "Novels of Ingenuity." On the face of it, little apart from the heading unites these three novels. *Desperate Remedies* and *A Laodicean* contain some of the conventional elements of 1860s sensation fiction, including characters with mysterious pasts, plotting villains, and heroines whose marriages are the focal point of the plots. In *The Hand of Ethelberta*, which announces itself as a comedy in its subtitle, the courtship plot is central and villains and murky pasts are largely absent. Even the connections that do stand out on a cursory survey (no manuscript survives for any of them; a large country house or castle is a crucial setting in each; they all come from Hardy's first decade as a novelist) are apt to seem coincidental.

Hardy gives characteristically indeterminate reasons for deciding to classify his novels. At the beginning of the General Preface to the Wessex Edition he writes that he has "found an opportunity of classifying the novels under heads that show approximately the author's aim, if not his achievement, in each book of the series at the date of its composition" (Orel 1966: 44). The almost casual tone makes the classification seem merely a small detail he had been meaning to see to; that tone is also evident in his April 1912 remark that the classification would give "journalists something to discuss" (*CL* IV: 209). In his first extant reference to the classification, though, he sounds more committed to it, as a defensive move. In 1911 he told Sir Frederick Macmillan:

> My idea for a long time has been to divide the novels into two groups, putting into the second group 4 or 5 of the more superficial & experimental ones, written just for the moment, critics having a way of pitching upon one or other of these lighter ones as typical of the whole. (*CL* IV: 160)

The "ostensibly descriptive but effectively judgemental" categories (Millgate 1992: 119) imply gradations of value, as do the General Preface's unspecific comments that some novels have a "lower" aim, and others, with a "primarily high" aim, were modified by "force of circumstances (among which the chief were the necessities of magazine publication)" (Orel 1966: 44). The "Novels of Character and Environment" category (containing most of Hardy's best-known works) is the first, and evidently intended to be pre-eminent; on the other hand, Hardy's remark that the novels in it "approach most nearly to uninfluenced works" (Orel 1966: 44) provides only muted (and rather opaque) praise.

Whatever its purpose, the 1912 classification had far-reaching effects. By privileging the "Novels of Character and Environment," it led to nearly a century's neglect of the rest, especially the "Novels of Ingenuity." If *Desperate Remedies, The Hand of Ethelberta*, and *A Laodicean* were often criticized in reviews and in studies of Hardy's fiction before 1912, in the wake of the Wessex Edition they began a slide towards near-oblivion. For much of the twentieth century they were left out of studies of Hardy's fiction, or dismissed with brief mentions. Rarely reprinted except as parts of complete editions, they dropped from most readers' sight altogether for many years. Since the mid-1980s they have received somewhat more attention, but readers other than Hardy specialists or enthusiasts are still unlikely to recognize even their titles. In the light of this history, disposing of the 1912 classification can seem almost a prerequisite for taking any of these three novels seriously, and several critics have taken this route. Peter Widdowson calls it "basically factitious" (Widdowson 1989: 49), and to Charles Lock the "Ingenuity" label in particular has little validity: it simply gave Hardy "a convenient term with which to push into the background the three novels which had probably attracted the least notice, and which were most often cited with pejorative intent" (Lock 1992: 51).

Despite its unfortunate results, though, the "Novels of Ingenuity" label can provide a useful lens for examining the three novels Hardy grouped under that heading, as long as its implicit value judgments are set aside. To begin with, we may note that in 1911 Hardy proposed a two-part division which put "lighter" novels in the subsidiary group. In the end, however, he divided the novels into three categories. (He actually lists four, but the fourth ["Mixed Novels"] contains only a single volume of short stories.) At least some of the novels in the second, "Romances and Fantasies" (see CHAPTER 19, HARDY'S "ROMANCES AND FANTASIES") were presumably once placed in "the second group" with those later called Novels of Ingenuity. Evidently, then, Hardy began to think not only of which critically vulnerable novels he wished to separate from his "best" work, but also of the specific characteristics of the novels he was grouping: "ingenuity" may connote more than "lightness," and the experience of re-reading the novels as he prepared them for the new edition may have made him newly aware of distinctions and commonalities that were less clear to him when he first proposed the classification.

Ingenuity, Realism, and Hardy's Prefaces

The *OED* (1989) notes several older, positive senses of "ingenuity," such as "High or distinguished intellectual capacity; genius, talent, quickness of wit." As these fell out of currency towards the middle of the nineteenth century, the word began to pick up more pejorative overtones, connected to the sense of "ingenious" as "aptitude for curious device rather than solid inventiveness or skill": examples cited by the *OED* include one from 1822, William Hazlitt's "Ingenuity is genius in trifles," and one from 1875, Benjamin Jowett's "Coincidences too subtle to have been invented by the ingenuity of any imitator." "Ingenuity" also has class resonances, for in senses such as "skill or cleverness in contriving or making something" it is often applied to artisans' hand-work. Hardy likely had the pejorative overtones of "ingenuity" in mind as he made his classification; in 1888, in "The Profitable Reading of Fiction," he had used "ingenious" mockingly in a reference to a "young and ingenious, though not very profound, critic" who thought novels about the upper classes necessarily made for the best reading (*THPV* 86). In the General Preface too the concept is associated with work that lacks profundity. Echoing his letter to Macmillan, Hardy claims that the Novels of Ingenuity "were written for the nonce simply"; they "show a not infrequent disregard of the probable in the chain of events, and depend for their interest mainly on the incidents themselves" (Orel 1966: 45). On the other hand, Hardy also calls them "Experiments," a term with more positive, scientific overtones, and he is willing to make claims for their realism, since "despite the artificiality of their fable some of their scenes are not without fidelity to life" (Orel 1966: 45).

A strange combination of aesthetic principles emerges here in connection with the ingenuity label. If these books really were "written for the nonce," why would such ephemera be part of a collected edition? If realism is important ("fidelity to life" as opposed to "artificiality" and "disregard of the probable"), what about a willingness to experiment? Even though Hardy's 1911 letter to Macmillan associates the experimental with the superficial, the word retains some of its scientific glamour in the General Preface. The idea that the novels are weak because generally they lack "fidelity to life" raises questions, for it has always been hard to know exactly how important realism was to Hardy. In his 1890 essay "Candour in English Fiction," for instance, one heavily inflected by his problems in getting *Tess of the d'Urbervilles* published, he asserts that "in representations of the world, the passions ought to be proportioned as in the world itself" (*THPV* 97). Yet he was always aware that art necessarily mediates, and a year later, in the less polemical essay "The Science of Fiction," he defines "realism" as "an artificiality distilled from the fruits of closest observation" (*THPV* 108). Once realism itself is recognized as an "artificiality," then ingenuity becomes a legitimate tool even of the realist.

Hardy's prefaces to the individual Novels of Ingenuity are as mixed as the General Preface in their assumptions about realism and their attitudes towards the books. In the 1889 preface to *Desperate Remedies*, after saying that he was "feeling his way to a method" in it, he notes that some of its scenes and characters "have been deemed not unworthy of a little longer preservation" (*DR* 448). Though hardly a strong endorsement, these remarks do suggest *Desperate Remedies'* experimental bent as well as the inexperience of its author, and the passive voice implies that others too have deemed parts of the novel worth preserving. In 1895 Hardy calls *The Hand of Ethelberta* "somewhat frivolous," but then asserts its realist claims by noting that the characters were "meant to be consistent and human" (*HE* 3). He also implies that the novel was ahead of its time, for if making servants central characters was a "delicate task" in 1876, by 1895 it had become a "more welcome" move (*HE* 3); in 1912 he could say that the novel's upstairs/downstairs situations, "eccentric and almost impossible" to many of its first readers, were being "paralleled on the stage and in novels, and accepted as reasonable and interesting pictures of life" (*HE* 4). The plot devices may seem "curious," but Hardy does not seem to deny them "solid inventiveness," and implicitly shifts the blame for their reception onto readers who failed to appreciate them.

More overt criticisms of novel-readers' limitations appear in the prefaces to *A Laodicean*. The 1896 preface refers to the illness Hardy suffered while writing the novel, and the strain of having to push on to the "predetermined cheerful ending" (*AL* 380); it also suggests that the book may "help to while away an idle afternoon of the comfortable ones whose lines have fallen to them in pleasant places" (*AL* 380). Hardy directs the put-downs at unthinking consumers at least as much as at *A Laodicean*, and the same holds for his definition of the book's ideal audience as the sheltered young, "to whom marriage is the pilgrim's Eternal City, and not a milestone on the way" (*AL* 380). In the 1912 preface he takes a different approach, locating characterization as a redeeming feature of *A Laodicean* and oddly offering the "really lovable" Paula Power, who is "individualized with some clearness," as a "compensation" for the unsatisfactory topography, which cannot be mapped onto the real contours of Dorset because so many of the novel's settings are "but the baseless fabrics of a vision" (*AL* 380–1). The blend of realist and anti-realist assumptions stands out here: the topography is apparently without any physical referent, but the fictional heroine is "real," even to the extent that she has flirted with the author, and "tantalized" him "by eluding his grasp for some time" (*AL* 381).

Both the General Preface and the prefaces to these three novels demonstrate Hardy's awareness that what is accepted as realistic or "reasonable" in fiction depends on the audience's expectations. Do they read for topographic detail, and the satisfaction of recognizing real "originals" in representations of landscape? Do they seek escapist reading for "hygienic purposes," as Hardy slyly puts it in "The Profitable Reading of Fiction" (*THPV* 76)? Do they want "lovable" characters or "human" ones – or do they simply want conventional entertainment and happy endings to help them pass the time pleasantly? Are heroines fictional constructs or quasi-human entities authors and readers can fall in love with? If he sees "verisimilitude in general treatment and detail" (Orel 1966: 44) as a defining characteristic of a "Novel of Character and Environment," Hardy also recognizes that verisimilitude is a contingent impression, so that an "almost impossible" representation can become "reasonable and interesting" to a later readership with different assumptions. Tim Dolin has pointed out, with reference to *The Hand of Ethelberta*, that the realist claim is misleading, since those who "judged it by the standard of realism . . . unsurprisingly found it wanting," and wrote it off as one of Hardy's worst (*HE* xxi): the same argument could apply to the realist claims made for the other Novels of Ingenuity. Yet the slippery and contradictory public pronouncements Hardy made about their realism have an ingenuity of their own, designed more to tease than to elucidate, or perhaps designed to distract readers from what Joe Fisher calls the "subversive complexities" of the Novels of Ingenuity (Fisher 1992: 3).

Ingenuity and the Ingenious

As he re-read his novels for the Wessex Edition, the recurrence of the actual words "ingenious" and "ingenuity," especially in *The Hand of Ethelberta* and *A Laodicean*, may have given Hardy the idea for the term "Novels of Ingenuity." Although the term occurs only twice in *Desperate Remedies*, both these appearances have particular significance. The first is a reference to "Mr James Sparkman, an ingenious joiner and decorator" (*DR* 70), who has made Miss Aldclyffe's dressing-table to her exacting specifications; his name echoes that of Hardy's uncle, James Sparks, a cabinet-maker who lived near the "original" of Miss Aldclyffe's manor-house and near Hardy's own birthplace. For Hardy to plant such a personal trace suggests a link in his mind between the ingenious artisan, who has accomplished his task "after months of painful toil" (*DR* 70), and the ingenious writer, who labors to transform memory into art while disguising its personal origins. Here, at least covertly, Hardy seems willing to claim kin, as it were, with the ingenuity of hand-work (see CHAPTER 11, HARDY AND CLASS). Significantly, Sparkman's task is an exercise in concealment, for his ingenuity has converted old cabinets into a piece that, like all the furniture in Miss Aldclyffe's dressing room, disguises its function, resembling "something between a high altar and a cabinet piano" (*DR* 70) rather than a dressing-table.

The second occurrence of "ingenious" in *Desperate Remedies* focuses more directly on writers, authors of "ingenious and cruel satires" which have been "stuck like knives into womankind" (*DR* 316). The comment follows the description of the Harpies quoted from Book III of Virgil's *Aeneid*, a stock misogynist passage, and introduces the narrator's claim that no satire can be "so lacerating to [women], and to us who love them, as the trite old fact, that the most wretched of men can, in the twinkling of an eye, find a wife ready to be more wretched still for the sake of his company" (*DR* 316). As Kristin Brady points out, this statement registers the narrator's "complacent sense that he and his reader stand outside the biological group he speaks of with such clinical authority" (Brady 1993: 92). Yet the passage also convicts author and narrator, those who control the novel's words, of complicity with the lacerating satires and the knives. After all, who has gratuitously introduced the Harpies to describe Mrs. Higgins's Dutch clock, and then focused a voyeur's gaze on Mrs. Higgins, a woman who has made herself "more wretched" by marriage, and whose dress is so disarranged as to be "almost useless as a screen to the bosom" (*DR* 316)? Surely the narrator, despite claiming to be himself lacerated by ingenious misogynist satires, is actually indulging in them? The sense of self-indulgence is stronger because almost all this episode is extraneous to the detective work Edward Springrove is engaged upon when he encounters Mrs. Higgins: neither she nor the episode is referred to again. The abrupt shift back to the story with "Edward hastened to dispatch his errand" (*DR* 316) underlines the narrative delay the digression has caused.

Ingenuity in *Desperate Remedies* is an uncomfortable concept, then, associated with personal and class affiliations that Hardy both acknowledges and shuns (he cut Sparkman's name after the first edition), with good workmanship used to make one thing look like another, and with writers' covert invocations of what they supposedly deplore. In *The Hand of Ethelberta* words related to "ingenuity" tend to have more positive connotations, especially as applied to Ethelberta Petherwin herself. Some of the men occasionally attempt ingenuity, but without marked success: Christopher Julian's note, demanding a meeting and falsely claiming that there will not be time for Ethelberta to send a reply, is "an ingenious suggestion to her not to be so cruel as to forbid him" (*HE* 155). The strategy collapses, though, and the meeting does not happen. Making desultory conversation after Ethelberta's marriage, the painter Ladywell tells Christopher that he sees the shore near her Knollsea house as demonstrating gendered forms of grandeur. Christopher calls this lame idea "very ingenious . . . and perfectly true" (*HE* 369), but his prior contempt for Ladywell as man and artist, and the clear implication that Ladywell has been using his pseudo-artistic concept as an excuse to sketch in Ethelberta's neighborhood, give an ironic edge to the compliment. Neither man can compete with "the ingenious Ethelberta" (*HE* 287), who controls virtually every social situation she encounters, and tells her sister Picotee that "Women who use public proverbs as a guide through events are those who have not ingenuity enough to make private ones as each event occurs" (*HE* 145). Ethelberta even manages to support Lord Mountclere on a steep incline, though his infirm "slips and totterings" tax "her strength heavily, and her ingenuity more, to appear as the supported and not the supporter" (*HE* 244).

In *A Laodicean* ingenuity has more clearly pejorative overtones, because it is normally associated with the tricks William Dare and his "illegitimate father" (*AL* 324) Captain De Stancy use and/or acquiesce in. De Stancy is occasionally capable of ingenuity on his own account, as in his "ingenious relinquishment of his part" (*AL* 218) in *Love's Labour's Lost* when he discovers that Paula is no longer playing the Princess, but it is generally his unscrupulous son, "the ingenious Dare" (*AL* 172), who works the plots to dispose of George Somerset as Paula's suitor and replace him with De Stancy. In the armed stand-off which results in Abner Power's defeat and departure, Dare and Power call each other "ingenious" (*AL* 324, 325); in this context, the word conveys a mixture of admiration and condescension in both the young schemer and the former terrorist. Commenting on his skill at altering photographs, the photographer in Markton calls Dare "very ingenious" (*AL* 337), and the architect Havill, despite his moral scruples, remarks on the "ingenuity" (*AL* 116) of Dare's plot to get rid of Somerset by cheating in the architectural competition for the castle restoration. Dare's ingenuity does falter, though, when he works on human material. Havill gives way to guilt and relinquishes his ill-gotten part of the castle commission; likewise, Dare manipulates De Stancy into giving up his teetotalism and his celibacy, only to find that his transformed father has become much less tractable. Dare's "ingenuity in vamping up a Frankenstein for his ambitious experiments [seems] likely to be rewarded by his discomfiture at the hands of his own creature" (*AL* 170).

Ingenuity in *A Laodicean* has few lasting successes. The only plot Dare completes is the destruction of Stancy Castle, one that enacts revenge rather than making a profit; ironically, Paula has privately planned to give the De Stancys the paintings Dare uses as fire-starters. His other plots, like Abner Power's ingenious explosive devices, also end up turning back on himself. De Stancy, to save Dare from arrest, informs Paula that Dare is his illegitimate son, and so puts an end to his own imminent marriage – the same marriage that Dare has tried so hard to bring about. The only sort of ingenuity that seems to have staying power in the novel is the kind that expresses itself in stone, whether it be John Power's railway tunnel or the castle itself, whose Norman walls, with their "vaulting of exceptional and massive ingenuity" (*AL* 24) survive the fire. Somerset's "original" and "fascinating" (*AL* 122) design for "a palace, with a ruinous castle annexed as a curiosity" (*AL* 123) also survives in his revised plan to "build a new house from the ground, eclectic in style" (*AL* 378) next to the ivied ruin, with the small difference that the castle is more ruinous than it was, and that the house will presumably not be attached to the ruin. Though it is not actually called "ingenious," his design clearly responds to and matches the ingenuity of the original architects and builders. Perhaps more importantly, his ingenuity works visibly to juxtapose two things rather than to conceal one or the other.

Despite their diversity, these uses of "ingenuity" and "ingenious" do form a partial pattern. From Sparkman's dressing-table to Dare's cheats to Ethelberta's attempt to support Lord Mountclere while appearing to let him support her, they generally involve covert activity, or the desire to disguise one thing as another. They also require considerable skill, whether artisanal, technical, athletic, criminal, or social. Finally, there are clear parallels between the artful manipulations of material objects and situations, and the ingenuity of another sort of plot-maker and workman, namely the novelist. As Jane Thomas has argued, *The Hand of Ethelberta* and *A Laodicean* (I would add *Desperate Remedies* as well) set out "not merely to reflect reality, but to show how reality and truth are discursively produced" (Thomas 1999: 96). Ingenious devices of various kinds comment on that discursive production, and we need not follow Fisher in seeing the Novels of Ingenuity as "dares" (Fisher 1992: 19) to understand that they center on conflicts between concealment and revelation, artifice and truth-telling, that have obvious resonance for the novelist.

Plotting: Fictional and Mechanical Devices

In any novel the presence of plotting characters is a reminder that plots, whether of con-artists or of novelists, are "artificialities." In each of the Novels of Ingenuity, the plotters' contrivances point to the master plotter who has contrived the whole, and occasionally even draws our attention to the workings of his own plot. Cytherea Graye, for instance, actually discusses the improbable coincidences that have brought her together with her dead father's old love: she accounts for them by invoking Providence, and concluding that there must be "invisible means at work" (*DR* 155), but readers with the novel in their hands are more likely to see those means as the author's. (For a more detailed examination of the way plots are discussed in *Desperate Remedies*, see my introduction to that novel, *DR* xxii–xxiii.)

The plotters' strategies tend to get less attention while they are closing in on their victims: as long as Miss Aldclyffe and her illegitimate son Aeneas Manston are tricking and pressuring Cytherea into marrying Manston, the narrative interest lies largely with Cytherea and the question of whether she will escape or not. Later on, when Owen Graye and Edward launch a counter-plot or "game" (*DR* 305), the novel increasingly centers on the defensive moves made by Manston and his allies, right down to their manipulation of physical objects. Hardy devotes considerable space to such episodes as Manston's interception and alteration of a letter from Edward to Owen, his attempt to drug his accomplice Anne Seaway – and Anne's inspired counter-move of pouring the drugged wine down the (presumably both capacious and corseted) bosom of her dress. In the often-cited watching scene, where three people spy on Manston and on each other as he uncovers and then buries the body of his first wife, fascination with the material object comes through all the more clearly because in the darkness everything has to be perceived by touch or hearing, as when Anne's fingers encounter "A warm foot, covered with a polished boot," that belongs to one of the other watchers (*DR* 371). The last volume of the novel focuses on the recalcitrant physicality of things, and the constant calls on the plotters' ingenuity as they try to mold those things to fit their plots.

While Cytherea remains largely passive in the midst of the plots, saying at one point that it is beneath her "dignity as a woman" (*DR* 308) to join the "game," Ethelberta has no such scruples, and in *The Hand of Ethelberta* the narrative interest goes with her both as heroine and as a "rare hand at contrivances" (*HE* 217). As a butler's daughter who fools fashionable London society into accepting her as a born lady, makes a precarious living by public storytelling, and employs her own family as servants and workmen, she necessarily plots much of her own life, including the novel's "happy" ending in which she deliberately suppresses her love for Christopher to marry the rich, aging, and corrupt Lord Mountclere. She accordingly has "quite enough machinery in her hands to keep decently going" (*HE* 211). "Machinery" suggests that both author and heroine can see their ingenious plots ironically, as mechanical contrivances; in "The Profitable Reading of Fiction" Hardy uses the word to describe the awkward plotting that reveals its "wheels and wires and carpentry" in novels which are "the product of cleverness rather than of intuition" (*THPV* 78).

It has become a critical commonplace to note the many correspondences between Hardy and Ethelberta, as writers of poetry and fictions, and as figures who rise from lower-class backgrounds to be accepted in fashionable drawing-rooms. By introducing a storytelling character with hidden servant-class origins and perhaps, like Ethelberta's father, by taking pride in the "superb audacity" (*HE* 221) with which she plays her role as a lady, even in the very house where her father works, Hardy created a covert sense of correspondence between himself and his heroine. That correspondence may suggest why Ethelberta is a more self-aware plotter than Manston, say. She operates the overlapping structure of fictions *as* a structure, a game played not to unmask a villain or win a lover but to try the skill of her "hand." Discussing her London life and storytelling project with Christopher, she refers to the "battle" of life as a game of chess:

> there is no seriousness in it; it may be put an end to at any inconvenient moment by owning yourself beaten with a careless "Ha-ha!" and sweeping your pieces into the box. Experimentally, I care to succeed in society; but at the bottom of my heart, I don't care. (*HE* 128)

Toru Sasaki suggests that Ethelberta's detachment is incomplete, since she never does own herself beaten (1998: xxii), but her ability to will herself into detachment is crucial to her success. When she discovers Mountclere's live-in mistress on the afternoon of her wedding day, and attempts escape only to be foiled by Mountclere's counter-plot, she gives way to laughter which has a "wild unnatural sound" (*HE* 394) only briefly, and recovers her poise by congratulating Mountclere as if they had indeed been playing chess: "It was stratagem against stratagem. Mine was ingenious; yours was masterly. Accept my acknowledgement. We will enter upon an armed neutrality" (*HE* 395). In the end, we discover, Ethelberta will actually rule Enckworth Court and Mountclere himself. She wins in part because she is "put upon her mettle" (*HE* 403), as her father comments, but this last direct view of her as she deflects defeat by denying its seriousness suggests that detachment – perhaps another trait she shares with her creator (Sasaki 1998: xxiii) – is at least as important a factor in her victory.

In her attempt to escape from Mountclere Ethelberta uses the stereotypical plotter's tools, secret notes and hidden accomplices; earlier in the novel, however, her plotting is more complex. She manipulates a complex set of class markers, and subverts the servant system by clandestinely employing her own family as her domestics and workmen. Dressing like a lady, and living in a fashionable house with a "family" of servants as any lady would, she appears to *be* a lady – except of course that in her case the servants really are members of her family. Even her lovers become, in a sense, part of her script as she shifts addresses, clothing, and companions to accommodate her changing personae: honest with Mountclere about her family, she deceives him about her love for Christopher and uses Christopher's and Picotee's simultaneous faints as a tableau to convince him that the love story involves those two instead.

Ethelberta's social success mirrors that of her storytelling, which persuades audiences to believe that the exotic events she narrates are based on her own experience. She tells Christopher that as a child she could always engage other children "by recounting adventures which had never happened; and men and women are but children enlarged a little" (*HE* 106). At the first performance, Faith Julian observes this process, noticing in particular the old lady who listens "with her face up and lips parted like a little child of six" (*HE* 122). Ethelberta's ingenious manipulation of the audience's perceptions creates a real risk for her if she is found out. As her mother points out, people rarely like recognizing that they have been childishly credulous, especially if they have been duped by someone of a lower class; she tells Ethelberta, "People will find you out as one of a family of servants, and their pride will be stung at having gone to hear your romancing" (*HE* 167). Unlike Manston and Dare, Ethelberta will not be threatened by the hangman or even the constable, despite sleeping as if she has "committed a murder" (*HE* 285). She does however risk social and artistic extinction, because so much of her ingenuity has been spent on creating illusions about herself: a revelation of the "wheels and wires and carpentry" in her case might stop the "machinery" permanently.

In *A Laodicean* as in *Desperate Remedies*, the antagonists do most of the plotting: Dare's complicated schemes on behalf of De Stancy drive much of the narrative, and Abner Power, with his scarred face and hidden revolutionary past, deepens the sense of danger that Dare brings into the novel. Dare stage-manages many crucial scenes, such as the one where De Stancy spies on Paula's gymnastic exercise in her revealing "pink flannel costume" (*AL* 152) and is seized with desire for her. His ingenious tricks often involve technology: he sends a telegram under a false name, doctors photographs, and uses photography as an excuse to hang around Stancy Castle. Dare is not alone in his technical skill, although he is in his fraudulent use of it: John Schad has pointed out the degree to which the telegraph is associated with women in the novel (*AL* xxv), and Jay Clayton sees the feminine (and lesbian) realm of the telegraph, which communicates by sound, as comparing favorably with the fraud, voyeurism, and aggression linked to men and the visual realm in *A Laodicean* (1997: 220–2). Significantly, it is Charlotte de Stancy, one of the few characters competent to "gather the message" (*AL* 35) from the telegraph, who begins to unravel the mystery of Dare's false message, and reveals it to Paula in time to stop her marriage to De Stancy.

Curiously contrasted with Dare's manipulation and falsification of documents is his use of his own body to record the truth, as insurance against that "treacherous book of reference" the memory (*AL* 124). Tattooed on his chest is the name "DE STANCY," placed there so that his body, in the case of "delirium, disease or death," can speak the truth of his descent, the same truth that he and his father are so careful to conceal. The truth this living document holds is not only the occasion for a whole series of false and forged documents; it is also one Dare will even kill to keep hidden (*AL* 126). Like Ethelberta's letter to Christopher, which claims to be "frank" but actually replaces a destroyed one in which she reveals her true origins (*HE* 83–4), Dare's tattoo inscribes the truth only to keep it securely hidden.

The Plotting of Love and Marriage

The courtship and marriage plot was an element of almost every eighteenth- and nineteenth-century novel, including the Gothic and sensation fiction that these books borrow from, and marriage is central to much of the plotting in the Novels of Ingenuity. Gothic and sensation novels typically interrupt the protagonists' love story by separating the lovers and deploying a range of sexual threats against the often captive heroine: versions of that pattern turn up in all three books. In *Desperate Remedies*, Manston and Miss Aldclyffe act the villains' parts, working to detach Cytherea from Edward and make her accept Manston instead; in *A Laodicean* Dare, De Stancy, and Abner Power try to detach Paula from Somerset and make her marry De Stancy. In both cases the plotters are linked by a hidden relationship, a version of the family "secret" Gothic and sensation fiction often turns on. Manston and Dare conceal their connection to their biological parents at the same time as they seek to exercise their filial rights, if necessary by blackmailing their respective parents. Marriage is key to their schemes because the women become the conduits for the wealth the illegitimate offspring cannot inherit directly. Miss Aldclyffe leaves her land and money to *"the wife of Aeneas Manston"* (*DR* 405), a way of benefiting her son without naming him as such, and Dare hopes that De Stancy's marriage to Paula will indirectly enrich him. Both marriages apparently offer what Abner Power calls "a splendid whole" (*AL* 309): Manston would get the woman he desires; Miss Aldclyffe, the pleasure of seeing the daughter of her old flame well married; Cytherea, a chance to regain the middle-class standing she has lost; Paula, a title and integration into an ancient family; and De Stancy, his ancestral seat and the wealth to go with it. Yet these conventionally appropriate plot resolutions mask not only the brides' wayward desires for other men, but also the sexual secrets of the previous generation. Once again apparent revelations – public acts of respectable marriage – are actually based on concealments. Without Dare's and Manston's plotting, and without the protection De Stancy and Miss Aldclyffe give their respective offspring, neither marriage would happen, or come to the brink of happening.

The Hand of Ethelberta goes further still by parodying the courtship plot. Critics such as Penny Boumelha and Edward Neill have identified echoes of Jane Austen's *Pride and Prejudice* in particular (Boumelha 1993: 245–8; Neill 2003: 32–7), but the sensation novel's version of the courtship plot is also being parodied, for Ethelberta forces herself into a marriage of convenience, much as others force Cytherea. She is her own villain, plotting her relinquishment of Christopher, whom she loves, and her marriage to Mountclere, who in most courtship plots would be decidedly the "wrong" choice. Moreover, she has a secret, though it is not illegitimacy; rather, it is the still more "shameful" one of her legitimate descent from a happily married butler. The real secret in *The Hand of Ethelberta* is that servants are human beings: late in the novel, when Chickerel audibly reacts to the news that his daughter is about to marry Lord Mountclere, his shocked employer asks "Did you speak?" (*HE* 335), as though she were addressing a domestic animal which had suddenly acquired human language.

Ethelberta's arranged marriage, rather than being undone before it happens or almost immediately thereafter, as in *A Laodicean* or *Desperate Remedies*, both takes place and endures, despite a suspenseful effort to prevent it, and extensive plot business surrounding her attempted escape after it. Yet though the novel elides the process by jumping from the wedding-night to the "Sequel" over two years later, the final outcome seems to be a degree of success that few eighteenth- or nineteenth-century novels would allow to such a loveless marriage. Ethelberta makes Mountclere persevere in getting rid of his mistress; she controls his drinking, his social engagements, and his entire estate, and she forces his family and the neighboring gentry to acknowledge her as Lady Mountclere. If we cannot gauge her degree of content with these victories, we cannot assume her unhappiness either, since our last access to her own perspective comes when we realize that Mountclere has thwarted her escape plan. Our final impression, in the "Sequel," is not of her feelings but of her ability to control others, as her husband, her family, and Christopher all acquiesce in the plans she has made for them, with varying degrees of awareness and reluctance.

The fictional assumptions about true love and marriage that Gothic, sensation, and courtship novels tend to invoke in their conclusions, though often after destabilizing them in the rest of the book, are further undermined in the Novels of Ingenuity by a recurrent emphasis on the artifice of love-talk. Manston's courtship of Cytherea, with its mixture of "bewitching flattery" (*DR* 221), reflections on "the evanescence of female beauty" (*DR* 221), and emotional manipulation, is a carefully planned construct from start to finish, despite his real desire for Cytherea. Similarly, although Edward's letter to Cytherea is not exactly false, the narrator remarks that a man like Edward, "unconsciously clever in his letters . . . may write himself up to a hero in the mind of a young woman who loves him without knowing much about him" (*DR* 61). Ethelberta shapes love-language to her own ends more deliberately than Edward or even Manston, and adds body-language to the mix: without actually lying to her suitors, she makes "little words in a low tone . . . express a great deal," by accompanying them with "a peculiar gaze into imaginary far-away distance" (*HE* 43).

A Laodicean contains especially incisive analysis of love-talk, principally by Paula. Understatement is Paula's personal preference, as in the letter to Somerset where she argues against the excessive value assigned to "the verbal *I love you*" (*AL* 239), and goes on to suggest that divining his beloved's feelings before she does ought to charm him more than "a reiterated confession of passion." Paula advocates a disquieting voyeurism here, envisioning a male lover who can peer into his lover's heart, "rejoice in secret over what she will not recognise" and derive "pleasure indeed" from his sense of possessing her heart without her knowledge and against her will. Yet her next sentence, where she refers to women's "great difficulties" and consequent need to make their lovers "hope, fear, pray and beseech," shows her awareness of the power imbalance in the fantasy she has just imagined (*AL* 239). Her vision of the gloating voyeur-lover may actually ironize and resist the Victorian notion that female desire can only be an "innocent" response to male desire: not yet trusting Somerset to be more than a typical member of his "dreadfully encroaching sex" (*AL* 174), she indirectly suggests that he wishes to leave her no space of her own.

Reluctant to believe utterances that may be exaggerated or posed, Paula continually checks her suitors' "expostulations" (*AL* 225) and "exclamations and transports" (*AL* 301). Speaking to Somerset at one point, she prefaces a half-promise to "make good come" of their relationship with a doubtful glance at his often-avowed love for her: "If you really do feel for me only half what you say . . ." (*AL* 224). She also shows impatience with her lovers' melancholy, telling Somerset, "don't be so morbid in your reproaches!" (*AL* 225), and later chiding his "forebodings" and "faint-hearted" (*AL* 237) fears. When De Stancy responds to her refusals with sighs and gloom she dismisses them, telling him that his "discontent is constitutional, and would go on just the same" whether she accepts him or not; her refusal of him, she asserts, "is purely an imaginary grievance." Indeed, his response, "Not if I think otherwise" (*AL* 316), suggests that she may be right, that his lovesickness is at least partly something he has thought himself into.

Except for the one reference to De Stancy's "ingenious relinquishment of his part" (*AL* 218) in the play, ingenuity is not usually attributed directly to the lovers in *A Laodicean*, but the lovers' "exclamations and transports," as rhetorical structures set up to persuade the beloved, do echo Dare's plots: certainly they have the common aim of pressing Paula to abandon her reserve and commit herself. In this novel more clearly than in the other two, ingenuity – in plotting, technological trickery, love-language, and representation of all kinds – becomes a threat, and to the extent that the author himself is identified with "ingenious" artisans and plotters, the fictional project itself appears dubious. If Dare can alter Somerset's picture to give him "the distorted features and wild attitude of a man advanced in intoxication" (*AL* 281), and if a lover can deceive even himself by his rhetoric, the courtship plot and the realist novel seem perilously close to clever fraud or self-delusion (see CHAPTER 13, HARDY AND ROMANTIC LOVE).

Conclusion

Ingenuity as it figures in these three novels refers to painstaking workmanship, the falsification and deliberate misreading of documents and of speech, lovers' stratagems, plots both fictive and villainous, and attempts at once to hide and to claim everything from a dead body to a relationship with a parent. In different ways, each novel demonstrates the pitfalls of a range of discourses and the malleability of discourse in the hands of anyone with the ingenuity to manipulate it. Hardy was clearly interested in the ingenious contrivances of his characters, and the dense plotting of all three novels suggests that he had a considerable investment in such contrivances himself. At the same time he was wary of identifying too closely with ingenuity, perhaps because to do so came too close to exposing the "machinery" of his own fiction-making. Just as James Sparkman's creation, despite the toil and skill he has spent on it, is after all neither a high altar nor even a cabinet piano but only a dressing-table, so fiction-making may be merely a matter of "wheels and wires and carpentry": telling the truth about it may alienate the audience, who will be embarrassed at having gone along with the "romancing" like children.

Bracketing off these books as "Novels of Ingenuity," written only "for the nonce" yet perhaps still worth reading, is one more instance of a revelation which at the same time conceals: the novels are there, included in the Wessex Edition, but placed in a category that pushes them largely out of sight so that even when they are read they will be taken less seriously than the others. Accordingly, their uneasy comments on the production of fictions are both available and submerged, as is their suggestion that language generally misrepresents and conceals even (or especially) when it seems to be revealing something.

References and Further Reading

Ball, David (1986). Hardy's Experimental Fiction. *English: The Journal of the English Association*, 35, 27–36.

Boumelha, Penny (1993). "A complicated position for a woman": *The Hand of Ethelberta*. In Margaret Higonnet (ed.), *The Sense of Sex: Feminist Perspectives on Hardy* (pp. 242–59). Urbana: University of Illinois Press.

Brady, Kristin (1993). Textual Hysteria: Hardy's Narrator on Women. In Margaret Higonnet (ed.), *The Sense of Sex: Feminist Perspectives on Hardy* (pp. 87–106). Urbana: University of Illinois Press.

Bullen, J. B. (1986). *The Expressive Eye: Fiction and Perception in the Work of Thomas Hardy*. Oxford: Clarendon Press.

Clayton, Jay (1997). The Voice in the Machine: Hazlitt, Hardy, James. In Jeffrey Masten et al. (eds.), *Language Machines: Technologies of Literary and Cultural Production* (pp. 209–32). New York: English Institute.

Dutta, Shanta (2000). *Ambivalence in Hardy: A Study of his Attitude to Women*. Basingstoke: Macmillan.

Ebbatson, Roger (1993). *Hardy: The Margin of the Unexpressed*. Sheffield: Sheffield Academic Press.

Ebbatson, Roger (2004). *A Laodicean*: Hardy and the Philosophy of Money. In Tim Dolin and Peter Widdowson (eds.), *Thomas Hardy and Contemporary Literary Studies* (pp. 80–98). Basingstoke: Palgrave Macmillan.

Fisher, Joe (1992). *The Hidden Hardy*. Basingstoke: Macmillan.

Gatrell, Simon (2003). *Thomas Hardy's Vision of Wessex*. Basingstoke: Palgrave Macmillan.

Goode, John (1988). *Thomas Hardy: The Offensive Truth*. Oxford: Blackwell.

Hardy, Thomas ([1871] 1998). *Desperate Remedies: A Novel*, ed. Mary Rimmer. London: Penguin.

Hardy, Thomas ([1876] 1996). *The Hand of Ethelberta: A Comedy in Chapters*, ed. Tim Dolin. London: Penguin.

Hardy, Thomas ([1881] 1997). *A Laodicean; Or, The Castle of the De Stancys: A Story of To-day*, ed. John Schad. London: Penguin.

Hiscoe, Carol Ball (1990). The Economic Construction of Taste in Thomas Hardy's "Novels of Ingenuity." Diss. Duke University.

Ingham, Patricia (1989). *Thomas Hardy: Feminist Readings*. Hemel Hempstead: Harvester Wheatsheaf.

Lock, Charles (1992). *Thomas Hardy*. Criticism in Focus. London: Bristol Classical.

Millgate, Michael (1992). *Testamentary Acts: Browning, Tennyson, James, Hardy*. Oxford: Clarendon Press.

Millgate, Michael (1994). *Thomas Hardy: His Career as a Novelist*, rev. edn. Basingstoke: Macmillan.

Millgate, Michael (ed.) (2001). *Thomas Hardy's Public Voice: The Essays, Speeches and Miscellaneous Prose*. Oxford: Clarendon Press.

Millgate, Michael (2004). *Thomas Hardy: A Biography Revisited*. Oxford: Oxford University Press.

Mistichelli, William J. (1992). The Comedy of Survival in Thomas Hardy's *The Hand of Ethelberta*. *Modern Language Studies*, 22(4), 88–104.

Neill, Edward (2003). *The Secret Life of Thomas Hardy: Retaliatory Fiction*. Aldershot: Ashgate.

OED (1989). *Oxford English Dictionary*, 2nd edn. *OED Online*. Oxford: Oxford University Press. Accessed Dec. 26, 2007: "Ingenious *a.*" <http://dictionary.oed.com.proxy.hil.unb.ca/cgi/entry/50116705>; "Ingenuity *n.*" <http://dictionary.oed.com.proxy.hil.unb.ca/cgi/entry/50116722>.

Orel, Harold (ed.) (1966). *Thomas Hardy's Personal Writings*. Lawrence: University of Kansas Press.

Pite, Ralph (2002). *Hardy's Geography: Wessex and the Regional Novel*. Basingstoke: Palgrave Macmillan.

Purdy, Richard Little, and Michael Millgate (eds.) (1978–88). *The Collected Letters of Thomas Hardy*, 7 vols. Oxford: Clarendon Press.

Sasaki, Toru (1998). Introduction to Thomas Hardy, *The Hand of Ethelberta* (pp. xxi–xxix). London: Everyman.

Taylor, Richard H. (1982). *The Neglected Hardy: Thomas Hardy's Lesser Novels*. London and Basingstoke: Macmillan.

Thomas, Jane (1999). *Thomas Hardy, Femininity and Dissent: Reassessing the "Minor" Novels*. Basingstoke: Macmillan.

Turner, Paul (1998). *The Life of Thomas Hardy: A Critical Biography*. Oxford: Blackwell.

Widdowson, Peter (1989). *Hardy in History: A Study in Literary Sociology*. London and New York: Routledge.

19

Hardy's "Romances and Fantasies"

A Pair of Blue Eyes, The Trumpet-Major, Two on a Tower, and *The Well-Beloved*: Experiments in Metafiction

Jane Thomas

Hardy's retrospective classification of his novels in the General Preface to the 1912 Wessex Edition is unhelpful to the general reader in many respects. Interpreted as the author's opinion on their aesthetic merit, it initiated the vexed division of his novels into "major" and "minor" works and contributed to the comparative critical neglect of nearly half of his fictional oeuvre. In addition, as Peter Widdowson has demonstrated, it encouraged critics to establish the "homogeneity" of Hardy's fiction, "to smooth and refine his work, rather than recognizing its fractured and dissonant discourses, its potentially *anti*-realist thrust" (Widdowson 2007: 16).

Hardy's modern critics have attempted to define or even excuse the controversial relationship to realism that these so-called "minor" novels clearly exhibit. Penny Boumelha notes how the vitality of their central female characters "provokes an uncertainty of genre and tone which unsettles the fictional modes in a disturbing and often productive manner" (Boumelha 1982: 30) but avoids this tantalizing issue entirely in her otherwise excellent study. *A Pair of Blue Eyes* is described as a poetic "tragi-comedy" in which Hardy was "feeling his way to a method" (Taylor 1982: 29); *The Trumpet-Major* as a historical and a comic novel that "utilizes" and "undercuts" both genres (Nemesvari 1991: xiii), a post-Darwinian combination of "elegy" with "record" (Barbara Hardy 1974: 12); *Two on a Tower* "reflects an impulse towards the experimental" (Taylor 1982: 121), whereas *The Well-Beloved* is "a story in which the bones of the narrative . . . show through its skin," an "autobiography" occasionally "strained by too unnatural devices" (Hetherington 1986: xxiv). One way out of this Polonius-like critical tergiversation might lie in the term "metafiction": a form of work that "explicitly and overtly lays bare its condition of artifice, and which thereby explores the problematic relationship between life and fiction" and draws attention to that dialogue of competing forms of communication within every novel that realism seeks to suppress (Waugh 1993: 4).

Hardy's taxonomy appears to relate to a somewhat conservative concept of realism. However, in "The Profitable Reading of Fiction" (New York *Forum*, March 1888), he declares that "the best fiction . . . is more true . . . than history or nature can be" (Orel 1967: 117). In "The Science of Fiction" (*New Review*, April 1891), he claims that art applies to the "phantasmagoria of experience" the "Daedalian faculty for selection and cunning manipulation" with the aim of being "more truthful than truth," and suggests that "a blindness to material particulars often accompanies a quick perception of the more ethereal characteristics of humanity" (Orel 1967: 134–7). In August 1890 he wrote:

> Art is a disproportioning – (i.e., distorting, throwing out of proportion) – of realities, to show more clearly the features that matter in those realities, which, if merely copied or reported inventorially, might possibly be observed, but would more probably be overlooked. Hence "realism" is not Art. (*LW* 239)

It seems strange, then, that the "Novels of Character and Environment" should be distinguished from the "Romances and Fantasies" by their "verisimilitude in general treatment and detail," whereas the "Novels of Ingenuity" are labeled "Experiments" with some "fidelity to life" (Orel 1967: 44–5).

Hardy doesn't elaborate on his use of "Romances and Fantasies" for *A Pair of Blue Eyes*, *The Trumpet-Major*, *Two on a Tower*, *The Well-Beloved*, and the volume of stories *A Group of Noble Dames* (for discussion of which, see CHAPTER 24, HARDY'S SHORT STORIES), deeming it "sufficiently descriptive" (Orel 1967: 44) but, like "Novels of Ingenuity," the term has a faintly dismissive ring to it, as if these texts are inferior to the "Novels of Character and Environment" because they are more fanciful, imaginative, more *fictional*. As Widdowson suggests, Hardy was extremely sensitive to criticism of his novels on the grounds of their " 'improbability', 'implausibility', lack of 'conviction', of 'credibility', of 'naturalness,' " all of which are "reflexes of a predilection for a seamless realism in fictional art" (Widdowson 2007: 12). It is as if by identifying his "flaws" Hardy sought to place himself, retrospectively, in the mainstream of the realist tradition and play down the diversity and experimentalism – the very "artfulness" – of his fictional output.

Interestingly, all four of these novels have at their center a specific and verifiable historical or scientific event or cultural movement around which the romance, or in Pierston's case the "fantasy," coheres. The action of *A Pair of Blue Eyes* is motivated by what Hardy calls "the craze for indiscriminate church-restoration" raging at the time of its composition (Orel 1967: 7), deplored by William Morris, just four years after the publication of the novel, in the manifesto of the Society for the Protection of Ancient Buildings (1877). For Morris, fifty years of attention to "these ancient monuments of art . . . have done more for their destruction than all the foregoing centuries of revolution, violence and contempt" (Morris [1877] 1936: 109). In the preface to the novel Hardy explains that this craze had just reached "the remotest nooks of western England," where the wild and tragic features of the coast had long combined in perfect harmony with the crude Gothic Art of the ecclesiastical buildings scattered along it, throwing into extraordinary discord all architectural attempts at newness there. To restore the grey carcases of a mediaevalism whose spirit had fled seemed a not less incongruous act than to set about renovating the adjoining crags themselves. (Orel 1967: 7)

An architect at the time of the novel's composition and publication, Hardy was aware of the controversy surrounding the issue of restoration and his preface echoes Morris's plea to architects to consider the "the living spirit" of buildings which "was an inseparable part of that religion and thought and those past manners" that had shaped their construction and which was threatened by indiscriminate tampering with their architectural fabric (Morris [1877] 1936: 111). In 1906 Hardy read a paper at the general meeting of SPAB which was markedly in sympathy with the society's manifesto and in which he looked back "in a contrite spirit at my own brief experience as a church-restorer." Making veiled reference to his visit to St. Juliot, where he had been sent by the architect's firm of G. R. Crickmay to supervise the restoration of the church where Emma's brother-in-law was rector (Millgate 2004: 112–28), he expressed the hope that "recalling instances of the drastic treatment we then dealt out with light hearts to the unlucky fanes that fell into our hands, [might] possibly help to prevent its repetition on the few yet left untouched" ("Memories of Church Restoration," Orel 1967: 205). However, it is not the vandalizing architect Stephen Smith who is censured in *A Pair of Blue Eyes* but the writer and critic Henry Knight, a purveyor of the spirit of the age who applies his knowledge and attention to Elfride Swancourt with a similarly destructive effect on her own living spirit.

A Pair of Blue Eyes was also inspired by the circumstances surrounding Hardy's courtship of his first wife Emma in 1870, in the romantic surroundings of the north Cornwall coast. It is this, perhaps, that led him to place this novel in the category of "Romances and Fantasies" for

The place is pre-eminently (for one person at least) the region of dream and mystery. The ghostly birds, the pall-like sea, the frothy wind, the eternal soliloquy of the waters, the bloom of dark purple cast that seems to exhale from the shoreward precipices, in themselves lend to the scene an atmosphere like the twilight of a night vision. (Orel 1967: 7)

However, Hardy's language seems more appropriate to a description of the setting of the "Poems of 1912–13," the highly evocative elegies he wrote after Emma's death in 1912. The "bloom of purple cast" features strikingly in "Beeny Cliff," dated March 1870–March 1913 (Millgate 2004: 291), and "After a Journey" movingly describes what is, quite literally, "a night vision": 'Soon you will have, Dear, to vanish from me, / For the stars close their shutters and the dawn whitens hazily' (*CPV* 349). This suggests that Hardy's imaginative re-creation of Emma's landscape was in process many years before her death and, more importantly, that the significance of both the

"Poems of 1912–13" and *A Pair of Blue Eyes* lies not in their biographical provenance but in how Hardy turns this raw material into art, employing that "Daedalian faculty for selection and cunning manipulation" that he prized so highly ("The Science of Fiction," Orel 1967: 134). In his subtle interweaving of the architectural and the romantic Hardy creates a moving indictment of the way in which patriarchal knowledge-producing discourses seek to fashion and refashion "the living spirit" to deadening effect. The landscape is merely the dramatic backdrop to the destruction of Elfride's spirit by the moral exigencies of her solipsistic lover, who is strikingly representative of the class and age that produced him.

The Trumpet-Major is set during the period of the Napoleonic and Peninsular Wars of 1803–15, when the southwest coast of England was galvanized against the expected incursion of the French army. Invasion is the dominant theme here and, as in *A Pair of Blue Eyes*, Hardy uses historical events to comment on the personal and individual. Beginning with the broader national issue of the threatened annexation of the British Isles by a foreign power, Hardy focuses on the invasion of ordinary lives by the forces of history and change, as the defending troops occupy the down and village of Overcombe. More specifically, the novel turns on the irruption of the forces of love and sexuality in the body and psyche of the heroine Anne Garland.

Two on a Tower follows a similar pattern to its predecessors in that the romance at its heart is set against a larger backdrop: the stellar universe. Unlike the plot of *The Trumpet-Major*, however, the events around which the action revolves were extremely topical at the time. A transit of Venus, following on from one in 1874, was expected in December 1882, just two months after the publication of *Two on a Tower* in novel form. Hardy may have hoped to cash in on the interest generated by the organization of global expeditions to observe and collect data on this momentous astrological event. The transit of Venus has symbolic significance in the novel, in that it describes the apparent movement of Venus across the sun. Swithin St. Cleeve, the young astronomer who excites the desires of the lonely lady of the manor from whose tower he observes the stars, is frequently described using solar imagery (Shuttleworth 1999: xxiii). The novel explores both the effect of his first encounter with love and sexual desire and the fickleness of love itself as it passes across and beyond his perspective. This novel, with its phallic imagery and compromised morals, is blatant in its examination of the vexed relationship of sexual desire to the social formation and, like *A Pair of Blue Eyes* and *The Trumpet-Major*, makes an eloquent plea for moral tolerance in the larger context of time, space, and imminent extinction.

The Well-Beloved, in its revised form at least, was Hardy's last novel, and it is a distillation of the major themes that had occupied him throughout his career as a writer of fiction. A "fantasy" in more ways than one, the novel also explores the aesthetics of femininity, an apt subject for a novelist who had consistently placed women at the center of his fiction. Although set some forty years before its date of publication in 1897 (WB 23), *The Well-Beloved* engages with one of the most topical issues of the day, the relationship between art and life, which lay at the heart of *fin-de-siècle* aestheticism and formed the central motif of novels such as Vernon Lee's *Miss Brown* (1884),

Oscar Wilde's *The Picture of Dorian Gray* (1891), and George Du Maurier's *Trilby* (1894), as well as Henry James' "The Real Thing" (1894) and Oscar Wilde's "The Decay of Lying" (1891). Covering the forty years between Jocelyn Pierston's virile entry into professional life as a sculptor and his descent into sexual and creative impotence, the novel also partakes in the general critical reassessment of Pre-Raphaelitism in the mid-1890s (Thomas 2004: 124–38). As in *A Pair of Blue Eyes, The Trumpet-Major,* and *Two on a Tower,* Hardy is concerned to explore the formative effects of dominant cultural, moral, and gender discourses on their feminine subjects (Thomas 1999: 131–46).

A Pair of Blue Eyes illustrates a major theme in Hardy's fiction: how individual expressions of desire are compromised and frustrated by the (conservative) social structures in which they are forced to articulate themselves. In reaction to the implications of Darwinian and Spencerian notions of the "survival of the fittest," Hardy's novels also cite difference and deviation not as "imperfections" that must be eradicated from the type, but as vital elements in the development of these structures. In the SPAB Manifesto, Morris criticizes the nineteenth century for having "no style of its own amidst its wide knowledge of the styles of other centuries," which leads "restorers" to strip away the "harsh and visible," though interesting, historical changes to a building in a mistaken attempt to bring it back to what they assume was "the best time of its history." In so doing they have no guide "but each his own individual whim to point out to them what is admirable and what contemptible" resulting in the production of "a feeble and lifeless forgery" (Morris [1877] 1936: 110). In applying their "individual whims" regarding masculine class status and feminine sexual purity, the Reverend Swancourt and Henry Knight force both Stephen Smith and Elfride into false positions. On discovering that Smith is the son of the village mason rather than a descendant of one of the most ancient West Country families, Swancourt declares "He appeared a young man with well-to-do friends, and a little property; but having neither, he is another man" (*PBE* 78). On discovering Elfride's failed elopement with Stephen, Knight tells her "I looked into your eyes, and thought I saw there truth and innocence as pure and perfect as ever embodied by God in the flesh of woman" (*PBE* 309) and reasons: "if she could but be again his own Elfride – the woman she had seemed to be – but that woman was dead and buried, and he knew her no more" (*PBE* 317).

Very early in the novel Stephen Smith notices how "intensely living and full of movement" Elfride looks "as she came into the old silent" church (*PBE* 27). It is Knight's refashioning of her according to a solipsistic, life-denying model of femininity that reduces her from the "proud equestrienne" to a corpse in a "light-coloured coffin of satin-wood, brightly polished, and without a nail" (*PBE* 346) and removes her from the pulpit of West Endelstow church, where she added her own unique touch of life and spirit to her father's outmoded sermons, to a niche in its vaults.

In his comparison of the "grey carcases of mediaevalism" to "the adjoining crags" (Orel 1967: 7), Hardy brings together architecture and geology in relation to the human. Churches and cliffs carry the evidence of their history in their architecture.

As Morris asserts, every change wrought to a building in the past "whatever history it destroyed, left history in the gap, and was alive with the spirit of the deeds done midst its fashioning" (Morris [1877] 1936: 110). As Knight hangs from the uniformly desolate "Cliff with No Name" he stares into the lifeless eyes of a fossilized trilobite "the single instance within reach of his vision of anything that had ever been alive and had had a body to save" (*PBE* 200). For John Ruskin it was the natural and honest imperfections of Gothic architecture, as opposed to the cold perfection of the classical style, that gave its buildings vigor, or what he calls "wolfish life" (Ruskin [1853] 2004: 37). The crude naturalism of the savage sculptures and grotesque gargoyles through which the medieval craftsman expressed his individuality "all admit irregularity as they imply change; and to banish imperfection is to destroy expression, to check exertion, to paralyze vitality" (Ruskin [1853] 2004: 49). Ruskin exhorts his readers to read the sculpture, and Knight does just this with the trilobite in the rock face, his imagination roving through "the varied scenes that had had their day between this creature's epoch and his own": "Time closed up like a fan before him. He saw himself at one extremity of the years, face to face with the beginning and all the intermediate centuries simultaneously" (*PBE* 200). But while the experience brings vividly home to him his own "smallness" in relation to the immense lapses of time recorded in the geological layers of rock, he fails to register the significance of the trilobite itself: an imperfection in the smooth black "bloom" of the cliff face but evidence, indeed the only evidence, of something that had once been alive in that now barren and lifeless environment.

A Pair of Blue Eyes is an eloquent and moving plea for the tolerance, even the appreciation, of "imperfection," especially moral imperfection, and in this respect it anticipates Hardy's fuller treatment of the idea in *Tess of the d'Urbervilles* – the "later book" of which this novel "exhibits the romantic stage" (Orel 1967: 8). It also argues against the deadening reduction of all forms to a recognizable and universal "type," and for the right of individuals to develop and articulate themselves in relation, rather than in thrall, to the truth-producing discourses of the time. The novel has been criticized for its narrator's misogynistic generalizations on the nature of women (Boumelha 1982: 32; Morgan 1988: 10), but these must be set in the context of its condemnation of Henry Knight for living his personal and intellectual life according to "a mass of generalities" "drawn forth from a large store ready-made" (*PBE* 124, 146), for having, as William Morris would say, no style of his own.

Elfride's attempt to enter literary discourse through the publication of a novelette is dismissed by both Knight and Mrs. Swancourt as a fraudulent attempt at mental respectability in that "it rather resembles the melancholy ruse of throwing loaves over castle-walls at besiegers, and suggests desperation rather than plenty inside" (*PBE* 118). As Jo Devereux suggests, "Elfride is not to be the creator of her own fictions but the passive receptacle of [Knight's]" (Devereux 1992: 20). However, Elfride's ill-fated attempt to author her own fictions is later successfully carried through by Ethelberta, who subverts the masculine discourse of the epic poem in order to articulate her own distinctive and devalued feminine voice.

Elfride describes her romance, *The Court of King Arthur's Castle*, as "A sweetener of history for young people, who might thereby acquire a taste for what went on in their own country hundreds of years ago, and be tempted to dive deeper into the subject" (*PBE* 141). Hardy's *The Trumpet-Major* may have been motivated by a similar impulse. This novel is more of a "romance" than a "fantasy" in the sense that its scenes and incidents are removed from ordinary life by its historical setting, which places the action around 1804–5, some eighty years earlier than the date of its publication. As a child Hardy was fascinated by the stories of the threat of the invasion of the south coast of England by Napoleon's forces told to the family by his paternal grandmother Mary Head Hardy, and by a periodical covering the Napoleonic Wars subscribed to by his grandfather, a private in the Puddletown Volunteer Light Infantry at the time: "The torn pages . . . with their melodramatic prints of serried ranks, crossed bayonets, huge knapsacks, and dead bodies, were the first to set him on the train of ideas that led to *The Trumpet-Major* and *The Dynasts*" (*LW* 21). This "worm-eaten magazine of ideas" features in the novel as an ironic metaphor for the mind of the "military relic" Simon Burden, who stares at the newly arrived cavalry "with a concern that people often show about temporal phenomena when such matters can affect them but a short time longer" (*TM* 12). On the sixtieth anniversary of the battle of Waterloo, Hardy and his first wife visited veterans in the Chelsea Hospital, where Emma was treated to first-hand accounts of the haze of smoke that so obscured the battlefield that "all that could be discerned was 'anything that shined', such as bayonets, helmets, and swords" (*LW* 109). The landscape and environment of Hardy's childhood still bore witness to preparations for the anticipated invasion:

> An outhouse door riddled with bullet-holes . . . extemporized by a solitary man as a target for firelock practice . . . a heap of bricks and clods on a beacon-hill . . . worm-eaten shafts and iron heads of pikes . . . ridges on the down thrown up during the encampment, fragments of volunteer uniform . . . brought to my imagination in early childhood the state of affairs at the date of the war more vividly than volumes of history could have done. (Orel 1967: 14)

An added emotional interest lay in his putative family connection with Thomas Masterman Hardy, flag captain to Admiral Nelson of the *Victory* at Trafalgar in 1805, under whose command Bob Loveday serves.

The novel demonstrates Hardy's trademark tenderness for the remarkable, but largely unremarked, lives of ordinary people briefly touched by the living stream of history (Ebbatson 1993: 46). His recognizably Victorian historical consciousness is expressed by Anne Garland, watching the soldiers mount guard for King George III on the esplanade at Budmouth, who

> now felt herself close to and looking into the stream of recorded history, within whose banks the littlest things are great, and outside which she and the general bulk of the human race were content to live on as an unreckoned, unheeded superfluity. (*TM* 108)

John Lovejoy provides the emotional link with the "international tragedy," joining Clym, Henchard, Giles Winterborne, Tess, and Jude to reinforce Hardy's abiding message concerning "the passing of the good, defeated by the fickle and the mediocre, into undeserved oblivion" (Taylor 1982: 81).

However history seems merely a temporary "domestic backcloth or setting" to the real action of *The Trumpet-Major* (Barbara Hardy 1974: 20–1). Though dynasties rise and fall somewhere far off in the distance, the inhabitants of Overcombe live out their smaller personal dramas of love and death as they have done for centuries. This sentiment is echoed in Hardy's poem "In Time of 'The Breaking of Nations,'" written during the First World War but harking back to the Franco-Prussian War of 1870–1: "War's annals will cloud into night / Ere their story die" (*CPV* 543).

The Trumpet-Major is more concerned with time than with history, or perhaps more accurately with the relationship between the two and the place of the individual man or woman within both. At noon, "the turning moment of the day," Anne Garland looks up from the heap of brightly colored worsted she is measuring into lengths for a rug to see two cavalry soldiers riding proudly over the down "as if nothing less than crowns and empires ever concerned their magnificent minds" (*TM* 10). They are followed, in one of the novel's strikingly filmic moments, by "a whole column of cavalry in marching order" moving as one body in a cloud of dust, illuminated here and there by the sun reflecting on their arms and accouterments in "faint flashes, stars, and streaks of light" (*TM* 11). The military precision of the troops setting up camp on the distant hill is contrasted with Anne's homely rug-making, the chromatic brilliance of the strips of fabric echoed in the colorful and varied uniforms of the different battalions on the down. The impermanence of the military encampment, raised and struck in a matter of hours and marked by only a tracery of ditches and humps, is compared with the durability of the miller's house, and the paving of its passage "which was worn into a gutter by the ebb and flow of feet that had been going on there ever since Tudor times" (*TM* 31). Even the humble, unconsidered rug carries the record of its making in its fabric, "the wools of the beginning bec[oming] faded and historical before the end was reached" (*TM* 9), while the brilliant uniforms of the soldiers will molder into dust, along with their wearers, on the battlefields of "Talavera, Albuera, Salamanca, Vittoria, Toulouse, and Waterloo; some in home churchyards; and a few small handfuls in royal vaults" (*TM* 106). However, the little and the great, those who lie in "unvisited tombs" (*Middlemarch*, 896) and those whose tombs become national monuments, are all subject to the leveling effects of time and death. This is one of the many lessons that Hardy took from history.

In another filmic moment we pan out from Anne watching "Those three or four thousand men of one machine-like movement," to take in "the glances of birds and other wild creatures, men in distant gardens, women in orchards and at cottage doors, shepherds on remote hills, turnip-hoers in blue-green enclosures miles away, captains with spyglasses out at sea," all of them "regarding the picture keenly" (*TM* 14). The captains with their spyglasses suggest Captain Hardy and Nelson on the battleship *Victory* at the battle of Trafalgar and also Nelson notoriously raising his telescope to his blind eye in order to ignore Admiral Hyde Parker's order to withdraw from the battle of Copenhagen four years earlier. If history turns a blind eye to the lives of the inhabitants of Overcombe, Hardy seeks to redress the balance, focusing on the brief invasion of ordinary lives by momentous historical events, and the more devastating invasion of time, change, and chancefulness.

The weathercock, subject to the vagaries of the wind and showing beneath its blue sailor's garb the red uniform of a soldier, is an apt metaphor not just for the fickleness of lovers but for the contingent nature of love itself:

> The image had, in fact, been John . . . and was then turned into Robert. . . . This revolving piece of statuary could not, however, be relied on as a vane, owing to the neighbouring hill, which formed variable currents in the wind. (*TM* 17)

The Trumpet-Major examines these "variable currents" and their effect upon the individuals whose emotions and desires are directed by them. These include sexual availability, class position, material circumstances, and opportunism. The advent of the brilliantly uniformed and glamorous soldiers affords the village girls "unbounded possibilities of adoring and being adored, and to the young men an embarrassment of dashing acquaintances which quite superseded falling in love" (*TM* 21). Some soldiers are followed by their wives, an altogether different breed of woman from the wives of the village, whose dress rivals the uniforms of their husbands in its quaint chromatic brilliance (*TM* 22). These chattering, starling wives bring their own ribald sexual experience into the village, and Hardy is comically ironic on the nature of the various "campaigns" in which they have been involved. Anne's sexual curiosity is roused by one of the new arrivals, a "houseless treasury of experience" with "a rosy nose and a slight thickness of voice which, as Anne said, she couldn't help, poor thing" who, despite Anne's sympathy, "was obliged to look for quarters" other than Mrs. Garland's "narrow" rooms (*TM* 22).

Allied to the soldiers' wives are the camp followers, such as the actress Matilda Johnson: "the lovely and virtuous young maiden" (*TM* 115) who is intimately acquainted not only with Bob but also with John Loveday, Captain Jolly, Captain Beauboy, Mr. Flight, and possibly the entire company of "the —th Dragoons." On the night of John's successful routing of Matilda from the Loveday household, Anne lies awake musing on the traits of the new friend who has come to her neighbor's house and "the rare qualities" in Miss Johnson's mind and person that have led Bob, "with his world-wide experience," to single her out "from among all other women, herself included" (*TM* 153). Chief among these "rare qualities" is sexuality, which is still nascent in the mind and person of Anne Garland despite her bewitching little curls and cap ribbons. As Barbara Hardy suggests, Bob's rebuke to John that, despite her history and conduct, Matilda would have been good enough for him, "is an endearing instance of Hardy's lack of over-intensity about sexual conduct." Although Matilda is far from exhibiting the "inner purity" exemplified by Tess Durbeyfield, *The Trumpet-Major* likewise comments wryly on the prevailing sexual double standards of Matilda's time and of Hardy's own (Barbara Hardy 1974: 30–1).

Despite its concern with factual accuracy, *The Trumpet-Major* deploys anti-realist strategies such as comedy and farce in order to comment, sometimes quite forcibly, on serious and contentious issues. These include sexual inconstancy; the complex realities underlying the pastoral and the romantic idyll; the materialistic base of sexuality; power relations between the genders; the disruptive nature of sexual desire, which leads individuals to sacrifice prudence to inclination; and the relative insignificance of considerations of class and sexual morality when set against the larger issue of war.

Two on a Tower extends Hardy's disquisition on the inconsequentiality of temporal moral codes in the larger context by setting, in the words of his preface, "the emotional history of two infinitesimal lives against the stupendous background of the stellar universe" (Orel 1967: 16). As in the previous two novels, Hardy's concern here is with the individual woman as the site of conflict between sexual desire and the social formations that seek to regulate it. The novel was criticized for its impropriety and its perceived satire on the Established Church, charges which Hardy refuted somewhat disingenuously in 1895, citing what he called the "scrupulous propriety" of the novel in that "there is hardly a single caress . . . outside legal matrimony, or what was intended so to be" (Orel 1967: 17). The issue of conjugal or non-conjugal embraces is emphatically overshadowed by the novel's blatant examination of sexual desire, and in particular female sexual desire, and the rigid constraints imposed upon it by considerations of class, gender appropriateness, and social position. Even Hardy's attempt to excuse Viviette's blatant passion for a much younger man and her decision to release him from the moral obligation to remarry her as an example of a kind of Comtean feminine "divine tenderness" "not unprofitable to the growth of the social sympathies" fails to convince entirely (Orel 1967: 17). Viviette's love for Swithin St. Cleeve is driven by predominantly sexual and selfish (though not dishonorable) motives rather than communal, spiritual considerations. Sensitized perhaps by the negative reception of *Tess of the d'Urbervilles* and *Jude the Obscure*, Hardy sought in the 1912 preface to weaken the radical charge of one of his most startlingly outspoken novels.

Placing *Two on a Tower* in the category of "Romances and Fantasies" neutralizes it still further, as does Hardy's definition of it as a "slightly-built romance" (Orel 1967: 16). The collision of the "real" with the romantic is at the very heart of this novel. Swithin catches sight of the devoted and expectant Lady Constantine (whose desire for him will lead her to compromise herself irrevocably) framed on the platform by the window of his railway carriage. The narrator comments "To both the situation seemed like a beautiful allegory, not to be examined too closely, lest its defects of correspondence with real life should be apparent" (*TT* 116), and on receipt of her brother Louis' coolly practical letter on the eve of her intended marriage to Swithin, Viviette laments "the deep glow of enchantment shed by the idea of a private union with her beautiful young lover killed in the pale light of cold reasoning" (*TT* 105).

Viviette and Swithin conduct their love affair in splendid but precarious isolation from the wider social community, on the top of a tower known as Rings-Hill Speer, on a "secluded fir tree island" cut off from the rest of Welland by a near-impassable ploughed field. The early days of their "married" life are spent in a primitive hut at the base of the tower awaiting the healing of the mark on her cheek that is "a clue to [Louis'] discovery of our secret" (*TT* 122). They dine on songbirds and water from the brook and eat their breakfast in the "sweet resinous air from the firs" as birds hop around the open door: "'I could be happy here for ever,' said she, clasping his hand. . . . 'Poverty of this sort is not unpleasant at any rate'"(*TT* 124–5). But such a relationship can only survive if insulated from the inevitable incursions of social and biological realities.

However self-deceived these particular lovers are, the narrator suggests that the desire they experience is as ancient as the prehistoric mound upon which their tower and hut sit, as is its social regulation by matrimony. As Swithin prepares for his marriage the narrator speculates on the events that had taken place in that camp and concludes:

> the primitive simplicity of the young man's preparations accorded well with the prehistoric spot on which they were made. Embedded under his feet were possibly even now rude trinkets that had been worn at bridal ceremonies of the early inhabitants. (*TT* 110–11)

The novel sets up a comparison between the microcosmic world of the individual (in thrall to the larger forces of desire and time) and what Tess was later to call the "blighted star" on which this conflict is acted out, which is itself subject to the immense forces of the universe, suggesting "that of these contrasting magnitudes the smaller might be the greater to them as men" (Orel 1967: 16). At the same time the star upon which Viviette and Swithin find themselves shows evidence, on its surface at least, of the human layering of history that gives continuity and meaning to the incidents in the life of a single man or woman. The novel continually strives to balance the cosmic and the human, and does so by challenging the "separate spheres" ideology that underpinned the Victorian understanding of gender difference. As Swithin almost literally loses himself in the immensities of space Viviette brings him back to earth with a slight touch on his arm:

> "Do come out of it" she coaxed, with a softness in her voice which any man but unpractised Swithin would have felt to be exquisite. "I feel that I have been so foolish as to put in your hands an instrument to effect my own annihilation." (*TT* 58)

Swithin is symbolically emancipated from his "trammelling" body by his telescope, but in the process he loses the ability to empathize and connect with what is meaningful in the human realm.

As in *A Pair of Blue Eyes*, this novel also interrogates the misogynistic gender discourses that its plot seems, at times, to endorse. Jocelyn St. Cleeve, like Henry Knight, articulates the prevailing association of the feminine with the physical and material rather than the spiritual or intellectual realm. Women and their "trumpery eyes" trap men into losing sight of their aspirations and their potentialities by ensnaring them with sex. Their brains are not made for "assisting at any profound science," and woman "sits down before each [man] as his destiny, and too frequently enervates his purpose, till he abandons the most promising course ever conceived" (*TT* 114–15). Here Hardy is rehearsing ideas that will receive fuller and more considered treatment in *Jude the Obscure*, with which this novel shares a number of themes. Arabella's crude distraction of Jude from his intellectual pursuits is suggested by Viviette's equally compelling, if more subtle and sympathetic, attempt to bring Swithin "down to earth." As in the later novel, *Two on a Tower* seems unresolved on the issue of whether, as Jude puts it, "the women are to blame" or whether it is "the artificial system of things, under which the normal sex-impulses are turned into devilish domestic gins and springes to noose and hold back those who want to progress" (*JO* 228). Viviette's surreptitious "rape" of a golden curl from the head of the sleeping Swithin suggests the story of Samson and Delilah and the picture that hangs on the wall of the "inn of inferior class" where Jude and Arabella drink beer on their first outing together (*JO* 43). But what this illustrates is the way in which pre-existing signifying systems articulate their own "truth," structuring reality into forms intelligible to a patriarchal social system, or as Viviette declares, quoting Shakespeare's Hamlet: "There is nothing either good or bad but thinking makes it so" (*TT* 100).

Throughout the novel Viviette strives to anchor herself within a recognizable and "legitimate" female identity. As Granny Martin declares: "The state she finds herself in – neither maid, wife, nor widow, as you might say – is not the primest form of life for keeping in good spirits" (*TT* 17). Later, on writing a letter declining the bishop's proposal of marriage, Viviette cannot settle on an appropriate form for her signature:

> "Viviette what?" she exclaimed hopelessly, as she flung down the pen.
>
>   A sudden revulsion from the subterfuge of signing herself "Viviette Constantine", in a letter of this serious sort, and the impracticability of using another signature for the present, wrought in her mind a feeling of dissatisfaction with the whole epistle, and pushing it aside she allowed it to remain unsubscribed. (*TT* 191)

As Sally Shuttleworth suggests, the numerous changes he made to the manuscript at this point signify "Hardy's own unease with the complex status he has conferred on his heroine" (1999: 280n2). But Viviette uses her liminal status to challenge the available female subject positions through an exercise of the kind of logic cheerfully adopted by later heroines such as Arabella in *Jude the Obscure* and Marcia Bencombe in *The Well-Beloved*. On discovering that her marriage to Swithin is not legal she considers whether she should "secure her own honour at any price to him" (*TT* 212). In a passage that also anticipates Tess Durbeyfield's situation after the death of baby Sorrow, the narrator surmises:

Women the most delicate get used to strange moral situations. Eve probably regained her normal sweet composure about a week after the Fall. On first learning of her anomalous position, Lady Constantine had blushed hot, and her pure instincts had prompted her to legalize her marriage without a moment's delay. Heaven and earth were to be moved at once to effect it. Day after day had passed; her union had remained unsecured, and the idea of its nullity had gradually ceased to be strange to her; till it became of little account beside her bold resolve for the young man's sake (*TT* 217)

As so many of Hardy's novels demonstrate, it is often the biological consequences of illegitimate desire that force women into confining "social moulds" (*JO* 215). Viviette's attempt, like Tess, to "veil bygones" (*TD* 99) is thwarted by her last rebellious sexual contact with Swithin, which places her back within the field of visibility by leaving her pregnant. The language of censure redefines her as "loose" and "fallen" rather than a passionate woman with a right to sexual self-expression (Thomas 1999: 114). Again Hardy's subsequent alterations demonstrate his increasing dissatisfaction with prevailing feminine stereotypes. In the first edition of the novel (1891) the narrator defends Viviette's deception of the bishop as "Nature . . . forcing her hand at this game; and to what will not nature compel her weaker victims, in extremes?" (*TT* 242). In the 1912 edition Hardy changes "Nature" to "Convention", suggesting that women's behavior is not the result of their biology but of their social situation.

Two on a Tower is a strenuous critique of the way in which sexual desire is legitimized by marriage. Viviette and Swithin's situation is ironically paralleled by the rustic Anthony Green who, despite his inclination, is unable to "hold out against the custom of the country, and the woman wanting ye to stand by her and save her from unborn shame" (*TT* 82). Viviette's hoodwinking of the bishop is her equally reluctant concession to the custom of the country as her hand is forced, quite literally, by the realities of the world outside the one she seeks to inhabit.

In Hardy's last novel, *The Well-Beloved* (1897), ideas on the relationship between the real and the ideal, art versus nature, and romance (or fantasy) versus realism cohere in what must also be one of his most experimentally "artful" novels. In the 1912 preface to the novel Hardy declares:

As for the story itself, it may be worth while to remark that, differing from all or most others of the series in that the interest aimed at it is of an ideal or subjective nature, and frankly imaginative, verisimilitude in the sequence of events has been subordinated to the said aim. (Orel 1967: 37)

In labeling it a "fantasy" Hardy draws attention to the novel's deliberate engagement with the imaginative. The Isle of Slingers, the location for much of the action, is linked to the body of the mainland by a "long thin neck of pebbles" (*WB* 9) making it, in anthropomorphic terms, the head or seat of the imagination itself. Its island status insulates it from actual contemporary realities (just as the Rings-Hill Speer

tower is marooned by the plowed field, *The Trumpet-Major*'s Overcombe is distanced
by history, and Endelstow by its legendary and romantic situation), thus allowing its
creator to indulge in imaginative "free-play." Hardy writes of it:

> The peninsula carved by Time out of a single stone . . . has been for centuries immemor-
> ial the home of a curious and well-nigh distinct people, cherishing strange beliefs and
> singular customs. . . . Fancies, like certain soft-wooded plants which cannot bear the
> silent inland frosts, but thrive by the sea in the roughest of weather, seem to grow up
> naturally here, in particular amongst those natives who have no active concern in the
> labours of the "Isle." (Orel 1967: 36)

The Isle of Slingers (Portland Island) is a place for artists or, as Hardy calls
Pierston, "Fantasts": visionary, capricious people given to flights of the imagination
who seek, through their art, to give material substance to the Platonic (or Neoplatonic) "Real." Indeed Hardy expresses surprise that the place "has not been more
frequently chosen as the retreat of artists and poets in search of inspiration"
(Orel 1967: 37). His imagery is interesting. The "silent frosts" of the mainland are
not conducive to the survival of "fancies" which thrive even in the roughest weather
of the island. We can detect here, perhaps, a comment on the hostile effect of prevailing realist evaluations of art on the more fanciful elements of his own fictional oeuvre
which, like an illicit love-affair, can only flourish in isolation from dominant moral
and cultural codes.

The Well-Beloved is Hardy's most "artful" novel in terms of its style and its subject
matter. It is a work of art about art and the artist (Miller 1975) and is insistently
self-referential. It is also schematic, its plot is artificial and manipulated, and its events
have been deliberately selected to illustrate an idea: that "underlying the fantasy followed by the visionary artist [is] the truth that all men are pursuing a shadow, the
Unattainable" (*LW* 304). The novel retains and develops the critique of the masculine
gaze and its power to define the female subject which is fundamental to *A Pair of
Blue Eyes*, but unlike Elfride Swancourt all three Avices manage to avoid Pierston's
aesthetic and sexual arrogation of their bodies.

As a sculptor of the Neoplatonic school (Ousby 1982), Pierston employs the very
"Daedalean" processes that Hardy claimed were common to all artists, in that cunning
manipulation of the raw stone with the chisel is necessary to the apprehension and
realization of the beauty locked within it. In "Memories of Church Restoration,"
Hardy argues that the "essence or soul" of an ancient Gothic building lies not in the
stone or timber that it is built from but in the forms into which these materials have
been shaped:

> Those limestones or sandstones have passed into its form; yet it is an idea independent
> of them – an aesthetic phantom without solidarity, which might just as suitably have
> chosen millions of other stones from the quarry whereon to display its beauties.

This, Hardy continues, is "the actual process of organic nature herself, which is one continuous substitution. She is always discarding the matter, while retaining the form" (Orel 1967: 214). It is precisely this "aesthetic phantom" or "form" that Pierston pursues in both his professional and his romantic life:

> "I have always been faithful to the elusive creature whom I have never been able to get a firm hold of, unless I have done so now. And let me tell you that her flitting from each to each individual has been anything but a pleasure for me – certainly not a wanton game of my instigation. To see the creature who has hitherto been perfect, divine, lose under your very gaze the divinity which has informed her, grow commonplace, turn from flame to ashes, from a radiant vitality to a relic, is anything but a pleasure for any man." (*WB* 40)

It is ironic perhaps that the stones that Jocelyn's father quarries from the island will be used in the very process of church restoration that Morris and Hardy so deplored. It is also ironic, in this commercial age, that while Jocelyn has earned twelve thousand pounds from "modelling and chipping his ephemeral fancies into perennial shapes" his father has amassed eighty thousand pounds from sending "his spoil to all parts of Great Britain" (*WB* 55).

The narrator appears to link the "organic" processes of nature with the aesthetic processes of the artist, suggesting that the "truth" each reveals to the visionary eye is universal, archetypal, and divinely inspired. Just as Pierston carves his representations of the "Well-Beloved" out of marble so time has carved out the Isle of Slingers from a single stone and nature shapes the Avices out of the gene pool of the "roan mare" Caros (*WB* 10). In explaining his preference for "a pretty island girl" to a woman of society, Pierston tells his friend Somers: "I know the perfect and pure quarry she was dug from" (*WB* 108). However, the increasing distance between narrator and male protagonists that Patricia Ingham notes in Hardy's novels is at its greatest here (Ingham 2003: 100). Unlike the Pre-Raphaelites, to whose aesthetic values Pierston subscribes, Hardy believed that art was a product of culture not nature, and that notions of "Beauty" were not universal. The narrator criticizes Pierston for failing to recognize that his "Well-Beloved "was a subjective phenomenon vivified by the weird influences of his descent and birthplace" (*WB* 16). The "Well-Beloved" derives from Pierston's imagination, generated from the rocks and ruined temples of the island of his birth. The novel is characteristically critical of the negative effects of prevailing patriarchal cultural constructions of physical and moral beauty. Most of all, it criticizes the cultural primitivism that underpinned Pre-Raphaelite aesthetics and the idealization of rural or working-class women that reduced their infinite variety to a single, uniform "type." Pierston's, Henry Knight's, and Angel Clare's ill-informed association of rural seclusion with sexual innocence mirrors the Pre-Raphaelite association of working-class women with freedom from cultural contamination, leading to their reduction to aesthetic icons with no life or personality of their own. As Pierston observes Ann Avice he surmises:

it was not the washerwoman that he saw now. In front of her, on the surface of her, was shining out that more real, more inter-penetrating being whom he knew so well! The occupation of the subserving minion, the blemishes of the temporary creature who formed the background, were of the same account in the presentation of the indispensable one as the supporting posts and framework in a pyrotechnic display. (*WB* 89)

The uneducated Ann Avice is contrasted favorably with her mother, who in Pierston's eyes exhibited the "tendency of the age" "to get her away mentally as far as possible from her natural and individual life . . . to make her an exact copy of tens of thousands of other people, in whose circumstances there was nothing special, distinctive, or picturesque" (*WB* 19).

In his own attempts to give "objective continuity and a name to a delicate dream" (Orel 1967: 36–7), Pierston merely manages to produce plaster "forgeries" whose popularity threatens his reputation as a serious artist. In connecting his "Lucys," "Janes," "Floras," and "Evangelines" (*WB* 16) with his "Aphrodites," "Freyas," "Junos," "Lilliths," "Minervas," and "Psyches," Pierston is committing the cardinal sin of confusing life with art and, as Hardy declares in "Memories of Church Restoration," "Life . . . is more than art, and that which appealed to us in the (may be) clumsy outlines of some structure . . . outweighs the more subtle recognition, if any, of architectural qualities" (Orel 1967: 215).

In common with *A Pair of Blue Eyes*, *The Trumpet-Major*, and *Two on a Tower*, *The Well-Beloved* champions the flawed human over the perfect ideal and mounts a strong critique of prevailing patriarchal moral and aesthetic judgments. It is exactly the "blemishes of the temporary creature" that make up the "living spirit" of Hardy's female protagonists. All three Avices, but perhaps especially Ann Avice and her daughter, insistently proclaim their right to a degree of self-determination and, without belonging to what the narrator of *Two on a Tower* archly calls "the phalanx of Wonderful Women who have sternly resolved to eclipse masculine genius altogether, and humiliate the brutal sex to the dust" (*TT* 256), the third Avice's bid for independence deals a fatal blow to the old order and gestures towards the "New Woman's" iconoclastic potential. It is as if Hardy felt that new forms of feminine subjectivity demanded new modes of representation, but not, perhaps, from his pen.

The Well-Beloved offers an important perspective on Hardy's fiction. It is a valedictory novel which critically examines the role of the artist and the aesthetic process itself, and a fascinating experiment in metafiction. If realism wasn't art for Hardy, and if the production of art was his ultimate goal, then the "Romances and Fantasies," along with the "Novels of Ingenuity," should attract more serious critical attention than has hitherto been the case, because they demonstrate Hardy's radical rather than his "flawed" aesthetic. It is worth noting that the "subgenres" of romance, fantasy, and historical fiction excite critical interest today precisely for the ways in which they draw attention to the tensions and oppositions inherent in more apparently "seamless" forms of aesthetic practice.

Hardy claimed that he abandoned fiction because the novel was "gradually losing artistic form . . . and becoming a spasmodic inventory of items, which has nothing to do with art." He declared that his aim had been "to keep his narratives close to natural life, and as near to poetry in their subject as the conditions would allow, and had often regretted that those conditions would not let him keep them nearer still" (*LW* 309–10).

In 1897, as he began revising *The Well-Beloved*, his most experimental and, along with *A Pair of Blue Eyes*, his most "poetical" novel (Ingham 2003: 70–1; Taylor 1982: 32), he speculated whether poetry might be a more suitable vehicle for aesthetic expression than the novel (*LW* 302), allowing him more scope, perhaps, "to intensify the expression of things . . . so that the heart and inner meaning is made vividly visible" (*LW* 183). It is a pity that by 1912 he seems to have lost the courage of his convictions and undervalued what is surely some of his most stylistically inventive and artful work.

REFERENCES AND FURTHER READING

Beatty, C. J. P. (ed.) ([1966] 2007). *The Architectural Notebook of Thomas Hardy*, rev. edn. Dorchester: Dorset Natural History and Archaeological Society.

Boumelha, Penny (1982). *Thomas Hardy and Women: Sexual Ideology and Narrative Form*. Brighton: Harvester Press.

Bullen, J. B. (1994). Hardy's *The Well-Beloved*, Sex, and Theories of Germ Plasm. In Phillip V. Mallett and Ronald P. Draper (eds.), *A Spacious Vision: Essays on Hardy* (pp. 79–88). Newmill: Patten Press.

Cecil, Lord David (1976). Hardy the Historian. In Margaret Drabble (ed.), *The Genius of Thomas Hardy* (pp. 154–61). London: Weidenfeld & Nicolson.

Davidson, Arnold, E. (1987). On Reading *The Well-Beloved* as a Parable of Art. *The Thomas Hardy Yearbook*, 14, 14–17.

Devereux, Jo (1992). Thomas Hardy's *A Pair of Blue Eyes*: The Heroine as Text. *Victorian Newsletter*, 81, 20–3.

Ebbatson, Roger (1993). *Hardy: The Margin of the Unexpressed*. Sheffield: Sheffield Academic Press.

Eliot, George ([1874] 1973). *Middlemarch*, ed. W. J. Harvey. Harmondsworth: Penguin.

Elliott, Ralph W. V. (1987). The Infatuated Artist: Thomas Hardy and *The Well-Beloved*. *Thomas Hardy Journal*, 3(2), 20–33.

Green, Laura (1995). "Strange [In]difference of Sex": Thomas Hardy, the Victorian Man of Letters, and the Temptations of Androgyny. *Victorian Studies*, 38, 523–50.

Hardy, Barbara (1974). Introduction to Thomas Hardy, *The Trumpet-Major* (pp. 11–33). Oxford: Oxford University Press,

Hardy, Thomas ([1873] 2005). *A Pair of Blue Eyes*, ed. Alan Manford. Oxford: Oxford University Press.

Hardy, Thomas ([1880] 1991). *The Trumpet-Major*, ed. Richard Nemesvari. Oxford: Oxford University Press.

Hardy, Thomas ([1882] 1999). *Two on a Tower*, ed. Sally Shuttleworth. London: Penguin.

Hardy, Thomas ([1891] 2003). *Tess of the d'Urbervilles*, ed. Tim Dolin. London: Penguin.

Hardy, Thomas ([1896] 1985). *Jude the Obscure*, ed. Patricia Ingham. Oxford: Oxford University Press.

Hardy, Thomas ([1897] 1986). *The Well-Beloved*, ed. Tom Hetherington. Oxford: Oxford University Press.

Hardy, Thomas (1979). *The Variorum Edition of the Complete Poems of Thomas Hardy*, ed. James Gibson. London: Macmillan.

Hardy, Thomas (1984). *The Life and Work of Thomas Hardy*, ed. Michael Millgate. London: Macmillan.

Hetherington, Tom (1986). Introduction to Thomas Hardy, *The Well-Beloved* (pp. xi–xxvii). Oxford: Oxford University Press.

Ingham, Patricia (2003). *Authors in Context: Thomas Hardy*. Oxford: Oxford University Press.

Miller, J. Hillis (1975). Introduction to Thomas Hardy, *The Well-Beloved* (pp. 11–21). London: Macmillan.

Millgate, Michael (2004). *Thomas Hardy: A Biography Revisited*. Oxford: Oxford University Press.

Morgan, Rosemarie (1988). *Women and Sexuality in the Novels of Thomas Hardy*. London and New York: Routledge.

Morris, William ([1877] 1936). Manifesto of the S.P.A.B. In *William Morris, Artist, Writer, Socialist*, ed. May Morris, 2 vols. (vol. I, pp. 109–11). Oxford: Basil Blackwell.

Nemesvari, Richard (1991). Introduction to Thomas Hardy, *The Trumpet Major* (pp. xi–xxii). Oxford: Oxford University Press,.

Orel, Harold (ed.) (1967). *Thomas Hardy's Personal Writings*. London: Macmillan.

Ousby, Ian (1982). "The Convergence of the Twain": Hardy's Alteration of Plato's Parable. *Modern Language Review*, 77(4), 780–96.

Richardson, Angelique (1998). "Some science underlies all art": The Dramatization of Sexual Selection and Racial Biology in Thomas Hardy's *A Pair of Blue Eyes* and *The Well-Beloved*. *Journal of Victorian Culture*, 3, 302–38.

Rimmer, Mary (1993). Club Laws: Chess and the Construction of Gender in *A Pair of Blue Eyes*. In Margaret R. Higonnet (ed.), *The Sense of Sex: Feminist Perspectives on Hardy* (pp. 203–20). Urbana: University of Illinois Press.

Ruskin, John ([1853] 2004). The Nature of Gothic from *The Stones of Venice*, II. In *John Ruskin Selected Writings*, ed. Dinah Birch (pp. 32–63). Oxford: Oxford University Press.

Ryan, Michael (1979). One Name of Many Shapes: *The Well-Beloved*. In Dale Kramer (ed.), *Critical Approaches to the Fiction of Thomas Hardy* (pp. 172–92). London: Macmillan.

Shuttleworth, Sally (1999). Introduction to Thomas Hardy, *Two on a Tower* (pp. xvi–xxxi). London: Penguin.

Sumner, Rosemary (1982). The Experimental and the Absurd in *Two on a Tower*. In Norman Page (ed.), *Thomas Hardy Annual No. 1* (pp. 71–81). London and Basingstoke: Macmillan.

Taylor, Richard H (1982). *The Neglected Hardy: Thomas Hardy's Lesser Novels*. London and Basingstoke: Macmillan.

Thomas, Jane (1999). *Thomas Hardy, Femininity and Dissent: Reassessing the "Minor" Novels*. Basingstoke: Macmillan.

Thomas, Jane (2004). Thomas Hardy, Thomas Woolner and *The Well-Beloved*: An Aesthetic Debate. *Thomas Hardy Journal*, 20(3), 124–38.

Ward, Paul (1973). The Artist's Dilemma: an Interpretation of *The Well-Beloved*. *The Thomas Hardy Yearbook*, 3, 31–3.

Ward, Paul (1975). *A Pair of Blue Eyes* and *The Descent of Man*. *The Thomas Hardy Yearbook*, 5, 47–55.

Ward, Paul (1978). *Two on a Tower*: A Critical Re-evaluation. *The Thomas Hardy Yearbook*, 8, 29–34.

Waugh, Patricia (1993). *Metafiction: The Theory and Practice of Self-Conscious Fiction*. London: Routledge.

Widdowson, Peter (2007). *Thomas Hardy*. Devon: Northcote House.

Wing, George (1987). Hardy's Star-Cross'd Lovers in *Two on a Tower*. *The Thomas Hardy Yearbook*, 14, 35–44.

20

The Haunted Structures of
The Mayor of Casterbridge

Julian Wolfreys

Texts, ideas, the traces of historical and cultural forces: all take time to arrive. If they arrive at all, they are never on time. The arrival of the trace is radically disordered from the start. If interpreted precipitately, texts miss being read and so remain to be received. Yet the reader cannot help but be precipitate, overly anxious, or laggardly. Moreover, any reception of some past trace always involves loss in translation, impoverishment through transmission. Thomas Hardy understood this more than most, and gave expression to it in a commentary on the Dorset dialect poetry of William Barnes. Interpreting, explaining, or annotating dialect words Hardy claimed, provided only "a sorry substitute for the full significance the original words bear . . . without translation" (Barnes 1908: vii). From another perspective, Hardy knew that words and signs arrive with a velocity that inevitably produces indirect, sensuous apprehension, thereby causing "a feeling before it gets defined" (Taylor 1993: 306). In this apprehension, Hardy marks a distance from realist forms of narrative. Instead, he marks himself a novelist of, and for, future generations. Hardy is only ever available as other to the times in which he wrote. In this, he remains the novelist of the nineteenth century who, more than any other, affirms the past as always arriving. He is the novelist and poet of cultural memory and the times of the other. In their transmission and critical reception Hardy's novels come to act on certain of their readers in a manner analogous with the effect that the many missives, telegrams, signs, paintings, and other modes of communication that pepper his texts produce on and in his characters.

The historicized, historicizing modes of representation that inform Hardy's writing mark and remark the time of their having taken place. They thus record both image and mental image, the world and mental reflection on or image of that world. In this, Hardy's historicizing records are themselves the traces of so many *memento mori*, so many archived and archiving (re)collections of heterogeneous traces. They are researches into, remembrances of, times past. They affirm the ruins of the innumerable pasts that crowd the present of so many of Hardy's novels, signaling and sending themselves into an unprogrammable future, and risking everything on reading or unreadability.

Whilst it has become something of a commonplace to speak of Hardy as a cinematic novelist, it is more accurate to remark that he shares with the technology of photography the ability to bear the burden of memory through the inscription of the haunting trace, as Tim Armstrong makes clear in his study of Hardy's poetry. Of photography, Armstrong observes: "alongside its status as an index of the real, the photograph itself becomes ghostly; it comes to represent mourning, abstracting and estranging its subject-matter" (Armstrong 2000: 59). Such estrangement and abstraction give one the sense of how intimately close and yet impossibly far Hardy is from our time, from the time we consider ours. To make us feel, rather than to make us see, except by that indirect vision of insight, this it might be said is Hardy's desire, his narrative and historical obsession. Hence, a complex textual weave emerges, comprising so many folds, and threads, so many echoes in different registers. Once a note is sounded in Hardy, an impossible number of others resonate for the patient reader, attentive to the difference of historicity, its signs and traits.

If we are to be attentive to the signs, traces, and marks of history and the ways in which the past leaves its remainders on our identities and our memories, we would do well to acknowledge that "We two kept house, the Past and I," as Hardy puts it in "The Ghost of the Past" (*CPV* 308). This is to confess to nothing less than the fact that ours is a ghost-ridden culture. We inhabit and share a modernity and a collective identity in which we dwell and which we find to be haunted everywhere, by what Hardy is pleased to call "the persistence of the unforeseen." Nowhere in Hardy's work is this insistent revenance acknowledged more persistently or blatantly at various cultural, historical, and personal levels than in *The Mayor of Casterbridge*. Specters are everywhere in what must be Hardy's most densely spectral novel and certainly the novel that comes closest to being a ghost story. The dead and their spectral manifestations appear even in the faces or actions of the living. The town of Casterbridge is a haunted place, its topographical, architectural, and archaeological structures resonating with the traces of the spectral. The ghosts of other textual forms, of which the tragic is only the most persistent or obvious, haunt the very structure of the novel. Michael Henchard especially is troubled by the past, by certain spectral returns that determine the direction of his life and the choices or decisions he believes he makes for himself. In this chapter therefore, I wish to examine how the various manifestations of spectral revenance, in their transgression of place, present, and representational narrative stability, transform one's understanding of time, place, and identity.

From one perspective, haunting is best, if provisionally, determined as the ability of forces that remain unseen to make themselves felt in everyday life. Such interruption in the everyday causes us to anticipate, to fear, to act, or to respond in ways that we do not fully comprehend, supposing that we understand them at all. As Keith Wilson suggests of the novel, "all the major characters reveal a capacity . . . of responding to experience as the working-out of inevitable courses" (Wilson 1997: xxxi). This assessment catches the sense of a spectral movement of the invisible within the visible. Such haunting can also cause us to feel unsafe, uneasy, in places where we had always felt at home. Haunting creates, then, the sense of the unfamiliar within the familiar. Its operation is thus a structural as well as a temporal disturbance. Haunting inhabits and, in creating an uncanny response, manifests itself as not arriving from elsewhere, but instead makes itself felt, as Mark Wigley suggests, "surfacing . . . in a return of the repressed as a foreign element that strangely seems to belong to the very domain that renders it foreign" (Wigley 1993: 108). As we shall see, haunting, ghosting, spectrality are all necessary traces in the structures of *The Mayor of Casterbridge*. Barely comprehensible, they inhere, haunting with an aggressive immanence the very places, narratives, and forms they serve to articulate.

The persistence of the past in the narrative present of *The Mayor of Casterbridge*, that unsettling or uncanny recurrence of the past trace described by Ned Lukacher as "a strange peculiarity in the presence of the present" (Lukacher 1998: 156–7), produces also in the disturbed subject the structural sense of uncanny displacement and doubling, that "uneasy sense of the unfamiliar within the familiar, the unhomely within the home" (Wigley 1993: 108). Suzanne Keen draws the structural and temporal strands together, offering a sustained consideration of "the return of the repressed" in relation to "centuries-old tradition." She considers also the persistence of "residual" customs and forms, along with the "archaic survival" of equally "archaic practices" as a temporal trace within the social spaces of Casterbridge and its environs in the novel's present (Keen 1998: 127, 132, 134, 140). Tess O' Toole's study of genealogical patterns and familial structures in Hardy also acknowledges the haunting trace: "as a 'spectre,' the genetic product is at once the reincarnation of a figure from the past and an image that has been raised by a guilty party's imagination" (O'Toole 1997: 18–19). Moreover, the spectral inhabits structure or identity in such a way as to displace or disrupt the propriety of the form from within. "Hardy's is a haunted art . . . [in which] material reality is displaced as the goal of representation by shadowy and spectral unrealities," as Jim Reilly avers (1993: 65), reading Hardy as working within a fictional paradigm that, though indebted to mimetic realism, nevertheless disrupts that realism repeatedly and violently from within its own conventions.

One prominent dimension of the spectral is that manifestation of the past in the present, as I have said. The ghost of and from the past leaves its trace in the structures of the present of *The Mayor of Casterbridge*. When we speak of the "past" in relation to *The Mayor of Casterbridge*, this might signal equally a number of traces, none with any precedence over any others. Of personal returns and manifestations of the past there are those who come back from Henchard's personal past: Susan, Lucetta, Elizabeth-Jane, even Newson. There is also the furmity woman, through whom the wife-sale returns to haunt Henchard's public identity, even as it has perpetually haunted his private sense of self. The impersonal past of Casterbridge is acknowledged in a number of ways, not least the mayoral office, and the surrounding land (the Ring, Mai Dun, Diana Multimammia, the history of the mayoral office). A rural past is acknowledged through and traced in the return of events such as the fair at Weydon Priors or the skimmington ride. Then there are the "past" texts that inform the structure of the novel – Greek and Shakespearian tragedy, the Old Testament, references to French novels, to Miltonic monsters, or the novels of Walter Scott, and Gothic fiction. Such traces, or "remains" as Nicholas Royle describes them, are not "the remains of something that was once present." They are, instead, that which, in being spectral, prevents "any present, and any experience of the presence, from being completely itself" (Royle 1995: 61). This ghostly trace has the ability to disrupt not only the present moment but also any sense of identity. It may even write itself as "dead men's traits" in the sleeping face of Elizabeth-Jane (*MC* 126).

This is not a simple or single instance in itself. It reiterates in part an earlier moment in the novel, when Susan and her daughter return to Weydon Priors, the mother's features being figured imperfectly in the daughter's as the manifestation of "Nature's powers of continuity" (*MC* 21). Thus, ghosting returns, while the return is always ghostly. Furthermore, the earlier scene that anticipates the haunting of Elizabeth-Jane is itself a return. The question of the return is not limited to the reiteration noted between the faces of the two women, as the text suggests. For as Hardy tells the reader, "The scene in its broad aspect had so much of its previous character . . . that it might . . . have been the afternoon following the previously recorded episode" (*MC* 21). This is but one instance of the persistence of return as evidenced through "particularities within a continuum," which in turn establishes "the anthropology of a location . . . explicitly relating the behaviour of present individuals to that of countless predecessors" (Kramer 1987: xxiii, xxii).

In that we can read a doubling movement of revenance, where movement haunts moment, we can suggest that the entire order of the novel is predicated on the troping of return as the spectral persistence disordering order and identity from within, as an otherness within the text. Even as Elizabeth-Jane's face is haunted by Susan's, and even as this recalls the earlier moment of return on the part of the two women, so that moment of return, in recalling the supposedly "initial" scene of arrival at the fair and the subsequent wife-sale, implies the continuous structural movement of displacement and disjointing. To this can be added a reading of the wife-sale, not as some simple or single originary event generating the unfolding of the narrative but as itself a moment of a form of "archaic survival" that, in turn, belongs to forms of economic "traffic" that "structure the novel" (Keen 1998: 140). This "structuring" is also at the same time a disturbance that inhabits the structure, disordering as the necessity of an ordered form, as an internal "other" that haunts and makes possible the very form itself. It disturbs the unity or identity of all structures, whether we are speaking of the human subject, an architectural form, the mapping of the town, or the form of the novel.

The spectral can be seen on occasions in acts of uncanny doubling, a form of return. For example, Elizabeth-Jane, on visiting her mother's grave, encounters a figure "in mourning like herself . . . [who] might have been her wraith or double" (*MC* 134). Lucetta – she is the "wraith" – is also an uncanny double of Susan Newson/Henchard on one occasion, the "double of the first" (p. 250). Elizabeth-Jane is herself a double of sorts. Not Henchard's but Newson's Elizabeth-Jane, she doubles even as she is haunted by the dead child whose place she has taken, whose identity is signed and simultaneously displaced in the reiteration of the name. That "Elizabeth-Jane" is a proper name given to two characters sharing the same mother (whose features "ghost" the second daughter's face) is important. For it alerts us to the importance of textual haunting, of haunting as textual, where even the act of writing can return, though never quite signifying that which it had done. This is a sign of repetition *and* displacement, return *and* disturbance. In addition, Henchard sees in Farfrae's face the double of his dead brother (p. 49), and this has an "uncanny appeal for Henchard" (Wilson 1997: xxv). Finally, Henchard is doubled (as is Lucetta) by the skimmington ride effigy that, as Suzanne Keen so appositely suggests, comes "back to haunt him" (Keen 1998: 140).

Keith Wilson speaks of the effects and figures of doubling in his introduction to the novel (Wilson 1997: xxviii). Such patterns and the "phantasms" of which they are composed (for all involve the images and memories of the dead) do nothing so much as signify the operations of each other, rather than intimating either a "reality" beyond the text or an origin or source of which the text is a copy. Indeed, the uncanny mo(ve)ment of revenance and disturbing reiteration comes from within a figure or face to disturb identity and disconcert the subject. In this operation, the ghostly trace, which in reiterating constantly operates in a manner similar to the simulacrum, "calls into question the authority and legitimacy of its model" (Durham 1998: 3). Such doubling and the rhythm of return of which it is a part destabilize more than the identity of particular characters. It is disruptive of "distinct domains and temporalities . . . [to] the extent to which they increasingly appear as the echoes or doubles of one another" (Durham 1998: 16). To put this another way, with direct reference to *The Mayor of Casterbridge*, it is not only a question of particular characters being haunted. The various spatial and temporal boundaries of the novel that are found increasingly to be permeable and capable of being transgressed signify one another's functions and potential interpretive roles in the novel.

This is the case wherever one is speaking of the "haunting" of the present by the past, signaled in the numerous returns discussed above, all of which permeate arbitrarily defined temporal boundaries. This can be read at the level of particular words themselves. Through archaic, untimely words such as "burgh and champaign" (*MC* 30), the present of the narrative is disrupted. Words such as "furmity" and "skimmington" also signify an anachronic haunting; traces of other times and other modes of expression, they remain ruinous and fragmentary, giving no access to some originary discourse. There is also spatial movement across boundaries, which involves a temporal emergence of residual archaic practices, as in the eruption of Mixen Lane into the "proper" or familiar space of Casterbridge (Keen 1998: 132).

Keen successfully reads the structure and space of Mixen Lane as the "other" of Casterbridge. Structurally internal to the town, part of it, this liminal site haunts the town and yet returns itself through the manifestation of "archaic practices of an ancient environ" (Keen 1998: 132). Its return is untimely and therefore uncanny, displacing the familiarity and domesticity of Casterbridge that Hardy has worked so hard to project. Yet Mixen Lane is but one figure in the novel simultaneously "at once removed from and infinitely proximate to" (Durham 1998: 17) what we consider to be the novel's present moment and its present action. Thus the world of Michael Henchard and the world of Casterbridge are disturbed in their identities from within by the articulation of alternative structures – others of, within, and as a condition of textual form – that signify, and thereby double, the operations of each other. Hardy's "use of place resonates with personal and social significance" (Greenslade 1994: 55), but such resonance is internally unstable, even as it destabilizes the form in which it emerges.

While a form of return, such haunting is not simply a straightforward temporal arrival from some identifiable prior past. As J. Hillis Miller puts it, "These are under-ground doublings which arise from differential interrelations among elements which are all on the same plane. This lack of ground in some paradigm or archetype means that there is something ghostly about the effects of this . . . type of repetition" (Miller 1982: 6). Speaking of Hardy's fiction in general, Miller motions towards a reading that acknowledges the reiterative, the reciprocally interanimated, and the effect of doubling that articulates Hardy's text. There is that which returns, though never as itself. In its untimely, not to say anachronistic, fashion, this spectral trace articulates – or, rather, disarticulates ahead of either our comprehension or ability to see this disturbance – a dissymmetry comprising a non-identity within identity.

The phantom-text is everywhere. Not particularly Gothic in itself, though none-theless appearing as the trace of a reference, there is the doxical acknowledgment of Susan as " 'The Ghost' " (*MC* 83), a "mere skellinton" (p. 85). Almost immediately upon her death, Susan is reported as having something of a headstone appearance by Mrs. Cuxsom: "And she was as white as marble-stone" (p.120). Susan is immediately replaced in this comment, her face equated with – and ghosted by – the second- or third-hand signification of a material which will form the architectural symbol of her being dead. Of Henchard, Nance Mockridge comments, in that knowing, pre-scient manner peculiar to working women in Gothic novels, "There's a bluebeardy look about en; and 'twill out in time" (p. 86). Not of course, that the Mayor has a dungeon, nor does he chain Susan in it, yet his figure is haunted with a powerful Gothic resonance. Moreover, Nance's prediction points to the "persistence of the unforeseen" (p. 334), as Hardy will put it on almost the final page (which statement, I would argue, is where all the spectral traces return from and to where they might be read as leading us). Her phrase is both economical and excessive: it is an utterance belonging to the cheapest of Gothic thrills, while also resonating in a somewhat uncanny, if not haunted, fashion. Structurally, therefore, her phrase, having to do with time, is disturbed from within, being both timely and untimely, having to do with the persistence of unreadable traces as a condition of temporal disturbance, with which the novel is so concerned.

Other characters are also marked in ways that suggest Gothic convention. Newson is given a ghostly quality in relation to the question of the return. Specifically, he disturbs Henchard: "The apparition of Newson haunted him. He would surely return" (*MC* 300). Conjuror Fall lives outside the town, and therefore outside the boundaries of society, as is typical of figures associated with alchemy and the black arts. His habitation and narrative preparation for the encounter between Henchard and Fall confuse discursive boundaries, intermixing the Gothic, the folkloric, and fairy-tale. The way to Fall's house is "crooked and miry" (p. 185), and Henchard's approach to Fall's home is suggestively eerie: "One evening when it was raining . . . heavily . . . a shrouded figure on foot might have been perceived travelling in the direction of the hazel copse which dripped over the prophet's cot" (pp. 185–6). Even the furmity woman gets in on the Gothic act, for, upon her return, it is remarked that she "had mysteriously hinted . . . that she knew a queer thing or two" (p. 202). Of course, what she knows is merely the information concerning Henchard's past, but her return is part of the general movement of return in the text, while Hardy carefully frames her ominous comment in a manner designed to amplify its portentous aspect.

What will return in this instance is the narrative that already haunts Henchard, as the furmity dealer's citation. While the old woman returns, what returns through her is the trace of the past and, with that, the suppressed truth as that which haunts. Indeed, Hardy engages in a narrative economy of recurrence, by which truth is apprehended as always revenant and revelatory. To put this differently, truth is always spectral and is only known in its iterable appearances, as such, regardless of the logic or rationality of a given narrative moment. The Gothic is one mode of production that allows for an economy of explanation, a logic of representation, to order and rationalize, even as it relies on the non-rational. Yet within that mechanism, there is always the spectral element. Gothic convention is precisely this: convention, structure, and law. Within such convention, however, is that which is irreducible by explanation. What cannot be explained is that the return happens, and that it happens moreover not as the return of some presence to the present, but as the haunted trace. The truth of Henchard's past is coincidental to the general movement of spectral revenance, which the Mayor of Casterbridge is incapable of reading, and which *The Mayor of Casterbridge* barely glimpses.

The technique of repetition at work throughout the novel provides this barely seen spectral condition, even while, within the structures of the text, such reiteration is locally domesticated through the recourse to particularly familiar textual forms, such as the Gothic. Not only are characters read and written as if in a Gothic context, therefore. They behave as though they were characters from a Gothic novel, even as the narrative voice mimics or is haunted by the trace of the Gothic. Elizabeth-Jane is "startled by the apparition of Farfrae" (*MC* 136). Lucetta's face is altered by an encounter with Farfrae also: her face "became – as a woman's face becomes when the man she loves rises upon her gaze like an apparition" (p. 178). There is something decidedly strange, *uncanny*, about Farfrae, that his appearance to two women should be described as an apparition, on both occasions. It even disturbs Hardy in the act of writing, for notice that pause signaled silently in the dash as the writer seeks the most appropriate simile. However, we will have to leave the Scot for a moment.

There are other Gothic traces, too, improper references and ghostly citations without specific origins. The keystone-mask above Lucetta's door (*MC* 142) and the decaying sign of the Three Mariners (pp. 42–3) have a certain Gothic appeal. Furthermore, their ruined, decaying qualities hint at the uncanny, the unfamiliar within the familiar. Suggesting forms of temporal persistence, of the past's ability to return and to disturb, they both signify a certain sinister ineffability that gives the lie to the familiarity and homeliness of the structures – the public house and Lucetta's home – of which they are synecdochic figures. Both serve economically in tracing that "structural slippage from *heimliche* [homely] to *unheimliche* [unhomely] [in which] that which supposedly lies outside the familiar comfort of the home turns out to be inhabiting it all along" (Wigley 1993: 108). Most immediately however, their function is to create that frisson so typically desired in the Gothic. Both the sign and the keystone serve a textual, that is to say a haunting, function, in that they remind us that a "house is not simply an object that may be represented, but is itself a mechanism of representation" (Wigley 1993: 163), whereby in the perception of an image, one encounters a structure of iteration.

We can read such effects at work when we are told how Jopp's cottage is "built of old stones from the long-dismantled priory, scraps of tracery, moulded window-jambs, and arch-labels, being mixed in with the rubble of the walls" (*MC* 221). Those scraps, the ruins of the priory, long since gone, operate as references in a number of ways. Priories are, of course, favorite ruined sites, often haunted, in Gothic discourse. There is in this image, with its fragments of clauses, the return of the past in the present structure once more, the structure of the cottage and the structure of the sentence. The former is structurally (dis-)composed by the material traces of a former structure; the latter is structurally (dis-)composed by the haunting traces of Gothic discourse that, in their phantomatic inscription, enact a ghostly transference in the image of the cottage, from its being simply an object to be represented, to being a mechanism of representation. In this, the text does nothing so much as displace itself, endlessly. For the operation of haunting signals not simply a prior moment, if that is even the purpose. Instead, it serves to signal a certain spectral dislocation that belongs to the novel as a whole, signaling the ruins of other ruins, the keystone, the decaying sign, the Ring (chapter 11), even as they in turn signify other traces, and the other of the trace. This movement, the Gothic "oscillation," is not merely an intertextual feature; it is of a different order.

The priory stones are therefore readable, as are other structural and architectonic features, in a manner similar to more explicitly narrowly textual referents, such as those from the Old Testament or tragedy, as we have already suggested. The "stones," in being the traces of an absent discourse, being performative fragments and ruins, are not there to suggest that the reader simply turn back to the literary past, to some prior form as the novel's inheritance or what might, too blithely, be described as "context." Instead, they acknowledge an inescapably haunted quality within the structure of any textual form. In this, they may be read as signifying those other momentary, fleeting textual traces, such as Hardy's reference to "The *misérables* who would pause on the remoter bridge" (*MC* 224). There is also that reference to Henchard's face and the "rich *rouge et noir* of his countenance" (p. 67). *The Mayor of Casterbridge* is peppered with French words and phrases, enough certainly that criticism of the 1950s and 1960s would doubtless have read such usage as part of Hardy's overreaching pretensions and a sign of the text's lack of coherence. However, such "foreign" elements while disjointing the text by their obvious, fragmentary "return" (they come to us from somewhere that is neither Hardy's Wessex, nor his English), also, in the two examples above, appear to signal other novels, albeit in the most fleeting and undecidable manner. Are these references to Hugo and Stendhal? Can we tell, can we be certain? The answer cannot be an unequivocal rejection of such a notion, any more than it can be an affirmative response. The momentary inscription of another language appears to install possible textual reference but, equally, remains undecidable as to its purpose, and thus haunts the structure of the text. Both references do, however, have a somewhat Gothic resonance. The *misérables* are those who *haunt* the marginally located bridges, already mentioned above. *Rouge et noir*, the coloring of red and black, is "Satanic" and is associated with Henchard throughout the novel (p. 351n67).

There still remains, though, a question pertaining to the trace of the Gothic, which we can only acknowledge for the moment before moving on. Why does the Gothic persist in Hardy's text? This may well be undecidable and thus belongs to that order of disturbance within the structure of identity which the haunting anachronic trace within the time of the novel causes to occur. What can be remarked, though, is that Gothic discourse relies on the external sign – decaying ruins, mad monks, skeletons, ghosts – disturbing the subject internally. The Gothic is in part a structure of representation that generates unease, discomfort, and foreboding. One's self is disturbed, haunted, by that which appears outside the self. Nevertheless, as in any good Gothic tale, the frightened subject, for all the unsettling sensations, frequently becomes obsessed with finding what might be behind those apparitions, those manifestations. We might suggest that this in part is the Gothic tale that haunts *The Mayor of Casterbridge*, for, inaugurated by a primitive act of the wife-sale, the novel is doomed to become haunted by this first moment, becoming in turn a story of uncanny obsession, namely Henchard's, who finds significant signs everywhere. Without pursuing this further, merely to hint at a possible way of reading events, it is important nonetheless to register the internal disturbance, the production of the uncanny precisely in the place where one should feel most like oneself – at home. When Henchard feels himself most at home, as the titular mayor and symbolic figurehead of the town, then haunting begins, the past returns, and everywhere the forces of doubling and iterability erupt.

We have seen already how devices of doubling and repetition, which are intrinsic to the novel's structure and identity, articulate *The Mayor of Casterbridge*, and yet disturb that very form from within. Thus, arguably, the entire novel may be considered as an exploration of the uncanny. There are numerous local and immediate instances of the experience of the uncanny in the novel. Henchard feels haunted by Newson, as we know already. Moreover, the reader is told repeatedly that he is a superstitious man. Henchard is first revealed as "superstitious" through his decision to visit Conjuror Fall (*MC* 185). Though this moment is not in itself uncanny (though arguably Henchard's trip to Fall is meant to induce an uncanny sensation in the reader), the next instance of Henchard's superstitiousness is, and deliberately so. Henchard is ruminating on his misfortune over the reckless crop selling:

> The movements of his mind seemed to tend to the thought that some power was working against him.

"I wonder," he asked himself with eerie misgiving; "I wonder if it can be that somebody has been roasting a waxen image of me, or stirring an unholy brew to confound me! I don't believe in such power; and yet – what if they should ha' been doing it!" . . . These isolated hours of superstition came to Henchard in time of moody depression . . . (*MC* 190–1)

While we may read the passage as remarking the residue of a superstition imbued with the discourse of folkloric mythology, the passage is notable nonetheless for its sense of the uncanny, of that internal power and the sensation of "eerie misgiving." Later, following the skimmington ride, we are told that "the sense of the supernatural was strong in this unhappy man" (*MC* 297). In this assessment of Henchard's response to the effigy there is the sense that Hardy may be read as explaining away the uncanny feeling through recourse to the idea of superstition, even as Henchard experiences it. Yet uncannily, perhaps, that earlier speculation concerning the waxen image may also be read as one more example of the "persistence of the unforeseen," while the effigy marks a form of return of Henchard's fear, even as it physically returns via the river.

Freud acknowledges that the writer, any writer, in creating uncanny effects in a narrative world otherwise predicated on "common reality" through the use of events that "never or rarely happen in fact," appeals to the "superstitiousness" that we have allegedly left behind (Freud 1997: 227). In a novel concerned so much with residual forms of haunting, however, the very trope of superstition as archaic pre-modern residue is readable as the uncanny manifestation of the haunting trace. Hardy's narrative is constructed so as to reveal Henchard as haunted by superstition, while playing on the possible residue of superstition in the reader, and yet maintaining a distance from such irrational sensations by doubting whether "anything should be called curious in concatenations of phenomena" (*MC* 204).

There are, however, clearly uncanny moments for Henchard that have little or nothing to do with superstition. Towards the end of his life Henchard is described thus: "He rose to his feet, and stood like a dark ruin, obscured by 'the shade from his own soul upthrown'" (*MC* 326). One of the most complex and overdetermined of sentences in the novel, this delineation of Henchard addresses both his own being haunted, suffering from the disturbance of the uncanny, and the uncanny haunting to which *The Mayor* is prone. The ghostly citation with which the sentence concludes traces a double movement at least. It comes from Shelley's *Revolt of Islam*, as does the phrase "dark ruin." While reading a citation, and one that, in its signifying operation, refers us to those other ghostly citations, we are impressed by the figure, not merely of the soul, but of the "shade" also. Conventionally, the reading of that "shade" should imply a shadow. However, there is also at work in this image the more archaic sense of "shade," meaning "ghost" or "specter." The phrase "dark ruin" is itself a ruin, a fragment, an improper citation that haunts the sentence and that does service as a simile for Henchard, even as it echoes beyond the image of Henchard, or, indeed, any animate creature, to hint at the Ring and other architectural sites and remnants out of which Casterbridge is composed, and by which it is haunted.

Not long prior to this moment, at which the return of Newson prompts Henchard's sense of being haunted once again, Henchard returns to the place from where the novel begins (*MC* 318–19). In this instance of reciprocal return – Henchard's return is counter-signed by the return of place – Susan's own words return to Henchard, and, uncannily, to the reader also: for her words are reported directly, from her own initial utterance, while they are also adrift from her, from the grave as it were, as a disembodied voice, the voice of the other, haunting Henchard's memory (p. 319). The sense of the uncanny is quite startling here, for even as we read the words on the page, so we hear and see those words imprinted in the memory, arriving from some other place, and yet from within at the same time. In this, Susan's voice is doubly haunting, for in its movement of return and address that, shockingly – uncannily – places the reader in the place of Henchard as addressee, it carries in it the anticipation of Henchard's will, which is reprinted on to the page, and there for every successive generation of readers (p. 333). J. Hillis Miller has provided an eloquent reading of the will as a "terrifying series of negative performances, spoken from the grave," and as a "kind of ghostly negative that . . . has positive existence" (Miller 1998: 110, 112). The will, directly before us, comes back as a fragment of Henchard's voice that, despite its commands to forget him, haunts us all the more.

"That Elizabeth-Jane Farfrae be not told of my death, or made to grieve on account of me.
"& that I be not bury'd in consecrated ground.
"& that no sexton be asked to toll the bell.
"& that nobody is wished to see my dead body.
"& that no murners walk behind me at my funeral.
"& that no flours be planted on my grave.
"& that no man remember me.
"To this I put my name.
                    "Michael Henchard" (*MC* 333)

What this act of narration from beyond the grave suggests to Miller, quite correctly in my view, is the ghostly condition of all narrative: "all narration is a murmur from beyond the grave . . . killing it as living speech and resurrecting it at the same time as ghostly, remembered speech" (Miller 1998: 112). Henchard's address provides exemplary and undeniable proof of, on the one hand, the fact of his death and, on the other, the return of his death, the paradoxical iterability of his finitude that also and at the same time turns us back to, and returns to us, as other than itself, the text of *The Mayor of Casterbridge* awaiting the act of reading, while signaling in this movement and spacing (that spacing which is the effect of haunting) that reading is always an endless work, remaining to come, again and again, as part of the structural openness and instability of historicity. It is through this that the sense of the uncanny is produced, the specter glimpsed. Through this redoubling, displacing, and regenerative rhythm, the ghost survives, and we as readers are uncannily transformed, destined to be the addressees, the recipients, of the will.

If the will offers a formal example of the temporal troubling of writing within itself through the difference on which it relies to communicate beyond any initial context or intention, Hardy does not limit the haunting experience of iterable eruption to the act of writing. We read so many instances in *The Mayor* in which something appears to come back or anticipate a return to come. So many events and signs remind us of so many others, and of our having experienced them before, that we may well read the text with a growing sense of that tedious, even oppressive, familiarity. However, perhaps this is the point, structurally at least. There is still the question of structure haunting us here, with which we began. To return to the question of return: what cannot be stressed too often is the proposition that, whether we are speaking of the proper name, the matter of architecture or archaeology, the question of textual traces or cultural events, the office of the mayor in relation to the social order, or a communal identity based on the supposed stasis of civic office, each figure repeats every other. Consider the resounding bells heard by Susan and Elizabeth-Jane on entering the town as one exemplary moment in the novel:

> They came to a grizzled church, whose massive square tower rose unbroken into the darkening sky. . . . From this tower the clock struck eight, and thereupon a bell began to toll with a peremptory clang. The curfew was still rung in Casterbridge . . .
> Other clocks struck eight from time to time – one gloomily from the gaol, another from the gable of an alms-house . . . a row of tall varnished case-clocks . . . joined in one after another . . . then chimes were heard stammering out . . . so that chronologists of the advanced school were appreciably on their way to the next hour before the whole business of the old one was satisfactorily wound up. (*MC* 31)

Each sound reiterates every other in this, even though time is "out of joint," so to speak. The passage, in its movement from clock to clock, from chime to chime, performs the gradual and erratic sounding of the hour, as the narrative moves. The hour is displaced from and within itself, even as each clock re-sounds the temporal punctuation of every other, and spaces the very idea of time. This one scene uncannily suggests the structure of the novel itself, where every form of return or reduplication signifies nothing so much as every other similar form. The clocks set the tone, if you will. Moreover in this temporal disjointing, the performance of which hints that there is no time like the present, there is no single present moment not always already divided, the spectral structure makes itself felt in that residual trace of another time sounding within the present, the medieval curfew bell. Furthermore, the chimes in this scene anticipate and return in the moment, just prior to the election of Farfrae as mayor, when the clocks strike half past eight, and the streets are "curiously silent" (*MC* 151).

The resounding of the time out of time with itself figures aurally both spacing and strata, as well as inevitable temporal registration. The clocks trace the spatial and temporal movements that haunt the town, but also analogically offer a figure for the composition of the novel, in its understanding of subjectivity and historicity. The architectonic resonance is common, and worked out in a particularly rich way in the opening of chapter 11, when Hardy describes Casterbridge:

Casterbridge announced old Rome in every street, alley and precinct . . . It was impossible to dig more than a foot or two deep about the town fields and gardens without coming upon some tall soldier or other . . .

Imaginative inhabitants who would have felt an unpleasantness at the discovery of a comparatively modern skeleton in their gardens, were quite unmoved by these hoary shapes . . . (*MC* 70)

In the same chapter, the Roman amphitheatre, the Ring, is discussed, in particular, the history of recurrence associated with the ruin:

Apart from the sanguinary nature of the games originally played therein, such incidents attached to its past as these; that for scores of years the town gallows had stood at one corner; that in 1705 a woman who had murdered her husband was half strangled and then burnt there . . . In addition to these old tragedies pugilistic encounters almost to the death had come off down to recent dates in that secluded arena . . . though close to the turnpike-road crimes might be perpetrated there unseen at mid-day. (*MC* 71)

What is merely suggested in the first passage by the mention of architectural and archaeological detail is made clearer in the second. The past persists as trace, setting the tone through its ghostly persistence in and disturbance of the present. The remains of architectural detail are "announced" through the present structure of the town, so that the present is represented as disturbed by such traces; the land itself is built upon the remains and return of the past. In the case of the Ring, it is not a question of architectural structure or archaeological remainder. Rather, the persistence is of a particularly spectral kind. Events of a similar nature recur within the same space, so that, as Hardy gradually dematerializes the return of the past – moving from overt structure, to what is hidden or sedimented, and then to forms of recurrence that are altogether more haunting – so he traces a temporal structure of revenance and insistence, of iteration, that is all the more disturbing and uncanny for the return of violence to the same location, as an effective figure of spectral dislocation.

What haunts here, whether one is speaking of the sound of the bells, the description of the town, or the history of the Ring, is the ineluctable recurrence of a ghostly trace. The motif is spectral precisely because it disturbs any sense of presence or the present, any sense of undifferentiated moment or identity. It announces difference and iteration. It is therefore structural, a question of the structure, to repeat myself once more. In this, the novel is less a narrative than a haunted archive, in which the structure is haunted by virtue of the fact that every trace in its return refers to every other trace having the power to do the same, and so overdetermine the present. Hardy capitalizes on the force of repetition, on the returns that he accumulates in a mode of writing as archivization, whereby the numerous traces, citations, references, allusions are gathered. That the novel may be read as having the power to create uncanny feelings in its readers through the endless and differentiated reminders that the present is the storehouse of past echoes and elements is one sign of its being haunted. That every subsequent generation of readers is enjoined to forget Michael Henchard by his will and yet receives his communication so unforgettably is another sign. The haunting condition is that effect by which language effaces itself even as its trace and injunction remain, whether by "language" we signify spoken or written signs or the material traces of other human remains. If we do not read these remains in their disseminating signification of one another and the ways in which they both structure and discompose identity within a given moment and across history, we run the risk of misunderstanding to what extent this is a phantom-text. A haunted and haunting space, *The Mayor of Casterbridge* offers a disorientating experience by which we enter into the true revelation of the historical and one's subjective production as a properly conceived historical being. Not perceiving this, we risk missing Hardy's ghostly communication, and so doom ourselves to live out haunted lives, much as is the case with Michael Henchard.

References and Further Reading

Armstrong, Tim (2000). *Haunted Hardy: Poetry, History, Memory*. Basingstoke: Palgrave.

Barnes, William (1908). *Selected Poems*, ed. Thomas Hardy. London: Henry Frowde.

Durham, Scott (1998). *Phantom Communities: The Simulacrum and the Limits of Postmodernism*. Stanford: Stanford University Press.

Freud, Sigmund (1997). The "Uncanny." In Neil Hertz (ed.), *Writings on Art and Literature* (pp. 193–224). Stanford: Stanford University Press.

Greenslade, William (1994). *Degeneration, Culture and the Novel*. Cambridge: Cambridge University Press.

Hardy, Thomas ([1886] 1987). *The Mayor of Casterbridge*, ed. Dale Kramer. Oxford: Oxford University Press.

Hardy, Thomas (1979). *The Variorum Edition of the Complete Poems of Thomas Hardy*, ed. James Gibson. London: Macmillan.

Keen, Suzanne (1998). *Victorian Renovations of the Novel: Narrative Annexes and the Boundaries of Representation*. Cambridge: Cambridge University Press.

Kramer, Dale (1987). Introduction to Thomas Hardy, *The Mayor of Casterbridge* (pp. xi–xxix). Oxford: Oxford University Press.

Lukacher, Ned (1998). *Time-Fetishes: The Secret History of Eternal Recurrence*. Durham, NC: Duke University Press.

Miller, J. Hillis (1982). *Fiction and Repetition: Seven English Novels*. Cambridge, MA: Harvard University Press.

Miller, J. Hillis (1998). *Reading Narrative*. Norman: University of Oklahoma Press.

O'Toole, Tess (1997). *Genealogy and Fiction: Family Lineage and Narrative Lines*. Basingstoke: Macmillan.

Reilly, Jim (1993). *Shadowtime: History and Representation in Hardy, Conrad and George Eliot*. London: Routledge.

Royle, Nicholas (1995). *After Derrida*. Manchester: Manchester University Press.

Taylor, Dennis (1993). *Hardy's Literary Language and Victorian Philology*. Oxford: Clarendon Press.

Wigley, Mark (1993). *The Architecture of Deconstruction: Derrida's Haunt*. Cambridge, MA: MIT Press.

Wilson, Keith (1997). Introduction to Thomas Hardy, *The Mayor of Casterbridge* (pp. xxi–xli). London: Penguin.

21

Dethroning the High Priest of Nature in *The Woodlanders*

Andrew Radford

Being a bachelor of rather retiring habits the whole of the preparations devolved upon {Giles Winterborne} and his trusty man and familiar Robert Creedle, who did everything that required doing, from making Giles's bed to catching moles in the field. He was a survival from the days when Giles's father held the homestead and Giles was a playing boy. (W 64)

Woven into the verbal texture of *The Woodlanders* (1887) are myriad "survivals" that reflect the residue of a moribund mythology no longer operant in the sheltered recesses of Little Hintock. Robert Creedle is referred to facetiously as a fossilized relic – a quaint but well-intentioned vestige of bygone "days." However, his master Giles Winterborne illustrates the meaning of a "survival" in all its complex tragicomic force as Hardy charts how anthropological myth has atrophied into hollow rhetoric, the principled use of imagination into mannered whimsy, and passionate sympathy into a projective narcissism. *The Woodlanders* articulates a more harrowing recognition than do Hardy's previous novels of an attenuated rural locale in the degree to which its traditional custodian Winterborne, the "priest" of the forest and its archaic culture, is "unmanned" by a socially constructed consciousness. Edward Burnett Tylor, an eminent ethnographer contemporary with Hardy, coined the term "survivals" in his seminal two-volume opus *Primitive Culture* (1871) to designate those mental and physical heirlooms of the distant past which obdurately linger into a later stage of civilization.

Among evidence aiding us to trace the course which the civilization of the world has actually followed, is that great class of facts to denote which I have found it convenient to introduce the term "survivals." These are processes, customs, opinions, and so forth, which have been carried on by force of habit into a new state of society different from that in which they had their original home, and they thus remain as proofs and examples of an older condition of culture out of which a newer has evolved. (Tylor 1903 I: 16)

Hardy's reinflection of Tylor's formulation throws into sharp relief the theme of local attachment to which *The Woodlanders* obsessively returns – a question dominating the fiction and sociology of the nineteenth century and after. At the outset of his literary career, Hardy tries to uncover in folklore a kernel of human response that the prevailing practices of an age cannot entirely smother. He relishes the outlandish pre-Christian practices secretly cherished and maintained by the rural peasantry among whom he grew up – the occult remnants so at odds with the "enlightened" views of the educated classes. However, *The Woodlanders* connotes a discernible darkening of Hardy's artistic vision, since he redefines Tylor's coinage to signify how Winterborne himself is a "survival" whose venerable and unique skills are rendered redundant by "a new state of society" and its avatars, Edred Fitzpiers and Grace Melbury. A glimpse of Winterborne's vocation from "an older condition of culture" is vouchsafed by Hardy's previous published novel, *The Mayor of Casterbridge* (1886):

> It happened that to-day there rose in the midst of them all two or three tall apple trees standing as if they grew on the spot; till it was perceived that they were held by men from the cider districts who came here to sell them, bringing the clay of their county on their boots. (*MC* 154)

When Winterborne is sent to Sherton Abbas to collect the newly educated Grace, whose arrival he awaits with tremulous hope, he carries with him to the muddy market a ten-foot high specimen "appletree" (*W* 34), which not only functions as his heraldic emblem but also invokes the "Wild Man" character of the medieval mummers' play (traditionally portrayed holding a tree). Winterborne, however, possesses neither the untrammeled belligerence nor the perverse lubricity of his medieval counterpart. This "bachelor of rather retiring habits" is everywhere exposed as a figure of static and pathetically vulnerable disconnection, beset by nagging doubts as he moves deeper into regions of hallucination and failure.

Winterborne's crippling constraint is accentuated by the "warming" party he and his "trusty man" Creedle provide for Grace. The Wessex novels are replete with analogous feast occasions: Bathsheba's shearing-supper in *Far From the Madding Crowd*, the "good supper" organized by Mrs. Yeobright to commemorate the return from Paris of her only son Clym (*The Return of the Native*). Normally, the act of feasting would symbolize the reanimating potential of togetherness, a ritualized interaction regulating and renewing social bonds. However, Winterborne senses that his own "homeliness" offends Grace's "acquired tastes" (*W* 176) and the feast is an unmitigated disaster, signaling not only his shortcomings as a host on that evening, but deeper problems which go to the heart of the novel's anthropological dissection of an archaic community in crisis:

> After supper there was a dance, the bandsmen from Great Hintock having arrived some time before. Grace had been away from home so long, and was so drilled in new dances, that she had forgotten the old figures, and hence did not join in the movement. Then

Giles felt that all was over. As for her, she was thinking, as she watched the gyrations, of a very different measure that she had been accustomed to tread with a bevy of sylph-like creatures in muslin in the music-room of a large house, most of whom were now moving in scenes widely removed from this, both as regarded place, and character. (*W* 70)

What was conceived as an opportunity for Winterborne's Hintock neighbors to rejoice in their own well-being, unfazed by a sense of class anxiety, only discloses glaring social gaps and regionally based power-relations. Old Melbury tries to distance himself from his "homelier" guests and so has little appreciation for the sacrament of solidarity which feasting epitomizes. Winterborne is complicit in his own downfall by inspecting himself through the distorting "lens" of what he believes to be Grace's patronizing attitude to the "folk" as peasant, poor, self-trained, and marginal. What is at issue here, as elsewhere in *The Woodlanders*, is Winterborne's capability to promote social cohesion through what the narrator terms his "gentle conjuror's touch." Hardy inquires who is empowered to revive the ceremonies of sylvan faith that are irretrievably waning in Little Hintock.

The fecund, quasi-mystical connection supposed to exist between Winterborne and his lush environment is what *The Woodlanders* crafts a mystical craving for, even as it repeatedly confounds and punishes the taciturn countryman for this rare affinity. When he descends from the great elm on which John South is fixated in his final illness, it is like a tree-spirit detaching itself: "the tree seemed to shiver, then to heave a sigh: a movement was audible, and Winterborne dropped almost noiselessly to the ground" (*W* 87). Although his "gentle conjuror's touch" with the orchards implies he may be best situated to counteract Old South's forlorn and terrified obsessiveness, Winterborne is usurped by the ambitious young physician Edred Fitzpiers, whose Arthurian-Norman name implies cultivation and urbanity in its modish antiquity. Fitzpiers is fascinated by arcane and exotic cases of psychic derangement induced by woodland isolation. Henry Joseph Moule, a respected antiquarian who became curator of the Dorset County Museum, refers to the source of Old South's dread in a letter to Hardy as the "elm-tree totem." The word "totem" first appeared in John Long's *Voyages and Travels of an Indian Interpreter and Trader* (1791), where it was employed to delineate the Chippewa belief in a guardian spirit that assumed the form of a particular animal (e.g., a bear, elk, or moose) that the Chippewa thereafter refused to eat and kill.

The real efflorescence of interest in totemism began with John Ferguson McLennan's *Primitive Marriage* (1865), and especially his essay on "The Worship of Animals and Plants" (1869–70), which Hardy may have read. The terms "totem" and "totemism" passed into general circulation in English when Sir James Frazer published his seminal survey *Totemism* in 1887, the same year as Hardy's *Woodlanders*. Marty South explains how her ailing father perceives the elm outside their cottage as "an evil spirit," "exactly his own age" sprouting up "when he was born on purpose to rule him, and keep him as its slave" (*W* 93). In the section of *Primitive Culture* devoted to animistic "survivals," E. B. Tylor details how tree-worship stubbornly persists in remote rural settlements:

The peasant folklore of Europe still knows of willows that bleed and weep and speak when hewn, of the fairy maiden that sits within the fir-tree, of that old tree in Rugaard forest that must not be felled, for an elf dwells within, of that old tree on the Heinzenberg near Zell, which uttered its complaint when the woodman cut it down, for in it was Our Lady, whose chapel now stands upon the spot. (Tylor 1903 II: 201)

Old South keeps time to the movements of his elm – "As the tree waved South waved his head, making it his fugleman with abject obedience," and believes it will fall on him. His destructive fixation on the tree in its temporal and ever-decaying condition renders him a being impaired; "Nurse nature" no longer has the capacity to heal a wounded spirit: "There [it] stands, threatening my life every minute that the wind do blow" (*W* 84). His insistence on his magical tree does not supply him with an increment of independence but an accentuated reliance which leads to his own debilitation and death, and it becomes a perverse source of suffering for his two dependants, Winterborne and Marty. When asked about Old South's condition, Winterborne tells Fitzpiers that "Others have been like it afore in Hintock" (*W* 151). Here a visionary connection or a phenomenal relationship with a natural locality has lapsed into a neurotic fancy, not a sacred faith. As a consequence, Old South has become estranged from his life-supporting woodland labor and, ultimately, from the Hintock community because of his fixation. Hardy underlines this point of deracination through arboreal paranoia by showing how Winterborne's destructive operation on the elm, whose lower boughs are lopped off before it is cut down ("shrouding" as it is called in Little Hintock), is inextricably intertwined with the falling in of lives which restricts his tenure of the cottages where the Souths also dwell, because Old South is the last life in the life-holding. Half his income, and Marty's modest residence, is taken away at a stroke.

The link between Old South and the elm swaying outside his window is a macabre parody of Winterborne's "sympathy between himself and the fir, oak, or beech" (*W* 58): a quasi-mystical correspondence between woodlander and trees has degenerated into neurasthenic torment which contorts and exhausts the spirit instead of ennobling it. When demanding that South's tree be cut down, Fitzpiers argues "what's a tree beside a life!" (*W* 93). Winterborne warns that the tree is Mrs. Charmond's property, but the doctor ripostes that he will inaugurate "a new era forthwith" (*W* 93) by cutting down the tree. He exists in ironic relation to his own origin as a member of an ancient local family whose name invokes the most traditional of English trees: the Fitzpierses of Oakbury-Fitzpiers. Thus the determined rationality of a scientist and decadent aesthete supersedes tradition and demands the institution of a fresh method of doing things: the worthless lumber of old faiths that have fallen into pernicious superstition must be cleared away.

Winterborne, acting on Fitzpiers' counsel, fells the elm, but when the deranged patient sees the vacant patch of sky left behind he has a fit and dies of shock. Fitzpiers' blindness to the virulence of the elm inadvertently kills the old man. By having the tree removed, Fitzpiers modernizes South's perception by showing him the very absence which the old man has been at pains to repress in and through his totem fantasy. The felling of John South's elm enacts the notion of dissociating traditional affiliation and the institution of artificial liaisons in their place, which not only comprises Old Melbury's lucrative livelihood but also imbues a narrative of romantic severance initiated by Barber Percomb's cutting of Marty's chestnut hair – the daughter tempted by material necessity to sell her natural adornment to support an ailing parent. The consequences of felling South's tree, an act whose seriousness Winterborne cannot as yet fully apprehend, clashes with the blackly comic effect of Fitzpiers' crass exclamation, "Damned if my remedy hasn't killed him!" (*W* 94). Fitzpiers kills off what he should preserve by his excessive reasoning upon the intricate mechanisms and agencies of the irrational and the inspirational. In the novel felling the elm becomes a criminal act (technically a theft), since it is performed without the authorization of their prosperous neighbor Mrs. Charmond. The civilized and rational law that safeguards her rights as estate owner would have the effect of protecting this "survival" of tree-worship, which was historically a persistent subversion of Christianity.

The confrontation between Fitzpiers and Winterborne intensifies on Midsummer Eve when the village maidens participate in the pagan "survival" of sowing hemp seed under moonlight to cast a spell that will bring forth a reaper (lover) into material form:

> [Grace Melbury] flew round the fatal bush where the undergrowth narrowed to a gorge. Marty arrived at her heels just in time to see the result. Fitzpiers had quickly stepped forward in front of Winterborne, who, disdaining to shift his position had turned on his heel; and then the surgeon did what he would not have thought of doing but for Mrs Melbury's encouragement and the sentiment of an eve which effaced conventionality. Stretching out his arms as the white figure burst upon him he captured her in a moment, as if she had been a bird. (*W* 133)

Grace Melbury's impetuous foray into this "low" culture of nature worship ironically results in capture by a louche member of "high" society. Hardy's pointed use of the word "captured" may be read in the light of the social evolutionary tradition of anthropological research, typified by J. F. McLennan's *Primitive Marriage: An Inquiry into the Origin of the Form of Capture in Marriage Ceremonies* (1865). The two chief sources of information about the early history of civil society, McLennan claimed at the outset of *Primitive Marriage*, were studies of existing primitive peoples and those of the "symbols" of more advanced nations. Here McLennan introduced his own "method of survivals": we "trace everywhere, disguised under a variety of symbolical forms in the higher layers of civilisation, the rude modes of life and forms of law with which the examination of the lower makes us familiar" (McLennan [1865] 1970: 11–12). *Primitive Marriage* is centrally concerned with "bride capture" – the ancient custom whereby, after a contract of marriage, the bridegroom or his companions were required to feign stealing the bride, carrying her off from her family by superior force.

By contrast with cases of real abduction, McLennan observed, the symbol was distinguished by the preceding marriage contract, which was then validated by the organized, concerted act of capturing the bride. Initially, McLennan posited, it appeared that bride capture was the survival of earlier periods of lawlessness in which women, like other forms of property, were seized by the most powerful men. The idea of Grace Melbury as a piece of "property" acquires bitterly sardonic force in *The Woodlanders*. As she indignantly notes, even her doting father Melbury seems to consider her a mere "chattel" (*W* 135), and the two forms of possession are closely related. Later Robert Creedle will agonizingly describe his master Winterborne's failure to secure Grace entirely in terms of her father's other material possessions: "Ye've lost a hundred load o' timber well seasoned; ye've lost five hundred pound in good money; ye've lost a stone-windered house that's big enough to hold a dozen families" (*W* 229).

It is the native Winterborne, the man most closely involved with the Hintock trade in trees and their by-products (apples, bark, spars), who should be, in McLennan's terminology, the most "powerful" man throughout this scene. Winterborne's affiliation with the Hintock trees evokes communal obligations rooted in locality and a profound comprehension of his temporal heritage, which is opposed to deracinating ambition and the emergent fashion of "sight-seeing." Fitzpiers, in restless search of romantic sensations, should be at a considerable disadvantage here, lacking any sense of the embeddedness of this community's history in its environment. His capacity for enjoyment and woodland appreciation stems from the established difference between himself and those he observes. Fitzpiers dreads and avoids any familiarity with the woods, which he finds alternately either revolting or stultifying. But it is this rakish interloper who captures Grace in the turmoil of the husband-conjuring ceremony and not Winterborne, who paradoxically appears both literally and metaphorically out of touch because he is stymied (and ultimately destroyed) by the *chivalrous* traits we would expect Fitzpiers to personify in a conventional social structure. These two male figures embody contrasting perceptions of power at play in the dense, all-enclosing forest setting. Winterborne's inability to protect his childhood sweetheart from the ruses of his more insouciant romantic rival reveals how easily the ethos of the predatory cosmopolite can infiltrate this seemingly sheltered corner and oust its traditional forms and custodians.

Winterborne's "manliness" in this scene is an ever-withering sexless force, in stark contrast to the exploitative sensualism of Fitzpiers, for whom the dynamics of desire are neither sympathetic nor lasting, but variable and momentary. Winterborne's meditative isolation only highlights the decadent excess to which Fitzpiers is repeatedly prone. The contradiction in him of the roles of Platonic idealist and incurable materialist seeking the next immoral escapade or fleeting frisson makes him a distinct, less principled variation on the type that includes Angel Clare and *The Well-Beloved's* Jocelyn Pierston (there is a kinship in name). Fitzpiers struggles to release himself from the physical grip of the natural milieu yet is dragged back by sexual imperatives into a satyrean cycle of seduction and abandonment. The primitive urge for license, of which he is both reluctant victim and triumphant hierophant, overwhelms his pseudo-scientific aspiration to ascertain by dissection the point at which the ideal touches the real. Hardy perceives the sexual force inhabiting Fitzpiers to be the dominant natural energy at play in human affairs. Moreover, his infidelities are not just casual but, in the entire pattern of *The Woodlanders*, crystallize a profound imbalance in the natural order which weakens and demoralizes Winterborne himself.

Within minutes of seizing Grace and proclaiming that he will keep her there forever, Fitzpiers transfers his attention to the hoydenish Suke Damson, whom he chases across the fields. The patrician Fitzpiers predictably codes Suke as the proverbial country wench – trope of the female laborer's potentially corrosive sexuality coupled with its witch-like attraction. He re-enacts with her the "superstitious sowing" in a hay mead under the full moon. D. H. Lawrence's *Study of Thomas Hardy* (1914) misconstrues Fitzpiers' impudent daring by dismissing him as "a weak, pitiable person," whose return to nature is at best specular, trivial, and touristic. The scalding irony which Lawrence fails to register is that the physician's languid disdain for social norms that dictate presumptuously to experience enables him to woo Grace away from a local beau and realize his desires through emphatic action. He is neither interested in nor discouraged by the mores of his woodland world, and he effortlessly violates its pagan rituals and its women. Indeed, his unfeigned delight in playing the role of recklessly flamboyant bohemian demonstrates an ability not only to survive, but to thrive, unlike the resigned stoic Winterborne, who is supposedly "perfectly at home in the woods" yet thwarted by civilized inhibition. While Winterborne "pursues doggedly a downward path to a miserable grave," compelled by Grace Melbury to espouse the chivalric maxim that counsels repression of sexual appetites, Fitzpiers deliberately indulges his "grosser passions." This extrovert virility allows him to deal with the vicissitudes that his own disruptive energies stir into action on Midsummer Eve.

That Fitzpiers is able to manipulate the midsummer "survival" evidences to what degree this festivity has lost whatever religious prestige it might once have possessed. The sowing has become an "ungodly performance" (*W* 132) – tawdry, injurious and ill adapted to the exigencies of contemporary life. In the complex experience that is Hardy's promiscuous discovery of time and its circumstance in his fictions, he is quick to divulge the threadbare vestiges of a community's former vigor as an integrated social structure, and seems doubtful as to whether it is possible, or even desirable, to revive mysterious beliefs such as those which form the ancient core of sowing. Whereas his friend William Barnes habitually saw the newest views of life intruding with predatory pervasiveness on the ordered calm of his poetic landscape, Hardy reacts with a sophisticated skepticism as to the true worth of these arcane folk customs.

The ritual of scattering hemp seed was originally related to a primitive conception of marriage designed to render the vegetation fecund by a process of "imitative" magic; that is to say, actual sexual union was intended to induce fertility in humans, crops, and animals. Fitzpiers indulges his irrepressible sexuality partly out of a malicious boredom, and there is an irony here that Hardy exploits with malevolent relish.

Given that these midsummer ceremonials were originally anchored in orgiastic fertility rites, Fitzpiers may be the only one acting in this anthropological context with faultless propriety! His predilection for German Idealist philosophy which privileges the interior rhythms of the mind above seasonal fluctuations empowers him to view only the life of his desire cast onto things, notably young women. To retire to a haycock with the compliant Suke Damson is an appropriate narrative resolution, however distasteful and blameworthy it may seem from a late Victorian bourgeois standpoint. Winterborne, on the other hand, about to be dispossessed of his cottage, epitomizes the diffidence that falters, and stands empty-handed. His need to conform to Grace's newly acquired standards of decorous propriety leads on Midsummer Eve to erotic frustration and perpetual futility rather than to cathartic release. He peers fitfully at his environment instead of dwelling steadily within it. Winterborne is too "noble" to fulfill his baser promptings: if his caste had been "higher" his morality might have been beneficially "lower." Perhaps, Hardy hints, Winterborne's sexual passivity and his delicate, deferential chivalry are as reprehensible at this juncture as Fitzpiers' willful pose of narcissistic detachment.

So the memorable image of Winterborne and his heraldic emblem of a "specimen appletree," far from implying a proud embodiment of the earth's overflowing ripeness, acquires a sobering pathos in the aftermath of the felling of Old South's totem-elm and the Midsummer Eve "survival." Winterborne's "gentle conjuror's touch," if permitted free rein, might have saved John South (and the cottages) whereas the remedial effects of Fitzpiers' empirical science only precipitated his death. Yet Winterborne's "marvellous power of making trees grow" (*W* 58) as a magical possession of the vibrant physical milieu is continually problematized, especially when he is transmuted by Grace Melbury into a whimsical wood-god at the end of chapter 28, a pivotal point in the novel. As she watches her husband Fitzpiers going off to meet his mistress Felice Charmond on the docile mare given to her by Winterborne, the man himself emerges out of the valley. Rays of the declining sun, which irradiated the white coat of Fitzpiers' horse as he disappeared into the distance, now burnish the blades of Winterborne's cider-making apparatus. With a resurgence of affection for what she presumes are his untarnished country virtues, Grace views Winterborne as the mystical beneficiary of the Hintocks in all its thriving abundance and variety. She desperately wants to believe that her childhood companion has been transfigured by the season:

> He looked and smelt like Autumn's very brother, his face being sunburnt to wheat-colour, his eyes blue as corn-flowers, his sleeves and leggings dyed with fruit stains, his hands clammy with the sweet juice of apples, his hat sprinkled with pips, and everywhere about him that atmosphere of cider which at its first return each season has such an indescribable fascination for those who have been born and bred among the orchards. Her heart rose from its late sadness like a released bough; her senses revelled in the sudden lapse back to Nature unadorned. The consciousness of having to be genteel because of her husband's profession, the veneer of artificiality which she had acquired at the fashionable schools, were thrown off, and she became the crude country girl of her latent, early instincts.

Nature was bountiful, she thought. No sooner had she been cast aside by Edred Fitz-piers, than another being, impersonating chivalrous and undiluted manliness, had arisen out of the earth, ready to her hand. This, however, was an excursion of the imagination which she did not wish to encourage, and she said suddenly, to disguise the confused regard which had followed her thoughts, "Did you meet my husband?" (*W* 185–6)

This is not uneducated vision, however, but Grace's effort to contain the threat of Winterborne's difference by resituating him within the cozy category of idealized peasant. The man who collected Grace from Sherton Abbas market standing under his specimen apple tree is now coated with traces of his vocation, the pips and flecks of apple flesh. Instead of being filled with a sense of personal distress, brooding over how "some kernels" in White-Hart Vale are "as unsound as her own situation" (*W* 184), Grace thinks "Nature is bountiful" after Winterborne's emergence. Her weaving around Winterborne's form wispy poeticisms hints at a failure rationally to regulate her conduct by balancing the flighty and fantastical with a clear-sighted view of the restricted possibilities of married life.

Grace's indulgence of "imagination" during this scene, as opposed to mature and measured scrutiny, marks her out as an embryonic transcendentalist destined for the arms of Fitzpiers, who seeks to mediate nature through technology. Through the suspiciously sub-Keatsian flourishes and literary generalizations, it seems that for Grace the Hintocks are no longer a tangible locale but rather a sylvan topos. Far from recovering a sharpened awareness of the particularities of her immediate surroundings, Grace distances herself from its grimier associations by aggressively stylizing Winterborne and the tools of his trade. Caught between a frivolous nostalgia for treading the old tracks and a keen desire for rapid cultural advancement, Grace endows the countryman with a prelapsarian innocence, striving to sublimate her attraction; for she does enjoy Winterborne sexually, but only as a psychological enigma always outside her rarefied social sphere.

As Hardy registers here, Grace's constructions of idealized purity are fraught with fears of previous contact (and thereby contamination) and worries of possible rebellion or threat. Hardy's narrative participates in and enables, while simultaneously contesting, such forms of pastoral representation and appropriation. Grace at the outset of this "moment of vision" recalls the suburbs, a new kind of living-space, a simulacrum of the tranquil country retreat within the ambit of the bustling metropolis, where manicured lawns and imported ornamental evergreens stand in for Hintock meadows and pasture. Grace "cultivates" this vision of Winterborne from a suburban perspective, fed by a flippant residual Romanticism, picked up from her fashionable finishing school, which makes her unwilling, or unable, to privilege clear outward perception over the erratic promptings of solipsistic inwardness.

Grace's "excursion of the imagination" not only alludes to Wordsworth's long poem but also underlines to what extent "imagination" has lapsed from a means of fostering a healthy, therapeutic relationship with nature to whimsies which are trite, insubstantial, and transient. Grace's exercise of "imagination" is not a positive sign of social integration or spiritual aspiration but an index of the perceptual aberrations to which her callow mind is repeatedly prone. Her re-vision of Winterborne as a resplendent figure who not only appears to merge with but presides over the region shows how vulnerable she is to dizzy raptures that evade, stifle, or negate altogether the realm of concrete commitment. Geoffrey Thurley remarks that "Giles is a Dionysiac worshipper of the earth and the seasons . . . a pagan" (Thurley 1975: 119). It is difficult to imagine Winterborne as a "Dionysiac worshipper" at this point, given his lonely self-absorption, while his "pagan" status is undercut by Grace's view of him rising like a new Adam out of the earth, "impersonating chivalrous and undiluted manliness" (*W* 186).

Just as Barber Percomb transmutes Marty South's natural adornment into the artifice that will safeguard Mrs. Charmond's appearance from the wasting effects of age, so Grace converts Winterborne's intelligently natural culture into an aesthetic conceit, fixing it as a "timeless" construct. Hardy also exploits the irony that if Grace's extravagant identification of Winterborne with the cider-making process is carried to its logical denouement, then this figure of ostensible natural fruition must surely be vulnerable to John Barleycorn's fate, or to being pressed like his own apples. In the autumn rites harvesting is associated with mortality. Hardy implies that we must accept the inevitable decline and disappearance of the old year-spirit, and its replacement, achieved by often vicious means, by a redoubtable new force. Winterborne *should* be dislodged – only, of course, Fitzpiers is grotesquely unfit to be crowned Little Hintock's new priest of nature.

Grace's fey pastoral thought-adventure conjures up an Emersonian "Nature" where "all mean egotism vanishes" and the "greatest delight which the fields and woods minister to is the suggestion of an occult relation between man and the vegetable" (Emerson 1971–87 I: 140). Yet her rapt regard completely smothers the fact that Winterborne typifies a genuinely humane knowledge to which her modish finishing school and Fitzpiers' ominous dabbling into esoteric lore could never lay claim. The hallucinatory intensity of her "Autumn's very brother" gloss evinces more about her status as an irremediably *split* person than it does about Winterborne, whose peculiarities are ignored while she indulges her fantasies of a Hintock tutelary spirit with sunburnt face and cornflower-colored eyes. However much she wishes to participate in and observe the Hintock rhythms and rituals, she simultaneously relapses into traditional privileged constructions of self and otherness which reify and make a fetish of Winterborne.

Grace is consistently depicted as an imperfectly manufactured product of polite culture, a sentimental tourist in her own homeland caught "as it were in mid-air between two storeys of society" (*W* 195), this "impressionable creature who combined modern nerves with primitive feelings" (*W* 265). She is precariously poised somewhere in social space, and the dynamic of Hardy's narrative derives from radical indeterminacies and equivocations over genteel decorum, the compulsive calibration of caste and status so often mistaken for personal worth. Grace is a pivotal figure between woodland and aesthetic culture; her marriage to Fitzpiers effectively ratifies and seals her divorce from the Hintocks. Although she feels as if she has returned to a momentous, dynamic relationship with her surroundings, the newly bourgeois Grace can never revert to being a "crude country girl" like Marty South, who occupies the lowest social and economic rung of rural life. Grace half-heartedly rebels against the "artificiality" paid for by wealth generated from her father's business of exploiting the forest (cutting down trees for timber). Grace's nostalgic dream of being restored through Winterborne to the untutored native she once was is a delusion only equaled by her father's hope that a recent divorce law will make a "grown" Grace "wholesome" again, eradicating the "stain" of her humiliating entanglement with Fitzpiers. As Edward Neill remarks, "with George Melbury . . . as its linchpin, *The Woodlanders* deals with the fruits of snobbery no less than the production of apples by nature and cider by men" (Neill 2004: 58).

If Grace's febrile but facile evocation of "Autumn's very brother" evinces how much she wishes to see Winterborne as the epitome of an organic relationship between man and the potency of nature, his inhibiting self-restraint is still painfully apparent because of the gentility she has imposed on him and with which she secretly feels most comfortable. Winterborne apes a "chivalrous . . . manliness": the very trait she exploits in One-Chimney Hut at the climax of the novel, effectively killing him by her own superfine moral scruples. The unnatural role Winterborne must play when Grace is present ends, as on Midsummer Eve, in dourness and detachment.

Later in the novel, when Grace is recuperating from her first illness, Winterborne "rose upon her memory as the fruit-god and the wood-god in alternation . . . sometimes leafy, and smeared with green lichen . . . sometimes cider-stained and starred with apple-pips" (*W* 249). However, Winterborne is a far cry from the regenerative figure of Grace's fancy because he, like his workmate Marty South, epitomizes a ruined and exploited human nature which cannot evolve *naturally* if it is compelled to minister to the demands of a new bourgeois culture and its false consciousness of decorum, chivalry, and sexual "correctness." In the bitter recognition that Grace "manufactures" Winterborne, and that his status as "wood-god" can be at best only a brittle poetic guise, Hardy charts the demise of a potent and benevolent nature spirit whose reality can no longer profoundly be entertained in the imagination. Crucially, he has his own naturally informed culture which is betrayed by Grace and Old Melbury. Winterborne and Marty South possess an affinity with the forest expressed in terms of their shared intuitive comprehension of a secret "script" unique to Little Hintock. For the scholar-gypsy Fitzpiers, the task of "reading" this ethnographic script is like trying to decode a foreign and faded manuscript, replete with ellipses and tendentious emendations. But for Marty and Giles the translation of these "runic" inscriptions is seemingly effortless, a gift rendered almost as extinct as the other fossil "survivals" in Little Hintock, ousted by the refined arts of which Grace and her husband are the dubious beneficiaries:

The casual glimpses which the ordinary population bestowed upon that wondrous world of sap and leaves called the Hintock woods had been with these two, Giles and Marty, a clear gaze. They had been possessed of its finer mysteries as of commonplace knowledge; had been able to read its hieroglyphs as ordinary writing; to them the sights and sounds of night . . . amid those dense boughs . . . were simple occurrences whose origin, continuance, and laws they foreknew . . . they had, with the run of the years, mentally collected those remoter signs and symbols which seen in few were of runic obscurity, but all together made an alphabet . . . The artifices of the seasons were seen by them from the conjuror's own point of view. (*W* 297–8)

Winterborne, unlike Michael Henchard, who visits a "conjuror" (Wide-Oh Fall) in *The Mayor of Casterbridge*, is himself endowed with "a gentle conjuror's touch in spreading the roots of each little tree, resulting in a sort of caress, under which the delicate fibres all laid themselves out in their proper directions for growth" (*W* 59). His caress, quite spontaneous and unconscious, is intended to nurture the young trees. Yet when he strokes the flower worn by Grace in the "Autumn's very brother" episode (*W* 187), Winterborne's "caress" intimates only stammering inadequacy and sexual repression.

Winterborne's apparent possession of the "finer mysteries" of Little Hintock is also complicated by the horrific accounts of the detrimental operation of natural forces within the forest. Winterborne, the whimsical "wood-god" of Grace's fantasies, can do little to resuscitate the creative potential of his birthplace. His inability to defend his locale from ugly decay shows in the myriad depictions of stunted and mutilated tree life. It is dangerous, Hardy suggests, to set much store by Grace's perceptions of the Hintock plantations and copses, for they signal more her nagging anxieties than the actual condition of the physical world – for instance, the "trees close together" she notices when alone at Winterborne's One-Chimney Hut, "wrestling for existence, their branches disfigured with wounds resulting from their mutual rubbings"; and the "dead boughs . . . scattered about like ichthyosauri in a museum" (*W* 280). Only Grace could compare features of a natural setting to a familiar urban location, especially one considered a hallmark of civility, synonymous with intellectual and moral edification. Also, the seasonal cycle and effects of shadow, sunbeams, mist, and storm all conspire to evoke a fictional milieu unceasingly and ominously changing. However, the presentation of trees in terms of the "Unfulfilled Intention" is a portrayal whose sheer starkness cannot be attributed to chiaroscuro or to Grace's fickle observation. We are deliberately enticed into the pastoral prettiness of the opening image before being exposed to the numerous disturbing features awaiting those who tread further into the forest depths:

They went noiselessly over mats of starry moss, rustled through interspersed tracts of leaves, skirted trunks with spreading roots whose mossed rinds made them like hands wearing green gloves, elbowed old elms and ashes with great forks in which stood pools of water that overflowed on rainy days and ran down their stems in green cascades. On older trees . . . huge lobes of fungi grew like lungs. Here, as everywhere, the Unfulfilled

Intention, which makes life what it is, was as obvious as it could be among the depraved crowds of a city-slum. The leaf was deformed, the curve was crippled, the taper was interrupted; the lichen ate the vigour of the stalk, and the ivy slowly strangled to death the promising sapling. (*W* 48)

The increasingly grotesque somatic imagery – which Hardy repeats for trees in the "wilder recesses" of Mrs. Charmond's park with its ugly fungoid and parasitic growths – is a far cry from *Under the Greenwood Tree* (1872), whose narrator evinces a rapt reverence for the woods. Hardy draws an analogy, and attributes the state of both Little Hintock and urban civilization to a common cause, the "Unfulfilled Intention." This abstract formulation implies the extreme and unrelenting cruelty that nature imposes upon itself when engaged in a Darwinian struggle for survival. The violence of the disfigurement that Hintock trees inflict on one another is the key element of Hardy's rural wasteland. One species seems to devour another; ivy slowly strangles "the promising sapling," indicating the relationship between malformation and ruthless exploitation. Little Hintock is no better than the vast modern metropolis, whose bleak associations of crime, infant mortality, and "roofs of slated hideousness" are famously described by Tennyson's disenchanted elderly speaker in "Locksley Hall Sixty Years After" (Tennyson 1987 III: 230). The "Unfulfilled Intention" also applies to Winterborne, who cannot halt the spread of disease in this district. Hardy reveals that individual beings and their plans are as vulnerable to social and psychological forces as saplings are to ivy.

It is fitting that Winterborne should be allied with autumn because the season owes its distinctive color and profusion to dying vegetation. The cider-maker and tree-planter who in Grace Melbury's eyes rises out of the earth like a new Adam in chapter 28 is eerily consumed by unhusbanded nature in chapters 41 and 42. This time, however, instead of bringing sunshine, autumn "was coming in with rains" (*W* 272). Once allied with the prodigal fecundity of the Hintocks, the delirious Winterborne dissolves into the sylvan surroundings by imperceptible degrees. His enfeeblement and absorption back into the forest is not the true source of tragedy here, for in the full cycle of nature, growth and decay, sowing and reaping, are equally necessary. Hardy's acute sense of disaster stems from the fact that the tree-planter and cider-maker has not been *fertile* in his time: the galling irony is that Winterborne completes the cycle of life without fulfilling his priestly function. His role has been seized by Fitzpiers, who cannot fulfill it either, as the grim farce involving Old South's elm tree attests. Winterborne's ritual death is marked by successive steps down the evolutionary ladder:

[There] were low mutterings; at first like persons in conversation, but gradually resolving themselves into varieties of one voice. It was an endless monologue, like that we sometimes hear from inanimate nature in deep secret places where water flows, or where ivy leaves flap against stones; but by degrees [Grace] was convinced that the voice was Winterborne's. (*W* 281)

Winterborne's cough sounds like "a squirrel or a bird" (*W* 275), then his voice floats upon the weather "as though a part of it" (*W* 278), and finally becomes indistinguishable, "an endless monologue, like that we sometimes hear from inanimate nature in deep secret places." He becomes first part of the animal kingdom, then of the inanimate world of water, wind, and stone. But the process of dying continues: Winterborne's final murmurs are "like a comet; erratic, inapprehensible, untraceable" (*W* 282). Hardy draws on (with an unsettling blend of heartfelt sincerity and stinging irony) the traditions of pastoral elegy in having all nature perform rites of mourning for the death of a god: "The whole wood seemed to be a house of death, pervaded by loss to its uttermost length and breadth. Winterborne was gone and the copses seemed to show the want of him; those young trees, so many of which he had planted . . . were . . . sending out their roots in the direction that he had given them with his subtle hand" (*W* 293). The novel closes with a shorn Marty South delivering a threnody to the unmanned warden of the Hintock orchards. Her tragically desiccated nostalgia is the only recognition we get from within Winterborne's locale of his singular capabilities. This tutelary nymph of Little Hintock, whose feminine contours are "so undeveloped as to be scarcely perceptible in her" (*W* 331), is a representative, like the man she loves, of "Unfulfilled Intentions" and the barren asexual current running through society in the forest. Her devotion is not only unrequited but the very source of her suffering rather than a means of her redemption. Critics have identified in this speech a simple, unadorned lyricism, neither self-conscious nor stilted, which works as a counterpoint to Grace Melbury's exaggerated perception of Winterborne as fertility figure. However, Hardy, instead of intimating the quality of enlightened endurance, hints instead at the masochistic and self-mutilating strains imbuing Marty's ritual of loss. Her longing for the imagined health of the past must be a sign of sickness in the modern moment. And it is by no means clear whether Marty sees Winterborne for what he really is, given that few others do in a novel that makes his visibility peculiarly problematic, and which debunks his status as a character promising the constancy and continuity of heartfelt connections between man and nature:

> "Whenever I plant the young larches I'll think that none can plant as you planted; and whenever I split a gad, and whenever I turn the cider wring, I'll say none could do it like you. If ever I forget your name let me forget home and heaven! . . . But no, no, my love, I never can forget 'ee; for you was a good man, and did good things!" (*W* 331)

The Woodlanders shows that Winterborne's status as a "good man" is not enough to restore any kind of harmony and happiness to those left behind. The macabre absurdity of the novel's resolution is reflected in how Fitzpiers' perseverance is rewarded as he flouts bourgeois norms and still claims Grace, in whom he experiences a renewed interest. Her proclaimed infidelity with Winterborne is ironically the stimulus for his inconstant, idealizing desire. Fitzpiers' corrosively cynical attitude intimates the final and irreversible erosion of faith in the capability of elemental potencies to inform and inspire the human world by a destructive dilettantism that dishonors their traditional mythological representation.

REFERENCES AND FURTHER READING

Ball, David (1987). Tragic Contradiction in Hardy's *The Woodlanders*. *ARIEL: A Review of International English Literature*, 18(1), 17–25.

Cates, Baldridge (1993). Observation and Domination in Hardy's *The Woodlanders*. In John Maynard, et al. (eds.), *Victorian Literature and Culture* (pp. 191–209). New York: AMS Press.

Davis, William A. (2003). *Thomas Hardy and the Law*. Newark: University of Delaware Press.

Dorson, Richard M. (1968). *Peasant Customs and Savage Myths. Selections from the British Folklorists*, 2 vols. Chicago: University of Chicago Press.

Dutta, Shanta (2000). Tree Obsession in Hardy and O. Henry. In Rosemarie Morgan (ed.), *Days to Recollect* (pp. 73–80). New Haven, CT: Hardy Association.

Emerson, Ralph Waldo (1971–87). *The Complete Works of Ralph Waldo Emerson*, 4 vols. Cambridge, MA: Harvard University Press.

Fisher, Joe (1992). *Hidden Hardy*. Basingstoke: Macmillan.

Garlock, David (1998). Entangled Genders: Plasticity, Indeterminacy, and Constructs of Sexuality in Darwin and Hardy. *Dickens Studies Annual*, 27, 287–305.

Garson, Marjorie (1991). *Hardy's Fables of Integrity: Woman, Body, Text*. Oxford: Clarendon Press.

Gatrell, Simon (2005). Wessex on Film. In T. R. Wright (ed.), *Thomas Hardy on Screen* (pp. 37–49). Cambridge: Cambridge University Press.

Fincham, Anthony (2005). Hardy, Death and the Psychosomatic. *Thomas Hardy Journal*, 21, 58–93.

Hardy, Thomas ([1886] 1987). *The Mayor of Casterbridge*, ed. Dale Kramer. Oxford: Oxford University Press.

Hardy, Thomas ([1887] 2005). *The Woodlanders*, ed. Dale Kramer, introd. Penny Boumelha. Oxford: Oxford University Press.

Hughes, John (2002). "For old association's sake": Narrative, History and Hardy's *The Woodlanders*. *Thomas Hardy Journal*, 18(2), 57–64.

Kiely, Robert (1995). The Menace of Solitude: The Politics and Aesthetics of Exclusion in *The Woodlanders*. In Margaret R. Higonnet (ed.), *The Sense of Sex: Feminist Perspectives on Hardy* (pp. 188–202). Urbana: University of Illinois Press.

Kramer, Dale (2004). *The Woodlanders*: The Conflicting Visions of Phil Agland and Thomas Hardy. In T. R. Wright (ed.), *Thomas Hardy on Screen* (pp. 140–52). Cambridge: Cambridge University Press.

Lawrence, D. H. ([1914] 1987). *Study of Thomas Hardy*, ed. Bruce Steele. Cambridge: Cambridge University Press.

McLennan, J. F. ([1865] 1970). *Primitive Marriage: An Inquiry into the Origin of the Form of Capture in Marriage Ceremonies*, ed. Peter Rivière. Chicago: University of Chicago Press.

McLennan John F. (1866). Bride-Catching. *Argosy*, 2, 37–42.

Neill, Edward (2004). *The Secret Life of Thomas Hardy*. Aldershot: Ashgate.

Stave, Shirley A. (1995). *The Decline of the Goddess: Nature, Culture and Women in Thomas Hardy's Fiction*. Westport, CT: Greenwood Press.

Stocking, George W. (1987). *Victorian Anthropology*. New York: Free Press.

Stocking, George W. (1998). *After Tylor*. London: Athlone Press.

Tennyson, Alfred Lord (1987). *The Poems of Tennyson*, ed. Christopher Ricks, 3 vols. Harlow: Longman.

Thurley Geoffrey (1975). *The Psychology of Hardy's Novels: The Nervous and the Statuesque*. St. Lucia, Queensland: University of Queensland Press.

Tylor, E. B. (1903). *Primitive Culture: Researches into the Development of Mythology, Philosophy, Religion, Art, and Custom*, 4th edn., 2 vols. London: John Murray.

22

Melodrama, Vision, and Modernity: *Tess of the d'Urbervilles*

Tim Dolin

In *The Life and Work of Thomas Hardy*, his predominantly self-authored biography, Hardy recounts an episode from his youth the significance of which might justly be described as primal:

> One summer morning at Bockhampton, just before he sat down to breakfast, he remembered that a man [James Seale] was to be hanged at eight o'clock at Dorchester. He took up the big brass telescope that had been handed on in the family, and hastened to a hill on the heath a quarter of a mile from the house, whence he looked towards the town. The sun behind his back shone straight on the white stone façade of the gaol, the gallows upon it, and the form of the murderer in white fustian, the executioner and officials in dark clothing, and the crowd below, being invisible at this distance of three miles. At the moment of his placing the glass to his eye the white figure dropped downwards, and the faint note of the town clock struck eight.
>
> The whole thing had been so sudden that the glass nearly fell from Hardy's hands. He seemed alone on the heath with the hanged man; and he crept homeward wishing he had not been so curious. It was the second and last execution he witnessed, the first having been that of a woman two or three years earlier, when he stood close to the gallows. (*LW* 32–3)

The woman was Martha Brown, convicted of murdering her husband and executed outside Dorchester gaol on August 9, 1856, where the 16-year-old Hardy must have arrived very early to secure a place near the front of a crowd of three or four thousand people, and where he was aroused by the woman's swinging body, tight in its rain-soaked black silk gown, and the wet canvas bag that stuck to her face (*CL* VII: 5). His memory of her death is rightly given as an important influence on *Tess of the d'Urbervilles* (1891), and rightly taken to be emblematic of the sexualization and violence with which men regard women in Hardy (see e.g. Nunokawa 1992). Looking back as an old man he admitted to being ashamed of his young self, but told the story so often and with such relish as to suggest that an old-world public hanging, if it stirred up guilty feelings of *eros* and *thanatos*, was also somehow innocent: ritualized, customary, and communal. Yet the later incident, often overlooked, is also significant – for *Tess* and for Hardy's writing more generally. Magnified out of all human proportion, unmediated by ceremony, the putting to death of James Seale invades the unsuspecting youth's field of vision. Gone is the composure of perspectival space, depth of field, and the mimetic and referential codes that hold observer and observed in their separate and settled places. Death is at once immense and intimate, as if the rational, institutionalized violence of modernity had been channeled weirdly and silently through the antique lens and up onto the ancient heath. The technological elimination of time and space becomes one with the elimination of life: the glass focuses as the clock strikes as the neck breaks. Vision becomes "inseparable from transience – that is, from new temporalities, speeds, experiences of flux and obsolescence, a new density and sedimentation of the structure of visual memory" (Crary 1990: 21).

The same jolt that nearly caused Hardy to drop the telescope would be felt across Europe and America four decades later, in the mid-1890s, when a sensational new form of entertainment, the Lumières' *Cinématographe*, captivated and frightened audiences with its "actualities" – segments of moving images depicting everyday modern life and faraway places.[1] An assemblage of single shots, each perhaps half a minute long, the twenty-minute show flickered from the mundane to the breathtaking, from slapstick gags to terrifying illusions: workers leaving a factory; a gardener creating havoc with a hose; glorious alpine scenery; and (most notoriously, because it panicked some viewers) the approaching arrival of a train at a railway station. The *Cinématographe* exploited the contemporary taste for extravagantly realistic theatrical spectacle: "train wrecks, car races, storms at sea, collapsing hot-air balloons, tornados, Alpine avalanches, and burning buildings" (Felski 2003: 508) were all routinely manufactured for the popular stage. But nothing prepared theater-goers for the visceral immediacy, the sheer aggressiveness, with which "The Most Perfect Device Yet Invented for the Photographic Portrayal of Life in Motion" (Kennedy 1999: 32) projected the mundane, the exotic, and comical up onto the big screen.

As a way of introducing its audiences to cinema, Proctor's Pleasure Palace in New York screened the first actualities as short items interspersed between various live burlesque acts. One of the most popular was Marie Dressler's "farcical spasm," *Tess of the Vaudevilles* (Postlewait 1999: 163), a satirical attack on the hit stage adaptation of Hardy's novel then playing on Broadway (Kennedy 1999: 32). This unexpected conjunction of *Tess*, the sensational advent of the moving picture, and the affective extremities of popular theater remind us that when we call Hardy a cinematic novelist we do not only mean that he "presents his materials in primarily visual terms" or that his visualizations "correspond in some significant respect to the visual effects characteristic of film" (Lodge 1981: 96). When he created "a visualised world that is both recognisably 'real' and yet more vivid, intense and dramatically charged than our ordinary perception of the real world" (1981: 96), Hardy was also exploiting the "aesthetics of astonishment" (Brooks 1976) that he experienced up on the heath as a boy: an aesthetics which culminated in the intensification and amplification of cinematic techniques, but which was already integral to popular culture by the mid-nineteenth century.

Many of Hardy's first readers were struck, as the magazine editor Frederick Green-wood was, by "the peculiarity of [his] genius." He has "an eye lensed like a micro-scope," Greenwood declared: a "comprehensive intensity of vision" that takes in the widest landscape and the smallest detail (Greenwood 1892: 431). But that "enlarging eye" was vulnerable to distorting what it saw, and Greenwood noted parenthetically that Hardy's writing was occasionally marred by "an exaggerated hand." The relation-ship between his "idiosyncratic mode of regard" (*LW* 235) and the idiosyncrasies of writing to which Greenwood delicately alludes – the improbabilities and coinci-dences, lapses into Latinism, and other forms of vulgar stylistic exhibitionism, pessi-mism, and fatalism – is a vital one. For the intensity of Hardy's vision is a *melodramatic* intensity, producing a distinctive aesthetics of astonishment wherein extreme inner conflicts and contradictions of social identity and consciousness are extroverted onto an expressionistic semiotics of landscapes and bodies. Not surprisingly, it had its origins in the era of sensationalism, the 1860s, when the highly suggestible young architect lived in London and was "simultaneously beguiled by the excitement of the theatre and repelled by its artifice" (Millgate 2004: 95), fell in love with Italian grand opera, and came under the lasting influence of the fashionable sensation fiction of Wilkie Collins and Mary Elizabeth Braddon.

Hardy's first novels were flagrantly sensationalist, full of outlandish characters, tortuous plots, and high emotionalism, and one does not have to look very far in his mature fiction for stagy villains, outrageous incidents, cliff-hanger suspense, sensational revelations, and implausible coincidences. Even *Tess* was described by one reviewer dismissively as having "the plot of Mr H. A. Jones" (Cox 1970: 180, referring to the early melodramatic phase of Henry Arthur Jones' career as a popular playwright in the 1880s), and Tess herself, another review noted, was "suggestive of the carefully-studied simplicity of the theatre, and not at all of the carelessness of the fields" (Cox 1970: 188). Yet Hardy's melodramatic imagination does not declare itself principally in character or plot, where it must ultimately be subordinated to tragedy, but in his genius for spectacle: striking "picture stories" (Gledhill 1987: 21–2), vivid tableaux combining detailed and lyrical descriptions of landscape with elements of symbolic non-verbal performance. As the word suggests, melodramas were originally "romantic and sensational in plot, and interspersed with songs" (*OED*), and Hardy's fictions may be characterized as prose narratives, romantic or sensational in plot, and interspersed with highly colored lyric-dramatic scenes. As he remarked in his own biography, he "almost always" noticed any "strangely bizarre effect" (*LW* 240) – "looking down at the young women dancing the *cancan*" at the Moulin Rouge one night, for example, and seeing past them through a window at the back to Montmartre cemetery, the "resting-place of so many similar gay Parisians silent under the moonlight" (p. 240). Hardy's is a scenic imagination in the double sense that it dwells in the detail of the world as it presents itself to his eye, and finds there a *setting* – a Hardy scene is always a scene *of* something. Even his use of metaphor, in this sense, exploits the sensational potential of the melodramatic situation, defined as the "startling reversal or twist of events that creates a dramatic impasse, a momentary paralysis stemming from a deadlock or dilemma or predicament that constrains the protagonist's ability to respond immediately" (Singer 2001: 41). During those early years in London Hardy wrote mostly poetry and thought of himself as a poet, and he practiced the art of verse by training himself to think metaphorically through a process of violent linguistic re-association, generating poetry out of the forced juxtaposition of isolated words and phrases he found in the dictionary, Palgrave's *Golden Treasury*, and standard volumes of the English poets. The energy of these exercises in catachresis – the strained synthesis of the "uncommon and the ordinary" (*LW* 154) – is openly erotic. Using a plain sequence of words from the dictionary, for instance, he extemporizes: "the / biting want: catch of lip by lip: long / kisses & short ceasings: sweet chafe / of . . . chills: close circuits of me" (Dalziel and Millgate 1994: 61). The "marvellous juxtapositions" (*THPV* 76) that appealed so much to his visual imagination, in other words, also motivated his linguistic experimentalism.

Roger Ebbatson has observed how in Hardy's earlier novels visual intensity and linguistic disruption work together. In *A Pair of Blue Eyes*, he argues, the momentum of the story is repeatedly stalled by some "rivetingly irrelevant detail" in which proliferating sense-data are given primacy over meaning. The "free-play of language . . . interrupts or dislocates the narrative line" (Ebbatson 1986: 31) and leads to a "breakdown of life into expressive moments" (1986: 32). One of Ebbatson's examples describes Stephen Smith staring into a summer-house at night:

> The scratch of a striking light was heard, and a bright glow radiated from the interior of the building. The light gave birth to dancing leaf-shadows, stem-shadows, lustrous streaks, dots, sparkles, and threads of silver sheen of all imaginable variety and transience. It awakened gnats, which flew towards it, revealed shiny gossamer threads, disturbed earthworms. (*PBE* 301)

Ebbatson adds that "the more determined exigencies of the major novels" disallow any such distractions or any such "radical independence of . . . sentences" (1986: 31); yet the gap between sense-data and meaning – between vision and insight – remained an acute problem for Hardy. In *Tess of the d'Urbervilles*, his tour de force of poetic fiction, it is difficult to distinguish the objective physical world from the "highly-charged mental atmosphere" (*TD* 213). Consider this scene, in which Tess and Angel stand together before a November sunset, Tess happy in her "perpetual betrothal," Angel anxious for her to name the wedding-day:

> Looking over the damp sod in the direction of the sun, a glistening ripple of gossamer webs was visible to their eyes under the luminary, like the track of moonlight on the sea. Gnats, knowing nothing of their brief glorification, wandered across the air in this pathway, irradiated as if they bore fire within them, then passed out of its line, and were quite extinct. (*TD* 200)

Ebbatson is right: far from being irrelevant, almost the entire novel is condensed into this one scene. I'm not thinking just of its ironical foreshadowings (the hopeful young lovers transfixed by an autumn sunset; the moral unenlightenment of Tess's "luminary," Angel; the dazzling and dazzled heroine's wanderings and ultimate extinction), nor of its place in the complex pattern of images of radiance and darkness in the novel, including a number of closely related twilight scenes. The dramatic shifts between Romantic hyperbole and irony in the representation of nature in the passage – it swerves between the Turneresque grandiosity of the sunset and the bathos of the insects indifferently flitting into and out of the band of light – accentuate the crisis of subjective experience being explored in the novel. The sardonic allusion to the Holy Spirit and the Acts of the Apostles expresses in shorthand many of the central ideas: that the numinous is merely an accidental epiphenomenon of unconscious natural processes, and offers no "track" or "pathway" to enlightenment; that beauty and truth are not inherent but are effects of perception; and that the post-Romantic passion for an absolute correspondence between inner being and the outer world isolates individuals in a monadic subjectivity that limits and damages human relationships.

How is it valid to speak of the melodramatism of such a Hardyan "moment of vision"? Hardy's melodramatic imagination is reminiscent of, yet finally very different from, that defined by Peter Brooks in his foundational study of the mode. For Brooks, melodrama offers Balzac and Henry James a means of access to a lost primary psyche and spirit, a "substratum of myth" absent in the post-Enlightenment, post-sacred West (Brooks 1976: 14). A symptom of modernity, it is also linked to the rise of modern art: melodrama is "an intensified, primary, and exemplary version of what the most ambitious art, since the beginning of Romanticism, has been about" (1976: 21–2), an art "constructed on, and over, the void, postulating meanings and symbolic systems which have no certain justification because they are backed by no theology and no universally accepted code" (1976: 21). Predicated on the conviction "that life does make reference to a moral occult that is the realm of eventual value" (1976: 22), melodrama is a way of "pressuring the surface of reality (the surface of [the] text) in order to make it yield the full, true terms of [the] story" (1976: 1–2), opening the narrative to "the abyss of occulted meanings" (1976: 198) in its eruptive moments of excess: moments of outrage, pathos, or hyperbole.

For Brooks, the melodramatic is one of the routes an incipient modernism takes to escape the material complacencies of realism – a familiar claim for Hardy, too, who uses melodrama strategically as, in Terry Eagleton's words, "part of the *contradictory* constitution of his artistic practice" (Eagleton 1981: 73); it is one form of the bad writing that aims to expose the ideological fault-lines of "fine writing." Regrettably there isn't space here to pursue in detail the complex questions of Hardy's realism and anti-realism. Without wishing to suggest that melodrama is interchangeable with other non-realist registers in unproblematically "disrupting" the classic realist narrative, nevertheless melodramatic spectacle, which developed historically (using non-verbal means such as dumb-show and music) as a way of sidestepping the class prohibition on spoken dialogue in theater (Gledhill 1987: 17), offered Hardy a powerful semiotics for circumventing the proscriptions of the mainstream Victorian novel. What follows, therefore, is a discussion of the specific relationship between melodrama, visuality, and modernity in *Tess*, which explores the uses of melodramatic spectacle in those passages of his finest writing, "passages of astonishing beauty and force which are to be found," as Virginia Woolf remarked, "in every book" (Woolf [1932] 1960: 224). In her essay on Hardy in *The Common Reader*, Woolf marvels at how "a single scene breaks off from the rest" with "a sudden quickening of power which we cannot foretell, nor he, it seems, control." What we most remember, she says, are "the bloated sheep struggling among the clover" in *Far From the Madding Crowd*, Troy's flashing swordplay, and "the wagon with Fanny's dead body inside travelling along the road under the dripping trees." And such scenes are everywhere in Hardy: how clearly we see and hear the Mellstock choir greeting each other, even in the utterly black midnight at the start of *Under the Greenwood Tree*; or the figure of Eustacia high on the barrow, silhouetted against the sky in *The Return of the Native*; or Sue and Phillotson walking awkwardly under one umbrella along "the wet and deserted lane" in *Jude the Obscure*. "Vivid to the eye, but not to the eye alone, for every sense participates," these scenes are full of a "wild power," Woolf affirms, but it is a power that "goes as it comes." Against her ideal of a sustained lyric intensity of expression, the moment of vision was simply and regrettably of the nature of Hardy's genius, which was "uneven in accomplishment." Most of his writing, she remarks bluntly, is "lumpish and dull and inexpressive," and he transcends it, as Dickens and Scott did, only by accident. With a condescension that is oddly reminiscent of the Victorians' faint praise of women novelists, and especially the Brontës, Woolf writes off Hardy's imagination as a sheer force of nature, unaided by "craft or skill." The moment of vision is experienced and communicated, she concludes, in a "blur of unconsciousness" ([1932] 1960: 224–5).

But of course the unconscious is close to the ineffable for Woolf. The "margin of the unexpressed" ([1932] 1960: 225) is her memorable phrase for the way rational language and thought are momentarily obscured by the dazzling clarity and vitality of Hardy's visualized world: his blind spots of time. But Hardy himself sought no such Kantian retreat from the unresolvable contradictions of social and cultural narratives. The "breakdown of life into expressive moments" (Ebbatson 1986: 32) was not a failure of art, but a *condition* for art in modernity. The best we can hope for, he concluded, was what he called in the preface to *Jude the Obscure* "a series of seemings, or personal impressions" without consistency or permanence (*JO* xxxv–xxxvi). A contemporary reviewer of *Moments of Vision*, the volume of poems published in 1917, observed that life, in Hardy's view of it, was nothing more than a series of impressions, each "given to us for what it is worth, as an experience of which we must make what we can, with no certainty that wrong will be righted" (McDowall 1917: 605). This the reviewer calls Hardy's "waiting attitude." It is the root of his philosophical laodiceanism and his essentially tragic view of the nature of things. Genuinely "baffled by the cries and counter-cries of a confused age," Hardy rejected both "an absolute moral law" and the progressive industrial spirit of his fellow Victorians (Graves 1923:

451). Mistrustful of frameworks of explanation, narrative coherence, moral certitude, or happiness, he waits and sees; or rather, sees and waits.

The melodramatic impulse in Hardy is therefore a symptom of what Weber famously called the "disenchantment of the world." It is a recourse to the irrational and instinctual – proverbially feminine qualities, as I discuss below – and an expressive form of the anomie and restlessness produced by industrial modernization: the process "by which capitalism uproots and makes mobile [what] is grounded," including "bodies, signs, images, languages, kinship relations, religious practices, and nationalities, as [well as] commodities, wealth, and labor power" (Crary 1990: 10). Hardy's "visualising language" (Berger 1990: xi) is thus a product of the social and cultural upheavals which are also the subjects of his fiction: economic migration; the class system and social mobility; the nature of femininity and the role of women; the debunking of the world of tradition and superstition; and the perpetual moral and intellectual uncertainty of modern life. His melodramatic visual imagination therefore develops in response to a wider crisis of vision and language being felt right across late Victorian cultural practices and movements, elite and popular, literary and visual. At one extreme it was felt in the breakdown of established canons of artistic representation and the rise of new theories, practices, and movements: Impressionism, Aestheticism, Decadence and counter-Decadence, Naturalism, Symbolism. At the other extreme, the crisis was felt in the "sensory violence" of everyday urban life (Singer 2001: 62), where, as Ben Singer has shown, the nerves, shaken by the chaos of human and animal traffic and the constant threat of crime, injury or death, are over-stimulated by an unrelenting assault of visual and linguistic signs, in advertising and in the increasingly sensational and melodramatic forms of popular entertainment referred to above.

Through the 1880s Hardy spent much of his time in London during a period of intense debate over the nature of art, and his slowly forming conception of Wessex – as real place and imagined place, where observation ends and art begins (*LN* II: 68) – emerges from his reassessment of his artistic concerns and practices against established and emerging aesthetic standards and principles: the competing convictions that "art should be grounded in the natural world and that it should be edifying"; and that its value "lies in the autonomy of its formal and decorative effects" (Harrison et al. 1998: 834). These debates lie at the heart of *Tess*'s melodramatics, in Hardy's polemical outrage against the villainous forces of moral hypocrisy and artistic compromise. When it appeared in three volumes in December 1891 *Tess* was instantly acclaimed as Hardy's greatest novel and censured for its hostility to the moral and literary establishment: the editors, publishers, booksellers, critics, and readers who, the novel implied, upheld and defended the hypocritical values and institutions that had doomed the unhappy heroine to her death. Hardy had become increasingly frustrated with the moral constraints of English fiction and was wearying of the surreptitious tactics needed to counteract the docile self-censorship to which he was forced to submit with evident loathing. But in *Tess* he went public for the first time with his anger and disapproval, and took his readers by surprise. This novel has overt polemical designs on us, as John Goode has remarked: it sits apart from its predecessors in meaning deliberately to give offense, and it does so by turning melodrama's characteristic mode of excess to purposive ends (Goode 1988: 110–11). Make no mistake: as the novel's first critics well saw, Tess Durbeyfield suffers excessively, and does so, they felt, for a cause of her angry author's. Thomas Hardy, the faithful presenter of the title page, accuses us of the deliberate "misrecognition of the innocence of the central protagonist" (Gledhill 1987: 30) and dares us to lose faith in her virtue. If the melodramatic plot retails the persecution of innocence and the triumph of virtue, the "defiant blazon" of the "Pure Woman" (Cox 1970: 212) is Hardy's declaration of the triumph of virtue *beyond* the realm of plot.

In the aggrieved "Preface to the Fifth and Later Editions" (1892) Hardy argued that *Tess* "was intended to be neither didactic nor aggressive, but in the scenic parts to be representative simply, and in the contemplative to be oftener charged with impressions than with opinions" (*TD* 462). He was ready to stand up against the injustices of the sexual double standard and the social inequalities that underpin it in *Tess*, but he was not ready to see his novel reduced to a *Tendenz-Roman* or "novel with a purpose." Nor was he happy with those who would "pervert plain meanings" (p. 464). Angered by the misconstruction or willful misrepresentation of his intentions by critics, he set about complicating and obfuscating the motives and actions of all the principal characters.[2] After successive revisions for each new edition, no decisive "moral argument" could be abstracted from either the events or their narration. Convictions dissolve into impressions, entangling readers in the hermeneutic complexities so central to the tragedy: we all see what happens, but we don't know for sure what it means (see Dolin 1998; Gatrell 1988; Jacobus 1978; Laird 1975).

The other effect of Hardy's revisions (still being made in 1912) was to obscure the novel's more egregious affinities with the popular stage, blatant in the Broadway adaptation of *Tess* and even more so in the parodic *Tess of the Vaudevilles*: the extreme virtue and innocence, as well as the passivity, of the beautiful, victimized young heroine; the narrative logic of persecution, the impossibility of escape, and the constant impediments to happiness; the stifling atmosphere of extreme emotional tribulation; the stagy villainy of the villain and the insipidity of the hero; the device of the heroine's vow, which imposes silence and submissiveness on her in the face of terrible adversity; the belated recognition of error by the absent hero; and the ultimate triumph of purity over the casual cruelty of the arch-melodramatic President of the Immortals. Everywhere in *Tess* we find melodrama's "psychic traps . . . waiting to be sprung" (Kirby 1980: xiv), and more so as the heroine's destiny begins to close in on her, and her world narrows down to a handful of people whom she cannot escape. There is an almost paranoid insistence in this novel on the return of the repressed: in the coincidental reappearances not only of the converted Alec but of the boorish Trantridge farmer, Groby, whom Angel had punched, and the two Amazonian Darch sisters.

"Melodrama always sides with the powerless" (Vicinus 1981: 130), and in *Tess* Hardy modifies the pastoral tragedy with conventions that speak forcefully to class oppression in modern urban, industrialized, secular, and rational societies. To do so, Hardy was obliged to complicate and ironize theatrical conventions. In place of the expected aristocratic villain, he conjures up the bogus Alec, whose "Victorian lucre" pays for the "Norman blood" (*TD* 17) he feigns, and who preys on the noble-hearted aristocrat-in-exile, Tess. And in case we should miss the point, Hardy has young Tess's young brother Abraham ask innocently why the villain keeps "putting his hand up to his mistarshers" and making his diamond ring twinkle (p. 47). He also rejects the schematic Manichaeism of the stage and the penny magazine. There is no providentially regulated universe to which Tess in her powerlessness can appeal. Acts and events are morally incomprehensible, and Hardy relentlessly arouses powerful feelings of agitation and suspense, and sets up moral polarizations to arouse feelings of pity and outrage against injustice.

He could not, however, eliminate more elemental affinities to melodrama in the novel's "nonclassical narrative mechanics" (Singer 2001: 46). *Tess*'s episodic structure sets up the familiar tension between the semantic power of scene or situation and the semantic power of narrative. The most conspicuous melodramatic situations function simultaneously as symbolic blazons and parodies of the lurid imagery of newspaper sensationalism and the theater of horrors. The most obvious of them are the death of Prince in the terrible collision with the anonymous forces of modernity – a speeding, noiseless mail-cart – captured in the sensational image of the spout of blood "falling with a hiss into the road" and splashing Tess's white dress with "crimson drops" (*TD* 33); and its counterpart, the climactic murder scene in the bright, unsavory seaside lodging-house, to which the reader bears witness obliquely through the pantomime of the landlady and the heart-shaped bloodstain on the white ceiling. (The narrator, like the landlady, is transfixed for a moment by the ludicrous, utterly compelling image of the ace of hearts, and the melodrama switches, as it often does in Hardy, to its obverse, farce.[3]) To these we might add others: the portraits of the grotesque d'Urberville dames; Angel's ghostly sleepwalking; the scene of the fugitive lovers in the great stage-set of Stonehenge; and the text-painter's "hot" messages in lurid blood-red – "THY, DAMNATION, SLUMBERETH, NOT" – whose commas drive each word "well home to the reader's heart" (p. 79) by disrupting their syntactic connection and relation in the same way that, at the level of narrative, the melodramatic situation threatens to disrupt the syntactic connections and relations between the elements of the unfolding story.

The melodrama of those expressive moments which delay the progress of the narrative in *Tess* is intimately tied up with the heroine herself. It has often been argued that Hardy's women characters are "treated as an allegory, idealized or demonized, the Other, while simultaneously accused of being deceptive, quintessentially duplicitous or unstable in [their] meaning, so that [they become] a trope of figural language itself" (Bronfen 1993: 69). Tess, however, is "as different as possible from those fickle and elusive young women . . . in some of his other tales" (Cox 1970: 187), and is consequently overburdened with allegorical meanings as she is overladen with Alec's roses and strawberries. Set apart from her "rustic associates" (*TD* 218) by her d'Urberville lineage and striking looks, she has "that touch of rarity about her" (p. 124). She is "a peasant by position, not by nature" (p. 232): "though untrained," she is "instinctively refined" (p. 181). The novel's title captures the paradox of the simple dairymaid hampered by the mythology of female heroism. Tess d'Urberville is no Jeanne d'Arc, but "the great campaign of the heroine" (p. 462) puts her by turns into the role of saintly visionary, child of nature, and warrior queen. A contraction of Theresa, Tess's name obliquely allies her with the saint and martyr whose unattainable example frames the fable of bourgeois female heroism in George Eliot's *Middlemarch*. Indeed, *Tess of the d'Urbervilles* may be read as a revision of Eliot's epic of domestic compromise.

When Angel describes Tess as "brim-full of poetry – actualized poetry . . . She *lives* what paper-poets only write" (*TD* 164), he echoes what Will Ladislaw pronounces to Dorothea Brooke in chapter 22 of *Middlemarch*: "You *are* a poem –and that is to be the best part of a poet" (Eliot [1871–2] 1986: 218). In this way Ladislaw aestheticizes what Eliot had called in an earlier story, "Amos Barton," the "serene dignity of [feminine] *being*" released from "the assiduous unrest of *doing*" (Eliot [1858] 1985: 19), and what Casaubon ominously calls a woman's "capability of an ardent self-sacrificing affection" ([1871–2] 1986: 50). Tess, on the other hand, is bracketed off, as Hardy's poetic scenes are bracketed off, from the narrative. Her heroism can only be represented aesthetically: she is heroic not in what she manages to achieve but in the steadfastness of her magnificent nature, which, called upon only to remain uncorrupted, radiates out of her as physical beauty. Many reviewers of the novel complained that Tess was not "faithful to her own sense of duty" (Cox 1970: 192). What "are the higher things to which this poor creature eventually rises?" demanded one reviewer: "She rises through seduction to adultery, murder, and the gallows" (1970: 219). This was not held up simply as a flaw in Tess's character but as a strenuous objection to the very principles and aims of Hardy's art. The proper function of art was moral teaching, and Hardy affected to expound "a great moral law" while treating the reader to the doings of a heroine who was incapable of rising to "a higher level of thought and feeling" (1970: 218). In creating Tess, however, Hardy had set out to rebuke "everything that constitutes the 'reality principle,' all its censorships, accommodations, tonings-down" (Brooks 1976: 41). The melodramatic violence of Alec's murder accordingly explodes at the end of a novel where all pathways to moral development and self-knowledge through experience have been blocked off to the heroine. For Angel, experience is liberalizing – he undergoes a man's "liberal education" (*TD* 99). For Tess, by contrast, experience is incapacitating and sinful: like Eve, she eats "of the tree of knowledge" (p. 103). And although her "passing corporeal blight had been her mental harvest" (p. 124), as the narrator claims, transforming her from a "simple girl" into a "complex woman" (p. 99), she is given no opportunity to express that complexity: to tell her story (p. 180). Defeated by Alec's relentless sexual advances, she is ultimately worn down, too, by Angel's unyielding aesthetic advances. Yet she does not flinch. For she must remain "the same, but not the same" (p. 89) – all essence, no experience; an unsophisticated girl uncorrupted by history.

Ignorant and incurious as he is, Angel is therefore surprised to discover the "ache of modernism" – "feelings which might almost have been called those of the age" – in the "sad imaginings" of this unsophisticated girl (*TD* 124). Yet perhaps, he reflects, "what are called advanced ideas are really in great part but the latest fashion in definition – a more accurate expression, by words in *logy* and *ism*, of sensations which men and women have vaguely grasped for centuries" (p. 124). Ironically, Angel cannot recognize Tess as a fellow modern. Yet even as a young girl she sees "how matters stood" (p. 37), and, no waiter on providence, she is ambitious, seeking in a village education a means to "what lay beyond her judgment" (she speaks local dialect and the standard English of the cities and towns, and hopes to be a teacher). She believes she can make her own future. She is immediately attracted to the nicely-spoken stranger on the green. She is conscious of the blightedness of her life and the absurdity of any romance that would have her made rich by marrying a gentleman. And she is, of course, that icon of Victorian urban despair, the fallen woman.

What Angel sees instead is an unexpected continuity between modernity and primitivism which becomes for Hardy an essential part of his melodramatic vision. Tess is a figure for poetry itself (and by extension for the victimized and marginalized poet), which Hardy connected with what Marianna Torgovnick calls "primitive passions," where "the primitive is the sign and symbol of desires the West has sought to repress – desires for direct correspondences between bodies and things, direct correspondences between experience and language, direct correspondences between individual beings and the collective life force" (1997: 8). Torgovnick is interested in the heyday of primitivism in anthropology and the arts in the 1910s and 1920s, but, as she notes, the idealization of the primitive, "with its aura of unchangeability, voicelessness, mystery, and difference" (1990: 20), emerges in the nineteenth century of Darwinism, racial science, and empire.

In December 1890, when *Tess* was appearing in the *Graphic*, Hardy made note of a conversation with his friend Edward Clodd, an amateur ethnologist who

> gives an excellently neat answer to my question why the superstitions of a remote Asiatic and a Dorset labourer are the same; "The attitude of man", he says, "at corresponding levels of culture, before like phenomena, is pretty much the same, your Dorset peasants representing the persistence of the barbaric idea which confuses persons and things, and founds wide generalizations on the slenderest analogies." (*LW* 241)

In parenthesis, Hardy adds: "(This 'barbaric idea which confuses persons and things' is, by the way, also common to the highest imaginative genius – that of the poet)" (*LW* 241). Hardy was familiar with the "Poetical fancies of primitive peoples" from his reading of Herbert Spencer (*LN* I: 160) and George Campbell's *Philosophy of Rhetoric* (1776).[4] Campbell argued that "all the words made use of to denote spiritual and intellectual things are in their origin metaphors, taken from the objects of sense" (Campbell 1860: 326). Metaphor belongs to an earlier stage of human development, where a language of "things animate" (or sentient) was used to express "things lifeless" (or intellectual or abstract). What in advanced cultures takes the form of *ideas*, in primitive cultures takes the form of *sensations*.

The rhetoric of primitivism in *Tess of the d'Urbervilles* has been noted in recent critical discussions of the links between Hardy's heroine and Victorian racial and social theory (see Brady 1999: 95–6). Havelock Ellis, reviewing *Tess*, likened "the solitary lives on these Dorset heaths" to "a primitive phase of society," and likened "the absence of moral feeling, the instinctiveness" of Hardy's women to their "direct relation to the wild and solitary character of their environment" (Cox 1970: 130). This is what attracts Angel Clare, who is taking the traveling cure, fleeing like so many of the late Victorians the psychic suffering and disaffection of their lives for primitive simplicity – except that Angel does not (at first) seek his cure in the tropics or deserts, but in Dorset. Like one of Conan Doyle's heroes, coming across a utopian lost world in the valley of the great dairies he goes native: he loses culture, as the narrator puts it, among "the Talbothays nymphs and swains" (*TD* 159).

What in later editions Angel first notices in Tess is "a fresh and virginal daughter of Nature" (*TD* 120). In the manuscript Hardy tried "superb," "true," and "real," and in the first volume edition "genuine", all stressing the relationship between sexual purity and racial authenticity. Angel is attracted to "unsophistication" (p. 203). Purity for him is a life entirely untouched by "the world," modern or traditional (he desires Tess's "supposed untraditional newness," p. 128), and Tess and the other dairymaids must, in this fantasy, be virginally English: unspoiled stock of the true race. The sign of their authenticity is what Torgovnick calls the "phenomenon of merging" (Torgovnick 1997: 9), an intense, sexualized nostalgia for the "emotions and sensations of relatedness and interdependence," which include "effacement of the self and the intuition of profound connections between humans and land, humans and animals" (1997: 4): a longing for those "'irrational' or 'mystical' aspects of the Western self" rejected in western Europe (or projected onto women and marginalized racial groups such as Gypsies). Angel's passion for the "new tribes from below" (*TD* 260) therefore leads him to make "close acquaintance with phenomena which he had before known but darkly – the seasons in their moods, morning and evening, night and noon in their temperaments, winds in their several dispositions, trees, waters and clouds, shades and silences, *ignes-fatui*, constellations, and the voices of inanimate things" (p. 118). "[W]onderfully free from the chronic melancholy which is taking hold of the civilized races with the decline of belief in a beneficent Power" (p. 118), Tess carries him back "into a joyous and unforeseeing past, before the necessity of taking thought had made the heavens gray" (p. 120), where he experiences, among the "impassioned, summer-saturated heathens" (p. 156–7), "the great passionate pulse of existence, unwarped, uncontorted, untrammelled by those creeds which futilely attempt to check what wisdom would be content to regulate" (p. 158).

Tess is repeatedly associated with images of the effacement of the self and the merging of the soul with the collective life force. On the fateful night drive with the beehives, the "mute procession past her of trees and hedges became attached to fantastic scenes outside reality, and the occasional heave of the wind became the sigh of some

immense sad soul, conterminous with the universe in space, and with history in time"
(*TD* 32). At Talbothays Angel is first bewitched by her "fluty" voice saying:

> "I don't know about ghosts . . . but I do know that our souls can be made to go outside
> our bodies when we are alive. . . . A very easy way to feel 'em go . . . is to lie on the
> grass at night and look straight up at some big bright star; and, by fixing your mind
> upon it, you will soon find that you are hundreds and hundreds o' miles away from your
> body, which you don't seem to want at all." (p. 120)

In the famous scene in which Tess is "fascinated" by Angel's harp music in the "damp
and rank" uncultivated part of the Talbothays garden (p. 122), she experiences that
same "exaltation": "conscious of neither time nor space," she undulates "upon the thin
notes," floating like the pollen that "seemed to be his notes made visible" (p. 123).[5]
In the twilit mornings in the pastures, too, Tess's face, "which was the focus of his
eyes, rising above the mist stratum, seemed to have a sort of phosphorescence upon
it. She looked ghostly, as if she were merely a soul at large" (p. 130); and in the
evening twilight, "the atmosphere [was] in such delicate equilibrium and so transmissive that inanimate objects seemed endowed with two or three senses, if not five. There
was no distinction between the near and the far, and an auditor felt close to everything
within the horizon" (p. 122). On the lonely hills and dales, "her quiescent glide was
of a piece with the element she moved in. Her flexuous and stealthy figure became
an integral part of the scene" (p. 85). In this last, however, it is the narrator who
participates in the primitivist fantasies that will lead Angel astray; and who goes on
to observe, with anthropological authority, that "a field-woman is a portion of the
field; she has somehow lost her own margin, imbibed the essence of her surrounding,
and assimilated herself with it" (p. 88). Once again, though, Tess is different, and her
difference is her fate. She is not "a figure which is part of the landscape", nor "a field-
woman pure and simple" (p. 280), until in desperation she covers her face and cuts
off her eyebrows to avoid the unwelcome attentions of men.

More significantly still, Tess, her family, and workmates – moderns all – inevitably
succumb to their own fantasies of oceanic unity, seeking a sedative serenity in day-
dreams, sleep, alcohol, romantic love, and sexual passion. When Tess falls in love with
Angel, she feels as her parents had felt when "a sort of halo, an occidental glow, came
over life." Then, troubles "and other realities took on themselves a metaphysical
impalpability, sinking to minor cerebral phenomena for quiet contemplation, in place
of standing as pressing concretions which chafe body and soul" (*TD* 23). At Talbothays, her new love envelops her "as a photosphere," irradiating her into "forgetfulness
of her past sorrows, keeping back the gloomy spectres that would persist in their
attempts to touch her – doubt, fear, moodiness, care, shame" (p. 195). But to submit
to the seductions of forgetfulness in this novel is to invite terrible material retribution.
Earlier, the fateful events in the Chase had been similarly foreshadowed by, and
enshrouded in, an almost opaque atmosphere of ecstasy and delusion. The "blue nar-
cotic haze" of Alec's smoke (p. 42), which smothers Tess in the first scene at the

poultry farm, thickens, as it were, into the "mist of yellow radiance" in the Ovidian hay-trusser's shed at Trantridge (p. 500), and the drunkenness of the homecomers imagining "themselves and surrounding nature forming an organism of which all the parts harmoniously and joyously interpenetrated each other. They were as sublime as the moon and stars above them, and the moon and stars were as ardent as they" (p. 69). When Tess becomes entangled in the "webs of vapour" which "formed veils between the trees" in the foggy Chase (p. 73), she is overcome by "drowsiness" (p. 70), and in that "moment of oblivion" (p. 70), the "coarse pattern" (p. 74) of Alec's casual sexual violence is traced on her body.

If Tess is a figure for a Romantic ideal of the poetic apprehension of "emotions and sensations of relatedness and interdependence," then the novel posits a connection between poetic desire, pastoral nostalgia, and tragedy. As Rey Chow argues, the primitive is interchangeable with the countryside in the sense that both "*stand in* for that 'original' something that has been lost" (Chow 1995: 22) – that has *already* been lost. Tess is a victim both of violent historical change, therefore, and of the *suppression* of the violence of history. She is ruined by successive rationalist fantasies of social transcendence: inborn nobility; feminine nature; racial integrity and purity; country life. Yet, and here the contradictions begin to multiply, she is simultaneously sanctified for the very same transcendence not only by the narrator – who is in love with her queenly character, feminine constancy, and staunch Englishness – but by the author, who makes her carry the whole weight of the novel's claims about art itself: that it transcends the local conditions of social life, and strives to capture the transhistorical essence of human nature. This involves author, narrator, and reader (both the male reader implied by the narrative, and the novel's actual readers, male and female) in a shared "erotic commitment" (Boumelha 1982: 54) to Tess as a figure for the endurance of the aesthetic. Violent change cannot alter what is intrinsic: she is a pure woman, in spite of rape, adultery, murder; she is a Norman d'Urberville, in spite of the long deterioration of her family line.

If moments of vision are obscuring, they are also delaying, and Hardy's visual imagination and tragic worldview may be said to coincide in a chronotope of delay in *Tess*. The "maladroit delay" from which the "anxieties, disappointments, shocks, catastrophes, and passing-strange destinies" spring is also expressed in the novel as a time-space of "strange and solemn" intervals: twilight (*TD* 129), that point of "delicate equilibrium" when there is "no distinction between the near and the far" (p. 122), and "when the light and the darkness are so evenly balanced that the constraint of day and the suspense of night neutralize each other, leaving absolute mental liberty" (p. 85). In *Tess* the tragedy happens in times and spaces where clear-sightedness is not possible (because of youth or weakness or tiredness or love or alcohol or weather) and subjective experience continually distorts the world it sees and tries to understand. Far from being a Bloomsbury epiphany, then, the Hardyan moment of vision is a melodramatic exclamation of postponement and longing which carries the reader "through and beyond the surface of things to what lies behind . . . which is the true scene of the highly colored drama" (Brooks 1976: 2); but the true scene is not "spiritual reality" but a still incomplete world, "charged with impressions" (*TD* 462) that are always on the verge of dissolving into the mist. The turmoil of passions, confused ideas, contested beliefs, and suppressed ideals cannot be left behind: the eruption of the poetic into the narrative transforms and resolves nothing.

Tess is therefore the exemplary heroine of the "psychical" sensation novel Hardy imagined in 1888 when *Tess of the d'Urbervilles* was beginning to take shape (*LW* 213): a novel where suspense and suffering take place in the mental lives of the characters.[6] Tess does not become "an integral part of the scene" at all; the world she becomes one with "is only a psychological phenomenon" – it *is* her inner life. She has so intensified natural processes that they seem a part of her own story (*TD* 85), but she is isolated in that world she creates, where she is not "an existence, an experience, a passion, a structure of sensations, to anybody but herself" (p. 91). All she can communicate of herself is captured in the disembodied voice that floats across the dark Sunday evening air when "her impulsive speeches" are "ecstacized to fragments," and all that is audible is "the spasmodic catch in her remarks, broken into syllables by the leapings of her heart" (pp. 194–5). Hers is the impassioned, fitful speech of the poetic imagination trying and failing to transcend history, creating only a mute force-field for all the incongruities, ambivalences, and crises that collect there from the momentarily suspended, traumatized social world. That is the melodrama of the Hardyan moment of vision.

NOTES

1   Louis and Auguste Lumière first exhibited the Cinématographe – a combination 35mm cine camera, printer, and projector – at the Grand Café in Paris in December 1895. It was first shown in London in March 1896 and in New York in June 1896.

2   Interestingly, Hardy's preface echoes Oscar Wilde's preface to the revised *Picture of Dorian Gray*, first published in the *Fortnightly Review* in March 1891: "Those who find ugly meanings in beautiful things are corrupt without being charming."

3   "If you look beneath the surface of any farce you see a tragedy; and, on the contrary, if you blind yourself to the deeper issues of a tragedy, you see a farce" (*LW* 224).

4   Hardy owned a copy of the 11th edition (London, 1841); there are "copious notes throughout the text and on the last two blank leaves." (*LN* I: 269; see also Taylor 1993: 76–8).

5   Charles Bernheimer argues that Hardy, who "had nothing to do with the English decadent movement and evinced no interest in . . . Wilde," dramatized in these passages the opposition between "natural process and aesthetic creation": "a version of the conflict that motivates the decadent choice to privilege art over life" (2002: 81).

6   "January 14. A 'sensation-novel' is possible in which the sensationalism is not casualty but evolution; not physical but psychical. . . . The difference between the latter kind of novel and the novel of physical sensationalism – i.e., personal adventure, etc., – is this: that whereas in the physical the adventure itself is the subject of interest, the psychical results being passed over as commonplace, in the psychical the casualty or adventure is held to be of no intrinsic interest, but the effect upon the faculties is the important matter to be depicted" (*LW* 213).

REFERENCES AND FURTHER READING

Berger, Sheila (1990). *Thomas Hardy and Visual Structures: Framing, Disruption, Process*. New York: New York University Press.

Bernheimer, Charles (2002). *Decadent Subjects: The Idea of Decadence in Art, Literature, Philosophy, and Culture of the Fin de Siècle in Europe*. Baltimore: Johns Hopkins University Press.

Björk, Lennart A. (ed.) (1985). *The Literary Notebooks of Thomas Hardy*. London and Basingstoke: Macmillan.

Boumelha, Penny (1982). *Thomas Hardy and Women: Sexual Ideology and Narrative Form*. Brighton: Harvester Press.

Brady, Kristin (1999). Thomas Hardy and Matters of Gender. In Dale Kramer (ed.), *The Cambridge Companion to Thomas Hardy* (pp. 93–111). Cambridge: Cambridge University Press.

Bronfen, Elisabeth (1993). Pay as You Go: On the Exchange of Bodies and Signs. In Margaret R. Higonnet (ed.), *The Sense of Sex: Feminist Perspectives on Hardy* (pp. 66–86). Urbana: University of Illinois Press.

Brooks, Peter (1976). *The Melodramatic Imagination: Balzac, Henry James, Melodrama, and the Mode of Excess*. New Haven: Yale University Press.

Campbell, George (1860). *The Philosophy of Rhetoric*. New York: Harper & Brothers.

Chow, Rey (1995). *Primitive Passions: Visuality, Sexuality, Ethnography, and Contemporary Chinese Cinema*. New York: Columbia University Press.

Cox, R. G. (ed.) (1970). *Thomas Hardy: The Critical Heritage*. London: Routledge & Kegan Paul.

Crary, Jonathan (1990). *Techniques of the Observer: On Vision and Modernity in the Nineteenth Century*. Cambridge, MA: MIT Press.

Dalziel, Pamela, and Michael Millgate (eds.) (1994). *Thomas Hardy's "Studies, Specimens &c." Notebook*. Oxford: Clarendon Press.

Dolin, Tim (1998). A History of the Text. In Tim Dolin (ed.), *Tess of the d'Urbervilles* (pp. xliv–lxviii). London: Penguin.

Eagleton, Terry (1981). *Walter Benjamin, or, Towards a Revolutionary Criticism*. London: Verso.

Ebbatson, Roger (1986). Introduction. In Roger Ebbatson (ed.), *A Pair of Blue Eyes* (pp. 13–38). Harmondsworth: Penguin.

Eliot, George ([1858] 1985). Amos Barton. In *Scenes of Clerical Life*, ed. Thomas A. Noble. Oxford: Clarendon Press.

Eliot, George ([1871–2] 1986). *Middlemarch*, ed. David Carroll. Oxford: Clarendon Press.

Felski, Rita (2003). Modernist Studies and Cultural Studies: Reflections on Method. *Modernism/Modernity*, 10(3), 501–17.

Gatrell, S. (1988). *Hardy, the Creator: A Textual Biography*. Oxford: Clarendon Press.

Gledhill, Christine (1987). *Home Is Where the Heart Is: Studies in Melodrama and the Woman's Film*. London: British Film Institute.

Goode, John (1988). *Thomas Hardy: The Offensive Truth*. Oxford: Blackwell.

Graves, Robert (1923). Mr. Hardy and the Pleated Skirt. *The Nation and Athenaeum*, July 7, 451–2.

Greenwood, Frederick (1892). The Genius of Thomas Hardy. *Illustrated London News*, Oct. 1, 431.

Hardy, Thomas ([1873] 1986). *A Pair of Blue Eyes*, ed. Roger Ebbatson. Harmondsworth: Penguin.

Hardy, Thomas. ([1891] 1998). *Tess of the d'Urbervilles*, ed. Tim Dolin. London: Penguin.

Hardy, Thomas ([1895] 1985). *Jude the Obscure*, ed. Patricia Ingham. Oxford: Oxford University Press.

Hardy, Thomas (1984). *The Life and Work of Thomas Hardy*, ed. Michael Millgate. London: Macmillan.

Harrison, Charles, Paul Wood, and Jason Gaiger (1998). *Art in Theory, 1815–1900: An Anthology of Changing Ideas*. Oxford: Blackwell.

Jacobus, Mary (1978). Tess: The Making of a Pure Woman. In Susan Lipshitz (ed.), *Tearing the Veil: Essays on Femininity* (pp. 77–92). London: Routledge & Kegan Paul.

Kennedy, Matthew (1999). *Marie Dressler: A Biography. With a Listing of Major Stage Performances, a Filmography, and a Discography*. Jefferson, NC: McFarland.

Kirby, Michael (1980). Melodrama Manifesto of Structuralism. In Daniel Charles Gerould (ed.), *Melodrama* (p. xiv). New York: New York Literary Forum.

Laird, J. T. (1975). *The Shaping of Tess of the d'Urbervilles*. Oxford: Clarendon Press.

Lodge, David (1981). *Working with Structuralism: Essays and Reviews on Nineteenth- and Twentieth-Century Literature*. London: Routledge & Kegan Paul.

McDowall, Arthur Sydney (1917). The Poetry of Thomas Hardy. *Times Literary Supplement*, Dec. 13, 603.

Millgate, Michael (2004). *Thomas Hardy: A Biography Revisited*. Oxford: Oxford University Press.

Millgate, Michael (ed.) (2001). *Thomas Hardy's Public Voice: The Essays, Speeches, and Miscellaneous Prose*. Oxford: Clarendon Press.

Nunokawa, Jeff (1992). Tess, Tourism and the Spectacle of the Woman. In Linda M. Shires (ed.), *Rewriting the Victorians: Theory, History, and the Politics of Gender* (pp. 70–86). London: Routledge.

Postlewait, Thomas (1999). The Hieroglyphic Stage: American Theatre and Society, Post-Civil War to 1945. In Don B. Wilmeth and C. W. E. Bigsby (eds.), *The Cambridge History of American Theatre*, vol. II: *1870–1945* (pp. 107–95). Cambridge: Cambridge University Press.

Purdy, Richard Little, and Michael Millgate (eds.) (1978–88). *The Collected Letters of Thomas Hardy*. 7 vols. Oxford: Clarendon Press.

Singer, Ben (2001). *Melodrama and Modernity: Early Sensational Cinema and its Contexts*. New York: Columbia University Press.

Taylor, Dennis (1993). *Hardy's Literary Language and Victorian Philology*. Oxford: Clarendon Press.

Torgovnick, Marianna (1990). *Gone Primitive: Savage Intellects, Modern Lives*. Chicago: University of Chicago Press.

Torgovnick, Marianna (1997). *Primitive Passions: Men, Women, and the Quest for Ecstasy*. New York: Alfred A. Knopf.

Vicinus, Martha (1981). Helpless and Unfriended: Nineteenth-Century Domestic Melodrama. *New Literary History*, 13(1), 127–43.

Widdowson, Peter (1989). *Hardy in History: A Study in Literary Sociology*. London: Routledge.

Woolf, Virginia ([1932] 1960). *The Second Common Reader*. New York: Harcourt Brace Jovanovich.

23

Jude the Obscure and English National Identity: The Religious Striations of Wessex

Dennis Taylor

No one is more prized as a national English author than Thomas Hardy, "the incomparable chronicler of his Wessex" as Raymond Williams somewhat wryly observed (1970: 97). Hardy would seem to be the prime embodiment of Englishness, rendered through his regional novels, with their cohesive national past reaching back into myth and history. Wessex might naturally be inscribed on the English flag. The biannual Thomas Hardy conference in Dorchester is practically as much an exercise in patriotism as in literary discussion. It attracts both tourists and scholars, and after the papers are read, tours are conducted of the "Wessex" countryside. Nationhood has been called an "imaginary political community" by Benedict Anderson and other cultural historians; so, Wessex is a created imaginary regional community, which would seem to line up well with the larger imaginary community of England itself.

Michael Millgate, Simon Gatrell, and others have discussed the geographical creation of Wessex, and its gradual formalization in Hardy's mind, until it became a full-blown region connecting the various novels. Merryn Williams, Peter Widdowson, and others have chipped away at the idyllic character of Wessex, showing that Hardy dramatizes, and is also shaped by, powerful economic and class interests. Such critics have pointed to the dark side of Wessex, its social and economic injustices. There has been some chipping away of the myth of English cohesiveness from the point of view of the working classes, of women, and various marginal groups; and it has been argued that Hardy's portrait of England in fact acknowledges and records the existence of these marginalized facets of English life. But the basic coherence of Hardy's Wessex as a geographical region with a coherent ancient history has not been challenged. It is normally assumed that the religious component of that history is the Church of England.

English national identity has often been described as English national Protestant identity. The role of the Church of England, which is distinctively defined as "of England," has traditionally been seen as essential for the construction of English identity, but in recent revisionist scholarship the fragility of that construction has been emphasized. Such scholarship has portrayed the idea of English national religious identity as an imaginary entity that has papered over many realities.

Some Hardy novels tend to present Wessex as a place with the Church of England at its center. Hardy's first pastoral novel, *Under the Greenwood Tree*, assumed an orthodox Anglican world; it may include conflict between the older more lackadaisical eighteenth-century church with its chorus and fiddlers, and the newer post-Tractarian minister with his preference for the organ. But the conflict is safely in-house, and the novel presents us with an English pastoral landscape where the village church is almost a natural growth. Ancientness is Church of England ancientness, with the hymn "Remember Adam's Fall" referred to as "an ancient and time-worn hymn, embodying a quaint Christianity in words orally transmitted from father to son through several generations" (*UGT* 60). The hymn was first printed in 1611, long after the establishment of the Church of England. This version of the Wessex historical world in *Under the Greenwood Tree* is drawn on, though with qualifications, in *Far From the Madding Crowd*, *The Mayor of Casterbridge*, and *The Woodlanders*, and forms a major component of the myth of Wessex for which Hardy is noted. If Wessex reaches further back into medieval times in these novels, it does so seamlessly, like the Weatherbury Barn that orientates *Far From the Madding Crowd*: "It not only emulated the form of the neighbouring church of the parish, but vied with it in antiquity. Whether the barn had ever formed one of a group of conventual buildings nobody seemed to be aware; no trace of such surroundings remained" (*FFMC* 126). When Bathsheba reintegrates herself into this timeless pastoral community, she does so to the tune of Newman's "Lead kindly Light" (*FFMC* 342) with no sense of inappropriateness.

Hardy described himself as "churchy; not in an intellectual sense, but in so far as instincts and emotions ruled" (*LW* 407), by which he meant "Church of England churchy." He and his Hardy forebears went to the local Stinsford parish church, which had been conventionally high and dry during the eighteenth century and had then settled into a form of moderate high church Anglo-Catholicism in the nineteenth century. Hardy also had evangelical and Baptist friends and associations in Dorchester, but he maintained his more conservative Anglican roots, until he lost his faith in London in the 1860s. However, he would continue to haunt Anglican churches throughout his life. (see CHAPTER 5, HARDY AND THE CHURCH)

Jude the Obscure is Hardy's great end-of-the-century novel. It is his final novelistic meditation on the nature of the world of Wessex. *Jude* is important also because in it Hardy confronts head-on the religious component of the history of Wessex. In *Jude*, the religious origins of Wessex are explored, but the results are extremely problematic. My argument is that in this novel Hardy challenges the identification of Englishness with the Church of England, and undoes the Protestant coherence of Wessex.

A key passage is the novel's description of Shaston (Shaftesbury), a passage that Hardy felt important enough to move from its initial imbedding in the middle of part 3 to stand as the introduction to part 4 of the novel. The passage reads:

> Shaston, the ancient British Palladour,
> "From whose foundation first such strange reports arise,"

(as Drayton sang it), was, and is, in itself the city of a dream. Vague imaginings of its castle, its three mints, its magnificent apsidal Abbey, the chief glory of South Wessex, its twelve churches, its shrines, chantries, hospitals, its gabled freestone mansions – all now ruthlessly swept away – throw the visitor, even against his will, into a pensive melancholy, which the stimulating atmosphere and limitless landscape around him can scarcely dispel. The spot was the burial-place of a king and a queen, of abbots and abbesses, saints and bishops, knights and squires. The bones of King Edward "the Martyr," carefully removed hither for holy preservation, brought Shaston a renown which made it the resort of pilgrims from every part of Europe, and enabled it to maintain a reputation extending far beyond English shores. To this fair creation of the great Middle-Age the Dissolution was, as historians tell us, the death-knell. With the destruction of the enormous abbey the whole place collapsed in a general ruin: the Martyr's bones met with the fate of the sacred pile that held them, and not a stone is now left to tell where they lie.

   The natural picturesqueness and singularity of the town still remain; but strange to say these qualities which were noted by many writers in ages when scenic beauty is said to have been unappreciated, are passed over in this, and one of the queerest and quaintest spots in England stands virtually unvisited to-day. (*JO* 199)

The passage, coming almost exactly midway in this novel about England's religious past, is remarkable for its deceptive clarity. How does Hardy see medieval Shaston? As something simply continuous with nineteenth-century Anglicanism? As the remote ancient history of that Anglicanism? The use of the word "Dissolution" rather than "Reformation" is interesting, and could reflect Anglo-Catholic minimizing of the Reformation break, with regret at the destruction it caused. Or it could reflect a Roman Catholic view of the Reformation as a fundamental trauma and historical break in English religious history. The description of Shaston and its itinerants as vigorous and generous (as in the way they defend Phillotson [*JO* 248]) recalls Cobbett's defense of the working class in *Rural Rides* and of corporate medievalism in his influential work, *A History of the Protestant Reformation in England and Ireland; Showing how the Event has Impoverished the Main Body of the People in those countries*: "It was not a reformation, but a devastation of England" (1824–7: 18). Raymond Williams, in *The Country and the City*, has traced the "tradition: Cobbett, Arch, Ashby; late Jefferies; Thomas Hardy" (1973: 196). We might also describe this as the tradition from Cobbett's *Rural Rides* (1830) to Barnes's *Poems of Rural Life* (1844) and on to Hardy's celebration of Barnes. (A rare explicit notice of Cobbett by Hardy is his marking of a Cobbett passage, from *Advice to young men*, in his early copy of *Half-Hours of French Translation* [1863: 267].) All that is left of the Merry England of Shaston's Catholic past is the roistering of the Shaston itinerants who resist the imposition of Puritan morality. That Cobbett was not Catholic, but a combination of "radical" and Anglican, muddies that picture as well.

   The Shaston passage comes at a key moment in Jude's religious evolution. *Jude the Obscure* is, among other things, a conversion novel in the nineteenth-century tradition of pilgrims' progresses charted memorably by Margaret Maison in *The Victorian Vision*. "*From Oxford to Rome* and *The Nemesis of Faith* measure the extremes of this class" (Tillotson 1956: 130). Conversions in these novels, and in parallel autobiographies, narrative poems, and many other genres, may proceed in high, low, and broad direction; or in their offshoots, Catholic, Evangelical, or Liberal directions. Indeed, *Jude* synthesizes various types of conversion novel. Young Jude proceeds toward a high (Anglican) church conclusion, but eventually converts to a kind of humanistic anti-church liberalism; Sue has preceded Jude in attaining a similar liberalism, though with more pagan and aesthetic elements, in the manner of Swinburne. At the end she converts to a high church penitential mode. Conversion to dissenting evangelicalism is reserved for Arabella though, as in the case of Alec d'Urberville, Hardy does not take it seriously. Hardy respects the evangelical Aunt Drusilla (whom the Reverend James Clare, in *Tess of the d'Urbervilles*, would have included in his congregation). But the great polarities of the novel are high church religion, which we need to define, and the liberal agnosticism or atheism of the same period. Hardy acknowledged the Foxian Protestant theory, which he gave to the Baptist minister in *A Laodicean*, that "the authentic, pre-Reformation Church of England is an essentially Protestant Church" (O'Malley 2000: 656; 2006: 204), but he had no interest in it (*contra* O'Malley), though the question of the new-fangledness of Anglo-Catholicism, with its relation to Roman Catholicism, is very much an issue.

Thus in his boyhood Jude comes under the influence of Richard Phillotson, who presumably keeps to an orthodox Anglican direction implicit in his ambition to go to Oxford and succeed as a clergyman. Jude himself moves toward clericalism as a vehicle of social advancement and hopes to imitate Phillotson. Jude's earliest religious affiliations seem to be with eighteenth-century Anglicanism, moderately Calvinist, against which the Methodists and later the Tractarians reacted. Jude probably began with "such stock works as Paley and Butler" (*JO* 136); but he becomes gradually more influenced by "the religious school called Tractarian: the well-known three, the enthusiast, the poet, and the formularist" (p. 80), namely Newman, Keble, and Pusey, the three ghosts he imagines at Christminster, and "the echoes of whose teachings had influenced him even in his obscure home" of Marygreen. Three chapters later he will describe Christminster as a place where "Newman, Pusey, Ward, Keble, loom so large!" (p. 103). And later, "As a relaxation from the Fathers, and such stock works as Paley and Butler, he read Newman, Pusey, and many other modern lights" (p. 136). Then he moves "deep" into "Pusey's Library of the Fathers" (p. 143) and Sue soon teases him for being in "the Tractarian stage" (p. 151). When Jude gives up his religion and burns his books, he burns them in historical sequence from eighteenth-century Anglican through Tractarian to Catholic: "Jeremy Taylor, Butler, Doddridge, Paley, Pusey, Newman and the rest had gone to ashes" (p. 218).

Sue Bridehead, meanwhile, has gone in the reverse direction, in her own version of the conversion novel. When we see her, she has become a liberal, even though she works in a shop which Jude describes as ritualistic. Her purchase of the statues of Venus and Apollo reflects the urbanity of Arnold's *Culture and Anarchy* and the more hedonistic culture of Pater, Swinburne, and Wilde. But she undergoes a sudden 180-degree turn at the death of her children, and reverts to a religious primitivism associated with the same ritualism that Jude had come to reject. She prostrates herself before the "Latin cross" (*JO* 349) (i.e., with an elongated stem, slightly higher perhaps than a plain Protestant cross, but not as high as a Roman Catholic crucifix) at St. Silas church. St. Silas is a "ceremonial church" (p. 95) in the ritualist tradition. (The actual church is St. Barnabas, still high, in the Jericho district of Oxford, designed by A. W. Blomfield, Hardy's employer when he was a Gothic architect.) Hardy had said: "I felt that by the heroine's recantation of all her views, at the end of the story, & becoming a penance-seeking Christian, I was almost too High-Churchy" (*CL* II: 97–8). It is hard to believe that Hardy is not being disingenuous in disclaiming a negative judgment, unless we see him as true to his aesthetic of rendering "impressions," particularly impressions of Wessex and, in this case, its historical religious components.

What does all this have to do with the history of Wessex? Jude and Sue's careers are determined by their relationship to English Christianity. But what Christianity is it? Hardy says that before Jude's de-conversion he "did not at that time see that mediaevalism was as dead as a fern-leaf in a lump of coal; that other developments were shaping in the world around him, in which Gothic architecture and its associations had no place" (*JO* 85). Earlier Jude had felt his way round the dark alleys of Christminster, with their "porticoes, oriels, doorways of enriched and florid middle-age design, their extinct air being accentuated by the rottenness of the stones. It seemed impossible that modern thought could house itself in such decrepit and superseded chambers" (p. 79). Shaston seems to represent a time when "mediaevalism" and its "associations" were alive, a green fern, before being fossilized. When did the fossilization occur? And when was it ever alive? Elsewhere in the novel, Hardy describes how "the outer walls of Sarcophagus College – silent, black and windowless – threw their four centuries of gloom, bigotry, and decay into the little room" (p. 332). This takes us back to the end of the fourteenth century, long after the deposit of Edward the Martyr's bones around 980 in Shaftesbury, Hardy's Shaston. So the nature of Christianity in early medieval Shaston becomes the issue, and brings in the complication of the role of Roman Catholicism in English life.

One complication with idealizing Shaston is that the novel often conveys the sense that fossilization applies to Christianity itself, from the very beginnings, in its holding to supernaturalism, the Commandments, sin, and all the rest. (This theory of primal fossilization is oddly parallel to the evangelical theory of primal purity.) Had Christianity then always been deathly? Hardy sometimes held this view. A year after publishing *Jude*, Hardy wrote a letter to Edward Clodd concerning his book *Pioneers of Evolution from Thales to Huxley*: "What seems to me the most striking idea dwelt upon is that of the arrest of light & reason by theology for 16,00 [*sic*] years" (*CL* II: 143). In his (and Florence Henniker's) copy of George Egerton's *Keynotes* (Yale collection), Hardy marked and wrote "good!" next to a passage reading: "It seems as if all the religions, all the advancement, all the culture of the past, has only been a forging of chains to cripple posterity, a laborious building up of moral and legal prisons based on false conceptions of sin and shame, to cramp men's minds and hearts and souls, not to speak of women's" (Egerton 1893: 40–1). So the Shaston passage in *Jude* is something of an anomaly, though a frequent anomaly in Hardy, repeated in those poems of medieval nostalgia written in the years just following the publication of *Jude*. Again, this inconsistent nostalgia may be associated with high Anglicanism, except that it is hard to reconcile it with Hardy's anger at the contemporary Anglican Church.

Hardy's attitude to that most marginalized of English entities, Roman Catholicism, is interesting. In *The Woodlanders*, Hardy reflects the influence of Edward Gibbon, "the sly author of the Immortal chapter on Christianity" (*W* 82), for whom Catholicism and atheism were the final antagonists, a binary reflected wryly in Dr. Fitzpiers' remark: "My neighbours think I am an atheist, except those who think I am a Roman Catholic" (*W* 244). In *Life and Work*, Hardy cites the Jacobite connections of his ancestors (*LW* 10–11). In 1862 Horace Moule took him to visit the Farm Street chapel "built by Pugin," and Hardy found the service "very impressive" (*LW* 503). Among his earliest "Literary Notes" were excerpts from Newman. Of course, Hardy is famous for his later assessment of Newman that "there is no first link to his excellent chain of reasoning, and down you come headlong" (*LW* 50–1). When Jude had been initially drawn to Oxford as a "city of light" (*JO* 25), Hardy was at least indirectly thinking of Newman. Hardy associated Oxford's "ineffable charm" with Arnold's characterization of it as "whispering from her towers the last enchantments of the Middle Age," and "calling us nearer . . . to the ideal, to perfection," thus "the home of lost causes" (Arnold 1884: xi). Hardy quoted the last two phrases but not the first (*JO* 81). In a later essay, "Emerson," Arnold put Newman and his "charm" (Arnold 1885: 139) at the heart of the Oxford ethos and associated it with his earlier "the last enchantments of the Middle Age" (1885: 142) and now with Newman's "solution which, to speak frankly, is impossible" (1885: 139). Arnold's frankly impossible solution may be reflected in Hardy's "no first link to his excellent chain of reasoning."

Hardy also found himself "deeply impressed" by the opening ceremony for the new Catholic Westminster Cathedral, though he was careful to add: "he had no leanings to Roman Catholicism" (*LW* 285). According to an entry in Arthur Benson's diary for 1904, "Hardy talked rather interestingly of Newman; he has read the *Apologia*, & I *thought* he said 'I joined the RC church for a time, but it has left no impression whatever on me now' " (quoted in Tomalin 2006: 284). This comment has the offhand status of another reportedly made by Hardy, that he wished he "had lived in the Middle Ages, when the Church was supreme and unquestioned. Life must have been very sweet and beautiful then, before doubts had arisen" (*CL* III: 157–8). Interestingly it is such sentiment that gives rise to various poems like "The Lost Pyx" (printed 1903) that Hardy wrote after *Jude*.

Generally, Hardy had a certain kind of Anglican obliviousness to the claims of the Roman Catholic Church, and to the great Reformation arguments that had characterized English church theology with varying intensity through its history. Jędrzejewski has argued, provocatively but not unpersuasively, that Hardy hardly distinguished Roman Catholicism from high church Anglicanism: "he seems to have paid very little attention to the numerous differences . . . failing, as a result[,] to see some of the complexities inherent in the problem of the understanding of Christianity as a whole" (Jędrzejewski 1993: 28). Hardy tended to see the Reformation as a minor historical blip in the history of the English Church. The Gunpowder Plot is referenced in *The Return of the Native*, but not as anti-papal statement but as remains of an ancient folk festival, with its bonfires on Egdon Heath. In *Life and Work*, Hardy refers to his childhood and seeing "the burning in effigy of the Pope and Cardinal Wiseman in the old Roman Amphitheatre at Dorchester during the No-Popery Riots. The sight to young Hardy was most lurid, and he never forgot it" (*LW* 26); but the event is described more as a thing of lurid curiosity, from an Ainsworthian point of view, with no identification with the anti-Catholic point of view. Hardy's later attendance at the foundation of Westminster Cathedral shows no dismay at what was so religiously traumatic to Victorian England, the "Papal Aggression" of 1850.

Thus there is little anti-Catholic animus in Hardy, even though anti-Catholicism had traditionally been a key component of post-Reformation English national identity, and of many English historical novels that preceded Hardy. If Jędrzejewski is right, it is hard to decide if Hardy is ecumenical, wise, or simply obtuse. It is likely that Hardy, especially given his wife's ferocious reminders about her Protestant enmity to Catholicism (see Kay-Robinson 1979: 200–1), was quite alert to the importance of the Reformation divisions but transcended them. He did so, I am arguing, in order to engage a more comprehensive notion of "Wessex." Roman Catholicism is an odd entity in Hardy; it can be subsumed under Anglicanism, it can be an exotic Continental entity, it can have an interesting continuity with medievalism. It is an unsorted piece of furniture in the Hardy landscape. But it helps point us to the way Hardy takes on more than he can fully handle, a critique of English religious national identity.

An interesting influence on Hardy in this regard was William Harrison Ainsworth. Ainsworth reflected a number of mid-nineteenth-century developments that were revising English attitudes toward its medieval Catholic past, and complicating the English sense of their Church of England history. Indeed, this gives Ainsworth's novels a significance that has not been accorded him in the critical tradition, where he is dismissed as a popular sensationalist (see among many others Tillotson 1956: 140). Ainsworth had a powerful effect on Hardy's boyhood imagination, especially through the historical novels that focus on Protestant and Catholic themes in English religious history. These novels show an interesting progression from *Rookwood* (1834), with its conventionally conniving Jesuit, to the later historical novels, *The Tower of London* (1840), *Old St. Paul's* (1841), *Windsor Castle* (1843) (from which Hardy took "Cardinal College"), and *Tower Hill* (1871). These show the influence of the Catholic revisionist historian John Lingard (also a key influence on Cobbett), who is acknowledged in the preface to Ainsworth's *Guy Fawkes* (1841). The result of Lingard's influence was that Ainsworth, a novelist of great popularity, took the medievalizing of Scott and pushed it in a direction favorable to the papists. He highlighted the persecution of Catholics, and the high honor and integrity of Catholic families. His portrait of Herne the Hunter in *Windsor Castle* is remarkable, because Herne is a complex phantom figure who reflects the moral complexity of the dangerously impulsive Henry VIII; Herne appears at moments when Henry is about to kill another wife. When Jude, after gazing at Christminster one evening, fears being chased by Herne the Hunter, it is tempting to reflect on Ainsworth's attitude to the import of this specter – except again that Hardy's views are so undifferentiated that we cannot make too much of Herne, as we cannot make too much of Shaston. The influence of Ainsworth on Hardy's novels is extensive (see Weber 1966 for starters), and thus may have influenced Hardy's attitudes toward the Church of England and its relation to the Church of Rome.

Wessex, I would argue, becomes a more complicated historical entity for Hardy because of its contested religious description. He begins to complexify Wessex early in his career. Egdon Heath in *The Return of the Native* is offered as an ancient setting, in contrast with the deracinated early 1840s intellectualism of Clym Yeobright. But that ancient setting is characterized by the following elements (I exclude classical, biblical, and other analogies): ancient geology, ascetics and "Egdon eremites" (*RN* 175) and hermitages (p. 200) ("The most thorough-going ascetic could feel that he had a natural right to wander on Egdon," p. 5), the Domesday Book of 1086 (p. 5), "the great western road of the Romans" (p. 6), "prehistoric times" (p. 6), Celtic barrows (p. 11), ancient ritual bonfires for the Gunpowder Plot but more relevantly evoking "Druidical rites and Saxon ceremonies" and also Thor and Woden (p. 15), old ballads from Percy's *Reliques* (p. 16), seventeenth-century dances (p. 132), the time of threatened Napoleonic invasions (p. 141), "a very curious Druidical stone" (p. 188), witches and hexes, "that traditionary King of Wessex – King Lear" (p. 444), this historical mishmash climaxing with the May Day ceremony compared to "fragments of Teutonic rites to divinities whose names are forgotten" (p. 390). "The instincts of merry England lingered on here with exceptional vitality, and the symbolic customs which tradition has attached to each season of the year were yet a reality on Egdon" (pp. 389–90). Here merry England is an entity older than church history, in the light of which the Reformation is a mere detail.

The curiously extensive but compacted history evoked by the novel is symbolized in the Mummers' performance of the play of St. George, an action that is ancient, nominally Christian, pagan, and even geological: "This unweeting manner of performance is the true ring by which, in this refurbishing age, a fossilized survival may be known from a spurious reproduction" (*RN* 122). Egdon's ancientness has long been acknowledged by critics, but not its layeredness, its combination of multiple historical levels, from ancient geology to medieval Catholic, all contained in the "seamed and antique features" as Clym describes the heath. This layered pastness is very different from the domestic old-fashioned Church of England past of *Under the Greenwood Tree*. Post-Reformation English church history is simply bracketed in Hardy's description of Egdon Heath, and only intrudes in the allusions to churches and marriage legalisms in Anglebury and Weatherbury and Budmouth, on the outer fringes of the heath.

Thus when Hardy refers to the ancientness, "ancient" can be druidical or early nineteenth-century. The "ancient" church can be (a) the pre-Reformation medieval church, early or late medieval, and conceived as Roman or as proto-Anglican; (b) the Elizabethan Church of England because it is old; (c) the Caroline Anglicanism of the Stuarts; (d) the eighteenth-century church; (e) something continuous with the Anglo-Catholicism of the nineteenth century; (f) the Roman Catholic Church.

The same layered striations of a complex history are at work in *Tess of the d'Urbervilles*. Here Hardy envisions another form of ancientness, in all its garbled confusion. The very title points to an awkwardness, in connecting a country girl to an ancient family with an odd French name. What kind of ancientness do the d'Urbervilles represent? The first d'Urberville, Sir Pagan d'Urberville, wonderfully named, came over with the Normans, and then the family was associated with the Cavaliers, in a standard medieval Catholic to Anglican progression. The conflation of pagan and medieval Catholic is consistent with Protestant views, reflected in Mrs. Durbeyfield's description of the family as "reaching all back long before Oliver Grumble's times – to the days of the Pagan Turks – with monuments, and vaults, and crests" (*TD* 26), reflecting Falstaff's comical "Turk Gregory," conflating papal and pagan Turkish threat. Mrs. Durbeyfield's folk Christianity is itself described as "Jacobean" (p. 28). Baptizing her baby, Tess performs a medieval "*Benedicite* which she had lisped from infancy," and her rite was a "Fetichistic" exercise more like "the Pagan fantasy of their remote forefathers than of the systematized religion taught their race at later date" (p. 109). A time of Catholic faith and a time of pagan myth are conflated. *Tess of the d'Urbervilles* displays that characteristic Protestant attraction to and condemnation of medieval mores: attraction to the May Day dance, the White Hart, the votive sisterhood, the story of William Dewy and the kneeling cows (p. 115), evoking the medieval association with miracle and faith as in Hardy's poem "The Oxen"; this medievalism is associated with pastoral innocence "before the necessity of taking thought has made the Heavens grey" (p. 124).

The same fascination with an unsorted medievalism is reflected in the novel's repulsion from the Chase, with its "Druidical mistletoe" (*TD* 41), the rapes conducted by Tess's "mailed ancestors," witchery and magic evoked at Talbothays, decadent old families (condemned by Angel), and the "fetchizing" of female virginity which Angel has inherited "with the creed of mysticism" (p. 330); all this is contrasted to the nouveau riche Stokes who have usurped the ancient name. The medieval romance climaxes with Angel's sleepwalking and carrying Tess to the ruined Cistercian abbey (p. 230). The tombs of the d'Urbervilles where Tess and her family find shelter are made analogous in this romance of ancientness to the stones of Stonehenge, and the old medieval stress on ritual sacrifice is conflated with the pagan sacrifice of Tess at Stonehenge. The final scene of Tess's execution is accompanied by the view of Wintoncester ("aforetime capital of Wessex") and its cathedral with its "Norman windows," "the ancient hospice, where to this day the pilgrim may receive his dole of bread and ale," "the quaint irregularities of the Gothic erections" (pp. 383–4). The whole picture, with its contrasting red-brick prison, is reminiscent of Pugin's *Contrasts* (see Taylor 1989: 84–5) with a dash of Cobbett. The scene focuses on Angel and Liza-Lu, as like "Giotto's Two Apostles" (p. 383); and the novel ends with the Aeschylean

"'Justice' was done" followed by sentences beginning "And the d'Urberville knights and dames slept on in their tombs unknowing. The two speechless gazers bent themselves down to the earth, as if in prayer . . ." Pagan and Catholic elements mingle in this evocation of ancientness which frames the oddly twisted prayerfulness of these two modern people, as though bent under a history that they cannot fathom.

At this point, we might distinguish three kinds of novel in Hardy: the novel of the homely recent post-Reformation English past in *Under the Greenwood Tree*, where the ancient past is a Church of England past; the novel of the ancient pre-Reformation or a-Reformation past in *The Return of the Native* and *Tess*; and the novel of pre- and post-Reformation English church history in *A Laodicean*, and *Jude*, where Hardy tries to clarify for himself the two competing versions of English history: the Protestant and Catholic versions, the former reflecting the triumphal Protestantism of the Reformation and its final cementing into English, actually British, identity in the eighteenth century (see Colley 2005), the latter reflecting a history of fragmentation and loss of the medieval unity pictured in the Shaston passage. What complicates these binaries is the so-called *via media* of Anglicanism and Anglo-Catholicism. Sorting out the Church of England, Anglo-Catholicism, and Roman Catholicism is one of the most vexed historical questions of our time. It is more than an academic question; it is a question about what it means to be English in traditional religious terms. It is a major question about English national identity, a question which has assumed great relevance in today's global world (for a recent colorful argument, see Jones 1998). It is question of who claims that world described in the Shaston passage. Patrick O'Malley is a rare critic who has grappled with the problem: "What is the past, what Hardy's narrator calls 'the ghostly past' [p. 83] . . . that intrudes upon the present? What, for example, is England's authentic religious heritage?" (O'Malley 2000: 655).

These issues are so ineluctable that Hardy strains to clarify them for himself, notably in *A Laodicean*. The heroine has rejected her Baptist alternative, much as Hardy did. As the novel draws to its end Paula experiences the French town of St. Jacques:

> She was transported to the Middle Ages . . . She had never supposed such a street to exist outside the imaginations of antiquarians. Smells direct from the sixteenth century hung in the air . . . The faces of the people . . . seemed those of individuals who habitually gazed on the great Francis, and spoke of Henry the Eighth as the King across the sea . . . (*AL* 460)

as though two great polities were not in conflict but merge in an homogenized medievalism. This picture, and Paula's and George's meetings in the dark French Catholic churches, are followed by the announcement that Lady de Stancy is retiring to a "Protestant Sisterhood," "Whatever shortcomings may be found in such a community" (*AL* 495); it is uncertain whether this kind of conversion is parallel or contrasting to the experience of the French church; this is one of the few places anywhere

where Hardy uses the word "Protestant." A related place is where Angel Clare's mother challenges him on his way to Brazil: "Brazil! Why they are all Roman Catholics there, surely!" (*TD* 255), and later, when Angel speaks of cloisters (comparing his Brazil exile) and Roman Catholicism, Mercy Chant exclaims "*I* glory in my Protestantism" (*TD* 260). Nevertheless, Hardy hardly ever uses the sectarian terms "Protestant" and "Catholic." In *Jude*, one senses Hardy searching for a term that doesn't exist when he has Jude mistakenly suppose that Miss Fontover, breaking Sue's statuary, found them "Too Catholic-Apostolic for her, I suppose? No doubt she called them Popish images and talked of the invocation of saints" (*JO* 103). (This is possibly, but not clearly, a reference to the Protestant millenarian sect the "Catholic-Apostolic Church," founded in the 1830s and associated with Edward Irving and Henry Drummond, noted by Hardy in *LW* 80, 208). When Jude screams at Sue "You make me hate Christianity, or mysticism, or Sacerdotalism, or whatever it may be called" (*JO* 350), the problem of nomenclature persists, not that different from what perplexed Paula in *A Laodicean*.

Paula's statement, that ends the novel – "I wish my castle wasn't burnt; and I wish you were a De Stancy" – reflects ambiguously a desire to return to feudalism or to go over to high church Anglicanism, or Episcopalianism as the Baptist minister earlier calls it (*AL* 70). The Baptist minister had sounded the old note when he worried about the De Stancy towers: "The spirit of old papistical times still lingers in the nooks of those silent walls, like a bad odour in a still atmosphere, dulling the iconoclastic emotions of the true Puritan" (p. 70). (Not to worry, though: Paula settles for laodiceanism (p. 496) and then Arnold's "modern spirit," p. 499). In fact the ambiguity is irresolvable, as Paula indicates when George challenges her, "You are not at enmity with Anglicanism, I am sure?" to which Paula's response is: "I want not to be. I want to be – what – ," and George speaks for her, "What the De Stancys were, and are" (p. 126). But what the De Stancys were, and are, is a buried and fragmented history. Paula is teased for going to "a service of the unreformed Church" in France, but replies "In a foreign country it is different from home" (p. 406), as though the home church were too complicated an entity to be simply explained.

There is a wonderful passage in *The Woodlanders* that expresses this opaque and cross-striated ancientness. Giles Winterborne has followed the woodland track into Sherton Abbas and driven into the streets,

> the churches, the abbey, and other mediaeval buildings on this clear bright morning having the linear distinctness of architectural drawings, as if the original dream and vision of the conceiving master-mason were for a brief hour flashed down through the centuries to an unappreciative age. Giles saw their eloquent look on this day of transparency, but could not construe it. (*W* 75–6)

Not only Giles, but also Jude, Paula Power, and the others cannot construe it. Nor do I think quite can Hardy. Nor do I think can we yet, so enmeshed as we are in this criss-crossing religious history.

The competing striations of this English religious history can be seen in the movement that was central to Hardy's early life, and forefronted in Jude: namely, the
Gothic revival in architecture. Jude, for his living, becomes a stonemason: "somehow
medieval art in any material was a trade for which he had rather a fancy" (*JO* 35).
The revival has its origins in perennial English antiquarianism, in the nostalgia for
medievalism in the eighteenth century, in Walter Scott, in the Romantic poets, in
Ruskin and Pugin. In 1836 Pugin published his *Contrasts or, a Parallel between the
Noble Edifices of the Middle Ages, and Corresponding Buildings of the Present Day; Shewing
the Present Decay of Taste*, a revised edition appearing in 1841, with contrasting plates
of "Catholic Town in 1440" and "The Same Town in 1840." Pugin, a Catholic convert,
and Ruskin, patriotically Protestant, can stand for the uneasily interwoven strands of
Catholicism and Anglicanism present in the revival from the beginning (Ruskin came
closer and closer to Catholicism, but is most remembered perhaps for Protestantizing
the Gothic craftsman in "The Nature of Gothic"). When Jude has his workshop illumination, there are echoes of Ruskin, but also echoes of Cobbett, and of the Shastonian
tinkers. In the first chapter of the novel, nouveau Gothic, which Ruskin despised and
felt guilty for inspiring, is contrasted with something much older.

> Above all, the original church, hump-backed, wood-turreted, and quaintly hipped, had
> been taken down, and either cracked up into heaps of road-metal in the lane, or utilized
> as pig-sty walls, garden seats, guard-stones to fences, and rockeries in the flower-beds
> of the neighbourhood. In place of it a tall new building of German-Gothic design,
> unfamiliar to English eyes, had been erected on a new piece of ground by a certain
> obliterator of historic records who had run down from London and back in a day. The
> site whereon so long had stood the ancient temple to the Christian divinities was not
> even recorded on the green and level grass-plot that had immemorially been the church-
> yard, the obliterated graves being commemorated by ninepenny cast-iron crosses
> warranted to last five years. (*JO* 12)

(George Edmund Street, a prominent Gothic revival architect like those Hardy
worked for, is the "obiliterator."). How old is that hump-backed church? That "original church," analogized to an "ancient temple," evokes the real thing, medieval
Gothic; but its wood towers suggest it is much more recent. *A Guide to the Church of
St. Mary the Virgin and the Two Fawleys*, by Ruth Lumley-Smith, begins by saying:
"The present church of St Mary the Virgin replaced an older part-medieval and part-
seventeenth century church." When Hardy studied or traced original church designs,
like the moldings at Rheims or the Early English ornamentation at Tintagel or the
"highly carved seat-ends [possibly Saxon] and other details that have disappeared" at
St. Juliot, he sought to counter "the obliteration of . . . the church's history" (Taylor
1989: 57; *LW* 82).

Elsewhere I have discussed Hardy's fascination with Gothic patterns and with the
striated, sedimented layers of history present in language and thought (see Taylor
1989: ch. 2; 1993: ch. 5). Early in life he was fascinated by his parish church at

Stinsford, "an interesting old church of various styles from Transition-Norman to late Perpendicular" (*LW* 13). Years later, still under Ruskin's influence, Hardy visited Rome and said he "began to feel . . . its measureless layers of history to lie upon him like a physical weight" (*LW* 195). I am interested in the distinctive weight of that history, in how its religious variegation presses on Hardy and results in his distinctive layered bricolage of historical eras: "bricolage" because Hardy's history is not only stratified, but made up of competing ways of interpreting that history, especially since the Reformation.

There is another tradition relevant to *Jude* and with a similar odd mixture of Catholic and Protestant elements. The tradition of the Gothic novel had begun in 1765 with Walpole's *The Castle of Otranto*, and continued through Charles Maturin's *Melmoth the Wanderer* (1820) and beyond. Maria Monk's fictional memoir, *Awful Disclosures of Maria Monk, as Exhibited in a Narrative of Her Sufferings During a Residence of Five Years as a Novice, and Two Years as a Black Nun, in the Hotel Dieu Nunnery at Montreal* (1836), climaxed the old conventions. (Interestingly this is the year when Pugin's *Contrasts* was published, beginning the more sympathetic Gothic revival.) Since its beginnings in 1765, the Gothic novel had displayed abhorrence and fascination with Catholic elements, as in the muring up of maidens in monasteries and nunneries. *Jude the Obscure* is yet another novel showing the influence of the Gothic novel (see O'Malley 2000), but with a twist. The monk abusing the maiden is Richard Phillotson, a mild Anglican schoolmaster, and the maiden kidnapped is Sue abasing herself before the Anglican cross in the ritualist church of St. Silas. Sue's sexual submission to Phillotson is gothicly horrible. Following *Jude*, three novels were written to defend the immolation of personality by high church religion, almost as if in answer to Hardy: Mrs. Wilfrid Ward's *One Poor Scruple* (1899), Evelyn Waugh's *Brideshead Revisited* (1946), and Graham Greene's *The End of the Affair* (1951). It is interesting that these are all Roman Catholic novels.

In *Jude*, various traditions come together in an intertwined reliquary episode whose significance has not been remarked before, Jude and Sue's excursion in Wiltshire (part 3, chapter 2). They debate where they want to go.

> ". . . Not ruins, Jude – I don't care for them."
>
> "Well – Wardour Castle. And then we can do Fonthill if we like – all in the same afternoon."
>
> "Wardour is Gothic ruins – and I hate Gothic!"
>
> "No. Quite otherwise. It is a classic building – Corinthian, I think; with a lot of pictures."
>
> "Ah – that will do. I like the sound of Corinthian . . ." (*JO* 136)

Jude picks up Sue at the Training College and notes "her emergence in a nunlike simplicity of costume that was rather enforced than desired." At Wardour, they wandered through the picture-galleries, Jude stopping by preference in front of the devotional pictures by Del Sarto, Guido Reni, Spagnoletto, Sassoferrato, Carlo Dolci, and others. Sue paused patiently beside him, and stole critical looks into his face as, regarding the Virgins, Holy Families, and Saints, it grew reverent and abstracted. When she had thoroughly estimated him at this, she would move on and wait for him before a Lely or Reynolds. It was evident that her cousin deeply interested her, as one might be interested in a man puzzling out his way along a labyrinth from which one had one's self escaped. (*JO* 137)

In the light of the labyrinth we have been exploring, there is much to remark in this overdetermined segment. A little attention to English guidebooks will help. Wardour Castle is the home of the Arundells, a notable Catholic family in England; the original castle was destroyed during the Civil War, and a new grand castle built, in classical Palladian or "Corinthian" style during the 1770s, and was a major Catholic center. This hall contains the mixture of sacred and secular art, religious and classical, that characterized high Renaissance and Baroque Catholic culture. (In the twentieth century Wardour became a girl's school, then luxury condominiums.) Fonthill Abbey nearby has nothing to do with this ancient Catholic history, but in fact is a neo-Gothic nineteenth-century abbey constructed by William Beckford, author of *Vathek*, a notable Gothic novel. The bricolage of factors here boggles the mind.

We could end our story here, with Hardy reflecting, in part consciously and in part unconsciously, on the complex religious history of England, with its competing high church and low church divisions, its competing English and Roman church claims to own English history, and its overdetermined medievalism. But there is one last step to my argument. As *Jude the Obscure* concludes, Hardy circles back to a liberalized Catholicism that draws on medieval sources for its foundation. *Jude* would seem to end with the end of religion, despite Hardy's protest to his friends: "you can imagine my surprise at the *Guardian* saying that everything sacred is brought into contempt" (*CL* II: 98). Again, Hardy can be seen as disingenuous, unless he is interested in recuperating some notion of religion, as I think he is. This recuperation comes with Jude's arrival at a sort of Pauline humanism that parallels the Shaston idyll, in a way that forecasts the "Apology" of *Late Lyrics and Earlier*. Hardy revised out of the novel some of its more anti-religious statements in order to make Jude's ideas parallel, not contrast with, biblical ideas, notably those found in the book of Job and the Pauline epistles. For example, when Jude bemoans Sue's immolation as the "dear, sad, soft, most melancholy wreck of a promising human intellect" (*JO* 389), he had blamed it in manuscript on her being "besotted with a senseless mysticism which has led you on to a sickening degradation" (fo. 463), but Hardy deleted this phrase and clause in the book publication. In the manuscript, when Jude hears about Sue's sickening submission to Phillotson, he says: "Supernaturalism, supernaturalism, what vices & crimes you've to answer for!" (fo. 464), but Hardy deleted this in the book publication. A final example: in the manuscript, Widow Edlin describes Jude crying out against God on his deathbed and adds: "he's been doing what Job was afraid to do" (fo. 400). In the published version, Hardy deleted this reference, to keep Job parallel, not contrasting. In the published book version also, Hardy added the long, famous passage of Job quotations in the last chapter, beginning "Let the day perish wherein I was born," where Job and Jude are made fully parallel. (In a letter Hardy wrote that *Jude* was "almost the first book of mine of which I feared that the Job-cum-Ezekiel moralist loomed too largely behind the would-be artist," *CL* I: 96.) In their last meeting, Jude and Sue agree about St. Paul's "Charity seeketh not her own": "In that chapter we are at one, ever beloved darling . . . Its verses will stand fast when all the rest that you call religion has passed away" (p. 361–2). The dark night of Jude's end is the other side of the brighter religious portrait of Shaston. Jude has arrived at the bedrock reality of his dream, a sort of crucifixion that is strangely consistent with his life-long quest to find the reality of Christminster, and behind Christminster, Shaston. Thus Sue had earlier referred to him as "St. Stephen, who, while they were stoning him, could see Heaven opened" (p. 205).

Jude's deathbed scene has an interesting connection with the description of Shaston:

> An occasional word, as from some one making a speech, floated from the open windows of the Theatre across to this quiet corner, at which there seemed to be a smile of some sort upon the marble features of Jude; while the old, superseded, Delphin editions of Virgil and Homer, and the dog-eared Greek Testament on the neighbouring shelf, and the few other volumes of the sort that he had not parted with, roughened with stone-dust where he had been in the habit of catching them up for a few minutes between his labours, seemed to pale to a sickly cast at the sounds. The bells struck out joyously; and their reverberations travelled round the bedroom. (p. 407)

This scene recapitulates, in an allusive way, these evolving historical currents. The old Wessex is dead, but the ancient history, however it is to be interpreted, lives strangely on. The world "strange" is repeated at the beginning and the end of the Shaston passage:

> Shaston, the ancient British Palladour,
> "From whose foundation first such strange reports arise,"
> (as Drayton sang it), was, and is, in itself the city of a dream. . . . The natural pictures-queness and singularity of the town still remain; but strange to say these qualities which were noted by many writers in ages when scenic beauty is said to have been unappreciated, are passed over in this, and one of the queerest and quaintest spots in England stands virtually unvisited to-day. (p. 199)

At his death, Jude is placed in a new version of "one of the queerest and quaintest spots of England." He dies alone, "virtually unvisited." The history that he represents ends in this working-class deathbed chamber of Christminster where only the sounds of the "Remembrance Games" can be heard. These sounds come out of a long, complex, striated history of England. Jude's books, a combination of old classics and Greek Testament, are coated with Gothic dust, the last bare remnant of a long tradition, often interrupted and often revived. (We had not known that the post-religious Jude had kept up with such reading.) It is pleasant to realize that this stone-dust, produced by the regrettable restoration inflicted on ancient churches, is literally the last debris spun out from the destruction of castles, abbeys, churches, shrines, chantries, hospitals, mansions "all now ruthlessly swept away."

> With the destruction of the enormous abbey the whole place collapsed in a general ruin: the Martyr's bones met with the fate of the sacred pile that held them, and not a stone is now left to tell where they lie. (*JO* 199)

These scenes (at Shaston) "throw the visitor, even against his will, into a pensive melancholy, which the stimulating atmosphere and limitless landscape around him can scarcely dispel" (p. 199). So also with Jude's deathbed scene. In this scene, the contrasting "stimulating atmosphere" consists of the Christminster bells booming joyously through the room. In that outside world, honors are being given to the Duke of Hamptonshire, who, in Hardy's *A Group of Noble Dames*, is a hard, money-driven man and abusive husband, "little attracted by ancient chronicles in stone and metal" (*GND* 201). He is in fact one of the nouveau aristocrats in the line of those who prospered from the "Dissolution" at the expense of the poor (as Cobbett complained). Jude, a modern martyr (according to Sue) is left alone, somewhat as medieval Shaston is left alone "passed over . . . and . . . virtually unvisited to-day."

I propose the connection between the Shaston scene and the Jude deathbed scene only as one of a number of connections that come into what is a very overdetermined death. Shaston medievalism is a very ambiguous entity, filtered through centuries of Protestant–Catholic polemic, and periodic high Anglican reappropriations of the medieval. The nostalgic norm of medievalism keeps changing shape as we try to define it. Whatever it is or was, Hardy is most concerned to portray its later "systematization" into something cold and obsolete when it betrays Jude's deepest dream. Jude is in the midst of this overdetermined history, and we remember the poignant moment in the high Anglican "Cathedral-church of Cardinal College" when Jude hears the psalm from the Book of Common Prayer: "Wherewithal shall a young man cleanse his way?"

Discussions of Hardy and Catholicism curiously overlook a most important, if allusive, statement that he makes in the "Apology" (perhaps evoking Newman's "Apologia") to *Late Lyrics and Earlier* (1922). Indeed, the only person who has noted the reference in this passage was a Father James O'Rourke, in "The Orthodoxy of Thomas Hardy" (1929), whom Jędrzejewski teases for seeing Hardy as crypto-Catholic. Hardy writes:

> For since the historic and once august hierarchy of Rome some generation ago lost its chance of being the religion of the future by doing otherwise [than "removing those things that are shaken"], and throwing over the little band of New Catholics who were

making a struggle for continuity by applying the principle of evolution to their own faith, joining hands with modern science, and outflanking the hesitating English instinct toward liturgical restatement (a flank march which I at the time quite expected to witness, with the gathering of many millions of waiting agnostics into its fold); since then, one may ask, what other purely English establishment than the Church, of sufficient dignity and footing, with such strength of old association, such scope for transmutability, such architectural spell, is left in this country to keep the shreds of morality together?" (*CPV* 561)

(Hardy then footnotes his disappointment in the Church's recent development.) The passage refers to the modernist movement in Catholicism, condemned by Pope Pius X in 1907. The utopianism of Hardy's passage is astonishing; the flank march would be round all of post-Reformation English history. Despairing of the Catholics, Hardy then turns back to his beloved English, curiously using the expression "the Church" (presuming the adjective "English" also applying here). The passage reverts to the traditional celebration of the Church of England, as the national church. Hardy retained a certain love for that insular church of England in *Under the Greenwood Tree*.

Indeed he retained a certain love for Christianity itself, in its green form. Around the edges of the Christianity he condemned, Hardy finds elements he likes, folk religion, genuine piety, myth and story, Shaston, all of these ancient; but he also finds elements in the present, in the charm of Oxford, in Newman as seen by Arnold, and just barely in the scenes of Roman Catholicism. This Christianity, green at some point now or at Shaston, haunts the novel and reopens the strands of English religious history.

Jude's evolution, in connection with the Shaston passage, and in the light of the "Apology" to *Late Lyrics and Earlier*, is in the tradition of those broad church heroes who attempt in earlier Victorian literature to arrive at some synthesis of traditional and liberal currents. Jude arrives at a pristinely religious sense of suffering and charity. He is in a long line of such nineteenth-century questers, from George Eliot's Felix Holt (1866) (perhaps reflecting the famous "radical" Cobbett), to Disraeli's Lothair (1870), to Hardy's own Clym Yeobright (1878), to Shorthouse's John Inglesant (1881), and, climactically, to Mrs. Humphry Ward's Robert Elsmere (1888). It is notable that Hardy denounced the " 'Robert Elsmere' school" in connection with the sophistry that "everything is both true & false at the same time" (*CL* I: 176). He would later criticize Mrs. Ward's uncle for typifying the

besetting sin of modern literature . . . Half its utterances are qualified . . . by an aside, and this particularly in morals and religion. When dogma has to be balanced on its feet by such hair-splitting as the late Mr M. Arnold's it must be in a very bad way. (*LW* 224)

The prophetic Hardy would have none of such *via media*s. But in fact Hardy, like so many others in the Victorian period, did want it both ways; he wanted his humanism and his Catholicism, he wanted his modernity and his medievalism, he wanted the fruits of the Reformation without the costs. That this was impossible casts another light on the significance of Jude's tragedy. There was no wherewithal by which Jude could cleanse his way.

Hardy said he gave up novel-writing because of the furor raised over the novel by the churchmen and Mrs. Grundys of the time. The "Bishop of Wakefield announced in a letter to the papers that he had thrown Hardy's novel into the fire" (*LW* 294). The critical attacks, Hardy said, resulted in "completely curing me of further interest in novel-writing" (*JO* 466 [Postscript]). Hardy was about to embark on his second great career: "Perhaps I can express more fully in verse ideas and emotions which run counter to the inert crystallized opinion – hard as a rock –which the vast body of men have vested interests in supporting" (*LW* 302). The attack gave Hardy the excuse to do what he had wanted to do for thirty years, become a full-time poet. Simon Gatrell notes that Hardy's "sense . . . of the closure of Wessex as a living culture was central to his slow decision to end his career as a creator of fiction" (Gatrell 1999: 32). One part of the motive to end his career may have been the unresolved conundrum about the nature of Wessex in its historical religious national terms. A novel must take on an entire world, but a poem can concentrate on "Unadjusted impressions" (preface to *Poems of the Past and the Present, CPV* 84). Someone else would have to resolve the mystery of English national identity.

References and Further Reading

Anderson, Benedict (1983). *Imagined Communities: Reflections on the Origin and Spread of Nationalism.* London: Verso.

Arnold, Matthew (1884). *Essays in Criticism*, 1st series (1865), 4th edn. London: Macmillan.

Arnold, Matthew (1885). Emerson. In *Discourses in America* (pp. 138–207). London: Macmillan.

Barnes William (1844). *Poems of Rural Life in the Dorset dialect.* London: John Russell Smith.

Cobbett, William ([1824–7] 1842). *A History of the Protestant Reformation in England and Ireland; Showing how that Event has Impoverished and Degraded the Main Body of the People in those countries.* New York: Doyle.

Cobbett, William (1829). *Advice to young men and (incidentally) to young women, in the middle and higher ranks of life.* London: the author.

Cobbett, William (1830). *Rural Rides in the Counties of Surrey, Kent . . . with Economical and Political observations.* London: the author.

Colley, Linda (2005). *Britons: Forging the Nation 1707–1837*, 2nd edn. New Haven: Yale University Press.

Egerton, George (1893). *Keynotes.* London: Elkin Mathews.

Franchot, Jenny (1994). *Road to Rome: The Antebellum Protestant Encounter with Catholicism.* Berkeley: University of California Press.

Gatrell, Simon (1999). Wessex. In Dale Kramer (ed.), *The Cambridge Companion to Thomas Hardy* (pp. 19–37). Cambridge: Cambridge University Press.

Half-Hours of French Translation (1863). Compiled by Alphonse Mariette. 3rd edn. London: Williams and Norgate. Hardy's copy, signed 1865, at Colby College.

Hardy, Thomas ([1872] 1987). *Under the Greenwood Tree*, ed., David Wright. London: Penguin.

Hardy, Thomas ([1874] 2000). *Far From the Madding Crowd*, ed. Rosemarie Morgan. London: Penguin.

Hardy, Thomas ([1878] 1998). *The Return of the Native*, ed. Simon Gatrell. Oxford: Oxford University Press.

Hardy, Thomas ([1881] 1912). *A Laodicean*. Wessex Edition, vol. XVII. London: Macmillan.

Hardy, Thomas ([1887] 1986). *The Woodlanders*, ed. James Gibson. Harmondsworth: Penguin.

Hardy, Thomas ([1891] 1920). *A Group of Noble Dames*. London: Macmillan.

Hardy, Thomas ([1891] 1988). *Tess of the d'Urbervilles*, ed. Juliet Grindle and Simon Gatrell. Oxford: Oxford University Press.

Hardy, Thomas ([1895] 1998). *Jude the Obscure*, ed. Dennis Taylor. London: Penguin.

Hardy, Thomas (1979). *The Variorum Edition of the Complete Poems of Thomas Hardy*, ed. James Gibson. London: Macmillan.

Hardy, Thomas (1985). *The Life and Work of Thomas Hardy*, ed. Michael Millgate. Athens, Georgia: University of Georgia Press.

Jędrzejewski, Jan (1993). Thomas Hardy and Roman Catholicism. *Thomas Hardy Journal*, 9(1), 27–40.

Jędrzejewski, Jan (1996). *Thomas Hardy and the Church*. Basingstoke: Macmillan.

Jones, Edwin (1998). *The English Nation: The Great Myth*. Gloucestershire: Sutton.

Kay-Robinson, Denys (1979). *The First Mrs Thomas Hardy*. New York: St. Martin's Press.

Lumley-Smith, Ruth (1985). *A Guide to the Church of St. Mary the Virgin and the Two Fawleys*. Privately printed pamphlet.

Maison, Margaret (1961). *The Victorian Vision: Studies in the Religious Novel*. New York: Sheed & Ward.

Millgate, Michael (1971). *Thomas Hardy: His Career as a Novelist*. London: Bodley Head.

O'Malley, Patrick R. (2000). Oxford's Ghosts: *Jude the Obscure* and the End of the Gothic. *Modern Fiction Studies*, 46, 646–71.

O'Malley, Patrick R. (2006). *Catholicism, Sexual Deviance, and Victorian Gothic Culture*. Cambridge: Cambridge University Press.

O'Rourke, Revd James (1929). The Orthodoxy of Thomas Hardy. *Irish Ecclesiastical Record*, 33, 237–45.

Purdy, Richard Little, and Michael Millgate (eds.) (1978–88). *The Collected Letters of Thomas Hardy*. 7 vols. Oxford: Clarendon Press.

Taylor, Dennis (1989). *Hardy's Poetry 1860–1928*, 2nd edn. London: Macmillan.

Taylor, Dennis (1993). *Hardy's Literary Language and Victorian Philology*. Oxford: Clarendon Press.

Tillotson, Kathleen (1956). *Novels of the Eighteen-Forties*, corrected edn. Oxford: Oxford University Press.

Tomalin, Claire (2006). *Thomas Hardy: The Time-Torn Man*. London: Penguin.

Weber, Carl (1966). Ainsworth and Thomas Hardy. *Review of English Studies*, 17, 193–200.

Widdowson, Peter (1989). *Hardy in History: A Study in Literary Sociology*. London: Routledge.

Williams, Merryn (1972). *Thomas Hardy and Rural England*. London: Macmillan.

Williams, Raymond (1970). Thomas Hardy. In *The English Novel From Dickens to Lawrence* (pp. 95–118). New York: Oxford University Press.

Williams, Raymond (1973). *The Country and the City*. New York: Oxford University Press.

24

". . . into the hands of pure-minded English girls": Hardy's Short Stories and the Late Victorian Literary Marketplace

Peter Widdowson

Hardy published four sizeable volumes of short stories during his lifetime (*Wessex Tales* [1888], *A Group of Noble Dames* [1891], *Life's Little Ironies* [1894], and *A Changed Man and Other Tales* [1913]) – some thirty-seven stories in all. But for a large part of the twentieth century they suffered a similar critical fate to his so-called "minor novels," being comprehensively disregarded or disparaged as largely worthless (as late as 1970, for example, R. G. Cox's *Critical Heritage* volume on Hardy had no section at all on the short stories [Cox 1970], and J. I. M. Stewart's *Thomas Hardy: A Critical Biography* characterizes them as merely "pot-boilers" [Stewart 1971: 147]). Since then, the stories have been accorded fairly wide-ranging critical analysis and celebration in common with the general revival of interest in Hardy's work as a whole – most extensively in Kristin Brady's pioneering, *The Short Stories of Thomas Hardy: Tales of Past and Present*, which significantly opens in 1982 by saying: "Until recently, Thomas Hardy's short stories have been ignored by critics and readers alike" (Brady 1982: 1). Thereafter, critics of various contemporary theoretical persuasions have analyzed individual examples of the shorter fiction, although such studies often still barely surface in many recent monographs and compendia.

However, the most interesting latter-day development with regard to the short stories is that involving textual scholarship, combined with cultural-historical understanding of the modes of production and reception within which late nineteenth-century writers like Hardy worked – the point being that the stories, as much as if not more so than the novels, went through several textual incarnations between publication in various periodicals catering for what Hardy caustically called "household reading" (Hardy [1890] 1997: 257) and book publication at some later date. They offer, in other words, a particularly sharp insight at once into Hardy's authorial craft(iness), late Victorian editorial policy, conventional morality, and contemporary readerships. A key work here, following on from the numerous earlier studies of the "making" or "shaping" of Hardy's full-length novels, is Simon Gatrell's *Hardy the Creator: A Textual Biography* (1988), which in a chapter on "Hardy and the *Graphic*" discusses Hardy's problems with that magazine over the publication of the series of short stories, *A Group of Noble Dames*, in 1890 (it was also for the *Graphic* that the more famous bowdlerization of *Tess of the d'Urbervilles* occurred a year later). T. R. Wright's *Hardy and his Readers* (2003) also has a chapter on Hardy's dealings with the *Graphic*; and, pre-eminently, there is Martin Ray's *Thomas Hardy: A Textual Study of the Short Stories* (1997), an impressively comprehensive scholarly account of all the principal variants of all the short stories included in the volumes published by Hardy himself. It is to this work that the present essay will be extensively beholden. However, one other major work of textual scholarship should be acknowledged here, although its contribution lies beyond the scope of this essay: Pamela Dalziel's *Thomas Hardy: The Excluded and Collaborative Stories* (1992), which collects together and offers full textual commentary on the ten stories not included in Hardy's own volumes.

What the present essay proposes to do, then, is to sketch in the trajectory of Hardy's short-story-writing career in relation to his dealings with the periodicals that he published in, and then to look in a little more detail at two or three individual stories, plus more generally the sequence *A Group of Noble Dames*, in order to see what Hardy had to do, first, to get his stories published, and second, to restore them to their originally conceived state. In so doing, it will suggest the tensions and contradictions incident upon the fact that, while Hardy was indeed a journeyman writer producing material for the market in order to earn a living, he was also punctilious to a degree in pursuing his craft and staying close to his vision. His continuous tiny revisions to stories apparently knocked off in the first instance to satisfy market demand are surely witness to the underlying seriousness with which he regarded them. We should not be fooled by Hardy's own later snobbish deprecation of his prose fiction, and especially the short stories, as he sought to present himself as "really" always a poet: there is nothing slapdash and uncaring about a writer who, over thirty years after he first wrote and published "The Distracted Preacher," changed all twenty-one references in the story from what he had recently discovered to be the wrongly named "excisemen" to more correct terms such as "preventive-men" while preparing the story for the 1912 Wessex Edition of *Wessex Tales* (see Ray 1997: 57).

But before turning to the matters announced above, let me offer a perilously synoptic account of some of the characteristics of Hardy's short stories. They present themselves in fact as better described as "tales" than as "short stories" in the present critically received sense: in other words, they tend to be anecdotal – often ramblingly told by narrator-characters – and unambiguous, if anticlimactic, in outcome rather than displaying tautness of form and language (Edgar Allen Poe's "unity of effect") and self-consciously indeterminate closure. Nevertheless, irony – in the sense articulated by two of Hardy's own ironic titles *Life's Little Ironies* and *Satires of Circumstance* – is their pervasive mode, and indeed, theme. But although "Fate" or "Chance" may play a large part in the apparently inescapable circumstances that flatten the best-laid plans of women and men, producing a deep sense of frustration, futility and misery, it is the ambitions, obsessions, and passions of the men and women themselves that are central to the irony of unpremeditable disaster. And at the heart of these human drives, at least in Hardy's universe, are sex and class – either separately or, more dangerously, in combination – and especially when inflected as desire/jealousy or aspiration/envy. This is well recognized these days in respect of his full-length novels, but it is equally true of much of the short fiction: from tales of the macabre ("The Withered Arm") or social ambition ("Fellow-Townsmen"), through the grotesque stories of ruling-class obsession with lineage and succession (*A Group of Noble Dames*), to the ironic tragedies of stifled urban lives ("An Imaginative Woman," "The Son's Veto," "On the Western Circuit"). The problem was – at least as regards publication in the family magazines of late Victorian England – that a caustically ironic treatment of such human desires and fallibilities meant treading continually on forbidden ground – as Hardy learnt only too well. So that even with the relatively light-hearted tale of romance and smuggling in 1830s Dorset, "The Distracted Preacher," Hardy had to tone down the sexiness of his young widowed heroine, Lizzy, in the *New Quarterly Magazine* version (April 1879), while emphasizing it more strongly in the later book editions. In the former, for example, she refills the keg from which she has drawn off some spirits by producing a bottle of water "which she poured on the hole," whereas in later versions, "she took mouthfuls" from the bottle, "conveying each to the keg by putting her pretty lips to the hole" (*WT* 174 and note). Equally, in the magazine, when dressed in her late husband's clothes to go smuggling, she wears the less intimate leggings, not the breeches she has on later, and her excuses to the preacher for her disguise ("which is no harm, as he was my own husband" and "I have got my own dress under just the same – it is only tucked in," *WT* 192) are omitted but add to the enticing portrait of her as it appears in the collected editions of *Wessex Tales*. In addition, Hardy appends a significant note to the end of the story in the 1912 Wessex Edition:

> The ending of this story with the marriage of Lizzy and the minister was almost *de rigueur* in an English magazine at the time of writing. But at this late date, thirty years after, it may not be amiss to give the ending that would have been preferred by the writer to the convention used above. (*WT* 223)

– an ending in which Lizzy does not become "a minister's wife with praiseworthy assiduity" in a Midland county, but – "much to her credit in the author's opinion" – marries Jim the smuggler and emigrates with him to the United States (*WT* 223). One explanation for the fact that Hardy, in 1912, did not simply replace the ending as published with his preferred one may be that he was still smarting from his confrontations with the periodical editors and wanted to settle old scores by drawing attention to their strait-laced interference.

The fragment of a quotation in the title of the present essay is from a letter by a "mother" cited to Hardy by Mowbray Morris, the editor of *Macmillan's Magazine* during its serialization in 1886–7 of *The Woodlanders*: "A story which . . . is certainly not fit to be printed in a high-toned periodical and to be put into the hands of pure-minded English girls" (quoted in Wright 2003: 162). Curiously enough – but perhaps predictably – the same form of words is used by William Locker, son and assistant of Arthur Locker, editor of the *Graphic*, during the exchange over "A Group of Noble Dames," which was to be published in the magazine's Christmas special issue in 1890. Having suggested that these stories were "not at all suitable for the . . . delicate imaginations of young girls," he asks Hardy whether he really thinks it "advisable to put [such stories] into the hands of the Young Person" (quoted in Gatrell 1988: 82; that Locker self-consciously alludes here to Mr. Podsnap's signature phrase in Dickens' *Our Mutual Friend* does not detract from the fact that he means what he says). It is no coincidence, then, that in the same year Hardy published his essay "Candour in English Fiction," one of only three essays on fiction that he ever wrote, which drips with disgust at the control circulating libraries and family magazines exerted over what serious authors could write. Suiting themselves "to what is called household reading," they pandered to "adults who would desire true views for their own reading [but who] insist . . . upon false views for the reading of their young people." What this amounted to, he continues,

> is that the patrons of literature . . . acting under the censorship of prudery, rigorously exclude from the pages they regulate subjects that have been made, by general approval of the best judges, the bases of the finest imaginative compositions since literature rose to the dignity of an art.

The effect is that "If the true artist ever weeps it probably is . . . when he first discovers the fearful price that he has to pay for the privilege of writing in the English language" (Hardy [1890] 1997: 256–8).

Hardy published his short fiction in a wide variety of British periodicals between 1878 and 1900 (those stories published in the United States appeared in one or other of the *Harper's* stable of periodicals, several of which sold between 150,000 and 200,000 copies per issue [see Johanningsmeier 1997: 16]). Individual *Wessex Tales*, for example, as collected in volume IX of the 1912 Wessex Edition, were first published in *Blackwood's Edinburgh Magazine*, *New Quarterly Magazine*, *Longman's Magazine*, the *English Illustrated Magazine*, and the *Bristol Times and Mirror* (one of the provincial papers syndicated by Tillotson's Newspaper Fiction Bureau [see below]). The six stories entitled "A Group of Noble Dames" appeared in the Christmas number of the *Graphic* in 1890, and in *Harper's Weekly* during November and December the same year. The additional four stories that made up the first collected edition of *A Group of Noble Dames* (Osgood, McIlvaine, 1891, and then volume XIV of the Wessex Edition) were "The Duchess of Hamptonshire" (Hardy's first short story published in England, in April 1878), "The Honourable Laura," "The First Countess of Wessex," and "The Lady Penelope," all first appearing in British magazines and in Harper's in the USA. *Life's Little Ironies* was first published in book form by Osgood, McIlvaine and by Harper & Brothers in 1894, without "An Imaginative Woman," but including

"The Melancholy Hussar of the German Legion" and "A Tradition of Eighteen Hundred and Four," "An Imaginative Woman" being first collected in volume VIII of the *Wessex Edition*, and the latter two stories transferring to the *Wessex Tales* volume of that edition at the same time. All again had first appeared in such magazines as *Pall Mall Magazine*, the *Illustrated London News*, *Fortnightly Review*, *The Universal Review*, and the *English Illustrated Magazine*. "The Fiddler of the Reels" was first published in *Scribner's Magazine* (New York), and the sequence of nine sketches, "A Few Crusted Characters" (as "Wessex Folk"), in the US and European editions of *Harper's New Monthly Magazine*. *A Changed Man and Other Tales*, first published by both Macmillan and Harper & Brothers in 1913, is a volume of hitherto uncollected stories by Hardy, most of them written and published many years earlier before he gave up prose for poetry, although the title story itself, first published in 1900, was the last short story he wrote.

What the above detail should suggest, given that it entirely omits Hardy's concurrent periodical and then book-length publication of the novels, is just what an onerous and skilled trade he was engaged in during the last two decades of the nineteenth century, a period which saw a proliferation of periodicals of all kinds. He would have had to register the particular identities of the magazines he was writing for on both sides of the Atlantic and their target readerships (he was also popular in Australia, where his fiction was serialized in several papers throughout the 1880s [Morrison 1995: 312]); negotiate with their editors on both textual and financial issues; meet copy-dates, while simultaneously undertaking further stories; and deal with issues of copyright. In respect of the latter, for example, six of the stories in *A Changed Man* had been published before 1891 and hence were not covered by the International Copyright Act ("Chace Act") of that year, the first US Congressional law to extend limited protection to foreign copyright holders from select nations. While correcting the proofs for this volume in 1913, Hardy characteristically but significantly commented to a correspondent on

> a forthcoming volume of short stories of mine – mostly bad – published in periodicals 20 years & more ago, which I am unhappily obliged to include in my set of books [the Wessex Edition] because pirated editions of some, vilely printed, are in circulation in America, & imported into England by the curious. I heartily wish I could snuff out several of them, but my hand is forced . . . (*CL* IV: 300)

It is not surprising, therefore, that Hardy's correspondence is full of instances of his detailed negotiations with editors. For example, negotiating with Tillotson & Son (see below) in July 1881 over a story for the Christmas supplement of the *Bolton Weekly Journal* (the story was "Benighted Travellers," later retitled "The Honourable Laura" and included in *A Group of Noble Dames*), he writes: "My price would be six guineas per 1,000 words for the newspaper right to the same in the United Kingdom only – or eight guineas if American and Australian newspapers are included" (*CL* I: 93); in November 1885, during discussions with the New York

Independent over terms for *The Woodlanders'* serialization in the United States (in the event, it appeared in *Harper's Bazaar*), he explains:

> I could send you . . . advance sheets, marked in weekly divisions, the whole story extending over several months; at a price somewhat less than a specially written story – say 4 columns of the Independent, viz, 2,500 words, per week, at six pounds (£6) for the week's instalment. (*CL* I: 131, 138)

And in April 1886, writing to the publisher of the book edition of *The Mayor of Casterbridge*, Hardy reveals the complexities incident on serial publication:

> I have promised Messrs Harper [in the US] not to publish the complete story more than a fortnight before that time [15 May, when the serial ended in *Harper's Weekly*]; and a new story of mine [*The Woodlanders*] has been somewhat awkwardly fixed to begin in *Macmillan's* magazine for May. To avoid clashing with the latter it would . . . be advisable to let them get their magazine off before publishing: which would seem to suggest May 7th or 8th as our date. (*CL* I: 143)

A brief look at one prosperous business in particular with which Hardy had dealings will complete my sketch of the nature of the marketplace late Victorian writers had to operate in. Tillotson & Son, based in Bolton, published a number of journals in Lancashire, but also ran Tillotson's Newspaper Fiction Bureau, which purchased serial rights from authors and syndicated their fiction to magazines and especially to provincial newspapers both in the UK and abroad. William Frederic Tillotson, who set up the bureau, was a teetotaler and Congregationalist whose strait-laced views determined the kind of material his publications printed, while his editor, William Brimelow, was a minister in the Independent Methodist Church. A circular of 1911 suggests the kind of fiction Tillotson's liked: "fiction which shall be domestic without being mawkish, sensational without being vulgar, and in close correspondence with human nature, yet entirely wholesome" (quoted in Johanningsmeier 1997: 128; for extensive treatment of Tillotson & Son, see Law 2000). No wonder, then, that when proofs of the first sixteen chapters of *Too Late Beloved* (later *Tess of the d'Urbervilles*) – including the scene of Tess's violation and her baptism of Poor Sorrow – arrived on Brimelow's desk in early September 1889, trouble was brewing. William Tillotson, who had signed a 1,000-guinea contract with Hardy for a new novel in June 1887 without sight of title, story-line, or manuscript, had died some six months previously. In his place, Brimelow considered it unfit for publication in a family newspaper, and asked Hardy to reconsider; Hardy refused; Tillotson's flatly declined to publish the novel, but offered to pay the contracted sum; Hardy then proposed that the contract be cancelled, and an amicable agreement was reached. So much so, indeed, that he immediately sold the Fiction Bureau a short story, "The Melancholy Hussar," which was widely syndicated, and at the beginning of 1890, sent a prospectus to Tillotson's outlining a new short novel (it later became *The Pursuit of the Well-Beloved*), in which he shows that he is now fully aware of what would suit the company: "There is not a word or scene in the tale which can offend the most fastidious taste; & it is equally suited for the reading of young people, and for that of persons of maturer years" (quoted in Johanningsmeier 1997: 128). *Tess*, of course, was finally serialized in the *Graphic* – in heavily bowdlerized form.

Hardy's forced adaptability about how his stories should be made fit for periodical publication is also apparent in his letters. For instance, when the story "A Withered Arm" was completed in September 1887, Hardy sent it to *Longman's Magazine*, only to have it rejected by C. J. Longman as much too grim and unrelieved, "especially as I believe that the majority of magazine readers are girls" (letter of September 27, 1887 in Dorset County Museum; cf. *CL* VII: 106n, and Millgate 2004: 266). Hardy immediately sent the story off to *Blackwood's Edinburgh Magazine*, noting in the covering letter that "I think [it] might suit Blackwood's" (in a later letter, he adds that he felt "the story had a Blackwood flavour about it," *CL* I: 169) and that "the cardinal incidents are true, both the women who figure in the story having been known to me" (*CL* I: 168). The owner and editor, William Blackwood, accepted it with a few emendations he himself had suggested (there is no evidence of what these were), and to which Hardy readily agreed: "The oversights to which you kindly draw attention shall be corrected" (*CL* I: 170). The author received £24 for the story (*CL* I: 172n).

A particularly telling admission also occurs in a letter to Sir Douglas Straight, editor of the *Pall Mall Gazette*, as Hardy prepared "An Imaginative Woman" for publication (in April 1894):

> I have deleted the passage; which I do quite willingly: & may as well say once for all – in case I shd write again for you – that I always give editors *carte blanche* in these matters: as I invariably reprint from the original copy for the book-form of my novels. If there is anything else (I have not observed anything myself) please use your judgement freely. (*CL* II: 48)

While the cavalier remark "I always give editors *carte blanche*" is surely disingenuous in that Hardy deeply resented editorial tampering with his stories, the letter succinctly sums up his policy – seen most familiarly, perhaps, in relation to the publication history of *Tess of the d''Urbervilles* – of strategically adapting his work for the magazines and then restoring the original text (although often with further revision) for the book version. That he did this with prior intention is apparent in some of his manuscripts, typescripts, and galley proofs, where he marked up passages to be cut in the periodical in such a way (in effect, using "stet") that he could easily restore them later (see Gatrell 1988: 83ff). In the particular case of "An Imaginative Woman" here, Hardy does not indicate which "passage" was "deleted," but it must be one of the two substantive changes discernible across the various versions of the story – in particular the manuscript (where manuscripts survive, they supply evidence of Hardy's original conception) and book forms (especially the 1912 Wessex Edition). The first is the erotically coded scene when the "imaginative woman," Ella Marchmill, is lying in the bed of the poet she never meets, but with whom she is infatuated, in the seaside boarding house where she and her family are currently staying. She has a photograph of him propped up in front of her and is musing on some lines he has penciled on the wallpaper behind her head: "And now her hair was dragging where his arm had lain when he secured the fugitive fancies: she was sleeping on a poet's lips, immersed in the very essence of him, permeated by his spirit as by an ether" (*LLI* 19–20). At this moment her husband unexpectedly arrives, saying, in the periodical version, "'I want to get out at six o'clock tomorrow if I can . . . I shan't disturb you by my getting up,'" while the manuscript fills the ellipsis with several lines about him "pulling off his clothes" and Ella worrying which bed he is going to sleep in as "he showed no sign of withdrawing." Furthermore, after the line in the periodical, "And he stooped and kissed her," the Wessex Edition adds his understated if sexually charged remark: "'I wanted to be with you tonight'"(*LLI* 20), a sentence surely destined to inflame the imaginations of pure-minded English girls (for the detail here, see Ray 1997: 175ff). The second bowdlerized passage which may be the one in question is the complete omission from the magazine version of a couple of lines at the very end of the story. In the manuscript and in the 1912 edition, the husband, musing on the likeness of the small son whose birth has been the cause of his mother's death to the photograph of the poet which Ella had kept, murmurs: "'Then she *did* play me false with that fellow at the lodgings! Let me see: the dates – the second week in August . . . the third week in May . . . Yes . . . Yes'" (*LLI* 32). As Martin Ray wryly comments: "Obviously Marchmill's calculation of gestation must have been rather too clinical for the editor of the *Pall Mall Gazette*" (Ray 1997: 176). The dreadful "little irony" of Hardy's story finally is that Mr. Marchmill rejects his own son – the innocent result of his "wanting to be with" Ella that night the preceding August.

The first story in the volume versions of *A Group of Noble Dames*, "The First Countess of Wessex," was not one of the six original "Dames" published in the *Graphic* but appeared first in *Harper's New Monthly Magazine* in the US in December 1889. Although the manuscript is missing, we can make an approximate guess as to what the story originally looked like – and that Hardy probably self-bowdlerized it – by comparing the periodical version with the book forms, which tend not to vary significantly between themselves (although the Wessex Edition does make Betty's account to her mother of her secret meetings with her husband sound slightly more risqué). The story concerns "a girl of twelve or thirteen" (*GND* 3), Betty Dornell, who is married off by her mother to an older man, Stephen Reynard, against her father's wishes. Reynard agrees to wait to claim his bride until she is 18, but as that time approaches, Betty falls in love with a local man favored by her father, "young Phelipson." In order to thwart Reynard's imminent arrival and consummation of the marriage, Betty purposely causes herself to be infected with smallpox, while simultaneously agreeing to elope with Phelipson. By way of a ladder at her window and her lover on a horse hidden in a thicket, Betty rides off pillion to start her new life. However, when Phelipson discovers she is sickening for smallpox, his ardor rapidly cools and he delivers her back home by way of the ladder once more. Here it turns out, Reynard is waiting, and unlike the pusillanimous Phelipson, he "imprinted a deliberate kiss full upon her mouth" (*GND* 42) regardless of her illness. Betty's father then dies, and her contrite mother feels that poor Reynard should now wait even longer to claim his young wife, who is clearly beginning to recognize her husband's qualities, while he in the meantime is ennobled, so that he can offer her the title of Lady Ivell and future Countess of Wessex. What finally transpires is that, unbeknownst to her mother, husband and wife have been secretly meeting for some time and Betty is now pregnant – Mrs. Dornell suddenly being "struck by her child's figure" (*GND* 46). The story ends happily with the couple having "a numerous family" and Betty becoming in due course the first Countess of Wessex. In the magazine, however, there are none of these later happenings: Betty does not elope with Phelipson (he, in fact, breaks his neck falling out of the window from which the ladder has been moved); there is no kiss from Reynard (who is generally portrayed less sympathetically than the patient, honorable man of the book forms); there are no secret assignations and no pregnancy (we are told they finally get back together, but Reynard only stays for an hour – time enough for Betty to become pregnant no doubt, but a possibility in the circumstances unlikely to spring to the mind of even the most sophisticated adult reader). What Hardy does for his "household readers" is simply substitute some contrived plotting for the more complex tale of relations between sexually credible men and women.

What happens in respect of the central six "Noble Dames" stories published in the *Graphic* has been fully described by Simon Gatrell and Martin Ray, but a synoptic account may still be worth giving here. The *Graphic*, a weekly illustrated paper founded by William Luson Thomas, a wood engraver and social reformer, was first published on December 4, 1869. It exactly fits R. D. Altick's "formula for popular periodicals as it developed in the last quarter of the century . . . : a price of 6*d.* or lower; plenty of light fiction and amusing non-fiction; and as many illustrations as possible," although he also notes that "Genuine literary quality was not ruled out, as the roster of first-rank authors who contributed to the popular magazines attests" (Altick 1957: 363 and n32). The *Graphic*'s cover price was sixpence; it recruited a number of eminent Victorian visual artists (*inter alia* Luke Fildes, Hubert von Herkomer, and John Everett Millais); and it contained a miscellany of weekly items, including coverage of domestic and empire news, of fashionable society, royal occasions, national ceremonials and legal trials, of developments in science, notes on rural matters, obituaries of important people, sports reports, book and music reviews, and a weekly serial by a popular writer – Hardy amongst them. Clearly, the *Graphic* was aimed at a middle-class readership, becoming the first successful rival of the *Illustrated London News* (compared to which it was rather more bothered by "Mrs. Grundy" [see Law 2000: 192, 194]), and having subscribers all over the British empire and North America (some of its most popular issues sold upwards of 200,000 copies).

Hardy approached Arthur Locker, the then editor of the paper, towards the end of March 1889 asking if the latter could give him "any idea how much you would be disposed to pay for . . . a Christmas story," following this up on April 1 by stating:

My price for a *Graphic* Christmas story of the length of the Romantic Adventures of a Milkmaid [published in the paper six years previously] would be £125 – this to include the *Graphic* right only – the right to print the story simultaneously in America or elsewhere abroad to remain with author – also to issue it in book form at any time not less than a month after its appearance in the *Graphic*. (*CL* I: 189)

hence giving a further taste of a writer's need to match creativity with business acumen in the late Victorian marketplace.

A diary entry for May 9, 1890 (*LW* 236) notes that Hardy had sent off the manuscript of *A Group of Noble Dames* to the *Graphic* as promised. He then appears to have waited some six weeks before hearing anything further, but when he did it was the letter from William Locker already quoted earlier indicating that the directors of the paper (most especially its founder, William Luson Thomas) were unhappy with the stories, now in proof form, and required changes, since "Many fathers are accustomed to read . . . in their family circles the stories in the *Graphic*" (letter in Dorset County Museum; full text given in Gatrell 1988: 81–2, and Ray 1997: 72–3). The stories' hinging on childbirth and "those relations between the sexes over which conventionality is accustomed . . . to draw a veil" were the stumbling blocks, and Locker's letter goes on to list the problems in each story. "Barbara of the House of Grebe," while "not the least what Mrs. Grundy would call 'improper,'" is nonetheless "very horrible" and "unpleasant"; "The Marchioness of Stonehenge," though "milder," "still insists rather more than is perhaps advisable upon the childbirth business"; "Anna, Lady Baxby" "would not suffer at all" if a different ending replaced the discovery of Lord Baxby's "vulgar amour"; "all that wants cutting" from "The Lady Icenway" is the suggestion that the lady in question "intended to raise up seed unto her second husband by means of her first" (which is a nice way of saying that she would have had sex with her sick first husband in order to get pregnant on behalf of her second had she not left it too late). However, it is the remaining two stories, "Lady Mottisfont" and "Squire Petrick's Lady," that "seem to me [Locker] to be hopeless" and not to be "put into the hands of the Young Person," the former turning upon "the hysterical confession by a wife of an imaginary adultery," the other on "the manner in which a husband foists upon his wife the offspring of a former illicit connection." While all six stories were bowdlerized to some degree for the *Graphic*, it is these two, together with "Lady Baxby," which suffered the most. Locker concludes, in an insufferably high-handed tone, that he thinks it

very unfortunate that [the stories] should have been written for a paper with the peculiar clientele of the *Graphic*; and I am sure we should not be justified in printing them as they stand.

Now, what do you propose to do? Will you write us an entirely fresh story, or will you . . . alter them to suit our taste; which means slightly chastening 1, 2, 3 & 4; and substituting others for 5 & 6?

In the event, Hardy made changes to all of the stories in order, as he put it in his diary for June 23, 1890, to "smooth down these Directors somehow" (*LW* 237). But as Gatrell points out, "It seems . . . that there were two or three different layers of bowdlerization, some made voluntarily, and others under pressure from the editorial staff of the English journal" (Gatrell 1988: 83). Pointedly perhaps, when the six stories ran more or less simultaneously in *Harper's Weekly* in the US, they were as Hardy had originally composed them and as they were to appear in the first book edition (cf. Ray 1997: 73–4). Gatrell's close scrutiny of the various manuscript and proof versions of the stories suggests that Hardy tried to pre-empt censure by the *Graphic* by making cuts *before* submitting copy to the paper, but that the main deletions had to be made after his run-in with the Lockers outlined above. On some sheets of the manuscript where whole paragraphs are excised, but marked up for later retention, Hardy noted: "[N.B. The above lines were deleted against the author's wish, by compulsion of Mrs Grundy, as were all other passages marked in blue.]" (see Gatrell 1988: 83ff). What is clear is that Hardy recognized that his stories would run into difficulties with the custodians of Victorian family values; that he was willing to gut his stories of their psycho-sexual realism and of their central theme (the ruling class's Achilles heel in respect of its need to produce suitable heirs); that he had a low regard for the intelligence of his serial readers; and that he intended from the start to reinstate the original material once he had earned his money in the marketplace.

For a detailed description of the changes and omissions Hardy made for the *Graphic*, the interested reader can go to Gatrell and Ray, but a few samples here will establish just how damaging (even incredible to modern eyes) the bowdlerization was. In "Barbara of the House of Grebe," the heroine's revulsion at Willowes', her first husband's, disfigured visage is significantly lessened, and a sizeable part of her second husband's torturing of her by way of the mutilated statue of Willowes is omitted, as are any references to her inability to give Lord Uplandtowers a "lineal successor" and his blaming her for it. All of this loses much of the ironic animus of the tale. "The Marchioness of Stonehenge" shows Hardy cutting the references to Lady Caroline's secretly wedded husband visiting her in her rooms at night (also changing "supremely" to "presumably" in the description of the newlyweds as "both being supremely happy and content," with its suggestion of intense sexual fulfillment), and all references to her pregnancy.

"Lady Mottisfont" suffered the most destructive bowdlerization of all the stories because at the center of it was the unacceptable *donnée* of an illegitimate child. Hardy therefore had to change the Contessa from being Dorothy's mother to being her aunt, and by a contorted piece of narrating explain how Sir Ashley was her father. The effect of this is, as Gatrell (1988: 90) says, to make "a nonsense of the story" by effectively reversing the character of Sir Ashley from affectionate to callous husband and father, and by losing the irony of neither adoptive nor birth mother finally caring for their "daughter." The cancellations in "The Lady Icenway" again relate to extramarital sex and the problem of producing an heir. Lord Icenway's rant about not having a "lineal successor" is deleted, and the ending so rewritten by Hardy that Lady Icenway merely regrets not waiting to remarry her first husband, rather than – "blushing as she had blushed in her maiden days" (*GND* 148) – suggesting to him as he lies dying that they might between them produce a counterfeit heir for Lord Icenway. "Squire Petrick's Lady" is the wryly ironic tale of a man who is led to believe by his wife that their son is in fact a by-blow of an affair with a young nobleman, and who gradually delights in this because it means nobler blood than that running in his own family's veins. He is finally disabused of his fantasy by being told that his wife was chronically delusional, by discovering that the young nobleman was out of the country at the crucial moment, and by seeing his own lineage unmistakably present in his son's face as the latter matures. A large central chunk of this story is simply cut from the periodical version, thus reducing its length by about half: everything to do with the young nobleman is excised, and the wife's story to the squire now is that their son died soon after he was born and was substituted by a poor woman's baby. The ending, therefore, also had to be radically altered, with the ironic effect being lost of the squire recognizing his own family's physiognomy in that of his son and being disgusted by it. Finally, in "Anna, Lady Baxby," there is the simple excision of Lord Baxby's foiled assignation with an "intriguing damsel" from the local town (*GND* 172–3), and the substitution for it of rather more respectable reasons for Anna staying loyal to her husband and the royalist cause. What is lost, though, is the characteristically piquant Hardyan touch of having her, before lying down with her sleeping husband, tie a lock of his hair to their bedpost with one of her own staylaces – an action perhaps too curiously suggestive for "the Young Person."

Finally, we may take a look at one of Hardy's finest stories, "On the Western Circuit," and one which required the most complex processes of bowdlerization and subsequent revision, with Hardy making alterations of all kinds in the manuscript, in a typescript, in the two periodical versions, in the galley proofs for the 1894 first collected edition of *Life's Little Ironies*, and in the 1912 Wessex Edition (for detail here, see Ray 1997: ch. 22; *LLI*, editor's "Note on the Text" and Appendix B). It was first published in the *English Illustrated Magazine* in December 1891, and by *Harper's Weekly* in the US the previous month. The story as we now read it concerns an illiterate young woman, Anna, who is being trained as a servant in the "Melchester" household of Mrs. Harnham, the lonely and childless wife of an elderly wine merchant trapped in a loveless marriage. At a town fair, Anna meets a young lawyer from London, Charles Bradford Raye, who is currently out "on the Western Circuit" of assize courts, and who rapidly seduces her (an explicit revision in 1894 says that in a matter of days, he had "won her, body and soul," *LLI* 102). However, in the course of their first meeting, Edith Harnham, out looking for her tardy maid, finds herself, in the crush of people, "pressed against Anna's acquaintance without power to move away . . . [so that] his breath fanned her cheek as well as Anna's." During this moment, Raye, thinking he is seeking Anna's hand, clasps Edith's: "Not content with holding the hand, he playfully slipped two of his fingers inside her glove, against her palm." Afterwards, Edith muses: "'Anna is really very forward – and he very wicked and nice'" (*LLI* 99), and next morning, catching sight of him in church, she is described thus:

> Mrs Harnham, lonely, impressionable creature that she was, took no further interest in
> praising the Lord. She wished she had married a London man who knew the subtleties
> of love-making as they were evidently known to him who had mistakenly caressed her
> hand. (*LLI* 101)

Raye drops Anna a line when he is back in London, but receives no answer and writes
briefly again; this time he does receive a reply: "the most charming little missive he
had ever received from a woman" (*LLI* 103). What he doesn't know is that Anna
cannot read or write, and that the letter has been penned on Anna's behalf by Edith
Harnham.

The tale unfolds from there: Edith writing impassioned letters from "the bottom
of her soul" to a man she barely knows as though she were indeed his lover and not
poor Anna. Her marriage "had left her still a woman whose deeper nature had never
been stirred," and a significant addition on the proofs of the 1894 book edition makes
fully explicit her sexual desire for Raye: "That he was able to seduce another woman
in two days was his crowning though unrecognized fascination for her as the she-
animal" (*LLI* 107). Anna becomes pregnant, whereupon Edith murmurs to herself
(in the 1912 version): "'I wish his child was mine – I wish it was'" (*LLI* 109; the
periodical has only: "'I wish he was mine – I wish he was'"). The letters continue,
and Raye decides to do the honorable thing by Anna and marry her. It is just after
the wedding, which Edith has attended, that the whole subterfuge is exposed, Raye
realizing that his true soul-mate is Edith, but that he is now "chained to work for
the remainder of his life, with her [Anna], the unlettered peasant, chained to his side."
Edith goes sadly home, with – 1894 proof addition – "her lips still tingling from the
desperate pressure of his kiss," and whispers to herself when her husband greets her:
"'Ah – my husband – I forgot I had a husband'" (*LLI* 117), a statement restored from
the manuscript in the 1894 proofs, but missing, of course, in the periodical. Why "of
course"? Because it will surely now be clear to the reader that a Victorian family
magazine could not possibly print a story which hinges so centrally on extramarital
sex – both physical (Anna pregnant) and mental (Edith's fantasizing), the latter the
more unacceptable, perhaps, because it at once signals proximate adultery and active
female sexual desire. Hence, for the periodical versions, Edith becomes a respectable
widow who may quite properly harbor feelings for another man, and there is no hint
of Anna becoming pregnant, merely that she pines for her young man away in London.
Almost all of the erotic material outlined above, therefore, is also excised from the
magazine. What becomes apparent, though, is that, in addition to restoring bowdlerized passages for the book editions, Hardy made many further revisions which were
not the result of bowdlerization – in other words, when reinstating the "original"
story, he did not simply resort to the manuscript but rewrote passages anew – with
the effect, on the whole, of making the later versions more sexually explicit.

By the second decade of the twentieth century, then – which had in any event seen
a diminution of the lending libraries' and family magazines' grip on the literary
marketplace – Hardy no longer had to play the system. Free of the tension between

compliance and resentment which that system fostered, he felt able to publish more racy detail, as witnessed perhaps, in the 1913 Wessex Edition version of "A Changed Man," by his inclusion for the first time of a "night-dress" in the luggage-bag Mr. Maumbry's wife Laura had packed when planning to run off with her lover (*CM* 22). He must have felt the pure-minded English Young Person of the twentieth century could probably cope with that.

REFERENCES AND FURTHER READING

Altick, Richard D. (1957). *The English Common Reader: A Social History of the Mass Reading Public 1800–1900*. Chicago: University of Chicago Press.

Brady, Kristin (1982). *The Short Stories of Thomas Hardy: Tales of Past and Present*. London: Macmillan.

Cox, R. G. (ed.) (1970). *Thomas Hardy: The Critical Heritage*. London: Routledge & Kegan Paul.

Dalziel, Pamela (ed.) (1992). *Thomas Hardy: The Excluded and Collaborative Stories*. Oxford: Clarendon Press.

Gatrell, Simon (1988). *Hardy the Creator: A Textual Biography*. Oxford: Clarendon Press.

Hardy, Thomas ([1888] 1991). *Wessex Tales*, ed. Kathryn R. King. Oxford: Oxford University Press.

Hardy, Thomas ([1890] 1997). Candour in English Fiction. In Peter Widdowson (ed.), *Thomas Hardy: Selected Poetry and Non-Fictional Prose* (pp. 255–60). Basingstoke: Macmillan.

Hardy, Thomas ([1891] 1962). *A Group of Noble Dames*. London: Macmillan (Greenwood Edition).

Hardy, Thomas ([1894] 1996). *Life's Little Ironies*, ed. Alan Manford. Oxford: Oxford University Press.

Hardy, Thomas ([1913] 1971). *A Changed Man, The Waiting Supper and Other Tales*. London: Macmillan (Greenwood Edition).

Hardy, Thomas (1984). *The Life and Work of Thomas Hardy*, ed. Michael Millgate. London: Macmillan.

Johanningsmeier, Charles (1997). *Fiction and the American Literary Marketplace: The Role of Newspaper Syndicates, 1860–1900*. Cambridge: Cambridge University Press.

Law, Graham (2000). *Serializing Fiction in the Victorian Press*. Basingstoke: Palgrave.

Millgate, Michael (2004). *Thomas Hardy: A Biography Revisited*. Oxford: Oxford University Press.

Morrison, Elizabeth (1995). Serial Fiction in Australian Colonial Newspapers. In John O. Jordan and Robert L. Patten (eds.), *Literature in the Marketplace: Nineteenth-Century British Publishing and Reading Practices*. Cambridge: Cambridge University Press.

Purdy, Richard Little (1954). *Thomas Hardy: A Bibliographical Study*. Oxford: Clarendon Press.

Purdy, Richard Little, and Michael Millgate (eds.) (1978–88). *The Collected Letters of Thomas Hardy*, 7 vols. Oxford: Clarendon Press.

Ray, Martin (1997). *Thomas Hardy: A Textual Study of the Short Stories*. Aldershot: Ashgate.

Stewart, J. I. M. (1971). *Thomas Hardy: A Critical Biography*. London: Longmans.

Wright, T. R. (2003). *Hardy and his Readers*. Basingstoke: Palgrave Macmillan.

25

Sequence and Series in Hardy's Poetry

Tim Armstrong

There are things
We live among "and to see them
Is to know ourselves."

Occurrence, a part
Of an infinite series . . .

(George Oppen, "Of Being Numerous")

Hardy is, by definition, a late poet, beginning his career in his fifties (even if recycling some earlier drafts) and writing up to his death at 87. The question of in what ways Hardy can be said to have "developed" has therefore been a vexed one, and some readers have been willing to suggest that his poems have an unusual consistency, with few of the stylistic shifts or reinventions of poetic persona seen in other poets. That is wrong, in part because each volume of Hardy's poetry does create its own quite distinct world, but equally because Hardy is fascinated by time and the development of topics, by the sequence of poems on a subject, and by poems on linked sequences of events or separate presentations of the "same" event. Dennis Taylor has pointed out the centrality of pattern and evolution in Hardy's poetry, including the great series of "wind-and-water" poems in *Moments of Vision* (1917) (Taylor 1981). There are sequences of poems on the progress of grief; on the shape of a life; on birdsong as an emblem of endurance; on ballad-memory and Wessex; and on abandoned gods, among many other topics. Many of these sequences shape towards a culmination in Hardy's late work, a poem which seems to sum up the series. Elsewhere, mini-series of poems occur (for example six grouped winter poems in *Human Shows*).

The issue of the serial or sequential is the topic of this essay. It is a preoccupation for Hardy, in part stemming from his deep investment in Darwinism and the notion of generations as series of versions of a family "type"; in part from an understanding of the progress of desire through successive related objects (as in his "last" novel *The Well-Beloved*). But it is also, at one level, an issue which is more abstract, expressive of an interest in the understanding of time and function. It is for this reason that I will suggest that one, albeit loose, way of thinking about Hardy's fascination with sequences and returns is in terms of the mathematics of series. As with serialism in music (originally described as "twelve-tone technique" or *Reihenmusik*, row music), Hardy's series voice a modernity which explores the "beat" (a word he often returns to), the interval, and temporal development (see e.g. Meyer 1967).

Nothing has been written on Hardy and mathematics, and little has been written about mathematics and literature generally, beyond studies of numerology. Mathematics is not a topic particularly apparent in Hardy's extensive reading; there is little evidence that he was aware of the important developments in mathematics around the turn of the century. Nevertheless he was schooled in basic maths and would have been aware of such commonplaces as Zeno's paradoxes (discussed by Bergson in *Creative Evolution* and by other writers). He also made notes from texts in which the series was an issue, including R. B. Haldane's *The Pathway to Reality*. More generally, Hardy is fascinated by what Barbara Hardy calls "structural play," and by thresholds and limits (Barbara Hardy 2000: 214). Time for Hardy readily falls into sequences marked by repetition, difference, and ultimately by what we might call an awareness of the limit point or the general term of the series. Seriality is also a formal issue implicit in his thinking on meter and stanza form (he wrote two poems in medieval "sequence meter" for example). And some of Hardy's poems have little else to them beyond an abstract progress across a series of changes, as in "The Something that Saved Him":

> It was when
> Whirls of thick waters laved me
> Again and again,
> That something arose and saved me;
> Yea, it was then.

(CPV 522)

The "Something" is never specified; all we have is a series of "beatings" of time: "then," "that day," "long," "last."

In what follows, I will occasionally refer to the mathematics of sequences, but always in terms of a parallel which remains loose rather than in any sense governing; I will also briefly mention set theory, the major branch of mathematics heroically and controversially conjured into existence by Georg Cantor in the decade between 1874 and 1884.

Series, Sequence-Poems and Temporal Collapse

How does sequence work in Hardy? I will begin by putting aside for a moment poems written *in* sequences, and deal with poems in which linked series of events or images are shaped. The sequence-poem asks a set of questions about the structure of time: how is its passing and pattern marked? Is it opening or closing for the speaker? Most generally this is a problem which engaged Herbert Spencer and other nineteenth-century thinkers: how does *order* (or what Spencer called "rhythm") emerge from the chaos of matter? Spencer's *First Principles* repeatedly uses the notion of series to analyze consciousness. Spencer characterizes science as seeking the "co-existences and sequences" among phenomena:

> Now relations are of two orders – relations of sequence, and relations of coexistence; of which the one is original and the other derivative. The relation of sequence is given in every change of consciousness. The relation of co-existence, which cannot be originally given in a consciousness of which the states are serial, becomes distinguished only when it is found that certain relations of sequence have their terms presented in consciousness in either order with equal facility; while the others are presented only in one order. Relations of which the terms are not reversible, become recognized as sequences proper; while relations of which the terms occur indifferently in both directions, become recognized as co-existences. . . . The abstract of all sequences is Time. The abstract of all co-existences is Space. (Spencer 1862: 229)

This to suggest that seriality is the fundamental structure underlying consciousness. Spencer suggests in fact that there are two series involved: the "vivid series" of immediate experience and the "faint" series of self-conscious reflection, the latter characterized by an infinite regress when consciousness takes itself as object. But lurking in his formula is another possibility: that the retracing of the sequence in consciousness and memory might convert it into a "co-existence," spatializing the flow of time. This is, I will suggest, a possibility which Hardy explores.

Hardy's work also bears comparison, albeit less directly, with the mathematics of series as expounded in T. J. Bromwich's *An Introduction to the Theory of Infinite Series* (1908) – a study which remained authoritative for many decades. Bromwich defines a sequence in terms which are helpfully general:

> The rule defining the sequence may either be expressed by some formula (or formulae) giving a_n as an explicit function of n; or by some verbal statement which indicated how each term can be defined, either directly or from the preceding terms. (Bromwich 1908: 1)

Hardy's "verbally" defined series might include: think of your loves in turn; think of all your new years; think of your ancestors in line. The most fundamental concepts in the study of series for Bromwich are that of the limit and the distinction between convergent and divergent series, for example:

$$1+\frac{1}{2}+\frac{1}{4}+\frac{1}{8}+\ldots \text{ whose sum is, at the limit, 2}$$

and the (very slowly) divergent harmonic series:

$$1+\frac{1}{2}+\frac{1}{3}+\frac{1}{4}+\frac{1}{5}+\ldots \text{ whose sum is nevertheless infinite;}$$

or the more obviously divergent series 2^n:

$2 + 4 + 8 + 16 + 32 + 64 + \ldots$ whose sum is again infinite.

One might suggest in a crude way that Hardy's series tend to convergence rather than expansion: he tends to direct repetition to a point of diminution and culmination, conceived of in terms of Spencer's "faint" or self-conscious series. This is partly because he saw himself, in Darwinian terms, as the termination of an evolutionary process; with the human itself as a kind of dead end in which consciousness is painfully exposed. The word "continuator" (used in the drafts of "The Pedigree" and in "Wessex Heights") signals this relation; the sense of the self as the next term in a series. But as we will see, the sense of standing outside and watching the series, of abstractly considering its sum, is also important.

The most famous example of a convergent series is that involved in Zeno's paradox of Achilles and the tortoise. The speedy Greek warrior gives the tortoise a head start in a race, say 100 meters. In Zeno's story, when Achilles has reached the tortoise's starting point the tortoise has moved on, say 1 meter. When Achilles reaches that point, 101 meters, the tortoise has again moved on, to 101.01 meters – and so on. So Achilles never catches the tortoise. This is a paradox that has been refuted in various ways, but its underlying problem is the introduction of the infinitesimal into the analysis of space and time: to "stop" time as Zeno effectively does, to become involved in a series which diminishes, is to freeze the subject in place.

To this I would compare the kind of crippling temporal arrest Hardy experiences in his troubled poem "In Front of the Landscape," the poem which introduces *Satires of Circumstance* (1914). The poet describes himself wandering a desolate landscape, "Plunging and labouring on in a tide of visions," with a series of ghosts confronting him (the file of specters is one of the most powerful expressions of series in Hardy, culminating in the three figures that step out of the frame in "Family Portraits"). Here he writes:

> What were the infinite spectacles featuring foremost
> Under my sight,
> Hindering me to discern my paced advancement
> Lengthening to miles;
> What were the re-creations killing the daytime
> As by the night?

> (CPV 303)

"Infinite spectacles" is an obscure term here, but it seems to suggest, in a way that almost consciously parallels Zeno, a vision of time which inhibits progression ("paced advancement"). Visions of the past drag the speaker to a standstill, ultimately to the grave itself:

Hence wag the tongues of the passing people, saying
    In their surmise,
"Ah – whose is this dull form that perambulates, seeing nought
    Round him that looms
Whithersoever his footsteps turn in his farings,
    Save a few tombs?"

                                        (*CPV* 305)

The question of how to move on, to disentangle oneself from the past and from pursuing ghosts, generates much of the power of *Satires of Circumstance*: in this poem and its companion-piece "Wessex Heights"; in poems such as "The Ghost of the Past" and "Spectres that Grieve" (both involving "sundry phantoms of the gone"); and of course in a different way in the "Poems of 1912–13," which Hardy added to the volume on the death of his wife, and in which he both pursues and is pursued.

Hardy's major poems of sequence come after Emma's death, and typically convey the sense of a pattern unrolling and finally being recognized as existing under an organizing principle, whether fruition, loss, or prophecy fulfilled. But there are earlier examples. In "A Wasted Illness," published in *Poems of the Past and the Present* (1901), the speaker passes through "vaults of pain," disturbed by "garish spectres" (*CPV* 152). He approaches the "door to Death" before turning and retracing his steps to life, noting that he will have to pass through the same grim rooms once again on the day of his actual death. In such poems, a life-sequence takes on an abstract character: it can (as Spencer said of the "co-existent") be spatially rendered and traversed in both directions. Here, the "galleries" are the spaces of a life which Hardy often considers in his poems, akin to the stanza form itself, accommodating the poem's temporal pulse. A series of "ands" link moments without any context:

    And hammerings,
And quakes, and shoots, and stifling hotness, blent
With webby waxing things and waning things
    As on I went.

                                        (*CPV* 152)

We could compare "The Five Students" (*Moments of Vision*), one of Hardy's central series-poems. It describes five unnamed people who die in turn, leaving only the speaker (Hardy identified one as his friend Horace Moule; others probably include Emma Hardy and Helen Holder, his sister-in-law). The poem works through an almost mathematical arrangement of permutations: "Five of us; dark He, fair He, dark She, fair She, I, / All beating by" (*CPV* 493) – where "beating," as elsewhere in Hardy, represents the pulse of being; to be "on the beat" (in the complex metrical form) is to be alive, moving forward across time while diminishing in number and expectation. The time-shifters of the poem are seasonal and diurnal – from the spring to the winter of a life, from morning to evening – but continuity is reasserted by the fourth line of each stanza (the second line of the third stanza), which works like the "and" discussed above: "As strenuously we stride"; "We on our urgent way"; "And forward still we press"; "And yet on the beat are we"; "Yet I still stalk the course." Two unpublished stanzas in the manuscript included a posthumous comment by the dead, stepping over the limit represented by the poet's consciousness; these were omitted, one can hypothesize, because they broke the poem's pattern of continuation/diminishment.

In "The Five Students" the beat, with overtones of the poet's own productivity, is a temporality associated with loss and enclosure; with a diminution which is at the same time an accumulation of experience. The events described fall into a clear sequence, with individual terms assimilated to some notion of a final or limit point. Poems like "After Reading Psalms XXXIX, XL, etc." repeat this pattern, which can partly be seen as typological (see Armstrong 2000: 16–29, 126–9). Here citations from the Psalms act as an externally mandated reference point threading the moments together as the speaker heads towards a final awareness of the meaning of the psalm. Similarly in "During Wind and Rain" the developmental narrative in which time moves forward, via the chorus which links the poem's scenes from the life of a family, is mapped onto a series of separate and equally abstract images or markers of mortality: sick leaves, storm-birds, rotten rose, and finally rain on a gravestone (*CPV* 495–6). The series brings a narrowing which ends in isolation and death.

This pattern – which I have thus far depicted as an abstract and formalized rendering of individual experience as a series of encounters with temporal images – is mapped in turn onto Hardy's sense of evolutionary development. "A Night of Questionings" is a poem constructed around a line of ghosts who arise on All Soul's Day to ask whether the world has improved. The poem is a series of repeats in which the similarity of past and present is stressed: it happens "just as in your time"; "The same"; "little difference"; "selfsame" (used four times); "As you did" (*CPV* 726–7). The "selfsame" here signals that which goes "in a strange cyclic throe / Backward to type" – a vision linked to Hardy's understanding of E. B. Tylor's doctrine of "survivals" (see Radford 2003). Officially, the world is improving and eliminating evil (hence the hanging of felons); but in fact it is producing a series which is frozen. In the final long stanza the hanged are told that the world has not improved despite its "thus neck-knotting you" (*CPV* 728). The movement "backward" undoes hopes of progress; the residue of past losses is not recuperated. The "type" here is thus the general terms of a series which could be called "human nature," which does not mend.

Hardy uses the work "sequence" only twice in his poetry, each time describing a poetic form derived from the *Sarum Missal*. "Sine Prole" (subtitled "Mediaeval Latin Sequence-Metre") is an evocation, thematically and metrically, of Darwinian belatedness: the poet, as always conscious of his family's childlessness, sees the windings of his "line" and himself as "the last one – / Outcome of each spectral past one / Of that file, so many-manned!" (*CPV* 721). Moderns do not lament the end of the family line as they are "schooled by lengthier vision"; they accept chance and discontinuity where earlier peoples (Hardy often sees the Jews in these terms) needed historical continuity. The scholarly antiquarianism of Hardy's meters pulls the poem backwards; and in the first stanza the beating trochees and internal rhymes drag across a series of enjambments and parentheses which make the poem itself a "time-trail":

> Nothing in its time-trail marred it:
> As one long life I regard it
>   Throughout all the years till now,
> When it fain – the close seen coming –
> After annals past all plumbing –
>   Makes to Being its parting bow.
>
> (*CPV* 722)

The most potent example of this Darwinian vision is "The Pedigree," arguably Hardy's most mysterious and sublime poem. The speaker examines his pedigree by moonlight; its "branches" twist into the face of a "Mage" which "winked and tokened towards the window"; then

> It was a mirror now,
> And in it a long perspective I could trace
> Of my begetters, dwindling backward each past each
> All with the kindred look . . .
>
> (*CPV* 460)

The result for the speaker is a sense of inauthenticity and pain: the speaker sees that "every heave and coil and move I made / Within my brain" is already there, "forestalled" and "portrayed" in the glass. The series can be traced back to a point of lost origins: "The first of them, the primest fuglemen of my line, / Being fogged in far antiqueness past surmise and reason's reach" (a fugleman leads a file in military drill). The poem ends with a declaration of self-authorship, though one remaining in tension with the notion that his utterances are (as in the sequence-meter) repetition:

> Said I then, sunk in tone,
> "I am merest mimicker and counterfeit! –
>   Though thinking, *I am I,*
> *And what I do I do myself alone.*"
> – The cynic twist of the page thereat unknit
> Back to its normal figure, having wrought its purport wry,
>   The Mage's mirror left the window-square,
> And the stained moon and drift retook their places there.
>
> (*CPV* 461)

"The Pedigree" offers two possibilities: that of a sequence ending with the self realizing and voicing its inauthenticity; and that of self-origination in an act of self-conscious thought. But what enables the speaker to move between these possibilities? Does being caught in a series inevitably involve a sense of enclosure?

Debating Series: Bergson, Russell, and Royce

In answering these questions, we can turn to some of the contemporary debates on the nature of series and sets which provide an oblique point of reference for Hardy. They offer competing views on the question of the adequacy of the series to describe the "real" (including the set of Real numbers which stand, in this debate, for what mathematics calls the "continuum" of all possible numbers on a line). The first view is represented by the work of Henry Bergson, whom Hardy read with some care, while refuting what he saw as Bergson's dualism. For Bergson, the analysis of reality offered by *any* sequential analysis – particularly the series of "snapshots" of time which he associated with the cinematograph and with Zeno – was flawed because of what it left out: the time between, as it were; the real flow as opposed to a mechanistic analysis. A passage from *Creative Evolution* which Hardy copied into his notebooks describes the world so created:

> Du Bois = Reymond [says] "We can imagine the knowledge of nature arrived at a point where the universal process of the world might be represented by a single mathematical formula, by one immense system of simultaneous differential equations, from which could be deduced, for each moment, the position, direction & velocity of every atom of the world. (*LN* II: 221n2423, citing Bergson 1911: 38 with variations)

This is the world-as-mechanism which Hardy describes in "The Musical Box" (*CPV* 482). Zeno's paradoxes are, Bergson suggests, based on the misapprehension that any formalism could encompass the nature of continuous motion (1911: 208–10). In contrast, Bergson depicted Being as a vital, uninterrupted flow, the "*life* of the real" (1911: 343), a totality which can never be rendered as a formal series.

In his well-known 1912 critique of Bergson, Bertrand Russell attacked Bergson's spatialization of number, including his notion that reality cannot be rendered "cinematographically." Russell argues that "A cinematograph in which there are an infinite number of films, and in which there is never a *next* film because an infinite number came between any two, will perfectly represent a continuous motion" (1914: 18). Behind Russell's thinking here lurks the mathematical notion known as the "Dedekind cut," which can be used to reconcile the continuous nature of a number line and the discrete nature of individual numbers. For Russell, the mathematical "cut" is adequate to describe the totality of the continuum; or to put it crudely, existence can be subject to analysis, even if the "now" has to be constructed as an infinitely bunched series.

How does this relate to the collapse into self-consciousness and temporal arrest we have seen in Hardy's series? One aspect of Russell's argument roughly parallels Hardy's thinking on Bergson. Russell argues that "pleasure and pain" refute Bergson's theory that magnitude implies space; they are quantities without spatial extension, in which we are nevertheless detached from the flow of time (1914: 13). Hardy's objections to Bergson – made in letters to Caleb Saleeby after the latter had sent him a copy of *Creative Evolution* in 1914 – also relate to Bergson's being a philosopher who, as Russell put it, "considered happiness an effect of knowledge" (1914: 2). Hardy writes:

> But the most fatal objection to his view of creation *plus* propulsion seems to me to lie in the existence of pain. If nature were creative she would have created painlessness, or be in process of creating it – pain being the first thing we instinctively fly from. If on the other hand we cannot introduce into life what is not already there, and are bound to mere recombination of old materials, the persistence of pain is intelligible. (*LW* 452)

If this is in part a rephrasing of the attack on a God who tolerates evil, the new element is a sense of the tension between the same and the new: a "propulsion" or creative evolution associated with happiness; and a fall into non-progression associated with pain. For Bergson, we take only as much of the past with us as we need to create the future; for Hardy, the past has its own claim. In "On an Invitation to the United States" he wrote

> I shrink to seek a modern coast
> Whose riper times have yet to be;
> Where the new regions claim them free
> From that long drip of human tears
> Which peoples old in tragedy
> Have left upon the centuried years.
>
> (*CPV* 110)

"Shrink" is characteristic, a word he often uses to describe the passing of time. In the second stanza he refers to himself as "scored" by the past and notes that, though he has no children, "I trace the lives such scenes enshrine, / Give past exemplars present room, / And their experience count as mine." The "rooms" here are again time conceived as a spatial series; to count the past as your own is to see yourself as the final term, the point where all series converge. The repetitive or convergent sequence involves pain, then, as it collapses into a limit. Instead of the Bergsonian past, which is gathered up dynamically as the ground of freedom, Hardy's past writes the living, producing a painful self-consciousness like that in "The Pedigree."

Bergson and Russell are not the only thinkers who inhabit this territory. As I have suggested elsewhere, Hardy noted reviews of (and possibly read) R. B. Haldane's Gifford Lectures for 1902–4, *The Pathway to Reality*, and its imagery of windows and series seems to inform "The Pedigree" (Armstrong 2000: 41–3). Haldane was in turn influenced by and discussed Josiah Royce's Gifford lectures a few years earlier, published as *The World and the Individual* (1900–1), a text which places the notion of the series, derived from mathematicians including Richard Dedekind and Georg Cantor, at the center of its discussion of order.

For Royce, the mathematics of the sequence provides a model for thinking about consciousness as a process of self-mapping. He distinguishes between cardinality (the use of numbers to count something) and ordinality (the seriality of numbers which defined the "next" in the series) (Royce 1900–1 I: 528). Royce links ordinality to the notion of Law, as opposed to the merely contingently linked. But series that are not "well ordered" in this sense are problematic: his example is the series of the fractions, in which there is never a next term: between 1/98 and 1/99 there is an infinite set of other fractions. This corresponds, in Royce's mind, to the process of perceptual *discrimination*, which consists in finding objects between any two objects compared (Royce 1900–1 II: 88–90). The world as it appears to us is thus not well ordered. Nevertheless, as a good Hegelian Royce believes that ultimately "The true series of facts in the world must be a Well-Ordered Series, in which every fact has its next-following fact" (1900–1 II: 107). Indeed, he suggests tentatively that the Absolute may be "transfinite" in Cantor's sense (1900–1 II: 69n) – by which he seems to mean that it includes all possible sets, well ordered and others. (The reference here is to Cantor's revolutionary notion of "cardinality" or the ordering of differently numerous infinities. Cantor pointed out that the infinite series of Rational numbers – those which can be expressed as fractions – cannot be mapped onto the infinite series of Real numbers, which includes irrational numbers like π or $\sqrt{2}$). Indeed, Cantor saw his findings in a similar way: as a devout Lutheran, he saw his work as confirming rather than challenging man's distance from God's infinitude.

But one might wonder how the human subject gets beyond perception – the windows of Hardy's poem – to the Absolute? Using Dedekind's notion of the *Kette* or chain, that is a series determined by a single function, Royce links ordinality to what he calls "self-representation," the ability of consciousness to become its own object:

> Their formal order of first, second, and, in general, of *next*, is an image of the life of sustained, or, in the last analysis, of complete Reflection. Therefore this order is the natural expression of any recurrent process of thinking, and, above all, is due to the essential nature of the Self when viewed as a totality. (1900–1 II: 538)

Ultimately, this totality is that of the world: "The world is an endless *Kette*, whatever else it is" (1900–1 II: 588). Royce thus finds in consciousness evidence of order. Hardy's version of this is the backward glance provided by poems like "Mute Opinion," in which he sees the past in "its unfolding," and "in web unbroken" (*CPV* 127). We can again relate this to "The Pedigree," and particularly between the painful consciousness of repetition and seriality, on the one hand, and the possibilities of self-ownership on the other. If Hardy rejects Bergson's "propulsion" and registers the pain of regression, he nevertheless asserts a power derived from an awareness of the *Kette*.

In later articles, Royce returned to the issue of series, and stressed in particular the status of "Open Series." This is from his 1917 article on "Order":

Open series are of enormous importance for the whole theory of order. The events of time, so far as these are known to us, form open series. No event recurs. In like manner, any physical process which follows, more or less definitely, the course of an open line, be it straight or curved, presents the features of an open series. The movements of a man, when he walks once over a road and does not return, or cross his own tracks at any point, form an open series. All our business, all our plans of life, all that makes our life a progress or the reverse, all that gives ethical significance to a personality and its activities, are things dependent upon the character of the open series. (Royce 1917: 536)

The striking thing here is the extent to which the "crossed track" or return is characteristic of Hardy's poetry. It is as if Hardy is suggesting that it is only in the closed or alternating series – only in the painful temporal collisions of repetition – that meaning emerges. "Apostrophe to an Old Psalm Tune" is one of Hardy's most typological poems, evoking a central reference point, Psalm 69, cited in *A Pair of Blue Eyes* and elsewhere, and linked to Emma; this is the psalm sung every August 13. Hardy plots it as a sequence of hearings across his life, from youth to new "stirrings" of its tone in the midst of the Great War. Where he had seen its meanings as exhausted, he suggests, they are awakened by war:

> So, your quired oracles beat till they make me tremble
> As I discern your mien in the old attire,
> Here in these turmoiled years of belligerent fire
>   Living still on – and onward, maybe,
>   Till Doom's great day be!
>
> (*CPV* 432)

The power of the psalm to "hail" the author again and again, to drive a new impulse through the trembling body, is affirmed – a realization which is an understanding of the meaning of the series as a whole.

It is, then, the totality of a series that offers knowledge. One might take Hardy's poem "The Two Houses," in which a new house and an old consider the effect of successive inhabitants and their spectral presences (one of a number of such poems in the corpus of this former architect). The word used of this effect is "obsess" ("Babes new brought-forth / Obsess my rooms . . .", *CPV* 596), a word which historically means to both occupy and haunt, as well as the modern meaning of a mental capture. The new house is reduced from boasting of its "haler" state to an "awestruck" question as to whether "I shall lodge shades dim and dumb." The old house replies:

> " – That will it, boy;
>   Such shades will people thee,
>   Each in his misery, irk, or joy,
> And print on thee their presences as on me."
>
> (*CPV* 596)

The cumulative verse pattern ($a^2b^3a^4b^6$) literally builds a sense of gathered experience: the house is a spatialized form of memory. Imprinting here is a different kind of presence, a form of gathered experience as well as a haunting. It can work in this way, I would suggest, because the "obsession" is formalized; the house – which is of course the house of "The Pedigree" – is a space without a need for the human; a container for a series of occupants which is formal, without the burdens and possibilities of the individual locked into time. In this it is like the awareness of pattern which offers freedom for Royce, though for Hardy it only ceases to become haunting at the limit where it becomes objectified and detached from the embodied human subject, at the point where it becomes what Spencer called a "co-existence," the ordered spatial shape of a series of rooms or a poem.

Desire and the Series

If one version of the series is the Darwinian progress of the "type," another series is that created by the plot of desire – where, as Freud observed, desire for the ideal object resolves itself into a series, since nothing can match the original (maternal) object. This is the plot of Hardy's "last" (according to some criteria) novel, *The Well-Beloved*, where woman, daughter, and granddaughter are wooed in turn. In Book 2, chapter 9, the notion of the series takes a mathematical turn. The hero Pierston looks at the second Avice:

> he stood still, watching her as she panted up the way; for the moment an irradiated being, the epitome of a whole sex: by the beams of his own infatuation
>
> > ". . . robed in such exceeding glory
> > That he beheld her not;"
>
> beheld her not as she really was, as she was even to himself sometimes. But to the soldier what was she? Smaller and smaller she waned up the rigid mathematical road, still gazing at the soldier aloft, as Pierston gazed at her. (*WB* 107)

This is mimetic desire; but also desire which knows its own status as fixated on an idea and bound to a plot of diminishing returns. Shortly after this Pierston comments to his friend Somers that he has been "always following a phantom whom I saw in woman after woman"; he continues: "while she was at a distance, but vanishing away on close approach, was bad enough; but now the terrible thing is that the phantom does NOT vanish, but stays to tantalize me even when I am near enough to see what it is!" In *The Well-Beloved*, a doubled plot sees the aging protagonist idealize his love-object even as he must be increasingly idealized by her.

Hardy's rather strange allegory "The Chosen" seems to embody a Roycean vision of this progress. It has a lover who has five previous objects of desire, each inadequate in some way and seemingly discarded:

> I thought of the first with her eating eyes,
> And I thought of the second with hers, green-gray,
> And I thought of the third, experienced, wise,
> And I thought of the fourth who sang all day . . .

(CPV 676)

The revelation of her place in a series appalls his present love, who "swerves" away before stopping and returning, now with all the women incorporated within her: "Her face was all the five's . . . made one." The narrator does not see this as the fulfillment of desire, however, but as a figure for retrospect and redemption:

> I took the composite form she was,
> And carried her to an arbour small,
> Not passion-moved, but even because
> In one I could atone to all.

(CPV 678)

The final or "composite" form of the series is the occasion for a meditation on the structure of desire. The poem offers the lover little consciousness – she barely knows him after her "change" and "lies" and is "tend[ed]" in the final stanza – but in a sense this reinforces her status: as a general form, she has no being directed towards the future, compressed into the space ("arbour") of spent desire.

To speak in this way is to move quickly to the end of a process: to an old poet's meditations on love. It is as interesting to ask what begins desire; what sets in train the hopes it embodies and necessarily resolves into a series of lesser passions. One figure for interruption, for the mark of desire, is the meteor. In the Aristotelian tradition, a meteor is the basic unit of meteorology; an unusual occurrence beneath the skies, and thus a set which includes earthquakes, storms, fish falling from the skies, and volcanoes. A meteor disturbs the normal. In "The Second Night" the lover sees that "A mad star crossed the sky to the sea" (*CPV* 661), signaling his beloved's fall; in "A Procession of Dead Days" the moment of romance is "a meteor act, that left in its queue / A train of sparks my lifetime through" (*CPV* 644). Desire leaves a fiery trace.

The pursuit of that trace is of course the logic of Hardy's great mourning sequence the "Poems of 1912–13," in which he engages with a series of re-representations of Emma, first in Dorset and then Cornwall, the scene of romance. Here seriality as an assertion of continuity is less the issue than a series of swervings, negations, affirmations, and interruptions. Here too time takes on an abstract, rhythmical character in which Bergsonian flow is reconciled with an awareness of repetition, return, and limits. Nowhere is that more apparent than in "Beeny Cliff," which ends:

> – Still in all its chasmal beauty bulks old Beeny to the sky,
> And shall she and I not go there once again now March is nigh,
> And the sweet things said in that March say anew there by and by?

What if still in chasmal beauty looms that wild weird western shore,
The woman now is – elsewhere – whom the ambling pony bore,
And nor knows nor cares for Beeny, and will laugh there nevermore.

(CPV 351)

The flow of assonance, the returns to the "b," "s," and "w" sounds, the play between "anew," "nigh," "still," and "nevermore," the triple rhyme and heavy beats – temporal markers of sameness, difference, repetition, and an infinite perspective – all combine to suggest that time is an oceanic series of waves, sounded out in the poem. This is the Hardy of pulsations and flux praised by Deleuze and Guattari, evoking the turbulence of being (see Musselwhite 2003). But what is interesting about such passages is the way they work with sequence: the return of a figure (the "domestic" in Emma's ghost wandering around Max Gate; "romance" in Cornwall) with a difference which finally enables the speaker to see the progress of the series and locate it in space as well as time, as in "At Castle Boterel":

> And to me, though Time's unflinching rigour,
>   In mindless rote, has ruled from sight
> The substance now, one phantom figure
>   Remains on the slope, as when that night
>   Saw us alight.
>
> I look and see it there, shrinking, shrinking,
>   I look back at it amid the rain
> For the very last time; for my sand is sinking,
>   And I shall traverse old love's domain
>   Never again.

(CPV 352)

The diminishing figure may be his vision of Emma, or reciprocally the poet himself (though "He withers daily, / Time touches her not" in "The Phantom Horsewoman" [*CPV* 354], two poems on), but in each case its receding series involves a notion of the difference between the ideal figure and the time-bound, with the issues of pain, lost time, and self-knowledge again bound into that encounter.

Series of Poems: Writing as Repetition

I want, finally, to look at an example of the series of poems within Hardy's work, as an emblem of the way in which a kind of writerly self-consciousness emerges as the poet confronts his own work. His poems on the romantic trope of birdsong provide an example. He wrote, in my count, almost forty-five poems with significant references to birdsong. The series moves from poems which consciously evoke a romantic inheritance – early poems like "Shelley's Skylark" and "The Darkling Thrush" (with its

Miltonic and Keatsian allusions) – to poems in which birds might be described as the For-Itself of nature. They include a mini-sequence (four poems together in *Poems of the Past and the Present*) and a late formal thematic: Hardy's last three volumes have birds in their opening two poems, emblems of continued presence.

The career-sequence has moments where it seems to move onto new ground. "Starlings on the Roof" suddenly has birds commenting on human migration and return, for example: " 'They will find that as they were they are, / That every hearth has a ghost, alack . . .' " (*CPV* 390). At moments the sequence seems to become self-conscious: "The Blinded Bird" (*Moments of Vision*) sees the bird as an emblem of suffering in adversity, mapping it onto a favorite passage from 1 Corinthians 13:

> Who hath charity? This bird.
> Who suffereth long and is kind,
> Is not provoked, though blind
> And alive ensepulchured?
>
> (*CPV* 446)

Here birds signal mortality and loss – like "The Caged Goldfinch" (*CPV* 491), placed on the grave of an unknown man – but also seasonal renewal, since new birds and repeated birdsong return every spring as the "selfsame" (a word we have seen linked to Hardy's understanding of repetition). This is "The Selfsame Song":

> A bird sings the selfsame song,
> With never a fault in its flow,
> That we listened to here those long
>   Long years ago.
>
> A pleasing marvel is how
> A strain of such rapturous rote
> Should have gone on thus till now
>   Unchanged in a note!
>
> – But it's not the selfsame bird. –
> No: perished to dust is he. . . .
> As also are those who heard
>   That song with me.
>
> (*CPV* 598)

Birdsong arises from the earth as an organization of matter: indeed, I would want to say that for Hardy the bird is an emblem of the seriality of life; of the way in which memory is imprinted on the world. "Proud Songsters" is the second poem in Hardy's final volume, *Winter Words*:

> These are brand-new birds of twelve-months' growing,
> Which a year ago, or less than twain,
> No finches were, nor nightingales,

> Nor thrushes,
> But only particles of grain,
> And earth, and air, and rain.

(CPV 836)

Arguably the final poem in the series, the one which in a sense summarizes its meaning in Hardy's final volume, is "The Boy's Dream" — a poem which describes a boy who wishes "to have, next spring, / A real green linnet — his very own — / Like that one he had late heard sing" (*CPV* 918), that is, to take within himself that seasonal cycle of song. The desire to "own" song is analyzed and linked to debility and loss: the boy is poor, lame, anemic, cannot fight, but dreams of what the bird embodies, self-expression and self-renewal within a cage: "His face was beautified by the theme, / And wore the radiance of the morn." This is not quite the last appearance of the theme in Hardy: in "We Are Getting to the End," the penultimate poem of *Winter Words*, he writes of caged larks in a "latticed hearse" (*CPV* 929), a final bitter twist of the idea. But "The Boy's Dream" is more personal, linking it to an original loss and a moment at which the series arrives at a form of self-understanding.

I have perhaps tested the limits of a rather odd way of thinking about poetry and mathematics — and perhaps not convinced the reader that "series" signals anything beyond a broad thematics of repetition; or perhaps a demonstration of Dennis Taylor's important observation that Hardy's lyrics establish that "the way a man pursues a vision of the years is like the way a man pursues his thoughts during a meditation" (1981: 8). In some ways that seems enough in itself: repetition and self-awareness are vital topics for Hardy.

But I would want to say more: that in so far as he participates in a wider debate on forms of series — signaled by the images of mirrors within mirrors, by poems on series of rooms, poems of dropping away, sequence-meters, and the like — he engages with issues allied to those which energized mathematicians and philosophers at the turn of the century. At one level these are abstract: is the series adequate as a description of a movement through time? Can consciousness be seen in terms of a series? But in Hardy the question is often rather more specific: what does it mean to think of oneself as the product of a series, or of one's desire as serial? What happens when the diminishing space of a life is seen in terms of the limit? What does it mean to see the series as spatially located, and thus subject to a kind of fixation and "co-existence" in which it might be seen as a whole? Hardy's poetry does, surely, address these questions, making the poet a philosopher of ideas whose preoccupations touch on a wider world. In particular, he confronted the painful seriality of human experience and desire; its tendency to diminishment and loss. And the "answer" offered by the study of series, if that is the right term, is that humans do think of their lives in terms of sequence, but that the serial nature of writing — writing on a topic; writing again; confronting one's own obsessions as forming a pattern — offers an awareness of the patterns involved, potentially seen as a form of detachment and knowledge.

References and Further Reading

Armstrong, Tim (2000). *Haunted Hardy: Poetry, History, Memory*. Basingstoke: Palgrave.

Bergson, Henri (1911). *Creative Evolution*. Trans. Arthur Mitchell. New York: Henry Holt.

Björk, Lennart A. (ed.) (1985). *The Literary Notebooks of Thomas Hardy*, 2 vols. London and Basingstoke: Macmillan.

Bromwich, T. J. (1908). *An Introduction to the Theory of Infinite Series*. London: Macmillan.

Brooks, Jean (1971). *Thomas Hardy: The Poetic Structure*. Ithaca, NY: Cornell University Press.

Campbell, Matthew (1999). *Rhythm and Will in Victorian Poetry*. Cambridge: Cambridge University Press.

Davis, Philip (1983). *Memory and Writing: From Wordsworth to Lawrence*. Liverpool: Liverpool University Press.

Ebbatson, Roger (1982). *The Evolutionary Self: Hardy, Forster, Lawrence*. Brighton: Harvester.

Haldane, R. B. (1903–4). *The Pathway to Reality*, 2 vols. The Gifford Lectures 1902–4. London: John Murray.

Hardy, Barbara (2000). *Thomas Hardy Imagining Imagination. Hardy's Poetry and Fiction*. London: Athlone.

Hardy, Thomas ([1897] 1996). *The Well-Beloved*, ed. Tom Hetherington. Oxford: Oxford University Press.

Hardy, Thomas. (1979). *The Variorum Edition of the Complete Poems of Thomas Hardy*, ed. James Gibson. London: Macmillan.

Hardy, Thomas (1984). *The Life and Work of Thomas Hardy*, ed. Michael Millgate. Oxford: Oxford University Press.

Hynes, Samuel (1961). *The Pattern of Hardy's Poetry*. Chapel Hill: University of North Carolina Press.

Ingham, Patricia (1980). Hardy and "The Cell of Time." In Patricia Clements and J. Grindle (eds.), *The Poetry of Thomas Hardy* (pp. 119–36). London: Vision Press.

Jacobus, Mary (1982). Hardy's Magian Retrospective. *Essays in Criticism*, 82, 258–82.

Knoepflmacher, U. C. (1990). Hardy's Ruins: Female Spaces and Male Designs. *PMLA*, 105, 1055–70.

Lanzano, Ellen Anne (1999). *Hardy: The Temporal Poetics*. New York: Peter Lang.

Meyer, Leonard B. (1967). *Music, the Arts, and Ideas: Patterns and Predictions in Twentieth-Century Culture*. Chicago: University of Chicago Press.

Miller, J. Hillis (1970). *Thomas Hardy: Distance and Desire*. Cambridge, MA: The Belknap Press of Harvard University Press.

Musselwhite, David (2003). *Social Transformations in Hardy's Tragic Novels: Megamachines and Phantasms*. Basingstoke: Palgrave Macmillan.

Paulin, Tom (1975). *Thomas Hardy: The Poetry of Perception*. London and Basingstoke: Macmillan.

Radford, Andrew (2003). *Thomas Hardy and the Survivals of Time*. Aldershot: Ashgate.

Rosenthal, M. L., and Sally M. Gall (1983). *The Modern Poetic Sequence, Genius of Modern Poetry*. New York: Oxford University Press.

Russell, Bertrand (1914). *The Philosophy of Bergson. With a Reply by Mr. H. Wildon Carr, and a Rejoinder by Mr. Russell*. London: Bowes & Bowes for "The Heretics," Paper originally published in *The Monist*, July 1912.

Royce, Josiah (1900–1). *The World and the Individual*, 2 vols. The Gifford Lectures 1898–1900. New York: Macmillan.

Royce, Josiah (1917). Order. In James Hastings (ed.), *Encyclopaedia of Religion and Ethics*, vol. IX (pp. 533–40). New York: Charles Scribner.

Shaw, W. David (1987). *The Lucid Veil: Poetic Truth in the Victorian Age*. London: Athlone.

Spencer, Herbert (1862). *First Principles*. London: Williams and Norgate.

Taylor, Dennis (1975). The Patterns in Hardy's Poetry. *ELH*, 42(2), 258–75.

Taylor, Dennis (1981). *Hardy's Poetry, 1860–1928*. London: Macmillan. 2nd edn., 1989.

Taylor, Denis (1988). *Hardy's Metres and Victorian Prosody*. Oxford: Oxford University Press.

Witek. T. (1990). Repetition in a Land of Unlikeness: What "Life will not be baulked of" in Thomas Hardy's Poetry. *Victorian Poetry*, 28, 119–28.

Zeitlow, Paul (1974). *Moments of Vision: The Poetry of Thomas Hardy*. Cambridge, MA: Harvard University Press.

26

Hardy's Poems:
The Scholarly Situation

William W. Morgan

In August 1969, when I presented my Ph.D. dissertation on Thomas Hardy's reputation as a poet to my committee, academic libraries that were completely up to date held two critical books on Hardy's poems: James Granville Southworth's *The Poetry of Thomas Hardy* (1947) and Samuel Hynes' *The Pattern of Hardy's Poetry* (1961). An Interlibrary Loan office could probably have secured Elizabeth Cathcart Hickson's 1931 University of Pennsylvania dissertation on "The Versification of Thomas Hardy" for the really thorough scholar. Kenneth Marsden's *The Poems of Thomas Hardy: A Critical Introduction* (1969) had been announced but was not yet available. No one had seriously questioned the adequacy of the posthumous *Collected Poems* (1930) or its many reprints, despite their faint impression, increasingly broken type, and occasional misprints. In that same year, twenty of Hardy's poems announced his first appearance as a poet in the Major Authors Edition of the *Norton Anthology of English Literature*. A few years later on, I would necessarily have written a very different dissertation. Nearly forty years on, as we are now, the situation for readers, critics, and scholars of Hardy's poems is one of such surprising plenty that it hardly seems to be the legitimate descendant of those 1969 forebears.

But I don't mean to make the situation of the late 1960s sound entirely barren: even in 1969, the texture of the critical following for Hardy's poems was thicker and more interesting than the short list of book-length studies might indicate. As they had appeared between 1898 and 1928, his eight individual volumes of shorter poems and three volumes of *The Dynasts* had been reviewed nearly 150 times. At least a dozen general studies of his work and career, including some published before and others after his death, had taken account of his achievement in poetry. His poems held a place in ten or more general surveys of English poetry by respected critics. The 1940 centenary issue of *The Southern Review* had appeared, with stringent but largely approving essays by such prestigious poets and critics as John Crowe Ransom, W. H. Auden, F. R. Leavis, Delmore Schwartz, R. P. Blackmur, Allen Tate, and others, thus raising the bar for what counted as serious writing about Hardy's poems. Some forty or more essays on the poetry in general, on specific themes and techniques, and on individual poems had appeared in major journals. Four biographies had been published, all of them treating the poems with respect – some even with admiration. Richard Little Purdy's monumental *Thomas Hardy: A Bibliographical Study* (Clarendon Press, 1954, reprinted 1968) had presented the textual and publication history of the poems with full seriousness and had taken the second career as much more than simply a supplement to the first. Hardy the poet was not quite, as he is today, the rival of Hardy the novelist; but he had established what looked to be a secure – if possibly modest – place in critical history.

Still, it would have been difficult to imagine what riches – and complexities – twenty-first-century scholars of Hardy's poems would have to work with. In every major division of literary study, the scholarly situation in relation to Hardy's poems is now one of (sometimes perplexing) abundance, and his place in critical history is no longer modest. There are two critical editions of his shorter poems, and there is even one of *The Dynasts* and *The Queen of Cornwall*. His letters have been published in an outstanding edition, and several of his surviving notebooks have been or will shortly be published. He has been the subject of numerous thoughtful biographies. And there are now something in the neighborhood of thirty critical/interpretive books on his poetry, to say nothing of the scores of critical articles in scholarly journals. When I wrote the annual review of Hardy studies for *Victorian Poetry* for ten years between 1985 and 1995, I found it difficult to keep up with the steady flow of new work – and the situation has not changed since 1995. If anything, the flow has increased.

Editions of Hardy's Poems

Besides several smaller volumes of selected Hardy poems, there are four more or less complete editions of Hardy's shorter poems available. The old Macmillan *Collected Poems* has been reborn as *The Collected Poems of Thomas Hardy* (Wordsworth, 1994), and since 2002 it has featured an excellent introduction by Michael Irwin. This book is essentially a photographic reproduction of the 1962 printing of the Macmillan text, which went out of copyright and was allowed to go out of print when Macmillan commissioned James Gibson to prepare *The Complete Poems of Thomas Hardy* (1976). One has to admire the opportunistic resourcefulness of Wordsworth, even if the book is still in many ways unsatisfactory (broken type – particularly annoying are the tail-less commas that look like periods/full-stops – and faint printing, no scholarly textual apparatus, no notes, none of the Uncollected Poems, etc.). Even with its deficiencies, however, this may be the best buy on the market for the general, non-academic reader.

For students and scholars, the situation is better. The paperback version of James Gibson's edition of *Complete Poems* (the hardback is not at present available from the publisher, though used copies are to be found) is more than a step up on the scholarly scale. With it, one gets a much cleaner version of everything in the Wordsworth volume, plus Gibson's thoughtful and admiring introduction, as well as seventeen pages of informative notes on textual variants, on separate publication in magazines and newspapers, and on other matters of scholarly interest. And this edition offers twenty-eight Uncollected Poems (none of them, one might argue, among Hardy's best work, but all of them part of the whole picture of Hardy's work in verse). For students and scholars who are not Hardy specialists, this is the book to own. For specialists and university libraries, there are two further – and more expensive – editions to consider: James Gibson's *The Variorum Edition of the Complete Poems of Thomas Hardy* (Macmillan, 1979) and Samuel Hynes' five-volume *Complete Poetical Works of Thomas Hardy* (Clarendon Press, 1982, 1984, 1985, and 1995). Gibson's *Variorum*, sadly, is no longer in print, but used copies are available. Of Hynes's five volumes, only volumes IV and V, comprising *The Dynasts, The Queen of Cornwall*, and two shorter dramatic pieces in verse, are still available from the publisher, Both the Gibson *Variorum* and the first three volumes of the Hynes *Collected Poetical Works*, however, are to be found from booksellers and in academic libraries. These are the best scholarly editions of Hardy's poems – though it is important to understand their differences and their limitations.

Gibson's text in both his editions is strongly tied to the Macmillan *Collected Poems*. His *Complete Poems* is essentially a skillful and informed cleaning up of that earlier text. When he came to publish the *Variorum* (which he had been working on before he undertook *Complete Poems*), he was bound to his own *Complete Poems* as a copy-text, though he knew about and recorded variant readings from what amounts to a second line of descent in Hardy's poetic texts, the line represented by the Wessex Edition (1912 and following) and the Mellstock Edition (1919–20), and, to a lesser extent, by the changes Hardy made in his own copies of his poems. It is clear that Hardy made changes to poems for those two collected editions and in his own copies (mostly preserved in the Hardy Memorial Collection at the Dorset County Museum in Dorchester) that he did not, for reasons unknown, incorporate into subsequent editions of *Collected Poems*. Perhaps he forgot to gather in the changes; perhaps he decided against them. We will never know. At any rate, because of these stranded variant readings, *Collected Poems* and its Gibson successors, *Complete Poems* and the *Variorum*, may be challenged as Hardy's final word on the text of his poems.

Hynes' *Complete Poetical Works* articulates that challenge in its front matter and in its choice of copy-text. Rather than adopting *Collected Poems* as a starting-point, Hynes begins with the first editions of the eight volumes of verse. Variants from those early volumes are duly recorded and are incorporated into the reading text when they seem by their date to represent Hardy's second thoughts or other clear intent. Whenever the stranded variants from the two collected editions and from Hardy's annotations to his own copies of his works are at odds with the latest-known text of the poem in question, Hynes trusts his own sense of "Hardy's mature style" to make the call.

The result of these two very different approaches to constituting Hardy's definitive poetic texts is that in no fewer than 350 of the nearly 1,000 poems the two scholarly texts disagree. This was the conclusion drawn by Martin Ray when in 2001 he published "A Collation of the Gibson and Hynes Editions of Hardy's Poems," thereby calling attention to the differences in a way and to an extent that had not been previously appreciated. And some of Hynes's choices will be jarring to readers who have long been familiar with the old *Collected Poems* and Gibson's successor texts. Here are just a few sample differences:

Gibson	Hynes
	"The Impercipient"
O, doth a bird deprived of wings	O, doth a bird beshorn of wings
	"Shut Out That Moon"
She wears too much the guise she wore	She bears too much the guise she wore
	"Afterwards"
Till they rise again, as they were a new	Till they swell again, as they were a new

For a cogent and lucid comparison of the two editions and further examples of the differences between their final texts, see Dennis Taylor's "Editions of Hardy's Poetry" at the Thomas Hardy Association's Poetry Page (<http://www.ilstu.edu/~wwmorgan/Authoritative%20Texts.htm>).

I will return to the somewhat confused state of Hardy's poetic texts later in this survey when I undertake to suggest some directions for future work.

Letters

By 1969 a scattered few of Hardy's letters had been published here and there – in Viola Meynell's edition of *Friends of a Lifetime: Letters to Sydney Carlyle Cockerell* (1940) and in Charles Morgan's *The House of Macmillan* (1943), for example. But for substantial and dedicated books, I had two selections from Hardy's letters – one of them rather miscellaneous, the other biographically focused – at my disposal: *The Letters of Thomas Hardy*, edited by Carl J. Weber (1954) and *"Dearest Emmie": Thomas Hardy's Letters to his First Wife*, also edited by Carl J. Weber (1963). The first was, as its subtitle announced, a collection "Transcribed from the Original Autographs now in the Colby College Library," and comprised 116 letters of differing degrees of interest ranging in date from early 1873 to late summer 1927, just a few months before Hardy's death. But the book did introduce scholars of the period to Hardy's diligent management of the publication of his work (letters to editors and publishers of both his prose and his poetry dominate the collection). The same professional theme – references to forthcoming stories and poems, to meetings with editors and publishers, etc. – makes a solid appearance in the other book as well, alongside more mundane matters such as instructions for the servants at Max Gate, travel arrangements for himself and for his wife, his reports on the social engagements he has attended, people he has met, etc. *"Dearest Emmie"* contains seventy-four letters – most of them written from London to Emma at home in Dorset – dating from 1885 to 1911 (Emma died in November 1912), and besides the insight it offered into Hardy's professional and social life, it might be said to have given scholars our first direct look at the cooling of feelings that overtook the marriage in its later years. From this collection, we also gained our first knowledge of Hardy's eager interest in the famous and beautiful people he had begun to meet as his own fame increased.

One of those was the Hon. Mrs. Florence Ellen Hungerford Henniker (née Milnes), born in December 1855 and thus nearly fifteen years Hardy's junior. She was a beautiful woman, a talented writer of fiction, and the wife of the Hon. Arthur Henry Henniker-Major. Hardy met her in May 1893 at the Dublin home of her brother, Lord Houghton, Lord-Lieutenant of Ireland, and the pair remained friends until her death in 1923. The (probably) incomplete gathering of Hardy's letters to her over those thirty years appeared in 1972 as *One Rare Fair Woman: Thomas Hardy's Letters to Florence Henniker, 1893–1922*, edited by Evelyn Hardy and F. B. Pinion (1972). This is the first collection of Hardy's letters that gave readers some insight into his emotional life. Clearly he was smitten with Mrs. Henniker, and there are moments of playful flirting and scolding and even longing, especially in the earlier letters. But what began – on Hardy's side at least – as a serious flirtation tinged with hopelessness matured over the years into a solid and reliable friendship. For some time early on, Hardy was also reading and critiquing Mrs. Henniker's stories, and the letters give us a good sense of his understanding of the audience for fiction, of his barely contained contempt for the prevailing idea of fictional decorum, and of his sharp eye as a reader. Whereas the earlier collections of letters had suggested that for Hardy a letter was a rather routine matter and not another art form, this collection went some way towards changing that perception. And since the correspondence with Mrs. Henniker carried on into Hardy's career as a poet, these letters give us moments of insight into Hardy's poems and his self-image as a poet as well. For an example, I cite the following comments on "A Sunday Morning Tragedy" from Hardy's letter of December 31, 1907:

> I have had a ballad – what I consider rather a strong one – refused by the *Fortnightly* and the *Nation* (though they both wanted something of me) on the ground that those periodicals "are read in families" – The poem turns upon a tragedy that "families" read about in the newspapers every week. But I expected that it would be declined, so was not surprised to see it come back. Yet people complain nowadays that the authors of England have no strength like those of Elizabethan days. If they had it, they could not show it! (E. Hardy and Pinion 1972: 135)

But all three of these tantalizing selections have been eclipsed by a first-rate comprehensive edition: *The Collected Letters of Thomas Hardy*, in seven volumes, edited by Richard Little Purdy and Michael Millgate (1978, 1980, 1982, 1984, 1985, 1987, 1988). This is an extraordinary work of scholarship – arguably the finest edition of letters accorded any Victorian figure. Purdy had the goodwill of Florence Hardy from early in her widowhood and until her death in 1937 and had been for decades the presumptive editor of Hardy's collected letters (sometimes to the dismay of other scholars, such as Evelyn Hardy and F. B. Pinion, who wanted to and sometimes did publish volumes of selections). He had unparalleled access to both public and private collections of Hardy's letters and for years he worked in his quiet way on the project. But when Millgate joined him in the 1970s the pace picked up quickly, and the first volume came out in 1978 – to enthusiastic reviews. The others followed at regular intervals over the decade, and by 1988 the collection was provisionally complete. This edition is impressive in every way – scrupulously correct transcriptions, clear indications of the location and nature of the original (i.e., which private collection or public library it is to be found in, whether it is a pencil draft, original in ink, carbon copy, typed copy, etc.), unobtrusive but incisive and relevant notes, comprehensive index, etc. For students of the poems, the edition is particularly useful, since the number of Hardy letters that have survived from his years as a poet is, not surprisingly, higher than the number of those from his earlier, novel-writing years. The first volume (representing 1840–92) covers nearly the entirety of his career as a fiction writer; the other six are a goldmine of tidbits and fragments of insight into the work Hardy did in his second career and his attitudes towards that work. Note the following letter of thanks, for example, that Hardy sent to John Middleton Murry after Murry sent him payment for "According to the Mighty Working" (which had appeared in the *Athenaeum* of April 4, 1919) and asked for another poem for the journal:

Max Gate | 23: 2: 1920

Dear Mr Murry:

Many thanks. These things seem to come as a gift, for I cannot feel that such intangible ware as thought-beats can weigh against a solid commodity.

My mind is quite vacant of any new poem, nor can I find one already written, beyond some lines I have long promised. I will, of course, bear your wish in mind. I gather that the Athenaeum has quite caught on, & I am glad.

Yrs sincerely
Th: Hardy.

(*CL* VI: 9)

There is no great revelation here or in any other letter, but phrases such as "thought-beats" and images of the 80-year-old poet searching his study for a suitable poem accumulate into a portrait of his attitudes towards poetry and of his work habits. And just a few weeks later, Hardy did in fact "find" a suitable poem:

Max Gate | Dorchester | April 7th. 1920.

Dear Mr. Murry:

Since you wrote kindly asking me for another poem I have found some verses which at first I thought would only suit publication in a *daily* paper dated April 30th. But I find that by accident there will be an Athenaeum on April 30th. next, and therefore I shall have pleasure in sending you the verses for serial use in that number, if it is not already made up. It if should be I will wait till I can find something else for the opportunity of appearing in your pages, as the aforesaid poem would lose some of whatever point it may have if it were published at another date. I can let you have it at once if you say there is room on April 30.

Yours sincerely,
Thomas Hardy.

P. S. I am presupposing you will care for it! Th. H.

(*CL* VI: 12)

The poem in question was "The Maid of Keinton-Mandeville," subtitled "A Tribute to Sir Henry Bishop on the sixty-fifth anniversary of his death: April 30, 1855." Such careful management of timing is but one of the many themes in the life of Hardy the poet that are opened up – not in any blaze of revelation, but in bits and pieces – over the course of the years and years of letters.

Purdy died in 1990, but Millgate has continued to gather letters that eluded the editors' earlier cast-net, and there is a good likelihood that an eighth volume will appear in the next few years. Meanwhile scholars and libraries also have, in addition to the seven-volume print edition, access to an electronic version on CD or by subscription to the publisher's server. The electronic version is handy for word searches: it might be revealing, for instance, to find out with a few keystrokes how many times and in what situations Hardy used the word "public" or "audience." Two further editions of Hardy and Hardy-related letters are worthy of note: *Thomas Hardy: Selected Letters*, edited by Michael Millgate (Oxford: Clarendon Press, 1990) and *Letters of Emma and Florence Hardy*, edited by Michael Millgate (Oxford: Clarendon Press, 1996). The latter presents forty-seven letters from Emma to various correspondents and 251 from Florence (sixty-five from before Hardy's death and 186 from after), Florence's "share" being larger because far more of her letters have survived. His wives' letters do not offer any particular insight into Hardy's poems, but they do give a vivid sense, especially in the case of Florence, of what domestic life at Max Gate must have been like when Hardy was pursuing his second career. The volume of *Selected Letters* – comprising 349 specimens dating from 1862 to late 1927 – is judiciously done and gives a good sense of the flavor of the entire seven-volume set. Here, as in the full edition, letters from the poem-writing years outnumber those from the years as a fiction writer, but Millgate has altered the balance somewhat and has given something closer to equal weight to the two careers. In these two volumes, as in his other work, Millgate is an authoritative but non-intrusive editor, giving the reader just the right amount of relevant information to make clear the letters' points of reference. All Hardy readers and scholars are greatly in his debt.

Notebooks

Hardy was a habitual note-taker throughout his life as a writer. His surviving notebooks (see CHAPTER 6, HARDY'S NOTEBOOKS) are mostly literary in character, except for the "Schools of Painting" notebook, which Hardy began in 1863 and which seems to have been part of his self-education during his early years in London. His "Literary Notes I," "Literary Notes II," and the "1867" notebook are likewise records of his intensive reading and self-education, but this time the education is specifically pointed towards his career as a writer. While the "1867" notebook contains extracts of a specifically literary character (from poems, novels, reviews, etc.), both the volumes of "Literary Notes" are quite miscellaneous: philosophy, history, psychology, art history and criticism, as well as current events all show up. These notebooks have been published as *The Literary Notebooks of Thomas Hardy*, edited by Lennart A. Björk (Macmillan, 1985). Almost twenty years later, there appeared another of the notebooks, of a similar character, though concerning itself with different kinds of content: *Thomas Hardy's "Facts" Notebook: A Critical Edition*, edited by William Greenslade (2004). Except for some revealing passages showing the extent of Hardy's research into the background of his poem, "Panthera" and others that may inform "Barthélémon at Vauxhall" and perhaps a dozen other poems, the "Facts" notebook, like the other commonplace books, does not offer anything like a direct gloss on Hardy's poems. But it is fascinating to see how his imagination can take some inert "fact" from a prosaic source and turn it into part of a novel or a poem. As is the case with the letters, these literary notebooks do not contain any striking revelations about either Hardy the ambitious young poet of the 1860s or the seasoned fiction writer turned poet of the 1890s through the late 1920s. But to read through them is to gain much admiration for Hardy's diligence, his wide learning, and his intellectual seriousness – and, in turn, to come to the poems with an awareness of the intellectual ballast that, in some mysterious way we do not yet understand, made them possible.

There are, however, two surviving notebooks that bear directly on the work of Hardy the poet, one of them, called "Studies, Specimens, &c.," belonging to his early days as an aspiring poet, and the other, called "Poetical Matter," originating in the last decade of his life. Both have been published in first-rate scholarly editions prepared by Pamela Dalziel and Michael Millgate (1994, 2009). The title of the "Studies, Specimens, &c." notebook gives a reasonably accurate idea of the contents of its eighty-nine pages: it mostly comprises "specimens" of language (from poets and other sources as diverse as Swinburne, Scott, Spenser, Shakespeare, Byron, Wordsworth, Milton, Marvell, Tennyson, Burns, Barnes, Shelley, Jean Ingelow, the Bible, the Book of Common Prayer, and even the odd novel), and sometimes those "specimens" become the basis for Hardy's "studies" – that is, he marks up the passage to highlight its most striking language (presumably for purposes of vocabulary-building), and sometimes takes that language as the basis for an improvisation of his own. These last exercises he calls "Concoc" (for concoctions) or "Inv" (for inventions). For example, "Why dost thou shew me iniquity . . .?" from the book of Habakkuk becomes "She showed me smiles"; and ". . . spoiling and violence are before me," from the same source, becomes "Her red spoilt eyes." Such entries not only tell us something about what the young Hardy was reading during the years 1865–7, but they also give us a strikingly intimate glimpse into his diligent efforts to teach himself to be a writer. The second notebook, even though it survives only as a print from a microfilm, is complete and mostly legible and is equally interesting, since it shows us much more than we have known before about Hardy's compositional process late in his life, a process that apparently included prose outlines, verse skeletons, and partial drafts (often multiple) before a tentatively final manuscript appeared.

Biographies

Setting aside a dozen or more books of the genre usually called "critical biographies," in which the critic's main interest is in Hardy's works and in which he or she ties those works to the general course of Hardy's life, there are also a dozen or more full-blown, dedicated biographies – that is, books in which the main object is not to critique or analyze the works but to tell the life-story. In my touchstone year of 1969, I had four – or, one might better say, three and a half – biographies to rely on, two in the former category and one and a half in the latter, the category that concerns me here: a critical biography by Ernest Brennecke, Jr., *The Life of Thomas Hardy* (1925), Evelyn Hardy, *Thomas Hardy: A Critical Biography* (1954), Carl J. Weber, *Hardy of Wessex: His Life and Literary Career* (1940), and the revised second edition of the latter (1965). Brennecke's book has generally been understood to be fair-minded but under-informed. It was published before Hardy's death and very much against his wishes. More importantly, it was published before the critical moments when Florence Hardy published Hardy's disguised autobiography under her own name, in two volumes entitled *The Early Life of Thomas Hardy* (1928) and *The Later Years of Thomas Hardy* (1930). (The original text as intended by Hardy has since been made available under Hardy's own title, *The Life and Work of Thomas Hardy*, edited by Michael Millgate [1984].) It is no exaggeration to say that these two volumes, largely written by Hardy himself and presented to the public as the work of Florence, dominated our view of the facts of Hardy's life until the mid-1970s. But not quite our view of Hardy's poetry, despite the two volumes' urgent insistence that Hardy had been, by temperament, a poet all along and a novelist only by necessity. Weber's two biographies – certainly the standard works for my generation of beginning scholars in the late 1960s and early 1970s – took the poems seriously but resisted Hardy's prioritization of them. For Weber, Hardy was pre-eminently a fiction writer, indeed a master of the novel, who had also written some revealing and interesting poems. Weber's main contribution to the dominant narrative of Hardy's life was not to follow Hardy's own contention about the primacy of the poems over the fiction but instead to tease out – from letters mainly – the narrative of Hardy and Emma's gradual estrangement. For Weber, the *Early Life* and *Later Years* story was essentially complete, and his responsibility was to temper Hardy's own enthusiasm for his poems while honoring the novels and adding his own view that the marriage to Emma had been a tragic union of incompatible temperaments, whereas the marriage to Florence had been a blessing to literature, since Florence's loyal support had made it possible for Hardy to continue his creative work on into his late eighties.

Weber's view was probably the dominant one until Robert Gittings' two-volume biography, *Young Thomas Hardy* (1975) and *The Older Hardy* (1978). We had had a hint of something different to come when Michael Millgate published *Thomas Hardy: His Career as a Novelist* (1971), with its interleaved chapters on Hardy's life and the novels one by one as they appeared; it was clear even then that Millgate, though he was in this book principally interested in Hardy's novels, was a skilled biographer who would not be satisfied with the "official" version of Hardy's life in the ghosted autobiography. But *Thomas Hardy: His Career as a Novelist* stops at the end of Hardy's career as a writer of fiction, so it is not of direct use to students of the poems. Gittings' books, on the other hand, are both skeptical of Hardy's self-constructed life-narrative and celebratory about Hardy's poems. So his work introduces an entirely new tone to the history of Hardy biography, and Hardy comes off as quirky, inattentive to his wives (possibly unfaithful to the first with the woman who would become the second), mean with his money, short with his servants, protective of his relatives at Bockhampton, secretive, perhaps ashamed of his humble origins, a bit paranoid about public exposure, etc. – but through it all a great writer, especially a great poet. Although many in the Hardy community thought Gittings had been far too hard on Hardy personally, virtually everyone agreed that he was a first-rate critic of Hardy's poems. But his principal contribution to Hardy biography was to crack the façade of the official version of Hardy's life. He read and used the letters of Hardy's wives, the diaries and memories of those who knew him, his notebooks, and the early drafts of the *Early Life* and the *Later Years* and gave them equal authority with the finished version of Hardy's own ghosted autobiography. I would guess that Gittings' two books are not read very much today, but their effect on biographical scholarship on Hardy is still with us, and students of Hardy's poetry can be grateful to him for his courage and for some strikingly insightful readings.

In Michael Millgate's *Thomas Hardy: A Biography* (1982), one can feel the writer pushing back against Gittings' portrayal of Hardy the man. Millgate never refers to Gittings by name, but he clearly wants to right some balances (suggesting, for instance, that Hardy's perceived "meanness" was just country frugality). Millgate had no need to reply to Gittings, since he was in a much stronger position from which to understand the daily texture of Hardy's life as well as its scope and sweep: he had access to the mass of letters that Purdy had collected and that he was helping to edit, to the two Purdy-owned Hardy notebooks ("Studies, Specimens, &c." and "Poetical Matter"), to Purdy's correspondence with Florence, and to numbers of other documents. And, of course, like Gittings, he had done his homework by reading ancillary sources (such as the diary of Edward Clodd, which recorded Hardy's visits, sometimes with Florence as his companion, to Clodd's house at Aldeburgh) and was not inclined to take the official narrative of *Early Life* and *Later Years* as gospel. So he had every advantage that Gittings had, plus others. And he was, furthermore, less likely than Gittings to be excited by the whiff of scandal. His account of Hardy the man is sympathetic, balanced, and deeply informed. Virtually everyone, even some subsequent biographers, refer to Millgate's biography as definitive for a generation. This is true for James Gibson's *Thomas Hardy: A Literary Life* (1996) and Claire Tomalin's *Thomas*

Hardy: The Time-Torn Man (2006), both of which offer exceptional insight into the life of Hardy the poet and into individual poems, even while deferring admiringly to Millgate as the master of the facts of Hardy's life.

Such is not the case with Martin Seymour-Smith's *Hardy* (1994), an 886-page book with no original research, no notes or bibliography, and a lot of self-assurance. The book is badly disfigured by a nasty grudge against Millgate; Seymour-Smith takes every occasion to ridicule Millgate's account of Hardy's life and his interpretations of this or that work. His view of Hardy is admiring beyond measure: Hardy was so much smarter than any of his critics or biographers that their paltry efforts to understand him are nearly contemptible. Hardy was also always and totally in command of his pen and always knew exactly what he was doing. The effects in his books and in his poems are there because he put them there knowingly. Seymour-Smith wants to suggest that Millgate in particular is not capable of understanding or responding adequately to such a genius as Hardy was; and because he lacks the imagination to comprehend Hardy, he is not adequate to the task of writing the life of such a genius. There are certainly some good moments of interpretive criticism of the poems in the book, but on the whole it is likely to strike a reader as a self-indulgent oddity. Ralph Pite's *Thomas Hardy: The Guarded Life* (2006), the other recent biography that does not defer to Millgate, sets out to map Hardy's inner or emotional life – to give an account of the part of his life-story that Hardy most assiduously hid from the public, and even from his family and friends: how did he really feel about marrying Emma, about the death of his father, about the reviews of *Jude*, etc? Pite's answers to such questions cannot be verified, of course, so the tests of (1) plausibility and (2) persuasiveness are the only relevant ones to apply. Some readers may be convinced; many will probably think the book a well-intentioned failure. Meanwhile, Millgate has published *Thomas Hardy: A Biography Revisited* (2004), into which he has incorporated new materials and in which he has substantially revised much of the 1982 book.

For scholars and students of the poems, the tradition of Hardy biography is rich and useful. All the biographies are worth reading. For the reader with limited time, my advice would be to read Millgate for the facts and for a balanced view of Hardy the man and then to turn to Gittings, Gibson, and Tomalin for good readings of the poems. But such advice does not say it all. There is a worrisome thread in the numerous Hardy biographies that requires our vigilance: whereas most of the biographers treat the fiction as art, they are almost all inclined, when they don't consciously stop themselves from doing so, to treat the poems as direct personal revelation. In a manner of speaking, Hardy asked for this treatment: he always insisted that his poems were the more "individual" part of his literary work, and he even instructed Florence to say – rather provocatively – in a letter of 1919 that "Speaking generally there is more autobiography in a hundred lines of Mr Hardy's poetry than in all the novels . . ." (*CL* VII: 161). But biographers, like the rest of us, are obliged to remember that even in the poems, autobiography is mediated by art, and art of a very high order. Thus one of the tests we would do well to apply to biographies of Hardy is whether or not the biographer understands that when the personal and autobiographical are carried over into a poem, they are transformed.

Electronic Resources

Besides the electronic versions of *Collected Letters* that I mentioned earlier, there are other electronic resources that the student or scholar of Hardy's poems can turn to. At the top of the list is the website of the Thomas Hardy Association: <http://www.yale.edu/hardysoc/Welcome/welcomet.htm>. This general page is a gateway to a huge number of resources – links to the Hardy Memorial Collection at the Dorset County Museum, the Purdy Collection at Yale, the Hardy Society (UK), a first-rate checklist of scholarly publications on Hardy and his work, as well as pages devoted to Hardy's life, his novels, his dramatic writings, his short stories, and of course his poems: <http://www.yale.edu/hardysoc/Poetry/poetry.htm>. This page offers Dennis Taylor's description of the Gibson and Hynes editions, Mark Simons' guide to collecting Hardy's poetry, and a link to the TTHA's Poem of the Month discussion, an electronic conversation devoted to a different Hardy poem every month. And finally, there are three very useful CDs compiled by Martin Ray and available as a benefit of TTHA membership: *Thomas Hardy: A Variorum Concordance to the Complete Poems* (1999); *Thomas Hardy's The Dynasts: A Concordance* (1999); *The Life and Work of Thomas Hardy: Allusions and Annotations* (2003).

These CDs are easy to use, comprehensive, and strikingly accurate. Want to know how often and where Hardy used the word "love" and all its derivatives in his poems? The Variorum Concordance will tell you in a couple of keystrokes. Wondering about the word "war" and its derivatives in *The Dynasts*? Want to know more about the Mrs. Champ Clark of Washington, DC, who wrote to Hardy in the summer of 1918 to tell him of her husband's political adventures in the US House of Representatives? These CDs will satisfy your curiosity quickly and reliably. As will another CD, called simply *The Poetry of Thomas Hardy* (Chester: Chester College of Higher Education, 2001), and compiled by Sara Haslam with Glyn Turton. This one features an electronic edition of Gibson's *Complete Poems*, as well as a search engine, several audio readings, photographs, video footage of critical conversations about the poems, as well as critical essays. Both electronic publishing and electronic scholarship have more than a foothold in the community of those interested in Hardy's poems.

Critical and Interpretive Studies

The last forty years or so have seen a tremendous surge in what might be called documentary scholarship on Hardy – that is, the publication of textual studies, editions, letters, notebooks, etc . – the kind of work that deals with stubborn facts. We have immeasurably more information at our disposal now than we did when I set out. Critical and interpretive writing about the poems has likewise surged: we now have something over thirty critical books and hundreds of essays to turn to. For obvious reasons I won't be commenting on all of them, but I can suggest the various groups or categories into which they fall and give a few examples of each.

Several of the most useful books could be called "Critical Introductions" – books that take a general view of Hardy's work in verse and offer themselves as guides to the beginning reader. Two such are Trevor Johnson's *A Critical Introduction to the Poems of Thomas Hardy* (1991) and John Powell Ward's *Thomas Hardy's Poetry* (1993).

Then there are a half-dozen of what might be called "Appreciations" of Hardy the poet. Joanna Cullen Brown's books (such as *Figures in a Wessex Landscape* [1989a], *A Journey into Thomas Hardy's Poetry* [1989b], and *Let Me Enjoy the Earth* [1990], for example), are thoughtful celebrations of the beauty of the world evoked by Hardy's poems. But the spirit of admiring celebration can and does also dominate more philosophical books such as Manas Mukul Das's *Thomas Hardy: Poet of Tragic Vision* (1983) or Mallikarjun Patil's *Thomas Hardy's Poetry and Existentialism* (1999).

At the other end of the spectrum are what I would call "Appraisals" or "Assessments" – books that are concerned to evaluate Hardy's contribution to poetry. And typically, they are skeptical about the value of much of Hardy's canon in verse. In this group I'd include Kenneth Marsden's *The Poems of Thomas Hardy: A Critical Introduction* (1969), Donald Davie's *Thomas Hardy and British Poetry* (1972), and Tom Paulin's *Thomas Hardy: The Poetry of Perception* (1975). For this group, Hardy the poet has a small body of poetic masterpieces but has yet to be shown as a major poet beyond question.

Another broad grouping comprises the historical and biographical studies – books that proceed from the premise that the marks left on Hardy's poems by his particular life-story and by the times in which he lived and wrote are the most reliable guides to reading those poems. This group would include William E. Buckler's *The Poetry of Thomas Hardy: A Study in Art and Ideas* (1983), all three of Dennis Taylor's admirable studies – *Hardy's Poetry, 1860–1928* (1981), *Hardy's Metres and Victorian Prosody* (1988), and *Hardy's Literary Language and Victorian Philology* (1993) – as well as the two comprehensive, encyclopedic books that have something to say about each of Hardy's more than 900 poems: J. O. Bailey's *The Poetry of Thomas Hardy: A Handbook and Commentary* (1970) and F. B. Pinion's *A Commentary on the Poems of Thomas Hardy* (1976).

Then there are the books that take a single technique, preoccupation, or theme and attempt to show how it opens up Hardy's entire canon in verse to a fuller understanding. Samuel Hynes' *The Pattern of Hardy's Poetry* (1961), mentioned earlier, is the first of these and concerns itself with "the eternal conflict between irreconcilables" (p. vii) as an organizing figure in Hardy's poems. Paul Zietlow's *Moments of Vision: The Poetry of Thomas Hardy* (1974) sees the most revealing pattern as "the tension within [Hardy] himself between an impulse to withdraw and to participate" (p. x). Katherine Kearney Maynard's *Thomas Hardy's Tragic Poetry: The Lyrics and "The Dynasts"* (1991) takes Hardy's effort to establish a new genre, tragic poetry, as the most useful key to his body of poems. For Brian Green in his *Hardy's Lyrics: Pearls of Pity* (1996), Hardy's master-theme is the conflict between an uncaring, probably unknowing, universe and the ethical impulse by which the best of humanity attempt to live. For Ellen Anne Lanzano in her *Hardy: The Temporal Poetics* (1999), the most revealing single conflict in Hardy's poems is that between time as a kind of fatalism and human emotional attachments as a means of transcending it.

The "Theory Revolution" has left but a small mark on the study of Hardy's poems so far, but two theoretically informed books deserve mention: James Richardson's *Thomas Hardy: The Poetry of Necessity* (1977) and Tim Armstrong's *Haunted Hardy: Poetry, History, Memory* (2000). The former treats Hardy's recovery of possibility in a world where transcendent meaning has disappeared, and the latter uses Jacques Derrida and others to explain – and, ultimately, to celebrate – the haunting presences in Hardy's poems.

Finally, there are a half-dozen collections of essays devoted to Hardy's poems – collections such as *Thomas Hardy: Poems*, edited by James Gibson and Trevor Johnson (1979), the special issue of *Victorian Poetry* (1979), edited by Frank R. Giordano, Jr., *The Poetry of Thomas Hardy*, edited by Patricia Clements and Juliet Grindle (1980), and *Critical Essays on Thomas Hardy's Poetry*, edited by Harold Orel (1995).

My theme throughout this essay has been *plenty*, and here is plenty indeed. But it's not clear to me that the Hardy community has managed to bring its two strands – of documentary and interpretive scholarship – together: where are the books that bring a commanding understanding of the textual variants, the notebooks, the letters, etc. to an interpretation of Hardy's poems?

What of the Future?

But to speak of work that will bring together the weight of fact that has been our benison in the last forty years and the problems of interpretation that are presented by all that fact is to speculate about the future. What needs to be happening in the next ten to twenty years of scholarship on Hardy's poems? In my opinion, we need four new initiatives:

A new or corrected scholarly text of the poems;
A biographical study of Hardy the poet;
A study of Hardy's books of poems as books;
A new encyclopedic reference book, with commentary on each of Hardy's poems.

About the scholarly editions. It gives me no pleasure to say it, but neither the Gibson *Variorum* nor the Hynes *Complete Poetical Works* is satisfactory. Gibson's text is as close to error-free as we are likely to see in this kind of work, but it lacks several advantages of Hynes': Hynes records all the erasures in pre-publication versions of the poems (whereas Gibson includes only selected ones); Hynes honors the authority of the "other" line of descent in Hardy's poetic texts in presenting his reading text (whereas Gibson records the "other" variants but keeps *Complete Poems* as his reading text); Hynes includes the illustrations to *Wessex Poems* and one additional uncollected poem (from a Purdy typescript) that was not available to Gibson. But the error-count in Hynes' edition appears to be considerably higher than it is in Gibson's: Martin Ray (2001) notes a number of simple misprints in Hynes that account for many of the 350 differences between the two texts. And in a later study, Ray compares Hynes' published edition to one of its sources, the holograph of *Poems of the Past and the Present*, and finds a fair number of "inaccurate transcriptions of variant readings" (Ray 2003: 99). Ray's findings are alarming. What is at stake, of course, is the question of whether the Hynes edition is to be thought of as reliable. Ray's research would cast some doubt – enough doubt, in my opinion, that I would want to caution against trusting Hynes without also checking Gibson. But, alas, even cross-checking the two editions cannot produce full confidence: since most of us are not in a position to step around the corner and check the accuracy of this or that transcription against its source, we need a revised edition of *Complete Poetical Works* – or at least an errata list. If Hynes is not willing or able to produce it, Oxford University Press should appoint someone else to do it. Nothing is more fundamental or essential than full and accurate texts.

About the biographical study I would like to see: Hardy wrote and published poems exclusively (or nearly so) for something like thirty years. He was, of course, the same man, but he was living a different life – one that we don't know as much about as we should. For most of that period there exists a huge cache of detailed biographical information – letters to and from him and his two wives, his poetic holographs, notebooks, correspondence with his publishers and with editors, the drafts of *The Early Life* and *The Later Years* – that has yet to be integrated into our understanding of Hardy's second career or the poems it produced. In the Hardy Memorial Collection alone there are some 3,000 letters *to* Hardy, many of them from editors and colleagues. Nothing has been written, for example, on Hardy the poet's ambivalent relationship with the periodical press (he both sought to publish in magazines and newspapers and at the same time was doubtful about their value). The kind of book I'm imagining might, if the writer dared to steal Michael Millgate's title, be called something like *Thomas Hardy: His Career as a Poet*. And such a volume might also provide the opportunity for something else I wish we had: a study of Hardy's books of poems *as books*. I have written an essay on *Time's Laughingstocks* as a book (see Morgan 2006), but I am not aware of any other such study. Yet every one of Hardy's volumes of verse is in fact a book – something organized by the poet in a secondary act of creation. One of the odd facts of literary reputation is that the more well-known and accepted a poet becomes, the less likely we are to read his or her work in the form in which it first appeared. A study of Hardy's books of poems would go some way towards making that oddity a little less common and would reveal an aspect of his artistic work about which we now know little.

And finally, I would call for a new encyclopedic book of commentary on Hardy's poems, one by one. We have a number of admirable interpretive/analytical books on Hardy's poetry, but they all seem to me just a little premature: each of them, understandably, in order to sustain its thesis, leaves out a goodly slice of Hardy's poetic output. In my view, what we need is not more studies of his *Poetry* but instead some more careful attention to his *Poems*. In fact, I would claim that Hardy didn't produce a *Poetry* in the same sense in which, say, Yeats or Keats or Wordsworth or Wallace Stevens did – that is, a body of poems accountable to the coherent worldview of their maker. His stance toward the world, for good or ill, was more modest than theirs – and his poems recorded a series of "seemings," as he often said. I am proposing something like – but more contemporary and rigorous than – J. O. Bailey's *Handbook and Commentary* and F. B. Pinion's *Commentary*, both of which are seriously out of date. Such a book might be the work of a single author or a collective enterprise; it might be published in print form or electronically. Regardless, it would send us all back to the texts of the individual poems – never a bad thing. It would also better serve students, who constitute many if not most of Hardy's readers and who are most likely to take on Hardy's poems one or two at a time rather than *en masse*.

* * *

My theme has been plenty – the plenty that has characterized the past forty years of scholarly work on Hardy's poetry – and my conclusion is a call for renewal in the midst of that plenty: renewal in the form of better editions, better integration of biographical fact with interpretation, better attention to the way Hardy first presented his poems to the public, and better, fresher attention to the individual poems. Critics and scholars of Hardy's poetry have accomplished much, and there is much good work yet to do. That is a healthy situation to find ourselves in.

REFERENCES AND FURTHER READING

Armstrong, Tim (2000). *Haunted Hardy: Poetry, History, Memory*. Basingstoke: Palgrave Macmillan.

Bailey, J. O. (1970). *The Poetry of Thomas Hardy: A Handbook and Commentary*. Chapel Hill: University of North Carolina Press.

Björk, Lennart A. (ed.) (1985). *The Literary Notebooks of Thomas Hardy*, 2 vols. London and Basingstoke: Macmillan.

Brennecke, Ernest Jr. (1925). *The Life of Thomas Hardy*. New York: Greenberg.

Brown, Joanna Cullen (1989a). *Figures in a Wessex Landscape: Thomas Hardy's Picture of English Country Life*. London: Carol Publishing.

Brown, Joanna Cullen (1989b). *A Journey into Thomas Hardy's Poetry*. London: Allison & Busby.

Brown, Joanna Cullen (1990). *Let Me Enjoy the Earth: Thomas Hardy and Nature*. London: Allison & Busby.

Buckler, William E. (1983). *The Poetry of Thomas Hardy: A Study in Art and Ideas*. New York: New York University Press.

Clements, Patricia, and Juliet Grindle (eds.) (1980). *The Poetry of Thomas Hardy*. London: Vision Press.

Dalziel, Pamela, and Michael Millgate (eds.) (1994). *Thomas Hardy's "Studies, Specimens &c." Notebook*. Oxford: Clarendon Press.

Dalziel, Pamela, and Michael Millgate (eds.) (2009). *Thomas Hardy's "Poetical Matter" Notebook*. Oxford: Oxford University Press.

Das, Manas Mukul (1983). *Thomas Hardy: Poet of Tragic Vision*. Atlantic Highlands, NJ: Humanities Press.

Davie, Donald (1972). *Thomas Hardy and British Poetry*. New York: Oxford University Press.

Gibson, James (1996). *Thomas Hardy: A Literary Life*. Basingstoke and London: Palgrave Macmillan.

Gibson, James, and Trevor Johnson (eds.) (1979). *Thomas Hardy: Poems: A Casebook*. London: Macmillan.

Giordano, Frank R. Jr. (ed.) (1979). *The Poetry of Thomas Hardy: A Commemorative Issue*. *Victorian Poetry*, 17(1 and 2).

Gittings, Robert (1975). *Young Thomas Hardy*. London: Heinemann.

Gittings, Robert (1978). *The Older Hardy*. London: Heinemann.

Green, Brian (1996). *Hardy's Lyrics: Pearls of Pity*. Basingstoke and London: Palgrave Macmillan.

Greenslade, William (ed.) (2004). *Thomas Hardy's "Facts" Notebook: A Critical Edition*. Aldershot: Ashgate.

Hardy, Evelyn (1954). *Thomas Hardy: A Critical Biography*. London: Hogarth Press.

Hardy, Evelyn, and F. B. Pinion (eds.) (1972). *One Rare Fair Woman: Thomas Hardy's Letters to Florence Henniker, 1893–1922*. London: Macmillan, 1972.

Hardy, Florence Emily (1928). *The Early Life of Thomas Hardy*. London: Macmillan.

Hardy, Florence Emily (1930). *The Later Years of Thomas Hardy*. London: Macmillan.

Hardy, Thomas (1930). *Collected Poems*. London: Macmillan.

Hardy, Thomas (1976). *The Complete Poems of Thomas Hardy*, ed. James Gibson. London: Macmillan.

Hardy, Thomas (1979). *The Variorum Edition of the Complete Poems of Thomas Hardy*, ed. James Gibson. London: Macmillan.

Hardy, Thomas (1982–95). *The Complete Poetical Works of Thomas Hardy*, ed. Samuel Hynes, 5 vols. Oxford: Clarendon Press.

Hardy, Thomas (1984). *The Life and Work of Thomas Hardy*, ed. Michael Millgate. London: Macmillan.

Hardy, Thomas ([1994] 2002). *The Collected Poems of Thomas Hardy*. London: Wordsworth.

Haslam, Sara, with Glyn Turton (comp.) (2001). *The Poetry of Thomas Hardy* (CD). Chester: Chester College of Higher Education.

Hickson, Elizabeth Cathcart (1931). The Versification of Thomas Hardy. Ph.D. dissertation, University of Pennsylvania.

Hynes, Samuel (1961). *The Pattern of Hardy's Poetry*. Chapel Hill: University of North Carolina Press.

Johnson, Trevor (1991). *A Critical Introduction to the Poems of Thomas Hardy*. Basingstoke and London: Macmillan.

Lanzano, Ellen Anne (1999). *Hardy: The Temporal Poetics*. New York: Peter Lang.

Marsden, Kenneth (1969). *The Poems of Thomas Hardy: A Critical Introduction*. London: Athlone Press; New York: Oxford University Press.

Maynard, Katherine Kearney (1991). *Thomas Hardy's Tragic Poetry: The Lyrics and "The Dynasts."* Iowa City: University of Iowa Press.

Meynell, Viola (ed.) (1940). *Friends of a Lifetime: Letters to Sydney Carlyle Cockerell*. London: Jonathan Cape.

Millgate, Michael (1971). *Thomas Hardy: His Career as a Novelist*. London: Bodley Head.

Millgate, Michael (1982). *Thomas Hardy: A Biography*. New York: Random House.

Millgate, Michael (ed.) (1990). *Thomas Hardy: Selected Letters*. Oxford: Clarendon Press.

Millgate, Michael (ed.) (1996). *Letters of Emma and Florence Hardy*. Oxford: Clarendon Press.

Millgate, Michael (2004). *Thomas Hardy: A Biography Revisited*. Oxford: Oxford University Press.

Morgan, Charles (1943). *The House of Macmillan*. London: Macmillan.

Morgan, William W. (2006). Aesthetics and Thematics in Hardy's Volumes of Verse: The Example of *Time's Laughingstocks*. In Keith Wilson (ed.), *Thomas Hardy Reappraised: Essays in Honour of Michael Millgate* (pp. 219–44). Toronto: University of Toronto Press.

Orel, Harold (ed.) (1995). *Critical Essays on Thomas Hardy's Poetry*. New York: G. K. Hall.

Patil, Mallikarjun (1999). *Thomas Hardy's Poetry and Existentialism*. New Delhi: Atlantic Publishers.

Paulin, Tom (1975). *Thomas Hardy: The Poetry of Perception*. London and Basingstoke: Macmillan.

Pinion, F. B. (1976). *A Commentary on the Poems of Thomas Hardy*. London and Basingstoke: Macmillan.

Pite, Ralph (2006). *Thomas Hardy: The Guarded Life*. London: Picador.

Purdy, Richard Little ([1954] 1968). *Thomas Hardy: A Bibliographical Study*. Oxford: Clarendon Press.

Purdy, Richard Little, and Michael Millgate (eds.) (1978–88). *The Collected Letters of Thomas Hardy*, 7 vols. Oxford: Clarendon Press.

Ray, Martin (ed.) (1999a). *Thomas Hardy: A Variorum Concordance to the Complete Poems* (CD).

Ray, Martin (ed.) (1999b). *Thomas Hardy's The Dynasts: A Concordance* (CD).

Ray, Martin (2001). A Collation of the Gibson and Hynes Editions of Hardy's Poems. *The Hardy Review*, 4, 127–40.

Ray, Martin (2003). The Bodleian Manuscript of *Poems of the Past and the Present. The Hardy Review*, 6, 99–104.

Ray, Martin (ed.) (2003). *The Life and Work of Thomas Hardy: Allusions and Annotations* (CD).

Richardson, James (1977). *Thomas Hardy: The Poetry of Necessity*. Chicago: University of Chicago Press.

Seymour-Smith, Martin (1994). *Hardy*. London: Bloomsbury.

Southworth, James Granville (1947). *The Poetry of Thomas Hardy*. New York: Columbia University Press.

Taylor, Dennis (1981). *Hardy's Poetry, 1860–1928*. London: Macmillan.

Taylor, Dennis (1988). *Hardy's Metres and Victorian Prosody*. Oxford: Clarendon Press.

Taylor, Dennis (1993). *Hardy's Literary Language and Victorian Philology*. Oxford: Clarendon Press.

Taylor, Dennis. Editions of Hardy's Poetry. The Thomas Hardy Association Poetry Page. <http://www.ilstu.edu/~wwmorgan/Authoritative%20Texts.htm>.

Tomalin, Claire (2006). *Thomas Hardy: The Time-Torn Man*. London: Penguin.

Ward, John Powell (1993). *Thomas Hardy's Poetry*. Buckingham: Open University Press, 1993.

Weber, Carl J. ([1940] 1965). *Hardy of Wessex: His Life and Literary Career*. New York: Columbia University Press.

Weber, Carl J. (ed.) (1954). *The Letters of Thomas Hardy*. Waterville, Maine: Colby College Press.

Weber, Carl J. (ed.) (1963). *"Dearest Emmie": Thomas Hardy's Letters to his First Wife*. New York: St. Martin's Press.

Zietlow, Paul (1974). *Moments of Vision: The Poetry of Thomas Hardy*. Cambridge, MA: Harvard University Press.

27

That's Show Business: Spectacle, Narration, and Laughter in *The Dynasts*

G. Glen Wickens

The cover illustration for the 1965 Macmillan paperback edition of *The Dynasts* featured a stern Napoleon gazing through his spyglass, with some ships drawn on the exaggerated lens to represent what he sees. The emphasis was just right, including the touch of humor in making Napoleon a cartoon figure – large hat and small body – reminiscent of the historical caricatures of Boney. *The Dynasts* abounds in scenes of watching and engages the reader most memorably as, to quote Hardy's preface, a "Spectacle" or "panoramic show" (D 3, 6)[1] that is seldom without its laughing side.

All too often, however, visual readings of *The Dynasts* ignore the laughing word and end up reinforcing one of the main objections to Hardy's most ambitious work. Praise for his visual artistry still leaves the problem of his so-called deterministic philosophy or fatalistic idea of history, whether critics see *The Dynasts* as anticipating the techniques of the cinema or possibly drawing upon its pre-history. Susan Dean invokes the changing views of the diorama as an analogy to help explain the shifting perspectives of *The Dynasts*, three of which keep the center of the drama preoccupied by "its urgent vision of unfreedom" (Dean 1977: 258). Often called cinematic, the famous aerial views in which armies and processions look like insects only serve to emphasize Hardy's supposed "theme of the inconsequence of man" (Carpenter 1964: 197). In Joan Grundy's appreciative but sometimes baffling account of the cinematic Hardy, the problem of the downward gaze goes beyond content to include form. For her, *The Dynasts* finally leaves the impression of "looking down upon a cockpit, hence a fixed stage" (Grundy1979: 123), with the reader so conditioned by the Overworld commentary that the human actors appear to be mere automatons in a predetermined show. The dubious assertion that all the Spirits insist on the clockwork toy as their central image for understanding human affairs, when in fact all comparisons of people to puppets, mannikins, and jacks originate with the Spirit of the Years, leads her to argue that references to one kind of show, the moving mechanical figures that remained popular into early Victorian times, have a reductive effect on our view of *The Dynasts* as cinema.

Since Grundy's analysis has stood for years as the main cinematic reading of *The Dynasts*, I will use the difficulties she gets into as a way of introducing the context of optical entertainments that will allow us to reposition Hardy's visual effects and better understand the forms they take and the functions they serve. In terms of her central, evaluative opposition, we find *The Dynasts* either "expanding" into remarkable verbal cinema or "contracting" into a commonplace historical drama. At their worst, the Spirits correspond to a theater audience, at their best to a moving camera. Hardy also uses vision as if it were a camera in the "stage directions," though sometimes these are no more than the name suggests and so some scenes, particularly indoor ones like the Brussels ball, but also the whole Waterloo sequence, confront the reader directly as theater rather than cinema with no point of view at all. Grundy finds a sense of a camera eye maintained through the bird's-eye view of the island of Lobau and through the field glasses of the Emperor Francis and his staff during the battle of Wagram but ignores how Waterloo opens with "An aerial view of the battlefield at the time of sunrise" (p. 653; 3.7.1) or how space turns into fragmented narrative place, as in a classical Hollywood film, through the many characters who gaze in Hardy's representation of the crisis-ridden ball and battle.

Hardy himself thought of his scenes as having a point of view: "the events generally in The Dynasts had to be pulled together into dramatic scenes, to show themselves to the mental eye of the reader as a picture viewed from one point" (*CL* VI: 161). Indoors, a room sets the basic limit of what can be seen, outdoors, a particular or general location such as the French and English "positions" at Waterloo. In every scene, the mediating voice of the prose observer positions the reader as spectator (and listener). If there is a camera eye in *The Dynasts* it belongs to this observer, who usually begins a scene with an establishing "shot" of physical description that goes beyond what would normally be found in a screen or stage play. To call the Spirits a camera is more problematic. We never know what they literally see in an indoor scene and they contribute more of "inventories and names" (p. 274; 2.2.5) than sharp physical details to the battle scenes. The Spirits are strange threshold figures, still able to see, hear, and, in the case of the Shade of the Earth at Borodino, even smell: "The fumes of nitre and the reek of gore / Make my airs foul and fulsome unto me!" (p. 468; 3.1.5). While they add something to the naturalistic representation of events, no camera could photograph their visual seemings and impressions without some prior distortion of the *mise-en-scène*, like the sets in a German Expressionist film of the 1920s. The way the Spirits close up time and space, following, for example, the direction of Marmont's Aide across Europe but in a rush so that we jump from the field of Salamanca to the field of Borodino, can determine the next "camera" set-up, but their own showings easily pass from literal to figurative seeing.

There is another sense in which point of view is not just something that suddenly appears in cinematic scenes. Even on the few occasions when Hardy provides bare stage directions, he remains concerned with point of view in the deeper sense of an evaluative orientation toward the world or a way of understanding events. In the scene at the palace in Petersburg, introduced with a single descriptive sentence, we laugh as the Empress-mother admits she is a Romanoff merely by marriage, then condemns the "bourgeois" Napoleon for wanting to marry the Austrian Archduchess, Maria Louisa. The setting may be private but the scene remains centrifugal, forming part of "one compacted whole" (p. 461; 3.1.3) in which almost every scene represents or recalls a crisis, a turning-point, the line crossed or, as in the case of the Emperor Alexander, almost crossed, given how close his "friend" Napoleon comes to being his brother-in-law.

Like a good showman, Hardy even thought of advertising *The Dynasts* on the grounds that "It carries you on like an exciting novel" (*CL* VII: 145). "Exciting" might be a stretch for events whose outcome is known beforehand, but since he constructs *The Dynasts* to be "as readable as a novel" (*CL* III: 91) point of view remains tied to narration and narration goes far beyond the intermittent remarks of the prose observer. Hardy does not rely on the reader's familiarity with the subject to connect his scenic " 'ordinates' " (*D* 6) and map the ten-year period (1805–15) of Napoleonic history that *The Dynasts* covers. In the Overworld, the Recording Angels rehearse the political background of the first House of Commons debate; the Rumours do the same for the battle of Jena. In the historical world, much of the dialogue recounts or reports a sequence of events. A typical example is the way Hardy uses some captured French officers, their lips loosened by Wellington's wine, to tell the story of the retreat of Napoleon's army after the battle of Leipzig as a fall from military glory.

The very act of looking in *The Dynasts* also means that instead of one unbroken narrative we get many stories. As David Lodge argues, one of the signatures of Hardy's narrative style is the use of an unspecified observer in description (Lodge 1973–4: 250). In *The Dynasts*, this observer usually speaks from some elevated ground, but weather, the haze and smoke of battle, and the shape of the terrain obscure his vision and restrict what he can report. To assume an even higher perspective does not help. In the aerial view of Leipzig on the first day of fighting, the struggle ceases to look like a battle and our attention is drawn more to the form of representation than its historical content: "So massive is the contest that we soon fail to individualize the combatants as beings, and can only observe them as amorphous drifts, clouds, and waves of conscious atoms" (p. 519; 3.3.2). Since the Spirits must see to narrate, the "free trajection" of their "entities" (p. 23; Fore Scene) does not bring uninterrupted viewing. The "rolling brume" of clouds "unscreens by fits / The quality of the scene" (p. 478; 3.1.9) of the Grand Army retreating in Russia. In the Rumours' narration, "Fitfully flash strange sights" (p. 499; 3.2.2) in the distance at Vitoria and "Life struggles can be heard, seen but in peeps" (p. 643; 3.6.6) in the wood of Bossu. That we do not always know where the Spirits are or hear about what they see is symptomatic of the way Hardy represents narration as a series of partial – usually in both senses of the word – and discontinuous views (see Armstrong 1993: 488). In Berlin one of a group of anxious ladies drawn to the threshold of a window looks through her glass and reads aloud the bulletins that try to shape the way the nation should view the twin disasters at Jena and Auerstädt. The narration keeps getting passed on as the prose narrator discovers watchers within a scene. From a safe distance at Wagram, the Emperor Francis and his staff remain anxious at their glasses to narrate the way victory turns into defeat, the French army unexpectedly capturing the heights that the Austrians once controlled. Like the citizens "saucer-eyed from anxiety and sleeplessness" (p. 521; 3.3.3) who watch and narrate the battle of Leipzig from a tower, people in *The Dynasts* seem to live on the threshold in crisis time. On the last day of fighting there, the story of Napoleon's narrow escape gets told sympathetically in terms of what one citizen can see from the window of an inn and what another witnesses near the Rantstädt gate.

In the midst of battle events pass with difficulty into narrative shape. At Trafalgar, Magendie complains that "We may make signs, / But in the thickened air what signal's marked?" (p. 134; 1.5.3). Commanders depend on the eyes of others, but at Waterloo "So many of his aides are cut down that it is difficult for Wellington to get reports of what is happening afar" (p. 684; 3.7.7). On the French side, Napoleon, Soult, and three other marshals take turns looking through their telescopes and trying to interpret whether or not the moving shape on the horizon is a body of troops and, if troops, whether Grouchy's or Blücher's. Since no one has clear discernment, Hardy uses multiple perspectives to narrate the battles, except at Vimiero, represented as a Dumb Show, and even there our attention is drawn to another gazer within the scene who has been directing the English movements with the help of his telescope – Sir Arthur Wellesley. Generally, as the battles proceed the narration grows more complex, until at Leipzig and Waterloo Hardy summons every kind of narrator, from the Spirits and historical leaders to anonymous spectators like the servant in the woman's camp behind Mount Saint Jean, who adds to the sense of looming catastrophe with his story of Ney's frightening cavalry charges.

If the existence of watchers and interpreters within a scene is much more filmic than the simple presence of visualization as such, there is no need to turn to Hardy's fiction (as Grundy does) for a more complete cinematic experience than *The Dynasts* offers. Like Wellington and Marmont gazing at each other through their spyglasses and trying to read the other's intentions at Salamanca, everyone in *The Dynasts* is both watcher and watched. Even the Spirits become part of the spectacle that the prose narrator experiences. He reports their entrance in the Fore and After Scenes, narrates some of their movements when they take on human form, describes the appearance of Pity and the Years when they become white sea-birds watching Villeneuve with large, piercing eyes, and listens to the Phantoms chant monotonously as the British army retreats from Quatre Bras. As the reader "watches" and interprets *The Dynasts*, without, of course, ever producing a final reading, Hardy provides no view above all the others to disentangle the lines of vision and narration that converge and diverge like the threads of the Will.

When the comprehension of existence passes to the Overworld, the Years has to remind the Spirits of his "ruling . . . that we should witness things / And not dispute them" (p. 35; 1.1.1). They sometimes agree that they are watching a play, but where Pity sees a "tragedy" the Spirit Ironic finds a "comedy" (p. 25; Fore Scene), with some episodes being "frankly farcical" (p. 214; 2.1.2) to the Spirit Sinister. Life also appears to be a show of some kind, but this impression raises the crucial question of who the showman is. To impose his master-narrative of the "rapt Determinator" (p. 437;

2.6.7), a "tale of Will / And Life's impulsion by Incognizance" (p. 64; 1.1.6) that Pity cannot accept, "Father" Years makes the Will the equivalent of the Showman who controls the moving images of his optical entertainment. As the "Prime Mover of the gear," the Will winds up the "flesh-hinged mannikins" (pp. 27, 24; Fore Scene) in a mechanical theater that expands into a *Theatrum Mundi*. The Will is also like a puppeteer who "pulls the strings" (p. 27; Fore Scene) and a magic lanternist whose "all-compelling crystal pane but drags / Whither the showman wills" (p. 116; 1.4.5). The Years does not hesitate, as many London showmen did, between the claims of education and amusement. His revelations of the Will are all matters of instruction – "See, then, and learn" (p. 27; Fore Scene) – and offered with a seriousness that emphasizes their claim to objective truth-value. However worthless the historical spectacle may be in itself, it must be treated seriously because everything visible reveals the Will's "High Influence" (p. 39; 1.1.2). As the drama of vision unfolds in the Overworld, Hardy makes clear that the Years' showings are also attempts to maintain a "hierarchy of Intelligences" (p. 51; 1.1.3). To keep the other Spirits in their place, the Will's "official Spirit" (p. 195; 1.6.8) insists that he alone has the gift of "bounded prophecy" (p. 543; 3.4.2) and of visualizing the Will's mode of operation. He also tries to suppress the laughter that threatens his authority as seer. Yet having personified the Will as a showman, the Years can hardly blame Irony for suggesting in the final scene at Ulm that "The Will Itself might smile at this collapse / Of Austria's men-at-arms, so drolly done" (p. 117; 1.4.5).

In the scene at Courcelles that Hardy largely invents, laughter spirals upward and out of control, allowing a Chorus of Ironic Spirits to transfer the label of "Showman" from the Will to the Years. Hardy begins with Napoleon chuckling good-humoredly at the Soissons folk whose reception he has bypassed in his eagerness to embrace his wife-to-be. The laughter quickly spreads to include Napoleon as he and Murat greet the Austrian royal coach, only to have Marie-Louise mistake them for two highwaymen in a comic mix-up that ironically points ahead to the serious time just five years later when the Allies paper the whole of Europe with posters declaring Napoleon an outlaw. While Murat has to laugh silently at the sight of his brother-in-law playing the impetuous bridegroom, an Ironic Chorus erupts into a song worthy of Gilbert and Sullivan that adds their "Hoo-hoo!" to the scene. Provoked by the Years' moral earnestness – "What lewdness lip those wry-formed phantoms there?" – the Ironic Spirits call the Years a "Showman" (p. 383; 2.5.6), a term that, as Hardy well knew, is anything but flattering. "Editors," he once commented, "are like showmen: what will draw at the moment is their policy" (*CL* II: 125). In Richard Altick's words, "pictorial showmen had to bait their bills with anything that would attract and keep their clientele," with the result that "hyperbolic language and almost routine misrepresentation or suppression of facts" were common practices (Altick 1978: 209, 423).

There is certainly something hyperbolic about the Years' (mis)representation of the Will: "ITS slaves we are: ITS slaves must ever be!" (p. 195; 1.6.8). Not surprisingly, the other main Spirits refuse to separate the tale from the teller, the show from the showman. Words with conditions attached inform their responses to the Will. Pity wonders "If thy words, Ancient Phantom, token true" (p. 39; 1.1.2); Irony refers to the "groping tentativeness of an Immanent Will," then adds, "as grey old Years describes it" (p. 336; 2.4.5). What the Years wants Irony to see remains "Your [i.e. the Years'] phantasmagoric show" (p. 117; 1.4.5). Hardy, in turn, has a good deal of fun with a Spirit who never laughs, with the philosopher as showman. Eventually the Years' obsessive conversion of all historical difference to metaphysical sameness begins to sound funny. In one scene, for example, Hardy plays with history, a portrait of Marie Antoinette slipping down on its face just as Maria Louisa agrees to marry Napoleon, then has the Years try to cover up the "mischief" of the fallen portrait with the solemn declaration that "The Will must have Its way" (p. 370; 2.5.3). For all his high thinking, the Years belongs in part to the tradition of the wandering showman, but instead of carrying a peepbox or magic lantern on his back he creates a "migratory Proskenion" (p. 66; 1.2.1), moving the Spirits about to watch the Will's "inexplicable artistries" (p. 449; 3.1.1) made visible in the human shows.

As the Spirits watch the historical spectacle, the Years does not always succeed in diverting their attention to the unconscious and therefore blameless Will. They also see the dynasts as a bunch of disreputable showmen running affairs in Europe for their own gain. Both the Spirit of the Pities and the Spirit Sinister invoke optical entertainments in scenes that are themselves shows put on by the dynasts, who know the value of the pageant and the procession (frequent subjects of the moving panorama) to impress people with their power. In the scene at Tilsit, Napoleon and Alexander meet on a raft with a gorgeous pavilion in the middle of the river Niemen, to show the multitude of spectators on both banks that they are now equal partners in a new brotherly alliance that will allow them, as one British spy sardonically reports, to cut up Europe "like a plum-pudding." As prelude to this spectacle, a Semichorus of Pities sings about how Napoleon "shatters the moves of the loose-knit nations to curb his exploitful soul's ambitions, / And their great Confederacy dissolves like the diorama of a dream" (pp. 236, 234; 2.1.7). The old story that Napoleon and Alexander tell about English selfishness, greed, and duplicity applies to all the dynasts, whose shifting alliances seem to the Pities as insubstantial as a dream, and remind them of the dissolving views of the diorama, the show that Louis Daguerre and Charles Mouton introduced to London audiences in 1823. In its original form, the diorama consisted of several transparent cloth paintings, each mounted at the end of a tunnel containing screens and curtains that could vary the lighting and make parts of a scene appear or disappear. A platform that held the spectators rotated until its proscenium viewing frame became aligned with the window-like opening of a tunnel. The way the lighting gave the illusion of depth to the pictures and, when changed, suggested the passage of time, usually from day to night, soon made the diorama more popular than the panorama. In *The Dynasts*, political alliances change as often as the shows of London. A new alliance is like a new show and, as if to strengthen this connection, Hardy gives the mode of viewing at Tilsit some dioramic features: we look with some French officers through windows in Bonaparte's temporary quarters at a Dumb Show of the meeting of the two emperors until a screen blocks our view when they retire to the interior of the pavilion.

Napoleon mounts an even more impressive show, a spectacle of much magnificence, for the pick of imperial society at his wedding. While the guests await the "hour of performance," the Spirit Sinister derisively calls the high proceedings a "galanty-show" (p. 390; 2.5.8), a term that could refer to either a magic lantern or shadow show. During the early years of the nineteenth century, many of the itinerant magic lantern showmen were Italian. In England, their cry of "galante so" – "galante" the Italian word for "fine," "so" the foreigner's pronunciation of the English "show" – became translated as galanty (or galantee) show (Cook 1963: 81). By mid-Victorian times, the magic lantern show became a major form of public amusement, and in its most popular form included the showman's comic lecture or narrative to accompany the slides. In Hardy's scene, the Spirit Sinister provides a darkly humorous vision of Napoleon's wedding procession crossing the path that Louis XVI and his bride took on their way to the guillotine. Sinister's evocation of this grisly past is so effective that the Spirit of the Pities sees the headless figure of Marie Antoinette, like a ghost in another kind of magic lantern entertainment, the phantasmagoria, walking beside Marie Louise and making "frail attempts / To pluck her by the arm" (p. 392; 2.5.8). In case the reader is still not smiling, Hardy has the Spirit of the Years, in typically long-winded fashion, return Marie Antoinette to the grave by reducing her to dust. The scene then concludes with the Spirit Ironic's joke that the English Church, in contrast to the absent French cardinals, will appreciate Napoleon's wedding because marriage to a Hapsburg will leave nothing for the coarse English caricaturists to attack, though the whole point of Hardy's scene is that Napoleon and his followers are now no better than the rest of Europe's moldy-minded oligarchs.

In the nineteenth century, pictorial re-creations like the magic lantern show and the diorama were as much of an institution as the theater proper, and as popular as movies are today. They are not the sign, when Hardy's prose narrator or Spirits allude to them, of *The Dynasts* taking on the circumscribed character of a stage play, any more than a film belongs to the world of drama because it happens to be screened in a theater. To read *The Dynasts* is like entering the world of nineteenth-century show business, where optical entertainments competed or combined to attract the spectator. By looking back, Hardy invites the reader to recall the whole "regime of the spectacle and the gaze that transversed the nineteenth century" (Neale 1985: 30). At the start of this regime, one kind of theater had already become a display of "moving pictures" in a mechanical performance; by mid-century the spectacle sometimes took precedence over the spoken word on the Victorian stage. Hardy takes this process a step further. In the carefully chosen words of his preface, he calls *The Dynasts* a "Spectacle . . . presented to the mind's eye in the likeness of a Drama" (p. 3). What matters most, to borrow the Years' words, are the "pictures of the Play" (p. 696; 3.7.8).

In a work as self-consciously visual as *The Dynasts*, there is no attempt to hide the way the "pictures" get created. Hardy explicitly names the modes of visualization that he uses to represent history and philosophy in popular forms. When the Years tries to assert his authority with a "real" picture of the Will, all we see is another show, one that from the prose narrator's perspective strongly suggests the techniques of the diorama: "A new and penetrating light descends on the spectacle, enduing men and things with a seeming transparency, and exhibiting as one organism the anatomy of life and movement in all humanity and vitalized matter included in the display" (pp. 27–8; Fore Scene). As the diorama developed, its pictures were painted on both sides, creating, in effect, a superimposition that allowed one scene to dissolve into another when the light that struck the opaque colors on the front of the painting gave way to the light that shone through the transparent colors on the back. The transparencies that Hardy's narrator describes work in much the same way, with the Will becoming superimposed on the human spectacle until "The strange light passes" (p. 680; 3.7.7) and the preternatural scene "fades again back to the normal" (p. 499; 3.2.2).

Jonathan Crary cites the diorama as one of a number of optical entertainments that reflected a fundamental shift in the position of the observer during the period 1810 to 1840 (Crary 1992: 112). Scientific research on retinal after-images, peripheral and binocular vision, and thresholds of attention removed vision from the stable and incorporeal relations of the camera obscura and relocated it within the subjectivity of the human body with its unstable physiology and temporality. In the diorama, the spectator ceased to be an autonomous viewer, and vision was no longer subordinated to an exterior image of the true or right relations of things. The diorama's observer became part of the machinery of viewing, moved slowly on a circular platform to consume images of an "illusory" reality in the form of landscape or architectural scenes so skillfully lit they seemed to belong to the order of time as well as space. As a spectator in a dioramic show of his own making, the Spirit of the Years can describe the Will only in physiological terms that remind us of the constitutive role of the body in any apprehension of the visible world: "These are the Prime Volitions, – fibrils, veins, / Will-tissues, nerves, and pulses of the Cause," whose sum is "like the lobule of a Brain" (p. 28; Fore Scene). Ironically, this "anatomy" of a cosmic brain provides the Pities with some grounds for the hope that the dreaming Will might one day awaken to fashion all things fair.

Hardy also uses dioramic effects for the Prince Regent's festivity – the sunlight fades, the radiance from inside Carlton House spreads through the skylights, the walls of two nearby houses become transparent to reveal the Prince's two "wives," and finally the walls of his own residence open so we confront the revel – to parody the Years' showings of the Will. When the Spirit Ironic assumes the role of showman, ordering the Rumours to scatter whispers of the King's death and to fetch the abandoned spouses, the Years' complaint, "ye strain your powers unduly here" (p. 432; 2.6.7), recalls the "exhaustive strain and effort" (p. 27; Fore Scene) needed to produce his own transparencies. Instead of seeing the Will superimposed on a battle such as Austerlitz, Vitoria, or Waterloo, we watch the battle of the sexes make the Prince begin to loathe his "whole curst show." Irony's antics help make satirically transparent what no diorama would have shown: dressed as a field marshal and boasting "I was born for war" (pp. 432, 436; 2.6.7), the heir to the throne cares more about the women in his life than the outbreak of new hostilities in Europe. To put an end to the fooling and reassert his vision of the "Mighty Will's firm work," the Years takes the form of a hollow-eyed gentleman, uttering gloomy prophecies that unintentionally add to the scene's laughter. The poor Prime Minister, Spencer Percival, shrinks when he hears that the "tomb-worm may caress thee" before he sees the impact of the next war. The Years ends up sounding like a parody of an Old Testament prophet. "I expected to see him," says the witty Sheridan, "write on the wall, like the gentleman with the Hand at Belshazzar's Feast" (pp. 432, 435, 436; 2.6.7).

Although the impulse to take on the "feverish fleshings of Humanity" (p. 41; 1.1.3) is strongest in Pity, none of the main Spirits can resist assuming bodily form and when they do they become like the ghosts made visible in the phantasmagoria, even producing, in the case of Rumour, scare effects with shocking news about Napoleon. Popular immediately after the French Revolution and in the early 1800s, the phantasmagoria still attracted large crowds at the Polytechnic Institute in London as late as mid-century. Its most famous practitioner, Étienne Gaspard Robertson, moved his magic lantern mounted on wheels and adjusted its lens to make his ghosts grow larger or smaller as he projected them from behind on an eerie screen of smoke. In 1798 Robertson held seances at the Pavillion de l'Échiquier in Paris where he resurrected such famous dead figures as Voltaire, Rousseau, and Marat and made a skeleton appear at the end of each performance while he reminded the audience that the same fate awaited them (Quigley 1960: 78). In *The Dynasts*, the Spirit of the Years, who believes in "Vision's necromancy" (p. 460; 3.1.3), conjures the spirits of the dead before the fighting even begins at Quatre Bras and Waterloo, explaining to Pity that the shadows pirouetting before many of the British soldiers leaving the Brussels ball are multiplied shimmerings of his old friend Death. No sooner has the Years dismissed the Vitoria festival at Vauxhall as a "phantasmagoria," than he uses a magic lantern technique himself, "magically" (p. 508; 3.2.4) enlarging the Emperor Francis' letter containing his formal declaration of war against Napoleon, its three vast red seals signifying that more blood will be shed.

In spite of the "tedious conjuring" (p. 39; 1.1.2) of dynastic wars, *The Dynasts* has a playful dimension, especially in its layering of shows and showmen. As the ultimate showman, Hardy constructs the scene of the Congress of Vienna as a show within a show. The three main watchers – Marie Louise, Count Neipperg, and the Countess of Brignole – enter a gallery that commands a bird's-eye view of the great saloon, but instead of a panoramic scene we get a peepshow through a grille that screens the fallen Empress from the dynasts below. The dialogue leaves no doubt that Hardy intends the irony of viewing the grand scene in a way that pointedly recalls one of the humblest and most common entertainments of the street and fairground in the nineteenth century. Though "doomed to furtive peeps / At scenes her open presence would unhinge," Napoleon's wife feels grateful to have a "glimpse-hole for my curiosity." Essentially a perspective box fitted with mirrors and lit by candles, the peepshow did get large enough to accommodate the number of viewers in Hardy's scene. Some models had multiple eyesights, each fitted with a lens to magnify the images and enhance their three-dimensionality, and even contained moving clockwork figures. Like the showman pulling strings on the side of the peepbox to lower a new scene into place, Hardy has Madame de Brignole part the curtains on the grille so that the light from a thousand candles reveals another, larger group of spectators watching a show of a different kind. On a stage at one end of the great hall, "Tableaux Vivants are in progress . . . representing the history of the House of Austria, in which figure the most charming women of the Court" (pp. 582, 583; 3.5.2).

Before they became a popular form of entertainment in the Victorian period, ending up as a fixture on the variety bill of the music halls, *tableaux vivants* figured in court entertainments and in the theater practice of having a group of performers suddenly freeze in their positions on stage, usually at the end of a scene or act. Just when the Allies think that the curtain has come down on "act the last / For our and all men's foe" (p. 536; 3.3.6), news of Napoleon's escape from Elba spreads through the Congress, disrupting the living pictures that celebrate the Habsburg dynasty. If Hardy likes anything about Napoleon it is the way his movements continually upset the old dynastic order. The scene in Vienna fuses the serious and the comic in a way that typifies *The Dynasts* as a whole. Napoleon's escape may mean another war, but it also produces a series of reversals that Hardy seems to enjoy as much as do the rude English diplomatists who "shake shoulders with hid laughters." A festive occasion turns dark for the official minds who, in a delightful twist, seem to switch roles with the women on stage: while Count Metternich "Stares at Prince Talleyrand – no muscle moving" (pp. 584, 585; 3.5.2), the ladies of the Tableau "leave their place, / And mingle with the rest, and quite forget / That they are in masquerade" (p. 584; 3.5.2). At least they can still move. For the reader alert to the intratextual echo, Hardy has already created a grim parodic double of the *tableaux vivants*. When the pursuing Russians discover some French soldiers who do not move, one officer says to Kutuzov, "here's a curious picture. They are dead" yet "They all sit / As they were living still" (p. 487; 3.1.11). We are reminded that Hardy does more than just create pictures of the ruling elite; he remains concerned with "Souls passed to where History pens no page" (p. 484; 3.1.10).

At the same time, Hardy never just sees the common man as the victim of "the dynasts' craving for power and their perpetration of mass killing to achieve it" (Armstrong 1993: 486). Napoleon turns warfare into a mass experience, and the patriotism he awakens in the nations of Europe means that its people fight willingly in the dynastic battles. The appetite for patriotic spectacles within the historical world of *The Dynasts* suggests that patriotism cuts across class lines. On Durnover Green, Casterbridge, a great crowd of Wessex folk gathers to listen to the band playing "Lord Wellington's Hornpipe" and to watch an effigy of Boney burn as it hangs from a rough gallows. When a mail coach arrives, the guard reports how London has already turned Napoleon into satirical entertainment: "just as we left London a show was opened of Boney on horseback as large as life, hung up with his head downwards. Admission one shilling; children half-price. A truly patriot spectacle!" (p. 609; 3.5.6). At the other end of the social scale, the fashionable elite come to Vauxhall Gardens to celebrate Wellington's victory at Vitoria (1814). The sounds and sights of patriotism are everywhere: in the new air, "The Plains of Vitoria," that the band plays, in the blaze of lamps and candles that illuminate the names of peninsular victories, in the fireworks display, and in the transparencies representing scenes from the war.

Laughter enters the scene through the dialogue of two attachés, who notice that the struggle to gain admission "was as bad as the battle of Vitoria itself" (p. 505; 3.2.4). Indeed the festival at Vauxhall seems a parodic continuation of the battle's aftermath that already looks like a farcical upheaval, with the French a "flying brothel" (p. 501; 3.2.3) and the British infantry out of the control of their officers. The wagons and carriages that choke the road from Vitoria and turn the pursuing English soldiers into plunderers become the coaches struggling to get into the gardens, where the traditional cry, "Take care of your watches! Pickpockets!", sounds in the evening. While history turns into spectacle at Vauxhall, the show goes on among the dynasts. The theme of betrayal and desertion that runs all through *The Dynasts* sounds in a diplomatist's report of how the Princess of Wales could not gain entry into the royal box at Vauxhall and in the attachés' news of the "Rank treachery" (pp. 508, 507; 3.2.4) of the Emperor Francis, who joins the new league that English guineas knit against his son-in-law.

Historically, the transparencies of war at Vauxhall Gardens were mounted to compete with the urban show most associated with the emergent nationalisms of the nineteenth century – the panorama. "From 1798 on," as Stephan Oettermann explains, "the panorama ceased to be just one form of entertainment among others in the mind of the British public; it succeeded in linking itself with patriotism and national pride" (Oettermann [1980] 1997: 107). A painter, Robert Barker, received a patent for his invention of the panorama in 1787, and by 1794 had opened his own building in Leicester Square, London, where spectators could enjoy the sensation of being present within the scene of London as viewed from the Albion Mills. While viewers had to turn their heads to see the whole 360° painting in the early panoramas, showmen soon developed moving ones, with the canvas wound between two rollers. Hardy seems to allude to the moving kind when he has his narrator describe how cities "pass in panorama beneath us as the procession [of Maria Louisa and her attendants] is followed" (p. 380; 2.5.5) and when the focus of the scene follows the English army retreating from Quatre-Bras, "the highway and its margins panoramically gliding past the vision of the spectator" (p. 649; 3.6.8). To represent the movements of armies and people over such a large setting as Europe, Hardy needed the special mode of viewing that only the panorama with its wide vistas could provide. His panoramic method also has a historical appropriateness: the clash of peoples in *The Dynasts* belongs to the age of panoramas. Napoleon was interested enough in the new visual entertainment to meet Barker's son and partner, Henry, in Paris in 1802 and to visit Pierre Prévost's panorama of the battle of Wagram in 1810, afterwards giving instructions to have eight rotundas built on the Champs-Elysées where the great French victories of the revolution and the empire could be celebrated through the mass medium of the panorama (Hyde 1988: 59). As "Panoramas became the newsreels of the Napoleonic era" (Altick 1978: 136), showmen made most of their money translating the important events and places of the Napoleonic Wars – Waterloo was Barker's bestseller – into huge cylindrical pictures. Sometimes history got illustrated so quickly that a Berlin panorama depicted the burning of Moscow just three months after the actual event (Cook 1963: 33).

The spread of panoramas to the capitals of Europe gave each nation a visual means of appreciating its beautiful landscapes and cityscapes, like the magnificent view from St. Paul's that Thomas Hornor painted for the Colosseum in London's Regent Park, and for commemorating its military triumphs. In the years following Waterloo, battle scenes, especially from Napoleonic times, remained the panorama's most common subject and one that often received the endorsement of military figures who had been present at the engagements depicted. The Duke of Wellington, for example, regularly visited and approved the various panoramas of Waterloo at Leicester Square. As the panorama evolved to keep up with the rival diorama, Charles Marshall added narration, military music, the thunder of cannon, and the noises of battle to enhance the realism of his 1824 "Peristrephic" (i.e. moving) panoramas of Ligny, Les Quatre Bras, Waterloo, and Trafalgar. In France, Jean-Charles Langlois, a veteran of Wagram and Waterloo, combined in some shows the effects of the panorama, the diorama, the phantasmagoria, and three-dimensional objects to take the audience into the very midst of the Napoleonic battles that he went on displaying until 1857 (Cook 1963: 44). Panoramas remained a major form of popular entertainment until the early 1860s, but even as late as 1890 London's Ashley Place was still reliving the glory of Waterloo with a daily panorama.

Hardy's extensive use of panoramic techniques clearly locates *The Dynasts* in a popular tradition of entertainment, but less obvious are the ways in which his own "show" works to subvert the aims and conventions of the historical panorama. Many scenes play off ironically against the way panoramas treated their subjects to lure the gaze of the nineteenth-century spectator. Although part of Napoleon's famed campaign of 1805, the battle of Ulm in Part First wins for the city "a dingy fame, / Which centuries shall not bleach from her old name" (p. 117; 1.4.5). Instead of promoting a cityscape with a sweeping view, what the narrator twice refers to as a panorama turns out to be as "dingy" as the infamy of General Mack surrendering a whole Austrian army to Napoleon. In the first scene at Ulm, thick sheets of rain and the murk of evening quickly obscure the prospect and cloak its blurred lights and fires. In the second, Napoleon and his staff appear wet and plastered with mud, while the monastery and broken bridge in the nearby village of Elchingen wear a desolated look.

When the Grand Army finally reaches Moscow in Part Third, everyone wants to enjoy the moment as a panorama. Viewed from the Hill of Salutation, "the city appears as a splendid panorama, with its river, its gardens, and its curiously grotesque architecture of domes and spires." First Napoleon and his marshals gaze at the city; then "There is a far-extended clapping of hands . . . and companies of foot run in disorder towards high ground to behold the spectacle" (pp. 471, 472; 3.1.7). When the French descend into Moscow, they encounter the monstrous irony of a city deserted except for a few grinning wretches left in a Kremlin gaol. A scene that begins with roofs twinkling in the rays of the September sun ends with a fire – the specialty of the diorama – that irradiates the city at night and turns most of it into one huge furnace.

During the retreat from Moscow, Napoleon "can be discerned amid the rest, marching on foot through the snowflakes" (p. 481; 3.1.9), now part of a panoramic view from the clouds that is anything but splendid. The point of observation in panoramas did get higher than the tops of buildings or hills, reaching, for example, the bird's-eye view from a balloon, but even here success still depended on a realistic representation. In Hardy, the high perspectives reveal all sorts of unexpected shapes that defamiliarize the objects seen. The retreating French army takes the shape of a caterpillar that moves "as a single monster might" (p. 479; 3.1.9). From the Puebla Heights, the plain of Vitoria "looks like the palm of a monstrous right hand" (p. 498; 3.2.2). Watching the combatants below on the field of Ligny, the Spirit of the Pities sees "an unnatural Monster" with "limbs and eyes a hundred thousand strong, / And fifty thousand heads." "It is," explains the Showman Years, "the Monster Devastation" (p. 639; 3.6.5). In the context of war, the strange and grotesque sights of the showman's tent or booth, like the woman beheaded that Hardy once saw at a fair (*LW* 119), assume huge proportions that disturb the aesthetics of the panorama.

Just as the pantomime incorporated the moving panorama in the early decades of the nineteenth century, Hardy often combines a panoramic perspective with a Dumb Show in *The Dynasts*. As long as nothing seems to move in the panorama of the upper Rhine in 1814, the narrator can appreciate the bird's-eye view of the beautiful country traversed by the river as if he were a spectator at a show offering yet another romantic vista. The delayed decoding in the Dumb Show sets up the shock that the strange dark patches moving slowly in the landscape are in fact armies and that what we are watching is the invasion of France. War-geared humanity so disrupts the clarity of the panorama that the narrator cannot pin down the advancing armies to any one shape or form. They are "mostly snake-shaped" but occasionally have "batrachian and saurian outlines"; they also move "like water from a burst reservoir" (p. 539; 3.4.1), carrying the threat of inundation. Again, "Monsters of magnitude" (p. 702; After Scene) unsettle the contemplative fascination of panoramic seeing, leaving the narrator with a sense of foreboding at the immensity of the human mechanism that advances into France.

The grotesque realism of the high perspectives serves more than a negative purpose: it always reflects a world in the process of becoming as history turns into a spectacle of the mass movements of people across the body of Europe. The destructive consequences of war prevent the grotesque images of armies from becoming comical, but laughter begins to emerge when we follow the enormous procession of Austrian carriages and detachments of cavalry in a movement made for peace. The tone of the scene abruptly changes from sad to ridiculous when the point of sight changes from a close-up of Maria Louisa, her eyes red from recent weeping, to high in the air, where we leave behind the beautiful forest scenery near Vienna and see the grotesque image of a procession that now "looks no more than a file of ants crawling along a strip of garden-matting" (p. 379; 2.5.5). Here the comic grotesque is interwoven with the historic theme of the renewal of dynasties. When the procession reaches Brannau, Maria Louisa of Austria suddenly becomes Marie Louise of France, forced to marry the man she once hated and to carry the burden of paying for the peace with France. By the time the procession reaches Courcelles and the point of view descends to earth, ending the panoramic Dumb Show, we are prepared for the humorous encounter between the bride to be and the man she mistakes for a highway robber.

The visual editing in *The Dynasts* has a pronounced up-and-down rhythm within or across scenes that prevents any one perspective or evaluation from gaining control over the field of vision. The battle of Coruña begins with an aerial perspective that registers the way the little English army stiffens to resist the French; then the point of observation descends to the rear of the English position so we can listen to two anonymous stragglers comically debate the necessity of firmness since they might end up like the wounded Sir David Baird or Sir John Moore, whose shoulder has been "knocked to a bag of splinters" (p. 299; 2.3.3). As long as we view what is left of the French army in Russia as a wounded caterpillar suffering can be kept at a distance, but when the point of vision returns to the earth we witness a tragic Dumb Show at the Beresina river, where thousands of fugitives drown, freeze, or burn to death, some of their shrieks so loud as to be heard above the roar of the guns. In the scene of Napoleon's invasion of Belgium in 1815, two high panoramas frame the close-up viewing. Hardy begins with a bird's-eye prospect that reveals "one great movement, co-ordinated by one mind" (pp. 611–12; 3.6.1). Yet when the point of observation descends close to the scene of the French army passing through Charleroi, we see and hear how Napoleon's presence divides Europe. Cheers arise from some of the town's inhabitants, and when Napoleon looks at the Declaration of the Allies against him the narrator notices how the poster is half-defaced. Hardy has not the slightest interest in the psychology of his characters except in so far as their interior life can be made vividly visible. As Napoleon reads that he is now liable to public vengeance, "His flesh quivers, and he turns with a start, as if fancying that some one may be about to stab him in the back." The Dumb Show ends with the point of vision soaring to give a brief glimpse of the Allied armies advancing from all parts of Europe, their "long and sinister black files" crawling with an ambivalence, like harmless "slowworms through grass" (pp. 612, 613; 3.4.1), worthy of the Declaration and the way it wraps the call to war in a legal condemnation of Napoleon.

There is so much panoramic viewing in *The Dynasts* that even Napoleon's dream at Charleroi unfolds as a "moral panorama" with the Duke of Enghien, the Bourbon prince Napoleon had executed in 1804, as "showman": "Thereupon a vision passes before Napoleon as he lies, comprising hundreds of thousands of skeletons and corpses in divers stages of decay. They rise from his various battlefields, the flesh dropping from them, and gaze reproachfully at him" (p. 630; 3.6.3). The phantasmagoric uprising of skeletons, so huge that it requires a panorama, makes Napoleon jump up in a sweat from his sleep and forces him to retreat, as he so often does, behind the abstraction of Destiny so that he can go on fighting.

What briefly disturbs Napoleon haunts most of Hardy's scenes of war, making them very different than the historical panorama's glorification of patriotic battles. The panoramic viewpoint seldom gets so high as to hide the "ugly horror" (p. 467; 3.1.5) of war: decks "reeking with . . . gory shows" (p. 136. 1.5.3), fields strewn with the "hot bodies of grape-torn horses and men" (p. 684; 3.7.7), wounded men "entreating mates / To run them through and end their agony," boys "calling on their mothers," veterans

"Blaspheming God and man," maimed horses "tearing round / In maddening pangs" (p. 468; 3.1.5). As the "night grows clear and beautiful, and the moon shines musingly down" on the field of Waterloo, we seem on the verge of some final, consoling panorama until the narrator remarks that all the landscape has to offer now is "the stench of gunpowder," and a grotesque "muddy stew of crushed crops and gore" (p. 697; 3.7.8).

Many of the panoramic battle scenes also contain ironic reminders of the fellowship that should prevail instead of enmity. On the second day of fighting at Talavera, the Dumb Show takes an unexpected turn, at once sad and grotesquely humorous, when the thirsty soldiers from both sides drink together at a little stream and "get to grasping hands across the rill, / Sealing their sameness as earth's sojourners." By the end of the battle, "hurt and slain, / Opposed, opposers, in a common plight / Are scorched together on the dusk champaign" (pp. 335, 338; 2.4.5). The very distinctions that make fighting possible get erased in the crowd of dead and wounded. At Albuera, "Friends, foemen, mingle" and "Colonels, Captains, ranksmen lie, / Facing the earth or facing sky" (pp. 411, 410; 2.6.4). At Trafalgar both the day's dead and the night's survivors emphasize the same visual pattern. During the battle, Villeneuve sees "friends and foes all mixed" (p. 137; 1.5.3) in the waves. Later a boatman sings a new ballad that recalls how all the living, victors and vanquished, "Were rolled together on the deep that night at Trafalgár" (p. 159; 1.5.7).

The scenes of war might be said to unroll like a moving panorama, but most of the transitions from one scene to another belong to the magic lantern tradition. Whereas moving panoramas had no breaks between the pictures displayed, Hardy's scenes usually end with the kind of curtain drop, fade-out, or darkness that lanterns could produce. By adjusting two lanterns or the multiple lenses on one lantern, the showman could link his slides as a sequence of dissolving views, one picture gradually fading as another took its place. Different shutters also produced different transitions between scenes, with the Lancaster's shutter darkening the whole screen at once between slides, and the terpuoroscope creating the appearance of an opaque curtain descending on the scene each time the slide changed (Cook 1963: 95). In *The Dynasts*, a "curtain of cloud" (p. 53; 1.1.4) or "Curtain of Evening" (p. 250; 2.1.8) often covers a scene, but rain, snow, mist, fog, dust, haze, shadows, and smoke serve the same purpose, people and places gradually becoming obscured as when "The sun sets over the gardens and the scene fades" at Schönbrunn (p. 598; 3.5.4), or when Rainbarrow "seems to become involved in the smoke from the beacon, and slowly disappears" (p. 90; 1.2.5). A moving viewpoint can produce a similar fade-out. The House of Commons and Westminster "recede into the films of night" (p. 52; 1.1.3), and the cliffs of Boulogne sink behind the water-line (p. 77; 1.2.3) as the point of view shifts one way or another across the Channel. Sometimes the setting remains visible, but people or objects gradually move out of sight as a scene ends. The columns of the French army marching from Boulogne disappear over the eastern horizon (p. 99; 1.3.3), the crowd wastes away and the Spirit of Rumour vanishes in a Paris street scene (p. 191; 1.6.7), and Napoleon's ships sail over the horizon after leaving Elba (p. 581; 3.5.1).

Although a few indoor scenes conclude with just the exit of characters from a room, most end with an additional darkening or curtaining effect. In the palace of Godoy, "the taper burns to its socket, and the room becomes wrapt in the shades of night" (p. 264; 2.2.2); in his headquarters at Charleroi, Napoleon "puts out the last candle; and the scene is curtained by darkness" (p. 630; 3.6.3). The mother in the scene of the English army leaving Brussels draws some window-curtains and the scene ends (p. 635; 3.6.4); the Congress of Vienna scene disappears when "The curtain of the grille is dropped" and "The light is extinguished (p. 587; 3.5.2).

In other scenes, both indoor and outdoor, similar visual effects have no literal explanation, as when the mid-air view of the Austrian army creeping towards Ulm "fades to nebulousness and dissolves" (p. 99; 1.3.2). "A nebulous curtain draws slowly across" (p. 181; 1.6.5) the scene of the meeting of the emperors at Paleny; "A gauze of shadow overdraws" (p. 196; 1.6.8) when Pitt dies. Scenes darken mysteriously or, in a kind of shorthand for a curtain fall, the narrator simply says that a scene shuts, closes, is veiled or covered. We might still be in the realm of closet drama when the imaginary curtain drops or draws on outdoor scenes at Tilsit (p. 237; 2.1.7) and Vimiero (p. 283; 2.2.7), but when the cloud-curtain closes on indoor scenes in the cockpit of the *Victory* (p. 146; 1.5.4), the "Old Rooms" Inn (p. 159; 1.5.7), the Imperial Palace at Vienna (p. 372; 2.5.3), and the Salon-Carré in Paris (p. 394; 2.5.8), drama turns into optical entertainment.

The visual equivalent of cinematic cutting occurs infrequently in *The Dynasts*, with its only sustained use coming in the Waterloo section where the action is almost continuous and scenes end as the point of view abruptly changes in a shot-reverse-shot pattern, back and forth between the French and English positions. The three Trafalgar scenes leading up to Nelson's death do much the same, but two of these become enveloped in smoke before the point of view changes. Exceptions aside, Hardy creates a visual structure that approximates the dissolving views of the magic lantern show, like Harry Pouncy's "Hours in Hardyland" that the author enjoyed shortly after finishing *The Dynasts*. Strictly speaking, there is only one true dissolve in *The Dynasts*: as darkness spreads on the second day of fighting at Leipzig the next scene at the Thonberg windmill begins to appear as "The distant firelight becomes clearer and closer" (p. 524; 3.3.3). Nevertheless, so many scenes fade out in some way, often beginning at sunrise and ending at night, that the main visual pattern begins to resonate thematically, brief scenes of conscious purpose, though often with destructive consequences, passing before the mental eye of the reader before the return to darkness associated with the mainly unconscious Will. Since the evidence of a better world does not yet exist, the chorus of Pities can only hear, not see, the future as deliverance – "a stirring thrills the air / Like to sounds of joyance there" (p. 707; After Scene) – and so *The Dynasts* ends without a curtain of darkness or cloud, its universe remaining an unfinished place about which no final word can be spoken.

Hardy draws so heavily and deliberately on various shows that preceded the birth of film that to call cinematic technique his "greatest innovation" (Pinion 1968: 109) in *The Dynasts* can be misleading. What might seem to be a "novel way of treating European vistas" (*D* xix) owes a great deal to the panorama, while Hardy's scenic transformations and transitions reveal his familiarity with magic lantern practice and the diorama. Although Hardy mentions seeing only one film, the 1913 Famous Players' adaptation of *Tess of the d'Urbervilles* (*CL* IV: 305), his knowledge of the pre-history of cinema means that *The Dynasts* shares much in common with the kind of films that appeared during the ten-year period (1897–1907) he worked on it. The early film pioneers, many of whom, like Cecil Hepworth in England, came out of the magic lantern tradition, adopted the techniques and genres of the older optical entertainments, Hepworth filming the coronation of Edward VII much like the moving panorama had recreated Wellington's funeral procession. By way of a brief conclusion, then, I want to consider *The Dynasts* in relation to the early cinema that always gets overlooked when critics argue that Hardy's spectacle "anticipates the conventions of an art that had not yet been invented" (Wain 1965: ix).

After the point of view moves between scenes in *The Dynasts*, it assumes, like the camera in early films, a fixed position for the scenes themselves, acting as a surrogate for the spectator in a theater. Each scene maintains a strict unity of time and space, playing out from beginning to end. There is no crosscutting between scenes in the manner of D. W. Griffith, and though Hardy constructs some jarring contrasts between, and occasionally within, scenes there is no montage of the kind Sergei Eisenstein made famous through the rapid intercutting of disparate shots. What we view in Hardy's scenes has the deep focus that was used almost exclusively in the early years of film. If Hardy calls attention to observers within his scenes, some early films, such as G. A. Smith's *As Seen Through a Telescope* and *Gramma's Looking Glass* (1900), incorporated the presence of a voyeur. By 1901 there were tripods with swivel heads that allowed for smooth pans of the kind we get when a landscape is "swept by the eye" (p. 406; 2.6.4) of the prose narrator in *The Dynasts*. The main mode of acting on the silent screen, mime, also figures prominently in *The Dynasts* where, for example, Napoleon's restless movements, usually up and down or back and forth, seem to visualize the shape of a career full of unexpected reversals. Like Hardy's Spirits, a showman would have commented on the films displayed. Indeed the early film catalogues contained the kind of narration that helps make *The Dynasts* seem like a shooting script. With its strange Spirits and historically accurate events, *The Dynasts* even combines the two broadest generic categories of the early silent cinema, the fantasy and the actuality, the magic of Georges Méliès and the realism of Louis and Auguste Lumière.

To point out these parallels is no dispraise of *The Dynasts*. It remains Hardy's most stunning visual achievement, a "vision-drama" (*CL* IV: 5) in which vision itself is both the subject of representation and the means of narration. The multiple perspectives within scenes make the visual organization of *The Dynasts* much more complex than the scene-equals-shot formula of the early silent cinema. Even what the prose narrator describes from a single viewpoint sometimes contains by implication the kind of shots, relatively rare in early films, that look ahead to the *découpage* of classical filmmaking. In cinematic terms, there appears to be inserted a close-up of Napoleon's vulpine smile at Austerlitz, a tracking shot of Napoleon and Alexander as they move from one room to another in the second Tilsit scene, and a point of view shot when Napoleon watches the signal rockets of the Allies from a window in his headquarters at Leipzig. It is as if Hardy, in the process of bending the older optical entertainments to his own purposes, discovered what would become central to the longer fiction film: that the best way to narrate in moving pictures is to bind the spectator to the gaze of the characters and, instead of just displaying a scene in one continuous take, to direct the viewer's attention within it.

NOTE

1   Since readers are more likely to have access to Harold Orel's one-volume edition (Macmillan, 1978) of *The Dynasts* than to Samuel Hynes' expensive two-volume edition (Oxford University Press, 1995), I quote from the earlier edition. These two versions of *The Dynasts* do not substantially differ. Indeed, the passages I quote are exactly the same in both editions. To produce an uncluttered page that will not distract the reader, I follow the practice of most critics in spelling Napoleon's name without an accent and in standardizing the fully capitalized names of the stage directions and the italicized speeches of the Overworld. Parenthetical references to *The Dynasts* list the page number(s), followed by the part, act, and scene.

REFERENCES AND FURTHER READING

Altick, Richard D. (1978). *The Shows of London.* Cambridge, MA: Harvard University Press.

Armstrong, Isobel (1993). *Victorian Poetry: Poetry, Poetics and Politics.* London: Routledge.

Carpenter, Richard C. (1964). *Thomas Hardy.* New York: Twayne.

Chanan, Michael (1966). *The Dream That Kicks: The Prehistory and Early Years of Cinema in Britain.* London: Routledge.

Cook, Olive (1963). *Movement in Two Dimensions.* London: Hutchinson.

Crary, Jonathan (1992). *Techniques of the Observer: On Vision and Modernity in the Nineteenth Century.* Cambridge, MA: MIT Press.

Dean, Susan (1977). *Hardy's Poetic Vision in The Dynasts: The Diorama of a Dream.* Princeton: Princeton University Press.

Grundy, Joan (1979). *Hardy and the Sister Arts.* London: Macmillan.

Hardy, Thomas ([1903–8] 1978). *The Dynasts: An Epic-Drama of the War with Napoleon,* ed. Harold Orel. London: Macmillan.

Hardy, Thomas (1984). *The Life and Work of Thomas Hardy,* ed. Michael Millgate. London: Macmillan.

Hyde, Ralph (1988). *Panoramania! The Art and Entertainment of the "All-Embracing" View.* London: Trefoil.

Lodge, David (1973–4). Thomas Hardy and Cinematographic Form. *Novel,* 7, 246–54.

Neale, Steve (1985). *Cinema and Technology.* Bloomington: Indiana University Press.

Oettermann, Stephan ([1980] 1997). *The Panorama: History of a Mass Medium,* trans. Deborah Lucas Schneider. New York: Zone Books.

Orel, Harold (1978). Introduction to Thomas Hardy, *The Dynasts* (pp. vii–xxvii). London: Macmillan.

Pinion, F. B. (1968). *A Hardy Companion.* London: Macmillan.

Purdy, Richard Little, and Michael Millgate (eds.) (1978–88). *The Collected Letters of Thomas Hardy.* 7 vols. Oxford: Clarendon Press.

Quigley, Martin Jr. (1960). *Magic Shadows: The Story of the Origin of Motion Pictures.* New York: Quigley.

Seed, David (ed.) (2005). *Literature and the Visual Media.* Cambridge: D. S. Brewer.

Wain, John (1965). Introduction to Thomas Hardy, *The Dynasts* (pp. v–xix). London: Macmillan.

Wickens, G. Glen (2002). *Thomas Hardy, Monism, and the Carnival Tradition: The One and The Many in The Dynasts.* Toronto: University of Toronto Press.

Wright, T. R. (ed.) (2005). *Thomas Hardy on Screen.* Cambridge: Cambridge University Press.

PART V
Hardy the Modern

28

Modernist Hardy: Hand-Writing
in *The Mayor of Casterbridge*

J. Hillis Miller

Is Hardy a modernist writer? It depends on what one means by "modernist." Definitions of modernism abound, but they tend to be diverse and even contradictory (Berman 1982; de Man 1983). Modernist literature, taken as a putative "whole," is complex, reticulated, and heterogeneous. One would do well, in any case, to be suspicious of period designations in literary history, as well as of lists giving the distinctive features of a given historical period. All the distinctive features that have been identified as "modernist" can already be found in Cervantes or Sterne. Moreover, one needs to distinguish carefully between "modernism" as a certain set of historical changes or conditions and modernism as distinctive formal and thematic features of the literature written during that period. The former would identify modernism as a certain stage in capitalism, or as the flowering of Western imperialism, or as the development of new communication devices, or as increased urbanization and the concomitant dislocation of rural life. Though each "modernist" author experienced those social conditions and changes in one way or another, it is impossible from those contextual factors to predict what the writing of a given writer is going to be like. Nevertheless, certain formal and thematic features, features that can be found *mutatis mutandis* in Western literature of any period, tend to be more salient and to take special forms in literature of what we call the "modernist period." These features include: an increased sense of the isolation and incommunicability of individual human experience; a sense that community has been "dissolved," "dislocated," or "conflagrated," as Jean-Luc Nancy puts it (Nancy 1991: 1); an increasing religious skepticism, accompanied by a lingering nostalgia for religious belief; an increased complexity in narratological devices used, at least as compared to Victorian literature; an increased propensity for unhappy endings (you can be fairly sure, when you pick up a novel by Anthony Trollope, that it will end happily, whereas you can be pretty sure the opposite will be the case for Conrad, Forster, James, and Hardy); a more deliberate and self-conscious reflection on what literature is and on what it can do, as in Stéphane Mallarmé and Wallace Stevens; and a curious and somewhat contradictory combination of two thematic features. On the one hand, modernism involves an increased attention to the registering of "irrelevant details." These are features of daily life that just happen to be there and that are worth bearing witness to for their own sake. This may go along with a sense of those details' historical fragility in a time of rapid change. On the other hand, modernist works often involve the careful and deliberate synthesizing of a whole text around a complex system of recurrent metaphors and symbols, so that every detail counts. Examples of such details are the sandwich man in Joyce's *Ulysses* and the tire marks in the sand in Forster's *A Passage to India*.

Hardy's works fit many of the features of modernism I have listed, but not quite all. A sense of individual isolation and of community's conflagration they certainly have, as well as religious skepticism, along with nostalgia for religious belief. Hardy's work, however, lacks the narratological complexity of, say, Conrad's novels. Though Hardy reflected about the nature of literature, he can hardly be said to match Mallarmé or Stevens in the results of doing that. Nor, though motifs recur in a given work by Hardy, such as the color red in *Tess of the d'Urbervilles*, can his works easily be said to develop complex symbolic systems. Hardy's works, as I shall show in one notable example, tend rather to present a lot of what appear to be "irrelevant details" that are not really irrelevant. They tell their stories by way of recurring elements that cannot be defined as symbolic, as allegorical, as iconic, as parabolic, as figurative, or even as thematic, though they are more than just "realistic details." Nor are they motifs in the Wagnerian sense. Wagner's motifs are salient, ostentatious. The listener to *Die Meistersinger* says, "Ah ha! There is another repetition of the 'prize song motif.'" To use any of these terms would put Hardy back under the rubric of what we have learned to call "aesthetic ideology," whereas one feature of Hardy's writing that makes him "modernist" is the way his linguistic practice shakes or to some degree subverts aesthetic ideology. Our everyday ideas about "realism" are parts of aesthetic ideology, since they take for granted certain assumptions about reference to the extra-textual world in realist works.

The verbal details I am investigating in this essay have a curious kind of laconic, hardly noticeable "relevance" that is hard to define. This relevance is more a disconnect than a connect, since it is not likely to touch the reader. You can read *The Mayor of Casterbridge* carefully and well without ever noticing all the mentions of hands. So far as I know, no previous critical essay on the novel has called attention to the manifold recurrences of the word "hand" and of related words like "finger" in this novel. One might call this verbal strategy "notation," in the double sense of writing down and taking notice, as in the contrast between Robert Burns' line, "A child's amang you takin notes" (Burns 1901 I; 289), and Hardy's poignant wish, in the poem "Afterwards," that after his death people will say of him: "He was a man who used to notice such things" (*CPV* 553). The things in question include a hedgehog at night traveling furtively over the lawn, and a hawk at dusk flying across the field of vision to alight on a thorn tree. These details are not "symbolic." They are just things that happen to be there. They are, however, not insignificant or "irrelevant" either.

The reader must remember, nevertheless, that a novel by Hardy, *The Mayor of Casterbridge* for instance, is a work of fiction, a virtual reality, though it no doubt has all sorts of transfigured relations to nineteenth-century life in Dorset. All the notations

of hands in this novel exist nowhere but in the text. They are part of Hardy's imagination of imaginary characters. Hardy creates Henchard, Elizabeth-Jane, Farfrae, and
the rest out of words rather than copying them from some pre-existing external
persons. Hardy's hands are references without referents.

This essay explores relevant/irrelevant details and the general question of Hardy's
modernism by way of a close look at one admirable example, already identified: the
recurrence of hand-notations in *The Mayor of Casterbridge*. One reason for my hand-
reading is a somewhat contrary desire to approach Hardy widdershins, rubbing his
writings against the grain of the text, so to speak. A Hardy novel like *The Mayor of
Casterbridge* is so visibly visual in orientation, so cinematic, that many passages almost
read like an elaborate scenario for a film. *The Mayor* is presented from the perspective
of a somewhat detached spectator who sees what anyone who was there might have
seen, often as a kind of spy, voyeur, or invisible looker-on seeing from the outside in
or from the inside out. Hardy's narrator observes, on the first page, that the silence
and distance between Henchard and his wife "would have attracted the attention of
any casual observer otherwise disposed to overlook them" (*MC* 1–2). That gives the
note for the narrator's stance throughout. He, she, or it sees what "any casual [but
sharp-eyed] observer," one gifted, in addition, with an unusual ability to put the
visible into words, would have seen and said. Susan and Elizabeth-Jane's approach to
Casterbridge, two decades later, is presented as a slow zoom-in from a distant hilltop
view presented initially as, quite literally, a bird's eye view. Susan and Elizabeth-Jane
get their first glimpse of Henchard as mayor by looking in the hotel window from
the outside at the mayor's banquet, just as, at the end of the novel, the forlorn
Henchard, bereft of everything, looks through a doorway at the wedding dance, to
see Elizabeth-Jane dancing with her true father, Newson. In between are many scenes
of overlooking. These especially focus on Elizabeth-Jane as detached spectator. For
example (one example among many), as a dweller in Lucetta's house, Elizabeth-Jane
can oversee all that goes on in the marketplace below on market day, just as, earlier,
when she lives in Henchard's house, she can see what goes on in Henchard's corn-
dealing business. From both her bedrooms, at different times in her life, she can see
all Farfrae's comings and goings, without herself being seen. She sees, for example,
from Lucetta's house, his knowing inspection of that portentous innovation "the
new-fashioned agricultural implement called a horse-drill" (p. 191). What she sees,
however, it happens, is one example among many of hand-notations in *The Mayor*,
my primary subject in this essay: Farfrae "handled it [the horse-drill] as if he knew
something about its make" (p. 192). Hardy's work depends so much on seeing that
an approach to *The Mayor of Casterbridge*, or to his other work, including his poems,
by way of the function in them of references to that premier organ of touch, the hand,
seems perverse. My hypothesis, nevertheless, might be phrased as a particular form of
speech act, a wager: "I bet an investigation of how Hardy uses the word 'hand' will
bring into the open what is most distinctive about his writing." Whether I win or
lose this bet remains to be seen.

Hardy always had a sharp eye for the local specificities of body language. He noticed
such things. Saying that assumes, perhaps fallaciously, that Hardy's representations

of gesture speech are empirical rather than imaginary. That might be hard to prove or disprove. Hardy's admirable essay "The Dorsetshire Labourer" (1883) is, in a manner of speaking, an authoritative, even-handed, anthropological description of the changes during the mid-nineteenth century in Dorsetshire farm laborers' ways of life (see especially Hardy [1883] 1966: 168–71). This essay contains, however, no passages about the gesture speech of Dorsetshire farm workers that might confirm, or contradict, the historical accuracy of the passage in *The Mayor of Casterbridge* I am about to cite. I see no reason to doubt the accuracy of Hardy's description of gesture language, but nevertheless it is important to remember that we only have Hardy's unconfirmed word for it, since fictional representations all too often get transferred, without proper qualification, into putatively scientific anthropological or sociological accounts. We say, without much reflection: "Hardy reports how south of England farmers in the mid-nineteenth century spoke with their bodies."

A splendid example of Hardy's attention to gesture speech is his description, in *The Mayor of Casterbridge*, of Casterbridgeans on market day:

> The yeomen, farmers, dairymen, and townsfolk, who came to transact business in these ancient streets, spoke in other ways than by articulation. Not to hear the words of your interlocutor in metropolitan centres is to know nothing of his meaning. Here the face, the arms, the hat, the stick, the body throughout spoke equally with the tongue. To express satisfaction the Casterbridge market-man added to his utterance a broadening of the cheeks, a crevicing of the eyes, a throwing back of the shoulders, which was intelligible from the other end of the street. If he wondered, though all Henchard's carts and wagons were rattling past him, you knew it from perceiving the inside of his crimson mouth, and a target-like circling of his eyes. Deliberation caused sundry attacks on the moss of the adjoining walls with the end of his stick, a change of his hat from the horizontal to the less so; a sense of tediousness announced itself in a lowering of the person by spreading the knees to a lozenge-shaped aperture and contorting the arms. Chicanery, subterfuge, had hardly a place in the streets of this honest borough to all appearance; and it was said that the lawyers in the Court House hard by occasionally threw in strong arguments for the other side out of pure generosity (though apparently by mischance) when advancing their own. (*MC* 69–70)

This passage speaks for itself, as one says, but several features of Hardy's notation may be noted. One is the way gesture language is presented as a supplement or prosthesis to speech, though speech may sometimes be wholly supplanted by the "ecotechnical" of the body, to borrow Jean-Luc Nancy's term for the body as a set of tools made of extended and separable parts (Nancy 2006: 93–5; Derrida 2005: 55–7).

Another feature is the way the past tense throws the body gestures Hardy describes somewhat nostalgically into the past. Things were once this way, but are that way no longer. A footnote to a description in the previous paragraph of the way spaces in front of houses were used as pens for pigs offered for sale expresses this nostalgia. "The reader will scarcely need to be reminded," says Hardy, "that time and progress have obliterated from the town that suggested these descriptions [Dorchester] many or most of the old-fashioned features here enumerated" (*MC* 69). That, presumably, included the old-fashioned gestures described in the next paragraph, cited above.

A third feature of this paragraph is a little more odd. Hardy implies that while spoken language can prevaricate and be untruthful, and even get away with that, gesture speech cannot lie. The man who expresses satisfaction by broadening his cheeks, etc. cannot be pretending. What he is feeling and thinking inwardly, in the secret recesses of his consciousness, recesses that are unavailable to direct access by others, is spontaneously and truthfully "outered" in gesture and facial expression. A "crevicing of the eyes" never perjures inner feelings. This is an extremely dubious proposition. It would mean that these now vanished Casterbridgeans lived in a won-derful intersubjective openness by way of their truth-telling bodies, and even wanted to live that way. A lawyer, in those happy days, would throw in, as if by accident, an argument for the opposition. This suggests that for Hardy either Casterbridgean gesture speech is a transparent universal language that anyone from anywhere at any time would understand, or that it is a conventional language that members of the Casterbridge community have learned to understand. The hint is that it is the former. Anyone could understand the meaning of these gestures "from the other end of the street," that is, from the sort of discreet distance the narrator in this novel for the most part maintains. The secretive and solitary Elizabeth-Jane, who studiously hides her feelings, and is a mystery to those around her, is an ominous intrusion on this openness, while Henchard personifies it.

The Mayor of Casterbridge, like many other novels, short stories, and poems by Hardy, is about the losses incurred by "progress," modernization, and industrialization in nineteenth-century England, for example by the substitution of the church organ for the choir of instruments in rural churches in *Under the Greenwood Tree*, or, in *The Mayor of Casterbridge*, by the introduction of new farm machinery, or by Farfrae's replacement of Henchard's haphazard "*vivâ voce* system" by modern exact written notation of buying and selling:

> The old crude *vivâ voce* system of Henchard, in which everything depended upon his memory, and bargains were made by the tongue alone, was swept away. Letters and ledgers took the place of "I'll do't," and "you shall hae't"; and, as in all such cases of advance, the rugged picturesqueness of the old method disappeared with its inconve-niences. (*MC* 103)

The reader will note the example of the "ecotechnical" here in one phrase. Bargains were made not by the mind and will, nor even, paradoxically, by audible speech, but "by the tongue alone."

The passage in *The Mayor of Casterbridge* about body language contains no references to the use of hands in gesture speech, though "the face, the arms, the hat, the stick, the body throughout" are mentioned. The face and arms, the list suggests, are as much prosthetic gesturing devices, modes of "ecotechnicity," as are the hat and the stick. My topic in this essay, however, is hands.

References to hands are so constant a feature of Hardy's writing that his work might almost be called a "chirography," a writing by hand about the hand's function in social intercourse. *Kheir* is Greek for "hand." Such a hand-writing might require a "chiromancy," or palm-reading, to decipher. The word "hand" enters into almost innumerable common idioms in English, as in "hand off" for the way a quarterback in American football hands the ball to the running back, or as in "hands off," as a warning not to touch, or as in "*Hand* me slab," in Wittgenstein's example, in the *Philosophical Investigations* (Wittgenstein 1968: 9ᵉ), of a command in a primitive language game, or as in the old telephone company advertisement: "Reach out and touch someone," which implies touching with the hand. The list of hand idioms could go on and on.

Most poignantly of all, perhaps, my hand touching the hand of another person is a sign, so we assume, for bodily intimacy with that person, as well as the signal of an accord, for example in a handshake. Maurice Merleau-Ponty asserts, falsely claiming authority from Edmund Husserl, that one proof of my access to the subjectivity of another is that touching the hand of another is like touching my own hand, whereas Husserl maintains the opposite. Husserl confesses, against the grain of the basic intuitionist doctrine of his phenomenology, that though my right hand touching my left hand is a basic proof of my immediate bodily presence to myself, touching the hand of another does not have this kind of immediacy. We never have more than doubly indirect access, that is, access by what Husserl calls "analogical apperception" (Husserl 1960: 108–11), to the interiority of another person. Jacques Derrida, in *On Touching – Jean-Luc Nancy*, discusses hands in Merleau-Ponty and Husserl at length. Derrida goes one move beyond Husserl and puts in question even the immediacy of self-touch. Derrida dares, as he says,

> to extend rather than reduce the field of appresentation [i.e. indirect access as named by Husserl] and to recognize its irreducible gap even in the said touching- touched of my "own proper" hand, my own body proper as a human ego. . . . Even between me and me, if I may put it this way, between my body and my body, there is no such "original" contemporaneity, this "confusion" between the other's body and mine, that Merleau-Ponty believes he can recognize there, while pretending he is following Husserl. (Derrida 2005: 192–3)

A lot is at stake, as you can see, in the question of what happens when my right hand touches my left hand or when I touch the hand of another person.

Every novelist, no doubt, is likely to mention the hands of his characters and to use hand idioms, but each does so differently and more or less often. I claim that an assessment of the use of hands in a given novelist is a powerful way to identify what is most distinctive about that novelist's sense of individual and social life. Thomas Hardy makes unusually abundant use of hand references both in his poetry and in his fiction. (See Miller [forthcoming], for a discussion of hands in Hardy's poetry.) Investigating Hardy's "hand-writing" in *The Mayor of Casterbridge* is a good way to test out my claim. The abundance and hardly noticeable evanescence of hand-notations in the flow of Hardy's language or in the novel's narrative space, like fireflies at dusk punctuating the text, is, in my view, quite remarkable. I need to illustrate that in detail by making Hardy's hands stick out. I do that in order to have empirical data on which to base my palm-reading. Citations are proof, or at least a sort of proof, since what you are justified in making of them may be debatable.

The stages of the drama in *The Mayor of Casterbridge* can be charted by way of appearances of the word "hand." Hardy's hands are clues to what is going on as the story progresses, in that extended country dance, "a reel or fling of some sort" (*MC* 121), of approach and withdrawal, proximity and distance, that I long ago called "the dance of desire" (Miller 1970: 144–75). The figure of the dance is of course borrowed from the novel itself. Henchard is displeased when he sees Elizabeth-Jane dancing with Farfrae, to "a tune of a busy, vaulting, leaping sort" (p. 123). That displeasure leads him to fire Farfrae. At the denouement of the novel, Henchard is led to wander away to his death when he looks in on Elizabeth-Jane's and Farfrae's wedding celebration to see her dancing with "someone who out-Farfraed Farfrae in saltatory intenseness" (p. 375), her real father, Newson. From chapter to chapter of *The Mayor*, the characters clasp hands, or refrain from touching. They reach toward one another, or draw back, write to one another by hand, point with their fingers, or gesture in other ways with their hands. The narrator and the characters use many idiomatic hand metaphors.

Henchard's fiery impetuosity, as he reaches toward one character after another, only to turn away from them or be repulsed – Susan, Farfrae, Elizabeth-Jane, Lucetta – is the primary energy motivating this circulating dance from chapter to chapter. He moves toward the absolute desolation of having, so to speak, no one to touch or who touches him, as the narrator observes near the end of the novel, speaking for Henchard in indirect discourse:

> There would remain nobody for him to be proud of, nobody to fortify him; for Elizabeth-Jane would soon be but as a stranger, and worse. Susan, Farfrae, Lucetta, Elizabeth – all had gone from him, one after one, either by his fault or by his misfortune. (p. 341)

All the characters, in their movements of approach and withdrawal, demonstrate how implacable is that sad primary law of Hardy's world: "Love lives on propinquity, but dies of contact" (*LW* 230).

In the opening scene the gulf between Henchard and his wife Susan is indicated in the way they do not touch hands. Henchard, rather, is "reading, or pretending to read, a ballad sheet which he kept before his eyes with some difficulty by the hand that was passed through the basket strap" (p. 2). In the third chapter, on the contrary, nineteen years later, Susan and Elizabeth-Jane walk the same road, but: "They walked with joined hands, and it could be perceived that this was the act of simple affection" (p. 21). When Elizabeth-Jane enters the room she is sharing with her mother at the Three Mariners Inn: "At Elizabeth's entry [her mother] lifted her finger" (p. 51), to command silence so they can hear Henchard and Farfrae talking in the next room. Henchard and Farfrae seal Farfrae's promise to be Henchard's manager with a handshake: "The young man's hand remained steady in Henchard's for a moment or two. . . . His hand, which had lain lifeless in Henchard's, returned the latter's grasp. 'Done,' said Henchard. 'Done,' said Donald Farfrae" (pp. 72, 73). Note that the hand here seems to operate by itself. It is Farfrae's hand that returns Henchard's grasp, not Farfrae himself. A moment earlier, Henchard is shown "holding out his right hand and leaning with his left upon the wicket which protected the descent" (p. 72), to bid Farfrae goodbye forever, so he thinks. Holding Farfrae's hand leads Henchard to renew his offer of a job. Farfrae's new status in Henchard's place of business, after he has sealed his bargain with his new employer, is indicated when Elizabeth-Jane comes upon him "in the act of pouring some grains of wheat from one hand to the other" (p. 71). The interaction between Henchard and Susan, Elizabeth-Jane and Susan, and Henchard and Farfrae is notated, the reader can see, by a kind of manual ballet: hands grasping hands or refraining from doing so.

When Henchard thinks he is face to face with his long-lost daughter, Elizabeth-Jane, his emotion is shown in the way he "allowed his hands to hang between his knees, while he looked upon the carpet" (p. 77). A little later, Henchard "handed the packet" to Elizabeth-Jane containing not only a note to Susan but the five guineas that in effect buy her back (p. 78). Then: "He took her hand at parting, and held it so warmly that she, who had known so little friendship, was much affected" (p. 78). When Susan and Henchard meet in the old Roman amphitheater, Susan accepts her renewed relation to Henchard by saying, "I am quite in your hands, Michael" (p. 84). In the next chapter, Henchard is shown "spreading his great hand over the paper" (p. 87) that his new employee Farfrae is using to "overhaul" Henchard's business records. Henchard's forehead is "shaded by his hand" (p. 89) when he tells Farfrae the story of how he got drunk years before and sold his wife, later taking Lucetta as his mistress.

The interactions among the main characters in chapters 14 through 27 are charted by hand-notations, focusing especially on Elizabeth-Jane in her relations to Henchard, Susan, Farfrae, and Lucetta. When they are abstracted from the text and cited in a sequential cascade, as I am about to do, they produce a surreal masquerade of disembodied hands clasping, unclasping, failing to clasp, and performing other actions, such as writing a note. Elizabeth-Jane, for example, receives "a note by hand" (p. 106), sent secretly by her mother, bidding her to meet Farfrae at a granary on Durnover Hill. This is the beginning of their tentative love affair. The Councilmen "leave the matter in his hands" (p. 118), when Henchard sets up his ill-fated holiday amusements that compete so unsuccessfully with Farfrae's and are a first stage in their estrangement. Henchard writes "in a heavy hand to Farfrae" (p. 130), forbidding him to address his attentions to Elizabeth-Jane. He takes the letter from Lucetta "up in his hands" (p. 133). This is the letter that will put him in communication again with the woman he has wronged, wronging his wife at the same time. Still under the illusion that he is Elizabeth-Jane's real father, though she does not know it, Henchard, "grasping her wet hand" (p. 141), appeals to her to love him when she weeps at his mistaken revelation. This happens just before he opens the letter from the now-dead

Susan telling him that Elizabeth-Jane is Newson's daughter, not his. He then turns against Elizabeth-Jane, for example by deploring her unmaidenly "hand," in the sense of handwriting: "It was a splendid round, bold hand of her own conception, a style that would have stamped a woman as Minerva's own in more recent days," whereas "Henchard's creed was that proper young girls wrote ladies'-hand" (p. 149). The comparison to Minerva is a delicate way of saying Elizabeth-Jane's "hand" stamped her as an aggressive, masculine woman. This is perhaps not surprising, since Hardy, it may be, put something of his sense of himself into Elizabeth-Jane's characterization: her detached watchfulness, her lowered expectations, her conviction that "happiness was but the occasional episode in a general drama of pain" (p. 385). Elizabeth-Jane further offends Henchard by taking "shovel in hand" to clean up "when the cat overturn[s] the coal-scuttle" (p. 150), rather than letting the servant do it. Later "she clap[s] her hand to her mouth" (p. 155), when she spontaneously uses one of the dialect words that so offends Henchard as a sign of her low-class origin. In the next scene, she is shown "putting her hand to her face to hide a quick flush that had come" (p. 156), when Lucetta, not yet known to her, overhears her wishing that she were dead with her dear mother. Much of the characterization of Elizabeth-Jane, the reader can see, takes place by notations of her hand gestures. Lucetta's relative superficiality is indicated in the way she casually "wave[s] her hand towards the tombstone" of Elizabeth-Jane's mother (p. 156), when the two women meet in the churchyard.

Elizabeth-Jane's relation to Lucetta starts a new figure, with new momentary partners, Lucetta and Henchard, Elizabeth-Jane and Farfrae, Farfrae and Lucetta, in the novel's dance of approach and withdrawal. Henchard "seem[s] relieved to get [Elizabeth-Jane] off his hands" (p. 163), when she tells him she is leaving to live apart from him. When Elizabeth-Jane presents herself at Lucetta's house, Lucetta greets her by "taking hold of Elizabeth-Jane's hands (p. 172), in another of the actual handclasps that punctuate the novel and that indicate the fluctuating allegiances among the characters. Another explicit handshake is a notation of something seen by Lucetta and Farfrae in the marketplace below: "Two farmers met and shook hands" (p. 186). A little earlier, Casterbridge farmers are described as "thrusting their hands into the pockets of remote inner jackets," and they have ready money "in their large plump hands" (p. 175). The farmers' hand-gestures are infallible indices to their characters and to their class status. When Farfrae comes courting Elizabeth-Jane, but is instead enticed by Lucetta, who is enticed by him, he has "a silver-topped switch in his hand" (p. 180), an "ecotechnical" appendage that is a sign of his new prosperity as an independent corn-dealer. When Henchard is introduced to Lucetta by Elizabeth-Jane, who does not know they have been lovers, the narrator says he "put his hand to his hat, which he brought down with a great wave till it met his body at the knee" (p. 192). When Lucetta is stealing Farfrae away from her, Elizabeth-Jane has a vivid, and accurate, imagination of their meetings: "She depicted his impassioned manner; beheld the indecision of both between their lothness to separate and their desire not to be observed; depicted their shaking of hands . . ." (p. 196). When Lucetta confesses that she has just seen Farfrae, in confirmation of Elizabeth-Jane's imaginings, she "[takes] her friend's hands excitedly in her own" (p. 24). Lucetta's growing preference for Farfrae leads her to "[hold] out her hand to [Henchard] in . . . cool friendship" (p. 201), rather than with the passion he expects and wants. The love compact between Farfrae and Lucetta is sealed when he "take[s] her hand" (p. 224), and she speaks "through her hands" when she is steeling herself to break for good with Henchard (p. 225). Henchard takes Elizabeth-Jane's hand (p. 226) when he wants her as witness to his coercion of a marriage promise from Lucetta, but a few moments later Elizabeth-Jane "[holds] Lucetta's hand" (p. 227), in uncomprehending sympathy with Lucetta's plight. The interaction among the three is signaled by a kind of sleight of hand among disembodied hands that clasp and unclasp another hand and then clasp some different hand. I say "disembodied" because little notation is given of the rest of the characters' bodies, while much explicit emphasis is given to the movement of their hands.

I grant that by singling out all these examples of the word "hand" (by no means all occurrences of the word), I am abstracting them from the flow of the narrative, within which they might pass by without being noted. That, however, is just what I want to stress. I want to indicate how all these "hands" function as a subliminal, hardly noticeable, recurrent rhythmic, or rather arhythmic note, more like a continuous ground bass than like a leitmotif, or perhaps like a continuous half-hidden melody beneath the ostensible melody. All these hands touching or failing to touch are like what Gerard Manley Hopkins called an "underthought" (Hopkins 1956: 252–3) beneath the surface thought. Or they are like hiccoughs, interruptions, caesurae, or syncopes, missed heartbeats calling attention again and again to the essential function of touching or failing to touch in human intercourse, at least in Hardy's fictional world. Hardy's hands show the way in which, for him, we all live by way of what Nancy calls *se toucher toi* (Nancy 2006: 36), to touch oneself touching you, to self-touch you. I am what I am because my hand grasps another by the hand.

My citations have called attention to this almost intangible, apparently no more than contingent, linguistic feature of Hardy's narrative procedures. I call it almost intangible because it does not fit any of the usual categories we literary critics are taught to notice. As I said earlier, hands are not exactly a thematic motif, nor a figure, or if a figure, as in "have in hand," so worn away by use, by usury, that their figurative nature is hardly evident. Hardy's hands are so nearly literal as hardly to seem like a trope at all. Nor is the hand in Hardy a symbol, or a sign of allegory, or a catachresis of something otherwise unnamable. Hardy's hands are just hands, part of the "realistic" stylistic surface. They are, however, somehow also more than just hands, since they imply that men and women relate to one another, and to themselves, by a touch of the hands, or by a refraining from touch.

After this syncope, I take my sequence in hand again. Farfrae's successful courtship is indicated when the spying Henchard sees Farfrae in the cornfield "taking her hand" (p. 224). When Henchard is told Lucetta is not at home, "he [goes] away handling his beard with a nettled mien" (p. 233). If he cannot touch her, at least he can touch himself on one sign of his manhood, his beard. Later Henchard's attempt to retain possession of Lucetta is indicated when he "hold[s] her hand within his arm" (p. 240).

He does not yet know that she has already quietly married Farfrae when he tries to force her to marry him "off-hand" (p. 242), and then releases her from that promise when she protests. When Henchard is declared bankrupt, he sells his gold watch and "hand[s] the money" to "one among the smaller of his creditors" (p. 254), even though his watch has not been demanded of him.

My need often to change present participles ("handing") to present-tense verbs ("hands") in order to make grammatical sentences in my citations obscures the fact that doing something with the hands, in Hardy's locutions, is sometimes, though not always, expressed in a present participle. These participles indicate that the handing or hand-holding is the concomitant of some other action, often speech.

In a later scene, Henchard "[shakes] Farfrae abruptly by the hand" after saying "I – sometimes think I've wronged 'ee" (p. 262). The note from Lucetta to Henchard requesting the return of her letters to him is "put in Henchard's hand by the postman" (p. 273). Elizabeth Jane sees "her father slowly raise his hand to a level behind Farfrae's shoulders" (p. 274), when he is tempted to pitch Farfrae head foremost out the top floor open barn door to his death below. The happy marriage between Lucetta and Farfrae is indicated when "Lucetta, light as a sylph, [runs] forward and seize[s] his hands" (p. 278). Henchard "hand[s] [Jopp] a package in brown paper" (p. 292) to deliver to Lucetta. These are the fatal handwritten letters from Lucetta to Henchard. When Jopp reads them aloud at the inn called "Peter's Finger" (p. 295), they reveal her past liaison with Henchard. This leads to the "skimmity-ride" and to Lucetta's death. Jopp can open the packet without breaking the seal, "the pen and all its relations being awkward tools in Henchard's hands," and he has "affixed the seals without an impression" (p. 292).

"Peter's Finger," by the way, counts as another hand reference. It is an odd name for a tavern, perhaps, as the Norton Critical Edition of the novel claims in a footnote, a corruption of the name of a church, "St. Peter-ad-Vincula," "St. Peter in Chains" (Hardy [1886] 1977: 194). *The Mayor of Casterbridge* makes many biblical references, including at least one more to St. Peter: Lucetta avoids French words because they will betray her origins in the island of Jersey, just as St. Peter's speech betrays him when he denies knowing Jesus: "She shirked it [any French word] with the suddenness of the weak Apostle at the accusation: 'Thy speech bewrayeth thee!'" (*MC* 174; Matt. 26: 73). "Peter's Finger" has a slightly obscene overtone, as well as religious connotations of a pointing, admonitory, saintly or divine finger, as in those biblical references to the finger of God (for example Exod. 8: 19; Luke 11: 20), or in those Renaissance paintings of the risen Jesus' encounter with Mary Magdalene in which he points skyward as he says, "Touch me not; for I am not yet ascended to my Father" (John 20: 17), or in the scene in which Jesus "with his finger wrote on the ground" (John 8: 6), or in Jesus' invitation to Doubting Thomas to "Reach hither thy finger, and behold my hands" (John 20: 27). I have found no iconographic tradition involving St. Peter's finger.

Henchard is shown "laying his hand upon the green cloth" when he proposes to the town council that he wants to join in the reception of the royal visitor (p. 303).

He insists on welcoming the visitor, wandering out in the royal carriage's way with a Union Jack on a stick "in his hand" (p. 305), even though he has been forbidden to do so. He waves the flag to and fro "with his left hand while he blandly [holds] out his right to the Illustrious Personage" (p. 306). This leads to Henchard's public humiliation by Farfrae when Farfrae seizes the lapel of Henchard's coat and drags him away. Henchard later "put[s] his own hand there, as if he [can] hardly realize such an outrage from one who it had once been his wont to treat with ardent generosity" (p. 310). Farfrae is now mayor and married to Lucetta, having doubly displaced Henchard. Henchard's large, awkward hands are a prominent part of his bodily presence. The Illustrious Personage later "[shakes] hands with Lucetta as the Mayor's wife" (p. 308), and the reader is told that, later, "the shake of the Royal hand still linger[s] in her fingers" (p. 310). The whole episode is structured around a play of hands proffered and accepted or refused.

In the scene of the wrestling match between Henchard and Farfrae, Henchard uses his "right hand" (p. 311) to tie his left arm to his body to even the odds between himself and Farfrae, while the unsuspecting Farfrae appears on the scene "with one hand in his pocket, and humming a tune" (p. 312), Burns' "Auld Lang Syne," that he sang when he first appeared at the Three Mariners, "a poor young man," years before: "And here's a hand, my trusty fiere, / And gie's a hand o' thine" (p. 312). As the Norton edition note observes, Burns' poem has "there's" instead of "here's" (Hardy [1886] 1977: 208). Hardy's mistake makes a slight but unmistakable difference. "Here" keeps the hand to a greater degree in the hands of the one who proffers it. Burns' verses inhibit Henchard from killing Farfrae, as he had intended to do, by pushing him out the open window with his "only free hand" (p. 314), when he over-masters Farfrae. "Your life is in my hands" (p. 315), Henchard says when he has Farfrae hanging out the window.

In the skimmity-ride scene Lucetta "seize[s] Elizabeth-Jane by the hand, and [holds] up her finger" (p. 320), as they stand by the window while the effigies of her and Henchard tied back to back on a horse's back pass by the street below. Lucetta's sight of this leads to her epileptic fit, her miscarriage, and her death. Henchard is described "holding up his hand" (p. 328) to stop Farfrae when he (Henchard) goes out on the road to try unsuccessfully to get Farfrae to return to his mortally ill wife. Henchard recognizes that she is dead when he sees "the servant raise her hand to the knocker" (p. 333), to remove the cloth that had muffled it to prevent bothering the mortally ill Lucetta. I am doing this, the servant says, "because they may knock as loud as they will; she will never hear it any more" (p. 333).

When Elizabeth-Jane comes to comfort Henchard after Lucetta's death, she is invited to lie down to rest after her wakeful vigil beside Lucetta's deathbed. When she awakens from her nap just after Henchard has told his "mad lie" to Newson (that Elizabeth-Jane is dead), he is shown "taking her hand with anxious proprietorship" (p. 340): "Towards the young woman herself his affection grew more jealously strong with each new hazard to which his claim to her was exposed" (p. 339). This happens according to the cruel law that governs Hardy's world. What you have and can touch you do not want. You want only what you cannot lay hands on with a sense of full possession. "When I was rich," says Henchard after he has lost Lucetta to Farfrae, "I didn't need what I could have, and now I be poor I can't have what I need!" (p. 269). Now that Lucetta is dead and Henchard has Elizabeth-Jane in a sort of tenuous pseudo-possession, he makes breakfast for her "with [his] own hands," and, when she demurs, he asks "how should I live but by my own hands" (p. 340).

When the despairing Henchard goes out to drown himself, he stands "on the brink of the stream with his hands clasped in front of him" (p. 342). When he is diverted from suicide by seeing his own image from the skimmity-ride floating in the water where the denizens of Peter's Finger have thrown it, he says, "Who is such a reprobate as I! And yet it seems that even I be in Somebody's Hand!" (p. 345). The narrator ironically undercuts Henchard's belief by saying there is a "natural solution of the mystery Henchard . . . regarded . . . as an intervention that the figure should have been floating there" (p. 345). Here is an example of the skeptical modernist Hardy's fascination, in spite of his skepticism, with religious belief.

Jacques Derrida has devoted a whole section of *On Touching – Jean-Luc Nancy*, "Tangent V," to an elaborate discussion, in the context of Nancy's thought, of Jean-Louis Chrétien's argument, in *L'Appel et la réponse*, that "the 'merciful hand of the Father,' with which he touches us, is the Son," that is, Christ, the second person of the Trinity (Derrida 2005: 244), and that God's hand is the original, literal hand, of which all human hands are no more than figures (Derrida 2005: 244–62). I have no doubt that all these human hands touching and clasping, even in so skeptical a writer as Hardy, have latently within them the Christian doctrine of the Incarnation and the concomitant powerful belief that even the most reprobate among us is "in Somebody's Hand."

Henchard sees Newson's fateful return "glass in hand" (p. 357), that is, looking through a telescope. This makes explicit the constant motif in the novel of spying from a distance, seeing without being seen and without being able to touch. The seeing in this case, however, requires the prosthesis of a hand-held tool. Seeing Newson coming leads Henchard to wander off for good, leaving Farfrae to plan his wedding to Elizabeth-Jane. The two are now so intimate that "they [join] hands without ceremony" (p. 361), when they meet. Henchard goes off with "a scrap of [Elizabeth-Jane's] handwriting," among other fetishistic relics, including "gloves, shoes . . . a curl of her hair" (p. 366). Elizabeth-Jane's handwriting seems to Henchard as intimate a part of her as a lock of her hair. When he returns to witness her wedding, he carries a caged goldfinch as a wedding present "in his hand" (p. 372). In an irony characteristic of Hardy, the goldfinch is left unnoticed under a bush and dies in its cage when Henchard is repudiated by Elizabeth-Jane and wanders away to die, forgetting the caged bird. Henchard "wash[es] his hands at the riverside" (p. 373) in preparation for coming to the wedding. He "seize[s] [Elizabeth-Jane's] hand" (p. 376) imploringly at their last meeting. She "gently [draws] her hand away" in repudiation of him (p. 376), and he then goes off to his death. Only Abel Whittle follows him, and then attends him on his deathbed. Abel is the workman whom he had treated cruelly for being chronically late to work, though he had been kind and charitable to Abel's mother.

Henchard's handwritten last will does not mention hands, except to say that Farfrae "handed the paper to her [Elizabeth-Jane]" (p. 384), when they find it after Henchard's death. Henchard does, however, say in his will "& that nobody is wished to see my dead body," where "nobody" rhymes dissonantly with "body." His dead body would of course expose his hands, perhaps, along with the face, part of the "obscenity," in the sense of indecent exposure, of a pathetically defenseless corpse. The will ends with the record of an act of handwriting. This sentence is an explicit performative speech act or writing act: "To this I put my name. MICHAEL HENCHARD" (p. 384).

If *The Mayor of Casterbridge* ends with a handwritten document, the novel itself perjures what this performative inscription commands by invoking, against Henchard's will, his memory. "& that no man remember me," writes Henchard (p. 384). This calls the reader's attention to the way the novel itself is an inscription. The text is material words on the page that have such effect as they do have on the reader, but one effect they surely do have is to lead the reader to remember Henchard, fictitious invention though he is. This final example of hand-notations also may call attention to the inordinate role of handwritten documents in this novel. Many letters and notes are exchanged among the characters, often with unforeseen and disastrous consequences, such as the death of Lucetta, Henchard's distaste for Elizabeth-Jane's unlady-like handwriting, his taking a scrap of her handwriting with him when he goes off alone, and so on. It would be possible to claim that the novel is as much about the power of handwriting in the human world as it is about human hands and what they can do. Or, it might be better to say, the prosthetic or technical extension of the hand in handwriting is perhaps the most potent use of the human hand. Handwriting is even more powerful than the use of the hand to clasp another's hand, or than to clasp one's own other hand, or than the use of hands to manufacture or use tools. Tools, as I have already suggested, are another technical extension of the human hand, though one that we share with all the many tool-making and tool-using animals, but the pen is perhaps the most powerful of human tools.

I have now shown that hands clasping or not clasping, hands handing something over to someone, or receiving something from someone, hands pointing, hands writing, etc., plus a large repertoire of common figurative idioms using the words "hand" or "finger," punctuate *The Mayor of Casterbridge*, like an "underthought." I have also shown how the whole novel can be mapped, charted, or graphed by following through the occurrences of "hand," especially hands clasping or writing. These serve as points on the line of Henchard's approach and withdrawal from the people in his life, or their withdrawal from him. Sooner or later, all withdraw: "Susan, Farfrae, Lucetta, Elizabeth – all had gone from him, one after one, either by his fault or by his misfortune" (p. 341).

Well, so what? How is Hardy's use of hands different from hands in "real life," or in other works of fiction? What can the thoughtful reader conclude from all these clasping hands about the possibility of truly touching and holding the other, or of touching oneself, in Hardy's world?

It would appear at first that all these scenes of hands clasping hands indicate that Hardy believes you can really touch and hold the other, or yourself, however momentarily. I do not believe this is the case. *The Mayor of Casterbridge*, perhaps more than any other work by Hardy, demonstrates in a moving way the hard Hardy law I have already cited: "Love lives on propinquity, but dies of contact." What does Hardy mean by love? *The Mayor* indicates that love for Hardy is the jealous desire for total and exclusive possession of the other person, often, though not always, sexual possession. Henchard is Hardy's most hyperbolic embodiment of love in this sense. He is "the kind of man to whom some human object for pouring out his heat upon – [be] it emotive or [be] it choleric – is almost a necessity" (p. 142). At one turning-point in the novel, the narrator reports that "by an almost mechanical transfer the sentiments which had run to waste since his estrangement from Elizabeth-Jane and Donald Farfrae gathered around Lucetta before they had grown dry" (p. 171). Love in Hardy is exacerbated by propinquity, that is, by a closeness that is not yet having and holding. Propinquity is proximity that is, at best, touch without touch. As soon as contact, even a fleeting, tangential touch, occurs, love dies. Love dies of contact. When love has died, possession of the other person dies too. True touching, in all these transactions, never occurs. "Contact" perhaps, but not touching in the sense one often means it, that is, as a sign of intimacy and possession.

The Mayor of Casterbridge is the nightmarish dramatization, by way of Henchard's experience, of this failure to touch. When the reader first sees him, his love for Susan has already died of contact. Though Henchard is drawn so powerfully to Farfrae, Farfrae's reserve always keep a space between them. Henchard then turns toward Elizabeth-Jane with greedy possessiveness and tells her she is really his daughter, not Newson's, but he does this at just the moment he discovers she is, after all, no daughter of his. Thereafter he is cruelly cold to her. His attempt to make amends to Lucetta for their illicit affair is blocked when she falls in love with Farfrae. When Henchard ultimately turns back in possessive love to Elizabeth-Jane, who still mistakenly thinks Henchard is her father, this is just the moment Newson, her real father, returns. He tells Newson "mad lies like a child" (p. 338), informing him that Elizabeth-Jane is dead. This leads Newson to go away. Ultimately, Newson returns and then helps Farfrae celebrate his wedding to Elizabeth-Jane. This return seems inevitable, in Hardy's world of "Satires of Circumstance," or of "Life's Little Ironies," to borrow the titles of one of his poetry books and one of his short story collections. Whatever person Henchard reaches out to touch instantaneously slips from his grasp, eludes his touch, even if he grasps them by the hand. Henchard, like Elizabeth-Jane when she is present at the flirtations of Lucetta and Farfrae, is like a point that cannot be touched by the circle that brings other people in touch.

This is Hardy's version of the Girardian triangle of mediated desire (Girard 1965). The person I desire is possessed by another. That is why I desire him or her. I am excluded, however, from the line that touches the other two and joins them. I am always the odd man or woman out, the point that the circle cannot touch. It is not even possible, in Hardy's world, to touch oneself, since that touching, as of the left hand by the right hand, is always accompanied, in Hardy's notations, by a division of the self into two, the acting self and the spectator self watching the acting self from a distance. This motif appears in many poems, quite explicitly, for example, in "He Follows Himself" (*CPV* 645–6). Such doubling is, in *The Mayor of Casterbridge*, especially dramatized in the characteristic coldness and detachment of Elizabeth Jane. She is not only given to watching others at a distance. She also self-consciously watches herself from a distance, as many passages attest. An example is the passage listing the unanswerable questions Elizabeth-Jane asks herself as she sits by the bed of her dying mother:

> all this while the subtle-souled girl [was] asking herself why she was born, why sitting in a room, and blinking at the candle; why things around her had taken the shape they wore in preference to every other possible shape. Why they stared at her so helplessly, as if waiting for the touch of some wand that should release them from terrestrial constraint; what that chaos called consciousness, which spun in her at this moment like a top, tended to, and began in. (pp. 135–6)

Henchard's warm impulsiveness, which causes him so much suffering, seems the opposite of Elizabeth-Jane's cool detachment, but Henchard too is remarkably self-conscious. Like Elizabeth-Jane, he often separates himself from himself and watches himself acting. An example is the moment when he ultimately withdraws from all others, since, the narrator tells the reader, "He had no wish to make an arena a second time of a world that had become a mere painted scene to him" (p. 369).

I conclude, somewhat paradoxically and counter-intuitively, that what all those notations of hands in *The Mayor of Casterbridge* signify is the failure of getting in touch. Touch, for Hardy, vanishes at the moment of "contact" and therefore never really takes place, or, in a better formulation, touch, for Hardy, takes place without taking place. You can touch and grasp the hand of the other person all right, but you do not, for Hardy, touch the heart of that person through his or her hand. Some gap, impediment, reserve, or division always, for Hardy, forbids union by way of touching. It is as though the hands you clasp were, in a manner of speaking, disembodied, separated from the rest of the other person's body, as in all those explicitly disembodied hands in Hardy's poetry that I have investigated in another essay (Miller [forthcoming]).

Elizabeth-Jane's happy marriage to Farfrae, that ends the novel, might seem the opposite of Henchard's forlorn acceptance at his death of his separation from everyone ("& that no man remember me"), but Hardy's narrator is careful to specify that Elizabeth-Jane's possession of Farfrae and her final prosperous happiness is still shadowed by her "field-mouse's fear of the coulter of destiny" (p. 100), and by her own form, at least in her youth, of inveterate detachment from others. This is the way her youth had taught her, in a phrase already cited, that "happiness was but the occasional episode in a general drama of pain" (p. 386), though her happy adult life may lead her to forget that lesson.

I claim to have verified my initial claim and to have won my bet. I have shown that trying to get in touch with the motif of hands is a good way to get a handle on what is going on in Hardy. I also claim that the failure to touch or be touched that is at the center of such a novel as *The Mayor of Casterbridge* in various ways justifies including Hardy among "modernist" writers in English. Hardy's "hand-writing" confirms his sense of the individual's isolation and of the dissolution of community. It also demonstrates a certain use of irrelevant/relevant detail that may be a distinctive feature of modernism. The intangibility of the other person, and a use of hand-notations, may be discerned in modulated forms in all of Hardy's fiction and poetry, though it would take a book-length study to demonstrate the way that works, persuasively and in detail.

References and Further Reading

Berman, Marshall (1982), *All That Is Solid Melts into Air: The Experience of Modernity*. New York: Simon & Schuster.

Burns, Robert (1901). On the Late Captain Grose's Peregrinations Thro' Scotland: Collecting the Antiquities of That Kingdom. In Robert Burns, *The Poetry*, ed. William Ernest Henley and Thomas F. Henderson, Centenary Edition, 4 vols. (vol. I, pp. 289–92). Edinburgh: T. C. & E. C. Jack.

de Man, Paul (1983). Literary History and Literary Modernity. In Paul de Man, *Blindness and Insight: Essays in the Rhetoric of Contemporary Criticism* (pp. 142–65). Minneapolis: University of Minnesota Press.

Derrida, Jacques (2005). *On Touching – Jean-Luc Nancy*, trans. Christine Irizarry. Stanford: Stanford University Press. 1st published in French, 2000.

Girard, René (1965). *Deceit, Desire, and the Novel*, trans. Yvonne Freccero. Baltimore: Johns Hopkins Press. 1st published in French, 1961.

Hardy, Thomas ([1883] 1966) The Dorsetshire Labourer. In *Thomas Hardy's Personal Writings*, ed. Harold Orel (pp. 168–91). Lawrence: University of Kansas Press.

Hardy, Thomas ([1886] 1920). *The Life and Death of the Mayor of Casterbridge: A Story of a Man of Character*. New York: Harper; vol. V of the Anniversary Edition of *The Writings of Thomas Hardy in Prose and Verse*, a reprint of the original

Wessex Edition, with the same texts and pagination.

Hardy, Thomas ([1886] 1977). *The Mayor of Casterbridge*, ed. James K. Robinson. New York: W. W. Norton.

Hardy, Thomas (1979). *The Variorum Edition of the Complete Poems of Thomas Hardy*, ed. James Gibson. London: Macmillan.

Hardy, Thomas (1984). *The Life and Work of Thomas Hardy*, ed. Michael Millgate. London: Macmillan.

Hopkins, Gerard Manley (1956). *Further Letters*, ed. Claude Colleer Abbott. London: Oxford University Press.

Husserl, Edmund (1960). *Cartesian Meditations: An Introduction to Phenomenology*, trans. Dorion Cairns. The Hague: Martinus Nijhoff. 1st published in German, 1950.

Miller, J. Hillis (1970). *Thomas Hardy: Distance and Desire*. Cambridge, MA: The Belknap Press of Harvard University Press.

Miller, J. Hillis (forthcoming). Hands in Hardy.

Nancy, Jean-Luc (1991). *The Inoperative Community*, trans. Peter Conner, Lisa Garbus, Michael Holland, and Simona Sawhney. Minneapolis: University of Minnesota Press. 1st published in French, 2004.

Nancy, Jean-Luc (2006). *Corpus*. Paris: Éditions Métailié.

Wittgenstein, Ludwig (1968). *Philosophical Investigations*, trans. G. E. M. Anscombe. Oxford: Basil Blackwell.

29

Inhibiting the Voice: Thomas Hardy and Modern Poetics

Charles Lock

"Nobody has taught me anything about writing since Thomas Hardy died."
(Ezra Pound, letter of 1934 to W. H. Rouse [Hutchins 1968: 104])

"Mr Hardy seems to lose all sense of local and historical perspective in language, seeing all the words in the dictionary on one plane, so to speak, and regarding them all as equally available and appropriate for any and every literary purpose."
(William Archer, review of *Wessex Poems* [*Daily Chronicle*, December 21, 1898])

"Your happy phrase, 'seeing all the words of the dictionary on one plane' . . . touches, curiously enough, what I had thought over."
(Hardy to William Archer, December 21, 1898 [*CL* II: 207])

"I am glad to get a letter from such an original thinker on poetry – and in poetry, I should add – as yourself: which very few people are nowadays, more's the pity."
(Hardy to Ezra Pound, November 28, 1920 [*CL* VI: 47])

"Hardy shames our ignorance; as a prosodist . . . he was immensely learned, with a learning that seems to be lost beyond recovery."
(Donald Davie 1973: 15)

"In his {Hardy's} opinion, vers libre *could come to nothing in England"*
(Robert Graves 1929: 377)

On the poets of the 1890s: "I am blind to the merits of these people as I am to Thomas Hardy."
(T. S. Eliot to Ezra Pound, December 2, 1924
[unpublished letter cited in Eliot 1996: 395])

Of the "Georgian poets": "queer young men whose wrongnesses are interesting."
(Hardy to Edmund Gosse, October 5, 1913 [*CL* IV: 307])

"Mr Hardy's langwidg waz choicer."
(Ezra Pound to James Laughlin 1935 [Laughlin 1989: 94])

The history of modern English poetry is distorted by delay and deferral. Had "The Wreck of the *Deutschland*" appeared in 1877, and *Wessex Poems* (or, under whatever title, Hardy's first volume of verse) at about the same time, the impact of Ezra Pound and T. S. Eliot would appear less abrupt, less unprecedented, less a revolution than a modulation. That *Wessex Poems* appeared in 1898 has meant that Hardy has been neither quite of the nineteenth century nor of the twentieth, whereas the first publication of Hopkins in 1916–18 has ensured that Hopkins has always been given hospitality in the twentieth. (On the ill-fittedness of Hardy as a nineteenth-century poet see Armstrong 1993: 484–9, and Shires 2004: 255–6; for another view, see Taylor 1999.) The poetic tradition since the first generation of Romantics has canonized its major figures securely within each century's limits; an even more decisive limit is marked by 1914. As Peter Howarth has noted, Hardy's poetic dedication to the Napoleonic Wars, as manifested in *The Dynasts* (1904–8) acquired a fresh and topical importance in 1914, not least for those poets directly exposed to warfare (Howarth 2005: 5); yet the poetic revolution associated with the publishing (significantly, by non-combatants) of *Cathay* (1915) and *Prufrock and other observations* (1917) seemed to put Hardy's verse (even *Moments of Vision*, also of 1917) back somewhere not quite of the twentieth century.

Michael Roberts's *Faber Book of Modern Verse* (1936), among British critics and students the most influential of all such anthologies, begins with Hopkins and moves on to Yeats. Hardy is uncited, unmentioned, his absence meriting not even an explanation. By contrast Methuen's *An Anthology of Modern Verse* (1921), a much more popular and indeed complacent selection, not only features Hardy prominently but bears the dedication "To Thomas Hardy, O.M. | Greatest | of the Moderns." Each of these anthologies was reprinted virtually every year up until the 1950s and beyond, the Methuen in a school edition as well. Academic critics of modern poetry followed the Faber program, and Hardy languished in the company of W. E. Henley and Ralph Hodgson, to name those who follow him in the Methuen anthology's alphabetical presentation. (Between Hodgson and R. A. Hopwood there is a single poem by Gerard Manley Hopkins.) Influential anthologies shape both taste and history, both hierarchy and lineage. The history of modern English poetry can to some luminous extent be traced in the allegiances within and antagonism between these two volumes. More than by any individual critic or learned despiser, Hardy as poet has been burdened by anthological association. In similar case, Edward Thomas is found in Methuen but not in Faber; Robert Frost and Ivor Gurney are in neither. Yeats's *Oxford Book of Modern Verse* (1936) is as we might now say inclusive, but, though by no means partial to Hardy, remains closer in selection as in spirit to Methuen than to Faber.

The publication of *Wessex Poems* in 1898, followed by seven volumes over the next thirty years, gives a sense of compression, of unnatural forced growth: a long life's work comes to fruition in the years of retirement, after a career as a novelist over thirty-five years. As Michael Millgate has so comprehensively documented, first in the work of that subtitle (Millgate 1971), Hardy seldom wrote except for money, and never without a view to furthering his career and enhancing his prestige. When Ezra Pound spoke of "the harvest of having written 20 novels first" (Pound 1971: 242), he may have exaggerated the number of novels but he pointed to the sense of accumulation and aggregation that renders Hardy's authorial career so distinctive, not just within English literature but within the entire Western tradition.

Critics of Hardy have tended to range themselves as admirers either of the novels or of the poetry; monographs on Hardy tend to take on a dutiful tone when dealing with the less-favored genre, which is to say that the poetry is treated as an obligatory supplement. Those who favor the poetry tend to ignore the novels; no monograph on Hardy could afford to begin in reluctance. Yet the construction of Hardy's career assumes a continuity, that all the writings come from one cloth. The view that Hardy had lost all interest in fiction after the reception of *Jude the Obscure*, or that his novel-writing had been mere journey-work to provide an income, is not credible. This is apparent from Simon Gatrell's outstanding work of "textual biography", *Hardy the Creator* (1988). Though its focus is exclusively on the novels, we see that Hardy's interest in cultivating the fictional domain of Wessex, and of preparing a collected edition of all his novels, increased steadily after 1898, and never diminished. In September 1907 an odd closing phrase in a letter to the director of Macmillan, "I don't feel up to a novel at present!" (*CL* III: 274; Gatrell 1988: 242), gives the impression that Hardy might yet write another. Gatrell comments shrewdly on Hardy's many disparaging remarks about his fiction that these "must be derived in part from the continuing attention his novels and stories received . . . at the expense of his poetry." (Gatrell 1988: 245; see also "Mr Thomas Hardy denies the statement of a contemporary that he has given up writing novels" [*THPV* 170]). In 1906 Hardy had his publisher announce that until the completion of *The Dynasts* "no new novel by him – if, indeed, he writes any more fiction – need be expected" (*THPV* 229). In 1910 we could have read: "Readers have almost given up hoping for another novel, although Mr Hardy has never distinctly stated that this will not appear. He feels that a condensed form of expression, as in poetry, attracts him more as the years go on. He does not think it probable that the 150,000 words or so of a novel will ever again come from his pen" (*THPV* 315). In terms of energy and dedication it would seem that from 1898 Hardy was consistently and meticulously concerned with the promotion of his writings as a whole. Although he might, around 1895–96, have wished to renounce fiction entirely, within ten years he was creating a monument whose center would be formed by his novels (Millgate 1992).

Against the immense amount of attention that he gave to the revision of the novels for their reissue in the Wessex Edition in 1912, and again for the (limited) Mellstock Edition of 1920, there is no comparable interest in the gathering of the poems. The first eighteen volumes, divided into four sections, clearly constitute the Wessex

Edition; it is not clear whether the six volumes of poetry form part of the Wessex Edition or a supplement thereto. The first of these contains *Wessex Poems* and *Poems of the Past and the Present* (1912); the second contains two of the three parts of *The Dynasts* (1913). These two volumes bear respectively XIX and XX on the spine, extending the numerical sequence. But there is no indication of numerical sequence on the spines of the remaining four volumes (or elsewhere therein): *The Dynasts Part Third* plus *Time's Laughingstocks* (1913), *Satires of Circumstance* with *Moments of Vision* (1919), *Late Lyrics and Earlier* with *The Famous Tragedy of the Queen of Cornwall* (1926), and, posthumously, *Human Shows* with *Winter Words* (1931). Hardy took immense pains over the revision and the presentation of his novels and stories in an edition that remains, more than fifty years after Purdy's verdict, "in every sense the definitive edition of Hardy's work and the last authority in questions of text" (Purdy 1954: 286); yet his treatment of the poetry (after first publication in volume form) was, by contrast, almost perfunctory. While the Mellstock Edition was in the course of publication, Hardy wrote to his publisher: "It occurred to me a day or two ago that it would be better if Wessex Poems preceded Time's Laughingstocks in the Mellstock Edition, being more correct chronologically; & that the suggestion might be in time I wrote straight to the printers, in case they should be taking it in hand" (*CL* VI: 20–1). The ordering of the volumes is thus determined with a startling degree of inattentiveness.

This bibliographical summary points to a problem: the relationship between Hardy's fiction and his verse is not the simple one of sequence that a chronological list of each volume by year of publication would suggest. Critics admiring of the verse have often cited Hardy's own words to establish an antagonistic relationship, with an assumed superiority of the poetry over the prose. The greater number of critics, admiring the novels, are inclined to regret that *Jude* was the last. Pound, whose high praise for Hardy's verse seems less eccentric and less extravagant with each passing decade, insisted on the intimate connection of the two: the verse as the harvest of the novels. Not in noting the connection, but in insisting on its importance, Pound has been virtually alone. (On Pound and Hardy see Hutchins 1968; Peck 1972; Davie 1973: 42–50; Taylor 1993: 372–7; Howarth 2005: 180–1). The oddity, awkwardness, clumsiness of Hardy's verse has been commented upon so frequently as to have become a commonplace. (For valuable summaries with references see Elliott 1984: 13–19; Taylor 1988: 199–204; Taylor 1993: 29–32). Likewise, critics seldom fail to point out the creaking plot and tendentious inevitabilities of the novels. But the two awkwardnesses usually remain unrelated, except in biographical terms, through invocation of the provincial autodidact. This essay will argue that Hardy's poetics are those of a novelist, of a particular kind. It was only after he had ceased to write fiction, and had devoted himself for some years exclusively to poetry, that Hardy realized the importance of his fiction, in its own right and as the prologue to, even the prerequisite of, the poetry: as if he had come to acknowledge that there ought to be commerce between them.

Many tributes have been paid to Hardy's poetry by distinguished critics as by eminent poets (Lock 1992: 91–100). Their observations have been sharp, their evaluations often generous. Yet the mode has tended to the concessive, as though Hardy were good in spite of himself. One exemplary and memorable instance is T. S. Eliot's in *After Strange Gods* (1934): Hardy's "style touches sublimity without ever having passed through the stage of being good" (cited in Elliott 1984: 15). More generous is R. P. Blackmur's memorable epithet on "The Walk" as a poem "reduced to riches" (Blackmur 1940: 47). None of this, either individually or collectively, made for the sense that Hardy was a great poet to be ranged with Yeats and Frost, Eliot and Stevens. Yet precisely such has been the claim of poets and critics as divergent as Harold Bloom and Philip Larkin. The awkwardness need not be entirely vitiating: it might somehow be converted into a quality.

A substantial and transforming work on Hardy's poetry has emerged over the past thirty years: Dennis Taylor's trilogy, *Hardy's Poetry 1860–1928* (1981), *Hardy's Metres and Victorian Prosody* (1988), and *Hardy's Literary Language and Victorian Philology* (1993), constitutes a scholarly engagement of considerable scope and painstaking detail. The work has yet to be absorbed in the entirety of its ambition by students of Hardy. Nor has it been properly appreciated by the historians and theorists of modern poetry, though Taylor's enterprise forms one of the finest and most learned treatments ever granted to any modern poet. The books remain difficult of access: a convenient one-volume edition is much needed if this work is to receive its due, and (hereby to pay a tribute of awkwardness) Hardy's poetry its.

While other critics have indulged in much special pleading, have even argued for the goodness of bad verse, for the grace of the graceless, for the split voice, the "broken-backed" poem, and have argued this with wit and subtlety as well as passion, Taylor asks us to reconfigure the very grounds of judgment. A hint might be taken from William Pritchard's elegant argument that what we find in Hardy's poetry is a presence rather than a voice:

> When the poet is Yeats one can hardly ignore the voice, or the changing voices, through which his poems speak to us, often speak very loudly to us. With Hardy, voice is dangerously easy to ignore, to the advantage of neither poem nor reader. (Pritchard 1980: 18)

This seems to respond to and endorse John Bayley's observation that Hardy's "presence is the reverse of a persona": "The use of a persona . . . is always inimical to the texture of Hardy's prose" for there is a "kind of eclipse which overshadows his text when the tone . . . becomes too consistent" (Bayley 1978: 194). Yet Hardy's novels conspicuously lack that generic characteristic defined by Bakhtin as novelistic discourse or the dialogical, also known as free indirect discourse, indicated by inconsistencies of tone, voice, and viewpoint (Lock 2004). Taylor supposes that "a Bakhtinian account of Hardy will soon appear" (Taylor 1993: 34; see now Wickens 2002) yet he is himself alert to the misfit. For what we have in the novels is an absence of distinctive voices, tones, idioms, and registers, though plenty of optical shiftings. We might say that we have silence, but not the ordinary silence of a novel, designed to be read without the voice: this is a silence for want of any voice, or voices. It is a silence to which the reader will be enjoined by the verse.

Bakhtin assumed poetry to be always and necessarily voiced: poetry must be read aloud. Yet that notion had been conspicuously flouted in a poem published in the same year as *Wessex Poems* (1898), Mallarmé's "Un coup de dès jamais n'abolira pas le hasard". Here all the complex effects of the typography and layout are lost when the poem is voiced. One might say the same of any poem with a visual form, such as a sonnet, but with a sonnet or any regular stanza one can visualize the poem with one's inner eye while listening to it through the outer ear. Hardy's poems have learnt from the novelist something of the tricks and potentials of silent reading. And where the dialogical depends on the "inner hearing" by silent reading of conflicting and contesting voices, Hardy's fictional prose allows for almost no hearing at all. When we can hear the tone, sonorous and resonant, as at the close of *Tess*, it is, as Bayley notes, "always inimical to the texture of Hardy's prose." Texture is a well-chosen word, for it commits us neither to the visual nor to the acoustic. We live close to the texture, and apprehend it in the appropriate way, with our hands and finger tips. In the novels this silence, this destruction or suppression of "voice", is achieved through a random instability of points of view. A voice needs to speak to us from a certain place, from which deixis (here, there, now, then, and so forth) derives its sense. The narrative voice in Hardy's fiction is spatially of no fixed abode, and therefore (this is Hardy's brilliant device, identified if not celebrated by Pritchard) the voice virtually fails to be registered.

Following Pound, Taylor traces the weave from novel to verse: "Hardy used his poetry to explore in a more concentrated and confined way the type of language critics complained about in his novels." (Taylor 1993: 48). To which we might add that he explores also the tricks of language that he had deployed in his novels without the critics having noticed much. In poetry he does this not by shifting viewpoint: the viewpoint of the poetic voice is precise and stable, enabling description by deixis, and is almost necessarily so in lyric whose rhetorical mode is apostrophe. In the novels the shifting viewpoint destabilizes a single vocal discourse. In the poetry, it is language, the words themselves, that do the work of unsettling the voice by denying the phrase, or frustrating it. That is to say that whereas in free indirect discourse the voice can change from clause to clause, even from phrase to phrase, in Hardy's verse it would have to shift from word to word: this occurs when there is no syntagm in a continuous register in which a voice might be found, or to which one might be given. When in silence we read a clause we hear its potential voicing; when we see a word in isolation, as in a dictionary, there is no attendant voicing. If the normal patterns of lexical collocation are broken, or unmet, we find ourselves reading a series of isolated words. This is most conspicuously felt as the great obstacle to reading *The Dynasts*: all those people are talking – it is a drama, after all – but the reader cannot hear them.

> Do now but note
> How cordial intercourse resolves itself
> To sparks of sharp debate! The lesser guests
> Are fain to steal unnoticed from a scene
> Wherein they feel themselves as surplusage
> Beside the official minds.
>
> (Part Third, V.ii.86–91, *CPW* V: 143)

The Countess of Brignole may have spoken in a manner of which this is a fair representation, but the Shakespearian pastiche of "fain to steal unnoticed from a scene" does not go with "surplusage." Yet "cordial intercourse" matches "sparks of sharp debate", rather as Macbeth's "multitudinous seas incarnadine" goes with "making the green one red." This is a lexical contrast (between words of Germanic and Latinate origin) often used by Hardy, as in setting "By hearts grown cold to me" against "With equanimity" (" 'I look into my glass' ", *CPW* I: 106), but it does not disturb the vocal continuity: English allows and even requires of all its speakers such lexical juxtapositions from unkinned word-hordes. (Hardy rejected the homogeneous lexical saxonizing of William Barnes). It is not at the philological level that Hardy's poetry disturbs. Many of Hardy's best-known and most anthologized poems (including "The Darkling Thrush" and "The Oxen") are plausibly one-voiced, and can be heard and read aloud as such. Close analysis may expose the lexical fractures: of "It Never Looks Like Summer" an early reviewer (in 1917) objected astutely that "it is not easy to lay a finger precisely on what is wrong with this vocabulary" but "all the phrasing is wrong." (Taylor 1993: 293–4); Linda Shires brings out the lexical weirdness, the contrasting valuation implied by certain words ("moonings", "blithely") in one of Hardy's most celebrated and oft-recited poems, "During Wind and Rain" (Shires 2004: 268–71). We may note the problem of "existlessness" and the substituted "wan wistlessness" in that much admired poem, "The Voice". Many of Hardy's poems, and all the famous ones, tend to be criticized for one or two awkward words: these are, almost inevitably, admired concessively as "otherwise perfect" poems.

The speeches throughout *The Dynasts* are consistently implausible, and therefore inaudible, and unutterable. For all the wittings and weenings, Hardy's is not a poor attempt at fustian, a clumsy falling short of the smooth effects achieved by Barham in the *Ingoldsby Legends* (1838): "Never I ween / Was a prouder seen . . .". Rather, Hardy's verse subverts the possibilities of voice. In Taylor's words, Hardy "implodes [voice] from within by means of the minute particulars of his diction" (Taylor 1993: 286). The consequences of this are far-reaching, and need to be traced through poets such as Pound and Williams. Taylor suggestively remarks that "Hardy's word combinations are like William Carlos Williams's line divisions; they are hardly ever what one expects" (Taylor 1993: 294). Often in Hardy we think we've found a poem that will sing to us, as in the one beginning "It never looks like summer", only to find ourselves, as we listen along, stumbling into a lexical ambush that counsels silence. Try this:

> We are budding, Master, budding,
> > We of your favourite tree;
> March drought and April flooding
> > Arouse us merrily,
> Our stemlets newly studding;
> > And yet you do not see!
> > > ("The Master and the Leaves", *CPW* II: 434)

The fifth line stops us on stemlets, and then asks us to move from stemlets to studding. Our focus is drawn to single words precisely because they are not collocated into phrases that we could identify, acknowledge, recognize and – the point of it all – voice.

Yet the first line is melodious to voice, and readers after c.1938 will find resonance in "We are dying, Egypt, dying" from MacNeice's "The Sunlight on the Garden". For poet and reader before MacNeice, the grammatical person would have been altered from Antony's "I am dying, Egypt, dying" (*Antony and Cleopatra* Act IV) as dying is succeeded by budding, leaving the dying to the one addressed, the Master. Stemlet sets up no suggestive echo, and is according to the *OED* a word of strictly botanical usage first recorded in 1838. There's a certain wit in this: if leaves are made to talk, their words might well be strictly botanical. "Studded", from the verb "to stud", is absurdly extended in semantic range: the buds appear on the stemlets as studs, though they have actually grown out from them, rather than being forced in, as a forced bonding of heterogeneous materials, which is the usual sense of studding. The effect in Hardy is to highlight the word and to leave the reader stranded with the word that refuses to be fitted into any tonal or syntactic context. Such words, we might parry, are thus his poems always studding. We may recall Walter de la Mare's remark of 1919 on Hardy's verse: "He forces, hammers poetry into his words." And he hammers words into his poems. (Howarth 2005: 152)

The effect of this studding is to stifle not only voice but also allusion. For allusion works by the phrase, as we see (and hear) in the opening line of "The Master and the Leaves". Yet it helps not at all to introduce *Antony and Cleopatra* into our thinking about the poem. The allusion is seldom the key and is usually a distraction. Kenneth Marsden reserves to an appendix a revealing discussion on "The Question of Influences" (Marsden 1969: 225–32). Influence cannot be equated with allusion, though allusion is certainly evidence (and acknowledgment) of influence. Marsden cites Cecil Day-Lewis: "Influence-spotters don't have a very happy time with him" (Marsden 1969: 225) and finds that this is not because influences cannot be spotted in Hardy's verse, but because the spotting yields so little. Marsden concludes that "many influences can be detected in Hardy's works, but few are important and none are very strong" (Marsden 1969: 231). This remains a truism in the criticism of Hardy's poetry, and one that has been seldom challenged. Pritchard notes that the critical emphasis on Hardy's "sincerity" (and its deceitful double, irony) is a way of coping with the problem of influence: instead of positioning Hardy within an allusive tradition, an inheritance of genres and tropes, one was resigned to confessing that Hardy told the truth as he perceived it, "sincerely", without regard to the poetic tradition.

The critical consensus was challenged by Donald Davie when in 1972 he identified the scale of the dilemma in a still exceptionally challenging essay, "Hardy's Virgilian Purples". The hemistich from "Beeny Cliff" – "and purples prinked the main" – is identified by Davie as an allusion to Virgil. Yet Hardy doesn't do that sort of thing: this ought to be simply an accurate perception of what the poet saw from the cliff-top. Davie takes up the cudgels of learning and allusion on Hardy's behalf:

we are determined to condescend to Hardy, to see in him what Yvor Winters saw – "a *naif.*" Even when we mean to praise, we patronize; when Hardy's "sincerity" is offered as a simple and straightforward value by F. R. Leavis and Douglas Brown . . . the implication is very plain that to Hardy – sturdily simple soul that he was – sincerity came more naturally than it did to his more sophisticated peers, or than it does (of course) to us. . . . Hardy on the contrary was a remarkably devious and tortuous man – just the sort of man who would at once convey and cloak his meanings with the allusive deviousness that I have been trying to demonstrate. (Davie 1972: 151)

The biographical appeal seems hollow, and gratuitous: for "devious and tortuous man" let us read "ingenious poet". On the phrase "allusive deviousness" one may however dwell, with delight. For it suggests that Hardy's deviousness is achieved or manifested through his allusiveness. Yet allusion does not manifest: it is itself a way of both conveying and cloaking a debt, or a note of thanks. How devious may allusiveness be before even the most learned readers fail to spot it?

Pritchard sees in Davie's argument the symptom of an academic quandary for critics schooled by Empson and Richards, Ransom and Tate: "If Yeats and Eliot were subtle, allusive, complex, and weighty, Hardy was, well . . . sincere." (Pritchard 1980: 18, authorial ellipsis). The one Hardy poem that students of English literature in American universities after 1945 were likely to have read was "The Darkling Thrush", a poem whose full-throated allusiveness could hardly be termed devious (Lock 1986). Pritchard's point (and Davie's) is that the obvious poems, those routinely anthologized, are the ones that most resemble our idea of poetry – and that these are exceptional rather than characteristic.

And the question remains. Even when we have identified the allusion to Virgil, in one of Hardy's most famous poems, closely studied by some exceedingly learned readers, all of them resistant until 1972 to noticing what would surely have been patent in Tennyson or Yeats or Eliot, we may still ask: Does the Virgilian allusion contribute anything to an understanding of "Beeny Cliff"? At this point Davie's case is weakened, for in order to assert the meaningfulness of the allusion he has to construct an elaborate topographical allegory that quite fails to persuade, and whose failure to persuade even Davie – "My story has an unhappy ending" – leads him around to some rather mean and condescending animadversions about Hardy's lack of poetic ambition (Davie 1972: 156).

Without reference to Davie, Taylor takes up the debate: "But I would argue that Hardy is generally not an allusive poet. . . . The subject of allusion deserves much more consideration . . . but I suspect that Hardy resists the urbanity of allusiveness which confirms a high culture of the best that is thought and wrote [*sic*]" (Taylor 1993: 293). Allusion has since been considered by Christopher Ricks, whose brilliant study *Allusion to the Poets* (2002) fails in its 300 pages to mention Hardy. The case of Davie's reading of "Beeny Cliff" might have been instructive, but the entire absence of Hardy is altogether more pointed.

Allusion works by the phrase and the clause, rather than by the single word. That is why we can all acknowledge the allusion in "We are dying, master, dying" but must retain some doubt over the single word "purples". (That it is from another language, Latin, complicates the question; but an intended allusion would signal its intention by a phrasal echo of, say, Dryden's English *Aeneis*.) Allusion may be visible lexically but it must be confirmed phonetically, and rhythmically. John Hollander's pioneering study of allusion is entitled *The Figure of Echo* (1981): Echo is the very being of allusion. A phrase set to a rhythm will echo from Shakespeare's Antony to Hardy to MacNeice. Each instance recalls a previous utterance. But a single word has no individuating rhythm, nor any voice at all. "Purples" may set up a theme, even a comparison, but in itself is no echo, nor can it, alone, allude. "Allusion is a matter of what we are to hear, and then to listen to." (Ricks 2002: 312). At least two words in collocation seem to be required if we are to enjoy the subtlety of allusion, both in conveying an echo and yet in covering that conveyance with its distinct and divergent syntagmatic purposes. A whole sentence or a stanza will cover, protect, encase the allusion: what conveys it (betrays it) will invariably be the specific turn of a phrase.

Hardy interrupts the voicing of the verse by drawing our attention to the isolated words with which it is studded. By this studding the normal conventional allusiveness of verse is frustrated. Taylor's argument is that each odd word draws attention not to a previous poetic citation of that word, but to the lexical status of the word as an item in the dictionary. The poem becomes a frame for the words that stud it: benighted, outleant, existlessness, domiciled, daysman, self-unheed, moils, magian, reticulations. By each of these words we can identify a poem, yet what identifies the poem is also an obstacle to its voicing. Consider "An Upbraiding" and try to voice: "Not differenced, as now," (*CPW* II: 282) or "existent" in "One We Knew" (where " 'poussetting' and 'allemanding' " seem by quotation marks to ask to be excused; *CPW* I: 331–32), or "outshapes" in "After the Last Breath":

> In view of which our momentary bereavement
>   Outshapes but small.
>
>   (*CPW* I: 327)

Sometimes, as in "Tess's Lament" (*CPW* I: 216–17), one finds the odd word – "unbe" – to be acceptable, even right, and one registers the unusualness of such eccentricity being redeemed, forgiven, even applauded. In "The Shadow on the Stone" (*CPW* II: 280) the verb "unvision" may also be rated a success in conventional vocal terms. One might add to the small list of vocally successful (or tolerable) eccentricities "skiey", though this adjective was confined to the manuscript of "The Garden Seat": "They are as light as skiey air!" In all printed versions, however, "skiey" is replaced by the far less interestful "upper" (*CPW* II: 331). And the reason may be that "skiey", though a curious stud in itself, alludes to Shelley's "Ode to the West Wind" and to uses in *Measure for Measure* and Carlyle's *Sartor Resartus*. (Hollander finds Milton suppressing allusion in making adjustments to "Lycidas" [Hollander 1981: 86–9].) "Skiey" is a single studding word, but one of purely literary usage, rather like "Darkling" in the title of that most openly and vocally allusive of Hardy's poems. Purely literary words, celebrated exemplars of "poetic diction", can do the work of allusion all on their own, if allusion can be silent. As Hardy knew well, using darkling in a title: for a title is

to be cited and looked at rather than articulated: to this titular use of the word
"darkling" one does not listen, nor when the poet does listen to the thrush's song
are we to be rewarded with an allusive and this time voiced occurrence of the word.
(On silence and voicing in Hardy, see Griffiths 1989: 216–36.)

Allusion is achieved by means of the phrase, very seldom by means of a single
word: "darkling" and "skiey" are exceptions. And recognition inheres in the voice. A
single word alludes not to another poet but rather to the dictionary, and Taylor's
argument could be rephrased in terms of an anxiety of lexical or even lexicographical
influence. The silence of Hardy's poetry may owe much to the silence in which novels
are read (and written), but it has become the silence of a list, of words arranged not
syntactically but paratactically. The parataxis is the list of all words which might be
substituted for the one written: a strange word deflects us from the syntactic axis and
sends us along the parataxis in search of a synonym, of another word which would
"make sense". We replace the odd word by one more familiar: "lived" or "dwelt" for
"domiciled", "at night" or "overtaken by darkness" for "benighted". Each paratactic
shift is motivated by a search for sense, yet it also draws our attention to what would
be lost if the word were actually replaced. This is a trick that we play on and with
and by ourselves, as readers, habitually. We may suppose that the choice of an unfamiliar word in poetry has been motivated by the demands of rhythm or rhyme. The
remarkable thing about Hardy's odd words is that they are seldom to be excused on
those grounds. To the contrary, the paratactic axis may often supply alternatives that
fit better, rhythmically or euphoniously, as well as being lexically familiar.

In "The Convergence of the Twain" there are a number of startlingly odd words,
welded in: "stilly couches she." Yet Hardy also likes to give his rhymes the feel of
being welded rather than "natural". Of the stanza

> Over the mirrors meant
> To glass the opulent
> The sea-worm crawls – grotesque, slimed, dumb, indifferent
>
> (*CPW* II: 11)

Howarth writes: "The welding of the rhymes is audible in the wrenched double stress
on 'indifferént' as if two things were being forced together and made to fit . . . the
form of the poem is indifferent to the normal pronunciation of 'indifferent,' and yet
that very indifference makes the word all too conscious of what it's doing" (Howarth
2005: 158). And so, if words are not themselves studded, unfitting, they are out of
their ordinariness distorted to fit the demands of rhyme or rhythm.

Taylor (1988) has analyzed in detail the range of the unmatched assortment of
stanzaic and metrical variation displayed in the *Collected Poems* and *The Dynasts*. The
visual variety of stanza forms can always be adduced, in the work of any poet, as an
argument for taking an interest in the look of a poem rather than its sound alone.
This is especially the case when, as in Hardy, the sounding or voicing of the poem is
not to be achieved without some difficulty. The metrical, syntactic, and lexical eccentricities are thus not unrelated to the exceptional variety of stanza-forms deployed by

Hardy: between the voiced awkwardness and the iconic (or architectural) assurance of the disposition of ink on the page, the reader, attentive in looking and voicing, may experience a dissonance approaching the sublime. Taylor defends the oddity of Hardy's meters in an ingenious manner, by suggesting that they anticipate modifications in English speech-patterns. Hardy recognized the flux in all things, not least in phonemes, and thus achieved "an accentual-syllabic form peculiarly consistent with a world in flux" (Taylor 1988: 121). Taylor continues: "Metrical form and current speech rhythms can never be identical. The patterns language assumes are momentary . . . they grow old, they bind us for a while in their obsolescing frames. In his metrical rhythms, Hardy captures the resonance of the life and death of forms. This resonance constitutes . . . the 'unique' music of Hardy's poetry."

The difficulties in voicing Hardy's poetry, what Richard Ellmann called "a serious impediment to articulation" (Taylor 1993: 32), may be a problem in synchronic terms, but it need not be so diachronically, in the long perspective. Clearly in the mid-twentieth century the rhythms of Yeats or Frost or Stevens struck the ear as "natural". Theirs is still a rhetorical poetry and so, like *Paradise Lost*, it is prone to a subsequent disjunction between meter and speech-rhythms. Changes in pronunciation, especially stress within words (e.g. "comfort", "research", "laboratory") as well as shifts of idiom and collocation, will only increase that disjunction. Archer's observation, that Hardy's language lacks historical perspective, should entail this: that the words, being laid out all on the one plane, are not limited to a particular instant or even one period of time. They start off disjunctively, their obsolescence already hammered in. The "free verse" of Pound or Williams (and to some extent of Eliot) may also be an attempt to hedge against the diachronic, because what we see is what we see rather than score for voicing: after Mallarmé one sees a poem, and acknowledges the significant look of a poem as an entirely legitimate inhibition on vocalization. Hardy's indifference to *vers libre* means that his poems look like poems (as Williams's tend not to), and thereby conceal their resistance to voicing. Yet as we move away from the phonetic system, the sound-patterning of English a hundred years ago, so we may find Hardy's poems at least no more awkward than they were. We might begin to hear something forced and "unnatural" in the poetry of Yeats (or in our voicing thereof), while Hardy's poetry, in moving through time, may acquire unexpectedly mellifluous passages or, at worst, some variation in the distribution of what's perceived as awkward.

This is indeed a radical solution to the *agon* of literary history. All the deprecations (even denunciations) of Hardy for his oddness, clumsiness, gaucheries, fall into place, or out of place and into time. In Howarth's view, what goes on in Hardy's verse "begins to look less like rural clumsiness, and rather more like the principled opposition to Romantic aesthetic unity" (Howarth 2005: 169). Taylor goes further, arguing that Hardy is the first poet to respond to what the *OED* demonstrates to be the shifting nature of words and their unstable pronunciation through history. We may propose that Hardy's is no local struggle within the recent poetic tradition, but one that strives towards a greater fracture: words and poetry have nothing "natural" in common, no bond, that is, as natural as the voice.

Hardy was persuaded to write two or three essays about fiction; about poetry he
limited his thoughts to the somewhat aggrieved and, in his own words, "uncalled
for . . . too cantankerous" "Apology" for *Late Lyrics and Earlier* (*CL* VI: 116, to Sydney
Cockerell, February 15, 1922; "Personally I think the preface a mistake," wrote Florence to Cockerell in April 1922: Millgate 1996: 181). Hardy there voices prophetic
concern at "the plethoric growth of knowledge simultaneously with the stunting of
wisdom" as symptom of "the precarious prospects of English verse at the present day"
and as harbinger of "a new Dark Age." (Hardy 1922: xiv). *Late Lyrics* was published
on May 23, 1922, *The Waste Land* on December 15. In the one, famously:

> I can connect
> Nothing with nothing

In the "Apology" appears this justification of discordant tones and themes: "But the
difficulties of arranging the themes in a graduated kinship of moods would have been
so great that irrelation was almost unavoidable with efforts so diverse." (Hardy 1922:
xiii) Even before *The Waste Land* Hardy can be parenthetically defiant, yet desperate:
"(if one may quote Tennyson in this century of free verse)." (Hardy 1922: xviii)[1] The
irrelation is not only among themes and tones within a collection of miscellaneous
poems composed over a number of years; there is a deeper irrelation, between words
and voices, sounds and letters, between all things and time, the time given by the
meter, as well as the time given to posterity, in whose time the meter may come to
creak, or cease to do so.

Whose is the more radical poetry, Eliot's or Hardy's? Pound's contribution to the
former, and his admiration for the latter, must stand as emblem for our dilemma, our
own precarious grasp of poetry in English over the past hundred years. Precarious (to
reiterate Hardy's word) in terms of both prosody and authority. For where the voice
is inhibited, the poet's authority is diminished. It is Tennyson or Yeats who bears the
authority of the poetic voice. Browning finds a way of concealing his voice within
another's; Pound and Eliot will tamper with the authority of their voices, will
somehow claim authority in a voice that is not the poet's but the critic's. Eliot alludes
by citation, learnedly, not always in English, and visibly rather than vocally: his is an
uneasy presence in Ricks's anatomy of allusion. Hardy, unmentioned by Ricks, makes
no claim to poetic authority, for the voice that would presume to eloquence, and thus
to the authority attained through a mastery of allusion, is always finding itself,
whether metrically or lexically, interrupted.

Davie himself identified exactly this, thirty-five years ago, when he spoke of
Hardy's "selling short of the poetic vocation" (Davie 1973: 40). Yet, reduced to its
riches, Hardy's poetry can be trusted; beyond all the seductive and authoritarian
abuses of the voice (not least, those of poets), this is a poetry of the word, true to each
of its words, bonded, welded, hammered, studded, outshown. By resisting voice, these
poems make it new, for they wear well, and wear time ever more lightly, their rhythms
and stresses as flexible and versatile as those of the revenants on the Garden Seat:

> With them the seat does not break down,
> Nor winter freeze them, nor floods drown,
> For they are as light as upper air,
> They are as light as upper air!

(CPW II: 331)

Hardy uses the voice, and obstacles to the voice, as a means of forging a disjunction between words and their utterance, between voices, rhythms and bodies. His interest in ghosts is no morbid obsession, but a way of figuring a poetics that might have a hold on posterity, a poetics of the precarious: that is, etymologically understood, a state of being insecure because reliant on another's voice, or on another's favor, or even on another's withholding of voice.

NOTE

1 The phrase "of free verse" may not be familiar in this context, even to Hardy scholars: it was dropped on the reprinting of *Late Lyrics and Earlier* in the Pocket Edition of 1923, and was never subsequently reinstated. The reasons for this omission have not to my knowledge been investigated. To beg the reader's permission merely to "quote Tennyson in this century" seems striving rather gratuitously to be considered unfashionable. But to "quote Tennyson in this century of free verse" is altogether more interesting, and more challenging. The publication in December 1922 of *The Waste Land* surely confirmed free verse as the characteristic mode of modern poetry. What else was published between February 1922 and early 1923 that might have led Hardy to revise and withhold his view that the twentieth century had surrendered to *vers libre*? Could it have been the immediate success and frequent reprintings, after the first issue on May 12, 1921, of Methuen's *Anthology of Modern Verse*?

REFERENCES AND FURTHER READING

Archer, William (1898). Review of *Wessex Poems*. *Daily Chronicle*, Dec. 21.

Armstrong, Isobel (1993). *Victorian Poetry: Poetry, Poetics and Politics*. London: Routledge.

Armstrong, Tim (2000). *Haunted Hardy: Poetry, History, Memory*. Basingstoke: Palgrave.

Bayley, John (1978). *An Essay on Hardy*. Cambridge: Cambridge University Press.

Blackmur, R. P. (1940). The Shorter Poems of Thomas Hardy. *Southern Review*, 6, 20–48.

Davie, Donald (ed.) (1972). *Agenda*. Thomas Hardy Special Issue 10.

Davie, Donald (1973). *Thomas Hardy and British Poetry*. London: Routledge.

Eliot, T. S. (1996). *Inventions of the March Hare: Poems 1909–1917*, ed. C. Ricks. London: Faber & Faber.

Elliott, Ralph W. V. (1984). *Thomas Hardy's English*. Oxford: Blackwell.

Gatrell, Simon (1988). *Hardy the Creator: A Textual Biography*. Oxford: Clarendon Press.

Graves, Robert (1929). *Goodbye To All That*. London: Jonathan Cape.

Griffiths, Eric (1989). *The Printed Voice of Victorian Poetry*. Oxford: Clarendon Press.

Gunn, Thom (1985). *The Occasions of Poetry*. San Francisco: North Point Press.

Hardy, Thomas (1922). *Late Lyrics and Earlier with many other verses*. London: Macmillan.

Hardy, Thomas (1982–95). *The Complete Poetical Works of Thomas Hardy*, ed. Samuel Hynes. 5 vols. Oxford: Clarendon Press.

Hollander, John (1981). *The Figure of Echo: a Mode of Allusion in Milton and after*. Berkeley: University of California Press.

Howarth, Peter (2005). *British Poetry in the Age of Modernism*. Cambridge: Cambridge University Press.

Hutchins, Patricia (1968). Ezra Pound and Thomas Hardy. *Southern Review*, 4, 190–204.

Laughlin, James (1989). *Pound as Wuz*. London: Peter Owen.

Lock, Charles (1986). "The Darkling Thrush" and the Habit of Singing. *Essays in Criticism*, 36, 120–41.

Lock, Charles (1992). *Thomas Hardy: Criticism in Focus*. New York: St. Martin's Press.

Lock, Charles (2004). Hardy and the Critics. In Phillip Mallett (ed.), *Thomas Hardy Studies* (pp. 14–37). Basingstoke: Palgrave.

Marsden, Kenneth (1969). *The Poems of Thomas Hardy: A Critical Introduction*. London: Athlone Press.

Methuen, A. (ed.) (1921). *An Anthology of Modern Verse*.

Millgate, Michael (1971). *Thomas Hardy: His Career as a Novelist*. London: Bodley Head; reissued Basingstoke: Macmillan, 1994.

Millgate, Michael (1992). *Testamentary Acts: Browning, Tennyson, James, Hardy*. Oxford: Clarendon Press.

Millgate, Michael (ed.) (1996). *Letters of Emma and Florence Hardy*. Oxford: Clarendon Press.

Millgate, Michael (ed.) (2001). *Thomas Hardy's Public Voice: The Essays, Speeches and Miscellaneous Prose*. Oxford: Clarendon Press.

Paulin, Tom (1986). *Thomas Hardy: The Poetry of Perception*. London: Macmillan.

Peck, John (1972). Pound and Hardy. In Donald Davie (ed.), *Agenda*. Thomas Hardy Special Issue 10, 3–10.

Pite, Ralph (2007). "Graver things . . . braver things": Hardy's War Poetry. In Tim Kendall (ed.), *British and Irish War Poetry* (pp. 34–50). Oxford: Oxford University Press.

Pound, Ezra (1971). *Selected Letters 1907–1941*, ed. D. D. Paige. New York: New Directions.

Pritchard, William H. (1980). *Lives of the Modern Poets*. New York: Oxford University Press.

Purdy, Richard Little ([1954] 1968). *Thomas Hardy: A Bibliographical Study*. Oxford: Clarendon Press.

Purdy, Richard Little, and Michael Millgate (eds.) (1978–88). *The Collected Letters of Thomas Hardy*, 7 vols. Oxford: Clarendon Press.

Ricks, Christopher (2002). *Allusion to the Poets*. Oxford: Oxford University Press.

Roberts, Michael (ed.) (1936). *The Faber Book of Modern Verse*. London: Faber & Faber.

Shires, Linda (2004). Hardy and Nineteenth-Century Poetry and Poetics. In Phillip Mallett (ed.), *Thomas Hardy Studies* (pp. 255–78). Basingstoke: Palgrave.

Taylor, Dennis (1981). *Hardy's Poetry 1860–1928*. Basingstoke: Macmillan; 2nd edn. 1989.

Taylor, Dennis (1988). *Hardy's Metres and Victorian Prosody*. Oxford: Clarendon Press.

Taylor, Dennis (1993). *Hardy's Literary Language and Victorian Philology*. Oxford: Clarendon Press.

Taylor, Dennis (1999). Hardy as a Nineteenth-Century Poet. In Dale Kramer (ed.), *The Cambridge Companion to Thomas Hardy* (pp. 183–203). Cambridge: Cambridge University Press.

Wickens, G. Glen (2002). *Thomas Hardy, Monism, and the Carnival Tradition: The One and the Many in* The Dynasts. Toronto: University of Toronto Press.

Yeats, W. B. (ed.) (1936). *The Oxford Book of Modern Verse 1892–1935*. Oxford: Clarendon Press.

30

Hardy's Heirs: D. H. Lawrence and John Cowper Powys

Terry R. Wright

To be an heir to a novelist as powerful and complex as Hardy is a double-edged bless-ing: it provides a writer with a bountiful legacy, a wealth of literary riches on which to draw, but it also lands the heir with an inhibiting model, a tradition not only to inherit but to live up to. Viewed positively, as it is by Rosemary Sumner, this influ-ence means that Hardy's novels, especially those of his final decade, provide "spring-boards for his twentieth-century successors" not only in terms of his "daring subject matter," his preparedness to address taboo areas such as sex, but in terms of his inno-vative narrative technique, gaps in the "logic" of realist characterization which draw attention to unconscious forces at work in his novels (Sumner 2000: 3–4). But literary influence, as Harold Bloom argued in a series of books beginning with *The Anxiety of Influence*, is never straightforward and rarely benign, leaving the younger author strug-gling for independence, rebelling against the poetic "father" and resisting too great a reliance upon him. Bloom provided a series of somewhat arcane terms to distinguish the various strategies to which writers turn in order to avoid excessive reliance upon their precursors: "clinamen" ("swerving" or reading correctively), "tessera" (using the same pieces of mosaic but rearranging them), "kenosis" (self-emptying in the manner of the Pauline Christ), and three other "revisionary ratios" (Bloom 1973: 14–15). I want to consider two very different heirs of Hardy, D. H. Lawrence and J. C. Powys, on the Bloomian assumption that we can learn a great deal about them, about Hardy, and about the process of writing from their creative reworking of him.

Both of these writers, along with Marcel Proust, John Fowles, Theodore Dreiser, and others, are included in the most sustained treatment of this topic, *Hardy's Influence on the Modern Novel* by Peter Casagrande. For him Lawrence illustrates the tensions within influence highlighted by Bloom while Powys more consciously locates himself within the same literary tradition. Both were critical of their precursor's pessimism but deeply attracted by his primary subject, "men and women passionately in love against a natural background at once beautiful and sinister" (Casagrande 1987: 33). Both can be seen in their own work to attempt to "correct" Hardy's problematic pessimism and, writing at a time when it was possible to be more explicit, to develop his writing about sexuality. These similarities, however, as I hope to demonstrate, should not disguise the huge difference between them in their relation to Hardy. Lawrence swerves violently away from Hardy while Powys writes self-consciously in his wake, rearranging very similar material.

Other critics who have written on Lawrence and Hardy claim that he tries to "complete" his primary precursor not only by extending Hardy's focus on sexuality but by exploring as he did the unconscious levels of personality, moving from characterization defined by conscious moral choice to an awareness of "states of being" beyond the conventions of the Victorian novel (Langbaum 1985: 69–70, 77). In terms of narrative technique, as Howard Mills points out, Hardy's polyphonic narrator "moves in and out of his fiction" while Lawrence is always himself "turbulently involved" in his work (Mills 1988: 16). Yet Hardy clearly provides not only Lawrence himself but also his readers with a model of a writer who constantly challenges them in the most dangerous areas of their self-understanding. Contemporary reviews of Lawrence's work highlighted the fact that he was "as dangerous to public morals as Hardy" (Draper 1970: 158–9). Others noted their shared tendency to polarize readers into "flaming disciples" or people who "shudder away from him as from the brink of a precipice" (Draper 1970: 252). In what follows I will consider first Lawrence's *Study of Thomas Hardy* (1936), and then how he can be said to have reworked him, most evidently in the novels completed immediately before and after that work, *The Rainbow* (1915) and *Women in Love* (1920).

Hardy, according to Jessie Chambers, was "the only serious writer I heard him [Lawrence] speak of with respect" (Beards 1969: 210); in fact, it was probably through the Chambers family that Lawrence came to read him, since he had been a favorite of theirs since the 4-year-old Jessie first read *Tess* aloud to her mother from the version serialized in the *Nottinghamshire Guardian* in 1891 (Worthen 1991: 109). Lawrence's first novel, *The White Peacock* of 1911, has been found reminiscent of Hardy in its treatment of its heroine's anguish, in its melodrama (Worthen 1991: 139–40), and in its presentation of "a world of blind fatalism" (Swigg 1972: 33), while his second novel, *The Trespasser* (1912), also presents its characters beating blindly (and in the suicidal Siegmund's case, unsuccessfully) against their tragic fate (Swigg 1972: 37–9). *Sons and Lovers* (1912) battles harder against the view that "men and women are doomed to failure in relationship" (Swigg 1972: 43). But it was his critical engagement with Hardy in 1914 which appears to have made him self-consciously "swerve" away from his precursor in his next novel, *The Rainbow*.

When Lawrence was asked to write on Hardy for Nisbet's series Writers of Their Day in July 1914, he immediately asked Edward Marsh to lend him not only Hardy's novels but Lascelles Abercrombie's *Thomas Hardy: A Critical Study* (1912) which he had first encountered two years earlier (Boulton 1979–2000 II: 193, 198). Abercrombie argued that Hardy's strength as a novelist depended on his "deliberately putting the art of his fiction under the control of a metaphysic," in his case a tragic one, which gave him "conscious mastery" over his material. The "highest art," Abercrombie insisted, "must have a metaphysic" (Abercrombie 1912: 19). Lawrence, as we shall see, seems to have wanted not only to provide a critical account of Hardy but to forge an alternative metaphysic of his own. His letters during the progress of the *Study of*

Thomas Hardy in the last few months of 1914 acknowledge the personal dimension of the book, which became "a sort of *Story of My Heart*: or a Confessio Fidei" (Boulton 1979–2000 II: 242), "mostly philosophicalish – slightly about Hardy" (II: 292). But it was in reaction to Hardy that he was working out a way of writing that would enable him to turn the sprawling manuscript of "The Wedding Ring," returned to him as unpublishable by Methuen in August 1914, into what are arguably his greatest novels, *The Rainbow* and *Women in Love*. Thinking about Hardy, in other words, became a "testing ground" for his own ideas and for his development as a novelist (Kinkead-Weekes 1989: xxxii).

The *Study of Thomas Hardy* oscillates between generalizations about life, sex, art, and religion and more specific comments on Hardy's work in a manner which clearly infringes the conventions of academic literary criticism. It is possible, however, to see the relevance of Lawrence's generalizations about life to his thinking about Hardy's fiction (as well as his own). It is certainly difficult to think of a more sustained "study of one great writer by another" (Mills 1988: 39). John Worthen's complaint that it describes "the novels he would have written had he been Hardy" (Worthen 1979: 56) merely confirms that what Lawrence is doing is establishing how he can break away from the influence of his precursor and establish a career based upon his own more positive metaphysic.

The first two chapters outline Lawrence's theories of art in terms of a Nietzschean "Gai Savaire," the title Lawrence attached to the typescript of the *Study*, a translation into his own idiosyncratic version of the medieval French "gai saber," a positive affirmation of human creativity in the face of a sometimes hostile universe. Lawrence celebrates art as excess, the beautiful poppy rather than the functional cabbage. "The final aim of every living thing, creature, or being," he announces, "is the full achievement of itself" (Lawrence 1985: 12). Too many of us, he complains, fail to achieve "true individuality," hanging back in cautious "self-preservation," content to be cabbages rather than blossom into beautiful poppies (1985: 15–17). This is the temptation, he argues, with most of the characters of Hardy's novels, to which he turns in chapter 3. He accepts that Hardy's characters "do unreasonable things . . . These people of Wessex are always bursting out of bud and taking a wild flight into flower"; they are "people with a real, vital, potential self." But the problem is that the result of "such an outburst" in Hardy's fiction is normally tragic. The "established form of life" of the community, its conventional morality, proves so "impregnable" that the passionate "individual, trying to break forth from it," normally dies "of fear, of exhaustion, or of exposure." The moral therefore is to "remain quite within the convention" be "good, safe, and happy in the long run" or risk tragedy by attempting to escape the "walled prison" of convention (pp. 20–1).

Lawrence provides comic synopses of the first five of Hardy's novels, which represent his most conventional work. The "fleshly passionate" Manston in *Desperate Remedies*, for example, like the "darkly passionate, lawless Miss Aldclyffe," has to be killed off while the dull hero and heroine are happily united. Fancy Day reaches a similarly safe decision to settle for "steady, solid . . . married life," carrying into the future "many unopened buds that will die unflowered." Elfride in *A Pair of Blue Eyes* falls at "the first little hedge of convention," while Bathsheba too refuses "the flower of imaginative fine love" (Sergeant Troy), settling instead for the "good steady Gabriel." Finally, *The Hand of Ethelberta* "marks the zenith of a feeling in the Wessex novels . . . that the best thing to do is to kick out the craving for 'Love,' and substitute common-sense." This, however, marks the end of Hardy's most conventional phase, "the end of the happy endings" (pp. 22–3). From now on he turns towards tragedy, displaying clear sympathy with those characters who have the courage to question the conventional morality of their community.

The problem, however, as Lawrence sees it, is that even in this later work Hardy himself does not quite sustain the courage to challenge the community. He sympathizes with rebels such as Eustacia Vye but nevertheless allows her to be defeated. It may not be altogether clear what Eustacia wants "but it is evidently some form of self-realisation," which she is not permitted. She therefore dies while Hardy apparently validates Clym's self-sacrificing ideals, which are really "a deep very subtle cowardice, that makes him shirk his own being whilst apparently acting nobly" (pp. 23–4). Eustacia dreams that her powerful nature will "come to blossom" with "some strong-passioned, unconfined man" (p. 26). But Clym, although "the force of life was in him," suppresses its flowering and retreats within the confines of the "moral chart" or "map" which he imposes upon the tremendous reality represented by "dark, passionate Egdon" itself, forever untamed and unpruned by human systems (p. 28).

At this point the *Study of Thomas Hardy* broadens out to consider a whole range of factors which Lawrence considers to have contributed to the narrow morality he so despises, attacking the Protestant work ethic, the "money-tyranny" (p. 37), and the obsession with scientific knowledge which threatens to overcome the joy of "being . . . the living stuff of life itself" (p. 41). He then returns once more to Hardy, suggesting that in the later work there is a clear conflict between his artistic predilection for the aristocrat, the individual who remains untrammeled by conventional morality, and "a moral condemnation of him" which allows "bourgeois virtues" to triumph. It will not be until Tess and Jude, Lawrence suggests, that Hardy allows himself wholly to "sympathise with the aristocrat" (p. 45). In *The Return of the Native* and *The Mayor of Casterbridge* he detects the "first show of real sympathy" for the aristocratic individual; at least they are not complete villains, as in the early novels. Hardy's "private sympathy," Lawrence suggests, "is always with the individual," the person of "distinct being" seeking "his own fulfilment," but he nevertheless allows the community to destroy him (or her). Neither Troy, Clym, Tess, nor Jude are given sufficient "life-flow" to "break away from the old adhesion," while Tess even "sided with the community's condemnation of her" (pp. 49–50).

At this point Lawrence again steps back from Hardy for three more chapters exploring the broader cultural issues that produced these conflicts in his work, in particular sex and religion. Fresh from his marriage to Frieda in July 1914 (a week after being asked to write the *Study of Thomas Hardy*), Lawrence celebrates the male desire for a woman as the central element in his life (p. 56). More esoterically, he develops the theology that had first begun to appear in the foreword to *Sons and Lovers* in terms of a set of related oppositions between Female and Male, God the Father and God the Son, Law and Love, the Flesh and the Spirit. For Lawrence God the Father (counter-intuitively) is Female, the creator of life, while God the Son, Christ the Word, is Male, inherently suspicious of the body. Whereas Renaissance art glorified the Father, celebrating the Flesh, the Reformation had brought a violent reaction in favor of the Son, abjuring the Flesh in the interests of the Spirit. Ideally, the Male and Female principles should not struggle for dominance but remain in creative balance. In Hardy, however, as in Tolstoy, there is no such equilibrium; his metaphysic demands that the Female bow to the Male, the Flesh succumb to the Spirit.

What rescues Hardy as an artist, however, as Lawrence argues in the third and final chapter on his fiction, is that the artist in him undermines his own theoretical meta-physic. "The man is much stronger in feeling than in thought," his "sensuous under-standing . . . deeper than that perhaps of any other English novelist" (p. 93). Although Hardy's narrators may often denounce the Female, the Flesh, his characterization reveals a deep sympathy towards them, especially in the final novels. In *Tess*, for example, both Alec and Tess are natural aristocrats (even if the former has to buy his title while the latter has long since lost hers). Tess, according to Lawrence, has the "true aristocratic quality" of "self-acceptance." She also respects the individuality and selfhood of others, though they "do not respect her right to be" (p. 95). Alec, whose "female" qualities are totally dominant, exploits her physically, while Angel, to whom "the female in himself is detestable . . . the result of generations of ultra-Christian training" (p. 97), oppresses her spiritually, leaving Tess too "despising herself in the flesh, despising the deep Female she was" (p. 98).

Lawrence's reading of *Jude* detects a similar division in Hardy between his uncon-scious sympathies for Arabella, who is "under all her disguise of pig-fat and false hair . . . in character somewhere an aristocrat" (p. 102), possessing "great female force of character." Her "coarseness," however, is "exaggerated to make the moralist's case" (p. 106). Jude, by contrast, is dominated by "the male idea," desiring "not to live in the body" but "in his mentality" while Sue is "born with the female atrophied in her: she was almost male" (p. 107–8). Like Tess, she identifies "utterly with the male principle," with "the Word," for all her intellectual denial of Christianity (p. 110). She consequently drains all the men she encounters, including Jude. Their marriage therefore is bound to fail, leading to her final act of renunciation and self-hatred, the result of their "laying of all the stress on the Male, the Love, the Spirit, the Mind" at the expense of "the Female, the Law, the Soul, the Senses, the Feelings" (p. 121). Only when these forces are properly balanced and reconciled, Lawrence suggests, can a man produce "supreme art," "the art which recognises his own and the law of the wom-an . . . the art which knows the struggle between the two conflicting laws, and knows the final reconciliation" (p. 128). This, of course, is a description which just happens to fit *The Rainbow* and *Women in Love*, to which Lawrence returned immediately on completion of the *Study of Thomas Hardy*.

Already, however, in the final pages of the *Study*, Lawrence can be found creatively to rewrite Hardy in his own terms, employing his own vocabulary rather than Hardy's to answer some of the questions raised by the novel. Why, for example, considering the number of common-law marriages to be found in Britain, do Jude and Sue generate such hostility in their neighbors? The answer, he suggests, lies in "their own uneasy sense of wrong, of sin, which they communicated to other people" (p. 118). It is a plausible enough answer, I suggest, but Lawrence's rather than Hardy's. Another question Lawrence asks of *Jude* (as many have done since) is why Father Time is made to kill his two siblings. The answer he supplies is again his own, suggesting that young Jude picks up subconsciously from Sue that he is an "accident" or "false note" in her life (p. 120). Her reluctance to be a mother, the denial within her of her "female" role, causes the boy's sense of worthlessness. Again, I suggest, before Lawrence returned to his own creative writing, the *Study* has begun to rewrite Hardy in terms of his own metaphysic.

Lawrence's work on Hardy, according to Mark Kinkead-Weekes, contributed directly to his subsequent reworking of "The Wedding Ring" into *The Rainbow* and *Women in Love.* For the former it gave him a new way to begin and end, setting the Brangwens against the "great background" of the Nottinghamshire–Derbyshire border (equivalent to Hardy's Egdon Heath) and encouraging him to expand the novel into the earlier generations of creative conflict between men and women of the family which anticipate Ursula's own struggles to fulfill herself, to achieve her full potential, a struggle which continues in the second novel (Kinkead Weekes 1996: 163–7). The "aristocrats" who people Lawrence's fiction can be seen as a product of his reaction to Hardy (Beards 1969: 226). For "Lawrence's people, unlike Hardy's, develop according to the laws of their individual natures," remaining independent of "the community and its morality" (Casagrande 1987: 49, 61).

That this development is related to Hardy's work, "correcting" or "completing" it in terms of Lawrence's metaphysic, is confirmed by his consistent use in his novels of the same metaphors as those found in the *Study*: images of male–female conflict and reconciliation, of "aristocracy," of independence from the community, and of the characters' final flowering or blossoming into "poppies" rather than "cabbages." *The Rainbow* famously begins with the difference between the Brangwen men, who enjoy a "blood-intimacy" with the natural landscape, facing "inwards to the teeming life of creation" (paradoxically a "female" quality in the *Study*) while the women want "another form of life" above that of the cattle, a "male" life, exemplified by the vicar, which "comprised religion and love and morality . . . the restraining hand of God" (Lawrence [1915] 1997: 8, 17). In the first generation on which the novel focuses in detail, Ursula's grandfather Tom sees that he is "incomplete" without Lydia, while union with her "would bring him completeness and perfection" (pp. 38–9). His speech at Anna's wedding can be read as a comic version of Lawrence's argument in the *Study of Thomas Hardy*: "Marriage is what we're made for . . . for a man to be a man, it takes a woman. . . . And for a woman to be a woman, it takes a *man*" (p. 135). Lawrence allows him to be heckled by the guests, just as Birkin, preaching a similar message in *Women in Love*, is questioned by Ursula. But the message remains clear, as it is when Lydia explains to Ursula that her first marriage had failed to achieve this: Lensky "had never received what she could give him" while "he had never let me become myself"; only with Tom had "she come to her own self" (pp. 254–8).

The second generation of Brangwens, Will and Anna, have to learn a similar lesson of self-fulfillment through sexual relationship. Tom fears that Will is too "self-contained," too wrapped up in his own religious world, to be open to Anna's otherness (p. 113), but he becomes transformed, "translated . . . in her hands," abandoning his male maxims, the "Tablets of Stone" prized by the community (pp. 147–8). Anna and Will continue to argue, Anna fearing "they were opposites, not complements." She criticizes the male bias of Will's interpretation of the creation story of Genesis, which the *Study* calls a "female" story celebrating Adam and Eve as "one flesh" (Lawrence 1985: 64). In Will's carving, however, Eve is "a little marionette" and "Adam as big as God": (Lawrence [1915] 1997: 172). She continues to undermine his religion, pointing as Lawrence had in the *Study* to the way in which the individual carvings in his beloved cathedral undermine its supposed dogmatic unity, an example of the art of the Middle Ages undermining its metaphysic (p. 202). Will nevertheless achieves an individuality of his own at a personal, sexual level, Anna noting, in the imagery of the *Study*, that "he was blossoming out into his real self" (p. 232).

It is Ursula, however, who is the most celebrated aristocrat of the novel, becoming "a Tess without shame . . . freed to develop in love" (Casagrande 1987: 55, 61). Even as a child, "she was always herself," caring little about "the world outside" ([1915] 1997: 217), adhering "as little as possible to the moral world" (p. 232), alternately full of contempt for "petty people" and fearful of "the mob lying in wait for her, who was the exception" (pp. 262, 269). She dreams of being "the lady Ursula" dispensing charity to the poor from her high horse (p. 283). The fact that Skrebensky is a baron is part of his attractiveness to her, although it soon emerges that he is committed to the values of the community rather than the individual: "To his own intrinsic life he was dead" (pp. 326–7). Ursula for a while feels the need to succeed in "The Man's World" (the title of chapter 13), pursuing her career as a teacher and at college. It is there, however, studying a "plant-animal" through a microscope, that she recognizes its symbolic value, like the poppy in the *Study*, as an example of life beyond mere "self-preservation": "To be oneself," she sees, is the true goal of existence (p. 439).

For a while Ursula and Skrebensky succeed together in escaping social constraints, celebrating "their own consummate being" (p. 450). The lovers stay in a hotel in Piccadilly behaving as "sensuous aristocrats" in "a world of servants." Ursula delights in addressing Skrebensky as "*Monsieur le baron*," which leads to their being treated by both staff and guest "as titled people" (p. 452). She argues for "an aristocracy of birth" not "money" (p. 259), deploring his community values and finally discarding him (p. 492). She has to wait until *Women in Love* for the arrival of a true aristocrat in the shape of Rupert Birkin, who shares her disdain for "the common ruck" and their unquestioning acceptance of the values of the community. "Anybody who is anything," he insists, "can just be himself and do as he likes" (Lawrence [1920] 1998: 32). He argues both with Gerald, whose life is "artificially held together by the social mechanism" (p. 57), and with Ursula, whom he tries to persuade to deny her "common self" and to enter into "a strange conjunction" with him, "an equilibrium, a pure balance of two single beings" (pp. 151–2) of the kind Lawrence had advocated in the *Study*. Ursula initially resists Birkin's notions (or at least his arrogant mode of preaching them) but the marriage they achieve represents at least a partial fulfillment of the reconciliation of opposites towards which the two previous generations of her family have struggled and for which Lawrence had argued in the *Study*.

To recognize the extent to which Lawrence is one of Hardy's heirs requires close attention to the *Study* and its outspoken rejection of Hardy's metaphysic. Both in the *Study* and in the two novels to which Lawrence returned immediately after writing it, he can be seen to challenge the way his precursor's characters are bullied by their community. His own characters, in contrast, allow their individuality to flourish in the face of the "morality" that threatens to stifle them. The continuity between the way this process is seen to unfold in the *Study of Thomas Hardy* and in the novels allows us to identify Lawrence as self-consciously reworking Hardy, "swerving" from him and "correcting" him in classic Bloomian fashion.

John Cowper Powys is more instantly recognizable as one of Hardy's heirs. His fiction resounds with explicit references to him, easily identifiable echoes of his work, not just of the Wessex location but of the manner in which the landscape is described. It would be inaccurate to say that Powys is content simply to repeat the patterns of his predecessor; he transforms his precursor's dominant mood of tragedy, for example, to his own idiosyncratic and carnivalesque form of comedy. Where Hardy often laments the intractable problems created by our sexual instincts, Powys celebrates the diverse and sometimes bizarre sexuality of his extraordinary characters. His critical writing on Hardy may be less interesting than Lawrence's, certainly less sustained, but his reworking of elements of his precursor's work in his own engages in more precise and direct ways with textual details in Hardy. After a brief consideration of Powys' comments on Hardy in other forms of writing (letters, diaries and essays), I will focus on the way his own Wessex novels creatively rework elements of his precursor, especially in the area of sexuality.

The whole Powys family, especially the three brother-novelists, not just J. C. but T. F. and Llewellyn also, have been seen to have "collectively inherited Hardy's mantle" (Keith 2006: 272), though "it was John Cowper who owed the most to Hardy and who in his writings repaid the debt in kind" (Cavaliero 2006: 5). His *Autobiography* claims that "it was not until I left Cambridge" in 1894 "that I so much as even *heard* of . . . Thomas Hardy" (Powys [1934] 1982: 181). It was in Hove, a couple of years later, where he was happily teaching whole "schools of girls," that he recalls first encountering "a small, plain brown volume" of *Far From the Madding Crowd*, half of which he read "in a single walk" (p. 225). For the next ten years, travelling around England as a university extension lecturer, he read "all the novels I could lay hold of." Once home, he would sit up "for hours and hours" reading *The Return of the Native* or some other Wessex novel and eating chocolate while "the genius of Hardy would drive my demon [responsible for his 'devilish moods'] away" (pp. 307–9). Having sent an effusive poem "To Thomas Hardy" in 1896, he was invited to Max Gate, where, on being shown the manuscript of *Tess*, he instantly vowed "to write a good book" himself (Powys 1995: 8). Hardy, in other words, may have driven one demon away, only to replace it with another, that of emulation.

Hardy became one of the many subjects on which Powys would lecture in both England and the United States, where he began touring in 1904 and continued to tour until his return to Dorchester in 1934. These popular lectures – Williams records over 2,000 people in Chicago "rising to their feet" after two hours on Hardy and "demanding more" (Williams 1997: 52–3) – were not exercises in conventional literary criticism. On the page, as in his entry in *One Hundred Best Books* (1916), Powys' comments appear fairly bland, praising, for example Hardy's "grandeur of style" and "clairvoyant feeling for Nature" (Marks 2006: 16–17). Again, however, they reveal not only his enthusiasm for Hardy but his desire to emulate him. *Visions and Revisions: A Book of Literary Devotions* (1915), for example, acknowledges that his own "earliest 'writing-life'" was "intimately" linked with the work of Hardy (Powys [1915] 1955: xviii). The short chapter on Hardy highlights two "stops" of his "country pipe," the tragic (the "jest the gods play on us") and the sexual: "with one he challenges the Immortals on behalf of humanity; with the other he plays such a shrewd Priapian tune that all the Satyrs dance." The first is "infinitely sorrowful and tender," the second, which dominates his last two novels, "whimsical, elfish and malign" (pp. 162–3). Both these tones, of course, will emerge in Powys' own work.

Occasionally Powys is critical of his precursor, for instance in a letter to Phyllis Plater of December 1925, when he writes, after re-reading *Jude the Obscure*, of Hardy's "morbidity" and "unnaturalness" in the arrangement of the events and dialogue. He quickly returns, however, to extolling his morality and mental purity, and celebrating the way he "certainly can describe people loving each other" (Humfrey 1990: 2–3). Powys' diaries record lecturing on Hardy in the States to a variety of audiences (Powys 1995: 28, 34) though again his published comments, as in *The Pleasures of Literature* (1938), repeat commonplaces about Hardy's pessimism and his "indignant sympathy with a suffering world" (Powys 1938: 609). Only when Powys begins to write about Hardy's "imaginary love-affairs . . . so vivid, so enthralling, so heart-breaking" (p. 621), do we gain some real insight into what it is in Hardy that excites him.

It is in Powys' novels, I suggest, that his response to his precursor catches fire, beginning with his first novel *Wood and Stone* (1915) but finding its most interesting expression in the four major Wessex novels: *Wolf Solent* (1929), *A Glastonbury Romance* (1932), *Weymouth Sands* (first published in Britain as *Jobber Skald* in 1935) and *Maiden Castle* (1936). *Wood and Stone* parades Powys' allegiance to Hardy not only with its dedication to "the Greatest Poet and Novelist of Our Age" but in its preface, which, after claiming that "Hardy cannot be imitated," proceeds to plant his own standard "in the heart of Wessex" (Powys [1915] 1974: viii). Casagrande dismisses the novel itself as "a Hardy pastiche," full of references to fate and unfulfilled desire. Its good characters, such as James Anderson, like Jude an educated stonemason, read and enjoy Hardy's work, while its wicked ones, such as Gladys Romer, modeled upon Eustacia Vye, reject them. Casagrande analyzes some more detailed debts to Hardy in terms of the description of landscape, claiming that Powys will graduate in his later work "from pastiche to style, from imitation of Hardy to discovery of his own vision and method through his swervings from Hardy" (Casagrande 1987: 73). This, he claims, happens partly through an exploration of Hardy's pessimism in Powys' second novel *Rodmoor* (1916), whose characters are again placed by their attitude to his work: the doomed Renshaws see him as a "great writer" while the more optimistic Fingal Raughty moves on from him to Rabelais (1987: 74). Similarly in *Ducdame* (1925), Casagrande sees Powys as contrasting the attitudes of the two brothers of the House of Ashover, one of whom remains locked in Hardyesque pessimism while the other battles more positively against illness (1987: 77).

It is in Powys' four major Wessex novels, however, that this reworking of Hardy produces the most interesting results, and it is on these therefore that I will focus. *Wolf Solent*, like *Wood and Stone*, has explicit references to Hardy both in the preface, where he features as one of "the greatest novelists in the world" (Powys [1929] 1961: vi) and in the text, where the eponymous hero's mother works herself "into a fuss by reading Thomas Hardy" (p. 396). Wolf himself is one of Powys' many returning natives, beginning the novel by traveling back to Dorset after a decade in London in order to work on a project not too dissimilar from *A Group of Noble Dames*, a history of Wessex which will focus on "adulteries, murders, and fornications" (p. 34). Like Jude, he finds himself torn between two very different women, the delectable Gerda, "a very healthy young animal" (p. 85) associated with the smell of pigs (p. 263), who satisfies his physical needs, and the cerebral Christie, with her "delicate profile" (p. 79), who stimulates "the deepest emotion he was capable of" (p. 263). Wolf, whose perspective, like Jude's, dominates the novel, finds Christie and himself "exquisitely adapted to understand each other" (p. 237), but also finds himself "wanting to make rough, reckless love to her" (p. 226). She, by contrast, is "devoid of passion" (p. 263), demurely discussing literature while Wolf thinks only of undressing her (p. 436). There is something reminiscent of *The Well-Beloved* about the way Wolf lusts after both these women, being sent into "a species of erotic trance" by a photograph of Gerda astride a tombstone: "the thought of the cool whiteness of that girl's skin and its contact with the chiselled marble" (pp. 62, 66). But Powys goes further even than Hardy in portraying the sheer variety of lusts by which his characters are driven. At one point, for example, three men, including Wolf himself, are depicted ogling some naked boys bathing in a river (p. 284). There is a lesbian scene later in the novel in which Wolf is similarly excited by the "passionate perversity" of two local girls, which provides him with "a deadly-sweet drop of delicious fermentation" (p. 386).

Far from making him ashamed of this, however, or leading his flesh-torn hero to the tragic end which awaits Jude, Powys has him happily accept his sexuality. It's not that Wolf isn't serious – as in Hardy's work there is much philosophizing in the novel about the nature of reality. Wolf at one point, in a passage reminiscent of *The Dynasts*, resolves to defy "the Power behind life" that causes suffering, allying himself with "compassionate forces" to be found in the universe (p. 434). But there is nothing in Hardy like the ending of *Wolf Solent* in which, having reconciled himself to his wife's infidelity as she sits flirting on her latest lover's knee, he refuses to take his predicament tragically, returning home instead for a cup of tea (p. 614). The novel as a whole may make no secret of its debt to Hardy (especially *Jude*) but this ending exemplifies a refusal on Powys' part to remain within the tragic mode of his precursor's major novels.

Weymouth Sands is a similar mixture of the self-consciously Hardyesque and the idiosyncratic, at times whimsical, mood characteristic of Powys alone. It reads at times like a tour of Hardy country, both literally in terms of its locations, and in a literary sense, again referring to a range of Hardy's work. If *Wolf Solent* can be read as a reworking of *Jude*, *Weymouth Sands* offers a recasting of *The Well-Beloved*, extending Hardy's analysis of the sculptor-hero of his final novel, who expresses his desire through the medium of his native Portland stone, to a whole range of characters struggling with their sexual longings (see Casagrande 1987: 89). There is an explicit reference to this precursor text when Magnus Muir, the middle-aged teacher hopelessly infatuated with the unfaithful young Curly, finds himself seated on a bench on the esplanade at Weymouth next to "a youth with a neat hat on, who was reading Hardy's 'Well-Beloved.'" Magnus glances at the book, catching in particular the word "oolite" (Powys [1934] 1980: 473). This, of course, is the word for limestone, itself composed of the fossilized bones of previous generations of fish, which Hardy employs in his novel, celebrating the process of recycling from life to stone to art in his hero's sculpture (Hardy [1897] 1997: 11).

Another word from *The Well-Beloved* which Powys recycles in *Weymouth Sands* is "nympholepsy," the somewhat grand term Hardy's sculptor uses for his pursuit of three generations of women from the same Portland family (p. 70). In Powys it is applied to the elderly mystic Sylvanus Cobbold, who plays "the platonic nympholept" (Powys [1934] 1980: 402). Just as Hardy's sculptor at 60 still hankers over the latest incarnation of Avice, so Sylvanus lies with the young Marret, prolonging rather than bringing to a climax "the culmination of the erotic ecstasy . . . using her young warmth, even as the aged King David did that of the youthful Abishag" (p. 380). Even the biblical reference here echoes Hardy, of course; it is employed by him in describing the young Ethelberta seated next to the elderly Lord Mountclere in *The Hand of Ethelberta* (HE 372). Other echoes of Hardy are scattered throughout *Weymouth Sands*, whose narrator at one point, in imitation of the famous sentence at the end of *Tess*, has Sylvanus contemplate the abyss that will last until "the Original Jester himself repents Him of His Joke" (Powys [1934] 1980: 519). The novel even ends like *Jude the Obscure* with a character "crying out . . . as to the Ancient of Days, 'Oh, why was I born, why was I ever born?'" (p. 567).

Powys clearly wants readers to recognize his debt to Hardy, locating his own work very clearly in his wake. But *Weymouth Sands* too is a very different novel from anything Hardy wrote. For a start, of course, it has a much larger cast, focusing on a characteristically wide range of eccentric creatures united only by their susceptibility to desire. Also, as in *Wolf Solent*, Powys allows most of his characters to accept both their own sexuality and their fate. In the final chapter, for example, Magnus Muir, although abandoned by Curly, dwells with pleasure on the liberties she has allowed him. He must learn to live with "a fossiled [*sic*] life in his heart, that was more recent than any to be found in Portland" (p. 549), but he takes comfort in the natural beauty of Weymouth's West Bay. Jerry Cobbold, the actor and circus performer, settles with his co-worker Tossty while Perdita returns to the Jobber, albeit chastened by experience. Powys appears to be celebrating in them a resilience beyond tragedy.

The third of Powys' four major Wessex novels, *A Glastonbury Romance*, is rather surprisingly omitted from Casagrande's analysis of his reworking of Hardy, although he does quote its 1953 preface, in which Powys records not only his "intoxication" by "all the novels of . . . Hardy" among others (Powys [1932] 1955: x) but his desire to emulate them, "a desperate mania for trying to write the sort of long romances I have always loved so intensely to read" (p. xv; see Casagrande 1987: 94). It is true that the second half of the novel, which focuses on the new religion brought to this ancient sacred site, takes the novel away from traditional "Hardy country," but in many respects the novel's first half, again illustrating the extraordinary permutations of desire, reads at times as if it is put together from remembered fragments of Hardy's work. It begins with another returning native, John Crow, traveling from Paris towards his old home, torn like Clym Yeobright between loyalty to his lover and to his late mother. The fact that his mother is already dead, of course, marks a significant difference from Clym, as does the fact that his lover Mary is also his cousin. There are other resemblances to Jude in his extreme sensitivity to suffering – he tiptoes over the ground, "so fearful was he of hurting so much as the tiniest beetle or the smallest worm" (p. 109) – and in the way Nell Zoyland, possessed like Arabella of the most "beautiful breasts" (p. 131), manip- ulates her idealistic young lover Sam Dekker. Nell, like Sue (but less ingenuously), encourages Sam to think that her husband's "love-making was odious to her" (p. 133) while actually continuing to sleep with him. "Men," she insists, "because of something fastidious and idealistic in their own nature, are always prepared to be touched to the heart by the idea of a girl's physical loathing for another" (p. 139). Powys here seems simply to be rearranging elements recognizably derived from Hardy for his own less serious purposes.

Powys also has the narrator of this novel intrude in the manner of Hardy's narrators to lament "the cruelty of the First Cause" responsible for so much of human suffering (p. 377; cf. p. 78) and to make sometimes misogynistic generalizations about the nature of women, their "fatal susceptibility to passionate touch" (p. 296) or the "levels of feminine emotion in the state of love entirely and forever unknown to men" (p. 298). When Nell and Sam prepare finally to sleep together, Powys dramatizes the pitch of erotic intensity he reaches in a manner similar to Hardy's description of Tess making her way through the undergrowth towards Angel Clare: Sam is supremely "conscious of . . . fertility in the damp spring air and of the hidden stirrings of vege- table juices in roots and stalks as his feet sank in the soft turf of the river-bank" (p. 304). There is even a scene at Stonehenge at which John Crow senses the authentic sanctity of its ancient stones (p. 104). These echoes of Hardy, however, unlike those in Powys' other Wessex novels, although obvious to anyone familiar with his work, do not seem to contribute to the main thrust of the novel. They are certainly unrelated to the religious plot, which reaches its climax in the Passion Play performed at Glastonbury. His exploration of the many and various sexual temperaments of his characters, which include a fascination with sadism and pornography and a recognition of several same-sex relationships, goes further than that of his precursor, finding more explicit expression than was possible for Hardy. But the background of sexual desire against which the religious plot develops remains recognizably related to Hardy's fictional world.

The last of Powys' Wessex novels, *Maiden Castle*, was actually written in Dorchester, to which he returned in 1934 after nearly thirty years in the States. Its hero too is yet another returning native, Dud No-Man, a writer working on a novel about the execution of Mary Channing in Dorchester amphitheater for the murder of her husband. Both author and character, in other words, repeat the circumstances of Hardy's return to Dorchester in 1883 to write *The Mayor of Casterbridge*, of which there are several echoes in the novel, the most obvious being Dud's paying £18 for a young circus girl, a similarity he notes himself: "only Trenchard [*sic*] *sold* his woman and I bought mine" (Powys [1936] 2001: 255). There are several references in the course of the novel to "the great Wessex author" (pp. 9, 184, 304), whose statue is the center of a curious scene in which Dud adds the name of his late first wife to the sketch of a recently unearthed goddess which has been attached to the statue's back, illustrating for Casagrande the way Hardy is "the figure 'against' whom he [Powys] writes," both as "a paternal support and a creative antagonist" (Casagrande 1987: 106).

For the most part, however, it is the similarity between the two writers which *Maiden Castle* exemplifies. Even in this scene at Hardy's statue, Dud No-Man recognizes a shared fascination with women, speculating whether "he'd have been most interested" in the boyish Wizzie or another object of his own erotic interest, the stately Thuella (Powys [1936] 2001: 389). Like both Wessex writers, Powys and Hardy himself, as is apparent in both their autobiographies, No-Man suffers from (or enjoys) a "cerebral eroticism" (p. 72), more excited by "casual encounters" than actual consummation, "the glimpse of a lovely ankle, the turn of a soft neck, the swing of a girl's figure as she walked" (p. 5). He is frequently thrown into erotic trances by the sight of Wizzie or Thuella or, even more exciting, the two of them together (p. 148). And yet, as in Powys' earlier work, when he is finally abandoned by Wizzie for Thuella at the end of the novel, "a strange acquiescence" descends upon him as he "faces without flinching . . . the long ascending path" the future holds for him (p. 483). Dud's novel too is rejected by his publishers, but Powys again opts for a resigned stoical ending rather than a tragic one.

Lawrence and Powys, then, present Hardy with very different kinds of heir. Lawrence, although clearly just as familiar with Hardy's work, which he analyzes much more closely than Powys, bears much less resemblance to his poetic "father." Having seen what is "wrong" in Hardy, in particular the way his "aristocrats" allow themselves to be ground down by society, he creates in his own work characters who celebrate and attempt to fulfill their individuality. Powys' characters, it is fair to say, differ from Hardy's (they are more eccentric and bizarre than any of his) but his Wessex novels advertise their genetic inheritance in every feature. He is clearly proud to write in Hardy's footsteps, producing work which sees itself quite consciously to be continuing the Wessex tradition. Some children imitate their fathers, others rebel; their inheritance, however, still needs to be recognized.

References and Further Reading

Abercrombie, Lascelles (1912). *Thomas Hardy: A Critical Study*. London: Secker.

Beards, Richard D. (1969). D. H. Lawrence and the Study of Thomas Hardy, his Victorian Predecessor. *D. H. Lawrence Review*, 2, 210–29.

Bloom, Harold (1973). *The Anxiety of Influence*. Oxford: Oxford University Press.

Boulton, James T. et al. (eds.) (1979–2000). *The Letters of D. H. Lawrence*, 8 vols. Cambridge: Cambridge University Press.

Casagrande, Peter (1987). *Hardy's Influence on the Modern Novel*. Basingstoke: Macmillan.

Cavaliero, Glen (2006). Introduction to Stephen Powys Marks, *John Cowper Powys on Hardy* (pp. 1–2). Radstock: Fosseway Press.

Draper, R. P. (ed.) (1970). *D. H. Lawrence: The Critical Heritage*. London: Routledge & Kegan Paul.

Hardy, Thomas ([1876] 1996). *The Hand of Ethelberta*, ed. Tim Dolin. London: Penguin.

Hardy, Thomas ([serialized 1892; 1897] 1997). *The Pursuit of the Well-Beloved* and *The Well-Beloved*, ed. Patricia Ingham. London: Penguin.

Hardy, Thomas ([1895] 1998). *Jude the Obscure*, ed. Dennis Taylor. London: Penguin.

Humfrey, Belinda (ed.) (1990). *John Cowper Powys's* Wolf Solent. Cardiff: University of Wales Press.

Keith, W. J. (2006). Thomas Hardy and the Powyses. In Keith Wilson (ed.), *Thomas Hardy Reappraised: Essays in Honour of Michael Millgate* (pp. 270–85). Toronto: University of Toronto Press.

Kinkead-Weekes, Mark (1977). Lawrence on Hardy. In Lance St. John Butler (ed.), *Thomas Hardy after Fifty Years* (pp. 90–102). London: Macmillan.

Kinkead-Weekes, Mark (1989). Introduction to D. H. Lawrence, *The Rainbow* (pp. xix–lxxvi). Cambridge: Cambridge University Press.

Kinkead-Weekes, Mark (1996). *D. H. Lawrence: Triumph to Exile, 1912–1922*. Cambridge: Cambridge University Press.

Langbaum, Robert (1985). Lawrence and Hardy. In Jeffrey Meyers (ed.), *D. H. Lawrence and Tradition* (pp. 69–90). Amherst: University of Massachusetts Press.

Lawrence, D. H. ([1915] 1997). *The Rainbow*, ed. Kate Flint. Oxford: Oxford University Press.

Lawrence, D. H. ([1920] 1998). *Women in Love*, ed. David Bradshaw. Oxford: Oxford University Press.

Lawrence, D. H. (1985). *Study of Thomas Hardy and Other Essays*. Cambridge: Cambridge University Press.

Marks, Stephen Powys (2006). *John Cowper Powys on Hardy*. Radstock: Fosseway Press.

Mills, Howard (1988). "Slightly philosophicalish, mostly about Hardy": Study of Thomas Hardy. In David Ellis and Howard Mills (eds.), *D. H. Lawrence's Non-Fiction: Art, Thought and Genre* (pp. 11–39). Cambridge: Cambridge University Press.

Powys, J. C. ([1915] 1955). *Visions and Revisions: A Book of Literary Devotions*. London: Macdonald.

Powys, J. C. ([1915] 1974). *Wood and Stone*. London: Village Press.

Powys, J. C. ([1929] 1961). *Wolf Solent*. London: Macdonald.

Powys, J. C. ([1932] 1955). *A Glastonbury Romance*. London: Macdonald.

Powys, J. C. ([1934] 1982). *Autobiography*. London: Picador.

Powys, J. C. ([1934] 1980). *Weymouth Sands*. London: Picador.

Powys, J. C. ([1936] 2001). *Maiden Castle*. Woodstock: The Overlook Press.

Powys, J. C. (1938). *The Pleasures of Literature*. London: Cassell.

Powys, J. C. (1995). *Petrushka and the Dancer: The Diaries of John Cowper Powys 1929–39*, ed. Morine Krissdottir. Manchester: Carcanet.

Sumner, Rosemarie (2000). *A Route to Modernism: Hardy, Lawrence, Woolf*. Basingstoke: Palgrave Macmillan.

Swigg, Richard (1972). *Lawrence, Hardy, and American Literature*. London: Oxford University Press.

Williams, Herbert (1997). *John Cowper Powys*. Bridgend: Severn.

Worthen, John (1979). *D. H. Lawrence and the Idea of the Novel*. London: Macmillan.

Worthen, John (1991). *D. H. Lawrence: The Early Years, 1885–1912*. Cambridge: Cambridge University Press.

Index